Margaret E. (Hertzg (n)

May 1979

BETWEEN REALITY
AND FANTASY

f Congress Cataloging in Publication Data

reality and fantasy.

des bibliographies and index.
ychoanalysis.   2. Infant psychology.   3. Winnicott, Donald
 1896-1971.   I. Grolnick, Simon A., 1930-   II. Barkin,
d.   III. Muensterberger, Werner, 1913-   IV. Title:
tional objects and phenomena. [DNLM: 1. Psychoanalytic theory.
0 B565]
.B477   155.4'22   77-92335
0-87668-318-9

ifactured in the United States of America.

Squiggle drawing by D. W. Winnicott. Copyright © 1978 Clare Winnicott.

BETWEE
AND F

Transitional Obje

edite
Simon A. Gro
and
Leonard Bark
in collaboratio
Werner Muensterb

NEW YORK •  JASON ARONSON

D. W. W.

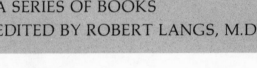

ARONSON

Library of Congress Cataloging in Publication Data

Between reality and fantasy.

    Includes bibliographies and index.
    1. Psychoanalysis.   2. Infant psychology.   3. Winnicott, Donald
Woods, 1896-1971.   I. Grolnick, Simon A., 1930-   II. Barkin,
Leonard.   III. Muensterberger, Werner, 1913-   IV. Title:
Transitional objects and phenomena. [DNLM: 1. Psychoanalytic theory.
WM460 B565]
BF173.B477   155.4'22   77-92335
ISBN 0-87668-318-9

Manufactured in the United States of America.

BETWEEN REALITY AND FANTASY

Transitional Objects and Phenomena

edited by
Simon A. Grolnick, M.D.
and
Leonard Barkin, M.D.
in collaboration with
Werner Muensterberger, Ph.D.

𝒜

NEW YORK   •   JASON ARONSON   •   LONDON

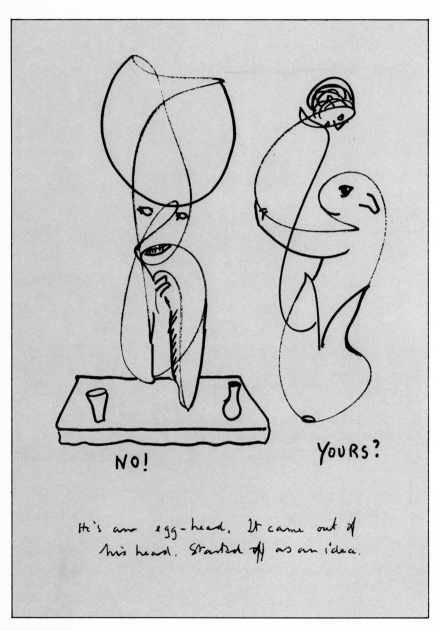

Squiggle drawing by D. W. Winnicott. Copyright © 1978 Clare Winnicott.

D. W. W.

Classical Psychoanalysis and Its Applications

A SERIES OF BOOKS
EDITED BY ROBERT LANGS, M.D.

Robert Langs
THE TECHNIQUE OF
PSYCHOANALYTIC
PSYCHOTHERAPY, VOLS. I AND II

THE THERAPEUTIC INTERACTION,
TWO-VOLUME SET

THE BIPERSONAL FIELD

THE THERAPEUTIC INTERACTION:
A SYNTHESIS

Judith Kestenberg
CHILDREN AND PARENTS:
PSYCHOANALYTIC STUDIES IN
DEVELOPMENT

Melitta Sperling
THE MAJOR NEUROSES AND
BEHAVIOR DISORDERS IN
CHILDREN

Peter L. Giovacchini
PSYCHOANALYSIS OF CHARACTER
DISORDERS

PSYCHOTHERAPY OF PRIMITIVE
MENTAL STATES

Otto Kernberg
BORDERLINE CONDITIONS AND
PATHOLOGICAL NARCISSISM

OBJECT-RELATIONS THEORY AND
CLINICAL PSYCHOANALYSIS

William A. Console
Richard D. Simons
Mark Rubinstein
THE FIRST ENCOUNTER

Humberto Nagera
FEMALE SEXUALITY AND THE
OEDIPUS COMPLEX

OBSESSIONAL NEUROSES:
DEVELOPMENTAL
PSYCHOPATHOLOGY

Willi Hoffer
THE EARLY DEVELOPMENT AND
EDUCATION OF THE CHILD

William Meissner
THE PARANOID PROCESS

Mardi Horowitz
STRESS RESPONSE SYNDROMES

HYSTERICAL PERSONALITY

Victor Rosen
STYLE, CHARACTER AND LANGUAGE

Charles Sarnoff
LATENCY

Heinz Lichtenstein
THE DILEMMA OF HUMAN IDENTITY

Simon Grolnick,
Leonard Barkin, Editors
in collaboration with
Werner Muensterberger,
BETWEEN FANTASY AND REALITY:
TRANSITIONAL OBJECTS AND
PHENOMENA

ARONSON

SERIES INTRODUCTION

For some years now, D. W. Winnicott's fascinating conception of transitional objects and phenomena has attracted wide interest and generated much creative thinking. There is a quality to the transitional concept that stirs the imagination, bridges conceptual gaps between seemingly disparate phenomena, and holds special promise for the understanding of such varied realms as infant and childhood development, psychopathology, the clinical interaction, and society and culture.

The present volume is not only a tribute to the creativity of Winnicott, but a means of expanding his initial thesis and demonstrating its pertinence to both basic clinical issues and broader cultural questions. The volume brings together three editors with extensive backgrounds in both clinical and applied psychoanalysis. International in scope, it unites and synthesizes contributions from both psychoanalysts and workers in related fields, thereby showing the relevance of transitional phenomena to many vital aspects of human life and endeavor. It is a volume, then, filled with the creativity that is the essence of the transitional concept and yet directed as well toward specific clinical and theoretical issues. As part of this series, it stands as an example of the contribution classical psychoanalysis can make to the widest possible range of human interests.

Robert Langs, M.D.

CONTENTS

PART III
Clinical Studies

PART VI
Concluding

PREFACE

The editors aim to show the growth and evolution of one of the most original concepts of modern psychoanalysis, that of transitional objects and phenomena. More than a quarter of a century after D. W. Winnicott described this neglected aspect of human behavior and development, the transitional process can now be seen as one of the basic organizing principles of the essential fabric of intrapsychic functioning. By now Winnicott has influenced workers not only in psychoanalysis but in related fields as well as in the arts. Many of these were most helpful to us, both by contributing to this volume and by aiding us in its organization.

It is now five years since one of us (S.G.), intrigued by the appearance of transitional objects and phenomena in so many adult patients, researched the literature and realized that there was no book available that attempted to synthesize the recent elaborations of Winnicott's concept. Extensive discussions with L.B. led to the mutual resolve to solicit original chapters from those working with and developing Winnicott's ideas. In this endeavor, it was inevitable that we would turn to our colleague and former teacher at the Downstate Psychoanalytic Institute for assistance, which he gave freely and enthusiastically. Werner Muensterberger had been writing about transitional objects and phenomena and their relation to the creative process since the early 1960s. As our senior editor, his unique combination of psychoanalyst, anthropologist, aesthetician, writer, and editor has added much to our joint effort at exploring this intriguing but often misunderstood area of psychoanalysis.

We want to thank our wives, Maxine and Ania, not only for their patience and understanding, but also for help with the book's contents and readability. Our editor, Michael Farrin, transcended that title. He rapidly grasped the concepts involved, and used his intellectual background, skill, and editorial experience in such a manner that his additions are interwoven throughout. Special thanks are offered to Clare Winnicott, Peter Giovacchini, Masud Khan, Judith Kestenberg, Gilbert Rose, and Robert Langs, who never stinted with their guidance and encouragement. There were many others, so many that a list would be inappropriately large, whose discussions, readings, tolerance, and inspiration allowed us to persevere in constructing a book about challenging and still controversial ideas.

SIMON A. GROLNICK
LEONARD BARKIN

BETWEEN REALITY
AND FANTASY

CHAPTER 1

BETWEEN REALITY AND FANTASY

Werner Muensterberger

The recognition of transitional phenomena and transitional objects has provided us one of the few critical, elucidating, and comprehensive concepts to have been elaborated in the course of psychoanalytic studies since Freud. The concept suggests an intermediate state of awareness preceding the infant's perception of I and non-I. This can be understood as a phase of transitional processes during which the baby's babbling, a s)ft cushiony toy, the edge of a blanket, or a lullaby provides a sense of cohesion. We could think of these items as instruments of an early delicate amenity vouchsafing continuance of touch or sound, and I mean continuance in the most elementary function. Ever since Donald Winnicott concerned himself with the things and events of these intermediate processes, his findings have achieved affirmation and, as the essays in this book show, led to further exploration.

Of all the personal reflections in Winnicott's work there is one which most eloquently captures the essence of his sensibility. Quoting a line from Tagore—"On the seashore of endless worlds, children play"—he said that this image has always intrigued him. It is a compelling image with a supernatural aura to which Winnicott (1971) responded in his characteristic way:

In my adolescence I had no idea what it could mean, but it found a place in me, and its imprint has not yet faded.

When I first became a Freudian I *knew* what it meant. The sea and the shore represented endless intercourse between man and woman, and the child emerged from this union to have a brief moment before becoming in turn adult or parent. Then, as a student of unconscious symbolism, I *knew* (one always *knows*) that the sea is the mother, and

Research and data of this essay are part of a larger study on the *Motivations of Collecting*, for which I received a fellowship from the John Simon Guggenheim Memorial Foundation and a grant-in-aid from the William A. Grant Foundation, Inc. I gratefully acknowledge their generosity.

onto the seashore the child is born. Babies come up out of the sea and are spewed out upon the land, like Jonah from the whale. So now the seashore was the mother's body, after the child is born and the mother and the now viable baby are getting to know each other.

Then I began to see that this employs a sophisticated concept of the parent-infant relationship and that there could be an unsophisticated infantile point of view, a different one from that of the mother or the observer, and that this infant's viewpoint could be profitably examined. For a long time my mind remained in a state of not-knowing, this state crystallizing into my formulation of the transitional phenomena. [Winnicott 1971, p. 95]

This was no formal knowledge but the root recognition of early instances of *experience* and *experiment* of the baby at the time of his first reaching out, his first aiming and quest for a bond and thus the first use of symbolic substitutes. We recognize impulses which presage emotional growth. Winnicott's advantage was his intimate work with children. The clinic in Paddington Green Children's Hospital in London was a convenient, cut-out place for what one might call a "field laboratory." Here thousands of infants with their mothers came under Winnicott's (1952) observation, and it was under the impact of these encounters that he made the blunt and appropriate claim: *There is no such thing as a baby.* In his poignant and unblurred manner he amplified: "If you show me a baby you certainly show me also someone caring for the baby, or at least a pram with someone's eyes and ears glued to it. One sees a 'nursing couple'" (1952, p. 99). In the clinic he had the raw material to study the visible signs and responses, the complexity and variety of infant-care. The hospital was a most suitable forum to investigate carefully patterns of cues and actions between mother and child or, more precisely, the infant between five and thirteen months of age. As his field technique, he had thought out his by now renowned spatula game:

I ask the mother to sit opposite me with the angle of the table coming between me and her. She sits down with the baby on her knee. As a routine, I place a right-angled shining tongue-depressor at the edge of the table and invite the mother to place the child in such a way that, if the child should wish to handle the spatula, it is possible. . . . You can imagine that mothers show by their ability or relative inability to follow this suggestion something of what they are like at home. . . .

Winnicott (1941) divided what follows into three distinct stages. First, the child, tempted by the shiny tool, touches the spatula, then hesitates

(Winnicott refers to a "period of hesitation") and after a moment's waiting puts it in his mouth "and chewing it with his gums . . . The baby now seems to feel that the spatula is in his possession, perhaps in his power. . . . In the third stage the baby first of all drops the spatula as if by mistake. If it is restored he is pleased, plays with it again, and drops it once more. . ." (Winnicott 1941).

We can scarcely fail to see the relevance of such detailed observation. All the features, even within each of the three phases, are part of a complex functional sequence. But to begin with their diagnostic evidence allows for insight into the constituent parts. The spatula may be just a thing the child can take or leave without connecting it with people. And Winnicott concludes that the child has not developed or has lost the capacity "for building up the whole person behind the part object. Or he may show that he sees me or mother behind the spatula" (1941, p. 64). If he does so "it is as if he took his mother's breast." This is sign language. It is articulation by means of symbolic equivalents, which concurs with Piaget's (1952) findings. But it would be naive to assume that the objective appearances are intelligible only in behavioral terms. Piaget saw, too, that moment of hesitation before the child takes the object or, in more than one sense, comes to grips with it. This is followed by inserting it in the mouth: certainly more than a vague intimation at taking it inside and holding it there. We could ask whether this is an attempt at cannibalistic annihilation, or, alternatively, whether the infant is making a point as a gesture of differentiation. Or again, is it his way of trying to undo separation? Doubtless, there is a spatula-breast equation, but its true significance resides "in the fact that the *full course of an experience is allowed*" (Winnicott 1941, p. 67). The step-by-step examination of the interplay with the spatula as an instructive experiment for diagnosis of the child as well as of the reciprocity between mother and offspring was an ingenious means of employing a concrete vehicle for preverbal communication. In enviable simplicity it revealed much of the little patient's own brand of budding selfhood, of emotional economy, of ready credence or distrust or aggressive-sadistic intentions.

Prior to dealing with the functional origin of transitional phenomena we should remember that Freud (1920) had noticed certain ritualistic routines in the behavior of his eighteen months old grandson. The little boy had got into the habit of throwing toys into a corner or under a bed. Moreover he had invented a game with a wooden reel to which a string had been attached. By throwing the reel over the edge of his cot it vanished into it, and he mourned its disappearance with a meaningful 'o-o-o-o-'-sound.

He then pulled the reel out of the cot again by the string and hailed its reappearance with a joyful "*da*" [there]. This, then, was the complete game—disappearance and return.

To this Freud added a footnote:

A further observation subsequently confirmed this interpretation fully. One day the child's mother had been away for several hours and on her return was met by the words "Baby o-o-o-o-!" which was at first incomprehensible. It soon turned out, however, that during this long period of solitude the child had found a method of making *himself* disappear. He had discovered his reflection in a full-length mirror which did not quite reach the ground, so that by crouching down he could make his mirror-image "gone."

The interpretation of the game then becomes obvious. It was related to the child's great cultural achievement—the instinctual renunciation . . . which he had made in allowing his mother to go away without protesting. He compensated himself for this, as it were, by staging the disappearance and return of the objects within his reach. . . . At the outset he was in a *passive* situation—he was overpowered by an experience; but by repeating it, unpleasurable though it was, as a game, he took on an active part. [Freud 1920, pp. 14-16] [1]

It was an exploratory endeavour by which the young child tried to work out a variety of emotions. In this connection I can indicate several functions though they do not cover the entire spectrum of meanings. There is his fear of having been left behind. There is retaliation by a gesture to exorcize the frustrating mother or even to throw her away, but then to bring her back again; there was, too, the identification with her, as the mirror game illustrates: he had incorporated her. He had "done away" with her but regained her in an act of magic reappearance. All these elements hint at the multiple function of the game. [2]

It can of course be said that temporary absence of the mother (or the caretaker) belongs to the expectable events in a baby's life, at least in those cultures from which we take our examples. In order to avoid renewed exposure to disillusionment, children discover means to diminish the hurt. They are never entirely effective, but the thumb can be used as a pacifier, or the teddy bear becomes an inseparable companion, or the wooden reel may serve to cover up the anxiety about the mother's disappearance. Still, the model we usually have in mind is that of the kind of child care we find in the Euro-American culture area. For example, we know of numerous societies in which infants are never left alone, or where mother and child are practically never separated and the pattern of socialization differs appreciably from our habits of child rearing. But whatever the combinations in the infant-mother interplay, one or the other variety of unpleasure seems unavoidable, if only because of the mother's inability to protect her baby from illness, pain, or discomfort. Moreover, innate maturational factors bring with them a natural tendency "to stand on one's own feet" and test one's capacity. All these courses of events are destined to be part of the internal logic of psychic orchestration.

Thus we can comprehend that regardless of gradations and variations in maternal concern there is bound to be a dialectic provocation between infant and mother because desire and forthcoming need-fulfillment are often on opposite sides of the scale.

If some of the consequences of the prolonged dependence of the human child had already become apparent to Freud, they were further pursued by Melanie Klein and her coworkers and by several psychoanalysts of the Budapest group, in particular by Hermann's (1936) seminal study *"Sich Anklammern—Auf Suche Gehen"* (To Cling—To Go in Search) and subsequently by Paul Schilder and Géza Róheim. It had been Hermann's position that due to the inevitable maternal frustrations the baby's sadistic impulses are mobilized, leading to regressive-narcissistic cathexes, and that in his need to cling he goes in search of substitute objects. To this Róheim (1943) added that we discover here a means of assurance, something that is part of the individual and at the same time a representative of the loved person. Hence people "will never be left completely alone because failing everything else they have these children of their minds to love." A developmental dilemma fosters the creation of substitutes, "dolls, property, money, etc., in fact, material culture." This, Róheim concluded, is "the theory of an 'intermediate' object as stabilization between a trend that oscillates between 'clinging' and 'going exploring' in Hermann's sense" (1943, p. 92). It would indicate that Róheim (1955) thought along similar lines when, about a decade later, he spoke of the twilight zone between the real and the imagined, the transitional phase which, as he described it, is *"located somewhere halfway* between the pure pleasure principle and the reality principle" (p. 10, italics mine).

I might add here that the close agreement between the Hermann-Róheim conceptualization and Winnicott's clinically derived conclusions is reminiscent of other almost simultaneously discovered facts or artistic creations. While Róheim spoke of the *location of magic* and considered the mother as the first environment, Winnicott (1967) explored "the location of cultural experience," which he designated as potential space.[3]

What Winnicott (1971) underlines is the eventual outcome of defenses and selfhood as rooted in the infant's experience and "confidence in the mother's reliability," regardless of the trauma of separation.

A baby can be *fed* without love, but lovelessness or impersonal *management* cannot succeed in producing a new autonomous human child. Here where there is trust and reliability is a potential space, one that can become an infinite area of separation, which the baby, child, adolescent, adult may creatively fill with playing, which in time becomes the enjoyment of the cultural heritage. [p. 108]

In his own way, Winnicott studied the reciprocity in what he liked to call "the nursing couple," thus creating an initial infraculture. Although *space* is primarily a metaphor of the ambience between mother and child (and eventually between the psychoanalyst and the patient), it is meant to be a resonant expanse associated with emotional substance, a "sense of trust matched with reliability." This has little to do with territoriality nor can it be operationally defined. It is the suspense of the absolute. Hence I would venture to say that phenomena such as "the experience of the first separatings" precede the tenuous cognition of objects. They might be thought of as impressions of a very brittle nature—as a proprioceptive consequence of endogenous and exogenous events, for we postulate that the infant is under the illusion that the mother's breast is part of him. What follows is an accumulation of sensations or, again, experiences with a wide variety of components—of pleasure or pain, of discomfort or dis-ease, of changes in temperature or light (to mention only a few), all stored and probably selectively processed. Logically, much of the baby's reaction to its separateness depends on the confidence in the mother's dependability.

We stand at the crossroads between the beginning of imaginative mastery or a neurotic sense of doubt or even despair; between a continued threat of projected danger or a genuine sense of selfhood or, in the current idiom, of "feeling together." Their empirical connection lies in the inevitability of disappointment, which is, after all, the very rudiment of a sense of identity.

The concept of identity is an ideal. I understand it as an awareness of one's boundaries vis-à-vis the outside world, beginning with the recognition of a body ego and eventually synthesizing identifications with the decisive persons in one's immediate environment, who in turn represent milieu-bound ideals and expectations. The study of infant care and particularly of infant care under varying sociocultural conditions makes clear that these milieu-bound ideals, moral sentiments, and dominant expectations themselves vary. I am thinking here of class and age differences within the same social system. Hence we must ask to what extent cultural patterns of mothering leave their mark on the creation and use of transitional phenomena.

To answer this question I must refer once more to our conventional conceptions of "inside" and "outside" or the recognition of I and non-I which is only fully accomplished by the time the child has reached the age of six or seven (Piaget). However, this estimation relies on work with children in the Euro-American culture area. Once we compare infant care in different surroundings, we see that the pace, the style, and in some respects the direction of development differ. As is well known, breast-feeding often lasts over several years, frequently far into the oedipal phase. There is an extended intimacy between mother and infant. Demand feeding is a matter of course. In some societies the next pregnancy is supposed to be postponed as long as the mother is lactating.

This is not the place to enter into descriptive details. But what should be said is that the extended symbiotic existence entails a considerable delay in the baby's forming of ego boundaries, only allowing for quite basic mechanisms of defense. As we know, such defenses use projection, ritualistic obsession, isolation, and collective identification as regulatory measures, and emotional independence from pregenital object-representations cannot be fully achieved. All of this concurs with adaptation which uses obsessional rituals, primitive fetishism or magic, and animistic beliefs—transitional objects and phenomena—as a reservoir against disillusionment (Muensterberger 1969). This mode of adapting maximal dependence to a derivative of not good enough mothering is of primary importance, for it sheds light on the effects of the mother-child relationship on the ensuing interpretation of reality.

Enough has been said to suggest that continued maternal provision, both at the various stages of development, from total helplessness to learning about separateness, and during the steps toward individuation has been crucial for a reliable sense of self.

This is an ideal. If the baby must turn to a doll or dummy he is making his first bargain. It is also a test, because on the basis of this compromise, he is sacrificing his demand for allness. Quite literally he agrees to a social contract. He does not demand *all*—and so far the mother, or perhaps only her breast, have been all—for he lets part of her go. This is a social as well as a cultural event (social in terms of his subsequent interaction, cultural as to be compatible with the relevant standards of his age and environment) because he is now on a course of displacements, inventions, and substitutions. These may entail failure or success. The substitutions may turn to, for example, bizarre, obsessional rituals or to "imaginative living" (to use Winnicott's expression), or the child may use toys of any sort as a device for gaining assurance. There can be all possible combinations between harmless infatuation and intoxicating compulsion.

The dread of separateness is thus at least partially cushioned by allowing for the use of objects or tunes. These are elementary acts in the process of self-organization. Only when the child is ready to distinguish between percept and concept do the doll and the lullaby turn from indispensable companions into playthings and enjoyable music. In an important sense they no longer have to serve as transitional phenomena. They may turn into favorite possessions.

The difference is essential because their presence is not imperative. They have lost their magic. What is more: if the object is dispensable and the child knows he can survive without it, there is also proof that it can be abandoned or left behind and so, in other words, can survive potential destruction without any trauma or loss to the child. He can use aggression constructively without risking harm. If we would think in animistic terms we could say that the object has lost its soul. It has also lost its magic efficacy, and the baby may henceforth experience life as a true individual within the shared reality of the world.

NOTES

1. See also: The interpretation of dreams, *Standard Edition* 5:461; Ernest Jones, *Life and Work of Sigmund Freud*, vol. 3, p. 41.
2. The various components show the usefulness of Waelder's "The Principle of Multiple Function" (1930). In a later paper, "The Psychoanalytic Theory of Play" (1932), Waelder alludes to a variety of functions, though without formulating the structural components involved.
3. I may refer here parenthetically to coincidences such as these, well-known in science, inventions, scholarship, and art. To give only one example: logarithms were evolved almost simultaneously by the Scotsman, Napier, in 1614, and by the Swiss, Bürgi, in 1620. A century later Su-li Ching-yün, a Chinese scholar, used them, and it is doubtful whether he had any information from Europe. (See A. L. Kroeber, *Configurations of Cultural Growth*, Berkeley, 1944, pp. 152-158; 202).

REFERENCES

Freud, S. (1920). Beyond the pleasure principle. *Standard Edition* 18:14–16.
Hermann, I. (1936). Sich Anklammern—Auf Suche gehen. *Internationale*

Zeitschrift für Psychoanalyse 22:365 ff. English translation: Clinging—going-in-search: a contrasting pair of instincts and their relation to sadism and masochism. *Psychoanalytic Quarterly* 45:5–36 (1976).

Jones, E. (1953). *The Life and Work of Sigmund Freud*, vol. 3. New York: Basic Books, p. 41.

Kroeber, A. L. (1944). *Configurations of Cultural Growth*. Berkeley: University of California Press, pp. 152 ff.

Muensterberger, W. (1969). Psyche and environment: variations in separation and individuation. *Psychoanalytic Quarterly* 38:191–216.

Piaget, J. (1952). *The Origins of Intelligence in Children*. New York: Norton, pp. 113–116, 273–303.

Róheim, G. (1943) *The Origin and Function of Culture*. New York: Nervous and Mental Diseases Monographs, p. 92.

——— (1955). *Magic and Schizophrenia*, ed. W. Muensterberger. New York: International Universities Press, p. 10.

Waelder, R. (1933). The psychoanalytic theory of play. *Psychoanalytic Quarterly* 2:208–224.

——— (1936). The principle of multiple function. *Psychoanalytic Quarterly* 5:45–62.

Winnicott, D. W. (1941). The observation of infants in a set situation. In *Through Paediatrics to Psycho-Analysis*, pp. 52–69. London: Tavistock, 1975.

———(1952). Anxiety associated with insecurity. In *Through Paediatrics to Psycho-Analysis*, pp. 97–100. London: Tavistock, 1975.

——— (1971). *Playing and Reality*. New York: Basic Books.

CHAPTER 2

makes me feel awful because so many of my friends and
oraries died in the first World War, and I have never been free
feeling that my being alive is a facet of some one thing of
eir deaths can be seen as other facets: some huge crystal, a
h integrity and shape intrinsical in it).

goes on to discuss the difficulty that a man has dying without a
aginatively kill and to survive him—"to provide the only
that men know. Women *are* continuous." This dilemma is
n terms of King Lear and his relationship to his daughters and
ar to the youngest daughter who should have been a boy.
hat these quotations give some idea of D. W. W.'s capacity to
rms with internal and external reality in a playful way, which
ity bearable to the individual, so that denial can be avoided and
ence of living can be as fully realized as possible. In his own
ying can be said to reach its own saturation point, which refers
acity to contain experience " (*Playing and Reality*, p. 52). He was
perience and he would have hated to miss the inner experience
lity of his own death, and he imaginatively achieved that
. In conversation he would often refer to his deathday in a
ed way, but I knew that he was trying to get me and himself
d to the idea that it would come.

started at the end of his life, I must now go back to the
s and relate something about his earlier years and about the
he and I spent together. I shall limit what I say to an attempt to
the theme of playing, because that was central to his life and

ust set the scene within which he grew up. It was an essentially
rovincial scene in Plymouth, Devon, and it was far from
ot merely in mileage, but in custom and convention. When we
lymouth from London he was always thrilled when we arrived
ce where the soil banked up at the side of the road changed in
e red soil of Devon. The richness of the soil brought back the
f his early life which he never lost touch with. Of course on the
urney, he was always equally pleased to be leaving it behind. But
oud of being a Devonian, and that there is a village of Winnicott
p of Devon. We never actually found the village, although we
eant to. It was enough that it was there.
innicott household was a large and lively one with plenty of
But there was space for everyone in the large garden and house
was no shortage of money. There was a vegetable garden, an
a croquet lawn, a tennis court and a pond, and high trees

D.W.W.: A REFLECTION

Clare Winnicott

The editors of this book have invited me to write something of a
personal nature about the man whose observations and experience led to
the concept of transitional objects and phenomena. In attempting to do
this I shall need to select only those aspects of his life and personality that
are relevant to the book. It could seem therefore as if these concepts
arose naturally and easily out of D. W. W.'s own way of life. In one sense
this is true; but it is only half the story. The rest concerns the periods of
doubt, uncertainty and confusion, out of which form and meaning
eventually emerged.

What was it about D. W. W. that made the exploration of this
transitional area inevitable, and made his use of it clinically productive? I
suggest that answers to these questions have to be looked for not simply
in a study of the development of his ideas as he went along, but
essentially in the kind of personality that was functioning behind them.
He could be excited by other people's ideas, but could use them and build
on them only after they had been through the refinery of his own
experience. By that time, unfortunately, he had often forgotten the
source, and he could, and did, alienate some people by his lack of
acknowledgement. While other people's ideas enriched D. W. W. as a
clinician and as a person, it was the working out of his own ideas that
really absorbed him and that he grappled with to the end of his life. This
was a creative process in which he was totally involved. In his clinical
work D. W. W. made it his aim to enter into every situation undefended
by his knowledge, so that he could be as exposed as possible to the impact
of the situation itself. From his point of view this was the only way in
which discovery was a possibility, both for himself and for his patients.
This approach was more than a stance; it was an essential discipline, and
it added a dimension to his life as vital to him as fresh air.

The question is sometimes asked as to why D. W. W. in his writings
seemed mainly concerned with exploring the area of the first two-person

relationship. Strictly speaking this is not true: he wrote on a wide range of topics, including adolescence and delinquency and other matters of medical and sociological concern, and the greater part of his psychoanalytic practice was with adults. However, it could be true to say that his main contribution is likely to turn out to be in the study of the earliest relationships, and its application to the etiology of psychosis and of the psychotic mechanisms in all of us. I suggest that his study took this direction from two sources. In the first place, he brought with him into psychoanalysis all that he had learnt and went on learning from pediatrics, and secondly, at the time he came to psychoanalysis the area of study just then opening up was that concerning the earliest experiences of life. Given his personality, his training and experience, and his urge for discovery, it seems inevitable that he would concentrate his researches on the so far comparatively unexplored area of earliest infancy and childhood. His findings, however, are recognised by many as having implications far beyond the immediate area of study. It is the expressed opinion of some that they throw light on all areas of living.

As I have suggested, the essential clue to D. W. W.'s work on transitional objects and phenomena is to be found in his own personality, in his way of relating and being related to, and in his whole life style. What I mean is that it was *his capacity to play* which never deserted him, that led him inevitably into the area of research that he conceptualised in terms of the transitional objects and phenomena. It is not my purpose here to discuss the details of his work, but it seems important to note that in his terms the capacity to play is equated with a *quality of living*. In his own words, "Playing is an experience, always a creative experience, and it is an experience in the space-time continuum, a basic form of living" (*Playing and Reality*, p. 50). This quality of living permeates all levels and aspects of experiencing and relating, up to and including the sophisticated level described in his paper "The Use of an Object" at which in his own words, "It is the destructive drive that creates the quality of externality"; and again,"this quality of 'always being destroyed' makes the reality of the surviving object felt as such, strengthens the feeling tone, and contributes to object constancy" (*Playing and Reality*, p. 93). For him, the destroying of the object in unconscious fantasy is like a cleansing process, which facilitates again and again the discovery of the object anew. It is a process of purification and renewal.

Having said that, I see my contribution to this book as an attempt to throw some light on D. W. W.'s capacity for playing. I expect that readers will be familiar enough with his writings on this subject to know that I am not talking about playing games. I am talking about the capacity for operating in the limitless intermediate area where external and internal

reality are compounded into the exper suggest that D. W. W. lived in a state of was far from the case. He often found li and depressed and angry, but given tir encompass these experiences in his own cluttered up with resentment and prejuc life the reality of his own death had to again gradually and in his own way. I wa autobiography because I felt that his sty such a task. He started to do this, but t typically he used this exercise to deal living, which was that of dying. I know I kept this notebook to himself and I did

The title of the autobiography was to l inner flap of the notebook reads as foll

T. S. Eliot   "Costing not less than ev
               Quartets]
T. S. Eliot   "What we call the beginni
               And to make an end is to
               The end is where we sta
               Quartets]

Prayer

D. W. W.   Oh God! May I be alive w

Following these words he started or imaginatively describing the end of his li

I died.

It was not very nice, and it took quite was only a moment in eternity).

There had been rehearsals (that's a had left out the "a." The hearse was

When the time came I knew all about the heart could not negotiate, so that the alveoli, and there was oxygen star fair enough, I had had a good inning gardener used to say. . . . .

Let me see. What was happening wh answered. I was alive when I died. That

it. (Th conter from which body

He the son to continui discusse in partic

I hope come to makes re the expe words " to the ca avid for of the r experien lighthea accuston

Havin beginnin years th illustrate work.

First I English London, drove to at the pl color to richness return j he was p on the n always

The V activity. and then orchard,

enclosed the whole garden. There was a special tree, in the branches of which Donald would do his homework in the days before he went to boarding school. Of the three children in the family Donald was the only boy, and his sisters, who still live in the house, were five and six years older than he. There is no doubt that the Winnicott parents were the center of their children's lives, and that the vitality and stability of the entire household emanated from them. Their mother was vivacious and outgoing and was able to show and express her feelings easily. Sir Frederick Winnicott (as he later became) was slim and tallish and had an old-fashioned quiet dignity and poise about him, and a deep sense of fun. Those who knew him speak of him as a person of high intelligence and sound judgment. Both parents had a sense of humor.

Across the road was another large Winnicott household which contained uncle Richard Winnicott (Frederick's elder brother) and his wife, and three boy cousins and two girls. The cousins were brought up almost as one family, so there was never a shortage of playmates. One of the sisters said recently that the question "What can I do?" was never asked in their house. There was always something to do—and space to do it in, and someone to do it with if needed. But more important, there was always the vitality and imagination in the children themselves for exploits of all kinds. Donald's family, including his parents, were musical, and one sister later became a gifted painter. The household always included a nanny and a governess, but they do not seem to have hampered the natural energies of the children in any unreasonable way. Perhaps it would be more correct to say that the Winnicott children successfully evaded being hampered. As a small child Donald was certainly devoted to his nanny, and one of the first things I remember doing with him years later in London was to seek her out and ensure that she was all right and living comfortably. We discovered that the most important person in her life then (1950) was her own nephew "Donald."

There is no doubt that from his earliest years Donald did not doubt that he was loved, and he experienced a security in the Winnicott home which he could take for granted. In a household of this size there were plenty of chances for many kinds of relationships, and there was scope for the inevitable tensions to be isolated and resolved within the total framework. From this basic position Donald was then free to explore all the available spaces in the house and garden around him and to fill the spaces with bits of himself and so gradually to make his world his own. This capacity *to be at home* served him well throughout his life. There is a pop song which goes, "Home is in my heart." That is certainly how Donald experienced it and this gave him an immense freedom which enabled him to feel at home anywhere. When we were traveling in France and staying in small wayside inns, at each place I would think to myself, "I wonder how long it will be before he's in the kitchen"—the kitchen of course being the centre of the establishment—and sure enough, he would almost always find his way there somehow. Actually, he loved kitchens, and when he was a child his mother complained that he spent more time with the cook in the kitchen than he did in the rest of the house.

Because Donald was so very much the youngest member of the Winnicott household (even the youngest boy cousin living opposite was older than he) and because he was so much loved, and was in himself lovable, it seems likely that a deliberate effort was made, particularly on the part of his mother and sisters, not to spoil him. While this did not deprive him of feeling loved, it did I think deprive him of some intimacy and closeness that he needed. But as Donald possessed (as do his sisters still) a natural ability to communicate with children of almost any age, the communication between children and adults in the Winnicott home must have been of a high order. Of course they all possessed an irrepressible sense of humor, and this, together with the happiness and safety of their background, meant that there were no "tragedies" in the Winnicott household—there were only amusing episodes. Not so many years ago, when the tank in the roof leaked, causing considerable flooding and damage, they were more excited and amused than alarmed by this unexpected happening.

At this point I should like to quote another page from Donald's autobiographical notes. Before doing so I should explain that the garden of the Winnicott home is on four levels. On the bottom level was the croquet lawn; then a steep slope (Mount Everest to a small child) leading to the pond level; next another slight slope leading to the lawn which was a tennis court; and, finally a flight of steps leading to the house level.

Now that slope up from the croquet lawn to the flat part where there is a pond and where there was once a huge clump of pampas grass between the weeping ash trees (by the way do you know what exciting noises a pampas grass makes on a hot Sunday afternoon, when people are lying out on rugs beside the pond, reading or snoozing?) That slope up is fraught, as people say, fraught with history. It was on that slope that I took my own private croquet mallet (handle about a foot long because I was only 3 years old) and I bashed flat the nose of the wax doll that belonged to my sisters and that had become a source of irritation in my life because it was over that doll that my father used to tease me. She was called Rosie. Parodying some popular song he used to say (taunting me by the voice he used)

> Rosie said to Donald
> I love you
> Donald said to Rosie
> I don't believe you do.

(Maybe the verses were the other way round, I forget) so I knew the doll had to be altered for the worse, and much of my life has been founded on the undoubted fact that I actually *did* this deed, not merely wished it and planned it.

I was perhaps somewhat relieved when my father took a series of matches and, warming up the wax nose enough, remoulded it so that the face once more became a face. This early demonstration of the restitutive and reparative act certainly made an impression on me, and perhaps made me able to accept the fact that I myself, dear innocent child, had actually become violent directly with a doll, but indirectly with my good-tempered father who was just then entering my conscious life.

Again, to quote further from the notebook:

Now my sisters were older than I, 5 and 6 years; so in a sense I was an only child with multiple mothers and with father extremely preoccupied in my younger years with town as well as business matters. He was mayor twice and was eventually knighted, and then was made a Freeman of the City (as it has now become) of Plymouth. He was sensitive about his lack of education (he had had learning difficulties) and he always said that because of this he had not aspired to Parliament, but had kept to local politics—lively enough in those days in far away Plymouth.

My father had a simple (religious) faith and once when I asked him a question that could have involved us in a long argument he just said: read the Bible and what you find there will be the true answer for you. So I was left, thank God, to get on with it myself.

But when (at 12 years) I one day came home to midday dinner and said "drat" my father looked pained as only he could look, blamed my mother for not seeing to it that I had decent friends, and from that moment he prepared himself to send me away to boarding school, which he did when I was 13.

"Drat" sounds very small as a swear word, but he was right; the boy who was my new friend was no good, and he and I could have got into trouble if left to our own devices.

The friendship was in fact broken up then and there and this show of strength on the part of his father was a significant factor in Donald's development. In his own words: "So my father was there to kill and be killed, but it is probably true that in the early years he left me too much to all my mothers. Things never quite righted themselves."

And so Donald went away to the Leys School, Cambridge, and was in his element. To his great delight the afternoons were free, and he ran, cycled and swam, played rugger, joined the School Scouts, and made friends and sang in the choir, and each night he read a story aloud to the boys in his dormitory. He read extremely well and years later I was to benefit from this accomplishment because we were never without a book that he was reading aloud to me, and one Christmas Eve sitting on the floor (we never sat on chairs) he read all night because the book was irresistible. He read in a dramatic way, savoring the writing to the full.

Donald described to me his going away to school. The whole family would be there to see him off, and he would wave and be sorry to leave until he was taken from their sight by the train's entering quite a long tunnel just outside Plymouth. All through this tunnel he settled down to the idea of leaving, but then out again the other side he left them behind and looked forward to going on to school. He often blessed that tunnel because he could honestly manage to feel sorry to leave right up to the moment of entering it.

I have in my possession a letter which Donald wrote to his mother from school which shows the kind of interplay that existed between members of the family:

My dearest Mother,

On September 2nd all true Scouts think of their mothers, since that was the birthday of Baden Powell's mother when she was alive.

And so when you get this letter I shall be thinking of you in particular, and I only hope you will get it in the morning.

But to please me very much I must trouble you to do me a little favour. Before turning over the page I want you to go up into my bedroom and in the right-hand cupboard find a small parcel. . . . . Now, have you opened it? Well I hope you will like it. You can change it at Pophams if you don't. Only if you do so, you must ask to see No. 1 who knows about it.

I have had a ripping holiday, and I cannot thank you enough for all you have done and for your donation to the Scouts.

My home is a beautiful home and I only wish I could live up to it. However I will do my best and work hard and that's all I can do at present.

D.W.W.: A REFLECTION

Clare Winnicott

The editors of this book have invited me to write something of a personal nature about the man whose observations and experience led to the concept of transitional objects and phenomena. In attempting to do this I shall need to select only those aspects of his life and personality that are relevant to the book. It could seem therefore as if these concepts arose naturally and easily out of D. W. W.'s own way of life. In one sense this is true; but it is only half the story. The rest concerns the periods of doubt, uncertainty and confusion, out of which form and meaning eventually emerged.

What was it about D. W. W. that made the exploration of this transitional area inevitable, and made his use of it clinically productive? I suggest that answers to these questions have to be looked for not simply in a study of the development of his ideas as he went along, but essentially in the kind of personality that was functioning behind them. He could be excited by other people's ideas, but could use them and build on them only after they had been through the refinery of his own experience. By that time, unfortunately, he had often forgotten the source, and he could, and did, alienate some people by his lack of acknowledgement. While other people's ideas enriched D. W. W. as a clinician and as a person, it was the working out of his own ideas that really absorbed him and that he grappled with to the end of his life. This was a creative process in which he was totally involved. In his clinical work D. W. W. made it his aim to enter into every situation undefended by his knowledge, so that he could be as exposed as possible to the impact of the situation itself. From his point of view this was the only way in which discovery was a possibility, both for himself and for his patients. This approach was more than a stance; it was an essential discipline, and it added a dimension to his life as vital to him as fresh air.

The question is sometimes asked as to why D. W. W. in his writings seemed mainly concerned with exploring the area of the first two-person relationship. Strictly speaking this is not true: he wrote on a wide range of topics, including adolescence and delinquency and other matters of medical and sociological concern, and the greater part of his psychoanalytic practice was with adults. However, it could be true to say that his main contribution is likely to turn out to be in the study of the earliest relationships, and its application to the etiology of psychosis and of the psychotic mechanisms in all of us. I suggest that his study took this direction from two sources. In the first place, he brought with him into psychoanalysis all that he had learnt and went on learning from pediatrics, and secondly, at the time he came to psychoanalysis the area of study just then opening up was that concerning the earliest experiences of life. Given his personality, his training and experience, and his urge for discovery, it seems inevitable that he would concentrate his researches on the so far comparatively unexplored area of earliest infancy and childhood. His findings, however, are recognised by many as having implications far beyond the immediate area of study. It is the expressed opinion of some that they throw light on all areas of living.

As I have suggested, the essential clue to D. W. W.'s work on transitional objects and phenomena is to be found in his own personality, in his way of relating and being related to, and in his whole life style. What I mean is that it was *his capacity to play* which never deserted him, that led him inevitably into the area of research that he conceptualised in terms of the transitional objects and phenomena. It is not my purpose here to discuss the details of his work, but it seems important to note that in his terms the capacity to play is equated with a *quality of living*. In his own words, "Playing is an experience, always a creative experience, and it is an experience in the space-time continuum, a basic form of living" (*Playing and Reality*, p. 50). This quality of living permeates all levels and aspects of experiencing and relating, up to and including the sophisticated level described in his paper "The Use of an Object" at which in his own words, "It is the destructive drive that creates the quality of externality"; and again,"this quality of 'always being destroyed' makes the reality of the surviving object felt as such, strengthens the feeling tone, and contributes to object constancy" (*Playing and Reality*, p. 93). For him, the destroying of the object in unconscious fantasy is like a cleansing process, which facilitates again and again the discovery of the object anew. It is a process of purification and renewal.

Having said that, I see my contribution to this book as an attempt to throw some light on D. W. W.'s capacity for playing. I expect that readers will be familiar enough with his writings on this subject to know that I am not talking about playing games. I am talking about the capacity for operating in the limitless intermediate area where external and internal reality are compounded into the experience of living. I hope I do not suggest that D. W. W. lived in a state of permanent elation because that was far from the case. He often found life hard and could be despondent and depressed and angry, but given time he could come through and encompass these experiences in his own way and free himself from being cluttered up with resentment and prejudices. During the last years of his life the reality of his own death had to be negotiated, and this he did, again gradually and in his own way. I was always urging him to write an autobiography because I felt that his style of writing would lend itself to such a task. He started to do this, but there are only a few pages, and typically he used this exercise to deal with his immediate problem of living, which was that of dying. I know he used it in this way because he kept this notebook to himself and I did not see it until after his death.

The title of the autobiography was to be *Not Less Than Everything* and the inner flap of the notebook reads as follows:

T. S. Eliot   "Costing not less than everything" [Little Gidding: *Four Quartets*]

T. S. Eliot   "What we call the beginning is often the end
And to make an end is to make a beginning.
The end is where we start from." [Little Gidding: *Four Quartets*]

Prayer

D. W. W.   Oh God! May I be alive when I die.

Following these words he started on the writing and it begins by imaginatively describing the end of his life. I shall quote his own words:

I died.

It was not very nice, and it took quite a long time as it seemed (but it was only a moment in eternity).

There had been rehearsals (that's a difficult word to spell. I found I had left out the "a." The hearse was cold and unfriendly.

When the time came I knew all about the lung heavy with water that the heart could not negotiate, so that not enough blood circulated in the alveoli, and there was oxygen starvation as well as drowning. But fair enough, I had had a good innings: mustn't grumble as our old gardener used to say. . . . .

Let me see. What was happening when I died? My prayer had been answered. I was alive when I died. That was all I had asked and I had got it. (This makes me feel awful because so many of my friends and contemporaries died in the first World War, and I have never been free from the feeling that my being alive is a facet of some one thing of which their deaths can be seen as other facets: some huge crystal, a body with integrity and shape intrinsical in it).

He then goes on to discuss the difficulty that a man has dying without a son to imaginatively kill and to survive him—"to provide the only continuity that men know. Women *are* continuous." This dilemma is discussed in terms of King Lear and his relationship to his daughters and in particular to the youngest daughter who should have been a boy.

I hope that these quotations give some idea of D. W. W.'s capacity to come to terms with internal and external reality in a playful way, which makes reality bearable to the individual, so that denial can be avoided and the experience of living can be as fully realized as possible. In his own words "playing can be said to reach its own saturation point, which refers to the capacity to contain experience " (*Playing and Reality*, p. 52). He was avid for experience and he would have hated to miss the inner experience of the reality of his own death, and he imaginatively achieved that experience. In conversation he would often refer to his deathday in a lighthearted way, but I knew that he was trying to get me and himself accustomed to the idea that it would come.

Having started at the end of his life, I must now go back to the beginnings and relate something about his earlier years and about the years that he and I spent together. I shall limit what I say to an attempt to illustrate the theme of playing, because that was central to his life and work.

First I must set the scene within which he grew up. It was an essentially English provincial scene in Plymouth, Devon, and it was far from London, not merely in mileage, but in custom and convention. When we drove to Plymouth from London he was always thrilled when we arrived at the place where the soil banked up at the side of the road changed in color to the red soil of Devon. The richness of the soil brought back the richness of his early life which he never lost touch with. Of course on the return journey, he was always equally pleased to be leaving it behind. But he was proud of being a Devonian, and that there is a village of Winnicott on the map of Devon. We never actually found the village, although we always meant to. It was enough that it was there.

The Winnicott household was a large and lively one with plenty of activity. But there was space for everyone in the large garden and house and there was no shortage of money. There was a vegetable garden, an orchard, a croquet lawn, a tennis court and a pond, and high trees

Give my love to the others: thank Dad for his games of billiards and V and K (sisters) for being so nice and silly so as to make me laugh. But, it being Mother's day, most love goes to you,
        from your loving boy
        Donald.

Some who read this abbreviated account of D. W. W.'s early life and family relationships may be inclined to think that it sounds too good to be true. But the truth is that it *was* good, and try as I will I cannot present it in any other light. Essentially he was a deeply happy person whose capacity for enjoyment never failed to triumph over the setbacks and disappointments that came his way. Moreover, there is a sense in which the quality of his early life and his appreciation of it did in itself present him with a major problem, that of freeing himself from the family, and of establishing his own separate life and identity without sacrificing the early richness. It took him a long time to do this.

It was when Donald was in the sick room at school, having broken his collar bone on the sports field, that he consolidated in his own mind the idea of becoming a doctor. Referring to that time he often said: "I could see that for the rest of my life I should have to depend on doctors if I damaged myself or became ill, and the only way out of this position was to become a doctor myself, and from then on the idea as a real proposition was always on my mind, although I know that father expected me to enter his flourishing business and eventually take over from him."

One of Donald's school friends, Stanley Ede (who remained a lifelong friend), had often stayed in the Winnicott household and was well known to all the family. Back at school after a visit to his home Donald, aged 16, wrote the following in a letter to the friend who had not yet returned to school:

Dear Stanley,
    Thank you so much for the lovely long letter you sent me in the week. It is awfully good of you to take such a lot of trouble and to want to. . . . .
    Father and I have been trying consciously and perhaps unconsciously to find out what the ambition of the other is in regard to my future. From what he had said I was *sure* that he wanted me more than anything else to go into his business. And so, again consciously and not, I have found every argument for the idea and have not thought much about anything else so that I should not be disappointed. And so I

have learned to cherish the business life with all my heart, and had intended to enter it and please my father and myself.

When your letter came yesterday you may have expected it to have disappointed me. But—I tell you all I feel—I was so excited that all the stored-up feelings about doctors which I have bottled up for so many years seemed to burst and bubble up at once. Do you know that—in the degree that Algy wanted to go into a monastery—I have for ever so long wanted to be a doctor. But I have always been afraid that my father did not want it, and so I have never mentioned it and—like Algy—even felt a repulsion at the thought.

This afternoon I went an eight mile walk to the Roman Road with Chandler, and we told each other all we felt, and especially I told him what I have told you now. O, Stanley!

> Your still sober and true—
> although seemingly intoxicated—
> but never-the-less devoted
> friend.
>   Donald.

It seems that Stanley, one year older than Donald, had taken the line that Donald should do what he himself wanted to do, and that he had offered to broach the question of Donald's future to his father and that he did so. There is a postcard to Stanley saying, "Thank you infinitely for having told father when and what you did. I have written Dad a letter which I think pretty nearly convinced him."

Donald recounts that when he summoned up courage to go to the Headmaster at school and tell him that he wanted to be a doctor, the Head grunted and looked at him long and hard before replying slowly: "Boy, not brilliant, but will do." And so he went to Jesus College, Cambridge, and took a degree in Biology. His room in College was popular as a meeting place, because he had hired a piano and played it unceasingly, and had a good tenor voice for singing.

But the first World War was on, and his first year as a medical student was spent helping in the Cambridge Colleges which had been turned into Military Hospitals. One of the patients, who became a lifelong friend remembers Donald in those days: "The first time I saw him was in hospital in Cambridge in 1916 in the first war; he was a medical student who liked to sing a comic song on Saturday evenings in the ward—and sang "Apple Dumplings" and cheered us all up."

It was a source of deep sorrow and conflict to Donald that all his friends went at once into the army, but that as a medical student he was exempt.

Many close friends were killed early in the war and his whole life was affected by this, because always he felt that he had a responsibility to live for those who died, as well as for himself.

The kind of relationship with friends that he had at that time in Cambridge is illustrated by a letter from a friend who had already joined up in the army and was on a course for officers in Oxford. It is written from Exeter College Oxford and dated 28/11/15:

What are you doing on Saturday for tea? Well, I'll tell you!! *You are going to provide a big Cambridge Tea for yourself, myself and Southwell* (of Caius) [Caius College Cambridge] whom you've met I think. He's a top-hole chap and has got a commission. If you haven't met him you ought to have, and anyway you've heard me speak of him.

Can you manage it? Blow footer etc. etc. or I'll blow you next time I see you. Try and manage it will you? Good man! It's sponging on you I know, but I also know you're a silly idiot and won't mind. Silly ass! Cheer O old son of a gun and get plenty of food.

Donald could not settle in Cambridge and was not satisfied until he was facing danger for himself, and, coming from Plymouth he of course wanted to go into the Navy. He applied for and was accepted as a Surgeon Probationer. He was drafted to a destroyer where he was one of the youngest men on board and the only Medical Officer in spite of his lack of training; fortunately, there was an experienced Medical Orderly. He was subject to a great deal of teasing in the Officers' Mess. Most of the officers had been through one or other of the Royal Naval Colleges and came from families with a naval tradition. They were astonished that Donald's father was a *merchant*. This was a novelty, and they made the most of it, and Donald seems to have made the most of their company and of the whole experience. He has often related with amusement the banter that went on at meal times. Although the ship was involved in enemy action and there were casualties, Donald had much free time, which he seems to have spent reading the novels of Henry James.

After the war Donald went straight to St. Bartholomew's Hospital in London to continue his medical training. He soaked himself in medicine and fully committed himself to the whole experience. This included writing for the hospital magazine and joining in the social life: singing sprees, dancing, occasional skiing holidays, and hurrying off at the last minute to hear operas for the first time, where he usually stood in his slippers at the back of the "Gods."

It is difficult to give any dates in relation to Donald's girl friends, but he had quite close attachments to friends of his sisters and later to others he met through his Cambridge friends. He came to the brink of marriage more than once but did not actually marry (for the first time) until the age of twenty-eight.

Donald had some great teachers at the hospital, and he always said that it was Lord Horder who taught him the importance of taking a careful case history, and to listen to what the patient said, rather than simply to ask questions. After qualification he stayed on at Bart's to work as Casualty Officer for a year. He literally worked almost all day and night but he would not have missed the experience for the world. It contained the challenge of the unexpected and provided the stimulation that he reveled in.

During his training Donald became ill with what turned out to be an abscess on the lung and was a patient in Bart's for three months. A friend who visited him there remembers it in these words: "It was a gigantic old ward with a high ceiling dwarfing the serried ranks of beds, patients and visitors. He was *intensely* amused and interested at being lost in a crowd and said 'I am convinced that every doctor ought to have been once in his life in a hospital bed as a patient.'"

Donald had always intended to become a general practitioner in a country area, but one day a friend lent him a book by Freud and so he discovered psychoanalysis; deciding that this was for him, he realized that he must therefore stay in London to undergo analysis. During his medical training he had become deeply interested in children's work and after taking his Membership examination, set up as a Consultant in Children's Medicine (there was no speciality in pediatrics in those days). In 1923 he obtained two hospital appointments, at The Queen's Hospital for Children and at Paddington Green Children's Hospital. The latter appointment he held for forty years. The development of his work at Paddington Green is a story in itself, and many colleagues from all over the world visited him there. Because of his own developing interests and skills over the years, his clinic gradually became a psychiatric clinic, and he used to refer to it as his "Psychiatric Snack Bar" or his clinic for dealing with parents' hypochondria. In 1923 he also acquired a room in the Harley Street area and set up a private consultant practice.

At the beginning he found Harley Street formidable because he had few patients, so in order to impress the very dignified porter who opened the door to patients for all the doctors in the house, he tells how he used to pay the fares of some of his hospital mothers and children so that they could visit him in Harley Street. Of course this procedure was not entirely on behalf of the porter, because he selected cases in which he was particularly interested and to which he wanted to give more time so that he could begin to explore the psychological aspects of illness.

The sheer pressure of the numbers attending his hospital clinics must have been important to him as an incentive to explore as fully as he did how to use the doctor-patient *space* as economically as possible for the therapeutic task. The ways in which he did this have been described in his writing.

However, there is one detail he does not describe, and which I observed both at his Paddington Green Clinic and in his work with evacuee children in Oxfordshire during the last war. He attempted to round off and make significant a child's visit to him by giving the child something to take away which could afterwards be used and/or destroyed or thrown away. He would quickly reach for a piece of paper and fold it into some shape, usually a dart or a fan, which he might play with for a moment and then give to the child as he said goodbye. I never saw this gesture refused by any child. It could be that this simple symbolic act contained the germ of ideas he developed in the "Use of an Object" paper written at the end of his life. There could also be a link here with the transitional object concept.

In attempting to give some idea of D.W.W.'s capacity to play, which in my view was central to his life and work, I have somehow slipped into an historical or biographical sequence of writing without intending to do so. This is in no way meant to be a biography. What I have been trying to do is to illustrate how he related to people at different stages of his life and in different situations. But I must now abandon the historical perspective which so far protected me, and bring him briefly into focus for myself and in relation to our life together. From now on "he" becomes "we" and I cannot disentangle us.

Many years ago a visitor staying in our home looked round thoughtfully and said: "You and Donald *play*." I remember being surprised at this new light that had been thrown on us. We had certainly never *set out* to play, there was nothing self-conscious and deliberate about it. It seems just to have happened that we lived that way, but I could see what our visitor meant. We played with *things*—our possessions—rearranging, acquiring, and discarding according to our mood. We played with ideas, tossing them about at random with the freedom of knowing that we need not agree, and that we were strong enough not to be hurt by each other. In fact the question of hurting each other did not arise because we were operating in the play area where everything is permissible. We each possessed a capacity for enjoyment, and it could take over in the most unlikely places and lead us into exploits we could not have anticipated. After Donald's death an American friend described us as "two crazy people who delighted each other and delighted their friends." Donald would have been pleased with this accolade, so reminiscent of his words: "We are poor indeed if we are only sane" (*Collected Papers*, p. 150, fn.).

Early in our relationship I had to settle for the idea that Donald was, and always would be, completely unpredictable in our private life, except for his punctuality at meal times, and the fact that he never failed to meet me at the station when I had been away. This unpredictability had its advantages, in that we could never settle back and take each other for granted in day-to-day living. What we could take for granted was something more basic that I can only describe as our recognition and acceptance of each other's separateness. In fact the strength of our unity lay in this recognition, and implicit in it is an acceptance of the unconscious ruthless and destructive drives which were discussed as the final development of his theories in the "Use of an Object" paper. Our separateness left us each free to do our own thing, to think our own thoughts, and possess our own dreams, and in so doing to strengthen the capacity of each of us to experience the joys and sorrows which we shared.

There were some things that were especially important to us, like the Christmas card that Donald drew each year, and which we both painted in hundreds, staying up until 2 A.M. in the days before Christmas. I remember once suggesting to him that the drawing looked better left as it was in black and white. He said, "Yes, I know, but I like painting." There were his endless squiggle drawings which were part of his daily routine. He would play the game with himself and produced some very fearful and some very funny drawings, which often had a powerful integrity of their own. If I was away for a night he would send a drawing through the post for me to receive in the morning, because my part in all this was to enjoy and appreciate his productions, which I certainly did, but sometimes I could wish that there were not quite so many of them.

Donald's knowledge and appreciation of music was a joy to both of us, but it was of particular importance to me because he introduced me to much that was new. He always had a special feeling for the music of Bach but at the end of his life it was the late Beethoven string quartets that absorbed and fascinated him. It seems as if the refinement and abstraction in the musical idiom of these works helped him to gather in and realise in himself the rich harvest of a lifetime. On quite another level he also greatly enjoyed the Beatles and bought all their recordings. Donald never had enough time to develop his own piano playing, but he would often dash up to the piano and play for a moment between patients, and invariably he celebrated the end of a day's work by a musical outburst fortissimo. He enjoyed the fact that I knew more about the poets than he did, and that I could say a Shakespeare sonnet or some Dylan Thomas or T.S. Eliot to him on demand. He particularly enjoyed Edward Lear's "The Owl and the Pussycat" and couldn't hear it often enough. In the end he memorized it himself.

Our favorite way of celebrating or of simply relaxing was to dress up and go out to a long, unhurried dinner in a candle-lit dining room not so far from where we lived. In the early days sometimes we danced. I remember him looking around this room one evening and saying: "Aren't we lucky. We still have things to say to each other."

For years two T.V. programs that we never missed were "Come Dancing" (a display of all kinds of ballroom dancing) and "Match of the Day," which was the reshowing of the best football or rugger match each Saturday, or in the summer it would be tennis.

I think that the only times when Donald actually showed that he was angry with me were on occasions when I damaged myself or became ill. He hated to have me as a patient, and not as his wife and playmate. He showed this one day when I damaged my foot and it became bruised and swollen. We had no crêpe bandage so he said he would go and buy one and I was to lie down until he returned. He was away for two hours and came back pleased with a gold expanding bracelet he had bought for me—but he had forgotten the bandage.

I was always speculating about Donald's own transitional object. He did not seem to remember one specifically, until suddenly he was able to get into touch with it. He described the experience to me in a letter written early in 1950: "Last night I got something quite unexpected, through dreaming, out of what you said. Suddenly you joined up with the nearest thing I can get to my transition object: it was something I have always known about but I lost the memory of it, at this moment I became conscious of it. There was a very early doll called Lily belonging to my younger sister and I was fond of it, and very distressed when it fell and broke. After Lily I hated *all* dolls. But I always knew that before Lily was a quelquechose of my own. I knew retrospectively that it must have been a doll. But it had never occurred to me that it wasn't just like myself, a person, that is to say it was a kind of other me, and a not-me female, and part of me and yet not, and absolutely inseparable from me. I don't know what happened to it. If I love you as I loved this (must I say?) doll, I love you all out. And I believe I do. Of course I love you all sorts of other ways, but this thing came new at me. I felt enriched, and felt once more like going on writing my paper on transition objects (postponed to October). (You don't mind do you—this about you and the T.O.?)."

It would not be right to give the impression that Donald and I shared only experiences that lay outside our work. It was our work that brought us together in the first place, and it remained central, and bound us inextricably together. Writing to me in December 1946 he said "In odd moments I have written quite a lot of the paper for the Psychoanalytical Society in February, and I spend a lot of time working it out. My work is really quite a lot associated with you. Your effect on me is to make me keen and productive and this is all the more awful—because when I am cut off from you I feel paralyzed for all action and originality."

In fact each of us was essential to the work of the other. During Donald's lifetime we worked in different spheres, and this was an added interest extending the boundaries of our joint existence. We were fortunate that through the years a wide circle of people came to be intimately included in our lives and work, and we in theirs. This was a strong binding force for all concerned because it provided the community of interest which is the pre-requisite for creative living. How lucky we were in those who shared our lives; how much we owe to them, and how much we enjoyed their company.

Throughout his life Donald never ceased to be in touch with his dream world and to continue his own analysis. It was the deep undercurrent of his life, the orchestral accompaniment to the main theme. His poem called "Sleep" is relevant here:

> Let down your tap root
> to the centre of your soul
> Suck up the sap
> from the infinite source
> of your unconscious
> And
> Be evergreen.

To conclude, I want to relate a dream about Donald which I had two and a half years after his death.

I dreamt that we were in our favorite shop in London, where there is a circular staircase to all floors. We were running up and down these stairs grabbing things from here, there, and everywhere as Christmas presents for our friends. We were really having a spending spree, knowing that as usual we would end up keeping many of the things ourselves. I suddenly realized that Donald was alive after all and I thought with relief, "Now I shan't have to worry about the Christmas card." Then we were sitting in the restaurant having our morning coffee as usual (in fact we always went out to morning coffee on Saturday). We were facing each other, elbows on the table, and I looked at him full in the face and said: "Donald there's something we have to say to each other, some truth that we have to say, what is it?" With his very blue eyes looking unflinchingly into mine he said: "That this is a dream." I replied slowly: "Oh yes, of course, you died, you died a year ago." He reiterated my words: "Yes, I died a year ago."

For me it was through this dream of playing that life and death, his and mine, could be experienced as a reality.

CHAPTER 3

D.W. WINNICOTT AND THE TWO-WAY JOURNEY

Marion Milner

Often, when I talked to people about D.W. Winnicott they would say, "Oh, but of course, he was a genius." I do not know what makes a genius. All I know is that I must take as my text for this paper something he once said to his students just before a lecture: "What you get out of me, you will have to pick out of chaos."

I want to describe the highlights of my contacts with him in matters of theory. I find this particularly hard to do, because I am one of those people who Freud reminded us exist, people who think in pictures. So what I want to say about Winnicott must center around certain visual images.

One night in 1957, driving through France, I saw a crowd in the marketplace of a little town, all gathered around an arc lamp where a trapeze had been set up by traveling acrobats. The star performers were there, in spotless white, doing wonderful turns and handstands on the bar. Below them was a little clown in a grey floppy coat too big for him, just fooling around while the others did their displays. Occasionally he made a fruitless attempt to jump up and reach the bar. Then, suddenly, he made a great leap and there he was, whirling around on the bar, all his clothes flying out, like a huge Catherine wheel, to roars of delight from the crowd.

This is my image of Winnicott. Often over the years when we had a gap of time and arranged to meet to discuss some theoretical problem, he would open the door, and there he would be, all over the place, whistling, forgetting something, running upstairs, making a general clatter, so that I would become impatient for him to settle down. Gradually, I came to see this as a necessary preliminary to those fiery flashes of his intuition that would always follow. He has actually written about the logic of this in one of his papers, where he talks of the necessity, when doing an analysis, of recognizing and allowing for phases of nonsense, when no thread ought to be searched for in the patient's material because what is going on is preliminary chaos, the first phase of the creative process.

After the whirling clown on the bar comes another image, an actual
Catherine wheel firework, nailed to a tree and lit by a small boy, in the
still dark of the countryside. The wheel at first splutters and misfires,
then gets going as a fizzing, fiery ring of light, sending off sparks into the
darkness around. I always have an image of the dark disk at the center
whenever I read in his writings about the unknowable core of the self.

My third image, woven into my thoughts for this chapter, is part of a
shared joke we had. During the war I had shown him a cartoon from the
New Yorker. It was of two hippopotamuses, their heads emerging from the
water, and one saying to the other, "I thought it was Thursday." It was
typical of him that he never forgot this joke. After all these years, I see
how it fits in with a dominant preoccupation of mine—the threshhold of
consciousness, the surface of the water as the place of submergence or
emergence.

And from this picture of the water's surface I come to one of his
images, that is, the quotation from Tagore that he put at the head of his
paper "The Location of Cultural Experience" (Winnicott 1971b): "On the
sea-shore of endless worlds children play." I too have had this line at the
back of my mind, ever since I first read it in 1915. Winnicott said that, for
him, the aphorism aided speculation upon the question, If play is neither
inside nor outside, where is it? For me it stirred thoughts of the coming
and going of the tides, the rhythmic daily submergence and smoothing
out of this place where children play.

Later in this paper about the place of cultural experience he uses
another image that we both had in common—only I had completely
forgotten about it. He is talking about how the baby comes to be able to
make use of the symbol of union and can begin to allow for and benefit
from separation, a separation that is not a separation, but a form of
union; and here he refers to a drawing that I had made, long ago in the
thirties, showing the interplay of the edges of two jugs. He says the
drawing conveyed to him the tremendous significance there can be in the
interplay of edges.

I too found myself using this same drawing as a visual symbol for his
concept of potential space. And it still has many overtones for me, since a
patient of mine used it constantly, in the more abstract form of two
overlapping circles which become two faces and then oscillate between
being two and being one.

So much for the images. Now for the actuality.

I first saw Winnicott when he was giving a public lecture in the late
thirties, talking about his work with mothers and babies and the famous
spatula game. He told how he would leave a spatula on the table in front

of the mother and baby, well within the baby's reach. Then he simply watched what the baby did with the spatula, watched for variations in the normal pattern of reaching for it, grabbing it, giving it a good suck and then chucking it away. He told how, out of this very simple experimental situation, he could work out, according to the observed blocks in the various stages, a diagnosis of the problems between the mother and the baby. As he talked, I was captivated by the mixture in him of deep seriousness and his love of little jokes, that is, the play aspect of his character, if one thinks of true play as transcending the opposites of serious and nonserious.

It was after this lecture that I began to attend his clinic as an observer, and I well remember the pleasure he took in this spatula game. I feel it was the neatness that satisfied both the artist and the scientist in the man, the formal qualities so simple and clear, providing a structure within which he made his observations. And this same feeling for aesthetic form continued in his therapeutic use with children of what he called the squiggle game. In fact, as described in his book on the subject (1971), he used these games to structure the therapeutic consultations. Each account of those drawing sessions with the child exemplifies as well his beautiful concept of potential space—an essentially pictorial concept, although he defines it as "what happens between two people when there is trust and reliability." Thus there is also the way the account of each session organizes time. Time stretches back, not only through the child's lifetime, but also through Winnicott's own years of psychoanalytic practice, so that he has at his fingertips the tools of psychoanalytic concepts, though using them here in a different setting.

Then there is what I have gained from his concept of the holding environment. I will not say much about this, for I have already given it extensive form in my book about a patient's drawings, having even embodied the idea in my title: *The Hands of the Living God* (Milner 1969). The phrase is in fact taken from a poem by D.H. Lawrence, a poem in which Lawrence describes the ghastly feelings of terror at falling forever when contact with the inner holding environment is lost.

I would in addition like to say something about Winnicott's comment, in his paper on play (1971a), on my 1952 paper on the play of a boy patient. Near the beginning of his paper Winnicott points out that I have related playing to concentration in adults, and that he has done the same thing. A little later he quotes my remark about "moments when the original poet in us created the world for us perhaps forgotten . . . because they were too much like visitations of the gods" (Milner 1952). His quoting this reminded me that one of the jumping-off places for my paper had been a growing preoccupation with certain moments in the boy's play, moments which seemed to both express and be accompanied by a special kind of concentration, moments actually symbolized, it seemed to me, by his continual play with lighted candles and fires in the dark, as well as by explicit play concerning visitations of the gods. All this seems to me now to link up with what Winnicott came to call "creative apperception," the coloring of external reality in a new way, a way that can give a feeling of great significance and can in fact, as he claims, make life feel worth living, even in the face of much instinct deprivation.

I realized too that this starting point for that paper of mine had also been the starting point for the first book I ever wrote, a book based on a diary I kept in 1926, about the sudden moments when one's whole perception of the world changes—changes that happen, sometimes apparently out of the blue, but sometimes as the result of a deliberate shift of attention, one that makes the whole world seem newly created. Although when I became an analyst I tried to fit these experiences into such psychoanalytic concepts as manic defenses against depression and so on, these ideas did not seem quite adequate to account for the phenomena. But then I found Winnicott making the distinction between the vicissitudes of instinct and what happens in creativity, which for him was the same as creative playing. This seemed to offer a more useful approach. Not that I found his way of putting his ideas about creativity entirely easy: sometimes he seemed to be talking about a way of looking at the world, sometimes about a way of doing something deliberately, and sometimes about simply enjoying a bodily activity, breathing, for instance, that just happens. I asked myself: In what sense are these all creative? Certainly they are different, as he says, from the making of anything, such as a house or a meal or a picture, though all these may include what he is talking about. Then I happened upon a statement that helped me clarify the problem. It was Martin Buber's remark about "productivity versus immediacy of the lived life." He was referring to what he called the dominant delusion of our time, that creativity (meaning, I supposed, *artistic* creativity) is the criterion of human worth. Buber went on to say that "the potentiality of form also accompanies every experience that befalls the nonartistic man and is given an issue as often as he lifts an image out of the stream of perception and inserts it into his memory as something single, definite and meaningful in itself" (Buber 1969). This phrase—lifting an image out of the stream of perception—clearly related to Winnicott's comment, "What you get out of me you must pick out of chaos." Thus one gets the idea of creativeness as not simply perceiving, but as deliberately relating ourselves to our perceiving. It is a perceiving that has an "I AM" element in it. And this brings me to Winnicott's use of the word *self*.

First, what does he say about the way self comes into being? He claims that the sense of self comes only from desultory formless activity or rudimentary play, and then only if reflected back; he adds that it is only in being creative that one discovers oneself. I have a difficulty here. I can understand him when he claims that the sense of self comes on the basis of the unintegrated state, but when he adds that this state is by definition not observable or communicable, I begin to wonder. Not communicable, yes. Not observable, I am not so sure. I think of the dark still center of the whirling Catherine wheel and feel fairly certain that it can, in the right setting, be related to by the conscious ego discovering that it can turn in upon itself, make contact with the core of its own being, and find there a renewal, a rebirth. In fact isn't Winnicott himself referring to this when he speaks of "quietude linked with stillness"? This reminds me of T.S. Eliot's "still point of the turning world" or "words after speech reach into silence."

Linked to this question of the discovery of the self is surely the discovery of one's own body. So the question arises, What is the relation of the sense of being, which Winnicott says must precede the finding of the self, to the awareness of one's own body? I think there is a hint about this when he speaks of the "summation or reverberation of experiences of relaxation in conditions of trust based on experience." For me this phrase stirs echoes throughout years of observation of how deliberate bodily relaxation brings with it, if one can wait for it, a reverberation from inside, something spreading in waves, something that brings an intense feeling of response from that bit of the outer world that is at the same time also oneself: one's own body. Here is what I think he means when he speaks of enjoying one's own breathing as an example of creativity.

As for his statements concerning the first toy, which he says we do not challenge as to its coming from inside or from outside (Winnicott 1953), these serve as a bridge for me, particularly to the special cultural field of religion. When I encounter, in a book entitled *The God I Want* (Williams 1967), the idea that to discover God as myself is also to discover Him as other than myself, when I read that receiving implies otherness and that at the same time what we receive is our own, I am reminded of the creative paradox so dear to Winnicott. And when he speaks of the transitional object as the symbol of a journey, it seems really to be a two-way journey: both to the finding of the objective reality of the object and to the finding of the objective reality of the subject—the I AM.

There was, as well as this word *creativity* and all its implications, another term that, since the late forties, had given me a lot of uneasiness, like a shoe beginning to feel too tight. The term was *primary process*. I had been taught that this was a form of archaic thinking that had to be outgrown. But slowly, over the years, *primary process* seems to have changed its meaning, so that it is now seen, certainly by some writers, as part of the integrating function of the ego: that is, it serves to join up experiences and assimilate them into the ego, in order to preserve the ego's wholeness. As such it is not something to be grown out of, but, rather, is complementary to secondary process functioning and as necessary to it as male and female are to each other. It is this primary process that enables one to accept paradox and contradiction, something that secondary process does not like at all, being itself bound by logic, which rejects contradiction. Although Winnicott hardly ever uses the term, I feel that given this new meaning, the concept of primary process is implicit in all of his work and integral to his idea of what it means to be healthy.

So what the hippopotamus joke means to me now is this: One must not try to make the hippo live only on land, because it is, by nature, incurably amphibious. And whatever it means to say that someone is a genius, I do wish to make clear that I believe Winnicott was on excellent terms with his primary process; it was an inner marriage to which there was very little impediment.

REFERENCES

Buber, M. (1969). *The Healthy Personality*, Readings edited by Hung-min Chiang and A. Maslow. London: Van Nostrand, Reinhold.

Milner, M., (1951). *On Not Being Able to Paint*. New York: International Universities Press, 1973.

——— (1952). Aspects of symbolism in comprehension of the not-self. *International Journal of Psycho-Analysis* 33:181–195.

——— (1969). *The Hands of the Living God*. London: Hogarth.

Williams, I.H.A., (1967). *The God I Want* (ed. James Mitchell). London: Constable.

Winnicott, D.W. (1953). Transitional objects and transitional phenomena. In *Collected Papers*. New York: Basic Books, 1958.

——— (1971a). Playing: a theoretical statement. In *Playing and Reality*. New York: Basic Books.

——— (1971b). The location of cultural experience. In *Playing and Reality*. New York: Basic Books.

——— (1971c). *Therapeutic Consultations in Child Psychiatry*. New York: Basic Books.

CHAPTER 4

Susan Deri contrasts Freud's dualistic conflict orientation with Winnicott's more dialectical developmental emphasis. While not unmindful of Freud's continued attempts at monistic formulations (André Green has recently noted that the drive concept is itself a bridge between psyche and soma; the 1895 Project is another case in point), Deri here elects to explain their differences in the framework of the topographic model, making frequent use of the terms *conscious, unconscious,* and *preconscious.* Agreeing with Lawrence Kubie, she thinks preconscious space the most helpful metaphor in understanding the genesis of the symbolic process and its later vicissitudes. Winnicott's developmental observations can be seen as additions to the structural, genetic, and adaptive points of view—an opinion shared by Albert Flarsheim in chapter 30.

In Deri's view, as in Kestenberg's (chapter 6) and Gaddini's (chapter 8), playing, inherent in the nursing situation, is utilized adaptively throughout development. The growing capacity for illusion and a creative symbolic world is correlated with developing ego strength; as differentiation proceeds, the corresponding ability to create transitional objects is dependent upon developing ego functions. These interwoven processes are facilitated by good enough mothering.

In a related chapter Gilbert Rose shows how creativity is used in everyday life for reality testing and adaptation, and how it contributes to the richness of our experience. Both he and Deri emphasize how the bridging of inner and outer reality includes the importance of the inanimate world, an idea developed extensively by Harold Searles in his *The Nonhuman Environment.*

L.B.

TRANSITIONAL PHENOMENA: VICISSITUDES OF SYMBOLIZATION AND CREATIVITY

Susan Deri

> If I assume that it is the smiling face and the guiding voice of
> infantile parent images which religion projects onto the
> benevolent sky, I have no apologies to render to an age
> which thinks of painting the moon red. Peace comes from
> the inner space.
> —Erik Erikson, Epilogue to *Young Man Luther*

The creative principle in human life, specifically as it derives from the
earliest relationship between infant and mother, deserves specific
consideration. Creativity is not treated systematically in the classical
psychoanalytic literature, where it tends to be subsumed as one method
of instinctual aim displacement under the heading of sublimation. It was
Winnicott who, within the framework of psychoanalysis, first appreciated the human urge for creativity from its earliest infantile manifestations to its highest forms in cultural life.

Freud's theory of mental functioning, based on the concept of tension-
reduction, can and should be synthesized with the theoretical stance
which sees the fundamental function of the human mind in the
organismic tendency toward form development. Since Winnicott is the
only psychoanalyst who represents the latter theory, this chapter will
concentrate on his contributions to the theory of the individual's healthy
development. Implications of this theory concerning the technique and
goals of psychoanalytic treatment can be drawn, but will be dealt with in
an expanded version of the present chapter.

I

Let us now examine Winnicott's contributions. Instead of debating
Freud's declared principles, Winnicott unfailingly picked out the gaps in
Freud's conceptual world and realized these "potential spaces" by filling
them with his own conceptual world. The gaps correspond to the lack of

certain concepts or categories of experience in Freud's theories—and possibly in his life.

A case in point is Winnicott's interest in how the enjoyment and love of reality come about, versus Freud's stress on the necessity to accept and adapt to reality. Another gap in Freudian theory was filled with the new concept of the "environmental mother" (versus the mother as the object of instinctual cravings). However, more important than other differences between the two men, and consequently between the two psychologies they offer, are their differing attitudes toward the possibility and desirability of mixing opposites, particularly features of inner and outer reality.

The question of inside-subjective versus outside-objective reality is of great concern to both Freud and Winnicott. While Freud concentrated on ascertaining the most effective methods of discriminating between the two, Winnicott delights in showing how well these two universes harmonize, intermingled within the same act, the same perception, or the same physical object. The word *real* is used by Freud only in referring to what is outside. The act of judgment, Freud (1925) says, must decide whether the thought refers to something "real," i.e., to something "out there," or to something "not real," to a product of the imagination. Freud certainly realized more than anyone before him the very "real" effects of fantasies, even unconscious fantasies, upon the individual's actual life; yet his dichotomizing Cartesian weltanschauung precluded the possibility of coining or using concepts of mixed category. Compare Freud's Cartesian strictness, his division of inside and outside, with the following quotations from Winnicott:

> In respect to these transitional objects the parents, as it were, conspire not to challenge the origin. They easily see that the thumb is part of the child and that the next toy or teddy bear or doll is a gift, but with regard to the object in question they undertake to refrain from challenging the infant as to its origin. There is madness here which is permissible. . . . The madness is that this object is created by the infant and *also* it was there in the environment for the infant's use. [Preface to Stevenson 1954]

In his original paper on transitional objects and phenomena (1953) the summary ends as follows:

> What emerges from these considerations is the further idea that paradox accepted can have positive value. The resolution of paradox leads to a defense organization which in the adult one can encounter as true and false self organization.

One more quotation (1953) and Winnicott's point should be clear:

> This intermediate area of experience, unchallenged in respect of its belonging to inner or external (shared) reality, constitutes the greater part of the infant's experience, and throughout life is retained in the intense experiencing that belongs to the arts and to religion and to imaginative living and to creative scientific work.

For Winnicott, creativity was not the production of art objects, but a "coloring of the whole attitude to external reality. ... It is creative-appreciation more than anything else that makes the individual feel that life is worth living" (1971, p. 65). These statements imply important new aims for psychoanalysis as well as a conception of mental health truly different from that of Freud.

Freud acknowledged that he felt unable to experience "aesthetic emotion," that his main interest in the visual arts was the subject matter (1914). He added that he "was almost incapable of obtaining any pleasure from music." I find this last statement particularly interesting because, as Susanne Langer (1942) writes, music is pure form; whatever the content might be, it is totally expressed through its form. Freud's interest, on the other hand, was always the *hidden*; the immediately perceivable in art or dreams was considered a "surface" or "disguise." The creative aspect of the manifest dream escaped him. Music eluded him, very possibly because no "surface" can be lifted without eliminating the whole work. On the other hand, the central significance that art held for Winnicott might well have been a subjective source of the development of his theory of transitional phenomena.

His insights regarding the significance of the very first physical contact between mother and child probably derived from the fact that most of his patients seem to have been borderline characters. These are patients with "unthinkable anxieties," patients who feel lost in the world, who do not develop a sense of having an "inside." Thus Winnicott observed a group of patients very different from those who led Freud to a theory of neurosis centering on the role of internal conflict.

II

I shall try now to deal with Winnicott's developmental theory and show how the mother's good versus bad management of each phase affects good or bad symbolization and creativity. However, the actual mother is not the only factor that influences the child's total development. He has his own constitutional, genetic givens, and we never know how much weight to ascribe to the genetic or environmental factors in the course of human development. It is safe to assume that the two extremes on the continuum, the seriously autistic child and the future creative genius, develop principally on the basis of their constitutional givens, relatively independent of their mother's management of their early life space. Beethoven's or Leonardo's genius may be influenced by but cannot be derived from early mother-infant interaction. In the case of autism, the mother can sometimes be trained to provide therapeutic guidance to compensate for her child's deficiencies (unfortunately, however, with autistic children, even the best professional treatment is not always successful). On the other hand, with a child of "average to talented" genetic endowment, certain aspects of the mother's care, as described below, will be most influential in facilitating or thwarting the satisfactory growth of life-creating activities.

The stage of dual-union. In the first phase, the infant and the mother are usually assumed to form an undifferentiated unit. I believe the term *dual-union* (Hermann 1936) is more appropriate. The function of the "good enough" mother in this stage is to protect the sense of unity and continuity of the infant's existence. For this purpose, the mother's empathic ability to treat the baby in harmony with his own biological rhythm is crucial. If hunger need is allowed to reach a certain point of tension, then the infant's sense of unity will be disrupted. Chaotic, ragelike discharge reactions can be assumed to accompany the experience of fragmentation or panic (it is hard to find words for the earliest life experiences). Besides the timing of feedings, tactile-kinesthetic communication is the most important determinant of the infant's well-being or lack of same. The infant's skin is the first concrete boundary or interface between him and the world. The rhythm, the intensity, and the undefinable ways of communicating love through touching and holding will determine whether this skin boundary is felt as good (as a source of pleasure) or as bad (as a source of discomfort). And the latter alternative is quite possibly the origin of not feeling at home either in one's skin or in the world. The "holding mother" is a salient concept in Winnicott's refreshingly concrete terminology. A mother who holds well gives her infant a feeling of unity within his skin (see Kestenberg, this volume). Loving and secure holding will lay the foundation for basic trust; bad-holding, for distrust and "unthinkable anxieties," such as sensations of falling into a bottomless abyss.

This stage might be decisive for the subsequent capacity for and love of symbolization. A libidinally cathected skin surface will pleasantly delineate the inside from the outside. Communication between the two areas lying on either side of the boundary will be felt as desirable; and symbolization *is* communication across a boundary (Deri 1965, 1974). A comfortingly wrapped up inside will lead to the experience of a good inner space (Erikson 1950). Later this inner space will be denoted as the mind, which, in terms of the "topographic model," (the model best suited for discussing symbolization), corresponds to the preconscious.[1] I also believe that the development of a "rich or poor" preconscious will depend on the primordial feeling quality in which the (equally primordial) inner space is experienced. Specifically, the process of internalization will be influenced by the feeling in which the infant experiences his inside. That an enjoyable sense of the outside facilitates the ease and quality of introjection goes without saying; but something is often overlooked: the feeling tone in which the inside is experienced is crucial for the *outcome* of introjective processes. If the inside is a good place, then it is worthwhile to fill it with good things. The internalized things, which are symbolic representations of outside objects, might also become imbued with the good qualities of the space in which they are stored.

The self's positive relationship to the preconscious—so crucial for healthily functioning symbolization—might well be rooted in the earliest tactile experiences offered to the infant by the holding mother. The borderline patient's feeling of emptiness, of no inside, of a lack of trust in the smooth functioning of his mind can have sources traceable to the earliest psychosomatic insecurities experienced in the arms of the nonempathic "holding mother."

The stage of hallucinatory wish fulfillment. We must assume at this stage that the structuring of the infant's mind has begun; otherwise hallucinatory wish fulfillment could not be hypothesized. Freud postulates this situation in the following terms: high need-tension present, but need-gratifying object (breast) absent. Through primary process functioning, the wish cathects the memory image of the breast with hallucinatory intensity. Freud explains this phenomenon by the primary need for tension discharge.

Winnicott (1958), on the other hand, describes the same phenomenon differently: "The creative potential of the individual arising out of need produces readiness for an hallucination. . . . The mother's love and her close identification with her infant make her aware of the infant's needs to the extent that she provides something . . . in the right place at the right time. This . . . starts off the infant's ability to use *illusion*, without which no contact is possible between the psyche and the environment." The empathic mother places the breast just where and when the infant created the illusion. In this manner, the mother facilitates the *illusion* that his need has created the breast. The infant at this point of development has only a vague sense of an inside and an outside. The mother's optimal adaptation to the infant's needs provides him with the *illusion* of an outside world that corresponds to his needs and to his capacity to create. The mother's ability to offer her breast at the height of the child's mounting need-tension provides him with the experience of magical control over the objects of the world. Winnicott believes that without this "primary illusion" of omnipotence, the growing infant and child cannot enjoy reality. Frustration can teach him to perceive and adapt to reality, but only the experience of fulfillment, coming from the outside but magically "created" by his wish, can foster a true love of reality.

In other words, a good mother's empathic provision of her breast offers her baby the world as a friendly, fulfilling place. The world will be cathected positively, and so will the act of wishing. Here is a good beginning for an optimistic, trusting attitude to the surround and a motivated connectedness toward its objects. The pleasure of "primary illusion" is likely to lead to the capacity for symbolic perception that lends rich coloring to seemingly ordinary objects. This does not imply a delusional attitude to the world, since, in the subsequent phases, good mothering inevitably includes well-dosed failures of gratification that allow reality perception and reality adaptation to develop.

The first self-created image leading to the absent need/love-object can be called the first protosymbol. It is at this point of mental development that Winnicott sees the origin of what he calls intermediate or transitional space. It is transitional between dream and reality, between inside and outside, the person and his environment. It is par excellence the dimension of connectedness or, even better, of mutual immanence. This is the space for creative symbol-formation, because it is the function of symbols to connect and unite opposites. This transitional space, a space for connectedness, accounts for an order in the world based on an *inner relatedness* instead of the Cartesian principle of dividedness. The processes taking place within this intermediate space eliminate the disruption of the life space between the person and his environment. The construction of the concept of transitional space and its value for mental health is Winnicott's unique contribution to psychoanalysis.

Thus, we can see how much the future vicissitudes of symbolization and creativity, activities conceptually localized in this intermediate space, will depend on the manner in which the mother hands over the world to the child. The paradigm of the "primary illusion" implies that new objects should be introduced into the child's life space so that he is provided with the experience that his wish virtually created them. How many times do we hear patients complain "they never gave me things I wanted *when* I really wanted them. By the time I got it, it didn't matter to me anymore." These are the children who always feel deprived, while their parents feel unappreciated; parental giving is poorly synchronized with the child's wishes. The result is a disruption between the child and the surrounding inanimate world as well as between him and his parents. The child can cease to wish, and his surroundings will feel meaningless, filled with useless, dead objects. Nothing will light up as a positive valence to strive for; this is the arid world of the anhedonic borderline character. Without the ability to formulate wishes, there can be no creativity. These eternally unfulfilled children do not know *how* to fulfill themselves, because there is no fulfilling, giving mother to be internalized. They will turn into angry, unhappy, alienated adults. Even if they are constitutionally endowed with creative talent, it cannot be used pleasurably. The dominance of destructive anger over Eros will prevent the creative formation of raw material into good Gestalts. Instead of containing usable wishes (a category connected to the functioning of the preconscious) these people experience their inside as a seething caldron of destructive, undefined cravings. A mother's mismanagement of this stage can provoke a primitive oral rage. Thwarted symbol-formation and creativity will in part be caused by the destructive oral rage which prevents the formation of the psychic structures necessary for progressive symbol-formation. If frustrations during this stage are too intense, the infant does not have enough capacity for "good illusion formation" to enter the next stage.

The stage of transitional objects. The creation and use of transitional objects assumes the existence of a "good enough mother."

A good enough mother intuitively knows when and for how long she can and should introduce a delay between the infant's needs and the fulfillment she can offer. The infant, who in the previous stage had the experience of magical creativity in the form of the primary illusion, can discover how to mend the gap in his life space that is produced by the absence of the gratifying mother. At this stage, the infant has a growing ability to recognize and accept reality. If his hallucinatory wish fulfillment previously coincided with the appearance of the real breast, then in the following stage, objects available in outside reality can be perceived and felt as receptive for illusory use. At first it can be the thumb or the fist, later a piece of soft material found near the crib, even later a soft stuffed animal, and finally, any toy which can fulfill the function of a good transitional object. From the baby's point of view, these are neither external objects nor pure wishful hallucinations: *they are both at the same time.* This is Winnicott's paradox, which he insists must be accepted and *not* resolved. Once resolved, the fatal Cartesian split between inside and outside will take place, and reality, even though "dealt with" adaptively, will never feel fully enjoyable. It can never feel as if it is partly created by the self. Perhaps this is the price one must pay for an excess of ego autonomy and "neutralized energy."

The baby, however, sucking and stroking himself with his good transitional object, does not yet suffer from too much ego autonomy; nevertheless, thanks to his creative semihallucination, he can obtain a measure of independence from his mother's physical presence. The transitional object is imbued with good mother-stuff and therefore undoes separation. Though still not a symbol *representing* mother, if environmental circumstances remain conducive, the object should lead to the successful use of symbolic means to bridge over to the desired but physically absent object. The creation of a good transitional object is predicated on the existence of a good enough mother whose child has the creative capacity to return equilibrium into his life space by means of a benevolent illusion.

Early good transitional objects can do more than open the way to symbolic, creative living in transitional space. They can also lead to an appreciation of the qualities of the objectively perceived real, outside world. Imagine the child playing with his teddy bear, which, while the mother is absent, is fused with the illusion of mother-qualities. Let us suppose that the mother returns within the span of time that the toy is still endowed with the illusion. Once the real mother is there, the toy loses its role in the semihallucinatory illusion of being *also* the mother, and becomes a real teddy bear with real, material features. The child has the mother for mother and the teddy bear for teddy bear. His objectively perceived world is thus enlarged. Knowledge of the nature of real objects is needed not only for the sake of the reality principle per se, but also for creative action, which requires knowledge and respect for the real nature of the raw material. Winnicott's conceptual localization of a transitional space lying *between* the space of dreams and the space of hard reality, is actually not correct. *Transitional space is not contiguous or even continuous with the Cartesian or Euclidean space of real reality, but is interwoven seamlessly with it; it can be lifted out only for the sake of conceptualization.*

The good transitional object can also help to enlarge the child's objectively perceived real world by serving as a trusty companion to hold on to while entering new territories (see Miller, this volume). The new, the unknown, by itself can be frightening for the small child (and to many adults); but carrying the faithful transitional object establishes a bridge between the old and known and the new and unknown. It helps to develop a feeling of familiarity within the unfamiliar.

In this sense, the transitional object is part of Piaget's "assimilative schema," without which accommodation to the new cannot meaningfully occur. The old, subjective "inside" contributors to perception make possible the assimilation of the truly new, so that instead of remaining a "foreign body" of knowledge it can become organically assimilated into the already existing world of the child—or of the adult.

A continuum exists between adult versions of good transitional objects and neurotically defensive fetishistic phenomena. A clinical example will explain. A female lawyer carries a ribbon in her coat pocket or pocketbook wherever she goes, and must secretly touch it whenever she is anxious in a professional situation. We can assume deep and unresolved infantile separation anxieties that are probably mingled with sadistic impulses. The same woman became completely confused following the smallest change in my office, waiting room, or schedule, or whenever I uttered a word she had not anticipated. For weeks she would engage in various repetitive, ritualistic acts during her sessions. Her favorite was playing with her pop-beads, pulling two apart and pushing them together again, an act lending itself to phallic interpretation; but in another sense she was practicing separating and joining together again. Her traumatic childhood kept her functioning at the level of defensive, repetitive self-destructive acts, in spite of her exceptional intellectual and good creative endowment.

Good transitional objects can deteriorate into fetish-objects if the mother does not reappear before longing turns into trauma. Seriously deprived children (such as institutional homeless children, feebleminded children, or children born blind and brought up in institutional settings) who were never able to create good transitional objects rigidly clutch their fetish-objects, without play, without enjoyment, without libido-investment in them. The only function of these objects is to supply a measure of defense against distressful anxiety. Greenacre (1971) neatly differentiates the positive developmental potentials of the transitional object from the arrested, frozen quality of the infantile fetish. She stresses that early body traumata, either experienced directly or witnessed, can lead to early acute castration fear, for which the fetish object serves as a "patch." Greenacre says that the "fetish...contains congealed anger, born of castration panic."

Whether the transitional object leads to good symbolization and a generally creative attitude to life or deteriorates into a rigidly frozen fetish and a hostile attitude to the very process of symbolization will depend upon the length of the mother's absences. The empathic mother reappears in time to prevent the metamorphosis of the good transitional object into a fetish-object. Such a metamorphosis is a dead-end, while with good enough mothering the good transitional object can transcend its original meaning by metamorphosing into broad, intermediate transitional space, where symbol-laden cultural activities and creative, imaginative living take place. Play, artistic creativity, and appreciation are the direct, natural successors to the early good transitional objects; all require the capacity for creative "magical illusion."

I think the infantile fetish can arise from early distress due to abandonment and not only from specific castration fear. Abandonment of the infant can result in narcissistic mortification of such intensity that its effect is most probably experienced as a mutilation of the incipient body-self. In the beginning, the "self" *is* the body-self. We can say that the infant's life space is in disequilibrium when it does not contain what he needs. This is so when the mother and all the things she can give are absent when needed by the infant. The intensity of ungratified need will result in a painful sense of incompleteness of the body-self. This state can be compared to the feeling of mutilation of the body-self, since at that early stage of development there is no sense of separation between the self and the needed gratifying objects. In the phallic stage, this same feeling might appear as castration fear. Thus, although the infantile fetish shows no developmental potential for symbol-formation and creativity, it does undergo changes in meaning corresponding to the sequential unfolding of the erotogenic zones.

A disappointing relationship between the young child and the mother can reduce the transitional object to various compulsive autoerotic activities, such as hair-pulling, protracted thumb-sucking, or compulsive masturbation. These fetishistic symptoms require intervention; they not only lead away from creativity but *actively inhibit* development of enjoyable play, learning, or any form of innovative symbolic activity. The amount of energy tied up in such symptoms precludes the freedom needed for creativity, because mental activity continues to be invested in the repetitive sadomasochistic fantasies that accompany them.

The stage of playing. The stage of transitional objects merges into what could be called the stage of playing. If everything proceeds optimally, the child can play, freely and creatively, and with concentrated dedication. The play will have form, with a beginning, a middle, and a natural end. It will be neither unimaginative and repetitive (reminiscent of fetishistic rituals), nor overexcited and disorganized, indicating the presence of raw instinctual forces. Probably no one has described the qualities of children's play better than Marion Milner in her paper "Aspects of Symbolism in Comprehension of the Not-Self" (Milner 1952).

A child who plays well demonstrates that illusion and reality were introduced beneficially into his life at an early time. Gratification and frustration were well timed and well dosed, resulting in smooth amalgamation between the basic instinctual forces, libido and aggression. Both are necessary for any form of creative activity, from play to artistic creation. Libido is needed for the building of good form, while the aggressive element is required for the capacity to destroy previous gestalts, without which innovative creation cannot take place. The child who cannot enjoy throwing over his building of blocks when he has finished playing with it, will not be able to begin a new one; all the constructive elements will be tied up in the old creation.

A child also requires good experience with the actual indestructability of his mother, who survives her symbolic destruction during periods of the child's frustration. Only after such reassuring experiences can the child use objects freely for his own creative enjoyment.

For the child to play with enjoyment, a good "playspace" must exist, i.e., the intermediate transitional space at that phase of development. This space is hospitable and generates symbol-formation; it is synonymous with Winnicott's "potential space" between mother and child. A good mother can turn this potential space into a good, creativity-bearing intermediate region, which both joins and separates mother and the playing child. In previous phases of development, the mother's good management of the child's needs resulted in his ability to form comforting illusions and transitional objects. During this playing stage, the mother's main task is to create a situation in which her child can play, yet be alone in her presence. These are the quiet times, when the child feels unpressured by instinctual needs and unchallenged by the demands of the environment: he can quietly "do his own thing" while knowing that the trustworthy, responsive mother is somewhere near, and available if necessary. In this situation, a calm "ego-relatedness" permeates the intermediate space between the child and what Winnicott calls the "environmental mother." The environmental mother is the continuation of the early holding mother, in contrast to the mother who is the object of instinctual cravings. The relatedness between the child and the environmental mother is gratifying in a nonparoxysmal and nonclimactic way. This is the original situation from which the capacity for tenderness and affection grows; it is unnecessary to derive these quiet, loving states from aim-inhibited instinctual drives or the neutralization of energy. The capacity for durable, tender love originates in the baby's enjoyment while being held firmly and lovingly during long intervals in which instinctual tensions are at their ebb.

It is the same instinctually unexcited, tension-free state in which the child enjoys playing alone in the presence of his mother. Here the mother "holds" the child safely, not in her arms, but within the securely "holding" intermediate space that she has created for the playing child. In this space the child can play safely, trusting his own creativity, the usability of objects for symbolic play and the durable dependability of the mother, even if she must leave for short periods.

III

What is the significance in psychology of ongoing "quiet" states versus the paroxysmal cycles of instinctual needs with regard to affect and cognitive development? Freudian psychoanalytic theory derives affect-development, as well as the impetus for ideational processes and the organization of reality experiences, from the effects of instinctual drive-tensions and their motivational corollary, the nervous system's inherent tendency to rid itself of excitation (Freud 1915).

Hermann (1936) introduced the nonclimactic, continuously effective "need for clinging (*sich anklammern*)" as a basically nonsexual, nonaggressive human "instinct" from which, under good circumstances, affectionate relationships can be directly derived. This heuristic modification of instinct theory was not assimilated into the main trend of psychoanalytic thinking (possibly because Hermann's works have only recently been translated). Besides Hermann, it was only Winnicott, among psychoanalysts, who saw in the child's nonparoxysmal instinctual relatedness to the mother the roots of secure, affectionate connectedness. This is the necessary matrix for the unfolding of the child's creative capacities.

Among non-Freudian theorists, this area received recognition within the framework of creativity by Bally (1945) and Schachtel (1959). Peter Wolff (1960) in his comparative study "The Developmental Psychologies of Jean Piaget and Psychoanalysis" differentiates the vantage points of these two theories: "Piaget . . . selected only those periods when the child performed at his optimum because organic tension was not interfering with his adaptive processes—while instinctual-drive-determined behavior was the core of Freud's developmental theory."

The "ego-related," good "environmental mother" knows how to create a safe atmosphere without exciting or impinging on the child's immediate world. She knows how to leave usable objects around without forcing them upon the child. He will find them when he needs them. Finding them will be as much a creative act as the discovery of *objets trouvés* for the artist, or driftwood for the beachcomber. Later, too, when the child has grown into an adult, he will have a way to unconsciously invest the world with parts of himself, so that when he "finds" new aspects of the world, they will appear not as foreign but as familiar places where he can find his own self. Whether this will happen also depends on the early "mirror-function" of the mother's face and eyes. As important as holding and tactile experience was for the growing sense of unity-within-his-skin for the infant, so is visual contact—mother and child looking at each other— for the playing child. Pleasurable skin feelings contribute to the delineation of a good inside space, which is then experienced as a vague feeling *within* the body. This inner space is the predecessor of the "mind," which corresponds more or less to what is called the preconscious, the storehouse of symbolic internal representations.

We can assume that the mother's internalized image is the first content of the slowly emerging preconscious. Her form can be viewed from many angles, but the eye to eye contact is the most significant. The mother's eyes look at the playing child while the child looks at the mother watching him play. The mother's eyes and face function as a mirror, reflecting the loved image of the child to the child. The child will internalize the image of the mother's eyes as it contained him. This reciprocal or serial mutual internalization will lead within the child's inner space (in his budding preconscious) to a sturdy, self-affirming structure. Its composition is analogous to the Russian wooden dolls; the largest doll contains another doll, which contains another, and so on. Just as the empathic mother knew intuitively how to offer her breast and how to offer objects for her child's creative use, she can look "creatively" and nonintrusively at the playing child. He receives the message that he exists in the world, that his existence is good and enjoyed by the mother. All this enters the child's inner space by introjecting the richness of the mother's mirroring face.

IV

The series of mother-child interactions, divided roughly into the four stages that have been described, will finally lead to *creativity*, or the lack of it, in *adult life*. Active creativity is predicated on the experience of the self containing a rich and fertile inner space. Erikson's concept of "generativity" seems to coincide with this subjective experience (Erikson 1950).

Describing the future fate of the child's good transitional object, Winnicott says:

Its fate is to be gradually allowed to be decathected....By this I mean that in health the transitional object does not "go inside" nor does the feeling about it...undergo repression. It is not forgotten and it is not mourned. It loses meaning...because the transitional phenomena ... have become spread out over the whole intermediate territory between "inner psychic reality" and "the external world as perceived by two persons in common," that is to say, over the whole cultural field. [Winnicott 1953]

This statement requires elaboration. The transitional object does not "go inside" in the sense of becoming a symbolic mental representation to cling to; in this case it would have turned into a frozen mental fetish. But, of course, it does "go inside" in the form of a pleasant memory image serving as a "fertilizer" of the preconscious. The preconscious becomes the internalized heir of the caring mother providing security and creativity—or of the bad mother. Internalization of experience is an ongoing process. The object-world around us is internalized in the preconscious by symbolically abstracted internal representations. On the other hand, to a great extent the symbols in the preconscious will determine how we perceive the world (Deri 1974). The use of projective techniques for personality diagnosis is based on this assumption.

The mother's physical holding and handling of the infant determines the feeling quality of the primordial inner space on the pleasure-unpleasure dimension. Later, the good mother builds a creative, fertile intermediate play space, which also contains her nurturing, mirroring face and eyes. The child perceives this whole situation by way of his syncretic mode of perception, and this complex percept will become internalized, thus contributing to the fashioning of the preconscious as an internal "playground" for symbolic creativity.

In contrast to the amorphous, disordered content of the unconscious and the barrage of perceptual stimulation from the external world, the preconscious is an ordered and ordering "zone." Memory images of perceptions are stored here. Memory images, as we know, are not one-to-one replicas of the infinitely complex external stimuli, but the outcome of organizing gestalt-perception. Memory images can be designated as symbolically abstracted internal representations since their gestalts reflect the *meaning* of the stimulus-pattern to the perceiver. Therefore, we can say that the object-world around us is symbolically internalized and stored in the preconscious.

The other, "inner" side of the preconscious is exposed to the barrage of instinctual stimulation originating in the unconscious id. This can be experienced as pressure; but only when "bound" into a preconscious form can it be experienced as a nameable and meaningful need or wish which can be communicated to the cognizing self and to the outer world. We call these gestalted, preconscious transformations of instinctual impulses *instinct-derivatives*. The quality, variety, and amplitude of the storehouse of symbolic forms in the preconscious will function analogously to day-residues in the shaping of the manifest dream, or to screen memories. The availability and quality of gestalted forms in the preconscious will determine how instinctual, emotional impulses can be experienced and expressed. Here we have finally explained how the creative process evolves through the mediation of the preconscious. Preconscious symbolic forms, visual or auditory, serve as structuring, formative, and expressive elements, giving shape and meaning to the created product.

Since the preconscious is that part of mental life which contains all that we know, all that is not repressed and consequently can be brought into consciousness without special effort, it does correspond phenomenologically to what we experience as our "mind." The mind can be experienced as rich or poor, empty or filled, dependable or not dependable in its function. These are the experiential, gestalt-qualities of "the mind" which will influence creativity in the narrower artistic sense, as well as in the wide, life space-creating sense. A trusting or nontrusting relationship to one's own mind will principally derive from the internalization of the mother's caretaking. Features of the child's self-representation will reflect the mother's early attitudes toward him. We could say that, in the beginning, the mother functions as the child's preconscious. In the course of mental development, her caretaking features and emotional attitudes are internalized by the child; they contribute to his mental structuralization, including his subjective attitude to his own mind. If he feels it is rich, that it functions dependably and is capable of producing the right word and the right concept at the right time, then we may assume that in early childhood the mother offered the objects of the world in a predictably benevolent manner.

Erikson's "Peace comes from inner space" can be amended: peace comes from the *creative* inner space that is the base for the symbolic function that bridges over the gaps of time and space, thus uniting what has been separated.

NOTE

1. In my view, the preconscious is the mental "territory" where form-creating processes take place. This largely coincides with Kubie's view (1958) that the creative process takes place through the mediation of the preconscious. However, this conceptualization and its use in this chapter require some metapsychological elucidation. According to Freud's "structural model," unformed instinctual energies are contained "in" the Id. In terms of levels of consciousness, the Id is all unconscious. In the Id unbound energy and consequently primary process functioning prevail. The ordering, form-giving functions of the psyche that obey the rules of secondary process and utilize "bound energy" are conceptualized as Ego-functions. Consequently, symbols, as *end-products* of formative processes and as such available to consciousness, have to be localized "within" the Ego. In his *Outline of Psychoanalysis* (1940) Freud states: "The inside of the Ego which comprises above all the intellectual processes has the quality of being preconscious." Thus, when dealing with intellectual processes, i.e., symbolic processes, Freud had recourse to the spatial metaphor of a container for the Ego, attributing to it an "inside" and an "outside." By referring to the "inside" as preconscious, he telescoped the topographic with the structural model. In other words, even when "officially" under the aegis of the structural model, Freud characterized the Ego as a "preconscious mental region" when referring to intellectual processes. But if *Ego* is used in this sense, then in fact we have returned to the "topographic model," since the structural theory views the Ego as a group of intercorrelated functions and *not* as a bounded region with an "inside" with specific psychological content. I think it more appropriate, then, to use the topographic model when dealing with problems of symbolization, such as language, intellectual processes, and creativity. Accordingly, in this chapter *preconscious* is used in the sense of a "mental territory" where symbols are stored. The concept of symbols comprises the subjective elaborations of internalized percepts, i.e., "memory-symbols" and internal representations, as well as the symbolic elaborations of instinctual urges, i.e., instinct-derivatives such as definable wishes. In the actual symbols subjective wishes and internalized images combine. The concept of "imago" in older psychoanalytic literature represented this state of affairs. Characterizing the symbols as preconscious or stored "within" the preconscious makes evident their communicative "bridging-over" function. We know from Freud (1915) that for the content of the unconscious to become conscious and communicable, it has to pass through and attach itself

to the word-symbols in the preconscious. Freud localized the preconscious between the unconscious and the conscious. The "inside boundary" of the preconscious faces the instinctual urges and the repressed unconscious material, while the "outer boundary" of the preconscious is in direct contact with "perception-consciousness."

REFERENCES

Bally, Gustav (1945). *Vom Ursprung und von den Grenzen der Freiheit: Eine Deutung des Spiels bei Tier und Mensch.* Basel: Benno Schwabe.

Deri, Susan (1965). The homeostatic and the representational function of the symbolic process with reference to the Rat Man's obssessive ideation. Paper read at the twenty-fourth International Psychoanalytic Congress, Amsterdam.

—— (1974). Symbolization in psychoanalysis and schicksals-analysis: a revised theory of symbolization. *Szondiana* 9. Bern: Hans Huber.

Erikson, Erik H. (1950). *Childhood and Society.* New York: W.W. Norton.

Freud, Sigmund (1914). The Moses of Michaelangelo. *Standard Edition* 23.

—— (1915). The unconscious. *Standard Edition* 24.

—— (1925). On negation. *Standard Edition* 19.

—— (1940). An outline of psychoanalysis. *Standard Edition* 23.

Greenacre, Phyllis (1958). The family romance of the artist. In *Emotional Growth,* vol. 2, pp. 505-532. New York: International Universities Press, 1971.

—— (1971). The fetish and the transitional object; The transitional object and the fetish: with special reference to the role of illusion. In *Emotional Growth,* vol. 1, pp. 315-334. New York: International Universities Press.

Hermann, Imre (1936). Sich Anklammern, Auf Suche Gehen. *Internationale Zeitschrift für Psychoanalyse.* Trans. *Psychoanalytic Quarterly* 45:5-36.

Kubie, Lawrence S. (1958). *Neurotic Distortions of the Creative Process.* Lawrence, Kansas: The University of Kansas Press.

Langer, Susanne K. (1942). *Philosophy in a New Key.* Cambridge: Harvard University Press.

Milner, Marion (1952). Aspects of symbolism in comprehension of the not-self. *International Journal of Psycho-Analysis* 33.

Schachtel, Ernest G. (1959). *Metamorphosis.* New York: Basic Books.

Stevenson, O. (1954). The first treasured possession: a study of the part played by specially loved objects and toys in the lives of certain children. Preface by D.W. Winnicott. *Psychoanalytic Study of the Child* 9.

Winnicott, D.W. (1953). Transitional objects and transitional phenomena. *International Journal of Psycho-Analysis* 34: 89-97.

—— (1958). *Collected Papers.* New York: Basic Books.

—— (1971). *Playing and Reality.* New York: Basic Books.

Wolff, Peter H. (1960). *The Developmental Psychologies of Jean Piaget and Psychoanalysis.* Psychological Issues, Vol. II. New York: International Universities Press.

CHAPTERS 5 and 6

Marion Milner has just shown how Donald Winnicott's metaphors capture the essence of the mother-child relationship. She has added depth to the terms *transitional object*, *good enough mother*, and *holding environment*, and has prepared the reader for the richness of the nursing situation described by Judith Kestenberg in chapters 5 and 6. Here the psychophysiological aspects of the nursing situation are viewed in their developmental significance, especially their role in the formation of transitional objects and body image.

In chapter 5, Judith Kestenberg, by means of neurophysiologic data, theorizes that the gamma nervous system acting along the body meridians is the basis of body image formation. The holding and play which occur in the intermediate zone between mother and child are related to both body image and transitional object formation.

In chapter 6, written with Joan Weinstein, Kestenberg concentrates on the nonnutritive functions of the nursing situation as the prototype of transitional object functions and develops her thesis that the transitional object is an adjunct to drive discharge.

L.B.

TRANSSENSUS-OUTGOINGNESS AND WINNICOTT'S INTERMEDIATE ZONE

Judith S. Kestenberg

The activity of the Gamma Nervous System builds the somatic base for all stirrings connected with psychic function.

—Glaser 1970, p. 219

Reaching out to the beginnings of psychic phenomena, we are hard put to find means of investigating the intermediate zone between soma and psyche. Freud (1914) postulated that there is a narcissistic investment in the id-ego from the start, but autoerotic practices precede this development. Mahler referred to the first postnatal stage as "autistic" (1968). Balint believed in the existence of primary object ties (1957), but on closer scrutiny, one discovers that he did not think of discrete objects but rather of environmental objects such as air or light, to which the human infant automatically turns. Our explorations of rhythms in the neonate (Kestenberg 1967, 1970, 1975, Kestenberg et al. 1971) suggest that feelings of security versus uneasiness combine with feelings of comfort and discomfort to give an affective base for coping with the inner and outer environment. The neonate operates primarily with reflexes regulated by the brain-stem, and it will take a long time before he can begin his life as a truly cortical animal. This has been widely used as an argument against the assumption that the id or ego nuclei are established before three months. Notwithstanding the claim of researchers that the child cannot differentiate between his mother and other people before five to six months of life, observant mothers have reported that their young infants can distinguish them by the way they are held, and by tone of voice.

M. at the age of four weeks could not easily be soothed by anyone besides his mother. L. at five and a half weeks would follow her mother's movements with her eyes until she disappeared from view.

She would not follow other people's movements in the same way. She could also recognize her mother's voice. When I held her at the age of seven and a half weeks, I could calm her only when she did not hear her mother talking.

· The progressive building up of psychic organization within the framework of early maternal care, is mediated via the Gamma Nervous System (GNS), which is controlled by the brain-stem. This system is the prime agent in the transformation of the dozing baby into an alert, awake human being whose sensorimotor experiences become activated by human touch (Ribble 1943, Montague 1971). Glaser calls it the "psychosomatic connection (*Bindeglied*)" (1967).

In this presentation, I shall summarize and amplify Glaser's and Veldman's views (1966) concerning the effect of touching and holding on the initiation of relationships. Following their direction, I shall show the influence of the GNS on the feeling tone of transsensus-outgoingness, which is at the root of the psychosomatic interaction between infant and caretaker. I shall propose that the GNS activation via the body meridians is the psychophysiological base of the body-image, which originates in the nonnutritive aspects of the nursing situation and is reproduced in the play with the transitional object. This will serve as an introduction to chapter 6, which deals with the functions and origin of the transitional object.

OUTGOINGNESS MEDIATED BY THE GNS

Glaser (1967) draws our attention to the fact that our movement representations are concerned with the stretching rather than with the flexing of the muscles responsible for changes of position. We stretch out our hand in greeting without even a passing thought to the fact that our finger-extensors are contracting to achieve the desired effect. If we simply hold out our hand during greeting, there is very little feeling of contact or warmth. The emphasis on stretching out (extending ourselves) enhances breathing and circulation, giving a human touch to the action. The affectomotor response is dependent on the mediation of the extracortical GNS.

The interplay between contraction and extension (shortening and lengthening) of muscles depends on the receptivity of the Golgi corpuscles, the muscle receptors—which can be called "feelers of tension"—and on the muscle spindles, which Glaser refers to as *Dehnung*, "feelers of distension." There is no proper translation for this German word, which implies that elasticity has been maintained and the stretching is reversible. The English word *distension* connotes an irreversible process; I therefore use the word, *extension* or *stretching out* as approximate translations. Muscle spindles have a double function:

1. When a muscle is stretched, the spindle emits impulses to the pyramidal tract via thick myelinated fibers. This spinal reflex effects a strong contraction of muscles, which remain at the same length (isometric). Provided there is no voluntary interference with the muscle contraction, its intensity can be maintained through central influence (isotonic).

2. The sensitivity of the spindle is additionally influenced by brainstem regulation. Within the spindle, the small intrafusal muscle, which is innervated by thin motor and sensory fibers of the GNS, responds to actual stretching or to the activation of appropriate areas of the brainstem in the same manner. By responding to the impulses from the brainstem it can signal an attitude of stretch in the muscle spindle, which prepares the corresponding area of muscle activity for movement. The action begins as if it were self-propelled, without much exertion and obeying the slightest directive. If a movement is already proceeding, it now becomes easier and more harmonious.

Under the influence of the GNS, movement flows freely and without anxiety, and is associated with growing out into the environment rather than shrinking from it (Kestenberg 1975). The body area that is most stretched out becomes imbued with a feeling of vitality, as if life were flowing through it. The elasticity of the tissues increases, and the attitudes of movement become endowed with expressiveness. Furthermore, the activation of the GNS through a stretch representation influences the whole body, every change of tension and shape necessitating a change in the whole configuration. Each activation of GNS has an influence on breathing. As movement becomes smoother and respiration becomes regular, a pneumogram reveals a swinging sinus rhythm in the interplay between the diaphragm and the abdominal muscles. Glaser's (1967) research indicates that this type of respiration underlies the attitude of trust the infant conveys when he lies happily and cozily in his crib. He describes the pleasure felt by the adult, who rests his hand on a "trusting" baby-belly. The abdomen seems to cuddle into the softly pressing hand.

TRANSSENSUS

Eutony (*Eutonie*) as described above is characteristic of infant and animal behavior. The adult is capable of achieving it when he can feel a primary outgoingness, a sense, which Glaser (1970) calls "transsensus," of going out of one's boundaries and incorporating others. The trustful attitude of "stretching toward" is not simply a reaction to a stimulus, but rather is an alert state of the total being. This extension may not lead to a visible movement, being confined instead to a muscle activity to which one hardly pays attention; this occurs in the case of the "cuddly baby-belly" described above. The eutony of the middle of the body makes one feel that an impulse arises from the center, flowing to the outside, seeking contact with a real or an imagined object. Transsensus enables us to experience the center and the expanding boundaries of the body as either seeking out or melting into an object. Through the activation of alertness, stretching-toward, and breathing, the GNS participates in the formation of the outer and inner configuration of the body-schema (Buytendijk 1956).

Transsensus must be dissociated from such higher cortical functions as secondary process thinking and voluntary actions. It is associated with "breathful flowing," spreading throughout the body and becoming succulent and warm (see chapter 6). It is a process which, through stretch action in the torso and/or hands, distributes the tonus far into the fingers and toes.

BODY MERIDIANS

In describing the basic forms of movement arising from transsensus, Glaser (1967) uses as guidelines the meridians of the body, which are identical with Chinese acupuncture lines:

> There are six meridians on each side of the body and four in the middle. The latter lead from the coccyx to the pubic bone, traversing the back and the front of the body. The former are divided into the outer, which are active on the outside of the limbs and end in the upper part of the torso or the face, and the inner, which run their course on the flexor side of the extremities and have no direct connection to the face.

In studying the meridians one can see that there is a continuity of tension lines between certain parts of the face and certain fingers and toes. For instance, the area between the nose and the upper lip is connected through long meridians both to the outer side of the index finger *and to the second toe*. Activation of one part creates tension changes through the entire meridian.[1] This principle, used in Chinese medicine, has been discovered independently by Glaser and Veldman (1966), by

Elizabeth Frost (1975), and by Janet Travel (1975). Frost, working in an anesthesiology department, found an exact correspondence between trigger points and reference zones. For instance, needles stuck into hands and feet would cause migraine headaches to disappear. Travel outlined hypothetical pathways of transfer from the trigger to the reference zone. She not only worked with skin areas, but also with muscles, using such techniques as local anesthesia and cold sprays. She aimed her therapy at reeducating muscles that produce pain through chronic spasm. Applying a strong barrage of sensory impulses to the skin of a reference zone allowed for the stretching and moving of muscles at the trigger points. Travel believes that the connections between trigger points are not direct, but occur through separate feedback loops in the central nervous sytem. The effectiveness of her therapy is based on the relaxation of muscles, which are restored to normal resting length.

Glaser and Veldman (1966) lay their hands on the appropriate places and remove spasms, discomforts, stiffness, and pain. Their psychotactile therapy is based on the principle of the re-formation of the body-image through transsensus. Patients are instructed to imagine that the physician's touching palm belongs to them as part of their body. This activates deep breathing and improves circulation. The entire trigger zone and the reference zones are connected by meridians, and become supple and elastic, with previously foreshortened and tense muscles returning to their normal length. Thus, several authors dealing with the same phenomena invented various healing methods based on the psychotactile stability of tension lines. The confluence of similar discoveries, by researchers from variant disciplines working independently of one another, enriched and deepened my understanding of early development.

In my brief work with Glaser (1967), I could experience firsthand how the illusion of incorporating another person's hand, arm, or entire body produces an invigoration of breath and increases the elasticity of tissues. Glaser demonstrated to me how a trained patient can feel the transsensus in relation to several people who are in contact with one another. This phenomenon allows us to understand the sensitivity of an infant who will only relate to people acceptable to his mother. He can "feel" his mother via the bridge of an accessory object who belongs, so to speak, to both of them (Kestenberg 1971; see also chapter 6). I have learned that babies and toddlers can participate in a very large group of mothers and children without anxiety, provided there is group cohesiveness and friendship between parents and staff. When there is dissent or distrust, the child withdraws and becomes asocial. When I learned to recognize, by observation of the shape and tension distribution in the patient's body, to what extent he was able to enlarge the scope of his body-image, I was impressed with the effect of the patient's transsensus on the therapist himself. His own breathing deepened and his contact with the patient extended over his entire body, even though his hand alone rested on the patient's back. My first thought was that I had witnessed the psychophysical evolution of transference and countertransference, which are founded in the mutual trust between mother and child—Glaser's transsensus.

There is great likelihood that transsensus operates through all senses, based as it is on GNS activation of the whole body. The modes of contact are many. For instance, we can often feel someone staring at us, or can sense that someone is approaching us from behind. This may well be prompted by an unconscious response to the increased stretching and breathing of another person. When we inhale deeply, taking someone else in and enlarging the image of our body-shape, we feel comfortable with the accepted object. Holding our breath—not giving up the acquisition—leads to inhibition and provokes anxiety. Deep exhalation, releasing what we took in, leaves us with a shrunken, deflated body-shape. After a brief pause, the process reverses itself. This constitutes the physical aspect of the rhythms of incorporation, associated with elation, and of projection, associated with a letdown, which are at the core of all relationships.

Glaser describes transsensus as an affective, pre-ideational conscious thought accompanying expressive movement. The mover may merely be aware of feeling comfortable. He easily can be taught to become aware of a feeling of flowing, invigoration, elasticity, and plasticity. It takes much more sophistication to become conscious of sequences of merging with someone else as a "me/non-me" possession which equates being and belonging, followed by a separation between "me" and "non-me." The rhythm of breathing and transsensus varies with changes in the basic relatedness between participants. These variations are conveyed to the onlooker through the expressiveness of movement patterns, stemming from minute alteration of body shape, as can be seen in slight smiling or frowning (Kestenberg 1967, 1975). Shape-changes are conveyed visually, kinesthetically, through heat radiation, and through touch, in the intimate (intermediate) zone between people joined in a loving embrace.[2]

THE BIRTH OF TRANSSENSUS

Applying what we have learned from Glasser and other researchers about trigger and reference zones with their tensile connections through stretch-meridians, and whose touch-pressure activates breathing and transsensus, we are mindful of the preparations for postnatal life the fetus undergoes in utero. Among the early movements of the fetus are Ahlfeld's breathing-movements which can be felt through the mother's body (Carmichael 1946). Small stretch-movements are experienced by the pregnant woman as kicking or pushing. Moving through the birth canal, after the water has broken, subjects the baby to pressure from the maternal tissues, which are stretched out by the child.[3] Being stretched and massaged over the entire body activates the entire GNS of the baby which, in turn, promotes breathing, alertness, and turning outward. As anticipated by Freud (1926) and Rank (1924) and documented by Greenacre (1945), the birth experience is a prototype for anxiety. This is predominantly based on the constriction involved in being squeezed out, and the high tension which precedes the first intake of breath. However, it is also a relief to be stretched out and to experience the first inhalation. The unity of breathing, elasticity, and transsensus-outgoingness suggests that the birth experience itself promotes the birth of feeling tones, which arise from sensing the stretch and the touch of air outside and inside the body.

Being wrapped, bathed, cleaned, massaged with a towel, and held for nursing seem to be continuations of GNS activations begun during the birth process. Holding the baby in a manner which coordinates best with his tonic neck reflex (see chapter 6), puts the back of his head into the nook of the maternal elbow, with the arm of the mother upholding almost the entire area of the not yet functioning antigravity muscles. The inside meridians of the mother's arm are stretched by the body of the child. When the child embraces his mother's back, his inner arm meridian is in touch with a relay zone in her body which transmits tensile states from the arm to the legs and to the head. The baby's other hand touches a similar area of transmission on the chest of the maternal body. By pressing the baby's frontal surface toward her body, the mother activates his middle frontal meridians. She may also support the outer surfaces of the child's arms and legs through her arms, legs, and pelvis. Her free hand adds touches to various parts of the child's body or her own breast area, in a manner which suggests that she knows which zone needs activation at a given time[4].

I have described the way maternal and infantile meridians are activated during nursing. Other holding positions enhance different types of interaction through a selective, light pressure on other parts of the body. Holding and being held, which covers large areas of the body, outlined by meridians, and digit-play, which acts as a trigger for transmission to corresponding body zones, combine to form an integrated body image. The stability of mutual support contributes to what Head (Schilder 1935) called the "postural model" of the body; finger-play adds to it the "kinesthetic-touch model." While the former helps create the three-dimensional shapes of mother and child, the latter highlights certain body-zones by revitalizing their activity. The well-being and transsensus, associated with feelings of elastic stretching and breathing together during mutual holding and touching, outlines the body-schema of the child like an affective shell. Finger and toe play, by periodically activating the GNS and its hypothalamic connections, keeps up the flow of maternal milk and prevents mother and child from falling asleep, in response to the monotonous sucking rhythm.

FROM TRANSSENSUS TO CREATION

There is a developmental progression from a flexed to a stretched out body attitude that culminates in human adult posture. Through the activations of the GNS during holding and being held, the baby stretches out. Play on the mother's body releases the grasp reflex, opens the fist and makes out of the active hand the principal tool of doing (being mobile) while the arms are holding (being stable). Through the meridian-connection between fingers and face, the hand becomes an extension of the mouth (Kestenberg et al. 1971), even when it is removed from it. The doing, playing hand becomes the foremost proponent of creativity: a bearer of communication (Saunders 1960) and a transmitter of culture (Almansi 1964).

Reproducing the closeness in the intermediate zone between mother and child while away from her, the child sucks one or more fingers of one hand. Only the other hand may be released for play; or the fingers not engaged in sucking will touch, rub or tickle certain accessible facial areas. The rhythm of these movements harmonize with sucking, but they change in various developmental phases to include the prevalent dominant rhythm (see chapter 6). This facilitates the inclusion of the face into all body-image changes during development. The hand that holds a transitional object is free to twist, pluck, rub, and stroke not only the snout area (Spitz 1965, Rangell 1954), but also any other accessible body part that is in special need of relibidinization. Frequently the fingers themselves are wrapped into the blanket and twisted around it in such a manner that it is hard to fathom which belongs to the child and which is a "non-me" possession.

Holding the transitional object, and imagining that it holds him, stroking it and making it stroke his face while sucking, are all conducive to the maintenance of a special state of consciousness, which is at the borderland between internal and external reality. The soothing rhythms of the sucking dull the sharp intrusion of reality, while the transsensus, based on being held and touched as well as on holding and touching, prevents the engulfment by the "nothingness" of sleep. The play action with the transitional object is the external manifestation of relatedness, the basic core of fantasy that weaves illusion into everyday life (Winnicott 1951). The building of the real and imaginary features of the body-image is based on the same principle (Schilder 1935). Each child has his own requirements for building and rebuilding the core of his body and his body boundaries, as they are framed by the near and far objects around him. When there is a feeling of loss of body integrity, some children call for their mothers to help them recoup their losses. For others, the transitional object—held and played with in a certain way—is a must for the comfort-giving reestablishment of an integrated body-image.

The transitional object gives the child confidence that through holding, possessing, and acting on it and with it, he is able to recreate himself and his mother. Therein lies the meaning of Winnicott's cryptic statement about an implicit agreement between mother and child that the transitional object is self-created rather than given by the mother. In this context, the transitional object becomes the prototype of the self-created baby who creates his own mother (Kestenberg 1975). The physiological base for this type of creativity in the intermediate zone between mother and child is the activation of the GNS, which, through its hypothalamic connection, regulates the hormonal, stimulating-dulling, and waking-sleep centers, as well as all other rhythmic regulators of bodily needs. Through its connections via the hypothalamus to the cortex, the comfort-giving, body-image building creativity becomes transformed into play and art—the individual's gift to society (Kestenberg and Robbins 1975). Transsensus, the ideomotor, affective component of body-image building, remains the core of all relationships. Transitional phenomena, the beloved possessions, allow the individual to dilute the intensity of his feelings for his love object and to make the rhythm of loss and retrieval of the object the principal ingredient of the uniquely human achievement—creativity based on sameness and leading to change (Muensterberger 1962).

NOTES

1. In Chinese medicine, the activation of these lines is said to affect the intestines.

2. Breathing in, in synchrony with another person, gives us the feeling of becoming very large and growing into the partner's body. Exhaling separates the partners and makes them feel smaller than before.

3. It is interesting to note that during labor and delivery, the mother's tissues are being stretched from inside. This impels her to breathe so deeply that distracting methods, advocating shallow breathing are needed to prevent premature expulsion and tearing of tissues. In one instance, a woman who actively "stretched herself" during the difficult period of transition experienced no pain and could breathe deeply without resorting to expelling actions which might injure her tissues. Through active stretching, based on the representation of being stretched by the baby and giving him room, the mother could experience comfort and feel related to the baby during labor. I shall return to this topic in a future publication.

4. The research concerning meridians and trigger zones on the mother's and the child's body has just begun. It may lead us further into an investigation of their connection with such somatic sources of infantile distress as colic, gas, asthma, and intestinal spasms (see Gaddini, chapter 8).

REFERENCES

Almansi, R. (1964). Egopsychological implications of a religious symbol. *Psychoanalytic Study of Society* 3:39-70.

Balint, M. (1957). *Problems of Human Pleasure and Behavior*. New York: Liveright.

Bing, E. (1967). *Six Practical Lessons for an Easier Childbirth: The Lamaze Method*. New York: Grosset and Dunlap.

Buytendijk, F. J. J. (1956). *Allgemeine Theorie der menschlichen Haltung und Bewegung*. Springer Verlag.

Carmichael, L. (1946). The onset of early development of behavior. In *Manual of Child Psychology*, ed. L. Carmichael, pp. 43-166. New York: Wiley.

Freud, S. (1914). On narcissism. *Standard Edition* 14:67-102.

——— (1926). Inhibitions, symptoms and anxiety. *Standard Edition* 20:77-181.

Frost, E. (1975). Acupunture referred: pain areas linked. *Medical Tribune* 1/29/1975, pp. 1, 8.

Glaser, V. (1967). *Sinnvolle Gymnastik*. Helfer Verlag.

——— (1970). Das Gamma-Nervenfaser System (GNS) als Psycho-Somatisches Bindeglied. *Atemschulung als Element der Psychotherapie*. Darmstadt: Wissenschaftliche Buchgesellschaft, pp. 210-221. Excerpts in text translated by J. K.

———, and Veldman, F. (1966). Psychotaktile Therapie. *Physik. Med. und Reh.* 10.

Greenacre, P. (1945). The biological economy of birth. *Psychoanalytic Study of the Child* 1:31-51.

Kestenberg, J. S. (1965). The role of movement patterns in development. I. Rhythms of movement. *Psychoanalytic Quarterly* 34:1-36.

—— (1967). The role of movement patterns in development. III. The control of shape. *Psychoanalytic Quarterly* 36:356-409.

—— (1970). Self-environment and objects as seen through the study of movement patterns. Unpublished (preliminary draft).

—— (1971). From organ-object imagery to self and object representation. In *Separation-Individuation*, pp. 75-99. New York: International Universities Press.

—— (1975). *Children and Parents: Psychoanalytic Studies in Development.* New York: Jason Aronson.

——, et al. (1971). Development of the young child as expressed through bodily movement. I. *Journal of the American Psychoanalytic Association* 19:746-764.

——, and Robbins, E. (1975). From early rhythms of socialization to the development of community spirit. In *Children and Parents: Psychoanalytic Studies in Development*, pp. 443-460. New York: Jason Aronson.

Mahler, M. (1968). *On Human Symbiosis and the Vicissitudes of the Separation-Individuation.* New York: International Universities Press.

Modell, A. (1970). The transitional object and the creative act. *Psychoanalytic Quarterly* 39:240-250.

Montague, A. (1971). *Touching.* New York: Columbia University Press.

Muensterberger, W. (1962). The creative process: its relation to object loss and fetishism. In *Psychoanalytic Study of Society* 2:161-185.

Rangell, L. (1954). The psychology of poise, with a special elaboration on the psychic significance on the snout or perioral region. *International Journal of Psycho-Analysis* 35:313-332.

Rank, O. (1924). *The Trauma of Birth.* New York: Harcourt Brace, 1929.

Ribble, M. A. (1943). *The Rights of Infants: Early Psychological Needs and Their Satisfaction.* New York: Columbia University Press.

Saunders, E. D. (1960). *Mudra. A Study of Symbolic Gestures in Japanese Buddhist Sculpture.* New York: Pantheon Books for Bollingen Foundation.

Schilder, P. (1935). *The Image and Appearance of the Human Body.* London: Kegan, Trench, Traubner.

Spitz, R. A. (1965). *The First Year of Life.* New York: International Universities Press.

Travel, J. (1975). Acupuncture referred: pain areas linked. *Medical Tribune* 1/29/1975, pp. 1, 8.

Winnicott, D. W. (1951). Transitional objects and transitional phenomena. In *Collected Papers: Through Pediatrics to Psychoanalysis*, pp. 229-242. New York: Basic Books, 1958.

TRANSITIONAL OBJECTS AND
BODY-IMAGE FORMATION

Judith S. Kestenberg
Joan Weinstein

> The postural model of the body is in perpetual inner self-construction and self-destruction. It is living in its continued differentiation and integration.
> —Schilder 1935, pp. 15-16

Winnicott (1951) discovered and named the transitional object, located it in an intermediate zone between mother and child, and subsumed it under the heading *transitional phenomena*. These phenomena, he felt, were the origin of creativity, at first expressed in illusion and play, and later in artistic contributions to culture. He pointed out that transitional objects wear away when they lose their usefulness, but that their influence fuses with and spreads into all that is created in the special psychic area lying in the borderland between perceptions of internal and of external reality. Tolpin (1971) suggested that transitional objects are not lost, but undergo progressive transmuting internalization (Kohut 1971). One of us (J. K. 1971) proposed that in each developmental phase, the child creates organic-object images out of a specific need for closeness between the dominant body-zone and the satisfying object. All external objects are used as bridges between organs and objects (Freud 1930, Searles 1960). The organs stand for the whole body, as for instance a mouth-

This study is based on material stemming from analyses of adults and children (by J.K.), and from direct observations of children in the Center,[1] as well as from reports and interviews with parents (by J.W.). At the time this material was gathered, Joan Weisntein attended the Center with her infant. The authors are grateful to Mrs. Buelte, codirector of the Center, to Drs. Berlowe and Marcus, and to the parents and children who helped in the present study.

body of the oral phase or a sphincter-body of the anal phase, and the corresponding objects are perceived as emanating from, respectively, the nursing and diapering areas of the maternal body. External objects are aids in the internalization of images into self- and object-representations. They can be people or things. J. K. (1971) classified them in accordance with their origin and function. Accessory objects are those people who care for the child in the mother's absence and supplement her functions. Intermediate objects are derived from body products, such as food, feces, and urine.[2] Bak (1974) referred to prosthetic objects which stand for a body part or its extension. Most tools are of this order. Via their common origin from organ-object images, they also substitute for maternal body parts. Transitional objects differ from all others because they contain elements of the past and present and are bridges to the future. They are cherished and loved as special possessions which bring comfort and solace, and they act as integrators of body parts (Kestenberg 1975a).

It is sometimes difficult to distinguish between transitional objects and fetishes (Wulff 1946, Greenacre 1969, 1970, Muensterberger 1962, Grolnick, chapter 14). Winnicott (1967) felt that play and creativity are derived from transitional phenomena, while repetitive, stereotyped uses of objects and ideas are "fossilized remnants of the past." Implicit in this point of view is the rigid defensiveness of fetishism, as compared with the outflowing illusion of the transitional world. A fetish is established in adulthood not only because of a split of the ego, stemming from the phallic phase, but also because of a prior failure in body-image formation (Greenacre 1970). Greenacre (1969) looked upon the transitional object as a temporary construction to aid the infant in the early stages of the building of reality and individuality. "In contrast," she said, "the fetish serves as a patch for a flaw in the genital area of the body image" (p. 163).

In this presentation, we shall circumscribe the functions of transitional objects and distinguish objects and phenomena used for either distracting or soothing from those which reproduce the stability and comfort first experienced in the arms of the mother, or which give solace by reinstating the child's capacity to play. We shall try to trace the transitional object as a cherished possession from the emerging feelings of possessing oneself and the mother. We will use the neurophysiological data reported in the preceding chapter to document the thesis that the infant's and the mother's nonnutritional activities during nursing lend themselves to the formation of psychic structure in the child; this Glaser calls "transsensus" (1967). We shall try to show that the transitional object is the successor to holding and playing during the nursing situation—these are at the core of the formation of organ-object images—and that the transitional object is an external aid in the integration of various body parts, rhythms, and shapes into a three-dimensional image of the body.

DISTRACTING, SOOTHING, CONSOLING, COMFORTING, DREAMING AND POSSESSING

Mothers and babies have distinct preferences in methods of alleviating distress. Some babies are distracted by a colorful object or light; others will seek out auditory stimuli or will even stop crying to listen to their own vocalizations. The distance receptors in the eyes and ears play a greater role in providing distraction than do the near receptors, such as touch and taste. Regular sucking, patting, and rubbing are rhythmic soothers or tranquilizers. Mothers have their own preferences for pacifying their infants. When a child is hurt, some mothers will rub, others will kiss the "boo-boo," and still others will blow it away. Offers of sweets and promises of good things are just as frequent. Distracting the child teaches him to ignore his bad feelings and shifts his attention elsewhere—methods which presage denial and repression. Soothing the baby usually involves a regular rhythmic repetition of ritual movement, derived from feeding and burping patterns[3] and leading to drive satisfaction. Most of the time, mothers and children work out a mutually satisfactory repertoire of distractors and soothers which they use habitually. Relying on the steadfastness of this repertoire, the "good enough mother" (Winnicott 1960) and the "good enough child" develop a mutual trust, born of the ability to predict the good outcome of a bad feeling. When a toddler is frustrated or hurt during his mother's absence, he may wait for her return before he will cry. The ability to wait for comforting rather than accepting another person's distractions and soothing, is a sign that the child derives fortitude (ego strength) from anticipating and waiting for the return of the mother. When the child complains to his mother only, her return signifies more than a reunion with a loved and loving person. The mother who gives comfort and solace to her aggrieved child is a prototype of a possession in Winnicott's sense. By letting him hold her and by holding him, she affirms the intactness of his body and of her own. By petting and caressing him while he cuddles, she restores to him the freedom to resume his interrupted play. The comfort and consolation she offers are joint creations of mother and child, and become models for self-possession, self-comforting and self-solace.

The transitional object is a very special bridge to the comforting and consoling mother. One of its distinctions is that it is rarely used for distraction from pain, as are other things and activities employed in the primitive defense of displacement from pain to pleasurable experiences. Neither is the transitional object a prime soother like the breast and thumb or a secondary soother like the bottle and the pacifier. These are all providers of direct drive satisfaction through the maintenance of regular rhythmic activity in the oral zone. The transitional object serves as an adjunct to a defense or a drive. When a young child feels abandoned by this mother, he feels defenseless and his transitional object loses its value as a comforter (A. Freud 1969). It becomes equally useless when drive discharge is hindered, because it can no longer function as bridge to the drive object and adjunct to drive activity. While some children suck their blankets or hold them without sucking at all, the majority need their transitional objects only when they suck their thumbs, pacifiers, or bottles for the purpose of self-soothing. When there is interference with these activities, the beloved object is not only devaluated, but its function as body-image builder is lost to the child.

Dora at the age of two was a thumbsucker; in addition she needed her bottle, sometimes during the day and always on going to sleep. While sucking she fondled her blanket, calling it by such endearing names as "Sweetie" and "Pettie." During a long vacation away from home, she became more and more attached to her bottle, which had been offered as a soother in strange surroundings. At two-and-a-half, she still asked for it whenever she was upset, and became greatly frustrated when it was not available. The blanket which she loved so dearly was of no help to her when her parents began to wean her and told her she was too big for a bottle. Whenever she was frustrated or offended, she would hide her face, her physical behavior betraying her feelings of being small, alone, and inaccessible to consolation. One day a staff member discussed this type of nonverbal behavior with all the children, explaining that babies needed to do it, but big children could talk about their feelings. A short time after, Dora approached her, pointing to a picture of an animal on her dress. She inquired about a crease between the animal's eyes and nose, asking whether this was a mouth. It was clear that she was trying to restore the image of her own face with the help of a teacher. The blanket would "sweeten" and "pet" her face when she had the bottle, but ceased to be a playmate and "face-restorer" without it.

Mary at the age of twenty-three months was mildly interested in her pacifier, which she sucked in conjunction with fingering her blanket. However, when she fell ill during her mother's absence, she became very dependent on the pacifier and less interested in her blanket. When Mary was two-and-a-half years old, she began to lose her pacifier frequently, each time demanding that her mother find one for her. She seemed to work through the loss of her mother and the loss of her body-integrity during the illness by repeated acting out of misplacing and retrieving the pacifier. She appreciated that the center staff had been helping her overcome both traumata. Without hesitation, she left her pacifier with a teacher, who kept it in a special place for her. At home, she cried and became very angry at her mother when she herself misplaced her pacifier. At the same time, she lost interest in her blanket. When her pacifier was returned to her in the center and at home, she began to suck her fingers at times and reconciled herself with her mother and her blanket. At that time, the mother noticed that Mary would fall asleep holding her toes and her blanket. This new behavior indicated that Mary was finding new ways of recovering control over her body.

The transitional object is neither a distractor nor a soother like a thumb or a pacifier. It is most frequently fingered and brought in contact with the face during sucking. Before falling asleep, babies may lie on top of it, bringing it in contact with a large part of the body. Walkers may drag a transitional object near their feet or wrap it around themselves. Our impression is that the deprived infant is unable to play and can use a blanket or soft animal for finger-play only when drive satisfactions is restored and the illusion of the reappearance of the oral, feeding mother is reinstated (Kestenberg 1969, 1971). The holding of the transitional object and the illusion of being held by it recreates the feeling of mutual embrace during the early feeding. The restoration of play makes the child capable of consoling himself; the feeling of support and security derived from holding strengthens his ability to comfort himself.

Transitional objects are very special possessions, endowed with powers to console and comfort. They can do this because of their special function as aids in the integration and reintegration of body parts into the totality of the child's body-image (as separate from that of the mother). They have acquired this capacity as adjuncts to drive satisfaction during nursing. However, as restorers and maintainers of body integrity, they may gain independence from drive aims and drive objects and are used by some children who do not engage in nonnutritive sucking. Sometimes their function becomes more clearly related to allaying anxiety and to the defensive working through of a loss.

Derek at ten months became attached to his blanket in the process of separating from his mother. Up to that point he had used her as a transitional object. He had to be nursed several times during the day and night. A precociously independent walker, he pulled his mother's hand and dragged her around on his "practicing" ventures (Mahler 1968). Derek had never fallen asleep in his crib; he would doze off at his mother's breast and be carried to bed. As soon as he awoke, he called for his mother.

Our first task, during an admission interview at the center, was to tell Derek that his mother would sit with us and that he could walk wherever he wanted to. Once this separation between mother and child was instituted, Derek, who had been afraid of strangers, began to play with either of the center directors. Soon he was able to play with other children and would come to the mother only for refueling (Mahler and Furer 1963). When we tried to put him in a crib, in which most children are comfortable, Derek was terrified. At our suggestion, Derek's mother began to put him into his crib before he fell asleep. At the same time, night nursing was discouraged. Gradually Derek learned to lie down in his crib, and after a few weeks he was able to play in it when he woke up. At the same time his blanket became a solace and a comforter to him. He would lie down on top of it or wrap himself into it standing up in his crib. When he saw Sol's blanket on the floor, he lay down on it and cuddled his face in it. However, he did not evidence the ecstatic pleasure Sol displayed on seeing his beloved "Bonnie" (his own name for the blanket).

It seemed to us that Derek's acceptance of separateness was facilitated by his "discovery" of a blanket which became a link between his mother's arm-space and his crib-space (Spitz 1965). While he was mourning the loss of his feeding mother and of himself as a nursing baby attached to her, the blanket became an external aid to his internal reorganization.

Jimmy may well have used his mother as a transitional object. He needed her for comfort almost incessantly until he became enamored of locomotion. When he then came into conflict between his desire to suck from the breast and his need to explore, he tried to take his mother's breast with him, pulling on it with his mouth as he walked off her lap. His mother told him he had a choice of sucking or walking, and he opted for the latter. He had called the nipples "rez"; now he became enamored of raisins. In the center he had been walking around with a little doll in his hand. At home he began to go to sleep with another tiny doll. These holding activities were so inconspicuous that they escaped our attention for some time. At seventeen months, shortly after weaning, Jimmy became acutely ill and had to be hospitalized on an emergency basis. Unfortunately the nurses on the ward became hostile to Jimmy's anxious parents and insisted on taking the child away from their arms for a minor surgical intervention. Because Jimmy could not sleep, the hospital staff decided to separate him from his parents at night and to sedate him. His parents had brought several familiar objects from home, among them a blanket which was previously an item of indifference to Jimmy. At this time he would not hold a little toy in his hand but, rather, would wrap himself in his blanket and each morning become a "complete blanket boy," with his body and face covered. Thus, he made himself invisible and made his parents disappear at will. Upon his return from the hospital, Jimmy was very angry with his parents and refused to go near the car which had taken him away. Covering himself with a blanket became a mixture of reliving the separation from his parents and a means of restoration of body boundaries; these had been seriously disrupted during his illness. It is interesting to note that Jimmy had begun to tear ("rip-off," Thompson 1974) the silk hem of his blanket with his teeth. The sharpness of these actions gave him a feeling of relief, while all along he retained either one or another of his two blankets, which he used interchangeably. It is tempting to speculate that Jimmy could rip and tear two objects in lieu of his father and mother and in lieu of feeling ripped by the febrile illness that literally shook him up. By holding on to these blankets, he could experience his fury and yet maintain the image of his love objects and of himself. Holding a little baby doll, covering it with his entire hand, used to help Jimmy to hold himself up and explore, or go to sleep in his crib. After his traumatic hospitalization, the blanket became a screen protecting his whole body against the dissolution he experienced during high fever. It served only secondarily as an aide in the working through of his separation from and anger with his parents, giving him the illusion of being held and embraced like a small baby, safe in his mother's arms.

Winnicott (1951) and Stevenson (1954) traced the transitional object from the nursing situation. Lewin (1950) contended that the dream screen was a replica of the maternal breast. Our observations of nursing and the use of blankets as screens suggest that the dream screen represents the outer limits of the horizon, provided by the nursing mother's body and face and by the confining, stable objects that in her absence hold the baby in place. Distractions interfere with stability and may prevent continuity in nursing and play. Characteristic of dreams is the stability of the dream screen upon which the dream action is projected. However, despite this stability there is frequently a shifting of shapes and places which reflects the shifting images of the dreamer's body and of the body of the object. Stability gives continuity to the basic framework of the body-image, while mobility facilitates reorganization. Grolnick (chapter 14) suggests that dreams utilize transitional phenomena to reconstitute from primitive organ-object imagery the self- and object-representations of the waking state. We proceed one step further by postulating that transitional phenomena (and transitional objects) play an important role in the building or reconstituting of the body-image (Kestenberg 1975a). Nightmares are failures not only of the wish-fulfilling function of the dream (Freud 1900-1901); they are failures also of the body-image-rebuilding function of the dream. A good dream screen is like a good blanket; it shields one from distraction and maintains one's identity as a requisite for undisturbed drive satisfaction. By providing a framework for memory and imagery, it ensures a harmonious integration between external and internal reality. By reuniting the dreamer with the original drive object, it facilitates continuity and yet gives free rein to illusory play with space, weight, and time.

When Derek protested against nighttime weaning, he remained awake for long stretches of time. When he finally fell asleep, he cried out in a manner which suggested he was having a nightmare. Once he could accept his blanket as an aide in falling asleep without nursing, he gradually began to sleep for longer stretches of time and his sleep became peaceful. Many children who have separated successfully and are free from anxiety will wake up at night and call for their mothers to cover them. They seem to need an external screen—a counterpart of the internal dream screen—to maintain the feeling of body integrity which originated during the nursing situation.

These and similar observations suggest that the transitional object is an external possession which reinforces the experiences of owning the drive object and the self as initiators of drive activity and drive-derivative play, fantasies, and dreams. The rhythmic rubbing and stroking of the blanket and/or the face is an adjunct to the real or imaginary sucking experience. It is derived from the finger and toe play of the nursling. From this play, fantasies and pretend-actions emerge to become a source of consolation. The holding of the transitional object reproduces the holding and being held during nursing; the illusion of mutual embrace gives comfort and engenders a feeling of security. Both, playing and holding, are the basic methods of building and maintaining the body-image.

THE NURSING SITUATION AS PROTOTYPE OF
THE FUNCTIONS OF THE TRANSITIONAL OBJECT

In this section we shall describe certain aspects of the nursing situation which contribute to the formation of the images of the mother's and the child's body as "non-me" and "me" possessions. In doing so, we shall differentiate between adjuncts to drive satisfaction, which lie at the core of the body ego, and the soothing, peace-giving attributes of drive satisfaction proper.

Rhythms of tension-flow. The young nursling falls asleep at the breast. This is due not only to the experience of satiation; the child may fall asleep before that. The sucking rhythm, which alternates evenly between the binding and freeing of tension (Kestenberg 1965), has a soporific effect. Consequently, nurses sometimes have to pinch or shake newborn children to get them to suck or resume sucking after they doze off during feeding The vegetative-sensorimotor disorganization of the neonate presents a challenge to the caretaker. She must aid him in the reintegration of his neurophysiological system, which is disrupted during the transition from intrauterine to extrauterine existence. The mother is a partner in this transition, as she readjusts from the state of pregnancy to that of motherhood. She had forebodings of her baby's preferences for rhythmic changes of tension when she perceived his fetal movements. She may now recognize and affirm through vision what she felt about her baby when he was inside her. She learns to maintain his sucking by synchronizing the flow of her milk to his sucking rhythm. She helps him to adjust to her tension changes. Here and there, she kneads her breast, touches or strokes the baby gently, or rocks him to reinforce the optimal sucking rhythm. Both her finger movement and his periodic play on her breast and back counteract the soporific effect of oral rhythms. The supplementary finger and toe rhythms, which coordinate nursing and states of alertness, do not serve as a prime soother but rather as an integrator and mediator between various body parts or functions and the mother (see chapter 5 for data on the activation of the Gamma Nervous System through touching). Without it, the nursing rhythm can be easily disturbed; the young baby can lose the nipple or doze off, and the older baby can become distracted. When the satiated baby falls asleep and relinquishes the nipple, hand and finger play as an adjunct of need satisfaction ceases as well.

Rhythms of shape-flow. The neonate is capable of sucking, but will perfect this function through interaction with the nursing mother. Similarly, he is capable of breathing, but will develop a regular breathing rhythm through body-contact with his mother (see chapter 5). We recognize the breathing rhythm because it results in changes of body-shape. Breathing in goes together with unfolding and growing of body shape and breathing out with folding and shrinking (Kestenberg 1967, 1975, Kestenberg et al. 1971). The flow of tension and the flow of shape are coordinated rhythms, with free flow related to growing and bound flow related to shrinking of body-shape. Rhythmic changes in tension are based on tissue elasticity and rhythmic changes in shape on tissue plasticity. The former vitalizes and soothes the tense baby[4], the latter gives structure to tension changes. When the mother embraces her child, she gives him enough support to keep him startle-free, but provides enough room for him to stroke her and to breathe without restraint. Within this context she helps him coordinate his needs with the support-giving, need-satisfying object. Such a coordination is based on reciprocity. The child's embrace of, and play with, his mother's body stimulates maternal breathing and circulation as well as milk production; this in turn organizes the child's breathing, circulation, and sucking. Both mother and child feel the closeness during inhalation and the slight separation during exhalation. Their bodies enlarge and shrink as they breathe in harmonizing shape-flow rhythms. Throughout life, inhaling retains its connection with taking in and exhaling with giving up, a rhythm which characterizes all relationships from the most primitive to the most advanced. Selective touching allows for the highlighting of special body-zones, some of which are more sensitive than others (Freud 1905-1906). It connects the touched zone with the touching object. Because the touch arises from the total breathing body of another, it does not evoke the sense of a part-object. The child that holds his mother s hand feels secure that he is held by her entire body, not merely by her extended limb. Breathing together lends a global quality of togetherness and separation which becomes the basis for feelings of possession and loss. The periodic play on selected areas of the mother's body and periodic maternal caresses have a differentiating effect, as they stimulate certain parts of the body which become more dominant than others. The upper part of the mother's body can thus be highlighted, giving rise to the equation of an expansive, generous mother with an aggrandized version of the breast. By the latter, the child means not only the milk-giving organ, but the whole mother whom he feels as pulsating and breathing between his embracing arms and legs, his touching expressive face, and his scrutinizing gaze. This constitutes the first version of a tridimensional possession. The ability to shape an object by play is derived from the sensations and experiences of playing with the mother's body.

We have described how rhythmic changes in tension and body-shape during nursing are reinforced by play activities which help the infant develop the image of a moving, elastic, and plastic body, his own and his mother's. This aspect of the body image has been called tensomobile and morphomobile (Blumenthal 1971). Schilder (1935) referred to it, saying that "the distinct surface of our skin is perceived only when we are in touch with reality and objects" (p. 86), and that "we do not feel our body so much when it is in rest; but we do get a clearer perception of it when it moves and when new sensations are obtained in contact with reality, that is to say with objects" (p. 87). However, the infant can only experience a sharing of rhythms within the supportive milieu of being held and holding, which provides the basis for a stable, tensostatic and morphostatic framework of the body-image. The provision of mutual support between the mother-child pair furnishes the requisite conditions for the development of transsensus (Glaser 1967) and trust to pursue undisturbed drive-satisfaction and play.

The transitional objects and phenomena which create and re-create rhythms and shapes within the context of touching and being touched, seeing and being looked at, and hearing and being heard carry with them a flux through which the individual can change, create, and recreate his body-image in relation to the image of his love object. The transitional object, probably more than transitional phenomena, re-creates the unity, which originated in the nursing situation, between the stability of holding and the mobility of play.

Being held and holding. "When our limbs are supported, they will feel different from when they are not supported, because the muscular tension is different" (Schilder 1935, p. 92). Through the influence of the vestibular apparatus, which is highly sensitive during the first two years of life, we perceive the position of the limbs as well as the addition or subtraction of physical masses to our body. To move a three dimensional image of our body into conscious awareness, we must first develop a framework into which we fit it (this corresponds to the dream-screen described in Lewin [1950] and discussed earlier in this chapter). It originates in the mutual holding experience of mother and child, whose prototype is the way they support one another during nursing (Soodak 1971, Kestenberg and Buelte 1971, 1974). To successfully adapt her body to build a stable yet movable human cradle for her child, the mother must have a "cradleable" baby who can hold her and turn to her while she hold him and turns to him. An example should clarify this point.

Ron was breastfed for the first few months. His devoted mother blamed herself for switching to the bottle when she noticed that Ron began to jerk away from her as soon as he was satiated. He would not look at her during feeding and was difficult to hold. One of us (J.K.) could show the mother how, through the utilization of the tonic neck reflex, she could sustain contact with Ron more easily. Still, he looked at his mother only rarely, but would not avert his gaze from his father. It reassured the mother when she understood that Ron's father approached him from the side while she tried to engage his gaze frontally. It became apparent that Ron had a deficit in his visual orientation and would not respond unless his attention was engaged laterally. Closer scrutiny revealed that the mother sensed the child's impairment and stopped breast feeding in response to it. She could not endure her baby's "rejection" of her. When she found a way to hold him and interact with him, she not only accepted him, but played an important role in helping to restore his functions.

There are several reflexes in the newborn which permit the child to respond to the mother's holding activity. The creeping reflex is utilized when the baby is held facing the shoulder. Righting reflexes play a role in positioning the child's limbs when his mother picks him up. The tonic neck reflex is particularly suited for what constitutes the baby's embrace of the mother during nursing (Robbins and Soodak 1973, personal communication[5]). When the baby's head is turned to the right, his left arm is flexed, reaching the breast area which he might hold or knead. His right arm is extended, embracing the back of the mother. The same is true of his legs, one is flexed and the other extended, forming an arc around the mother's body lower down. The baby's body is upheld by the mother's arm, which covers almost his entire spine area, especially the antigravity muscles. A counterpressure is exerted by the maternal chest. Either the leg or the other arm of the mother participate in keeping the baby stable in the optimal nursing position. Both mother and child give each other leeway for coming closer together and moving away a bit for suckling, sucking, breathing, and playing. Frequently stability is provided by sustained eye to eye contact (Spitz 1965).

Responding to one another by an increase in breathing and blood circulation, they feel a warmth that is associated with the body boundaries becoming succulent and growing, ready to admit another being into the dual symbiosis so fittingly described by Mahler (1968). Under conditions of mutual holding they "transcend" into each other and feel each other's existence (see chapter 5, which describes Glaser's concept of transsensus). These are the physical ingredients of emotional warmth.

A secure, cradling mother conveys to her child what can be later described as a feeling of security and trust. He will not be dropped and startled. He can proceed with sucking, breathing, and playing without the disorganizing effects of wobbling or dangling, or of being squeezed, jiggled, jostled, not given room to breathe, confused by contradictory stimuli. Secure holding provides the milieu for undisturbed drive satisfaction and the freedom to play. The feeling of mutual support facilitates the child's formation of a stable body-image, both of himself and of his nursing mother. This fosters the feeling of owning, of possessing both his own body and that of his mother.

Building a body-image while being gratified appears to be one of the infant's first psychic "acts." However, gratification per se is not conducive to the building of stable structures. The requisites for satisfaction (such as holding and being held) and the adjuncts of gratification (such as playing while sucking) are structure-building in the dual sense of providing both stability and mobility of structure. In this way, psychic schemata become indestructible on the one hand and amenable to reorganization on the other.

Suckling and rocking the young baby may make the young mother drowsy. In our culture, unless she is in bed with the baby, she must wake and replace her body-cradle with a crib.[6] Through her discontinuance of rocking and dozing, she teaches the child to wake after feeding and resettle in the crib, which is a substitute for her body.[7] This requires not only kinesthetic, touch, and temperature readjustment, but also a visual shift from the mother's face to the surfaces of inanimate objects, such as the crib, sheet and blanket. Having received good care while nursing in the maternal cradle, the infant then discovers various methods of substituting for this experience. He can use his thumb to suck and soothe himself by reevoking a sustained oral rhythm. This can occur as an inborn given which may interfere with or reinforce sucking at the breast (Hoffer 1949) or as primary identification with the suckling mother (Kris 1951). Throughout the many separations from the holding mother and her substitution by the holding inanimate object, the baby reenacts the security of the nursing situation with nonmother possessions. The older infant, who holds and plays with a transitional object before falling asleep, maintains the illusion of remaining in touch with his mother. This helps him reevoke the feeling of possessing her during sleep and dreaming (Kanzer 1955). On awakening, he can wait for his mother's appearance only when his crib and its accessories are familiar objects with which he can reconstitute his former "waking self." The stability and sameness of the crib within the larger spatial configuration of his room and its permanent furnishings bridge the distance that separates the child from his parents. In this sense, the crib with its contents is a transitional object. Because the child does not carry it around with him, its significance in his life may be overlooked.

Dan neither sucked his fingers nor was attached to any special object. He used his mother to comfort him and approached her several times a day asking her to hold him. He had been accustomed to sleeping without a blanket and never asked for one. At the age of twenty-one months, he was well coordinated and precocious in his motor development, yet he never climbed out of his crib. When he was given a new bed, he was happy about this sign of becoming a "big boy" like his brother. However, he was somewhat apprehensive. He not only demanded that he be covered by a blanket, but he also kept a small object in his hands while going to sleep. His mother had originally provided both the holding experience and the crib. Dan now transferred the stabilizing function to the blanket. It enclosed him, as had his mothers arms and the sides of the crib.

Johnny, at the age of one year, would chew a corner of the blanket before going to sleep. When he was given the blanket, he smiled and dragged it with him while creeping, but he never demanded it when he was out of his crib. Sol who loved his "Bonnie" with passion, needed it only when he was going to sleep.

Blankets, diapers and pillows are selected as transitional objects, not only because their soft texture and pliability remind the child of the maternal body, but also because they are usually crib-objects. In the mother's absence, the crib becomes the principal feature of the child's holding environment (Winnicott 1960, Kestenberg and Buelte 1974). Blankets envelop the child, giving the illusion of maternal arms; they can be held, fingered, and brought close to the face in a manner reminiscent of holding the mother and playing with her breast during nursing. Whether the transitional object is used in conjunction with sucking, or not, the child fingers it with an oral rhythm. As he begins to feel clear sensations emanating from the anal sphincter, he will combine the oral rhythm with an anal type. When other zones become dominant, their preferred rhythm is added to the repertoire of blanket play (Kestenberg 1971, 1975b). The child's mother may not be able to change her own tension qualities quickly enough to suit his. He may need to interpose the blanket between his body and hers in order to integrate sensations from all parts of his body. Visual and auditory rhythms and tunes, used to console the child when he is frustrated or hurt, are adjuncts to bodily rhythms. These supplementary rhythms are not prime soothers, but rather the coordinators and mediators between various body zones and the nursing mother.

In addition to being a fine instrument on which the child can harmonize, the transitional object such as blanket or a diaper is also a form-giving and form-receiving object. Usually soft and pliable, it is capable of assuming many shapes that follow the child's contours or is arranged in special ways in relation to his body. It can be squeezed and pressed flat and wrinkled to the face. It can be extended to its full length or dragged in a manner reminiscent of a mother holding her child's hand. It can be made into a ball and held like a small or a big baby or it can become a wrap for a baby. It can be endowed with an imaginary mouth that is fed when the child is fed. A corner or hem can become particularly important, maybe because it has sharper contours or is more reminiscent of the areola of the breast or the nipple. It may have qualities of the sphincter as the child experiences it. When used primarily in lieu of a body organ, the blanket, with its volume and weight, reinstates the feelings of maternal size, volume, and weight that the child can shape and mold in relation to his own body.

Edna became enamored of a very large, fancy blanket when she was eleven months old. Her mother became concerned lest she would damage this irreplaceable object and then miss it. She offered her a pillow covered with the same material, then a swatch from the pillow case, but neither was "just right" for Edna. Her mother then sewed up the blanket so that it became less unwieldy, its length now equaling the child's head and torso line, but its thickness and apparent volume doubled. Edna was quite satisfied.

Each child choses his transitional object in accordance with its consistency, texture, size, volume, shape and odor. In each instance, it is a three-dimensional, shaped, and shapable possession that can fuse with the child's shape or separate from it. It can be used as a bridge to the mother's total body or to highlight and differentiate dominant zones, which change with progressive development (Kestenberg et al. 1971). Despite the changes in rhythms of playing and rhythms of shapes created by the child, despite the changes in size and texture through wear and tear, the transitional object is capable of retaining its basic characteristics, thus proving itself an indestructible possession. It is probably more the parent than the child who feels distraught when a satin edge, the fuzz of a blanket, or a teddy bear becomes worn out. Analyses of children and adults whose parents removed the damaged transitional object, reveal that they loved the supposedly ruined possession and felt injured by its loss.[8] Some children consider such objects used up (Winnicott 1953) because they are no longer useful in the re-formation of the body image. Some remain loyal to their onetime friends and assign them a special place on the shelf. Others repress their early experiences with such objects or at least forget what happened to them. What remains internalized is not the image of the object, but its image-building, integrative function, now taken over by the ego.

CONCLUSIONS

When we extract from the varieties of transitional objects those qualities which are derived from the nursing situation, we are left with the conclusion that holding and the illusion of being held offers comfort and security. Rhythmic play, an original adjunct of sucking, gives solace through illusory interaction with the lost nursing mother. The same ingredients allow transitional objects to aid in the maintaining and rebuilding of the body image in relation to the image of the mother. *Holding* and *fingering* are the two aspects of creativity which evolve from the intermediate zone between mother and child. One provides the "holding environment" (Winnicott 1960) in which creativity flourishes; the other has its root in the early play which gives a touch of illusion to our "changing environment."

The essential loneliness of the creative experience is derived from the experience of the infant, who has lost touch with his mother. The yearning for reunion is overcome by illusions, fantasies, and body memories, all related to the first formation of psychic content (transsensus) in the intermediate area, which bridges the gap between internal and external reality. Transitional objects are created in loneliness. They are based on feeling alone, yearning for past intimacy, and the recreation of past togetherness, while weaving into it current wishes and hopes for the future.[9] Transitional objects restore lost objects. Through their mediation, children who might have become lost in autoerotic activity can dream and maintain contact with the environment. They are integrating agents which help make the child's total body come alive and feel intact, maintaining at the same time the integrity of the love object. They are external aids in the formation of an integrated body image.

NOTES

1. The Center, for Parents and Children, located in the suburban community of Port Washington, N.Y., creates a meeting ground for parents, children, researchers, trainees, and teachers, working together to provide a mutual support system through the interplay of several program components. Within this structure the primary focus is on preventive services to babies, toddlers, and expectant and current parents. Mothers, (and/or fathers) and children attend biweekly

sessions, geared toward a communal study of best methods of child care. The staff consists of psychoanalytically oriented observers, movement specialists, and teachers. The children are provided a variety of experiences which enrich their development and help socialize them. Particular attention is paid to the notation of movement patterns of parents and children. Movement profiles are constructed which serve as a base for the retraining of movement pattern as a nonverbal intervention, serving the best interests of parents and children. A milieu is created in which parents develop an awareness of each other's relationships with their children. All parents help to solve a particular problem in child rearing and all parents help when staff and one or two parents are engaged in research. By sharing their experiences and helping to invent better child rearing methods, parents are able to bridge over some of the sense of isolation characteristic of the nuclear family. Each parent's expertise is utilized to develop programs, curricula, and material to meet their children's needs. By assisting the staff, teaching adolescent trainees, and participating in child development courses and conferences (as well as by maintaining regular logbooks of their children's development), parents become increasingly aware of patterns of interaction between children and their peers and adults in the center and at home. Movement training courses attune them to nonverbal communications. The research component of the program is an integral part, where the theme of mutuality is put into operation. While parents understand that they and their children are subjects of observation, they actively contribute to the gathering of information, such as was necessary for the writing of this paper. From each new insight, derived from this type of communal research, there evolves an immediate benefit to parents and children, a sharpening of questions which remain unanswered, and thus a call for future research.

2. Buxbaum (1960) and Bak (1974) referred to these objects not created by the baby but given to the child by the mother as *intermediate* rather than *transitional*. All things are given to the young child by his parents; only some of these give him the illusion that he has created them. In our terminology, all body products which are the first "intermediate" (not transitional) objects are bridges between mother and child, and are subject to traffic both ways. The ten-month-old feeds his mother, who in turn feeds him. The older baby gives his excrement to his mother and is disappointed when she does not return it. In contrast to transitional objects, intermediate objects are easily destroyed and easily replaced. They are frequent forerunners of fetishes, whereby the object that stands for the maternal phallus has developed in analogy to the shape of the fecal column (Kestenberg 1970).

3. The word *soothing* is derived from *soth*, meaning *truth*. In this sense, a good mother is a soothsayer, who truthfully predicts "you will feel better soon." The experience of having been soothed by sucking and satiated by the mother's milk gives credence to her omipotent healing methods.

4. Tissue elasticity is severely impaired in illness, fatigue, and toxic states. A sick mother or a sick child are sometimes unable to attune to one another because, in illness, tension-changes suffer from loss of vitality. The body may feel limp or leaden rather than alive and pulsating. A mother who becomes active rather than depressed when her child suffers may vitalize the child's body by stimulating him to respond to and mirror her tension and shape changes. A tired mother can use her baby to vitalize herself. The ensuing alertness of the child may prevent his falling asleep.

5. Robbins and Soodak are members of Child Development Research who are collaborating in the Sidney L. Green Prenatal Project in the Long Island Jewish Hospital, New Hyde Park, N.Y. They discovered the significance of the tonic neck reflex for maternal care while teaching a course about movement patterns to the nurses of th ᵎ neonatal nursery.

6. Gaddini (1970) found that rural children who slept with their parents were less likely to use transitional objects than those city children who were confined to sleeping in their own cribs. Remaining in close proximity to the mother's body made the use of transitional objects superfluous (Muensterberger 1969). One must wonder whether there was a concomitant decrease in creativity.

7. The obligation of the good Western mother to provide the child with a crib is clearly expressed in a poem by Brentano (1778-1842).

> Ich Schau zu dir, so Tag als Nacht,
> Muss ewig zur dir schauen,
> Du musst mir, die mich zur Welt gebracht
> Auch nun die Wiege bauen
>
> I look to you through day and night
> I must look to you forever
> You, who had brought me into the world
> Must also build me a cradle.
> (translation by J.K.)

8. Psychoanalyses of parents whose children use transitional objects, interviews with parents of analyzed children, and supplementary discussions with parents in the center suggest that a parent's (especially the mother's) body-image changes in successive stages of parenthood (Kestenberg 1976). The most conspicuous change occurs during transition from pregancy to motherhood. Mothers' feelings about transitional objects vary in accordance with their own wishes for separation or rapprochement with the child (Bush et al. 1973). Many parents refuse to relinquish control of their children; they feel rejected when the child prefers the transitional object in stress situations. Others, feeling guilty over their own desire to desert the child, offer objects to be left in the crib with the lonely child. Parents are particularly threatened

when a child remains attached to a damaged, shedding object. In one such instance, the mother removed a worn lamb, saying: "It is either the lamb or me, one of us must go." She could not accept an intermediate-zone object which was damaged and messy. Children sometimes feel indifferent about the lost objects, but their analyses reveal that indifference is a cover for a feeling of loss which encompasses an estrangement from the love object, an incompleteness of the body image, and a stifled creativity. The feeling of loss is overdetermined, as the child recognizes the parent's fear of injury and mourns the loss of an intact love object. It will take us too far afield to discuss here how the mother uses the child and his transitional object as an aid in the reorganization of her body image. We shall return to this topic in a future publication.

9. Ich bin allein,   Hin zu dem Glanz
     Fort is die Erde   Der tiefsten Naechte,
     Nachts muss es sein,   Fort aus dem Raum
     Das Licht mir werde.   der Erdenschmerzen
     O fuehrt mich ganz   Durch Nacht und Traum
     Ihr innern Maechte!   Zum Mutterherzen.
     (from a poem by Justinus Kerner, 1786-1862)

I am alone   On to the radiance
The earth is gone   Of deepest night,
There must be night   Out of the space
For light to come.   Of earthly pain
Oh lead me whole   Through night and dream
You, inner powers!   To mother's heart.
(translation by J.K.)

REFERENCES

Bak, R.C. (1974). Distortions of the concept of fetishism. *Psychoanalytic Study of the Child* 29: 191-214.

Blumenthal, M. (1971). Discussion at workshop on metapsychology, L. Rubinstein, chairman New York Psychoanalytic Institute. Quoted in Kestenberg et al. (1971).

Brentano C. (1778-1842). In *Anthology of German Verse*, ed. Farber du Faur and K. Wolff, pp. 309–310. New York: Pantheon Books, 1949.

Busch, F. et al. (1973). Parental attitudes and the development of the primary transitional object. *Child Psychiatry and Human Development* 4:12–20.

Buxbaum, E. (1960). Hair pulling and fetishism. *Psychoanalytic Study of the Child* 15:243-260.

Freud, A. (1969). Film review of Robertson's film "John, Seventeen Months: Nine Days in a Residential Nursery." *Psychoanalytic Study of the Child* 24:138-143

Freud, S. (1900-01). Interpretation of dreams. *Standard Edition* 5.

—— (1905-06). Three essays on sexuality. *Standard Edition* 7:125-245.

—— (1927). Fetishism. *Standard Edition* 21: 149-157.

—— (1930). Civilization and its discontents. *Standard Edition* 21:59-145.

Gaddini, R. (1970). Transitional objects and the process of individuation: a study in three different social groups. *Journal of the American Academy of Child Psychiatry* 9:347-364.

Glaser, V. (1967). *Sinnvolle Gymnastik*. Helfer Verlag.

Greenacre, P. (1969). The fetish and the transitional object. *Psychoanalytic Study of the Child* 24:144-164.

—— (1970). The transitional object and the fetish: special reference to the role of illusion. Presented at meeting of New York Psychoanalytic Society, 17 March 1970.

Hoffer, W. (1949). Mouth, hand and ego-integration. *Psychoanalytic Study of the Child* 3:293-312.

Kanzer, M. (1955). The communicative function of the dream. *International Journal of Psycho-Analysis* 36:260-266.

Kerner, J. (1786-1862). In *Anthology of German Verse*, ed. Faber du Faur and K. Wolff, p. 325. New York: Pantheon Books, 1949.

Kestenberg, J.S. (1965). The role of movement patterns in development. I. Rhythms of movement. *Psychoanalytic Quarterly* 34:1-36.

—— (1967). Movement patterns in development. III. The control of shape. *Psychoanalytic Quarterly* 356-409.

—— (1969). Problems of technique of child analysis in relation to the various developmental stages: pre-latency. *Psychoanalytic Study of the Child* 24:358-383. New York: International Universities Press.

—— (1970). Discussion of Greenacre's paper "The Transitional Object and the Fetish: Special Reference to the Role of Illusion." Meeting of the New York Psychoanalytic Society, 3/17/1970.

—— (1971). From organ-object imagery to self and object representations. In *Separation Individuation*, pp. 75-99. New York: International Universities Press.

—— (1975a). Discussion of Grolnick's paper "Dreams and the Transitional Object." Meeting of Long Island Psychoanalytic Society, 3/3/1975.

—— (1975b). *Children and Parents: Psychoanalytic Studies in Development*. New York: Jason Aronson.

—— et al. (1971). Development of the young child as expressed through bodily movement. I. *Journal of the American Psychoanalytic Association* 19:746-764.

——, and Buelte, A. (1971). Holding the baby. Presented at the Dec. 1971 Meetings of the American Psychoanalytic Association.

——, and Buelte, A. (1974). Holding each other—holding oneself up. Presented at the International Congress of Child Psychiatry, Philadelphia, Pa.

Kohut, H. (1971). The analysis of the self. *Psychoanalytic Study of the Child, Monograph No. 4.*

Kris, E. (1951). Some comments and observations on early autoerotic activities. *Psychoanalytic Study of the Child* 6:95-116.

Lewin, B. (1950). *The Psychoanalysis of Elation.* New York: Norton.

Mahler, M. (1968). *On Human Symbiosis and the Vicissitudes of the Separation-Individuation.* New York: International Universities Press.

———, and Furer, M. (1963). Certain aspects of the separation-individuation phase. *Psychoanalytic Quarterly* 32:1-14.

Muensterberger, W. (1962). The creative process: its relation to object loss and fetishism. *Psychoanalytic Study of Society* 2:161-185.

——— (1969). Psyche and environment: sociocultural variations in separation and individuation. *Psychoanalytic Quarterly* 38:191-216.

Robbins, E., and Soodak, M. (1973). Personal communication. International Universities Press.

Schilder, P. (1935). *The Image and Appearance of the Human Body.* London: Kegan, Trench, Traubner.

Searles, F. H. (1960). *The Nonhuman Environment.* New York: International Universities Press.

Soodak, M. (1971). Retraining of movement. Presented at the Dec. 1971 meetings of the American Psychoanalytic Association.

Spitz, R. A. (1965). *The First Year of Life.* New York: International Universities Press.

Stevenson, O. (1954). The first treasured possession: a study of the part played by specially loved objects and toys in the lives of certain children. *Psychoanalytic Study of the Child* 9:199-217.

Thompson, P. G. (1974). Homeostasis disruptions. Unpublished.

Tolpin, M. (1971). On the beginnings of a cohesive self: an application of the concept of transmuting internalization of the study of the transitional object and signal anxiety. *Psychoanalytic Study of the Child* 26:316-354.

Winnicott, D. W. (1951). Transitional objects and transitional phenomena. In *Collected Papers: Through Paediatrics to Psycho-Analysis,* pp. 229-242. New York: Basic Books, 1958.

——— (1960). The theory of the parent-infant relationship. *International Jounal of Psycho-Analysis* 41:585-595.

——— (1967). Discussion of Kestenberg's paper "Acting Out in the Analysis of Children and Adults." International Psychoanalytic Congress, Copenhagen.

Wulff, M. (1946). Fetishism and object choice in early childhood. *Psychoanalytic Quarterly* 15:450-471.

CHAPTER 7

When the editors discussed with René Spitz their project for the further study of transitional objects and phenomena, he encouraged us and told us of his desire to contribute to the volume. The present chapter, written after his death by his close associate, Dr. David Metcalf, emerged from their study of early object relations and dreaming: it is understandable, then, that they should be able to specify the transitional object's organizing functions at a critical period in development. After all, Spitz had for decades made seminal contributions in this area, coining the term *psychic organizer* and conducting classic studies on the connection between mothering and optimal development.

Metcalf and Spitz go beyond Winnicott in postulating a transitional object stage in transitional object relations development "from recognition of a Sign Gestalt to evocation through a volitional act of mentation." Arnold Modell, reasoning from clinical data, has reached similar conclusions rooted more in the analysis of the borderline state and Mahler's work on separation-individuation.

The authors bring Winnicott's ideas more into the mainstream of developmental and ego psychology. They agree with Winnicott that the transitional object is both indicator and representative of the inception of the infant's complex symbolic functioning. They tie this to ego development, especially to object relations, and show the importance of recognition and evocative memory in achieving object constancy.

L.B.

THE TRANSITIONAL OBJECT: CRITICAL DEVELOPMENTAL PERIOD AND ORGANIZER OF THE PSYCHE

David R. Metcalf

René A. Spitz

The transitional object is the first evidence of the infant "clearly distinguishing between fantasy and fact, between inner objects and external objects, between primary creativity and perceptions." Winnicott (1951) expanded this creative formulation and discussed the development of language, the reality principle, active adaptive efforts by the infant, the infantile roots of creativity, and some psychopathological sequelae of fixation at or regression to this period.

A host of important developmental observations have stemmed from this work. The theory of psychoanalytic technique and psychoanalytic developmental theory have used the important interface concept provided by Winnicott's formulations as an aid in exploring and clarifying that troublesome and difficult area, the confluence and "cooperation" as Freud (1905) called it, between "the two methods," between data derived from the direct observation of infants and children, on the one hand, and the knowledge achieved by means of psychoanalytic genetic reconstructions, on the other. The need for finding acceptable, valid, and useful methods for appropriately balancing, imbricating, and interrelating

Editor's note: Dr. Spitz died September 14, 1974. He had a deep interest in this topic and had planned to contribute a chapter to this volume. The conceptualizations and views expressed here are an outgrowth of our many discussions about the role of transitional objects and transitional phenomena in the development of object relations. These formulations originated as one part of a monograph in the development of object relations and the inception of dreaming in infancy. It is difficult, at this time, to credit specifically one or the other author for ideas which evolved out of a collaborative effort. Suffice it to say that Spitz's creative flair never left him and is alive in these formulations. We wish to thank Dr. David Parrish for making us aware of the work of Drs. Metcalf and Spitz, an awareness which led to the inclusion of the present chapter in this volume.

retrospective genetic-psychoanalytic and developmental-observational (often prospective) material has never been greater, as psychoanalysis struggles both to redefine its possible "widening scope" and to more clearly and rationally define and maintain its "core identity" and cohesive sense of integrity and self.

Our interest in transitional objects and transitional phenomena was stimulated by work on the inception of dreaming during infancy (Spitz et al. 1970). We drew heavily at first on the emerging important and provocative knowledge (dating to the mid-1950s) on the physiology of sleep and dreaming. However, it becomes increasingly clear that this enlargement of our horizons raised almost as many questions as it clarified. Unresolved still is the persistent issue of the leap from soma to psyche; Spitz discussed this at length in "Bridges" (1972). Furthermore, the inception and ontogenesis of dreaming involves other aspects of human development, all of which have drawn attention for many years, some once again gaining the center of our attention as psychoanalysis becomes increasingly concerned with developmental problems (Metcalf 1976). We begin to gain a clearer picture of the limits, the valid applicability, and the dangers connected with "the widening scope" (Stone 1954, Strupp 1976). Among these important issues are the development of memory, of libidinal object constancy, and of the capacity for symbolization.

Separation-individuation (Mahler et al. 1975) can in part be conceptualized as involving a concatenation of these more separable aspects. They all overlap and interact in their functions and development, connected to a large degree through the principle of dependent development (Spitz 1959). It is surprising that transitional phenomena and transitional objects, their origins, developmental vicissitudes, and fate, and their functions and meanings have been relatively neglected when one considers that herein lies the key, as Winnicott (1951) noted, to the inception and unfolding of symbolic thinking, one of the foundations for the unique human mental activities of dreaming, fantasy, and creativity.

We take as our starting point the early development of memory in relation to the first two nodal periods of psychic organization, the smiling response at age 3 months (Spitz and Wolf 1946) and stranger anxiety (often overlapping with infantile separation anxiety) at 6 to 8 months (Benjamin 1963, Tennes and Lampl 1964, Spitz 1965). A delineation of memory development is a necessary prerequisite for understanding the inception and progression of "thing-permanence," of libidinal object constancy, of transitional phenomena, and of dreaming. Fraiberg (1969) clarified psychoanalytic and Piagetian views on libidinal object constancy, object constancy, and object ("thing") permanence. She differentiates recognition memory (memory in the presence of the thing or object stimulus) and evocative memory (in the absence of a need for the object, or the object's presence).

On the basis of mother-stranger differentiation (Tennes and Lampl 1964, Spitz 1965, Fraiberg 1969), recognition memory can be shown to be operating by 6 to 8 months. The smiling response in the third month is actually already a *recognition* in the sense that the percept of "privileged Gestalt" is recognized as the *signal* for need gratification. In the second half of the first year, smiling no longer takes place as the function of an actual need; what is now perceived and evoked is the representation of the face of a unique individual, different from all others. From the provider of relief from unpleasure, the percept of the libidinal object has become the object of complex dynamic exchanges and relations. But this is not yet the "recognition proper" of the libidinal object's perceived, specific, unique attributes. Stranger anxiety at about 6 to 8 months indicates that the approaching person is a nonobject. The nonobject does not correspond to the infant's needs of the moment. It evokes a complex mixture of libidinal and aggressive cathexes which characterize the "memory" of the libidinal object without leading to the closure which the recognition of the need-gratifying object would have provided. As Fraiberg implies, and as we will adumbrate, an existing need-state can serve as a stimulus for evoking the memory of a satisfaction. In this context it can be considered the equivalent of an exteroceptive perceptual stimulus.

This proposition also applies to the riddle of the transitional object in the evocation of the libidinal object. At this stage in development, the transitional object's percept can serve to evoke the dynamic formula of the libidinal object's memory. After very little progress along this developmental line, this memory can be evoked endogenously without the crutch of external perception or internal survival-insuring needs. We felt it important to distinguish the "primal needs" to which Fraiberg refers from the secondary development of what we have called "quasi-needs." From about 6 months to 12 months, the infant is still guided and controlled by primal needs, particularly at approximately the beginning of the inception of evocative memory at about 16 to 18 months (Piaget's "Stage 6"). Parenthetic to this discussion but central to our own interest is the fact that dreams have been verbally reported as early as 19 to 22 months; our studies of memory development and memory organization lead us to postulate a much *earlier* onset of dreaming proper but this argument is not focal to the current presentation.

The period in development during which evocative memory can be demonstrated is preceded by a period during which this well-organized, predictably demonstrable type of memory is actually *in the process* of being formed. This process should be clarified. *We maintain that on the way from recognition memory, active from about age 6 months, to the predominance of evocative memory, achieved toward the end of the second year of life, the establishment of "transitional phenomena" and the transitional object will represent a stage of its own.*

This shadowy and variable developmental period is one in which the conflict between autonomy and dependency is the central problem in the mother-child dyad. In the course of the vicissitudes of this conflict, situated at the beginning of the anal period, the child is striving to implement and actualize his recently acquired capacity for autonomy; the beginnings of reality testing are initiated. With its maturational impetus, this movement conflicts with the child's dependency and love attachment to the libidinal object, the mother. The two contradictory and opposite currents provoke an ongoing atmosphere of exchanges in which the predominance of the libidinal drive alternates with the predominance of the aggressive drive. It is our contention that this alternation and these exchanges establish the coherence, on the one hand, of the libidinal object as such, and, on the other, of the relationship of the child with the object. The outcome will be a coherent psychic structure, representing the mother, part objects, "ego nuclei," and previously fragmented relations of all sorts forming the constituent parts of this integrated whole. This structure, which serves need-gratification while providing the incitement for ongoing development, acquires through the process of reciprocal exchanges and conflict-solutions, a completely unique character containing an endless host of attributes. These attributes are partly compatible and partly contradictory. It is this strange, paradoxical, and unique structure that will permit the deepest emotionality of the feeling "mother" to accompany the individual throughout life. For at this stage "mother" is *absolute security* and *complete trust*; so much so that aggression against her becomes possible for that very reason—*because* she can be trusted.

When the need for the mother arises, the transitional object serves as a quasi-evocative stimulus. With the help of the completion gradient (Spitz 1959), this stimulus evokes the total affect-gestalt, "mother," with the unique meaning of security. It is out of this impact of developmental processes on ongoing maturation, that we observe the epigenesis of evocative memory. It is this process and this structuring that enables the child to endow one inanimate thing from his surround (a blanket, a soft toy, etc.) with an essential attribute of the libidinal object: *security.* A new structure arises, purely psychological and by nature devoid of all actual need-gratification: the *transitional object*. As a result of a psychological operation, the transitional object is transformed into a quasi-need.

The child has recourse to this device in situations of insecurity, which vary from child to child according to the subject's individual history. Among these situations, the state of going to sleep is of outstanding importance. In going to sleep, the ego, a recently and as yet not firmly established caretaker of the child, relinquishes its executive control (perception, motricity, and motility) of the drives. These, now uncontrolled, become threatening and have to be dealt with by an as yet barely established device; we have posited this device to be the attempts at solution of the completion gradient, the "problem solving" gratification in the dream. A delicate balance of regulatory switching must take place which can easily miscarry. In our opinion, such miscarriages are manifested in infantile sleep panic and, in extreme cases perhaps, by "sudden infant death." It is well known that the peak incidence of sudden infant death coincides with a major period of establishment of a psychic organizer, the beginning of the stage of the smiling response. This is attended by numerous physiological and primitive psychic organizational shifts.

The going to sleep transition represents a danger to the ego and demands the intervention of mother (a glass of water, a tuck-in, singing, presence), and when that is not available, the transitional object is called upon to evoke her memory and replace her. We call this developmental period *the stage of the establishment of the transitional object*.

What danger does going to sleep represent? The danger of relinquishing the control of the ego, just when ego-autonomy is in the process of being established with the help of a series of conflicts with the love object. Autonomy is experimentally acquired through the most archaic, and therefore most conflict-free, sector of the ego, namely the body ego. It is relatively conflict-free, not only because of its origin at the stage of nondifferentiation, but also because its performance and successes are rewarded by the praise of the presumptive love object. These attempts at problem solving are an unending source of the "aha" experience, with its high level of narcissistic gratification, mostly involving the love object's delighted participation. It is this inexhaustible source of narcissistic gratification which involves also the triumphant consciousness of the child becoming the caretaker of his own security; this, however, must be relinquished piecemeal while falling asleep.

Why is the transitional object a relatively successful protective device against the development of panic states which otherwise ensue during falling asleep or arousal? One is reminded of Winnicott's postulate that the transitional object is, among its many functions, one of the sources of art. On a much more advanced level, for instance in the adult or preliterate cultures, apotropaic devices (masks, magic wands, puppets, etc.) play a comparable role. The indispensable attribute of the transitional object is that it can be mouthed at an early stage of its development. All its other attributes are adventitious and determined by the history of the individual child. Accordingly, they may belong to the actual mouthing situation or may appear unrelated to the stage at which they are observed.[1] Herewith we return to the most profound source of security experienced by the body ego, and to the oral triad of Lewin (1950): to eat, to sleep, to die.

Spitz (1965) and I (1975) have described critical periods and organizers as representing asynchronic progression between maturation and development, leading to an inadequacy or imbalance of regulative devices; stimulus-provoked tensions can no longer be discharged with the help of available mechanisms. The organizer consists in the invention of a new discharge formula, a new modus operandi. The outstanding aspect of the *second organizer*, the eighth month's anxiety, is exactly that the unpleasure takes the form of *anxiety*; the transitional object's function consists in allaying this anxiety and, for instance, in making sleep possible. That the transitional object is originally mouthable is crucial; it takes us back to the earliest and most reliable device for the removal of unpleasure sensations originating in the body ego. It leads us back to the all-reassuring, be that food or a pacifier; it leads us back to the primal cavity (Spitz 1965) from which sleep originates, and again to Lewin's oral triad.

The period of the transitional object and its vicissitudes have not as yet been sufficiently investigated. Its natural history and chronology should offer us valuable information on the emergence of mentation, on questions concerning the detection of prototypes of dreams in the first year of life (we have termed these *protodreams*), and lastly, on the question as to when during development "predreams" followed by representational dreams can occur.

One unresolved question is the meaning of children's use of transitional objects in the mother's presence. It appears that the early stages of evocative memory correspond to the emergence of a categorically new type of psychic functioning. Cognitive elements, memory traces, are being organized into coherent units of a higher order of complexity. These units show the capacity for far more numerous interrelations than do the primitive relations preceding this stage. Again, we refer to a new modus operandi: the emerging capacity to bring about interchanges between cognitive mental structures in the form of thought processes and interactions between these mental structures and objects or individuals in the surround. It is at this stage that we would be inclined to place the inception of original creative mental activity of the child.

The *indicator of the onset* of this critical period in development is the emergence of the transitional object. We suspect an equivalence between the transitional objects of waking reality and the representational dream in the sleep state (see Grolnick, chapter 14). Verbal behavior after 15 months clearly demonstrates this in the progress from the one-word sentence ("global language") to the acquisition of a richer vocabulary and an idiosyncratic syntax. We see now that through chance and as a result of the vicissitudes of a given child's personal history, transitional objects become endowed with a significant part of the need-gratifying object's recognition cathexis. As a result, the transitional object becomes a constituent of the building memory structure, which represents the total gestalt of need-gratifying tension-reduction. This we might call the prototype of the future libidinal object. The prototype of the transitional object is seen in the dynamics of the functioning of the sign gestalt (the paradigmatic face) which evokes the smiling response at about age 3 months via the confluence of gratification, feeding, falling asleep, and tension-reduction. All these form a repetitive, coextensive patterning which interconnects mother's face, tension-building, and tension-relief.

It is evident that the transitional object is endowed with the libidinal cathexis belonging to a quasi-need. In this case, the transitional object becomes representative and substitutes for the libidinal object proper. However, in contradistinction to the libidinal object, the transitional object remains conflict-free. In exchanges with the libidinal object (the real, living mother) conflict arises incessantly and actually forms the fabric, the tissue, of object relations. But no conflict can arise with the transitional object; as long as it is there it complies.

Accordingly, it is to be expected that the transitional object will arise at a stage at which the constitution of the libidinal object proper is not yet complete. The transitional object will carry even over into the often tempestuous vicissitudes of object relations the climate of that golden age in which the unambivalent signal, "need-gratification," represented the relief of need-tension. We therefore feel justified in postulating the establishment of the transitional object as *a specific stage in the progress from recognition of a sign gestalt to evocation through a volitional act of mentation.* It is a stage in the natural history of object development.

It is perhaps due to this freedom from conflict as well as to its magic evocative power (of what we might loosely term *hallucinatory need-gratification*) that, notwithstanding the vaunted power of reality versus imagination, the transitional object survives in the course of the subsequent developmental stage—that of the libidinal object proper. The transitional object remains available as an aid and assistant to the libidinal object proper during the vicissitudes and struggles which lead the child through the storms of the formation (and dissolution) of the oedipus complex; we might therefore speak of the transitional object as a prosthesis for evocative memory. Further development of the transitional object will lead in two very different, seemingly paradoxical but actually dialectical directions. One, the development of evocative memory proper, involves the ability to relinquish the transitional object; the other the retention of the transitional object, can by way of a change in function (Hartmann and Loewenstein 1962) lead to the highest levels of imaginative objectification.

It is thus evident that the period for the inception, further development, unfolding, and organization of transitional phenomena and for the cathexis of transitional objects is prolonged and complex. This period has many of the characteristics of a critical period in development. It entails what we have termed (Spitz et al. 1970) "a new modus operandi"; its time of inception is marked by an *affective indicator*, the libidinal cathexis of a "thing." Although the inception of this period at a simple level of psychic organization is usually clear, its further development, maturation, and putative ending are lost in the escalating complexities of expanding psychic structure and mental functioning.

We believe that this critical period for transitional phenomena provides a necessary and unique bridge between the inner and the outer, between fantasy and reality. This bridge is unique because it serves a connecting function while also allowing a separation under ego-control. Thus, prior to this period the differentiation between outer reality and inner perception (drive, need, "hallucination") is indistinct and imperfect. After the inception of this period, reality testing matures and transitional objects become the vehicle for the development of fantasy, symbolization, and the myriad substitutions, displacements, and condensations which are the stuff of the dream-work. The inception of dreaming and its further evolution require the prior (or perhaps coterminous) inception and development of transitional phenomena. The beginning of dreaming and the flowering of the period of transitional phenomena also form a landmark in the establishment of psychic structure because it is in this complex and intertwined developmental line that creativity, under ego direction, has its origins. It is with the dream and with the cathexis of transitional objects and phenomena that "regression in the service of the ego" originates. From the confluence of these related but separate streams in psychic development arise some of the greatest accomplishments of man.

NOTE

1. To interpret smoking in the adult is relatively easy. To interpret the rabbit's foot in the pocket is a little more difficult, and to interpret the rheumatism protection of the potato in Bloom's back pocket in Joyce's *Ulysses* is even more difficult. However, these examples of the "genetic fallacy" (Langer 1942, Hartmann 1960) indicate a tempting trap.

REFERENCES

Benjamin, J.D. (1963). Further comments on some developmental aspects of anxiety. In *Counterpoint*, ed. H. Gaskill, pp. 121-153. New York: International Universities Press.

Fraiberg, S. (1969). Libidinal object constancy and mental representation. *Psychoanalytic Study of the Child* 24:9-47.

Freud, S. (1905). Three essays on the theory of sexuality. *Standard Edition* 7:125-243.

Hartmann, H. (1960). *Psychoanalysis and Moral Values*. New York: International Universities Press, page 93.

Hartmann, H. and Loewenstein, R.M. (1962). Notes on the superego. *Psychoanalytic Study of the Child* 17:42-81.

Langer, S.K. (1942). *Philosophy in a New Key*. 1974 ed. Cambridge: Harvard University Press.

Lewin, B.D. (1950). *Psychoanalysis of Elation*. New York: Norton.

Mahler, M.S., Pine, F., and Bergman, A. (1975). *The Psychological Birth of the Human Infant*. New York: Basic Books.

Metcalf, D.R. (1975). René Spitz and the biopsychology of early infant development: the inception of dreaming. Presented at a meeting of North Pacific District Branch, American Psychiatric Association, Vancouver, B.C., April 1975.

——— (1976). Some old and some new thoughts on psychoanalysis as a developmental psychology. Presented as The Sophia Mirviss Memorial Lecture, San Francisco Psychoanalytic Institute and Mount Zion Hospital and Medical Center, San Francisco, California, April 1976.

Spitz, R.A. (1959). A genetic field theory of ego formation. New York: The New York Psychoanalytic Institute and International Universities Press.

——— (1972). Bridges: on anticipation, duration and meaning. *Journal of the American Psychoanalytic Association* 20:721-735.

Spitz, R.A., and Cobliner, W.G. (1965). *The First Year of Life*. New York: International Universities Press.

Spitz, R.A., Emde, R.N., and Metcalf, D.R. (1970). Further prototypes of ego formation. *Psychoanalytic Study of the Child* 25:417-441.

Spitz, R.A., and Wolf, K. (1946). The smiling response. *Genetic Psychology Monographs* 34:57-125.

Stone, L. (1954). The widening scope of indications for psychoanalysis. *Journal of the American Psychoanalytic Association* 2:567-594.

Strupp, H.H. (1976). Some critical comments on the future of psychoanalytic therapy. *Bulletin of the Menninger Clinic* 40:238-247.

Tennes, K.H., and Lampl, E. (1964). Stranger and separation anxiety in infancy. *Journal of Nervous and Mental Diseases* 139:247-254.

Winnicott, D.W. (1951). Transitional objects and transitional phenomena. In *Collected Papers: Through Paediatrics to Psycho-Analysis*, pp. 229-242. New York: Basic Books, 1958.

CHAPTER 8

Winnicott's precursor objects, a concept elaborated here by Renata Gaddini, differ from transitional objects in that they are neither separate from the infant (e.g., the thumb) nor created by him (e.g., the pacifier). The infant must be able to bridge the rifts caused by developmental strains during the first six months. On Gaddini's view, precursor objects are not simply a casual aspect of the child's attempts at reestablishing an age-appropriate symbiotic union with the mother: rather, they enable an optimal symbiotic experience to develop, and set the stage for differentiation in the latter half of the first year. She postulates the use of precursor objects as a precondition for the development of transitional objects during the phase of differentiation.

Following Winnicott, she relates the precursor to the psychosomatic equilibrium of the early stages of life, and stresses the importance of good enough mothering. Where this mothering is deficient, where there is a breakdown of what Winnicott would call the holding and facilitating maternal environment, there somatizations can occur. The child fails to develop transitional objects and can be predisposed to fetishism. The concomitant failure of higher symbolization can lead to such bodily expressions as rocking, rumination, colic, dermatoses, and asthma. The rocking child "becomes" the mother, recreating a prenatal union, but is unable to deploy his energies for separation, individuation, and more mature object relations. Both rocking and rumination can create a sense of union with the holding, rocking mother of the nursing situation. Oral rhythms can play a role in both conditions, which Gaddini maintains should be considered as seriously as colic and asthma. In this volume Judith Kestenberg's discussion of the development of the body image with its focus on the nursing situation complements the views of Gaddini and Winnicott.

Though Melitta Sperling did not accept the concept of transitional objects, her descriptions of the breakdown of the mother-infant dyad parallel Gaddini's analysis of the earlier situation. There is a limit to the infant's capacity to use transitional object precursors as shock absorbers for the stresses and strains of maternal distancing; as a result, infantile aggressive surges cannot be bound, and failures occur in symbolization, differentiation, defense, body-image formation, and the delineation of self- and object-representation. Thus are found weakly established ego autonomies as well as impaired play and creativity. Sally Provence, in a number of classic studies in collaboration with other authors, has detailed much of this on the basis of clinical observations of infants who were subjected to moderately severe stress.

L.B.

TRANSITIONAL OBJECT ORIGINS AND THE PSYCHOSOMATIC SYMPTOM

Renata Gaddini

The problem of the translation of conflict and anxiety into somatic symptoms—what Freud called the mysterious leap between the mind and the body—has been approached in a variety of ways during the last thirty years. The pioneer researchers in the field—Cannon, Dunbar, and Alexander—all took the adult intrapsychic processes as the arena of their research. They included psychological specificity, organ choice, and mediation. Recently Greene (1958), Engel (1962), and others of the Rochester school have focused on the quality of the child's object relationships to understand the formation of the psychosomatic symptom. They conceptualize psychosomatic symptoms as generated on the basis of both, the nearness-separateness polarity and the interaction of mother and child dependence and independence. These researchers consider asthma with it typical dependency conflicts, the fear of being either too far or too close, to be a model for the process of psychosomatic symptom formation.

A NEGATIVE AND A POSITIVE MODE

In the last few years I have reconsidered, from this new vantage point, other psychosomatic symptoms occurring at an early developmental level: rumination, three-month colic, and asthma. *As a conceptual framework I propose to use the development of a transitional object (T.O.) in infancy as the sign of a positive mode, and the development of the psychosomatic symptom as its negative.* This is a view compatible with that of Winnicott (1966), who described psychosomatic illness as "the negative of a positive: the positive being the tendency towards integration" and as "the inherited tendency of each individual to achieve a unit of the psyche and the totality of physical functioning." To continue in Winnicott's words: "This stage in the integrating process is one that might be called the 'I am' stage.

Developmental failure results in an uncertainty of indwelling...the dwelling of the psyche in the personal soma and vice versa. Psychosomatic disorder implies a maternal failure which has left an infant without the essentials for the operation of the maturational processes."

An understanding of Winnicott's concept of the transitional area as a potential space between mother and child and between object and subject is essential for our clinical work. We must understand the quality of the relationship between the child and the object, and how his anxiety is shaped by object loss. Where mind-body integration has not taken place, where an experiential identity of the spirit or psyche and the totality of physical functioning has not been attained—as in psychosomatic illness—there we also find that a transitional area has not developed.

THE DEVELOPMENT OF THE TRANSITIONAL AREA AND ITS OBJECTS

The concept of transitional area implies the bridge which the infant constructs from pure subjectivity into objective, shared reality: the symbolic representation of the reunion with the mother after the separation at birth takes place in this transitional area. It may be "a bundle of wool, or the corner of a blanket or eiderdown, or a word or a tune, or a mannerism" (Winnicott 1971)—that is, a source of comfort. He can be with his T.O. continuously, reassuring himself of his union and oneness with his mother. "The point of the transitional object, however," warns Winnicott "is not its symbolic value so much as its actuality....It is an illusion, but it is also something real" (Winnicott 1951).

During the first months of life the infant cannot differentiate himself from the object. His intensely experienced feeling states correspond to internal and external events. He has not yet integrated any of these happenings into a gestalt, has not linked those which could combine into a pattern of understanding, nor has he emerged from the state of fusion with the mother[1] and said "I am." Until five or six months of age, the relationship of the infant with the object is highly subjective which makes the modification of a basic narcissistic organization a difficult one. As he outstrips the object, he finds himself in need of it; he "creates" it, provided, as in Winnicott's paradox (1969), "that the object be there waiting to be created and to become a cathected object." If the mother is present continuously, the infant remains narcissistic, as in the first month of life.[2] He begins to evolve the moment she appears: the first creation—the transitional object—takes place in the absence of the mother.

Since 1967, we (Gaddini and Gaddini) have been engaged in studying transitional objects and the process of individuation in three social groups. Research involving the study of the development of psychosomatic symptoms has shown that frustration, distress, and anxiety must be experienced in an optimum equilibrium with good enough mothering; otherwise the transitional object bridge is not built. In "good enough mothering" the mother denies her other interests, and does not disrupt her child's inner life. This creates a positive balance. But when the mother is too insistent upon giving "the object" to the baby and when there is an overemphasis on "the symbol," despair occurs, and the object is thrown away or decathected. The compulsive element involved in the creation of the T.O. may be seen in the adolescent who clings to the symbol, or observed in the hospitalized child who has been separated from his mother. In this clinging to the T.O. there is an element of deprivation, or the threat of a previously experienced deprivation. The attachment is an attempt to deny this, though it must be said that at times the T.O. becomes ineffectual.

The T.O. consists of aspects of the mother's environment which the infant has selected for representation, aspects he has experienced that were mediated through his own bodily sensations. This coincides with the time of increased strain related to growth, when speech and locomotion are being established simultaneously. *It became clear from our studies that the infant's security blanket substitutes for the wrapping blanket that mother used to protect him when nursing.* The bit of nylon and linen which the child manipulates while going to sleep is a remnant of the mother's robe, which might have caressed his cheek or other uncovered parts of his body (particularly around the face and oral area) during feeding. (It is interesting to note that our statistics indicate that babies born in autumn and winter more often have woolen objects, while spring and summer babies more often have linen or nylon objects; see Figure 1.) The reminiscence of the cutaneous perception he experienced while fused with the breast is evoked by the infant, and he reexperiences that protective fusion, a reunion. The object or the modality with which he finds reassurance itself evokes the reminiscence of somatic sensations (tactile and postural perceptions) which revive the happy time of postnatal reunion with the mother. In order to create this symbol of reunion, it is necessary that this happy time be lost *after* he has had the opportunity to experience it optimally. Skin sensations combined with kinesthetic stimulation derived from the holding situation are contained within this creation, providing models of somatic functions from which psychic models will later develop. Representations of skin and muscles

TYPE OF T.O. ADOPTED

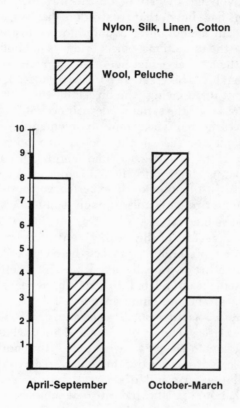

Fig. 1

together with the mouth area are the first libidinal concentration. Rado (1933) has referred to this as the narcissistic rind of the ego.

In our view, the organization of all perceptual experience emerges in relation to holding and feeding. It is on the basis of these early experiences that the T.O. appears, representing the first symbolic reunion with the mother. In other words, the capacity to have a symbol comes from the baby, *but environmental influence is crucial.*

The symbol contains the baby's contribution and "meets the mother in the T.O." (Winnicott 1969). As the mother is more difficult to retain the child can safely say of his T.O.: "This is my mother." If he is anxious about a dream, it can be recreated in a symbol that comes from his dream potential; it has his own self in it. *To be* in the symbol[3] rather than *to have* a symbol is probably the difference between the T.O. of the healthy child and the object of the hypochondriac or the stereotyped object of the psychotic. Separation anxiety, fantasies of reunion, the entire symbiotic phase, and the process of separation-individuation arise from the threat of loss. The need to insure his survival after object loss induces the child to create a T.O. It is not yet an object of external reality, but it has the *capacity* to be an object, in a symbolic sense. In fact, what matters "is not the object's reality, as it can be seen from the outside, but the way the child represents it internally. It is not the cloth or the teddy bear that the baby uses—not so much the object used as the use of the object" (Winnicott 1971).

PRECURSOR OBJECTS

At this point, a discussion of the various early forms of the T.O. will help clarify the origins of the infantile psychosomatic syndromes.

In agreement with Winnicott (1967), we have termed *precursors* (of transitional objects) those objects that, while they have the capacity to console the child, have not been discovered or invented by the child. *They are provided by the mother, or are parts of the child's or the mother's body.* Besides the tongue and fingers, the forerunners of transitional objects include (1) the pacifier, (2) the bottle used as a pacifier, (3) the child's wrist, (4) the mother's wrist, (5) the back of the child's hand, (6) the back of the mother's hand, and (7) the child's hair, ears, or nevi, which are touched or rubbed to produce a tactile sensation in association with the sucking or other combined actions. What usually happens with pacifiers, or "passifiers," as Winnicott liked to misspell it, is that mothers push them into the baby's mouth in such a manner that the baby has no alternative but to be pacified. "What is so completely absent in the pacifier technique is the baby's reaching out towards....In other words there is no allowance for the baby's creative capacity which shows in the way, for instance, that the hand may reach towards an object, or the mouth itself which may go towards an object in terms of saliva" (Winnicott 1968; see also Gaddini 1970).

It would be incorrect to designate a mother or grandmother's hand, ear, or hair, or a nevus (or their subsequent substitution by appendages of the child's own body) as true T.O.s. They do seem to have the exclusive talismanic value typical of transitional objects. However, Winnicott explicitly distinguishes the two: "It is lucky that the child uses this object

TABLE 1

Appearance of the Psychosomatic Symptom in Relationship
to the Development of the Transitional Object

	Maternal role	Infant role	Psychosomatic symptom
Psychosomatic symptom arises prior to development of T.O.	Abrupt termination of nursing	Mouth and incorporation have maximum investment	Rumination
Psychosomatic symptom arises during period T.O. precursor would develop	Maternal preoccupation decreasing in a general way	Rapid period of neuro-motor and sensory maturation	Colic
Psychosomatic symptom arises after period when T.O. would normally develop	Moves away or toward too quickly or intensely	Seeks support and feels independent	Asthma

(transitional object) and not the mother herself or the lobe of her ear or her hair" (Winnicott 1965).

As is well known, transitional objects and phenomena are basically symbols of union (union after separation) with the mother. These objects stand for part objects, notably for the breast, and only gradually do they represent the baby or the mother and father. "It is only on the basis of this symbolism of union that the object or the phenomenon can be exploited by the mother who is longing to get free" (Winnicott 1968).

CLASSIFICATION OF PRECURSOR OBJECTS

On the basis of our research we have made a tentative effort to differentiate two precursor object (P.O.) categories:

1. *The into-the-mouth P.O.* This corresponds to Bertram Lewin's oral stage of mental organization, at which mouth and incorporation have maximum investment (see Table 1). It is the basic P.O. which will provide the primal sensation of self and, later, of somatic integrity. A sudden loss or removal of this early P.O. can create the most severe somatic reactions and symptoms. We have often found this loss the basis for disintegration anxiety. As has been mentioned above, infantile fetishism can emerge from this early fear of disintegration or multilation.

2. *The skin contact and tactile sensation P.O.*[4] This category of P.O. appears somewhat later than the into-the-mouth variety, which in our studies is intimately related to the first month of life. A tactile P.O. never appears without the earlier into-the-mouth P.O. *The tactile P.O. is based on the skin sensations experienced by the infant within the breast's ambit; we see it as an expression of the mother's holding function.* Clearly, the infant's wrapping blanket, caressing his cheek or upper lip while sucking, is part and parcel of the tactile sensation obtained from the mother's body and the entire holding situation. At this early age, he cannot distinguish whether the sensation is produced by a part of the mother's body or is separate from it, or whether it is animate or inanimate.[5] He cannot "know" that a tactile sensation will create his tactile P.O., or which tactile P.O. will become his T.O.

In the course of development, the into-the-mouth P.O. is given up, and the tactile P.O. can become the transitional object. The T.O. originates from the tactile P.O. in those cases in which the latter belongs to neither the mother's nor the child's body but instead to the mother's ambit and her holding function. The T.O. is usually adopted by the child during the second part of the first year; it acquires value for him as a self-created reality and independent consoler. With weaning, the separation process begins and symbiotic ties to the mother weaken. Objects which are separate from both the mother's and the child's body become cathected, while the into-the-mouth P.O. loses its value or is gradually abandoned. The T.O. becomes the real talisman.

We find that the process of attachment to the T.O. (the symbolic representation of the reunion with the lost mother) takes place when the child feels deserted or lonely in the empty space and time between the developing self and mother (see Bergman, chapter 10). Soon the T.O. will serve as a powerful defense against anxiety arising from the threat of separation and abandonment, anxiety which arises particularly in relation to the detachment from reality and the separation from the object which occurs while falling asleep.

PSYCHOSOMATIC SYMPTOMS: RUMINATION

Psychosomatic symptom formation takes place along the same developmental continuum as does the creation of the T.O., but is a psychophysical rather than psychological resultant. As we have stated, a complementary relationship between the T.O. and the psychosomatic symptom has been established by both clinical and field observation. From the psychophysical point of view (table 1) we find that early psychosomatic symptoms arise in the infant as a defense against sudden loss, be it the loss of the breast (nipple) or the loss of the into-the-mouth P.O. at a time when the mouth and the mechanism of incorporation have maximum investment. The infant feels abandoned, with insufficient or absent protection, and in the somatic symptom, the infant seeks a semblance of reunion with his mother.

Considering rumination as an example of an early psychosomatic symptom, we feel that a sense of reunion with the mother (or a distorted model of reunion is suggested) in the manner the infant continues to reexperience the incorporation of milk and other foods. Rumination is a pathological model of a defense against sudden loss, a defense in which the infant continuously attempts to re-create the sensation of milk flowing into the mouth and being reswallowed. In the past, reports on rumination have been based on organ studies (stomach, pylorus, cardia): it is only since the recent conceptual advance from organ to infant, and from the infant to the mother-infant interaction, that we can understand this condition and attempt to alleviate it. Rumination has a particular nosological value in developmental psychosomatic studies. The capacity for rumination implies the presence of a transition from a physical to a psychophysical response, as well as the attainment of a certain level of maturation within a climate of sudden and marked deprivation. To use

Hoffer's description (1949) of the mental processes of early infancy, "they belong to the no man's land between biology and psychology, which Freud called 'Biological Psychology.'"

Thus from a nosological point of view, rumination may be regarded as a developmental failure due to sudden deprivation, whereas from a specific point of view, it is a pathological state related to the P.O. Initially, we see a frantic tongue sucking; the infant compensates from "inside" for the sudden loss of his P.O. A further element of incorporation is gradually added with the actual regurgitation and reswallowing of the food. From a developmental point of view, the P.O. is no longer the breast, but is not yet separated from the self. Because it is within the self which it helps to integrate, it is endowed with the extreme passivity and dependence associated with body language. This may be understood as the totally dependent human organism's extreme defense against separation. It exemplifies an objective dependence on an external world of which he knows nothing, as he cannot differentiate himself from the object; he therefore feels alone in the world. Later in infancy, in the more organized psychosomatic symptom, this extreme passivity and dependence is expressed in body language. The difference lies in the infant's more mature fantasy life at that time. The early stages of the capacity for symbolization in the seven to eight month old infant are necessary to the development of a T.O. on the psychological side or, on the psychophysical side, an attack of asthma. It is a time when a subjective psychic dependence on the external world develops in the child, a dependence linked to the relationship the infant now has with the object. This state intensifies the child's conflicts while he modifies his basic narcissistic organization.

INFANTILE COLIC AND ASTHMA

Colic is the earliest example of an organized psychosomatic disorder of infancy. It can occur by the third month if the infant has not developed a P.O. (the into-the-mouth type particularly), or if the P.O. the child has been provided (pacifier) or has found for himself (thumb, fingers, tongue) is not sufficient to absorb the anxiety stemming from the unbalanced interaction between him and his mother. This interaction becomes asynchronous because his rapid neuromotor development communicates to the mother that he has acquired a certain self-sufficiency, that he is no longer so dependent on her. She begins to seek other interests, as she feels there is less need to meet this dependence on her. The "to-and-fro" movement between dependence and independence, which characterizes the growing child's facilitating environment, is lost.

Thus there are times when the child still requires his mother, but finds her less dependent on him. This is the basis for occasional crises, and the provided or found P.O. is no longer sufficient to absorb and neutralize the mounting anxiety produced by the loss. During these crises, due to a decompensation of the demand/gratification ratio, the child "cries in colic." The entire process, from complete dependence to independence— except the compensating effect of the P.O.—is well described in Winnicott's "The Maturational Processes and the Facilitating Environment" (1965).

Asthma, an equally complex psychosomatic symptom, arises at the end of the first year (rarely before this age) or in the first years of life following the period of the normal development of the T.O. In these cases the mother apparently moves away too abruptly or harshly, and does not graduate adaptation to the changing and expanding needs of the child, whose growth processes impel him toward independence and adventure. When the mother fails to adapt to her child in instances where the child's need has not created a T.O. (reflecting the environmental failure to play its positive part), he can feel the threat of annihilation, and turn to such somatic manifestations as asthma.[6] *None of our asthmatic children of average or marked severity developed a transitional object.* This observation confirms the hypothesized reciprocal relationship between the T.O. and early psychosomatic illness.[7]

Both the T.O. and psychosomatic symptoms are psychic processes which can be studied from the genetic point of view. Hence, rumination coincides with the passing from the automatic organic response of vomiting to a more organized response (E. Gaddini 1969). The T.O. develops in the same manner, and it is often possible to determine the genetic steps of its formation as it evolves from the P.O.

SELF-ROCKING

Self-rocking, another powerful compensation for the union that is lost at birth, is usually found in infants who did not have an into-the-mouth P.O. It seems an equivalent of the latter. In this practice, the infant discovers a primitive way to evoke his rocking mother, to reproduce prenatal rocking (associated with the time he was carried intrautero), or to compensate for an insufficient postnatal rocking. Since incubator babies as well as those who have been in the hospital during the first months of life often demonstrate self-rocking (rhythmical movements of the body), this indicates that powerful intrauterine life rhythms have prevailed over an extrauterine postnatal reality not "good enough" for the child and therefore not sufficiently cathected. This leads us to view self-rocking, from an economic point of view, as an autistic solution; from a pathogenetic point of view, it signifies severe deprivation.

The moment an infant has adopted an autistic self-rocking, he cannot be contacted easily from the outside world. For him, self-rocking and all rhythmical movements of the body become a diffuse means of achieving motor discharge. They are also a powerful defense against the anxiety of separation; anything which tends to bring him in touch with reality and with the outside world will encounter this defense, as would occur with an autistic child. According to Winnicott (1968), self-rocking is "a squalid substitute that the child devises for himself imitating the absent mother; but in doing so, he becomes the rocking mother, and loses his identity."

The T.O. is a desirable step in normal development, whereas the psychosomatic symptom is a related but pathological structure. However, we must always keep in mind that the T.O. is conceptualized as a *psychic operation, not a real object.* The blanket is not a blanket, and the teddy is not a teddy. Although one is positive, and the other negative, the T.O. and the psychosomatic symptom are both psychic processes, the former turned toward the exterior, and the latter toward the interior. In this respect, self-rocking has a body-bound connotation which distinguishes it from typical transitional phenomena. It would seem that in self-rocking the *body as a whole* intertwines frustrated charges with autistic rhythms, attempting to master an environment which has failed to meet the need for dependency and rocking.

Defining the exact "location" of self-rocking is difficult; this body experience is *both* a transitional phenomenon and an early psychosomatic organization. The consistent link that exists between early physiological events and later development suggests that these early experiences are blueprints of the vicissitudes the infant undergoes in relation to the very early interactions between mother and child.

VICISSITUDES OF EARLY FEEDING

In our observations, we noticed that *every* young infant feels complete *only* at the moment of reunion with his mother's breast: otherwise he searches about and can even disorganize. This is suggested also by the fact that infants on demand feeding usually do not have an into-the-mouth P.O., nor do they compete with their fingers in the feeding process, in the manner which suggested to Winnicott (1965) that they are "holding on to self-created reality while using external reality." When the need for reunion arises, infants on demand feeding simply turn to the breast and, unless there has been an alternative object, bottle, or pacifier, seem content.

The complexity of an adult's personality can be understood only if followed from the moment when, as an infant, he interacts with something outside himself, usually the mother, and specifically that part of her which feeds him—the breast. On this matrix he originates, builds, and colors his relationship with the outside world. The intrauterine situation—ultimately disrupted by birth—is associated in the neonate with a sense of security and unity. The attempt to reestablish this union remains as a characteristic of the human condition—and perhaps not of the human alone.

External circumstances may have vital importance in the first object relationship. If birth is difficult, it may complicate the child's adaptation. In these cases difficulties in nursing may arise, and the sucking may take place vicariously. The manner in which the mother responds to signals of tension and to the need for comfort determines whether she will be a reliable object. *The vicissitudes of her infant's bodily functioning are the pivotal elements in the first communication between the child and the external world.* We have begun to realize how much nutritional problems in very early life influence the basic formation of personality structure. If it is true that even an optimal feeding will recompense the child only partly for the lost security of his prenatal union, it seems evident that difficult feeding, indicative as it is of problems in the mother-infant dyad, should express itself in an altered object relationship.

SOMATIC COMPLIANCE

Psychoanalysts and biologic researchers agree that every reaction and somatic behavior is counterpointed by an original bodily experience (either at birth or in the earliest part of life). Bridger and Reiser (1959) and Lipton et al. (1961) have studied behavior and the autonomic responses to stress in the neonate. This data (particularly that of Bridger) indicates an inverse relationship between behavior and the autonomic functioning, an active motor response being associated with decreased autonomic activity. The implications of the work of Bridger and his colleagues are clear for psychosomatic researchers: we must now consider all the parameters of the child's total experience (including weight, modality of birth, and characteristics at birth) before we can understand the various symptoms "adopted" in somatic pathology.

Clinical observation has not been integrated sufficiently into our research. We do not know how mothers perceive the first bodily experiences of their infants; we may, however, speculate on what happens to the growing child when initial somatic responses grade into the psychosomatic, as well as on what will occur subsequently, when psychic responses prevail (see Table 2). Prior to birth, the infant's responses are presumably feelings based on sensation, whereas after birth they are based on sense perception. Later, from a knowledge of these perceptions, ideas develop which are organized into thoughts. As Bion (1962) puts it, "Thinking is a process forced on us by sense perception." The first psychic activity has the capacity to create models which parallel functional physical patterns, thereby reproducing the underlying somatic models. However, this is not an automatic repetition. The somatic counterpart, and its concomitant anxiety are mastered during this translation onto the psychic plane. A well-known example of this process is the concept of introjection, which refers to a model of mental functioning paralleling incorporation, a model of physical functioning. Rumination is a paradigmatic example in this sense, as it begins quite early.

FURTHER OBSERVATIONS ON RUMINATION AND COLIC

For centuries, ruminators have been considered mentally retarded; effect was taken as cause. Actually, as mentioned earlier, rumination is a psychosomatic defensive organization (see Gaddini and Gaddini 1959). It may appear as early as the third month, two or three months being the

TABLE 2

Developmental moment	Dominant mode	Process
Until birth	Sensation based feelings	Autistic world of feeling
From birth	Infant enters world of sense perception, i.e., of relationship	In relating to object the infant is stimulated and kept alive
Later	Knowledge of perceptions organized in thoughts	Psychic development as a process of differentiation

minimum experiential period for the construction of a psychosomatic model of response. As we have mentioned, also, ruminators are typically infants who were breast-fed and then *suddenly* weaned. We can now understand the steps from repeated vomiting (a pure somatic response) to rumination (a psychosomatic response), in which vomiting is organized as a defense (E. Gaddini 1969). It is interesting that this displacement seems to decrease the mortality rate for these vomiting infants, who would otherwise quickly dehydrate and die. When vital defense mechanisms are not threatened, death occurs less frequently. We may therefore correlate the infant's early psychic activity (now operating as a defense, though a pathological one) with his survival, leaving aside the many complexities accompanying the acquisition of consciousness.

With rumination, colic is one of the most precocious psychosomatic syndromes. In the first months of life, colicky babies have sudden spells of screaming, with all the physical signs of pain and distress. The screaming and the mounting tension may last for hours, and they can become inconsolable. At four months, the same baby might accept a "soother" or a pacifier for consolation; at eight months he might acquire a blanket or a teddy for comfort; but at three months, he despairs.

We see two genetic moments in this condition; one relates to the child, and the other to the mother. The three-month-old can lift his head from the bed, from both the prone and supine positions, and can hold it steadily when sitting with support. Soon he will reach out for objects. His interest in the environment increases daily. Now an infinite space separates him from his neonatal days, when he was more apt to feel sensations derived from his internal organs and apparatuses than from sense organ perceptions carried from the external world (Table 2).

While this exciting development continues in the infant, "maternal preoccupation" begins to decrease. Now, with a sense of maternal nonavailability, a vaguely perceived threat of deprivation can cause the sudden expression of tension, which can be then translated into colic.

This response is transitory and localized to a moment in the developmental process which normally is rapidly mastered. We are convinced that the prolongation and the complications of this transitory syndrome may be caused by various interventions, some of them iatrogenic. This hypothesis is reinforced by the fact that the symptomatology disappears when the child receives physical attention, even from a maternal substitute. The basic difficulty, however, lies in the mother-child relationship: third-month colic is a somatic response to rage, the infant's "answer" to the experience of his mother's asynchronous unavailability.

SOME CONCLUSIONS

We have used the examples of rumination and third-month colic because they appear at an early time of life when there is insufficient integration between psyche and soma. The child is not yet capable of creating an object for himself. It can be said that the ruminator will have difficulty passing from *the imitation of the incorporation*, which he reiterates with his ruminating (E. Gaddini 1969), to a *symbolic representation of the reunion with his mother* (T.O.), which requires a level of development beyond the part object (breast, nipple). Third-month colic seems to be a transitory psychosomatic syndrome, which can be overcome if the deprived child experiences an optimal sense of loss, which, given a facilitating environment, enables him to create a symbol of reunion.

Thus, we may say that each time these psychosomatic symptoms appear, the child's use of the object has been affected adversely. We should emphasize here that the focus should be always on the *interaction* between mother and infant rather than on either one. In Winnicott's words (1971), "There is no such thing as a baby." If the interaction includes pathogenic, poor maternal functioning, the mother cannot know her baby empathically, and infant feeding (one of the most significant aspects of the mother-infant relationship) is jeopardized. The mother's help is needed to manage the awful transitions from the contentment of sleeping or walking to all-out greedy attacks. A poorly functioning mother is not available to mediate these transitions (this is indicated in Table 3 as *pathogenic environment*). An example of the mother's nonavailability can be found when the newborn is separated in the nursery, or when from birth it is on a rigid feeding schedule. In such conditions the infant is *let down*. He sucks his thumb or pacifier instead of being frustrated; this distracts him from an enriching sensory input.

If the child is let down all the time, at a later stage self-rocking or other rhythmical body movement will appear. The rocking child imitates his mother: but in so doing he feels annihilated, *becomes* a mother who rocks babies, losing himself in the process. Self-rocking is a sign of deprivation, the result of an inadequate maternal response to his earlier screaming and crying. Screaming, in fact, *is* a cry for the mother, and implies there is still hope.

In a *borderline environment* the mother does not let her infant down, but cannot adapt to his needs as "good enough mothers" can. Frustration must be timed optimally for the growing child. Depriving of frustration and spoiling the child who should be frustrated were, in Winnicott's view, signs of an incipient failure of the environment; "Children want to be spoiled and want to be frustrated" (Winnicott 1970). In an environment which has failed during the initial months, we find such

TABLE 3

**Pathogenic, Borderline, and Facilitating Environments,
Their Effects at Two Stages of Development**

Environment	Mother	Infant	Early Somatic Response	Later Response
Pathogenic	Not available Not predictable Feeding not reciprocating event Protective function lost Doesn't get to know her infant Separated from infant in nursery	Let Down Apathetic Non-protected transitions between sleep and waking, hunger and satiation Doesn't get to know mother	Vomiting Screaming crying Constant sleep	No transitional object Non-relating child Self-rocking Annihilated Psychotic No capacity for creative playing No abstract symbolization
Borderline	Spoils with untimely frustrations Resents dependence	Let down at times Resents non-availability Untimely experience of frustration	Regurgitation Three-month colic Sleeping difficulties Dermatosis	Language difficulties Masters meaning of symbols principally on somatic level Psychosomatic symbolization
Facilitating	Knows her infant Adapts to needs Frustrates when necessary	Knows mother Transitions clear between sleeping and waking, hunger and satiation	Extending world Development of transitional object or phenomena	Intermediate area between psychic reality and external reality Symbolic functioning Cultural experiences Creativity

psychosomatic responses as third-month colic, sleeping difficulties, and dermatoses; at a later stage, more mental difficulties appear, including impairments in the development of language and symbolization (see Lorenzer and Orban, chapter 28).

Within a *facilitating environment,* optimal functioning of mother-infant interaction occurs; the mother knows her infant and adapts to his needs. Here the child can create a T.O. as insurance against the fear or threat of loss. Later, at the "thinking stage," symbolization develops, accompanied by an intense investment in cultural experience. The child has the capacity to be concerned and to believe in; he can be creative and constructive even in distress.

PREVENTIVE CONSIDERATIONS

At the Thirteenth International Congress of Pediatrics, Kretchmer (1972) in his closing remarks stated that infant survival would improve considerably if we could recognize that the separation between obstetrics and pediatrics is only administrative. "In the study of the biology of the organism, the mother and child can be considered as one system." That system may safeguard the narcissistic needs of the child and may gradually, through a facilitating environment, draw narcissistic libido toward representations of the external environment. However, the atmosphere may be pathogenic rather than facilitating if it does not cater to the child's narcissistic needs. This asynchronization may start with pregnancy or with the process of birth, when it is the primary narcissism of the fetal, neonatal, and perinatal periods (Greenacre 1945) that is frustrated.[8]

Studies show that abnormal deliveries can adversely affect early infantile narcissism and the mother-infant relationship. We are currently engaged in research in which we hope to identify the earliest reliable indicators of less than optimal development. We also plan to examine any factors which may influence the growth process; it seems essential to know these from both the theoretical and the practical point of view.[9]

The comments by Jacobi made over eighty years ago remain pertinent (see Kretchmer 1972): "Indeed, the most interesting time and the one most difficult to understand, is that in which persistent development, increase, solidifications, and improvement are taking place. . . . The history of the embryo and foetus finds its legitimate termination in that of the infant and child. . . ." Out of the organic relationship between obstetrics and pediatrics emerge the principles which are the basis of the important innovative concept of perinatal medicine. We must explore the area of the early facilitating or nonfacilitating environment—so frequently administered by the pediatrician—if we desire rational, preventive, and noninterfering interventions in infantile psychosomatic disorders.

APPENDIX: THE SWEDISH STUDIES

In a previous paper we (Gaddini and Gaddini 1970) described our regret concerning the scarcity of systematic studies of transitional objects, and the more and more approximate use of the term *transitional object*. Recently the Swedes Ekecranz and Ruhde (1971) have studied the use of T.O.'s and transitional phenomena using a methodology consisting of interviews with 120 mothers (of families of three children). In these interviews, "transitional phenomena" were studied systematically, as were "various transitional objects: frequency, forms and functions." Their relation to variables, which the authors considered indicative of ego development, was considered, with apparent negative results.

The absence of this correlation contrasts markedly with the first results of our longitudinal study, necessitating a reconsideration of their methodology, as well as of ours. There are a number of points on which we do not agree, due to the differing interpretation the Swedish authors have given to the terms *transitional objects* and *transitional phenomena* and their various expressions. We introduced the concept of precursor after long discussions with Winnicott: the term *precursor object* in the context of the transitional area should be limited to the thumb or fingers, to the pacifier, or more rarely, to the tongue. From the developmental point of view, all these refer to an intermediate relationship between the self and the object. According to Ekecranz and Ruhde, the pacifier may be equivalent to the thumb (they are both P.O.'s); but, we believe, the bottle should not be confused with the breast, even though milk comes from both. In fact, no matter how primitive a relationship the child has with the P.O., it represents a developmental progression as compared to the infant's view of the breast itself in his early months. At that time, the breast is perceived as a part of the self, making it impossible for the infant to experience a true relationship. With the bottle, on the other hand, many characteristics of the breast and of breastfeeding are lacking.

Our second point of disagreement with the Swedish authors concerns their use of the concept of the mother as transitional object. They quote Winnicott and Greenacre on this matter, but we question whether their interpretation is correct. In each of our cases the mother herself is the greatest consolation ever wished for: it is only when she is *not there in person* that the child "creates" the transitional object. From this the now classic interpretation arises: it is the reunion with the mother as primary object that the child evokes when he feels lonesome and helpless.

A third point of disagreement with Ekecranz and Ruhde concerns the confusion in their paper between "transitional objects" and "transitional phenomena." To Winnicott these two concepts were always very close, but not equivalent. Some erroneously surmise that the term *transitional phenomena* includes the entire range of reunion symbolizations, while the term *object* refers to the particular object used in each case. The two terms, however, have never been used in this manner by Winnicott. The T.O. is in fact always exterior to the child's body, and instinctual elements play an insignificant role, whereas instinctual features *are* present in rocking[10], and in nearly all transitional phenomena. The confusion of these two concepts also complicates the evaluation of what seems a rather frequent use of transitional phenomena among the Swedish population—74% of all cases. It would be interesting to know how many of these cases involve objects and how many involve phenomena, as well as what percentage include self-rocking. They should try to specify each case, as the terms *object* and *phenomena* have different implications, particularly concerning automatic body movements in which the instinctual component replaces symbolization. It is exceedingly difficult to evaluate the object relationship of a given child when researchers apply the generic expression *transitional phenomenon* without specifying it an actual object, a human rhythm (rocking, in arms or cradle), or self-rocking.

NOTES

1. This fusion with the mother, which precedes the separation-individuation process, and in which experiences of mutuality are included, lasts until approximately the fifth month and represents Mahler's symbiotic stage.

2. In many of our cases it has been found that it is the mother's symbiotic tie to the baby which prevents him (or her) from symbolizing the reunion which occurs with her physical presence in the same bed, or room. When this is the case, one almost never finds that the child has "invented" a transitional object.

3. In a discussion, Dr. Satz suggested the idea of the child "crying in the symbol, and therefore being." The separated child, fearful and sobbing into his blanket, is able to attain a proxy reunion with the lost mother. The new dual unity creates a sense of being, of wholeness, from experiences of suffering and anxiety.

4. Fenichel refers to skin sensitivity and oral eroticism in his study "Neurotic disturbances of sleep" (1942).

5. Yet T. O. formation can be viewed as the psychological pathway along which the distinction between animate and inanimate objects is achieved (see Abrams and Neubauer, chapter 9); this may demonstrate how the inanimate must have previously been fused with the animate to have value for the developing infant.

6. Spitz (1965) sees the infant's incapacity to master eight month anxiety as a pathogenetic element leading to the ego's failure to build autonomous structure and adequate psychic defenses (p. 163).

7. In other words, each time we find that mind-body interaction has not occurred, and that "an experiential identity of the spirit or psyche and the totality of physical functioning has not reached" (Winnicott 1966), as in psychosomatic illness, the child does not develop a true transitional object.

8. Greenacre justifiably questions whether human birth among civilized people is ever "normal."

9. A family history of hereditarily based disease is a most interesting predisposing pathogenic factor. We intend to study it. Here the mother's preoccupation with her infant has an important influence on the child's perception of his body ego, and on its normal integration with psychic components. We already see a correlation between the way the mother experiences her infant's bodily functions and the type of somatic pathology the child will undergo. Winnicott's case of an ulcerative colitis child, who could not be helped because of "the splitting which was in the mother" can be cited.

10. Both in the rhythmical movement of the child's body (which we call self-rocking) and in rocking in cradles or while being held.

REFERENCES

Bion, W. H. (1962). *Learning from Experience*. London: Heinemann Medical Books.

Bridger, W. H., and Birnes, B. (1963). Neonate behavioral and autonomic responses to stress during soothing. In *Recent Advances in Biological Psychiatry*, vol. 5, pp. 1–7. New York: Plenum Press.

Bridger, W. H., and Reiser, M. F. (1959). Psychophysiological studies of the neonate: an approach toward the methodological and theoretical problems involved. *Psychosomatic Medicine* 21:265–276.

Ekecranz, L., and Ruhde, L. (1971). Transitional phenomena: frequency, forms and functions of specially loved objects. *Acta Psychiatrica Scandinavica* 48:261–273.

Engel, G. (1962). *Psychological Development in Health and Disease*. Philadelphia: W. B. Saunders.

Fenichel, O. (1942). Symposium on neurotic disturbances of sleep. *International Journal of Psycho-Analysis* 23:49–68.

Gaddini, E. and Gaddini, R. (1959). Rumination in infancy. In *Dynamic Psychopathology of Childhood*, ed. Jessner and Pavenstedt. New York: Grune & Stratton.

Gaddini, E. (1969). On imitation. *International Journal of Psycho-Analysis* 50:475–484.

Gaddini, R. (1970). Transitional objects and the process of individuation. *Journal of the American Academy of Child Psychiatry* 9: 347-365.

——— (1975). *On the Genesis of the Fetish*. In press.

Greenacre, P. (1945). The biological economy of birth. In *Psychoanalytic Study of the Child* 1:31–51.

Greene, W. A., Jr. (1958). The role of a vicarious object in the adaptation to object loss: use of a vicarious object as a means of adjustment to a separation from a significant person. *Psychosomatic Medicine* 20:124–144.

Hoffer, W. (1949). Mouth, hand and ego integration. *Psychoanalytic Study of the Child* 3/4:49–56.

Kimball, C. P. (1970). Conceptual development in psychosomatic medicine: 1939-1969. *Annals of Internal Medicine* 73:307-317.

Kretchmer, N. (1972). Growth and adaption of pediatrics. *Helvetica Paediatrica Acta*, Supp. 28:33–37.

Lewin, B. (1946). Sleep, the mouth and the dream screen. *Psychoanalytic Quarterly* 15:419–434.

Lipton, E. L., Steinschneider, A., and Richmond, J. B. (1961). Autonomic functions in the neonate. *Psychosomatic Medicine* 23.

Rado, S. (1933). Fear of castration in women. *Psychoanalytic Quarterly* 2:449.

Spitz, R. (1965). *The First Year of Life: a Psychoanalytic Study of Normal and Deviant Development of Object Relations*. New York: International Universities Press.

Winnicott, D. W. (1951). Transitional objects and transitional phenomena. *International Journal of Psycho-Analysis* 34 (1953).

——— (1965). *Maturational Processes and the Facilitating Environment* New York: International Universities Press.

——— (1966). Psychosomatic illness in its positive and negative aspects. *International Journal of Psycho-Analysis* 47:510–516.

——— (1967). Personal communication.

——— (1968). Personal communication.

——— (1969). Use of an object. *International Journal of Psycho-Analysis* 50:711–716.

——— (1970). Personal communication.

——— (1971). *Playing and Reality*. New York: Basic Books.

CHAPTER 9

In this chapter, Samuel Abrams and Peter Neubauer consider the functions of the transitional object in object relations, thus extending its bridging function. Their developmental and observational study focuses on the child's constitutional orientation to either the animate or the inanimate.

The transitional object is viewed here in the context of normal development. Human and nonhuman qualities invested in the object allow it to "stretch" the child's constitutional proclivity toward whichever side is neglected. This and other important functions have led to the increasing acceptance of the transitional object as a psychic organizer.

There is another important implication of this study. Some have held that the orientation of a child toward the inanimate world automatically connotes a pathological structure and a failure in the mothering process. This view is of course diametrically opposed to Winnicott's position on the normal developmental role of the transitional object. Abrams and Neubauer suggest that the child's orientation may in part be *constitutional*, sometimes having little to do with the mothering process. In such cases the role of the transitional object can be essential in extending the range of object relations and in furthering development in general.

L.B.

TRANSITIONAL OBJECTS: ANIMATE
AND INANIMATE

Samuel Abrams

Peter B. Neubauer

PSYCHOPATHOLOGY AND DEVELOPMENT:
THE TRANSITIONAL OBJECT AND THE FETISH

Psychoanalysis is a clinical endeavor as well as a general psychology. The study of a phenomenon from one of these perspectives occasionally complicates our view of it from the other. Perhaps this is nowhere better illustrated than with transitional phenomena.

Since the transitional object bears an obvious relationship to the fetish, it comes to the attention of the clinician. As it is also a facet of normal development, it is, as well, part of the general psychology of mental processes. A more precise cataloging should promote a greater understanding of these differences.

Psychopathology. In the realm of psychopathology, facts about the transitional object have often accrued as a consequence of its implicit link with the fetish. Contributions have accumulated from clinical experience with both adults and children. Addressing himself to sexual perversions in men, Freud (1927) noted that fetishism was linked to the castration complex: the fetish represented the illusory female penis. Some analysts have elaborated upon this relationship to the phallic-oedipal period (e.g., Gillespie 1956, Bak 1968, while others have stressed prephallic and preoedipal determinants, often implicating specific environmental influences (e.g., Abraham 1910, Dickes 1963, Greenacre 1960, 1969, M. Sperling 1963). In these instances the discoveries arose from the psychoanalytic situation, which provided the opportunity for retrospective perusal, reconstruction, and recall during the course of conflict resolution.

Data have also been gathered by direct observation of children. Wulff (1946) described what he called true infantile fetishes. He collected samples spanning a period from the first year of life to age four. These involved intimate alliances with blankets, a chamber pot, bibs, a handkerchief, and nightgowns, all objects used as sources of intense satisfaction or relief from anxiety. Wulff viewed these phenomena as pathological and hypothesized that these fetishes were extensions of the mother, explicitly challenging the earlier view implicating the castration complex. Roiphe (1968), on the basis of research observations, described the existence of a period of normal development of sexual arousal in children between the ages of 16 and 24 months. Subsequently Roiphe and Galenson (1973) suggested that symptoms arising from this early "phallic" interest, "free of any oedipal resonance," could be a determinant in the development of an infantile fetish. Such symptoms function to avoid castration anxiety. In moving genital arousal to an earlier period, they could restore the original dynamic proposed by Freud.

In summary, as a consequence of work with adults and children, support has been lent to the view that an early intensified and frequently protracted relationship to a central, selected object can become a vehicle for pathologic tendencies and serve dynamic, symbolic, and strategic expressions.

Development. Another sector of psychoanalytic literature has met the issue of this central, selected object from a different standpoint: its ordinary and regular occurrence as a feature in normal development. Winnicott (1953) spearheaded this interest. Acknowledging Wulff's 1946 contribution but clearly separating his own work from it, Winnicott emphasized the ubiquitous nature of the infant's relationship to this significant not-me possession. He stressed the value of the transitional object in separating from the breast of the mother, as an influence in the emergence of reality testing, as an aid in the experiencing of illusion, as a factor in creativity and as an implement in the movement from magical control to active manipulation. In addition, he noted the value of such phenomena in the development of symbol formation. In recounting a brief example of an infant *without* a transitional object, Winnicott implied that the child's subsequent development contained many pathological features. Thus, he clearly emphasized that the phenomena were normal, universal, and even necessary for health. Greenacre (1969) similarly stressed the developmental significance of the transitional object, hypothesizing that it functions by "promoting a kind of psychophysical homeostasis as individuation progresses." She too noted the role of the transitional object in creativity, reality testing, and object relationships and in addition reemphasized its importance in the mother-child interaction. "There seems little doubt that the early object most focused on is the mother. . . . It is chiefly the relation to the mother which can be relaxed or tightened up according to the baby's needs, by his use of the transitional object, with its enormous illusory value."

Busch et al. (1973), drawing from observational data, suggested that transitional phenomena may fall into two distinct developmental periods—the first during sucking and weaning, the second at the age of two or somewhat beyond. They propose to distinguish these as "primary transitional objects" and "secondary transitional objects" respectively. Unlike the pathologic fetishistic objects of childhood, which tend in their view to evoke excitation, "primary transitional objects" have a soothing effect. Developmentally appropriate objects are further distinguished from the psychopathologic by the following features: (1) they usually do not meet a direct oral or libidinal need; (2) they are "created" by the child rather than originating with the parents; and (3) they are clearly differentiated from the child's body. Bush et al. reflect and further promote the tendency in the literature to separate the developmentally significant from pathologic expressions.

In the following, research data will be offered to suggest yet another developmental function of transitional phenomena.

THE CATEGORY OF OBJECT ORIENTEDNESS

In the course of a systematic longitudinal study undertaken at the Child Development Center to follow children from infancy through adolescence, many variations in growth became apparent. Some of those variations—threshholds, activity levels, affective range, cognitive capacities, motoric skills, etc.—were anticipated; to receive them, conceptual categories were created in the original research design. However, an unexpected finding emerged, one which seemed strikingly relevant to any study of transitional phenomena: a variation appeared in the degree of leaning toward humans (the animate world) and toward things (the inanimate world). To receive and study this variation the category *object orientedness* was created and its central propositions offered (Abrams and Neubauer 1975):

There is a common pool of predispositions out of which currents of relatedness to people and to things emerge. Observation establishes the finding of individual variations in which there may be *significant* predominant early inclinations either toward the animate or the inanimate world. A comparison of matched samplings suggests that these tendencies may appear as early as the second or third month of life; they cast their impressions on the surrounds, or emerging phases and functions, on the continuing developmental process, and on character formation. These variations in leanings may possess this influence through their capacity to evoke a preferred style of processing percepts and situations.

Further study of this category of object orientedness suggested several additional propositions:

1. Where a leaning reaches a certain intensity, it appears to have its own set of developmental consequences; the peaks and valleys of each thrust have yet to be studied systematically at different periods of growth and during succeeding phases.
2. Since such variations become manifest so early, they may reflect predispositions of the personality. Inferences about "congenital" influences have been cataloged in an earlier work (Abrams and Neubauer 1975). A study of the literature even suggests that under certain conditions such leaning may be predictable before birth. For example, it has been reported that among monozygotic twins the heavier, usually the firstborn, is more human-oriented (e.g., Allen et al. 1971). Naturally, this does not exclude the possibility that such leanings can sometimes result from specific, regularly reinforced environmental preferences.
3. Certain developing functions appear to cluster about one or the other style of orientedness: for example, thing-oriented infants show evidence of enhanced gross motor abilities when compared to similar-age matched infants with a more "human" leaning. Other developing functions seem to bear no correlation to either disposition; for example, developmental landmarks such as the smile emerge at similar periods in either variation.
4. The initial leaning with its clustering casts its impression on the evolvement of increasingly complex functions. Thing-oriented infants, for example, are likely to move toward a surer development of specific conceptual abilities, while more human-oriented children move toward personal, interactional skills. Furthermore, the former may involve themselves with tasks and achievements, while the latter seem more inclined toward accomplishments within social relationships.
5. Finally, and not unexpectedly, an interrelationship between a leaning and the environment has been noted. In those instances where the disposition appears early, primary figures in the infant's milieu tend to respond selectively to it, and thereby reinforce the disposition. In

effect, it is cycled back into the psychic system and may help to foster specific traits of character or interests, as well as the form and content of conflicts or conflict resolutions.

TRANSITIONAL PHENOMENA

Any systematic longitudinal study generates both observational information and relevant hypotheses. It was natural that empirical data about transitional phenomena would come under scrutiny during the course of our developmental study. With the observation of variations in orientedness, this became even more likely. The possibility of correlating these leanings with transitional phenomena seemed especially promising.

During the study, observations accrued which related to the qualities of engagement of transitional objects: (1) it appeared that an early sensory preference for touch correlated positively with a subsequent high engagement; (2) increased erogenous zone activity (observationally measured, for example, by the intensity and persistence of mouthing) was not in itself an indicator of subsequent high involvement (this raises intriguing questions concerning the presumed relationship between orality and transitional phenomena); and (3) parenting styles in themselves do not emerge as definitive influences (however, since the sifting of the data dealing with parent-child interactions is still incomplete, this statement must be viewed as preliminary).

And what of the effect of variations of orientedness on transitional phenomena?

Against expectations, the data suggest that a dispositional leaning in itself appears to have no specific influence on the frequency, timing of emergence, or intensity of engagement with transitional objects. However, infants inclined toward one disposition or the other may utilize transitional phenomena for different developmental tasks.

It is generally acknowledged that transitional phenomena serve as bridges from the primary objects to the rest of the world. Transitional objects function as representatives of the absent mother, permitting the negotiation of separation and the illusion of control. Observations of infants inclined toward human or thing orientedness, however, suggest the following broadening of current hypotheses:

1. Transitional objects serve the interests of expansion for the infant. In more thing-oriented children, they may facilitate the movement toward the animate and hence toward interactional experiencing. For the more human-oriented, transitional phenomena may be vehicles to

things, tasks and achievements. Thus, such early treasured possessions can have the developmental function of facilitating expansion by bridging the separate currents of interests directed toward people and things. In examples of marked polar leanings, transitional phenomena may serve this bridging function regularly.

2. And what of the structural consequences of such processes? Transitional objects are generally recognized as steps in the development of stable mental representations of the primary human objects. This appears especially true in the more person-oriented children. It may be that the more inanimately inclined use transitional objects as a stage in the development toward stable *self* representations, i.e., relatedness to things and tasks become kernels of representation of the individual himself. Thus, the crossing-over process may be conceptualized as a movement either from the primary object toward a broadened self representation or from self-image to the enhanced representation of others.

ILLUSTRATIVE OBSERVATIONAL DATA

Benjamin. Benjamin showed a clear preference for human-orientedness. During the first year of his life, he was especially inclined to explore everything with his mouth; this was always more an expression of mouth pleasure than of interest in the object itself. No specific item kept his attention for long—neither the mouthing nor the fingering of it. An observer reported during a visit when Benjamin was 9 months that "nothing that I could offer him to play with had anything like the valence that the human face had. He would rather inspect me or follow his mother about with his eyes than attend to the cup, rattle, or so forth." At 15 months it was noted that Benjamin's involvement with tasks proved trying for him, and that he was inclined to summon human assistance quickly and frequently in the face of frustration. At about this time he acquired a strip of cloth which became part of a nighttime ritual. At 20 months, the cloth was still present. His interest in "things" and tasks appeared enhanced when they implied a specific interactional meaning. For example, he insisted on controlling the elevator button when someone important was about to leave the apartment. By 27 months there was evidence of an expansion of interest in tasks and achievements, although even then such interests invariably contained an interactional component. His cloth strip had evolved into a blanket or special edge of material, and appeared to parallel his increasing generalized exploration of the inanimate world. At 30 months he relinquished his requirement for the transitional object although he insisted that his mother hug or kiss him during his presleep ritual. His subsequent development reflected a more-than-subtle persistence of his orientedness to humans, although an increasing integration of the inanimate world had been achieved.

Alan. From his earliest months, Alan had a great interest in the inanimate world. At the age of 4½ months, it was noted that he could maintain attention to inanimate items for as long as twenty minutes, although no particular item or possession attracted him exclusively. By the age of 9 months, some leveling out of his predisposition was noted; however, his interest in motor activity and in inanimate objects continued to be a paramount feature of his growth. Although he required a nighttime bottle when retiring, a favored not-me possession was not chosen. At the 15 month observation, however, Alan required a strip of cloth in his evening presleep ritual. By the 20-24 month period, an expansion of the stream of human interaction was noted, reflected particularly in an increasing attachment to his father. By 20 months, he had developed a night ritual in which he touched his blanket and mouthed his fingers. During the next two years this ritual gradually expanded to include two plushy bears as well as his special blanket. Although still oriented toward the inanimate, clear evidence for enhanced contact with people was reported. He showed increasing interest in his sister and her friends along with the persistent preference for his father. Then, in the months that followed, his affection for the stuffed toy evolved into a close, special relationship with the family dog, who quickly became a central experience in his developing involvement with the animate world. An interplay evolved with the dog which was both affective and intimate; in his latency years he spoke of his dog as his "toy." The preference for the inanimate persisted in Alan, although human interaction and an increased potential for imagination was achieved and integrated into his personality.

DISCUSSION

These clinical vignettes are offered to illustrate the proposed additional developmental function of the transitional object. With Alan, the more thing-oriented boy, the relationship to the cloth and the plushy bears may have bridged his expansion to the animate world. The affectionate interaction with his dog appeared to evolve from the controlled relationship to the piece of cloth and his stuffed animals. A more familiar but related process is seen in Benjamin, the human-oriented infant. The transitional object facilitated his interest in inanimate things, permitting a movement away from the field of person interest and toward task and achievement orientations.

Where a leaning exists, the transitional object serves as a bridge of expansion facilitating a crossover to the other pathway. Each evolving developmental phase has its necessary expression in persons and processes; expansion requires the capacity to engage both sets of experiences.

The extent of the crossing-over varies. Its limitations may derive from an excessive strength of the original leaning, from an unremitting environmental reinforcement of the natural tilt, or from a restriction in the availability or use of transitional phenomena. Additional study will be necessary to determine the means by which such impediments may be overcome and the specific experience by which expansion along alternate routes might be encouraged or facilitated.

How is this related to character style? The thing-oriented child who is involved intensively with the control of inanimate possessions may develop related qualities in his subsequent human relationships: for example, a greater restriction of considerateness, or an insistence on domination. Where crossing-over or expansion has been limited, his human relationships may be characterized by treating persons as things within the framework of a carefully controlled sphere of interaction. On the other hand, a human-oriented child, familiar with the wider range of interaction characteristic of human relationships, may have difficulty in adjusting to the focused, limited interplay required for the attainment of specific goals or achievements. In all of this, the crossover function of transitional phenomena may be critical; further research into the manifestations of such phenomena may help establish the validity of these propositions and their implications.

These conclusions may be derived from instances of object orientedness arising from variations in equipment; similar implications may be extended in those instances where it is a consequence of deficiencies in stimulation, with a resulting emphasis in one line of relatedness. In such cases, the clustering of functions and emerging characteristics may parallel the observations made of congenitally determined variations in leaning. We question and will further study whether various transitional phenomena (including pets, for example) can provide reparative bridges to link the currents of relatedness required for other functions and for further development.

SUMMARY

A longitudinal study of children from birth offered the opportunity to observe variations in human and thing orientedness. Features of this category of behavior have been described.

It is suggested that when a leaning becomes significant, transitional objects may function as bridges of expansion in two ways: from the animate to the inanimate, and from the mental representation of others to the representation of the self. Some tentative hypotheses have been offered concerning polar leanings, emerging styles of engagement, the structural configuration of the underlying processes, and the effects of environmental influences.

REFERENCES

Abraham, K. (1910). Remarks on the psycho-analysis of a case of foot and corset fetishism. In *Selected Papers on Psycho-Analysis*, pp. 125-136. London: Hogarth Press, 1948.

Abrams, S., and Neubauer, P. B. (1975). Object orientedness: the person or the thing. *Psychoanalytic Quarterly* 45:73–99.

Allen, M., Pollin, W., and Hoffer, A. (1971). Parents, birth and infancy factors in infant twins. *American Journal of Psychiatry* 127:1597-1603.

Bak, R. C. (1968). The phallic woman: the ubiquitous fantasy in perversion. *Psychoanalytic Study of the Child* 23:15-36.

Busch, F., Nagera, H., McKnight, J., and Pezzarossi, G. (1973). Primary transitional objects. *Journal of the American Academy of Child Psychiatry* 12:193-214.

Dickes, R. (1963). Fetishistic behavior: a contribution to its complex development and significance. *Journal of the American Psychoanalytic Association* 11:303-332.

Freud, S. (1927). Fetishism. *Standard Edition* 21:149-157.

Gifford, S., Murawski, B. V., Brazelton, B., and Young, G. C. (1966). Differences in individual development within a pair of identical twins. *International Journal of Psycho-Analysis* 47:261-268.

Gillespie, W. M. (1956). The general theory of sexual perversion. *International Journal of Psycho-Analysis* 37:396-404.

Greenacre, P. (1960). Further notes on fetishism. *Psychoanalytic Study of the Child* 15:181-207.

——— (1969). The fetish and the transitional object. *Psychoanalytic Study of the Child* 24:144-164.

Roiphe, H. (1968). On an early genital phase. *Psychoanalytic Study of the Child* 23:348-365.

―――, and Galenson, E. (1973). The infantile fetish. *Psychoanalytic Study of the Child* 28:147-166.

Sperling, M. (1963). Fetishism in children. *Psychoanalytic Quarterly* 32:374-393.

Winnicott, D. W. (1953). Transitional objects and transitional phenomena. *International Journal of Psycho-Analysis* 34:89-97.

Wulff, M. (1946). Fetishism and object choice in early childhood. *Psychoanalytic Quarterly* 15:450-471.

CHAPTER 10

The experience of the intermediate state between fantasy and reality Winnicott described metaphorically; he called it *potential space*. Here are located man's nascent creative capacities. The budding awareness of separation brings sensory elements into relief, creating both the locus of transitional phenomena and the function of transitional objects. Here too are the roots of play as a first step toward exteriorization and the experience of culture.

Relying on considerations such as these, as well as on Mahler's observations regarding the vicissitudes of separation-individuation, Anni Bergman shows how the potential space metaphor can be usefully ensconced within the developmental framework.

Several chapters in this volume are devoted to a further study of transitional space. Simon Grolnick's chapter on the Etruscan religion concerns this metaphorical space between life and death, what is portrayed as a journey from the familiar land of the living to the unfamiliar land of the dead. In her chapter, Susan Deri notes that "transitional space is neither contiguous nor continuous with the space of reality, but is interwoven seamlessly with it." Masud Khan's chapter on the secret elaborates the theme of an inner space which is analogous to a transitional phenomenon.

L.B.

FROM MOTHER TO THE WORLD OUTSIDE: THE USE OF SPACE DURING THE SEPARATION-INDIVIDUATION PHASE

Anni Bergman

We shall not cease from exploration
And the end of all our exploring
Will be to arrive where we started
And know the place for the first time.
                    —T.S. Eliot, *Four Quartets*

The moment of birth propels the infant from the warm enclosure of the mother's body into the open space of the world. For the mother, the baby, who has been part of her body and a fantasy, now becomes a reality—a human being totally dependent upon her. The baby is born into his mother's expectant arms and can become one with her in a new way—in a symbiotic union. He must then once more emerge as a separate individual, undergoing a process Mahler, Pine and Bergman have termed the psychological birth of the human infant—the separation-individuation phase. This second, psychological birth, the hatching from the "common symbiotic membrane," the separation-individuation process, has been described in numerous publications (Mahler 1963, 1965, 1970, 1971, Mahler and Furer 1963, Mahler and LaPerriere 1965, and Mahler, Pine and Bergman 1975). At the end of this process, the infant has become a toddler with an awareness of himself as a separate being. This awareness involves not only himself, his body now separate from his mother, but includes as well the space surrounding him, space which has become a precious and protected possession. Winnicott (1971) says:

Whereas inner psychic reality has a kind of location in the mind or in the belly, or in the head or somewhere within the bounds of the individual's personality, and whereas what is called external reality is located outside these bounds, playing and cultural experience can be given a location if one uses the concept of the potential space between the mother and the baby. In the development of various individuals it has to be recognized that the third area of potential space between mother and baby is extremely valuable according to the experience of the child or adult who is being considered. [p. 53]

The space surrounding the self is not part of the self, but it is not part of others. It has the quality of being a possession and yet is not, as are other possessions, either tangible or definable. How far does it extend? With whom and under what circumstances can it be shared? When is it friendly and protective, and when frightening and vast? When does it isolate, when does it connect? When is it inaccessible, like a wall surrounding someone? When is it open to include others? And how does the space outside relate to the space within?

It is useful then to think of a third area of human living, one neither inside the individual nor outside in the world of shared reality. This intermediate living can be thought of as occupying a potential space, negating the idea of space and separation between the baby and the mother, and all developments derived from this phenomenon. This potential space varies greatly from individual to individual, and its foundation is the baby's trust in the mother experienced over a long enough period at the critical stage of the separation of the not-me from the me, when the establishment of an autonomous self is at the initial stage. [Winnicott 1971, p. 110]

Intrapsychic events are experienced within a space. We may be filled with joy, with expectation, or with fear and sadness. We may be empty, drained, or filled and complete; at times we may be overflowing, unable to contain our emotions. Sadness as well as happiness can make our tears flow over. Extremes of fear or pain can make us lose the contents of our bladder or bowels.

At the completion of the separation-individuation process, the child emerges as a separate small individual surrounded by space which both separates and unites him with his mother, a mother who now exists not only on the outside but also as an inner presence that regulates the sense of well-being and safety and enables the child to gradually exchange the omnipotence of the mother-infant unit for a growing sense of his autonomy and competence. If the process fails, the space that both separates and unites is not available, and the individual is threatened by engulfment or unbearable isolation. Asch (1966) holds that claustrophobia is not necessarily symptomatic of a phallic conflict. It is his belief that

> identification with the fetus inside the mother is associated with two fantasies of dread. One, the danger of being squeezed out passively, abandoned and flushed away like a bad, smelly stool; this involves the fantasy of birth as an anal process of separation from the mother; it is pre-genital and does not involve the father. Two, the danger of being passively chewed up, dissolved and digested, to be fused with the mother on the most primitive level, with a terrifying loss of identity. These are two distinct anxieties with mainly anal and oral drive derivatives. One is a fear of separation from mother while the other is its opposite, a fear of complete fusion. One involves abandonment by the object, while the latter consists of loss of the self-representation.

In this chapter I shall consider the space between mother and child as it constitutes itself and grows during the separation-individuation process. This results in space that becomes the possession of each individual, defining him, giving him room to grow, the possibility of coming and going, and the capacity to separate from and reunite with a loved object. I shall consider the use of space during the subphases of the separation-individuation process, space defined by the child's growing ability to both create it and bridge it. I shall give special consideration also to "transitional spaces." These are spaces of transition between a mother-world and a world outside. I am referring to spaces such as windows, thresholds, and doors, as well as to vehicles which carry us from one space to the other—cars, trains, airplanes—and about which we can develop strong feelings. Finally, I shall try to connect certain basic experiences of space with certain periods of early development. Observations to be cited were made during the course of a research study begun in 1959 by Dr. Margaret Mahler and her associates at the Masters Children's Center in New York. There normal mothers with normal babies six months to three years old were observed four times per week in a playgroundlike setting. The observations began at that point in development at which the child's psychological space coincides with actual space, and continued as processes of internalization gradually brought about the creation of inner space. This inner space is a metaphor denoting the location in which psychic events occur and in which object representations and self representations are held side by side but separate from each other.

CLOSENESS AND DISTANCE

Many authors have given attention to two opposing but essentially human needs: the need for closeness and the need for distance; the need for clinging and the need for separating; the need for being one with the mother and the need for becoming an individual in one's own right. Imre Hermann (1936) was the first psychoanalytic theorist who postulated a nonsexual primary object relation drive in the infant. He called it the "clinging instinct" (sich anklammern) and its dialectic opposite the "instinct to search" (auf die Suche gehen). Hermann considers the mother-child relationship the basic dual union, that is, the primary context from which the development of the individual emerges. Individuation for him starts with the trauma of the necessary dissolution of the primary mother-child union. At this point the child goes in search of new objects to cling to. Spitz, in No and Yes (1957), says:

> This tendency to separateness counteracts from the beginning the child's more obvious tendency of clinging to the mother. The simultaneous presence of diametrically opposed tendencies in the child, beginning with birth, cannot be sufficiently emphasized. They have their exact counterpart in the existence of similar tendencies in the mother. With the cutting of the umbilical cord a cleavage takes place between mother and child. They become discrete physical entities. At the same time he is driven by a desperate urge to reestablish the previous state, both mother and child strive for as close a contact as possible with each other, culminating in the nursing act. But at the end of nursing they are driven apart again, a cycle which is recaptured with each nursing act.

Mahler's conception differs from that of Spitz in that she does not recognize from the beginning a simultaneous tendency to cling and to separate. She distinguishes an autistic phase lasting about three weeks, during which sleeplike states account for far more of the infants time than do states of arousal. She finds this reminiscent of that "primal state of libido distribution that prevailed in intrauterine life, which resembles the model of a closed monadic system, self-sufficient in its hallucinatory wish fulfillment" (Mahler 1971, p. 7). At about three weeks, the autistic shell is replaced by "a quasi-semipermeable membrane enveloping both parts of the mother-infant dyad." From symbiosis the infant slowly disengages himself during the separation-individuation process, resulting in an intrapsychic separation of self and object.

Balint, in Thrills and Regressions (1959), describes two primitive disturbances in object relating; these are described in terms of the use of space, which, as we will see later, closely resembles its use during the subphases of separation-individuation. One disturbance is characterized by the need to cling to objects, and experiences the space between them as a threat. The other denies the need for objects and has an exaggerated need for open spaces. These, Balint says, are not opposites. Rather, "they are two different attitudes, possibly developing or, so to speak, branching off from the same stem" (p. 46). Both are reactions to the recognition that a blissful world without boundaries between mother and child is disturbed by the need to accept existence of objects with resistant, aggressive, and ambivalent qualities. Balint says that

> despite many gradations and changes, there are apparently two basic ways in which people respond to this traumatic discovery. One is to create an ocnophilic world based on the fantasy that firm objects are reliable and kind, that they will always be there when one needs them, and that they will never mind and never resist being used for support. The other is to create the philobatic world which goes back to life prior to the experience that objects emerge and destroy the harmony of the limitless, contourless expanses. . . . This world is colored by an unjustified optimism—originating in the earlier world of primary love—that enables the philobat to believe that his skills and his equipment will be sufficient to cope with the elements—the substances—as long as he can avoid hazardous objects. [p. 68]

We feel that these disturbances described by Balint originate during separation-individuation, the process of gradual disengagement from our symbiotic beginnings. Inasmuch as they are both disturbances in the use of space, they are of particular interest to us here.

There are two kinds of space, enclosed space and open space. The model of the enclosed space is the womb. Lewin, in his paper on claustrophobia (1935), states that true claustrophobia is regularly connected with fantasies of being in the womb and of one's own birth. Open space is the world outside following separation. Closed spaces are protected, open spaces are exposed. But either one without the other is terrifying. The enclosed space, no matter how beautiful, becomes prison or exiles us when we are denied or deny ourselves the possibility of leaving it. On the other hand, the open road leads nowhere. It becomes the plight of the refugee who is denied the essential human need for protection and belonging. In children's games the zone of security is often called "home," the symbol of the safe mother. However, children's games also contain the other element, that of the open space which must be conquered with skill and daring. Balint (1959) writes:

> All thrills entail the leaving and rejoining of security. The pleasure experienced in either of these two phases, that is, either when staying in security or when leaving it in order to return to it—are very primitive, self-evident and apparently in no need of explanation— although it must be stated that not every adult can enjoy them equally. [p. 26]

According to Mahler's theory of symbiotic child psychosis, the cause for this severe disturbance lies in the fact that though the infant is maturationally ready to take the first steps toward separation, he can be emotionally unable to do so, because of "a deficiency or a defect in the child's intrapsychic utilization of the mothering partner during the symbiotic phase, and his subsequent inability to internalize the representation of the mothering object for polarization" (Mahler 1971). This results in panic, the fear of engulfment and abandonment. In classical cases of symbiotic psychosis, the child is not comfortable with mother and often pushes her away vehemently. Yet he cannot function away from her. This intolerable state provokes the building of a wall of secondary autistic defense against all object relating.

All spaces are essential for human development: the enclosed mother space, the open, outside world spaces, and spaces of transition between the two. People move with varying degrees of ease between the two spaces. Although the wish to move, to travel, is ubiquitous, there is always some degree of reluctance at the moment of leaving, not to speak of the more severe forms of homesickness and travel phobia.

> In long-range planning for a trip, I think there is a private conviction that it won't happen. As the day approached, my warm bed and comfortable house grew increasingly desirable and my dear wife incalculably precious. To give these up for three months for the terrors of the uncomfortable and unknown seemed crazy. I didn't want to go. Something had to happen to forbid my going, but it didn't. [Steinbeck 1961, p. 19]

THE SPACE BETWEEN MOTHER AND CHILD

There is no space between the nursing infant and the mother. The infant at first has no knowledge of space, no knowledge of an outside world, or of the mother as a separate entity. During the symbiotic period, autonomous ego functions develop as the baby begins to find the breast, to gaze into mother's eyes, to listen to her footsteps, to look at bright colors or moving objects. All of these come and go; they come from somewhere and they go somewhere. They provide the first rudimentary experience of space, even though this space is not yet felt to be outside. By the age of five months, the beginning of the differentiation subphase, the infant starts to strain away from mother. As he does this, he has already acquired the means with which to bridge the space he is creating. He strains away from mother because the world out there lures him, but as he does this he can take in, feel the mother better from this distance he has created, and he can reach and grasp her body; he can grasp, but he cannot yet let go. The ability to let go of grasped objects develops somewhat later, providing a new lesson in space: objects fall, disappear, can be retrieved. During the differentiation subphase one can at times observe the conflict between the desire for mother and the breast, and the lure of the outside world; between the need for a space between himself and mother, and the desire to undo that space. An infant at that age often acts as though he wanted to devour the mother, to literally attack her with an open mouth—the ultimate undoing of the space between them.

Even before the infant has sufficient control of motility to be able to reach out, he can engage his mother actively with his eyes, and elicit a response from her. During the differentiation subphase, seeing itself, looking at people and things not mother, becomes a most pleasurable activity. The nursing baby under five months of age seems to gaze steadily into the mother's eyes; but from about five months on, the baby, after the first hunger is satiated, will actively look around and follow both visual and auditory stimuli. As soon as the first hunger is satisfied, the world out there competes with the breast. The world out there becomes an enticement and impetus, though the libidinal energy with which the urge to explore is invested is still supplied directly by the mother. The "undernourished" child does not have desire or energy to explore, or the explorations become painful rather than pleasurable, an aspect of early stranger or strangeness anxiety. The ability to distance visually precedes the ability to reach and explore tactilely, at first the body and face of the mother, but, increasingly during the differentiation subphase, the faces of others, as well as interesting objects in the environment, especially objects attached to people, such as jewelry and eyeglasses. The exploration of the "other's" face or body during the differentiation subphase is often followed by a return to close bodily contact with mother.

In our observational study of separation-individuation, certain infants would explore the environment most actively while in mother's lap, if given sufficient freedom to explore in the mother's vicinity. Others, especially those too closely enveloped by the mother, would actively push away from her, seemingly struggling for greater freedom. In an extreme case of this sort, we found one little boy who actually preferred to be held by adults other than his mother during this period. Other children while exploring from mother's lap seemed suddenly overcome by distress and simply could not integrate closeness to mother with the exploration of others; they could not give up one for the other. Steven, a child of this sort, rather early in life seemed to resolve the conflict by ignoring his need for closeness and turned his energies to exploration of the outside world. Interestingly, though, he especially liked to explore the inanimate world. It seemed a more neutral ground that would diminish the conflict between closeness and distance. Even early in life he seemed to prefer to explore through his play with toys (see Abrams and Neubauer, chapter 9). He would endlessly push cars and trains about, and would especially enjoy seeing them go in and out of tunnels. In addition to the more obvious meaning of actively playing at separation, the play also enacted the passage from closed to open spaces and vice versa.

Each phase of the separation-individuation process seems to have its own optimal distance between mother and child. While this varies with each mother-child pair, according to their temperament and predilection, one might possibly see these variations as the outcome of the process of mutual adaptation between mother and child. In other words, then, the optimal distance for each child during a given subphase would be a compromise between what might be optimal for a particular phase of development and what would be possible for a particular mother and child. To illustrate: during the differentiation subphase the available instruments for distancing and approaching are the eyes and the reaching-out arms and exploring hands. The optimal distance thus would be one allowing the infant maximal use of these instruments while preserving the maximal amount of closeness compatible with the emerging need for distancing. In order to distance, the baby has to be somewhat apart from his mother and yet close enough to be able to reapproach her. Thus, the optimal distance is no longer attained by the mother's holding the infant closely in her arms as during the symbiotic phase, but by holding the infant loosely enough to leave torso and arms free for exploration; in this position he can pull away from mother far enough to look at her from a greater distance. The infant held too closely will push away and, as a last resort, prefer to be held by others. The infant whose mother's hold is painful or uncomfortable will push away and prematurely try to be on his own. The infant placed at too great a distance by the mother will experience the distancing process as painful, will clamor to be held, and will cling. In all cases the infant begins to have a voice in determining distance or closeness during this first phase of the separation-individuation process. The space explored and created during the differentiation subphase, from about five to eight months, is a space between mother and child. The space surrounding the mother— especially her feet—as well as the space surrounding the child is essentially enclosed. Open spaces are as yet inaccessible.

THE SPACE "OUT THERE"

The differentiation subphase is at about age eight months succeeded by the practicing subphase. As his ability to bridge the space increases, the creeping and crawling infant creates a new space between himself and his mother. He can now bridge the space as well as create a space not only by looking and reaching, hearing or being heard; he can now bridge the space with his body, as he can actively leave his mother and then return. During the practicing subphase there is a great investment in developing ego functions, as well as in the world out there. The baby is relatively oblivious of the mother, as he is not yet fully aware of his separateness. Mother is the home base to which the baby periodically returns to restore his waning energies. However, there are times when he creates a distance greater than he can comfortably bridge. Then suddenly he can be overcome by the feeling that he cannot return to mother. Yet on the whole, if during the differentiation subphase the infant had operated largely within the mother-child space and had eventually learned to know and respond to her as a special person, during the practicing subphase the most important space is out there. The practicing infant seems almost compelled to seek out open space, and he does this in an elated mood. As the mother is still experienced as part of the self, the space is usually not frightening; the practicing infant is actually surprised when he falls and mother is not automatically at hand to rescue him. Balint (1959), in his description of the philobat, brings to mind the practicing infant:

The philobatic world consists of friendly expanses dotted more or less densely with dangerous and unpredictable objects. . . . The philobat's illusion is that apart from *his* own proper equipment he needs no objects, certainly no one particular object. . . . The philobat feels that using his equipment he can certainly cope with any situation; *the world as a whole will "click in"* and he will be able to avoid treacherous objects. . . . The philobat feels that it is within his power to "conquer the world." [pp. 34-35]

This description is most reminiscent of the description of the practicing subphase, the love affair with the world, the elated mood, the feeling of omnipotence emanating from the mother's still being experienced as part of the self.

While the optimal distance during the differentiation subphase was found on mother's lap or at mother's feet, the optimal distance during practicing is found in the space out there in the outside world. His mother is within reach of the distance modalities, close enough to be heard, to hear, to be seen, to be joined for emotional refueling in case of need or fatigue. The mother is needed as a stable point. She should not step in too quickly when a child finds himself in difficulty, but neither should she be unavailable in that situation. In other words, she should be neither intrusive nor aloof.

We may look at some children's attempts to adapt to situations in which optimal distance is unavailable. Susan, for instance, whose mother had been able to enjoy close physical contact but did not want to be bothered once the child started to move away, became more insistently demanding during the beginning practicing period. She insisted, for example, that her mother pick up a toy for her. What seems to have happened later is that Susan, since her mother would not give freely, was to some extent fixated at this level and continued to make demands upon her mother. This did not leave her free to relate to the other-than-mother world, and in particular made it difficult for her to relate to other children.

Doris manifested the opposite problem. Her mother allowed her ample freedom to explore, was always watchful, always ready to support and help with voice or action. However, she was unable to provide her daughter the gentle push that would convince her that her mother was confident she could function in the world outside. Doris showed some evidence of fixation at the level of needing her mother in case of trouble. She showed strong separation reactions and difficulties with new situations, a character trait which remained characteristic of her.

Jason was a boy who could not outgrow the elated state accompanying the feeling that he could conquer the world. He was a motor-minded little boy who started to walk freely at the early age of nine months. His mother was a depressed woman with a rather poor image of herself. It was most important that her son be precocious, a narcissistic completion of herself. She was in great awe of her little boy. She was burdened by his early walking, as prematurely walking toddlers are a burden to any mother. Jason's mother, in awe of her fledgling, was the very opposite of Doris's. The latter could not convey her confidence in her daughter's ability to manage on her own. Jason's mother, on the other hand, seemed to impart to her son the idea that he could manage no matter what. She did not temper his age-appropriate feeling of omnipotence with her own ability to be a rational judge of danger. She allowed him total freedom, and Jason never seemed to learn to be a judge of danger himself. Recklessly he would throw himself into space. He was forever falling, but, interestingly, he hardly ever cried. It was as if the sense of omnipotence and of his own invulnerability dwarfed his physical pain.

LEAVING AND RETURNING

At approximately fifteen months, the beginning of rapprochement, an important change occurs. In the course of practicing, the toddler becomes aware that his mother is not automatically at hand, that he cannot always get back to her when he wants, that she cannot automatically shield him from all pains and frustrations. In other words, after a period of practicing encounters with the outside world, as well as with his mother, the toddler is repeatedly faced with feelings of helplessness. Thus he becomes aware of his separateness. An important change occurs in the direction of his movement and experiences in space. While the practicing infant generally moved out in the direction of the big world, protected by the illusion of mother's magical presence, the rapprochement child moves back toward the mother. However, he does not return empty-handed. It is most characteristic of him to bring objects found in the big world back to mother and to deposit them in her lap. During differentiation, the space was confined to the space between mother and child and the space immediately surrounding them; during practicing the space seemed to have no limits; during rapprochement we see clearly for the first time the movement in space that becomes so important from then on, the movement that is truly essential, namely leaving home base (the mother) and returning. But this is by no means easily accomplished. Earlier, during the phase of differentiation, we described a conflict between the wish to incorporate the mother and to distance from her. During the rapproachement subphase, the conflict between wishing to be autonomous and separate, and yet wanting mother ever present and available becomes enlarged by the cognitive developments that require the toddler to relinquish his illusion of mother's presence in their shared omnipotence. During the rapprochement crisis, the toddler, who wants to have it both ways, often cannot bear either situation—to be close to mother forces him to be more passive than he likes, and to be away from her confronts him with feelings of helplessness and intense longing. Thus, during rapprochement, transitional spaces acquire extraordinary importance.

What is the optimal spatial distance during this period? No longer need the mother be within sight or earshot; now a space close by will suffice, where the toddler knows his mother to be, where he can find her and leave her again. Here, for the first time, the toddler discovers the thrill of leaving and refinding his mother. It is this leaving and refinding of the mother which allows her to be created anew each time she is found (Winnicott 1971). Each time the toddler finds her he brings along a new piece of the world outside, and each time he leaves her he takes with him a part of her. Increasingly this part is an image, but often it is concrete. Typically a child of this age will take something from his mother's pocketbook and run off with it. During rapprochement the intervening space becomes once again the space *connecting* mother and child. But this space is now enlarged by the toddler's growing capacity for locomotion, perception, and beginning symbolization and internalization.

In discussing the space between mother and child during differentiation, we mentioned that at times the infant seemed to be in conflict over closeness and distance. During rapprochement, in the enlarged space, the conflict over closeness and distance becomes central. The space between mother and child now turns into a space of conflict between them. At times the toddler insists on shadowing every move of his mother, knowing her whereabouts, controlling her; at times the opposite behavior, driving her away, becomes characteristic. The toddler is forever running away from mother, escaping, yet expecting to be swept up in her arms. Another characteristic pattern is that of veering away, going toward mother, and in the last moment changing direction. The period of rapprochement is one of indecision. On the one side is a fear of reengulfment; on the other side is the fear of abandonment. The optimal distance is thus one that allows for back and forth movement between toddler and mother, with all the pushes and pulls that this entails. It calls also for a place at some greater distance from her—a resting place where the toddler can exercise his newly emerging capacities and interests in the non-mother world, but where the mother is nevertheless available when he needs her.

A child caught up in the rapprochement struggle, unable to resolve his dilemma, is reminiscent of Balint's description of the person who clings to objects and cannot manage the spaces between them.

During the rapprochement subphase, which requires that the toddler reconcile his need for both mother and outside space, transitional spaces take on particular importance. These are spaces that allow the toddler to remain in both places at the same time. For example, before entering a room he might stand on the threshold, hesitant either to come or to leave. Alone in a room, away from his mother, he can console himself by looking out the window, which allows him to stay in a space away from mother and yet be in contact with an outside in which his mother can come and go. Then at certain times a toddler of this age might need to have the door open when he is away from mother; on the other hand, he might not be able to settle down unless it is closed. Playing with doors— closing and opening them, playing with the doorknobs—is another activity that seems important. At Masters Children's Center, where observational study of the separation-individuation process was conducted, a new space had to be created to meet the needs of toddlers at rapprochement age and beyond. The room where mothers, observers, and babies were together suddenly seemed too small. The toddlers gradually began to leave whenever the door was open. The staff created a toddler room across the hall, where toddlers could be without their mothers. This was a new and non-mother world. The door, the threshold and windows of that room became transitional spaces, spaces a child could enter when he missed his mother, but did not want to interrupt his non-mother play. Another room that took on special importance to him during this period was the cubby room, where mothers and children hung their coats when they arrived. It had a large window facing the play yard. This became a transitional space par excellence. Apparently prompted by a wish to find their mothers, children would often leave the toddler room. However, they would often change their minds and go to the transitional cubby room instead. There, in a symbolic manner, they could be close to the world of mother and home, since their mothers' coats were there; but they were also symbolically in the world outside, which they could watch through the tall window. Usually, after a short sojourn in the transitional room, they returned to the non-mother toddler room, which provided space for expanding ego functions and a respite from conflict with the mother.

Thus, as the sense of being a separate individual develops, so does the need for a variety of spaces (mother, outside, transitional), and so does a proprietary feeling toward such spaces. Now a child can push another child and fight for the special space of his mother's or a mother-substitute's lap. A child can now fight to sit next to a particular person or in a particular chair that he might consider his. Also at this time, certain moving objects, such as tricycles or kiddie cars, become the most treasured possession, and I believe, transitional spaces. These most coveted objects lend additional speed and power to the incessant coming and going, leaving and finding mother, and in addition become small home bases on wheels. Often the child who leaves them still considers them his property, his home base, and becomes upset if another child sits on his tricycle or kiddie car.

The rapprochement subphase coincides with the anal phase of psychosexual development. During the anal phase, awareness of inner spaces as well as transition from inside to outside is strengthened by the toddler's growing awareness that the contents of the bladder and bowel are his property to give or withhold. At the same time an inner representational world begins to have more and more power and reality.

The rapprochement subphase is followed by an initial attainment of object constancy. This implies a growing acceptance of separateness and an increasing internalization of the love object. Mother becomes more an internal presence, and the child between two and three can imagine and accept her being elsewhere. Thus the need for incessant coming and going is diminished. The child is better able to accept temporary separations, substitute adults, and can become absorbed in activities in the outside world. Symbolic play begins to substitute for the actual doing. A child of that age, instead of going to mother, can begin to play at being mother, father or baby. A child of this age can begin to play house or castle or cave, and so find symbolic representations of the enclosed mother space.

THE USE OF SPACE AS THERAPEUTIC COMMUNICATION

In a recent paper Furer (1974) maintained that the subphases of the separation-individuation process, while they cannot be directly recon-structed in the verbal content of analytic treatment, nevertheless play an important role in the establishment of the basic transference and therapeutic alliance. One would assume that the patient's use of space is an important communication to the analyst. This has been described by Winnicott (1971), Khan (1973), and Searles (1973).

I would like to give a few examples in the treatment of children where the use of space in the analyst's office was of special importance in working out problems arising from the separation-individuation process.

These were not verbalized in therapy, but served as the background music, the atmosphere in which the treatment took place. Peter came to treatment at the age of four. He suffered extreme separation anxiety and it was many months before he would come to his treatment sessions without his mother, even when she promised to wait for him in the waiting room. Peter also wet and soiled his pants, and was generally willful and uncontrollable. He was a cherished child, good-looking and intelligent. He had been an active baby and his mother had experienced his early motor development as a threat. She had been happy with him when he was an infant, but trouble began when, during the practicing and rapprochement subphases, his intimidated mother interpreted Peter's precocious activity as willfulness. Rather than being quietly available, she fought with him, unsuccessfully tried to control him, and frightened him with unpredictable outbursts of anger. When Peter was two, his baby brother was born, and Peter could not reconcile himself to having a rival. At the beginning of treatment he repeatedly acted out family scenes that ended in cataclysms of destruction. In these he was both the perpetrator of misfortune and the rescuer, identifying alternately with the victim and the aggressor. During a later phase of treatment, Peter became interested in books about space and time, the heavenly bodies, and prehistoric animals. He insisted his therapist read these to him while he sat on a swing, moving toward and away from the therapist, who had to sit in a fixed position. In this play he seemed to reenact experiences concerning his mother and outside space, experiences in which he controlled closeness and distance. This was not interpreted, but was allowed to unfold.

Jimmy was a boy whose sister was born when he was eighteen months old. From early on he had shown a strong, clinging attachment to his mother, who felt quite helpless in the face of it. She felt inadequate as a mother and feared that she, without wishing to, prevented Jimmy from becoming an individual. Jimmy was a quiet, withdrawn little boy who experienced treatment, especially any verbal intervention, as an invasion. It was almost impossible to find a workable distance. One Valentine's Day the therapist gave him a white chocolate lollipop. He asked the therapist to sit close to him but not to talk while he sucked the lollipop, which he said reminded him of milk. He remarked how hard it was to suck but not bite the lollipop. He said how good the session was and again implored the therapist not to talk. The session apparently recreated a symbiotic union, a good mother prior to separation. Again this experience was allowed to develop.

Maria[1] was a little girl with an intense ambivalent relationship to her mother. Her parents had separated after long and violent struggle. While at home with a baby-sitter, Maria had an accident in which she blinded herself in one eye. For a considerable period in therapy she regaled her therapist with insatiable demands for objects which would never satisfy her. Finally she invented a game in which she created a space under a table for herself, then hung blankets over it and demanded that the therapist supply various objects for it. This space had to be recreated for her by the therapist prior to each session. She played in it quietly by herself, while the therapist had to be watching and available outside. After many months of playing this game, Maria emerged. She no longer needed her special place, and she was now able to relate to her therapist in a new way, on a more mature level. She allowed some give and take, and recognized the therapist as a separate person rather than as an extension of herself.

These examples show how problems of space, of closeness and comfortable distance, of being able to come and go, are worked on by patients in the therapeutic situation as an accompaniment and counterpoint to what is said in words. Feelings of well-being and safety are achieved when feelings about space belonging to preverbal times are recreated by the child in actions or words, allowing for freedom to move with greater ease from enclosed mother space to the space out there. As the conflict is worked through, both spaces become more available. This does not imply that the problem is settled once and for all. Conflicts in this area will recur throughout life, but they are less overwhelming once the essential conflict of the rapprochement crisis is at least partly worked through and resolved.

We have shown how the baby moves in the course of the subphases from being one with mother to beginning awareness and eventual exploration of ever widening areas of the world outside. We have seen the toddler move back and forth from mother to the world outside. Eventually, a space within becomes available which allows for the fantasied creation of both spaces.

SOME THOUGHTS ON THE IMPORTANCE OF HOME SPACE

Throughout life, *where* one is and not just *with whom* affects one's mood and sense of well-being and safety, and people vary widely as to the varieties of space in which they feel most comfortable. From prehistoric times people have devoted time and energy to creating the home space. A young woman during her therapy described her home as a barometer of what was going on within her. More than the clothes she wore, the neatness or sloppiness of her house represented her feelings about herself. When she was a child, her family had moved from a country house which she remembered as sunny and spacious, and in which she had felt close to her mother, to a more expensive but smaller suburban home. She never came to love this new home and in it she began to feel more estranged from her family. In adulthood, she forever attempted to recreate the home of her early childhood.

And finally I would like to present a personal experience which demonstrated to me the importance of home space. On a hiking and camping trip in a faraway country, a group of people, most of them strangers to each other as well as to the country, started out together with the knowledge that they would be trekking for more than two weeks through totally unfamiliar mountain territory. A mood of anxiety prevailed on the first afternoon of the trip. After several hours, the first campsite was reached. As each person approached, he was greeted by a member of the working crew who handed each a small bunch of flowers and led him to his designated tent. This small gesture of hospitality in the wilderness provided much to change the mood of the group to one of confidence and friendliness, which helped everyone through the more difficult and strenuous moments that were bound to arise; no words of reassurance could have worked as well as a ready shelter and a bunch of flowers. Home was carried to the vast spaces of the faraway mountains, giving this group of people the reassurance that both of these essential spaces would still be available.

SUMMARY

During the first few weeks of life the human infant, through the nursing care of his mother, becomes united with her in symbiotic oneness. Slowly as the infant matures he begins to differentiate inside from outside, mother from others, himself from mother. As he does this, space between him and his mother has to be created and bridged. Each period of development during the separation-individuation process has an optimal distance between baby and mother. Exploration of different spaces—mother and world out there—eventually results in cognitive awareness of separation and relative helplessness. Thus during rapprochement there is a continuous need to traverse the space separating infant from mother. Yet at the same time, the space surrounding the self becomes a precious possession, and space within becomes a reality reinforced by toilet training and the ability to retain or deposit bowel and bladder products. With the advent of beginning object constancy, the inner world of thought and fantasy allows for the symbolic representation of experiences in space—thus widening the world outside as well as securing the home space.

As the realization of the irreconcilability of home and outside space becomes a reality, transitional spaces become a necessity for comfortable functioning. In the outside world these transitional spaces must contain elements of both mother and world outside: the home away from home, the home on wheels, the freedom to come and go, a place to play. It is more difficult to conceptualize the transitional space within the representational world, but it seems that the ability to think and to delay gratification creates a safe space within, mediating between passionate longings for mother and need for distance from her. The concept of transitional space based on observations in a toddler study is an extension of Winnicott's transitional object. The initial and primitive experiences of differentiation of self from mother seem to contain parts of both. Transitional spaces serve a similar function in the widening world of the toddler in his movements from mother to the world outside.

NOTE

1. I wish to thank Dr. Linda Gunsburg for sharing this material with me.

REFERENCES

Asch, S. S. (1966). Claustrophobia and depression. *Journal of the American Psychoanalytic Association* 14:711-729.

Balint, M. (1959). *Thrills and Regressions*. London: The Hogarth Press.

Eliot, T. S. (1943). *Four Quartets*. New York: Harcourt, Brace.

Furer, M. (1974). The psychoanalytic process, the therapeutic alliance and child observation. Paper presented at the Midwinter meeting of the American Psychoanalytic Association, New York, December, 1974.

Hermann, I. (1936). Clinging–going-in-search: a contrasting part of instincts and their relation to sadism and masochism. Trans. *Psychoanalytic Quarterly* 45(1976):5-36.

Khan, M. M. R. (1973). The role of illusion in the analytic space and process. *Annual of Psychoanalysis* 1:231-246.

Lewin, B. D. (1935). Claustrophobia. *Psychoanalytic Quarterly* 4:227-233.

Mahler, M. (1963). Thoughts about development and individuation. *Psychoanalytic Study of the Child* 18:307-324.

——— (1965). On the significance of the normal separation-individuation phase: with reference to research in symbiotic child psychosis. *Drives, Affects, Behavior,* edited by M. Shur. New York: International Universities Press.

——— (1970). *On Human Symbiosis and the Vicissitudes of Individuation: Volume I. Infantile Psychosis.* New York: International Universities Press.

——— (1971). A study of the separation-individuation process and its possible application to borderline phenomena in the psychoanalytic situation. *Psychoanalytic Study of the Child* 26:403-424.

———, and Furer, M. (1963). Certain aspects of the separation-individuation phase. *Psychoanalytic Quarterly* 32:1-14.

———, and LaPerriere, K. (1965). Mother-child interaction during separation-individuation. *Psychoanalytic Quarterly* 34:483-498.

———, Pine, F., and Bergman, A. (1975). *The Psychological Birth of the Human Infant: Symbiosis and Individuation.* New York: Basic Books.

Searles, H. F. (1973). Concerning therapeutic symbiosis. *Annual of Psychoanalysis* 1:247-262.

Spitz, R. A. (1957). *No and Yes: On the Genesis of Human Communication.* New York: International Universities Press.

Steinbeck, J. (1972). *Travels with Charley.* New York: Bantam.

Winnicott, D. W. (1971). *Playing and Reality.* New York: Basic Books.

CHAPTER 11

In our work we continually struggle to ascertain the nature of our patient's object relations and to this end pay close attention to their reflection in the transference. Additionally, much of the classic analytic theoretical structure has object relations theory as its foundation. In a chapter virtually delineating a philosophy of psychoanalysis, André Green considers with great sensitivity Winnicott's place in the history of analysis, especially with regard to the concept of the object. This has particular importance in view of Winnicott's successful and innovative attempts at treating borderline patients, attempts based on his picture of child development from the standpoint of transitional object formation.

Winnicott once said that he was always maneuvering with his patients to create an analytic situation. With borderlines as with children, the immaturity of ego structure necessitates changes in the basic technique. Green favors distortions or parameters leading to greater symbolizing capacity.

Green defines an analyzing object constructed of contributions from both patient and analyst, a construction suggestive, in its being a fusion of me/not-me, of Winnicott's transitional object. Theodore Greenbaum elaborates a similar view in chapter 12, using Isakower's metaphor of the analyzing instrument. In any such construction, play, creativity, and illusion become fundamental facets of the analytic process, facets rooted, however, in the ego and its developmental history.

L.B.

POTENTIAL SPACE IN PSYCHOANALYSIS:
THE OBJECT IN THE SETTING

André Green

THE OBJECT IN ANALYSIS,
THE ANALYSIS OF THE OBJECT,
THE OBJECT OF ANALYSIS

On several occasions, Freud was led to assert that psychoanalytic concepts have chiefly an heuristic value and that only secondarily can they be defined more rigorously or replaced by others. No concept since the founding of psychoanalysis has been more broadly utilized than that of the object. According to Littré, the French Academy Dictionary gives the same illustration in defining the word "subject" as it does in defining the word "object": natural bodies are the *subject* of physics; natural bodies are the *object* of physics. Rather than deplore the confusion that arises here, or protest against philosophies which would divide subject and object absolutely, I wish instead to emphasize that their relationship is one of symmetry or of complementarity: no object without a subject, no subject without an object. From Freud's time to ours psychoanalytic theory has not been able to avoid facing up to the truth of this.

Freud completely disrupted the old relation between subject and object. Instead of opposing to the object the subject as it was defined by philosophical tradition, he coupled the object to the drive—the *anti-subject*. For it is quite clear that the drive cannot assume a subjective function. In his theory, drive—and the agency which connotes it, the id—represents for Freud that which is the most impersonal, the least capable of an individual will: both because it is rooted in the body and because it is associated with the radical characteristics of the species as such. Although the drive of Freudian theory is sharply distinguished from the

Translated by Anita Kermode and Michele Sirègar.

classical notion of instinct, the two remain related by their fundamentally improper "nature"—that is, in their departure from the propriety of self-sameness of the subject. However, with the development of object relations theory, Freud's concept of the ego could no longer provide an adequate theoretical complement to newly emergent formulations of the object. Attempts to supply this deficiency led to the elaboration of such ego-related concepts as the "self," and the "I." Thus the subjectivity of the subject (which Freud had managed, as it were, to bracket off) makes its reappearance in contemporary analytic theory. It returns explicitly in Pasche who gives it an existential dimension, and in Lacan, who, following the structuralist movement, insists on its impersonal character and relates its effects to those of a nonrepresentable set of combinations which he calls the order of the Symbolic. Elsewhere, and from different cultural perspectives, Hartmann, Jacobson, Spitz, Winnicott, Kohut, and Lichtenstein have distinguished, for varying reasons, the ego of Freudian theory from the concept of the self. But the self, which approximates the academic notion of the subject, is unrelated to the function of the subject as viewed from a structuralist perspective.[1]

FREUD'S CONCEPTION OF THE OBJECT

The question of the object must therefore be posed in terms of its historical evolution, since the object in psychoanalysis, the analysis of the psychoanalytic object, and the object of psychoanalysis itself are closely interrelated issues. In Freud (1915) the object is part of a setting, a *montage*, to which it is simultaneously internal and external. It is internal insofar as it forms a constitutive element of this montage, as one of the components of the drive apparatus. For if there is a psychic apparatus, it is because there is a drive apparatus. The source, the pressure, the aim, and the object of the drive comprise this apparatus. However, the source and the pressure have a physical origin and as such are not displaceable; the displacement or the replacement of one source by another does not eliminate the problem of pressure at the original source. For example, one can try to cheat hunger by masturbating, or sexual desire by eating, but the hunger like the sexual desire will remain unappeased and the illusion can only briefly be sustained. Above all it is crucial to observe that such a displacement of source and such a displacement of pressure can be achieved only through the artifice of a change of aim (e.g., fellatio in the place of coitus) which may also be accompanied by a change of object (e.g., choosing a homoerotic or autoerotic object in the place of a heterosexual one). Autoeroticism is an obligatory solution, a replacement dictated by the discontinuity of the object's presence and, in the end, by the more or less belated awareness of its loss. The drive components are sharply separated into two polarities: the source as a somatic, internal element and the object as a nonsomatic and external one.

Thus the conceptual framework of the object in Freudian theory includes the following characteristics:

1. The object is part of the drive apparatus: the *included* object.
2. The object is external to the drive: the *excluded* object. At first the object of need, it becomes, by *leaning on* the need, the object of the desire (anaclisis).[2]
3. Of all the components of the drive apparatus, the object is that for which *substitutes* are most easily found. Thus it is eminently an object of transference.
4. The *absent* object can be replaced by another external object or by a part object taken either from the external object (e.g., the breast) or from one's own body (e.g., the thumb).
5. The object can be *incorporated* (as a familiar or as an alien, uncanny thing); it can be *introjected* (as a psychic process); it can be the object of *identification* (as the object which is both identified and identified-with in incorporation or introjection); it can be *internalized* (taken from the outside to the inside).
6. The object is initially *confused* with that which objectifies it and presents it *as* an object, i.e., with that which puts it forth (*ob-ject*). The result may be either a formless chaos where there is neither object nor *anti-object*; or, more often, a state of reversibility pertaining to both the object and the anti-object. (In this context, *anti-object* means *counter-object*, antagonistic yet at the same time close to the object.) Here we have the object of projection.
7. The distinction between object and non-object is made by way of the integration of *object loss*.[3] Its consequence is the creation of an *internal object* distinct from the *external object*. This evolution parallels the distinction between *part object* and *whole object*.
8. Corollary to the formation of the internal object is that of the *fantasied object*. Inversely, the fantasy is itself taken, in its turn, as object. Its opposite is the *real object*. The first is governed by the pleasure principle, the second by the reality principle. The fantasied object is located in an extraterritorial position within a psychic apparatus ruled by the reality principle.
9. The choice of object depends on multiple criteria. One of the basic

distinctions governing object-choice is that between the *narcissistic object*, formed on the model of the narcissism of the non-object, and the *anaclitic object*, based on the model of the objectal object. This difference is redoubled by the notion of *investment:* the narcissistic investment of the object, the objectal investment of the object—which suggests the importance of the economic transformation.

10. The play of differences which characterize the object may be situated, as we have just seen, along various axes. But two of them have a dominant role: on the one hand, separation of the *good* and the *bad* and, on the other, separation according to the *difference between the sexes*—the phallic versus the castrated object, the masculine versus the feminine object (penis/vagina), and the paternal versus the maternal object (in the Oedipus complex).

11. The object is bound both to *desire* and to *identification*—identification being the primary mode of relationship with the object, leading then to a secondary identification with the object of desire after its renunciation.

12. The object is in a *mediating position* with respect to *narcissism*: at once its agonist and antagonist.

13. The object can be a product of the *constructiveness or the destructiveness of the drives*. It can be either constructive or destructive for the non-object (i.e., for the ego or the self).

14. The *erotic object* (i.e., the object as invested by the constructive qualities of Eros in Freud's final theory of the drives) evolves toward sublimation; whereas the object of destructiveness evolves, not toward objectal chaos, but toward *objectal nothingness* (i.e., the zero point of excitation) because the object is always a source of excitation, whether external or internal, pleasurable or unpleasurable.

15. The study of object relations concerns the relationship *to* the object or *between* objects. The nature of the link is more important than the action which unites object to non-object or objects amongst themselves. This link is one of conjunction or of disjunction.

Thus the object, according to Freud, is by nature polymorphous and polysemous. Here it is vital to point out that in Freud's work the object never depends exclusively on its existence or its essence, its perception or its conception. It should be defined as neither form nor essence but rather as *a network of relationships with shifting boundaries and with variable investments which keeps the anti-object (or the anti-subject) awake and alive, i.e., in a state of desire.*[4]

THE COHERENCE OF FREUDIAN THEORY

The aim and object of psychoanalysis is, in short, the construction of the *analytic object*, which the analysand can carry away with him from the analysis and can make use of in the absence of the analyst, who is no longer the object of transference. Inversely, the detachment from the analyst of the analysand-as-object implies that the countertransference can be displaced onto another analysand and that the analysand is now capable of becoming another kind of object for the analyst, an *other*.

THE AVATARS OF THE OBJECT IN THE WORK OF FREUD'S DISCIPLES

Freud's disciples went on to tamper with this remarkable theoretical construction, adding on to or else whittling away the main edifice so as to impair, more often than not, the harmony of the whole. The empirical/theoretical gap, i.e., the disparity between facts encountered in practice and the theory which accounts for them, led to an overvaluation of one or another partial aspects of the theory. Thus, with Reich, the problems of character analysis gave rise to an emphasis on the relation to the external object. Then, with Abraham, the true pioneer of object relations theory, the genetic debate led to the specification of the subphases of development, going from the differentiation of the preambivalent part object through to that of the postambivalent genital whole object.

One of the consequences was a "genetic" psychoanalysis whose reduction of the structural dimensions of analytic thought to the merely genetic has seriously impoverished the complex temporal mechanisms of Freudian theory, suppressing, for instance, the crucial concept of deferred action. Psychoanalytic time became psychobiological time, distinguished by mere successiveness, evolutionary and normative (the genital relationship as the Ideal). Linear "development" replaced temporal dialectic. To be sure, Freud's scheme of libidinal development contributed a good deal to this situation. In consequence, analytic theory began to grow rather less psychoanalytic, rather more psychological. Attention shifted from libidinal development to the development of the ego, whose relationship to reality became (ideally) equivalent to the postambivalent genital relationship. (But it is certainly not among psychoanalysts that we will find this ideal illustrated.) Later on, a further step was taken when, with Hartmann, the ego gained a measure of autonomy, allowing the id to become autonomous in its turn (M. Schur). All that remained to complete the process was the introduction into analytic theory of Piaget, whose thought had formerly been entirely antithetical to it.

Given that Freud's work is open to multiple interpretation and thus is susceptible to divergent modes of development, it cannot be said that the orientation adopted by Hartmann and most of North American psychoanalysis is unjustifiable. And, after all, it tallies in many respects with that of Anna Freud. It would seem that psychoanalysis has yielded in large part to the fascinating ascendancy of child analysis. It has been inclined to rely not only on what has been learned from the *psychoanalysis of children*, but also on the *psychoanalytic understanding of the child* (Lebovici and Soule 1970), that is, on information gleaned from psychoanalytic applications in fields external to it: direct observation (Spitz); the genetic study of development (Mahler); and the study of the ego through its sensorial or cognitive tools, or through the observation of children brought up under unusual circumstances (D. Burlingham and A. Freud on infants without families). Melanie Klein took an altogether different approach, which has ended in the dissension we are all aware of. But here we must go back again, the better to understand this theoretical lineage.

Groddeck undermined Freud's radical dualism: the object was no longer "psychic." It became psychosomatic, and the id was made into a natural divinity. Rank and Ferenczi gave the object, in their turn, quite a different shape. The former emphasized the original separation—birth, which establishes the separation of mother and child and hence that of the object and the non-object. Freud rightly reminded him that this original separation is, at the time, only relative (biological), that it is repaired by the subsequent fusion of mother and child, and that only with the metaphorical loss of the breast does the difference between ego and object get properly established. As for Ferenczi, while calling back into question the split between psyche and soma, his essential contribution was to change the meaning of the transference by understanding it as a process of introjection (as well as of projection), and above all by stressing, in his final years, the significance of the analyst as object, thereby implicitly shifting the emphasis onto the role of the countertransference.

Abraham and Ferenczi were to influence various independent currents of thought. Balint, the spiritual heir of Ferenczi, emphasized *primary object love*, denying all autonomy to primary narcissism. Later on he gave much importance to the fact that Freud's work dealt essentially with clinical structures which had already achieved a more or less successful internalization of the object, whereas nonneurotic structures are characterized by a failure, more or less, of internalization. *Failure*, in this context, is no more than an approximate term, since what is at stake is rather a *fault*. The basic failure is actually a *basic fault*, a primordial defect giving rise to the fault which then devolves upon the primary love object and which the analyst must, in the course of treatment, replace by a "new beginning."

But Melanie Klein (who had undergone analyses with both Ferenczi and Abraham) was already in the process of developing a quite opposed theory of object relations, insofar as she focused on *internal* objects, *fantasied* objects (part or whole), relegating entirely to the background the role of the external object and appealing (like Freud) to the role of constitutional and innate factors, especially the destructive drives. However, she was not able to avoid a misunderstanding. The destructive drives—one should rather say the *instincts* of destruction—are directed onto the object first and foremost by projection. Although she recognized that this projection is not total (in other words, that some internal destructiveness remains in spite of projection), *she behaved as if only this projected part should be taken into consideration*. Note that it matters little whether the object is, in the present case, internal or external, since what counts in Melanie Klein's theory is the *centrifugal* orientation of projection; at all events, a centripetal orientation is never more than the consequence of the return upon himself of the subject's destructive projection (projective or introjective identification).

Ferenczi had his disciples, and Klein has hers as well, whether analyzed by her or not. Fairbairn resumes her approach when he deflects the aim of the object. For Freud, the drive sought satisfaction through the object; for Klein, the drive seeks chiefly to cope with destructiveness. For Fairbairn, the drive (but is there still such a thing as drive for Fairbairn?) seeks the object itself (object seeking). Finally Winnicott arrives on the scene. His contribution, derived from the analysis of borderline states, has a number of facets:

a. The baby all by himself does not exist; he is *coupled* with the object of maternal care.
b. Before the inauguration of the paranoid-schizoid phase, we must take into consideration the role of holding—i.e., the change involved in the transition from the intrauterine to the extrauterine condition. Nestling within the womb is replaced by nestling in the mother's arms. The phase of *holding* is followed by *handling* and finally by *object-presenting*.

c. The object is at first subjective (or the object subjectively perceived), and then becomes the objective object (or the object objectively perceived). *It is essential that the subjective object precede the objective object.*

d. The object is answered to by the *self*. The self is silent and secret, in a state of permanent noncommunication. It shelters the subjective objects and may experience states either of *disintegration* under the influence of anxiety (Winnicott called it "agony"), or of return to *nonintegration* (diffused states going from fusion all the way to nonexistence).

e. The mother/object's intolerance of the baby's spontaneity can bring about in the baby a dissociation between psyche and soma, or between the two components of bisexuality, or between one aspect of the drives (e.g., the destructive drives) as against the other. The creation of a *false self*, conforming to the image of the mother's desire, allows protection to the *true self*, which is kept in secrecy. Let us remember that we can communicate only indirectly with the true self.

f. The problem with these states is the problem of dependency. The analyst's attitude in the face of the patient's regression, especially his complicity in preventing regression, may lead to his collusion with the false self; an interminable analysis or a psychotic breakdown is likely to result.

g. The analyst's work consists in a *metaphorical* replacement of the deficiencies of maternal care, either through accepting the analysand's dependence or through accepting his need for fusion within the symbolic interplay—for the analyst does not represent the mother, he *is* the mother. The *analytic setting* represents maternal care. The analyst must also be able to accept his periodic destruction (along with the resultant hatred in the countertransference) as a condition of his periodic resurrection, so that the analysand may be able to *use* the analyst.

h. The *transitional object*, which is neither internal nor external but located in the intermediate area of *potential space*, comes to life and comes into use "in the beginning" of the separation between mother and baby. The transitional object invokes the idea of *transitional space*, which is extended into the cultural experience of sublimation.

i. The transitional object is coextensive with the category of *playing* and with the *capacity to be alone* (in the presence of the mother or of the analyst).

j. Analytic technique is directed toward bringing about the capacity for play with transitional objects. The essential feature is no longer interpreting, but enabling the subject to live out creative *experiences* of a new category of objects.

k. If the transitional object is a not-me possession, two other possibilities are involved:
   1. The noncreation of this object, through being excessively bound to experiences of either fusion or separation.
   2. The inversion of the sense of possession by the démarche: "All I have got is what I have not got." This suggests a somewhat different concept, which I have formulated as *negative satisfaction*.

It is easy to see that Winnicott has in fact described not so much an object as a space lending itself to the creation of objects. Here the line itself becomes a space; the metaphorical boundary dividing internal from external, that either/or in which the object has traditionally been entrapped, expands into the intermediate area and playground of transitional phenomena. In *Playing and Reality* Winnicott gives us glimpses into the private elaboration of this line of thinking: from his early fascination with the image of the seashore where children are playing, to his discovery in talks with Marion Milner of "the tremendous significance there can be in the interplay of the edges of two curtains," through to an even more personal, and yet thoroughly practical, extension and amplification of the line in his use of the squiggle-game.

French analysts have long held themselves aloof from this development, meanwhile splitting up into two main factions. Bouvet's work on object relations grows out of a theoretical blend in which a concept of defensive activity inspired by A. Freud, Reich, Federn, and Fenichel is augmented by Bouvet's own contributions, most significantly his concept of *distance from the object* as illustrated in the variations of the *rapprocher*. The economic dimension, always present in Bouvet, is salient as well in the work of the French psychosomatic school (Marty, Fain, De M'Uzan, David) and in those who stress the role of affect in technique, clinical description, and theory (Green). In opposition to these trends, Lacan has adopted a formalistic approach and has built up theoretical models in which the object (which he calls "the object (a)") is of great importance, especially in relation to the mirror-image. But it would be impossible, within the limits of the present chapter, to give a full account of all the functions of the object (a), as this would require an exposition of the whole Lacanian theory, which differs considerably from all those previously discussed (see, however, Green 1966).

Another, although quite different, formalistic approach is that of Bion, who addresses the problem of the object from a perspective unusual to modern psychoanalysis. Adapting to his own ends the Kantian concept of the thing-in-itself, he inserts it into the symbol "O" standing for that unknowable state of being forever and always inaccessible to being known in itself, and yet at the source of all knowledge, which will never constitute more than an approximation of "O." In this he rejoins the formulations of Freud's *Project for a Scientific Psychology*. Note that, just as in Winnicott, it is once again the *space* of thinking that takes precedence over the object. However, it is regrettable that in the work of both Winnicott and Bion the concept of analytic time is less well developed than that of analytic space. We may register our dissatisfaction with the constructions of genetically minded analysts, but we have as yet no theory to offer in their place.

Analytic experience has convinced me that the only way out of the impasse of empiricism versus intellectualism, or "realism" versus "abstraction," is through exploiting the technical and theoretical possibilities suggested by Winnicott's work, making all necessary modifications. And so I want now to examine more closely certain of Winnicott's propositions, of interest for the following reasons:

1. They emerge from the study of the analytic setting taken as reference point, which means that theory stays in direct touch with practice.
2. Practice here has to do with borderline patients who, more than classical neurotics, have become the paradigm cases for current analytic practice and theory.
3. The theory deriving from such work is the fruit of an imaginative elaboration deeply rooted in the countertransference feelings of the analyst. Thus the transference gives way to the countertransference as the center of attention.
4. Winnicott's thought may be open to criticism in many respects, but it reflects, above all, a richly alive experiencing rather than an erudite schematizing.
5. Winnicott's work poses, with remarkable acuteness, the question of the future of psychoanalysis. Rigidly maintaining its classical stance, psychoanalysis could on the one hand attach itself to an embalmed and stiffened corpse, failing to pursue a critical evaluation of its theories as challenged by present practice. In this case it would be pledged to the mere safeguarding of its acquisitions, without ever calling into question the theory sustaining them. The alternative is a psychoanalysis which, periodically renewing itself, strives to extend its range, to subject its concepts to radical rethinking, to commit itself to self-criticism. In which case it must run the risks entailed by such self-examination, from which the best as well as the worst may emerge.

ANALYTIC PLAY
AND ITS RELATIONSHIP TO THE OBJECT

A great creative thinker—and such Winnicott undoubtedly was, perhaps the greatest of the contemporary analytic epoch—provides endless proof of his gifts, I ought to say even of his genius, throughout his life's work. But often it is during the final stage of his career, struggling it may be against the threat of a fast-approaching death, that he rises to his full stature. I was deeply impressed by feelings of this kind while reading *Playing and Reality* (1971). I should like here to pay tribute to this book, elaborating in my own way what I brought away from it.

Winnicott's name will always be associated with the idea of the transitional object and transitional phenomena, of potential space, of playing and illusion. What has progressively emerged from his initial description of the transitional object—which was constantly being enriched as the years went by—is that Winnicott, in a series of observations which seemed harmless and unassuming enough, had in fact delineated a conceptual field of the highest importance, whose definition was based at one and the same time on child observation and the analytic situation. We must get one thing straight: in his case the observation of the child did not, as one might think, take priority over the observation of the analytic situation. On the contrary: it was because Winnicott was first analyzed, and then went on to become an analyst himself, that he was able, in looking at children, to notice what had been escaping everyone's attention. For we cannot say that the discovery of the transitional object brought to light some recondite and obscure reality. Freud once said that he had done nothing but discover the obvious. The same could be said of Winnicott. The least observant of mothers has always known that her child likes to fall asleep with his teddy bear, or while fondling a bit of cloth or a corner of his blanket. But before Winnicott no one had understood the importance of this, just as no one before Freud had ever been struck by the significance there might be in an eighteen-month-old's game, played during his mother's absence, of throwing away from him and then pulling back again a reel of cotton. Here too it had to be a psychoanalyst, the very first one, who could observe this spectacle with new eyes.

Thus, analytic experience seems to have been the determining factor in the formation of Winnicott's concepts, as it was in those of Freud. Nor is it by accident that it should be Winnicott and his students Khan, Milner, and Little who have provided us with the most fertile reflections on the *analytic setting*.

I have elsewhere proposed (Green 1975) the hypothesis that the analytic situation is characterized by the fact that each of its two partners produces a double of himself. What the analysand communicates is an analogue, a double of his affective and bodily experience; what the analyst communicates is a double of the effect produced on his own bodily, affective, and intellectual experience by the patient's communication. Thus the communication *between* analysand and analyst is an object made up of two parts, one constituted by the double of the analysand, the other by the double of the analyst. What is called the "therapeutic alliance" or "working alliance," which I prefer to call the *analytic association*, is, in my belief, founded on the possibility of creating an *analytic object* formed by these two halves. This corresponds precisely to the etymological definition, in Robert's *Dictionary*, of a symbol: "an object cut in two, constituting a sign of recognition when its bearers can put together the two separate pieces." In my opinion this is what occurs in the analytic setting. The analytic object is neither internal (to the analysand or to the analyst), nor external (to either the one or the other), but is situated *between* the two. So it corresponds exactly to Winnicott's definition of the transitional object and to its location in the intermediate area of *potential space*, the space of "overlap" demarcated by the analytic setting. When a patient terminates his analysis, it is not only that he has "internalized" the analytic interplay, but also that he can take away with him the potential space in order to reconstitute it in the outside world, through cultural experience, through sublimation and, more generally, through the possibility of pairing or (let us rather say) of coupling.

The analytic situation differs from the game of chess (to which Freud was fond of comparing it) in that it is *the analyst who determines the rules of the game*, as Viderman (1970) has rightly observed. In case of disagreement, arbitration is possible only if (in a juridical sense) the rules of law are contravened; but the law governing analysis remains in the hands of the analyst, who exercises both legislative and executive power. These rules which are laid down before the game begins confer a considerable advantage upon the analyst (1) because he has already been analysed and (2) because usually he has already conducted other analyses. All equality between the two parties is abolished.

But this spatial account of the game needs to be complemented by a temporal one. In analysis it is *always* the analysand who makes the first move. No analysis is conceivable in which, after the statement of the fundamental rule, the analyst speaks first. The analyst can only respond to the first move, which is always played by the patient and only when he decides on it. Similarly, it is always the analysand who makes the last move in the final farewell, the analyst taking leave of his patient only in answer to this farewell (although it may be only temporary).

This structure, which invokes the notion of the double, must also make room for the absent. The absent one in analysis is none other than the analyst's own analyst[5]—which goes to show that analysis always proceeds across generations. As I said before, even if it is his first analysis, the analyst has already been analyzed. In the analytic interplay, the absent metaphorically represented by the analyst's analyst is connected with two other modes of absence: that of past reality, inaccessible as such both to analyst and to analysand, and that of an equally inaccessible present reality. The analyst cannot get to *know* his patient's real life; he can only imagine it. And likewise the analysand can never know the analyst's life; he too can only imagine it. Both are reduced to approximations. Even as the analytic process unfolds, each partner communicates, through verbalization, only a part of his life experience. Here we get back to Winnicott's concept of the silent self, and a memorable sentence comes to mind: "each individual is an isolate, permanently noncommunicating, permanently unknown, in fact unfound" (1963). From this springs the importance of the capacity to be alone (in the presence of the mother or of the analyst) and its consequence: the analyst is always having to navigate between the risk of separation anxiety and that of anxiety concerning his intrusiveness.

Winnicott has formulated an essential paradox for us, one that, as he says, we must accept as it is and that is not for resolution. If the baby is in health, he "creates the object, but the object was there waiting to be created and to become a cathected object. I tried to draw attention to this aspect of transitional phenomena by claiming that in the rules of the game we all know we will never challenge the baby to elicit an answer to the question: did you create that or did you find it?" (*Playing and Reality*, p. 89). This paradox joins up with another: *the transitional object is and is not the self.*[6]

The qualities peculiar to the transitional object confront us with an unimpeachable double truth. *The analyst is not a real object; the analyst is not an imaginary object.* The analytic discourse is not the patient's discourse, nor is it that of the analyst, nor is it the sum of these two. The analytic discourse is the *relation* between two discourses which belong neither to the realm of the real nor to that of the imaginary. This may be described as a *potential relationship,* or, more precisely, as a *discourse of potential relationships,* in itself potential. Accordingly, the analytic discourse has, in regard to past and present alike, only a potential relationship to the truth. But this does not mean that the analytic discourse may consist in simply anything at all. It must bear an *homologous* relationship to imaginary (or psychic) reality; it forms its counterpart. This implies an approximate correspondence, but an affective approximation, *without which its effect would be nil.* The homology is one we are obliged to construct, for lack of positive evidence. Nevertheless, this construction is not arbitrary, since we cannot help but construct the real, even when it pleases us to think we are doing no more than perceiving it.

In one of his most fundamental papers, inspired by Lucan's 1953 work on the mirror phase (1966), Winnicott analyzes the function of the mother's face as the precursor of the mirror. Here he stresses the importance of the baby's initial communication not only with the breast but also with the mother's face. We know that the baby at the breast (or bottle) sucks while looking not at the breast but at his mother's face. Winnicott rightly points out that while this is going on the baby may see in the mother's gaze either himself or herself. If, too precociously, it is the face of the mother/object that he perceives, he cannot form the subjective object, but will prematurely evolve the object objectively perceived. The result is that he must organize a false self, as an image conforming to the mother's desire. He must then hide away, in secret, his true self, which cannot and indeed must not be allowed expression. With his false self, he can achieve only an external identity. But this is a pathological solution. In the normal progress of events, a compromise is obtained through the creation of the transitional area of experience.

"If the baby is in health . . ." said Winnicott. Some babies, we know, are not. And among these some will later impress us with the intensity of their negative therapeutic reaction. It is striking that Winnicott found it necessary to add, in *Playing and Reality,* a supplement to his original paper on the transitional object. The difference between these two pieces of work is considerable, the fruit of twenty years' experience. In the later version Winnicott discusses what he calls the *negative side of relationships.* In certain borderline cases, the absence of the mother is felt as equivalent to her death. Here the time factor must be duly weighed, since it is in terms of temporal accretion ($x + y + z$ quantity of deprivation, expressed as the accumulated moments of the mother's absence) that Winnicott imagines how the baby can move from distress to "unthinkable anxiety" by way of a traumatic break in life's continuity ("The Location of Cultural Experience"). For such infants *"the only real thing is the gap;* that is to say, the death or the absence [in the sense of nonexistence] or the amnesia" (*Playing and Reality,* p. 22 italics mine). While analyzing a patient of this kind, Winnicott arrived at the conclusion that from the point of view of the child *the mother was dead,* regardless of her absence or presence. It occurred to him that in the transference "the important communication for me to get was that there could be a blotting out, and that this blank could be the only fact and the only thing that was real" (Ibid). This remark bears out precisely my own observations about the importance in psychosis of the negative hallucination of the subject. For Winnicott's patient, who had had previous analysis, the negation of the first analyst was more important than the fact of the existence of the second analyst. "The negative of him is more real than the positive of you." Such vengefulness is particularly severe with respect to an object which has failed. Here retaliation is a negative response to a negative trauma; in other words, the trauma is not only something which has occurred—in the classical sense of a traumatization (through sexual seduction or an aggressive act)—but that which *did not occur, owing to an absence of response on the part of the mother/object.* "The real thing is the thing that is not there." A very true statement, revealing how the thing that is not there, the symbol, is taken as reality; which recalls Hanna Segal's idea of symbolic equation, but in an exactly contrary sense. In Segal's example, violin= penis. But in Winnicott's example, and here he meets up with Bion, *the non-object is the object.* The non-object, in this context, means not the representation of the object but the nonexistence of the object. Winnicott speaks of symbols which disappear. Patients in whom structures of this type are found can seem mentally deficient, and in my own initial encounters with such analysands I have come away with a strong impression of their psychic and intellectual poverty. Their motto is: "All I have got is what I have not got."

This line of speculation, which Winnicott adds in 1971 to his original hypothesis about transitional objects and not-me possessions, is crucial, as it opens the way to a new conceptual theme, *negative investment.* I have postulated (1967, 1969) the existence of a negative narcissistic structure characterized by the valorization of a state of nonbeing. Striving for that state of quietude which follows satisfaction with an object, but finding himself in a state where satisfaction has not occurred within limits tolerable for his psychic apparatus, the subject seeks to attain the same state as if satisfaction had been achieved, through the strategy of renouncing all hope of satisfaction, through inducing in himself a state of psychic death not unrelated to Jones's idea of *aphanisis.*

In his paper on the mirror-role of the mother's face, Winnicott uses the illustration of the patient who said to him, "Wouldn't it be awful if the child looked into the mirror and saw nothing?" The anxiety of the negative hallucination is truly unthinkable. In my opinion, all the defensive maneuvers described by Melanie Klein's advocates amount to nothing but an awesome strategy for avoiding this fundamental and primordial anxiety.

If "negative symbolization" can provide an extreme (and very costly) solution, another kind of solution is adopted in borderline cases. In my own experience, what I have most often observed is a need to hold on to and to preserve at all costs a bad internal object. It is as if, when the analyst succeeds in reducing the power of the bad object, the subject has no other recourse than to make it reappear, in fact to resurrect it, in its original or in an analogous form, as if the thing most dreaded were the *interval between the loss of the bad object and its replacement by a good object. This interval is experienced as a dead time, which the subject cannot survive. Hence the value for the patient of the negative therapeutic reaction, which ensures that the analyst will never be replaced, since the object which would succeed him might never appear or might only appear too late.*

In another section of *Playing and Reality,* "The Use of an Object and Relating through Identifications," Winnicott discusses the patient's ability to *use* the analyst. For this to be possible, the analyst must allow himself to be destroyed as frequently as the subject wishes, so that the latter may be reassured that the object has the capacity to survive his destruction of it. Winnicott makes the interesting comment that destructiveness of this kind is not related to aggressiveness. This states yet another paradoxical truth. It must be understood that what is here in question is not the fantasied activity of an experience of mentally acted-out destruction; rather it is a radical decathexis. Hence what we are concerned with is a succession of libidinal or aggressive cathexes and of decathexes which abolish the preceding cathexes and the objects linked to them. When carried to an extreme, such decathexes lead to psychic death, just as anarchic cathexes deeply pervaded by aggressiveness lead to delusion. Thus the fundamental dilemma becomes: delusion or death (physical or psychic). The work of the analyst is aimed at transforming these alternatives into something less extreme, so that delusion may become playing, and death absence. In this context absence does not mean loss, but *potential presence.* For absence, paradoxically, may signify either an imaginary presence, or else an unimaginable nonexistence. It is absence in this first sense which leads to the capacity to be alone (in the presence of the object) and to the activity of representation and of creating the imaginary: the transitional object, constructed within that space of illusion never violated by the question, Was the object created or was it found?

Freud, as I remarked above, sometimes compared the analytic situation to chess. If Winnicott is the master-player of psychoanalysis, it is surely not chess that he plays with his patient. It is a game with a cotton reel, with a piece of string, with a doll or teddy bear. Finally, with children Winnicott plays the squiggle-game, in which each partner takes a turn drawing a scribble, which is then modified by the other. The spontaneous movement of a hand which allows itself to be guided by the drive, a hand which does not act but rather expresses itself, traces a more or less insignificant and formless line, submitting it to the scrutiny of the other, who, deliberately, transforms it into a meaningful shape. What else do we do in the analysis of difficult cases? The beautiful clarity of the chess game, unfurling itself under the open light of day, is absent there. Instead we find ourselves in a murky night pierced by flashes of lightning and sudden storms. Meaning does not emerge complete as Aphrodite rising from the waves. It is for us to construct it. Viderman believes that, prior to the analytic situation, the meaning that we seek has never existed; it is the analytic process which constitutes it *as such* for the first time. Meaning is not discovered, it is created. I prefer to describe it as an absent meaning, a virtual sense which awaits its realization through the cuttings and shapings offered by analytic space (and time). It is a potential meaning. It would be wrong to think that like Sleeping Beauty it merely waits there to be aroused. It is constituted in and by the analytic situation; but if the analytic situation reveals it, it does not create it. It brings it from absence to potentiality, and then makes it actual. To actualize it means to call it into existence, not out of nothing (for there is no spontaneous generation), but out of the meeting of two discourses, and by way of that object which is the analyst, in order to construct the *analytic object*.

This theory implies that mental functioning has to be taken into consideration. In chess, there is only one kind of material at stake; the pieces have different *values* and an unchangeable mode of progression. The analytic situation, on the contrary, brings varying materials to light: drives, affects, representations (of things or of words), thoughts, actions. Their specific modes of functioning—to be the plaything of a drive (directed toward the body or toward the world), to feel, to imagine, to say, to think, to act—all these modes are capable of an ultimate exchange of function. The vectorization of drive into language is placed in check here. For speaking could become tantamount to acting, acting to evacuating, imagining to filling up a hole, and thinking could, at the extreme verge, become impossible (cf. *Blank Psychosis*, Donnet and Green 1973).

Here we have evidently reached the limits of Freudian practice and theory. There is urgent and growing need for another system of reference which gives pride of place to the countertransference and clarifies its elaborative potentialities. The analyst ought either to use his imagination, or resign, for the unconscious creates its own structure only by way of the Imaginary.

The importance of the analytic setting arises from the fact that it allows the development of a *metaphoric* regression which is a double, an analogue of infantile regression. In the same way, the response of the analyst, comparable to holding, is itself only a double of maternal care. It is as if, out of the totality of physical and psychic maternal care, only the psychic aspect were to be admitted into the analytic situation. The part which is not given play in analysis is the one that is missing when the analytic object is constituted. This object, which takes shape through the communication of psychic maternal care, leaves in abeyance any actual regression to the past on the part of the patient, and any physical care on the part of the analyst.

But we must go yet further. And here my agreement with Winnicott reaches its limit. When Winnicott pointed out that there is no such thing as a baby, reminding us of the couple that it forms together with its cradle or with its mother in the holding situation, his observation, as we know, caused quite a stir.

I would maintain, for my part, that there is no such entity as a baby with his mother. No mother-child couple exists without a father somewhere. For even if the father is hated or banished by the mother, erased from her mind in favor of somebody else, of her own mother or father, the child nevertheless is the product of the union of the father and mother. Of this union he is the *material, living, irrefutable* proof. There are mothers who want to wipe out any trace of the father in the child. And we know the result: a psychotic structure. Thus we can assert that ultimately *there is no dual relationship.* There can be no dual exchanges, but there is always some link establishing the possibility of duality, in the form of areas of reunion and separation within the dual relationships.

In the analytic situation, this third element is supplied by the analytic setting. *The work of the analytic setting is comparable to the mirror-work, without which it is impossible to form an image from an object.* This induces the thought that reflection is a fundamental human property. Probably this attribute is innate, but we do now know that an object is indispensable in order to transform this *innate potentiality into its actual realization, failing which, the potentiality dies out and is lost. The analyst is the object necessary to such a transformation, but he can bring it about only with the help of the work of the not-me, which is the analytic setting defined spatially and temporally. What answers for the setting is the combined discourse of the analysand and the analyst, doubles of their respective experience.* Without affect there is no effective language. Without language there is no effective affect. The unconscious is not structured like a language (Lacan); *it is structured like an affective language, or like an affectivity having the properties of language.*

Winnicott was much blamed, and is still being blamed, for his delight in distorting the classical analytic setting. Since I am not prepared to endorse any and every deformation of the analytic setting, I must distinguish between those I would find acceptable and those I would have to reject. It seems to me that the only acceptable variations of classical analysis are *those whose aim is to facilitate the creation of optimal conditions for symbolization.* For classical neurosis, classical analysis serves this function. With borderline patients (taking this term in its broadest sense), the analyst must preserve in each case the minimum conditions requisite to the maximum development of symbolization. Today the analyst's major difficulty lies in this area. No one can decide for him the modalities or the extent of the variations required by such cases. This predicament has several possible results:

1. The cynicism of the analyst who, exploiting for personal ends his patient's need for dependence, gains a pseudoindependence through such shameless manipulation.
2. The collusion involved in a mutual dependency.
3. Guilt connected with the feeling of having transgressed the implicit analytic law.
4. Freedom in analysis based upon the principle that analysis is the construction of the analytic object.

A protective device is necessary here: the analyst's constant awareness of his countertransference and his full employment of it by way of the transference of the analysand. By the term *countertransference* I mean to take into account not only the affective effects, positive or negative, of the analysand's transference, not only the analyst's capacities for antipathy or for sympathy, but also his total mental functioning, including his reading and his exchanges with colleagues. Having said this, I would still agree with the restrictions that Winnicott imposed upon the countertransference in limiting it to the professional attitude. However far we may wish to extend our identification with the patient, this human identification is still a professional one. Hypocrisy is quite out of place here. We terminate the session and do not yield to the patient who wishes it would go on indefinitely. We leave for vacation without him and are paid for our work. We do our best to listen to him, but we see and hear only what we are prepared to see and hear, just as the patient can only understand what he was already on the verge of understanding, although he could not arrive at it all by himself.

In our activity as analysts, our real work does not lie in a mere receptivity to what the patient is communicating, nor on the other hand is it wholly determined by those preconceptions and presuppositions which are necessarily prior to all communication. The analyst's creativity takes shape within the time and space of the communicative exchange where the analytic object is formed by continuously and discontinuously constructing itself.

Analysts listen more easily to their patients than they can to each other. Doubtless because—and this is the final paradox—a colleague is more an-other than he is an a-like, and a patient is more an a-like than he is an-other. Alter ego.

NOTES

1. As used here, the term *structuralist* belongs not to the perspective of Hartmann, Kris, and Loewenstein, but rather to that of F. de Saussure, R. Jakobson, C. Levi-Strauss, and J. Lacan.

2. The German term is *anlehnumg,* which suggests the idea of a supporting function—the sexual instincts as being supported by the instincts of self-preservation. For example, oral pleasure at first *leans upon* hunger (i.e., oral need) and later develops independently from it in the form of pleasure.

3. This implies that the object exists before it is lost, but that its very loss is what determines its existence as such.

4. This mobility of boundaries is discernible throughout the history of psychoanalysis. After Freud, Melanie Klein curtailed the territory of the external object while extending proportionately that of the internal object. But after Klein, Winnicott in his turn encroached on the domain of internal objects by putting back into the maternal environment—i.e., the external object,—what Klein had taken away from it. Nevertheless, this process has not been circular, since the result was to create a third object: the transitional object.

5. Hence the inequality and the heterogeneity of the double analytic discourse. The analyst relies upon a discourse with the absent, namely his own analyst, author of his difference from the analysand.

6. What Winnicott in fact said was that the transitional object is and is not the breast, but the same formulation may be applied to the self.

REFERENCES

This list is a selection of references. For a detailed bibliography, see Green 1973, 1975.

Donnet, J. L. and Green A., (1973). *L'enfant de Ca: La Psychose Blanche*. Paris: Editions de Minuit.

Freud, S., (1905). Three essays on the theory of sexuality. *Standard Edition* 7:135–245.

—— (1915). Instincts and their vicissitudes. *Standard Edition* 14:117–140.

—— (1925). Negation. *Standard Edition* 19:235–239.

Green, A. (1966). L'object (a) de J. Lacan, sa logique et la théorie freudienne. *Cahiers pour l'Analyse* 3. Paris: Le Seuil.

—— (1973). *La Discours Vivant* (La conception psychoanalytique de l'affect). Paris: P.U.F.

—— (1975). The analyst, symbolization and absence in the analytic setting. *International Journal of Psycho-Analysis* 56.

Lacan, J. (1966). *Ecrits*. Paris: Le Seuil.

Laplanche, J. and Pontalis, J. B. (1973). *The language of psychoanalysis*. London: Hogarth Press.

Lebovici, S. and Soule, M. (1970). La connaissance de l'enfant par la psychoanalyse. Paris: P.U.F.

Viderman, S. (1970). *La Construction de l'Espace Analytique*. Paris: Denoël.

Winnicott, D. W. (1963). Communicating and not communicating leading to a study of certain opposites. In *The Maturational Processes and the Facilitating Environment*. London: Hogarth Press.

—— (1951). Transitional objects and transitional phenomena. In *Playing and Reality*. London: Tavistock, 1971.

—— (1967). The location of cultural experience. In *Playing and Reality*. London: Tavistock, 1971.

—— (1967). Mirror role of mother and family in child development. In *Playing and Reality*. London: Tavistock, 1971.

—— (1971). The use of an object and relating through identifications. In *Playing and Reality*. London: Tavistock.

CHAPTER 12

Theodore Greenbaum has extended Isakower's analyzing instrument concept to both the analytic situation and the working alliance. He reveals it as functionally and structurally similar to Winnicott's transitional phenomenon (see also Green, chapter 11). A metaphorical instrument is created, a product of both therapist and patient, representing for both the me and the not-me something more than each yet different from either. The creative energies of both therapist and patient are evoked in place of the teacher-student opposition that all too often produces an intrusive and didactic analysis. Greenbaum identifies his views with those of Greenacre and Loewald and his picture of the analyst's experience transcends that of cognitive style. His emphasis highlights the creative aspects of the analytic process.

L.B.

THE "ANALYZING INSTRUMENT" AND THE "TRANSITIONAL OBJECT"

Theodore Greenbaum

In considering certain aspects of what Otto Isakower called "the analyzing instrument" (1963) one is struck by their correlation with "transitional objects and phenomena" as described by Winnicott in his classic paper (1953). This chapter will examine the interrelationship of these two concepts as a focus for a discussion of some current ideas on the psychoanalytic process, with the hope of providing an increased perspective on the psychoanalytic situation.

"The analyzing instrument" is a metaphor which Isakower used in teaching and supervising to convey what he believed to be the essence of psychoanalytic interaction. The heuristic value of this metaphor lies not only in its evocativeness, but also in its capacity to accommodate and highlight many of the concepts that analysts have developed about the psychoanalytic process. Isakower believed that the development of the analyzing instrument constitutes the metamorphosis of the novice into the genuine practitioner of psychoanalysis.[1] The optimally working analyzing instrument functions outside of conscious awareness. Opportunities to observe it arise when it goes awry or when it is "switched off" at the end of sessions—that is in retrospect. It functions when the analyst is "in rapport with the patient." It is a "composite consisting of two complementary halves"—one half functioning in the analyst, the other half in the patient. It is "a unique and specific setting in relation to a near identical or analogous constellation in a second person." It can make rapid and fluid transitions to varying levels of wakefulness between vividly visual impressions to highly abstract thinking. Freud (1912) alluded to it when he wrote that the analyst should "turn his own unconscious like a receptive organ towards the transmitting unconscious of the patient. . . . as a telephone receiver is adjusted to the transmitting microphone" (pp. 115–16). To quote Isakower:

The session is broken off, the patient is leaving the room; you, the analyst, are in the process of emerging out of the "analytic situation"— that near dreamlike state of hovering attention; the patient is being separated from you and you are left alone. In this short moment of the severance of the "team" you are left in mid-air and you become aware of the denuded raw surface of your half of the analyzing instrument, the surface which is opposite the patient's half. This surface now becomes accessible to observation because its cathexis is not bound to the surface of the patient's half of the apparatus. Now, you, in a slow-motion replica, can make observations. The slow-motion comes from the induced process of reintegration of that part of you within yourself, a reintegration required by the withdrawal of the patient's half. There is a re-distribution of cathexes, and while this is going on, you can, in fortunate instances, observe it. It can be observed because your observing function is no longer glued to its former object—the patient's "half." What can be observed now, I can only indicate here by giving a few scant examples from my own observation, to be regarded as nothing but rough tracings: (1) Visual representations of the content, that is, the manifest content of the patient's productions together with the content of what came up to meet them from within you. This includes verbalized and nonverbalized content, content put into actual words in talking to the patient and such other elements that were not put into actually so many words. (2) Auditory, acoustic representations of the same things, for example a word said by the patient which when it was heard, induced what may be called peculiar reverberations in the auditory sphere, and you immediately sensed its many facets and ambiguities and found yourself making bridges and switches. You now become consciously aware of all this. You may even visualize the spelled-out word before your inner literal eye. . . . When the operation is broken off, the integration of the analytic instrument is also broken up. A transitory disintegration takes place, to be followed quickly by the necessary reintegration, and we may see, like an "exploded view," the way things were fitted together.

If we pause now to consider Winnicott's concept of transitional phenomena (1953) we will find certain analogies to Isakower's description. Transitional phenomena occur during the phase in which the infant gradually becomes aware of the independent existence of true "not me" objects. Transitional objects are tangible objects to which the child becomes inordinately attached. They represent an externalized fusion of aspects of himself and his mother. The object is "affectionately cuddled as well as excitedly loved and mutilated." The infant relates to it as though it had a life of its own. Transitional phenomena are not tangible objects but function for the child similarly to transitional objects. An infant's babbling or an older child's repertory of songs can be transitional phenomena. Transitional objects and phenomena substitute for the dual unity of mother and child and help to alleviate the child's anxiety as he gradually adjusts to separations from his mother. With further development of identificatory processes, the child can finally tolerate separations without his reassuring transitional objects and phenomena. This phase is concurrent with, and an early part of, the development of the symbolizing function.

Transitional phenomena are at the core of such pathological developments as fetishism, but are also the basis for a wide variety of such derivative cultural activities as playing, religious experience, and artistic creativity, all of which can represent, at least in part, fused aspects of self and object. The transitional object develops normally where good enough mothering has occurred so that the child feels sufficiently secure to allow a blanket or a teddy bear to stand for her in her absence. Where mothering has been inadequate, transitional object formation becomes distorted or in certain cases is even absent. The good enough mother adapts adequately to the child's age-appropriate needs. She adapts almost completely to her infant's demands but gradually less so as his ability to tolerate frustration grows. His conceptualization of external reality develops simultaneously. A growing sense of process grows within him, which is the beginning of mental activity.

Winnicott believed these earliest interactions between infant and mother contain the roots of creativity. After initial experiences of need gratification from a good enough mother, when additional needs arise, the infant develops the *illusion* that he "creates" his object of fulfillment. Indeed, at this early stage of development, there is no ability to distinguish between need arising within the self and the object in which it finds satisfaction. This corresponds to Kestenberg's concept of organ-object unity (1971) and Ferenczi's stage of magic-hallucinatory wish-fulfillment in the development of a sense of reality (1913). With the inevitable gradual disillusionment which occurs, transitional objects and phenomena appear as substitute satisfactions. They are created by the child's adaptation of a part of the external world to conform to the configuration of his need. Since our needs are never completely satisfied, we are everlastingly preoccupied with attempts to adapt outer reality to inner need and express this in such "intermediate" forms of adult activity as artistic creativity. The transitional phase of development is made possible by the mother's unchallenging adaptability to her child's need for illusion formation.

A review of Isakower's descripton of the analyzing instrument impresses one with the similarity of the analyst's attunement to his patient to the good enough mother's adaptability to her child (Winnicott 1965). The involvement (ideally) is so thorough that there is no conscious awareness of it while it is in operation. It is "a unique and specific setting in relation to a near identical or analogous constellation in a second person." In order to be "with" the patient the analyst must experience a controlled partial regression. The good enough mother's adaptability to her child's needs also requires her to regress creatively. Specifically, Isakower notes what the analyst experiences at the moment of breaking off the session: "The patient is being separated from you and you are left alone. . . . You become aware of the denuded raw surface of your half of the analyzing instrument, the surface which is opposite the patient's half." Because of his own past history of separations the analyst is able to empathize with this moment of separation which stirs up the most deeply rooted anxieties in the patient. He then observes the emergence of something analogous to, or derivative of, transitional phenomena. In the moment of separation he has reached deeply into his *own* past where he has used transitional objects and phenomena to alleviate *his* early separation anxiety; but because of his present attunement to the patient in the service of the analysis, he conforms empathically to configurations of the patient's life. He senses that the patient experiences analogous transitional phenomena. This must be similar to what the good enough mother unconsciously experiences, again and again, during her child's transitional period of development.

It seems to me that Isakower attempted, through his promulgation of the "analyzing instrument" metaphor, to evoke, capitalize upon, and encourage the artistic potential of the nascent analyst. While fully cognizant of the importance of scientific abstraction in psychoanalytic theory, he felt that its overuse could be detrimental to the development of the sensitivity so essential to the clinical practice of psychoanalysis. He felt that the uniqueness of the individual can be lost as the student compulsively tries to "fit" him into a preconceived "scientific" category.[2] The "switching on" of the analyzing instrument implies the analyst's receptivity to regression while he is in a state of acute attunement to the patient. *This does not mean closing off "higher" levels of ego functioning;* in fact, the observing or scanning function is ceaselessly active. It is akin, if not identical, to the artist's "regression in the service of the ego," in which perceptivity is increased far beyond that of common sense observation. The historical model for both situations would seem to be the early mother-child relationship, where the mother provides a structure on which the child can objectify and satisfy his needs and gradually build his own structure. The early mother-child matrix becomes available in feeling states. Observation of transitional phenomena derivatives is possible if attention is directed to them. All levels in the developmental range become alive and, by selective focusing of the instrument, a rich variety of psychic phenomena becomes accessible.

We speak of the "evocativeness" of art. It seems to articulate feelings we are unaware of possessing; yet part of the pleasure of the esthetic experience is the deep sense of recognition it evokes. Through the constellation of sound, movement, or pigments which the artist has put together, a structure, a template has been presented; his appreciator can hang his own inner responses and feelings on it and, in a sense, objectify them. In this way mastery becomes part of the esthetic experience.

Something akin to this occurs in the analytic situation when the analyzing instrument is working smoothly. The analyst is receptive and attuned to his patient. Like the artist, he actively seeks to find forms (interpretations) in which these feelings can be expressed. These forms will be (ideally) composed only of elements which have gradually emerged in the unique setting between patient and analyst and will refer to the patient's inner experiences. On these forms the patient can objectify and elaborate the subtleties of his inner life.

Greenson (chapter 13) presents several instances in which patients on the way to more autonomous functioning used the analyst or the analytic situation as transitional objects. If the therapeutic alliance (or "working alliance" or "basic transference" or "basic trust" or "rapport") in analysis is indeed modeled upon the early mother-child relationship, then one might always expect to find remnants or derivatives of transitional phenomena as the patient gradually relinquishes his neurotic bonds to childhood. The following vignette of an overt "transitional transference experience" is presented in order to demonstrate the potential for a wider use of the analyzing instrument as well as to demonstrate by contrast the existence of the more typical silent transitional transference experience.

A thirty-five-year-old highly competent woman sought treatment because she felt lonely and isolated, and seemed unable to form close, meaningful relationships. Her mother had been severely depressed, embittered, and withdrawn and had never been able to provide sufficient warmth to her daughter. Her preoccupied father was thoroughly absorbed in his legal profession, and would emerge unpredictably from his isolation for periods of highly charged, erotically tinged interplay with the patient. There also had been a seductive relationship with an older male cousin. Not surprisingly, the patient suffered from insomnia and routinely sedated herself to sleep at night. She quickly formed an intensely erotized, idealized transference and immediately began to act upon it by a series of seductions of married men. Some of the underlying anger toward me and others was apparent to the patient from the start, but it was some time before she became aware of its intensity or pervasiveness. Her character had developed reactively; subdued, overly kind and sweet, she would approach a near panic state whenever the deep anger came close to the surface; bedtime, of course, was such a moment for her.

Her craving for close physical contact with me had many aspects. Nearest the surface was her desire to continue the highly charged but never culminated sexual interplay with her father and cousin (not to mention the erotomanic denial of homosexual impulses, penis envy, castrative wishes, etc.) More deeply, she desperately wanted maternal nurturing. But most strenuously repressed was the terrifying, overwhelming rage toward her mother; and she required a close, soothing relationship to keep this buried. Thus, her cravings were intense, and her need for response urgent and immediate. On one level of the transference, I had become a form of transitional object for her. She wanted to hold me, stroke me, carry me with her. As she would speak of these desires she would stroke a cushion or a wall rug adjacent to the couch. But from time to time she would want to bang on the wall, tear the cushion apart, or fling it at me.

While in this state of mind, she once remembered a clown doll with a pixie cap that she used to take to bed with her when she was little. She would fall asleep while sucking and chewing on the pointed cap. This transitional ojbect was a fused externalized representation of her mother and herself (as well as a condensation of phallic and fetishistic accretions). Rather than being a creative transition for her toward a larger world beyond, it became the first of a series of (human) transitional objects, of which I was the latest, in whose absence she experienced overwhelming anxiety. This occurred at bedtime especially, and she would then sedate herself to sleep. On other occasions of extreme anxiety she would attempt extraanalytic contacts with me by requesting additional sessions or by telephoning me.

My own response to this patient demonstrates the working of the analyzing instrument. For some time I did not understand the significance of her behavior, but I sensed her feelings of desperation and responded with a great deal of tolerance in my manner. Whatever value this tolerance had, it seemed to intensify her impulsivity. Ultimately I began to feel used—not as a person but almost as an inanimate object. It then occurred to me that I had become a sort of talisman for her—indeed a transitional objective derivative. At that point I made no interpretations about this, although I felt a personal relief, since much that I had not understood began to fall into place. However, my own attitude toward her began to change, and my indulgent manner was replaced by a more persistent inquiry into the meaning of her behavior. After an initial intensification of anxiety, she became calmer and freer in her associations as she spoke of her longings. It was here that the memory of the clown doll appeared, confirming my impression, and we could begin to develop reconstructions of certain aspects of her childhood from the point of view of derivatives of transitional objects. This opened up new vistas in the analysis. The analyzing instrument had worked, perhaps belatedly, in that my attunement to her had permitted me to experience her need for me in this special way, allowing us to fill in essential gaps in our understanding of her early development. The analysis had encompassed an area where the therapeutic alliance had lapsed.

Cases in which standard genetic interpretations fail to resolve a hardened negative transference indicate a serious disturbance of the therapeutic alliance. Cautious but persistent attempts should be made here to extend the analyzing instrument into the disturbed therapeutic alliance, even where there are serious problems in basic trust. This would mean careful, tentative, empathic attempts at rather early reconstructions, using the "regressive" techniques alluded to earlier. Often such patients bring in confirmatory and elaborative data, enlarging the analytic field, with a consequent restoration of alliance and hope.

In more "classical" cases, where problems rooted in the early preoedipal period are not of crucial pathological significance, the working of the analyzing instrument is usually smooth and silent and easily escapes observation. Yet it is possible to conceptualize its operation, especially in cases where the desire for autonomy is great and the therapeutic alliance consistent and strong (i.e., cases where secondary gain is minimal). The patient is lying on the couch deeply engrossed in his thoughts, memories, feelings, fantasies, etc. and intent upon conveying them to his listener. The analyst is thoroughly cathected to his "opposite number," attempting to receive and integrate, with every resource available to him, the messages from the patient. In the (symbolic) space between them, wherein their two working surfaces come into juxtaposition as the functioning analyzing instrument, a symbolic structure is gradually, cautiously, and painstakingly built through mutual interpretation, error, modification, reconstruction. This symbolic structure is a transitional object derivative. It is comprised of elements contributed by its two creators. It is carried away, thought about, played with tenderly or angrily, added to. It becomes the stepping stone, the transition to a richer, more fulfilling life.

The analyzing instrument works because the analyst "has been there before." Having been there before is obviously a prerequisite for empathy. The moment of separation at the close of a session can be conceived of as a derivative of transitional phenomena experience within the analyst himself. If the analyst's attunement to the patient has been close and precise, and corrections have been made for his idiosyncratic distortions and countertransferences, he can sense exquisitely how his patient needs him—even into the preverbal realm.[3]

Separation-individuation is never complete, and deep longings for reunion with the mother are struggled with throughout life. The good enough mother understands and adapts herself intuitively to her child's use of transitional objects because she also has been there before. Moreover, she has experienced her baby as part of herself and must deal with her own problems of separation along with her child. Thus, during the early years, she accumulates innumerable snapshots and home movies, keeps a diary, and gilds baby's shoes. All of these mementos serve to remind her that, for all of her pride in his growing autonomy, he once was a part of her and dependent on her. Through identifications with him she "knows" the significance of his transitional objects and she creates transitional objects and phenomena of her own. Precisely how she uses these is a measure of her own autonomy and creativity.

The artist's creations are derivatives of transitional phenomena. They are fusions between his own inner rhythms and his perceptions of aspects of the world around him. The analyst also copes creatively with his own problems of separation as his patient gradually relinquishes neurotic ties to him. He has created, with his patient's assistance, transitional phenomena—the interpretations and reconstructions— which help him work through the separation, thereby enriching the level of his own experience, even as he takes pleasure in his patient's growing autonomy.[4]

NOTES

1. For a discussion of the "analyzing instrument" from another point of view see A. Reich (1966).

2. Isakower warned that the analyst's attempt to make abstract formulations *during an actual session* such as, for example, "Now his negative oedipal is coming into the transference" could remove him excessively from the smooth organic operation of the "instrument." He believed that the analytic instrument provides the most profound access

into psychic reality. But his approach to the patient was that of the consummate artist. He would have agreed with Ernst Cassirer, (1944) who in *An Essay on Man* stated: "Science means abstraction, and abstraction is always an impoverishment of reality. . . . The artist does not portray or copy a certain empirical object—a landscape with its hills and mountains, its brooks and rivers. What he gives us is the individual and momentary physiognomy of the landscape. He wishes to express the atmosphere of things, the play of light and shadow. . . . Our aesthetic perception exhibits a much greater variety and belongs to a much more complex order than our ordinary sense perception. In sense perception we are content with apprehending the common and constant features of the objects of our surroundings. Aesthetic experience is incomparably richer. It is pregnant with infinite possibilities which remain unrealized in ordinary sense experience. In the work of the artist these possibilities become actualities; they are brought into the open and take on a definite shape. The revelation of this inexhaustibility of the aspects of things is one of the great privileges and one of the deepest charms of art" (p. 160).

3. Of course only confirmatory data with a corollary opening of new insights will create the necessary sense of conviction in both patient and analyst.

4. An important methodological point in comparing the "analyzing instrument" with "transitional phenomena" is that transitional phenomena encompass a vast variety of human experience. Artistic creativity is a highly developed, specialized, derivative form of transitional phenomena. Similarly, certain aspects of the "analyzing instrument," as conceptualized by Isakower and discussed in this paper, are specialized, highly developed *derivatives* of transitional phenomena; the two concepts should not be thought of as simply interchangeable.

REFERENCES

Cassirer, E. (1944). *An Essay on Man.* New York: Bantam, 1970.

Ferenczi, S. (1913). Stages in the development of sense of reality. In *Sex in Psycho-Analysis,* pp. 181–203. New York: Dover, 1956.

Freud, S. (1912). Recommendations for physicians on the psycho-analytic method of treatment. *Standard Edition* 12:109–120.

Isakower, O. (1963). Minutes of faculty meeting of the New York Psychoanalytic Institute. Unpublished.

Kestenberg, J. S. (1971). From organ-object imagery to self and object representations. In *Separation-Individuation: Essays in Honor of Margaret S. Mahler,* pp. 75–99. New York: International Universities Press.

Reich, A. (1966). Empathy and countertransference. In *Annie Reich: Psychoanalytic Contributions,* pp. 344–360. New York: International Universities Press, 1971.

Winnicott, D. W. (1953). Transitional objects and transitional phenomena. *International Journal of Psycho-Analysis* 34:89–97.

——— (1965). *The Maturational Processes and the Facilitating Environment.* New York: International Universities Press.

CHAPTER 13

Though often mentioned in passing, the use of the analyst as a transitional object is a topic Winnicott never directly addressed. In this chapter, Ralph Greenson explores the area, demonstrating how other features of the analytic situation, such as the office itself, can be used similarly. He explains how an analysis can be undermined by a transitional transference reaction in which the therapist is invested with a quality of magical reassurance. Greenson relates the feeling of possessing the analyst to identificatory processes, including projective identification. The transitional transference reaction can equally well attach itself to the less material aspects of the therapeutic situation, including the therapeutic process. Repetition and ritualization of the process can serve as a transitional phenomenon, often remaining silent during the course of analysis. Only as termination with its attendant separation approaches does it clamor for interpretation. It bears examination, however, where patients attend sessions religiously but are silent, or where therapeutic impasses occur. On the other hand, although it should ultimately be interpreted, such a reaction can lend support to any therapeutic process.

Greenson postulates that an analysis can traverse a pathway within the developmental framework set forth by Mahler. The analyst evolves from a symbiotic self object to a transitional object, and finally to a real person.

L.B.

ON TRANSITIONAL OBJECTS AND TRANSFERENCE

Ralph R. Greenson

Winnicott's "Transitional Objects and Transitional Phenomena" (1951) is one of those genial works that keeps growing in importance with the years; it has spawned many further insights. The transitional object is by now so well recognized a phenomenon that one is amazed it took so long for psychoanalysis to single it out for special attention. I shall use the term as he did, namely, as referring to the infant's first not-me possessions. This chapter will deal also with certain transference phenomena which can be understood as transitional phenomena in the Winnicottian sense.

A depressed thirty-five-year-old woman patient tells me how she misses the physical closeness of her recently lost lover. After much intense crying and noisy sobbing she slowly begins to quiet down, consoling herself with the belief that her analysis is helping her pull herself together. As she says this, I notice her gently and rhythmically stroking the burlap wallpaper alongside the couch with her fingertips, her eyes half-closed. There is a pause and then she says: "You are good to me, you really try to help." She continues to stroke the wall in silence. I too remain silent. After a few minutes the patient, now dry-eyed, stops stroking the wall, straightens her somewhat rumpled dress and says: "I feel better now, I don't know why, I just do. Maybe it was your silence. I felt it as warm and comforting, not cold as I sometimes do. I did not feel alone."

At first I did not realize that for my patient, at that moment, my office wall was a "transitional transference object." The stroking of the wall seemed to have many other meanings. For example, she was stroking the wall as she wanted to stroke and be stroked by her lover and by me. It was an acting out of a transference reaction. The stroking of the wall was also, I eventually discovered, a reenactment of something more infantile. The rhythmic movements, the half-closed eyes, and the soothing effect of my noninterference should have indicated to me that it might be a transitional transference experience for her.

This was confirmed when I began to speak to the patient. She quickly interrupted to say that my words seemed an intrusion. I waited and then said in a quiet voice that I had the impression that as she wept she let herself slip into the past; the stroking of the wall might have brought back an old sense of comfort from childhood. The woman replied: "I was only dimly aware of the stroking. Above all, I loved the tweedy quality of the wallpaper. It has little hairs like fur. Strange, I felt the wallpaper responding to me in a vague way." I answered, still not fully comprehending the transitional nature of her experience: "So you felt in your misery that being on the couch, stroking the wallpaper in my silent presence was like being comforted by a kind of mothering person." After a pause the patient replied: "You know I don't quite agree with you. This may sound strange to you, but it was stroking the wallpaper that helped—and also, I suppose, your letting me do it. It reminds me of crying myself to sleep as a child by petting my favorite panda bear. I kept that panda for years, in fact I have baby pictures with it. Of course, then it was quite furry and later it became smooth, but I always felt it as furry." (Later, this patient had dreams of me with black and white spots, traceable partly to her panda bear and partly to my beard, which she called furry.)

I believe that this clinical vignette illustrates how an inanimate object, the wallpaper, can become a transitional transference object for a patient. It was her primitive possession. She was stroking herself and felt loved in return by the wallpaper. The rhythm of her movements indicate its origin in such autoerotic acts as thumbsucking. However, the wallpaper is neither part of her nor is it her mother's breast. Yet it is related to and partakes of both while remaining quite distinct from each (Winnicott 1951, p. 242).

A transitional object serves as an intermediary for the infant's discovery of the difference between inside and outside. It is an actual object but also has symbolic meaning. It is the *not* being the breast or the mother that is as important as the fact that it stands for the breast or the mother (p. 233). A fully developed transitional object is temporarily more important than the mother for the child (p. 235). The patient I described felt my voice as an unpleasant intrusion; she preferred the wallpaper.

The transitional transference objects arising in the analysis of neurotics are felt to be, to a degree, alive; but the patients also know this to be an illusion. In contrast, Searles (1960) has described psychotic transference reactions to inanimate objects; these are delusional. In such patients, inanimate transference objects are usually malignant and terrifying (Klein 1952, Rosenfeld 1952). In neurotics, transitional objects may be hated besides being loved, but they must endure and they may not retaliate. In many ways the transitional object is like a talisman, as the following case illustrates.

I told an emotionally immature young woman patient, who had developed a very dependent transference to me, that I was going to attend an International Congress in Europe some three months hence. We worked intensively on the multiple determinants of her clinging dependence but made only insignificant progress. Then the situation changed dramatically when one day she announced that she had discovered something that would tide her over my absence. It was not some insight, nor was it a new personal relationship. It was a chess piece. The young woman had recently been given a carved ivory chess set. On the evening before her announcement, as she looked at the set through the sparkling light of a glass of champagne, it suddenly struck her that I looked like the white knight of her chess set. The realization immediately evoked in her a feeling of comfort, even of triumph. The white knight was a protector, it belonged to her; she could carry it wherever she went, it would look after her, and I could go on my merry way to Europe without having to worry about her.

I must confess that despite my misgivings, I also felt some relief. I was grateful for all the help I could get. The patient's major concern about the period of my absence was a public performance of great importance to her professionally. She now felt confident of success because she could conceal her white knight in her handkerchief or scarf; she was certain he would protect her from nervousness, anxiety, or bad luck. I was relieved and delighted to learn, while in Europe, that her performance had indeed been a smashing success. Shortly thereafter, however, I received several panicky transatlantic telephone calls from her. The patient had lost the white knight and was beside herself with terror and gloom, like a child who has lost her security blanket. A colleague of mine who saw her in that interval said that all his interventions were of no avail, and he reluctantly suggested I cut short my trip and return. I hated to interrupt my vacation and I doubted whether my return would be beneficial. Surprisingly, it was. I no sooner saw her than her anxiety and depression lifted. It then became possible to work for many months on how she had used me as a good luck charm rather than as an analyst. The talisman, the chess piece, served her as a magical means of averting bad luck or evil. It protected her against losing something precious.

If we review the transitional objects described thus far, it seems that the infant's security blanket provides comfort and soothing. As the infant matures he may discard this type of not-me possession and take on similar pleasure- and security-procuring objects. The talisman is a later derivative and seems to function more in the direction of warding off ill fortune. Only secondarily does it afford pleasure. The amulet has to be worn to be effective, but its objective is identical. There are many varieties and combinations of good luck charms which people cling to in later life. In times of dire stress and helplessness, even an adult may return to his original transitional object.

My final considerations deal with the different ways patients relate to their analysts. We see early "floating" transference reactions, as Glover (1965) called them, as well as the real object relations cited by Anna Freud (1954). Patients also react to "the analysis," instead of to the analyst (Greenson 1967). Even the analyst's office may take on extraordinary power in serving the patient as a haven against the dangers in the external and internal world. The analytic procedures may be taken by the patient as "my analysis," his possession. Such patients may seem to work hard in their analysis but their insights are all undermined by the magical and comforting effects they unconsciously attribute to the office or the analytic set-up. In these instances, we are dealing with transitional transference reactions. Reider (1953) has described similar reactions to institutions.

We also see a variety of identifications during analyses, some motivated by the libidinous wish to possess, others out of fear of the aggressor or the wish to control the analyst—the projective identification so frequently stressed by the Kleinians. All these identificatory reactions seem related to Winnicott's transitional phenomena: they contain a blurring of me/not-me and are possessive.

Some of Mahler's and Kestenberg's ideas on separation-individuation seem relevant here. Kestenberg (1971), following the lead of Mahler (1968) and her associates, hypothesizes about the various symbiotic bonds persisting throughout development between mother and child. She describes a united organ-object with a dominant organ, a zone-specific pleasure, and a phase-specific contact with the drive object. Each phase ends with new shapes of self and object representations. The separation of the pleasure-seeking organs and the satisfying object is experienced as a loss. Kestenberg believes that there are two basic mechanisms which maintain the integrity and continuity of self and object despite this loss. One method is to replace the lost unity with a less symbiotic bond. The other is to replace symbiotic bonds by bridges such as body products (intermediate objects), external possessions (Winnicott's transitional objects), and people (accessory objects). I believe this can be seen during the course of analyses

As the analysis progresses, the transference distortions become more transparent to the patient and lose their covering-up function. As a consequence, in the terminal phase of analysis one sees more realistic representations of the analyst in dreams and more realistic reactions to him in the analytic hour. In a recent paper, Oremland (1973) suggested that the undistorted portrayal of the analyst in dreams of the terminal phase indicate a successful analysis. I am tempted to say that for some patients in the course of a successful analysis, the analyst evolves from a symbiotic self-object to a transitional object and, finally, into a real person.

REFERENCES

Freud, A. (1954). The widening scope of indications for psychoanalysis: discussion. *Journal of the American Psychoanalytic Association* 2:607-670.

Glover, E. (1965). *The Technique of Psychoanalysis.* New York: International Universities Press.

Greenson, R. R. (1967). *The Technique and Practice of Psychoanalysis.* New York: International Universities Press.

Kestenberg, J. S. (1971). From organ-object imagery to self and object representations. In *Separation-Individuation: Essays in Honor of Margaret S. Mahler,* ed. J. McDevitt and C. Settlage, pp. 75-99. New York: International Universities Press.

Klein, M. (1952). The origins of transference. *International Journal of Psycho-Analysis* 33:433-438.

Mahler, M. S. (1968). *On Human Symbiosis and the Vicissitudes of Individuation, Volume 1: Infantile Psychosis.* New York: International Universities Press.

Oremland, J. D. (1973). A specific dream during the termination phase of successful psychoanalysis. *Journal of the American Psychoanalytic Association* 21:285-302.

Reider, N. (1953). A type of transference to institutions. *Bulletin of the Menninger Clinic* 17:58-63.

Rosenfeld, H. A. (1952). Transference phenomena and transference analysis in an acute catatonic schizophrenic patient. In *Psychotic States: A Psycho-Analytical Approach.* New York: International Universities Press, 1965.

Searles, H. (1960). *The Non-Human Environment in Normal Development and in Schizophrenia.* New York: International Universities Press.

Winnicott, D. W. (1951). Transitional objects and transitional phenomena. In *Collected Papers.* New York: Basic Books, 1958.

CHAPTER 14

Dreams, only briefly mentioned in Winnicott's basic paper a quarter century ago, are considered here by Simon Grolnick, who establishes the theoretical basis for dreams and dreaming as transitional phenomena. Using case study material, he shows how he was able to unravel a clinical puzzle in a patient who dreamed extensively, but whose dreams were inaccessible to analysis. When their use as transitional phenomena was taken into account, an analytic stalemate was broken in which the usual resistance interpretations had created only confusion and more resistance.

This case, part of a growing body of literature, epitomizes the therapeutic problem of patients whose early developmental misfortunes have led to regressive object relations and impaired formation of affective symbols. The therapeutic implication is that in addition to content, defense analysis, and cognitive insight, the therapeutic interaction must take into account the form of the limitation occasioned by developmental arrest.

L.B.

DREAMS AND DREAMING
AS TRANSITIONAL PHENOMENA

Simon A. Grolnick

I know how men in exile feed on dreams.
　—Aeschylus, *Agamemnon*

Had I the Heaven's embroidered cloths,
Enwrought with golden and silver light,
The blue and dim and the dark cloths
Of night and light and half-light,
I would spread the cloths under your feet:
But I, being poor, have only my dreams;
I have spread my dreams under your feet;
Tread softly because you tread on my dreams.
　—W.B. Yeats, "He Wishes for the Cloths of Heaven"

Since D. W. Winnicott's fundamental "Transitional Objects and Transitional Phenomena" (1951) was published, psychoanalysts on both sides of the ocean have been expanding, refining and integrating its ordinal concepts and clinical implications. This chapter is an attempt to confirm and to expand upon Winnicott's suggestion that dreaming is a transitional phenomenon. He explained that by the time the transitional object of the infant loses its meaning transitional phenomena have "become diffused, have become spread out over the whole intermediate territory between 'inner psychic reality' and 'the external world as perceived by two persons in common,' that is to say, over the whole cultural field." Then, to clarify further, after describing his concept of the "good enough" mother, he lists among the infant's intermediate or transitional means of coping with this maternal "failure" the following: "Remembering, reliving, fantasizing, dreaming; the integrating of past, present and future." Though he did not elaborate in the 1951 paper,

Winnicott had in a 1945 article noted that when the dream is remembered and communicated to another person, the "dissociation" of the "child asleep from the child awake" is fostered:

> In fact, the waking life of an infant can be perhaps described as a gradually developing dissociation from the sleeping state. Artistic creation gradually takes the place of dreams or supplements them, and is vitally important for the welfare of the individual and therefore for mankind.

Dreaming and transitional phenomena are both broad concepts; it is hoped that this discussion will clarify some of their interrelationships. Winnicott's suggestion will be illustrated, using the psychoanalytic literature and clinical material, but first it will be necessary to clarify the spectrum between daydreaming and dreaming. Following this the implications of dreaming as a transitional phenomenon will be discussed in an effort to understand certain resistances in the creation and reporting of dreams. The multileveled differences between "pleasant dreams" and nightmares will be taken up, as will the question whether both are active participants in the developmental process or are merely epiphenomena of it.

CLARIFICATION

The widely variant manifestations of the dream and dreaming are reflected both in the lexicon and in the psychoanalytic literature. Webster's New Twentieth Century Dictionary, for example, defines a "dream" as:

1. A sequence of sensations, images, thoughts, etc., passing through a sleeping person's mind
2. A fanciful vision or fancy of the conscious mind; daydream; reverie
3. The state, as of abstraction or reverie, in which such a daydream occurs
4. A fond hope or aspiration
5. Anything so lovely, charming, transitory, etc., as to seem dreamlike

These definitions correspond roughly to the hierarchic states of the dream-daydream continuum as described in the psychoanalytic literature. Kubie's statement, "We are never fully awake or asleep," sets the context, which Arlow elaborates in a recent paper (1969a): "In one part of our minds we are daydreaming all the time, or at least all the time we are awake and a good deal of the time we are asleep." In another paper (1969b), Arlow writes: "clinical experience demonstrates how daydreaming may intrude upon the conscious experience of the individual at all levels of wakefulness and somnolence." He refers also to the visual qualities in the fantasies of children and creative individuals, again accentuating the presence of a fluctuating, hierarchical continuum.

REVIEW AND DISCUSSION OF THE LITERATURE

Though the connection between transitional phenomena and dreaming was first suggested by Winnicott in 1951, the psychoanalytic literature had long before implicitly linked them. One of the clearest connections was in Freud's important early contribution to the understanding of the creative process, "Creative Writers and Daydreaming" (1908):

> Whoever understands the human mind knows that hardly anything is harder for a man than to give up pleasure which he has once experienced. Actually, we can never give anything up; we only exchange one thing for another. What appears to be a renunciation is really the formation of a substitute or surrogate. In the same way, the growing child, when he stops playing, gives up nothing but the link with real objects; instead of *playing,* he now *phantasies.* He builds castles in the air and creates what are called *daydreams.* [1]

At a time when there was no clear concept of the separation-individuation process or of transitional phenomena, Freud wrote about the intermediate states connecting narcissism with object relations, and the concrete with the abstract.

Ella Freeman Sharpe (1937) described a patient who dreamed that a piece of cotton in her mouth seemed to be attached to her inner organs. While pulling at the cotton, she awoke in terror. Several later variants of the dream culminated when "the patient again took a hair from her mouth." However, on this occasion it emerged easily, and no anxiety was felt in the dream. Sharpe stressed that the elements of "cotton," and "hair" had not only immense unconscious symbolic significance, but at the same time "bridged the unconscious fantasy with real experiences from earliest infancy to late childhood." This suggests textural, cottony transitional object qualities, the possibility of the mouth and inner organs serving as intermediate objects (Kestenberg 1971), and implies that a dream with its symbols can serve as a bridge between the present and the past (Kanzer 1955, Roland 1971), between fantasy experiences and realistic perceptions.[2]

In Ernest Jones's important essay on the nightmare (1911), he described the contributions of the dream to mysticism, religion, and, hence, illusory phenomena:

> What is the focus of essential importance is the conclusion that dream experiences have furnished significant contributions to the developing conception of the soul, whether of the individual or of supernatural beings, and especially to its characteristics of existence apart from the body.

Following Jones, Max Stern and John Mack have studied the bad dream or nightmare and have attempted to evaluate the effects of dreaming on the developmental process. In an article on pavor nocturnus, Stern (1951) suggested that as a result of the intermediate state between sleeping and waking "the sensation of the reality of the processes becomes transferred to the residual part of the dream hallucination. Thus, like real experiences, the hallucinatory dream experiences in pavor nocturnus exert formative influence throughout life." The very young child cannot distinguish intense dream from reality experiences, and it is reasonable to assume that dream trauma and real, repetitive trauma are treated similarly by the primitive ego. During the period at which early self- and object-representations are developing and not clearly separated, the nonhuman environment, the transitional object environment, and the nighttime dreaming environment become both identificatory building blocks and catalysts, which can progressively or regressively influence development. Mack (1965) reflects this concept, though he does not refer to transitional phenomena directly. Aside from facilitating instinctual discharge, the nightmare "may also be regarded as amongst the earliest defensive operations of the immature ego, a kind of 'desperate creativity' aimed at reducing and mastering instinctual tension." In his book *Nightmares and Human Conflict* Mack (1970) attempts to assess the nightmare's effects on the formation of psychic structure. Concerning the dream as a reflection of psychic activity, he is prepared to say:

> It is perhaps more useful theoretically to look upon the nightmare as a kind of end product, reflecting a great variety of other forces, some of which foster adaptation and integration, while others tend to bring about disintegration or disorganization. . . .

Nightmares, as we have seen, arise in the context of environmental threat, the revival of traumatic memories, or the thrust of developmental advance, but the *outcome* of the dream, whether or not it is followed by integration and mastery or disintegration and further regression, depends upon the complex interplay of *all* of the above forces as they interrelate uniquely in any given instance or individual situation.

He writes, "I would see the dream, the nightmare, and the psychosis more as basic psychic and psychological processes reflecting the state of the organism as a whole rather than as serving as such active instruments of adaptation." Yet Mack stresses how the manifest content of the dream tends to result "in the formation of *new* combinations of percepts and images from the present and from the recent and distant past." Impressed by the creativity in dreaming, he says, "This creative elaboration does not cease with the dream work, but proceeds during the telling of the dream in further imaginative embellishments, a process related to but extending beyond Freud's secondary revision." He concludes, "More research is needed regarding the various relationships between anxiety, dream formation, creativity, mastery, and the development of psychic structure."[3]

In contrast to the nightmare, "pleasant dreaming" has been more or less taken for granted, and the literature has reflected the view that pleasant dreams are resistive, or at least defensive operations. Lewin in the *Psychoanalysis of Elation* (1961), while speaking of the elated end of the happy dream spectrum writes: "Dreams with a manifest elated mood are well known; dreams which contain laughter or that palm themselves as happy dreams mean the reverse of what they seem to say. They contain patent death wishes or thoughts of one's own death." This is taken out of context to some extent and I doubt Lewin ultimately maintained a reductionistic view of the pleasant dream.

Transitional objects were linked with dreaming and with Lewin's (1961) concept of the dream screen in a paper by Ralph Greenson (1954). He described a patient who obsessively feared that he was making the sound *Mmm*. A dream fragment concerning a piece of velvet cloth led to associations of an active and current transitional object experience. Greenson wrote, "The manifest dream and latent dream thoughts seem to indicate that the velvet material could be understood as a dream screen in accordance with Lewin's ideas on the subject."

Greenson may not have been aware of Winnicott's contribution in 1954, as he did not refer to transitional objects as such; however, his idea is relevant and suggestive. The dream screen signifies a pure fulfillment of the wish to sleep. It is suggested that the dream screen shifts from self-breast fusion states and then through intermediary phases, during which visual, tactile, and kinesthetic perceptions of transitional objects are added to its representation. A patient of mine with inhibitions in creativity produced a beautiful, haunting dream image that appeared as if on a slide projector screen; he wondered how he could have created something so exquisite.[4] The dream (which will not be described in detail) began in a black and white darkness, in the shade of an elevated railroad. As the patient sensed he was actually awakening, a vivid technicolored country scene appeared. Gravestones with ancient inscriptions stood in a setting with a nostalgic, pastoral beauty. It is significant that the patient, who suffered early object loss, had been haunted from childhood by fears of death. His major sublimation had been photography. Associations to the dream directly identified fears of separation from past and present relationships as well as the fear of death. The patient experienced the dream as if he were being reborn and entering a new world. In one sense, he had been able to bridge the vale of darkness, sleep, and death with a progressive new integration within the transitional world of the dream, the by-product of which was a created, comforting phenomenon, transitional in nature. There seem to be important implications here can perhaps be developed in the future.[5]

Muensterberger (1961) in a fundamental paper entitled "The Creative Process" was fully aware of the close relationships among dreaming, creativity, and transitional phenomena. With clinical and anthropological evidence he demonstrates that the creative artist denies, as does the fetishist, both separation and castration. He sees the use of the transitional object as an opportunity to return to "the illusion of a long remembered and yet oblivious unity which transcends disconnection." Then he adds, "It is a paradox to which the dreamer inevitably returns or which the artist tries to undo." Taking dreaming as a general representational phenomenon, Muensterberger suggests a more specific connection among the precursors underlying dreaming, sleep, the imaginative process, and the creative act:

> I believe it can be shown that image formation and representation as well as the emotional prompting for mastery through magic serve to deny separation anxiety as well as castration anxiety. This contention will perhaps shed a brighter light on the creative process in general. It can be approached by observing the drowsy infant holding on to substitute representatives of his immediate environment, imaginary companions be they his thumb, a blanket, a pacifier, or a teddy bear.

In "The Communicative Function of the Dream" Kanzer (1955) explicitly traces the links between the dreams and transitional phenomena in terms of communication and the internalizing process (particularly the formation of introjects) and from the standpoint of object relations. To quote a pertinent passage:

> Falling asleep is not a simple narcissistic regression but the consumma-tion of a conflict in which the good (oedipal or preoedipal) parent is re-attached to the ego and the bad eliminated. In anxiety dreams these endeavors are unsuccessful. The sleeper therefore is not truly alone, but "sleeps with" his introjected good object. This is evidenced in the habits of sleepers—the physical demand of the child for his parent, of the adult for his sex partner, and of the neurotic for lights, toys and rituals as preliminary conditions for sleep.[6]

At this point Kanzer cites Winnicott's paper on the transitional object (1951) and makes the crucial distinction between interpersonal communication and communication with introjects. The former is seen typically in desires to tell dreams to others, usually someone in the latent content of the dream, as well as in the frequent dream form taken by many artistic, poetic, and mythological creations. More complex are the communications of the sleeper's ego with his introjected objects, communications involving the dream process itself. Observations made by other analysts are of interest here. In *Dream Analysis* Sharpe (1937) pointed to certain patients who tend to dream with images of parts of the body or of inanimate objects. After further development during the analytic process, "Instead of dreams the sole content of which is part of a whole we shall have instead whole persons whose 'parts' are important." Mack (1965) relates manifest imagery in dreams to the internalization process, describing how "shifts in the presentation of the parents can be observed in the dreams themselves. In the smaller children inanimate objects, and later animals may be the conveyors of terror, and the representation of the parents is rudimentary, or occurs according to certain of their qualities as the child perceives them."

It is entirely possible that a palette full of transitional images as well as narcissistic and part object images is available to the dreamer, certainly to the artist. In this sense, the dream is a refueling with representations first of the original fusions with the part-object breast, then of the mother, and finally of transitional objects; that is, regression in the dream occurs at all available developmental levels. Ideally, this royal road is replete with "comfort stations," each ready to supply a need ranging anywhere from fusion to object constancy. The transitional object level may be a major "resting place." The analytic material to be reported later on should be pertinent here.[7]

One of the most sophisticated discussions of transitional phenomena occurs in Judith Kestenberg's important "From Organ-Object Imagery to Self and Object Representations" (1971). She cogently warns us in a footnote, "Neither people nor the 'stuff' of transitional phenomena from which dreams are made can be reduced to the status of things. They are adjuncts of the drive object." Kestenberg divides transitional phenomena into accessory objects, intermediate objects, and true transitional objects. I believe that the dream, both as a whole and with reference to its introjects, can serve any of these functions. The accessory object (who assists the mother in the care of the infant) "is held onto as a temporal link of the past with the future ('when Nannie goes, mother will come')." Linking this with Kanzer's internalized parental images seems a natural step. Transitional objects are more than blankets (Kestenberg 1971); "Pets and people, sounds and words, melodies and rhythms, colors and shapes become part of the world of transitional phenomena and may be treasured as personal possessions which re-create 'something old' within the context of 'something new.'" According to Kestenberg, intermediate objects are bodily products which serve as "bridges" between the child and his mother. The inanimate and animate objects around the child are subsequently imbued with their qualities. "He treats them as if they too had come out of his body and externalizes them upon the qualities of feeling from the inside of his body. They too become intermediate objects." Dreams also can qualify here. They arise from the interior of the body and the self, can have good and bad, clean and unclean qualities, can be treasured, and also intermingle with the world of play and imagination, serving as nocturnal babysitters.

CLINICAL EVIDENCE

The data from a psychoanalysis should provide additional evidence for the premise of this chapter. A single engineer in his early forties sought out a city analyst after having been in analytically oriented therapy on the couch for several years, with what he considered good results. However, he realized he had not been able to control his anxiety adequately or improve his relationships sufficiently to marry. The change of therapists was attributed to a move into the city which precluded the late evening visits to his suburban psychiatrist.

The patient's difficulties were characterized as a limitation in his capacity to feel, episodic anxiety attacks accompanied by the fear of falling apart, a mild duodenal ulcer, difficulty in making decisions (which had a claustrophobic component) and an inability to find a permanent love partner. He dated frequently but whenever the relationship drifted toward the serious, he backed down. His rhetorical style included a forced expressiveness that nevertheless had its own basic flatness, with compulsive and stilted qualities.

Early in the analysis, his manner of experiencing, revealing, and working with his dreams became the principal feature of the manifest analytic content. I was treated to an elaborate network of intellectualized, learned dream interpretation; affect was defended against in the transference, especially the anxiety concerning his passive, helpless position in the analytic situation, with its homosexual implications.

My first reaction was one of measured skepticism concerning these secondary and tertiary elaborations and exegeses. I attempted to interpret the resistance against affect in general and against the transference specifically. Suggesting that his interpretations were created to ward off a fear of my words, I implied his need to control the analytic situation. If anything, his dream web tightened; he became protective of his version of *The Interpretation of Dreams*, as if I would censor it, distort it, deprecate it, even rob him of it. He accused me of a virtually inexcusable lack of empathy and understanding. I realized that he was correct.

From that point, I resisted the temptation to interpret, no matter how frustrating his pedantic journeys became. At last he was able to continue his story and therefore communicate its latent meaning. What unfolded was an annotated spoken text, with themes and counterthemes, a complex cross-reference system involving his previous dreams and their interpretations. Manifest content moved directly into explanation without free association. "Water dreams," "fire dreams," "female dreams," "homosexual dreams," "basketball dreams" were elaborately correlated and followed. Footnotes almost hovered over the couch.

Then a story line emerged, a series of developing themes, each converging toward an anticipated finale concurrent with the end of the analysis. A birth process was evident, of which he himself was aware. The patient frequently reassured both of us that the end was in sight. Dreams were omens, portents, signs of our progress. "We're a couple of good dreams away from my true feelings."

When I asked him to associate to this dream story, he recalled that he had treasured his father's telling of elaborate bedtime stories, both original and traditional. Apparently they were oases in a stormy relationship with his borderline mother, who alternated between seductiveness, hostility, and depression.

The plot thickened when he first mentioned that he recorded each dream upon awakening, keeping a "dream book" by his bedside, virtually at his pillow. As more background information emerged, I concluded that the operational "resistance" was his attempt to hold on to the concrete-abstract, fantasy-reality dream saga that both represented and *was* a transitional phenomenon. When I acknowledged my previously confiscative interpretations and shifted to a more empathic understanding of the adaptive and developmental aspects of his manner of dealing with his dreams, he seemed greatly relieved. He felt I understood at last. The frantic dream analysis waned significantly (though it returned periodically) in proportion to an increase in the depth of the therapeutic alliance. There were strong hints that the struggle we were having over his dreams recapitulated early battles concerning his use of transitional objects and parts of his body (penis and feces) which had transitional object significance. His mother who gradually emerged as an intrusive and perfectionistic Craig's wife, had trained the patient prematurely.

Dream stories, dream jottings, dream rememberings served to connect the various facets of his life while repression eliminated a sense of connection to his past, contributing to a defect in his sense of identity. One therapy was linked to the other by this exegetical bridge. Even the time between sessions was tied together with the silken strands of dream themes, just as the journey from the point of falling asleep to the moment of waking was connected by a pathway of dreams. A dreamless night was experienced as a frightening void.[8] In fact, the patient stated that he would prefer a night of painful dreams to a dreamless one. Dreams were time indicators, milestones, but were at times more ephemeral, like soap bubbles, or cartoon bubbles emanating from the couch.[9]

I have stressed this patient's characteristic manner of understanding, communicating, and associating to his dreams and their transitional object significance. But the manifest dream content itself seemed of equivalent importance. A fairy-tale, magical quality persisted. Burlap turned into silk in one dream; the theme of metamorphosis was recurrent. The following dreams will be discussed with special emphasis on the theses of this paper, with no attempt at covering all their aspects.

TWO DREAMS

The patient described one of his many animal dreams: "I was watching a man, a bird and a horse. The bird attacked the horse's testicles with his beak. Then I turned around and heard a sawing sound. When I looked, something was sawing away at the horse's penis." The patient spoke of how he had written down the dream. He had awakened, nearly in a panic, worried about having a heart attack. This reminded him that the previous day while playing tennis he had feared he might overexert himself and have a heart attack. The dream was "quite a nightmare." It reminded him of a dream in which he had asked for a helping hand, and of the phrase, "lend me a hand." When he spoke of the fear of the previous night that accompanied his awakening from the dream, he felt a pain in his chest. More indirect associations to the dream included his painful reactions to the impending threat of separation from his current girl friend. The bird was associated to his mother's having constantly told him that he ate like a bird, which recalled his struggles with her concerning his eating habits. After that the patient informed me that he was worried about his dream awakenings and wondered if I would prescribe a tranquilizer in case insomnia might lie ahead. He reminded me that he feels safe when he carries one and that his previous therapist had provided them whenever necessary. Then, when he realized they were not forthcoming, he began, rather characteristically, to recreate his earlier associative style, elaborating at length on the "castration dream" he had experienced and how this linked in with innumerable others.

I interrupted him, saying that the dream was peopled with both humans and animals, that the casting made it sound a little like a fairy tale. He responded that it did seem so, that he found the manner in which he was telling me the dream reminiscent of the beginnings of his father's bedtime stories. [10]

Clearly this multi-determined dream and its associative sequence can be "listened to" with a number of previously determined sets, ranging from a complete free-floating attention to a selective searching for specific themes (Spence and Lugo 1972). The patient's level of early regression and fixation and the clinical phenomena warrant a reading organized around the transitional object level of his experience. It can be reconstructed that as a child the patient experienced nightmares which were attempts to discharge affects and drives during a time when he was terrified of separation and of being engulfed and penetrated by a witchlike mother. His father, the fairy tales, and eventually the dreams and daydreams themselves served as safety valves and lifesavers in a sea of anxiety. My patient's dream and its related phenomena seem to be alloys of both the nightmare and his defensive efforts to bind the anxiety and turn it into a fairy tale, a euphemistic nightmare. Further inquiry about his statement that it was a nightmare did not reveal the typical symptoms described by Mack and Jones.

Many of this patient's dreams were well stocked with inanimate objects, abstractions, games (basketballs going through hoops, tennis balls passing back and forth over a net, a game with no players). He frequently dreamed of swimming with large, inflated rubber toys. This seemed related to suppressed memories of water play with actual rubber toys and probably surreptitious masturbation during a period of anxiety concerning bath and toilet experiences with his overwhelming mother.

On another occasion he described a "nightmare" which was actually experienced as a mild anxiety dream. "I was being chased by a woman in my room. I ran into my parents' bedroom and saw them in bed under the covers. I tried to get under the covers for consolation." At the time I was impressed by the vagueness of his description. When I asked him to clarify the images in the dream, it occurred to him that he could not actually see his parents. The bed could have been stuffed with pillows, and was covered with a pink blanket. It was tucked in so tight he could not enter his father's side of the bed. His associations related how his mother went to work when he was only nine months old. At other times she was not available for comfort. The pink blanket reminded him that even now, before sleep, he would continue to finger the satin edge of his blanket and that he had done this for as long as he could remember. This was the first time he had spoken of a direct current transitional object experience. Then he added that the same fingering motion occurred when he played with the "pinky" fingers of his girl friends. A soft, plump pinky especially pleased him.

DISCUSSION

The circle closed. The absent or nonconsoling mother is substituted for by blanket and pillow, and this transitional experience, not sufficiently internalized into structure (Tolpin 1971), is fetishistically displaced onto his love object in the present. The dream itself, aside from its specific content, enters the world of transitional phenomena and illusion, along with its "cover story," which renders it both a nightmare and not a nightmare; the vagueness of the experience provides an ambiguousness in which fairy tales can "come true." The secondary revision serves as a blanket; it is defensive, but simultaneously consoling and soothing, in the transitional object sense.

As the analysis progressed, I realized that on another level his dreams were anthropomorphized. They were friends, seers, guides used as magical clouds pointing him to a promised land.[11] "This dream says," or "that dream tells me that in a few months this problem will clear up." The dream companion was described as if it were his externalized penis, which he referred to as a separate person who could urinate, stand erect and virtually think. It seemed to possess its own volition. The penis was at once plaything and playmate, an object he toyed with while fantasying during his frequent childhood and adolescent masturbation. Now a good dream seemed like a good erection (the expected anal level good bowel movement did not appear at this time in his associations). He offered his dream to me as himself, but also as a play object for us. On another level it was his penis for me to play with. Yet it did not seem that the dream as a penis was both a phallic and a transitional object.

The "good" or potent dream as a good omen participated simultaneously as a magical phallic horse which would fly him to a bountiful, blissful world, but also functioned as a transitional bridge. He wanted to play with the dream blanket and to allow me to play with it by means of my interpretations. The homosexual aspect of this desire was certainly present, but the operational level appeared to be that of the mutual play between mother and child (Winnicott 1971, pp. 38-52). We could share the blanket and toys which served as a substitute; at the same time they could be used as a bridge back to the mother during the need for rapprochement. It would seem that the latent meaning of the preference for games and toys in the manifest content of his dreams was present in the communication, "play with me." In an intellectualized manner, the patient persistently interpreted the basketballs entering hoops and tennis balls colliding into nets as references to sexual acts; these he described as genital or phallic. Yet the operative level again seemed an earlier one, where the dreams occupied the intersubjective space of a symbiosis-separation-individuation continuum, serving alternatively as part of the self, a blanket, toys, and imaginary companions. The patient's use of genital symbolism to represent an earlier developmental level of union is reminiscent of the use of genital symbols and ritual coitus to represent a communion with the gods of primitive religions (Goldberg 1930).

FURTHER DISCUSSION AND CONCLUSIONS

My patient's dreams and dream elaborations served both defensive and transitional object needs. Bridges that served him well during his struggles with the separation-individuation process were revived when he was faced with the isolation and deprivation of the analytic situation. Of course the profuse dream production had a simultaneously anal, phallic and exhibitionistic significance. The dreams also were attempts at repairing a disrupted body image, i.e., the dreams themselves, in toto, had phallic, anal, and body meaning, as did their internal symbols.

The stress in this chapter, however, has been to demonstrate that dreams and secondary elaborations as well as the dream process itself provide nightly available transitional phenomena which offer a bridge between the self and the object, and a means of rejoining the comforting, "pleasant dreams" aspect of the parents. Conceivably, each night the dream, part introjected parent, part dreamer, is held, savored, and possibly recreated by the child's ego at a higher developmental level. Then it is given up and laid aside until the next evening, repeating the daytime use of transitional objects as developmental guide posts which assist the traversal of the difficult course between symbiosis and the establishment of object constancy. Once this latter stage is to some extent attained, the dream vehicle allows nightly ego regression to organ-object fusion, providing a refueling which helps to maintain stable self and object-representations (Kestenberg 1971).

My patient's special early development included an inconsistent mother who seriously delayed object constancy while her devouring and penetrating qualities led to both castration anxiety and the fear of body annihilation. The normal transitional functions of the dream were intensified and its recall and elaboration became obligatory and fetishistic in nature. To speculate further, it could be said that for this patient dreaming was so involved in a fetishistic-like service that it could not function as a bridge to creativity (Giovacchini 1966). Interestingly, some increased capacity for creative performing and experiencing did occur as the patient's dream world lost its intensity.

My patient presented a dream barrier that functioned simultaneously as a dream blanket, or a transitional phenomenon that made the analytic situation tolerable. As noted, his early developmental difficulties contributed to a special circumstance where dreaming approached a fetishistic phenomenon. However, to the extent the separation-individuation process never fully attains a "happy ending," dreaming can always serve a transitional phenomenon function, in either a healthy developmental sense or an obligatory one. If the analyst is aware of this, he is less likely to offer premature resistance interpretations and actually intensify a developmental "resistance" to the premature loss of a needed substitute object.

My patient required a period of time to work with his own dreams, even if on another level this functioned as a transference resistance to affect. My initial interpretations were experienced as if his transitional blanket had been appropriated, changed, even washed or purified before its loss could be tolerated. I believe our current mode of dream interpretation will be enhanced by taking this phenomenon into account.

NOTES

1. In the same paper Freud showed the continuum between daydreams and night dreaming.

2. Byron in his poem of unrequited love, loss and madness, "The Dream," writes of his dreams:

> They do divide our being; they become a
> Portion of ourselves as of our time,
> And look like heralds of eternity;
> They pass like spirits of the past—they speak
> Like sibils of the future. . . . . . .

3. In his intriguing analysis of universal mythological themes, Joseph Campbell in *The Hero With a Thousand Faces* allows the wisdom of the ages to suggest whether dreaming can promote growth and development. He describes the heroes' crossing of the return threshold from the other world, pointing out how he frequently returns unchanged from this metaphorical dream world. Rip Van Winkle awakens "with nothing to show for the experience" but his whiskers. The Irish hero, Oisin, returns from a long sojourn in the dream equivalent of the land of youth, but accidentally touches the earth with one foot. He immediately loses the steed that kept him in magical space, and turns into an old man. (The return from Shangri-La in Hilton's novel provokes a similar fate.) However, a contrasting view is presented in the Arabian Nights story, the Tale of Prince Kamar Al-Zaman. The Prince "experienced while awake the bliss of deep sleep, and returned to the light of day with such a convincing talisman of his unbelievable adventure that he was able to return his self-assurance in the face of every sobering disillusionment." The talisman was a ring that symbolized the heroes' attempt to unite the earthly and godly spheres.

4. Giovacchini (1966) and Kohut (1971) describe dreams which were experienced by their patients in a similar manner.

5. Hamilton (1969) has suggested that "object loss leads to a regressive fusion with the lost object and that the dream becomes an integral part of this process having originally been utilized by the infant to cope with the loss of direct oral gratification during sleep." He demonstrates in his paper on Keats how the poet externalized his dreams in the form of poems. "Because of the intense ambivalence and hypercathexis of the introject, this method was only partially successful and, having to be repeated over and over again, led to one of the richest, most profuse creative efforts in all of literature."

6. See an early pioneer in the understanding of dreams, folklorist-poet Charles Godfrey Leland, in his first book *The Poetry and Mystery of Dreams* (1856) for an interesting related point of view: "These instances, I

believe are neither few nor far between, in which dreams have given to the afflicted, positive comfort and encouragement during their waking hours. The features of the loved who have long been parted from us either by accident or death, are thus renewed or revivified far more sympathetically than can be done by the most accurate portrait, while to the lover despairing of his lady's favour, a pleasant dream often holds forth hopes not less stimulating than her smiles. All, it is true, are not gifted with such vivid imaginations as to frequently experience these sweet delusions, but they have in every age existed to such a degree that the world has never wanted races who held with religious faith that

> 'Departed spirits at their will
> Could from the Land of Souls pass to and fro,
> Coming to us in sleep when all is still.' "

7. Irving Harrison's "A Dream Followed by Elation," (1960) noted that "the windows, the white paper like a blank sheet, the picture frame and the pane of glass are all dream screen equivalents and all symbolize for the patient the breast (penis). Such regressive, hallucinatory revivals represent intermediate steps on the way to the blank screen."
It should be stated that some of the formulations in the literature and in this chapter use the manifest content of the dream. Conceivably during rapid developmental change or difficulty the manifest symbols in dreams more closely reflect the general state of object relations; i.e., "presymbolic images" may be present, providing direct gratification as well as reflecting primary process needs. This is not to contradict their simultaneous use as symbols with referents in the latent content of the dream. Symbols in dreams not only have "horizontal" ambiguity and multiple associative connections, but may be the apex of a "pyramid," with fusion levels "topped" by the substitute object, then the transitional object and ultimately the symbol, which itself includes the spectrum of concrete to abstract levels of meaning.
8. The night can be cold and threatening to the child and his parents, both of whom project their terrors into it. A culture provides rituals to help cope with this universal anxiety and offers transitional bridges between falling asleep and waking. The parent reassures that a pathway of dream stepping stones will be pleasant, secure ones. Popular songs, which rarely mention nightmares, tell us to dream when we are feeling blue. But the advice can be insufficient. Eugene Field (1949) said it humorously in "Seein' Things":

> Mother tells us Happy dreams! and takes away the light,
> An' leaves me lyin' alone 'an seein' things at night.

The attempted reassurance, "If I should die before I wake, I pray the Lord my soul to take," also falls short of success. Little Boy Blue, who looks after the sheep, is mercifully allowed to remain in his dream world:

Will you wake him, no, not I
For if I do he'll be sure to cry.

The child is asked to count sheep to protect him from lying awake and anxious at the brink, thus supplying him a cute, wooly companion during the night journey, just as during the day his actual stuffed animals and toys travel with him while shopping with mother or going to nursery school. The vampires, night fiends (Jones 1911), and witches on broomsticks that crisscross the night abyss vie with his friendly companions and steeds. Mary Webb in her novel, *Precious Bane* (1924), warns us to "saddle your dreams after you ride 'em," and Emily Dickinson's horses' heads are turned toward eternity, providing a comforting destination on the other side. Yeats's (1959) "Horses of Disaster" are hidden by the comfort of the twilight state in a relevant poem. In it he asks his lover to let "your hair fall on my breast/Drowning loves lonely hour in deep twilight of rest." It seems that the fears of the night, loneliness and separation including early conceptualizations of death are mollified by the parent, the child, and, in a special sense, the poet. Frightening animal symbols are transformed into comforting, furry domesticated ones, nocturnal counterparts to the stuffed and real pets of the day. The dream and its related phenomena are an arena for this struggle between the comforting and the terrifying. Winning provides a base for future, structured, internalized self-comfort (Tolpin 1971).

9. Winnicott (1945): "The subject of illusion is a very wide one that needs study; it will be found to provide the clue to a child's interest in bubbles and clouds and rainbows and all mysterious phenomena."

10. The patient could not recall any original or retold fairy tale with these characters. An interesting speculation, however, is The Little Green Frog, as described in Andrew Lang's *The Yellow Fairy Book* (1894). A king was despondent and ill grieving over the death of his queen. He had difficulty in breathing: "Perhaps the worst pain he had to bear was a sort of weight on his chest which made it very hard for him to breathe." The prince tried to save his father by stealing a magic horse in order to help him to find the magic bird, which was brilliantly colored and bejewelled. In an appointed place, the bird was not to be found but in its stead a maiden called Serpentine. At one time she had existed in the form of a frog who had been advising the prince. Finally the bird is captured with Serpentine's aid, and the king is cured in the nick of time. Then, at last, the bird is revealed as the lost queen and the two couples are reunited in a typical happy ending.

11. Lord Byron, who both savored and dreaded the black nightmare experience, personalized the dream similarly in "The Dream," Stanza 1:

Our life is twofold. Sleep hath its own world.
A boundary between the things misnamed
Death and existence: Sleep hath its own world,

And a wide realm of wild reality,
And dreams in their development have breath
And tears and tortures and the touch of joy.

Also see Leland (1856): In a fairy-tale sketch, God decides to give man the dream at the beseeching of Guardian Angel of the World. Because God feels that man is not all bad, at times his "heart is ready to receive the good which a light external aid might fix upon him!" God says to the Angel, "Give him the Dream." Then "the sweet Guardian flew over the world with his sister, the Dream. Far and wide they spread their gentle influence, and the hearts of life-weary mortals were rejoiced."

REFERENCES

Arlow, Jacob (1969a). Unconscious fantasy and disturbances of conscious experience. *Psychoanalytic Quarterly* 38:1–27.
——— (1969b). Fantasy, memory and reality testing. *Psychoanalytic Quarterly* 38:28–51.
Campbell, Joseph (1949). *The Hero With a Thousand Faces*, pp. 218-228. Princeton, N.J.: Princeton University Press.
Field, Eugene (1949). Seein' things. In *Home Book of Verse*, ed. Burton Egbert Stevenson. New York: Henry Holt.
Freud, Sigmund (1908). Creative writers and day-dreaming. *Standard Edition* 9:143–153.
Giovacchini, Peter (1966). Dreams and the creative process. *British Journal of Medical Psychology* 39:105–115.
Goldberg, B. Z. (1930). *The Sacred Fire: The Story of Sex in Religion*. New York: Liveright.
Greenson, Ralph (1954). About the sound "mm". *Psychoanalytic Quarterly* 23:234–239.
Hamilton, James (1969). Object loss, dreaming and creativity. *Psychoanalytic Study of the Child* 24:488–531.
Harrison, Irving (1960). A dream followed by elation. *Journal of the American Psychoanalytic Association* 8:270–280.
Jones, Ernest (1911). *On the Nightmare*. Part III, Chapter II. The Mare and the Mara: A Psychoanalytical Contribution to Etymology. II. The Horse and the Night Fiend. London: Hogarth Press, 1949.
Kanzer, Mark (1955). The communicative function of the dream. *International Journal of Psycho-Analysis* 36:260–266.
Kestenberg, Judith (1971). From organ-object imagery to self and object representations. In *Separation-Individuation: Essays in Honor or Margaret S. Mahler*, pp. 75–99. New York: International Universities Press. Also in Kestenberg, *Children and Parents: Psychoanalytic Studies in Development*, pp. 215–234. New York: Jason Aronson.

Kohut, Heinz (1971). The analysis of the self. *Psychoanalytic Study of the Child*, Monograph No. 4. New York: International Universities Press.

Lang, Andrew (1894). The little green frog. In *The Yellow Fairy Book*. New York: Dover, 1966.

Leland, Charles Godfrey (1856). *The Poetry and Mystery of Dreams*. Philadelphia: E. H. Butler.

Lewin, Bertram (1961). *The Psychoanalysis of Elation*. New York: Psychoanalytic Quarterly, Inc., p. 91.

Mack, John (1965). Nightmares, conflict and ego development in childhood. *International Journal of Psycho-Analysis* 46:403–428.

——— (1970). *Nightmares and Human Conflict*. Boston: Little, Brown.

Muensterberger, Werner (1961). The creative process: its relation to object loss and fetishism. *The Psychoanalytic Study of Society* 2:161–185.

Roland, Alan (1971). Imagery and symbolic expression in dreams and art. *International Journal of Psycho-Analysis* 53:531–539.

Rosen, V. (1964). Some effects of artistic talent on character style. *Psychoanalytic Quarterly* 33:1–24. Also in Rosen, *Style, Character and Language*, ed. S. Atkin and M. Jucovy, pp. 331–352. New York: Jason Aronson, 1977.

Sharpe, E. F. (1937). *Dream Analysis*. London: Hogarth Press, 1949.

Spence, D., and Lugo, M. (1972). The role of verbal clues in clinical listening. In *Psychoanalysis and Contemporary Science*, vol. 1, pp. 109–131. New York: Macmillan.

Stern, M. (1951). Pavor nocturnus. *International Journal of Psycho-Analysis* 32:302–309.

Tolpin, M. (1971). On the beginnings of a cohesive self: an application of the concept of transmuting internalization to the study of the transitional object and signal anxiety. *Psychoanalytic Study of the Child* 26:316–354.

Webb, Mary (1924). *Precious Bane*. New York: Random House.

Weissman, P. (1971). The artist and his objects. *International Journal of Psycho-Analysis* 34:89–97.

Winnicott, D. W. (1945). Primitive emotional development. In *Collected Papers: Through Pediatrics to Psychoanalysis*, pp. 145–156. New York: Basic Books.

——— (1951). Transitional objects and transitional phenomena. In *Collected Papers. Through Pediatrics to Psychoanalysis*, pp. 229–242. New York: Basic Books, (1958).

——— (1971). *Playing and Reality*. New York: Basic Books.

Yeats, W. B. (1959). *Collected Poems of W. B. Yeats*. New York: Macmillan.

CHAPTER 15

Winnicott originally felt that even though the transitional object could be cathected more strongly than the mother, it would be used to further normal development only so long as necessary. It would then be decathected, leaving no trace, and would fade away. In this first conception, there was no internalization of object representation or function. Another way of stating this is that there was no structuralization. Using Kohut's frame of reference and terminology, Tolpin suggested that the soothing function of the transitional object is internalized and structuralized, bit by bit, via a process called transmuting internalization. This process, not unique to the transitional object, occurs also with other maternal functions, part of and furthering normal development. The result is a self-soothing function permitting greater separation, growth, and individuation. This position eventually found acceptance with Winnicott, though it is only from personal discussions reported by Gaddini and Giovacchini that we know of the shift; it was never reflected in his writings.

Victor Rosen once wondered whether the relationship to the transitional object could be internalized, thus contributing to qualities of character and style. Henry Kaminer's study contributes, as do those of Giovacchini (chapter 21) and Parrish (chapter 18), to our understanding of these issues, and explores what happens with a failure of internalization of this soothing function.

Kaminer describes the effects of an intrusive parent, where the transitional object seems created and chosen by the parent. The object then appears more fetishistic than transitional. Less a resting place for normal development, it instead contributes to stereotyped attempts to cling, attach, and cope with an acute separation anxiety. Here there is more of the quality of a true addiction, with concomitant hostility, depression, and inhibition.

L.B.

TRANSITIONAL OBJECT COMPONENTS
IN SELF AND OBJECT RELATIONS

Henry Kaminer

Some excerpts will be presented from the analysis of a woman who made use of a transitional object in a clear and distinctive manner. Her predilection for a type of object relation normally associated with the stage of separation-individuation will be explored. Although the overt use of a transitional object was discrete and circumscribed, there was a corresponding pervasive influence on all her object relations, including the analytic relationship, which affected the perception of herself as an individual. Her analysis revealed the enormous impact of the transitional object and of the transitional mode (Winnicott 1953) on all aspects of her life.

The patient, Miss B., was a twenty-seven-year-old unmarried woman who had been in analysis for over a year. She had come into treatment because of depression and dissatisfaction with her situation in life. Living at home with her parents, she felt mired in a dull and routine existence. She had only casual involvements with men and felt closely tied to her parents, unable to build an independent life for herself. Her one sibling, a much-admired older brother, was happily married and successful in his career. The parents were of lower middle-class background and Miss B. felt alienated from her father, who was rather passive, formal, and emotionally distant. When she was four, for example, he accepted an out-of-state job and for an entire year saw the family only on weekends.

The main theme of her analysis centered on feelings of inadequacy and loneliness. At the same time, Miss B. felt that all men were stupid, pompous, and foolish. She and her girl friends could manipulate men so easily. An intense erotic transference developed quickly, and her ideas and feelings centered around her strong wish to possess me as a real object and her apprehension concerning the frustrations she would endure if she faced this desire without her characteristic jocular manner. In treatment she gradually recognized her need to cling to people, particularly to boyfriends, and began to realize her great fear of this intense desire. The patient dreaded that she would fall into a hopelessly dependent relationship, and then be rejected because she needed the man more than he needed her. Separations of any kind during the course of treatment were upsetting to her and she often attempted to deny them to avoid pain.

A few weeks before the beginning of my summer vacation, the patient was talking about how empty her life would be when both her friends and I would be away. A girl friend was driving to the West Coast and invited her to come along. Although the patient had often expressed a desire to visit the beautiful warm beaches of California, a free and expansive indulgence of her desires frightened her, and she decided not to accompany her friend. During a Friday session (just before the weekend, which usually was experienced as a painful separation), the patient announced that she was depressed. She held a small doll with a white cloth body, which she toyed with throughout the session, often clutching it to her breast. She quickly exclaimed, "Look, see this sleepy little doll. I bought it while shopping for a present for my niece." She then described how she had been shopping and arguing with her mother. She had been telling her mother not to be infantile, not to adopt the position of a martyr, but to be more independent. She laughed and said that would also be good advice for herself. She went on to say that she had sent her turtle to California with her girl friend. "He was sad—I felt it would cheer him up—besides, it's like you send an American flag up to the moon." (Only later in the session did she find it necessary to inform me that the turtle was a small toy, not a live pet.)

For the rest of the session the patient spoke about a man she was interested in but had not seen in some time, describing with some feeling how she was preoccupied with feeling lonely and wanting him. She also spoke of sexual desires, and how she was trying to remain cool and uninvolved to alleviate the frustration. Then, for the next three sessions, the patient talked about feeling bored and lonely. She bemoaned the fact that treatment was superficial and ineffectual, that she was getting nowhere. Each time I would interpret this as a reaction to my forthcoming vacation, she would feel even more depressed and apathetic, wondering if treatment were worth all the financial and emotional deprivation that went with it.

I noticed the doll and inquired further about it. She said it was just like one she had as a child. "Oh—I saw it in a store—I was *looking* for one—it's cute—it sleeps—I take it everywhere with me. I bought it the weekend I didn't go down to the shore to see my boyfriend. It stays in any position you put it. Look, you can turn it any way." At this point, I said that she made it seem as if it were a baby. (Months ago the patient had become aware of pregnancy fantasies and the wish to be fulfilled by becoming pregnant.) The patient responded, "Well, no, not exactly—it's like a toy— something to make me feel good—less lonely—to stick with me—it's not a pet—I have pets, a dog and a cat—pets you have to take care of—they make demands on you—this doll does what I tell it—I talk to it, I can do what I want with it, it listens and it doesn't make demands or contradict me and I don't have to walk it or feed it when I don't want to—and when I'm not in the mood for it, I just put it away and it just waits for me. I can turn it off when I want to."

This patient used small toys (the doll and possibly the turtle) as transitional objects. Her own description of the qualities of the little doll shows great similarity to Winnicott's description of a transitional object (Winnicott 1953). Her perception of the turtle as a representative of herself, and yet also as separate from herself, fits the concept of a transitional object as a "first not-me possession." She surrounded herself with small toys in her bedroom, and would hold them or think of them when she felt lonely or abandoned. Contact with them made her feel less empty, more complete. She would use them when she felt anxious and ignore them at other times. During one session, she became anxious talking about assuming adult responsibility, reached for a favorite ring, and could not find it. She was convinced it had rolled under my couch, but it was not there. Later she found it at home. When not in need of soothing, she was unaware of the location or presence of the transitional objects.

Ever since this patient was an infant, her mother had tried to maintain control of their relationship. The girl was to be compliant, uncomplaining and unassertive, and her mother would make decisions for her. Miss B. was expected to reflect favorably on her mother by success in dancing lessons, by an impeccable deportment, and by being pretty and polite—in other words, by being a doll. The family lived very near the elementary school, and the patient recalls vividly how she would arrive at her house after school and watch other children walking past on the way home. She yearned to play with them and would sit, quietly and primly on the porch, dressed neatly and attractively, hands clasped, hoping that someone would approach, admire her, and play with her. Needless to say, such satisfaction was infrequent. However, she clung to her mother's advice; all she had to do was to be restrained, neat and pretty, and everyone would come to her. She was, in effect, acting as her mother's doll— keeping out of the way until needed, and then passively receiving the attention of others. As an adult, the patient suffered greatly in her professional activities and in social situations, when it gradually became clear to her that this passive presentation of herself could not maintain an adequate social life. In the analysis, she had the fantasy that her mere presence was sufficient, that I should work on her, or analyze her, and tell her the results. My statement that this was not sufficient to help her evoked an indignant response, as if a basic rule of nature had been challenged.

The mother had boasted to the patient that during childhood she had never allowed her to become frustrated enough to cry. When shopping for example, she would buy her daughter a little toy or trinket as she entered the store, and the child would be content with this while the mother busied herself with trying on clothes or shopping. Thus the mother actively encouraged the continued use of inanimate possessions to avoid experiencing anxiety or other frustrations. (Dickes, chapter 20).

To this day, the importance of shopping together persists. The mother has always insisted the patient accompany her on shopping trips, and now depends on the patient for transportation. The mother has steadfastly refused to learn to drive, although the family lives in a suburban area, and expects the patient to be her chauffeur and shopping companion.

Later in treatment, the patient realized that there was infantile quality in her relationship with her latest boyfriend. He made no demands on her, constantly proclaimed his admiration, and waited on her like a devoted servant. She treated him with a casual indifference, enjoying the feeling of power and control. Eventually, she decided it would be better to end the relationship and try to develop a more mature involvement with other men. However, she could not carry out this resolve, explaining that before she could give someone up, she always "had to have a transition person" to turn to, so she wouldn't be lonely while looking for a new boyfriend.

The relationship between mother and daughter, each mutually seducing the other to gratify their dependency needs, obviously impeded the process of individuation. The practice of averting anxiety by giving tangible objects or gifts helped to perpetuate the use of transitional objects into adult life.

The patient tended to be possessive with people, and could not bear to relinquish their attention. It was difficult for her to conceive of a loving relationship where two people willingly wanted to give to each other. She imagined everyone was trying either to possess or to be possessed in order to be cared for and adored. Thus, her object relations involved seeing people as possessions, as things.

Miss B. had great difficulty making any important decisions. She had a circle of girl friends who were closely entwined in each other's lives, thoughts, and feelings; she would always discuss decisions with them. When she would have a clear idea of what she wanted, she presented her dilemma in such a way that the friends would respond by prescribing the course of action she had already chosen. She would then carry it out, relieved of the burden of responsibility. She not only saw other people as possessions to be used, but saw herself as a part-person, incomplete, needing someone strong and decisive to complete her. The dilemma, of course, was that she feared she would submerge herself in such a person and be totally controlled, which was frightening to her.

Miss B. performed a ritualistic action so subtle and fleeting that at first I was not sure it was anything more than a prolonged nonverbal goodbye. At the end of each session, she would arise from the couch, walk toward the door, turn, pause, look at me, smile an enigmatic smile, and leave. One day she hinted at the meaning of this ritual. As she turned and paused, she said, "You know, sometimes I feel that you don't exist when I leave—it's like if I say 'poof,' and you disappear in smoke, and you come back again when I need you." Then she smiled and left. The intensity of the wish to control the object, to be able to turn it on and off, to create or destroy it according to her need, is apparent in this brief vignette. It is similar to her description of her relationship with her little doll.

Miss B. had a talent for dancing and was encouraged by her parents. With fondness she remembered that her father would take her to dance lessons and wait patiently outside while she practiced. Although talented, she would regularly refuse to perform at home for friends or relatives. She could dance only when following a well-rehearsed routine, and could never be spontaneous or interpretive. Miss B. remarked that she was criticized by her teachers for not moving her arms and torso gracefully. She would "hang like a puppet from strings," though her legs would move well. At sixteen she had to decide whether to pursue dancing as a career. Aside from the phallic and exhibitionistic conflicts the choice represented to her, she felt that she lacked creativity, that she danced "like a wooden doll." Her teachers confimed this. In treatment she began to see that she was afraid of the active role involved in becoming a solo dancer, in contrast to being a member of the chorus line, which moved under the control of the director.

As can be seen from these excerpts, the defects in self- and object-representation posed particular problems in the analysis. Miss B. insisted on satisfaction of the transference wish that I become a part of her need-satisfying system. One aspect of this is illustrated by her speech pattern. Early in the analysis, I noticed that Miss B. would speak spontaneously, but avoided mentioning details. She would interrupt herself to get to the next idea, and then interrupt that one as well. When this was analyzed, we learned that "she couldn't be bothered with the details," and expected me to finish her sentences for her, as if I shared the idea and knew it already. This fantasy is often found in twins, who in many ways show signs of incomplete self-representation (Arlow 1960; see also Parrish, chapter 18).

Miss B. also would listen to my voice and feel soothed and comforted, as if the words flowed over her like a caress. At the same time she said she didn't like the ideas I was presenting and therefore did not hear them— only the soothing voice came through. The role of the mother's voice as a transitional phenomenon has been discussed by various authors (Gaddini and Gaddini 1970, Winnicott 1953).

DISCUSSION

Stevenson (1954) provided examples of a doll and other objects used by adults as transitional objects serving as adjuncts to a relationship between two people. My patient seems to have used the turtle to maintain a link with her friend who was leaving; but she also identified the turtle with herself. She was afraid of the beaches of California, which symbolized a hedonistic loss of control, but she sent the turtle to enjoy itself in her place. The doll was used in the more traditional way, to allay separation anxiety. These manifestations in adults are probably more common than is realized, since they can occur without attracting notice or causing difficulty. It required the stress of my summer vacation and the separation it entailed to bring this practice so sharply into focus.

A young woman treated by Nancy Spiegel (1968) persisted in using a shoelace as a comforting object from age two onward. Its importance seemed derived from her mother's beads, which fascinated her at nine months. This was also the time of weaning. The shoelace problem was presented in conjunction with masturbation fantasies and practices, and was part of a "good" ritual used to cleanse her from the "bad" ritual. It played the role of a transitional object in the sense that it reunited her with the good mother after she had "lost" the mother by her "bad" rituals (including masturbation). Spiegel's patient also demonstrates an area of confluence of the fetish and the transitional object, and the underlying magical thinking. This idea has been further developed by Greenacre (1970).

An interesting comparative study by the Gaddinis (1970), of child-rearing methods in rural Italy and urban Rome, examines the precursors of transitional objects. The authors describe articles or parts of the mother's or child's body which the mother offers the child in lieu of herself. These may then be used actively by the child as transitional objects. Songs and rocking rhythms are included.

A recent article by Busch, Nagera et al. (1973) emphasizes the difference between the primary transitional object—something discovered by the child and actually created by the child in the sense that the special significant meaning of the preexisting object is created by the child—and soothing objects supplied by the mother. One particular difference concerns the ability of the child to create a transitional object as an early but major step toward individuation. The extended use of objects provided by the parent involves encouraging a regression to a level of object relationship beyond that necessitated by the child's ability to tolerate separation. The child can use the externally provided object as a transitional object; but this will eventually impede individuation. Busch, Nagera et al. emphasize the complexity of the process of being weaned from a transitional object, demonstrating how it depends on a variety of factors, internal and external. Miss B. showed the results of an interference with the natural weaning or relinquishing process by her prolonged need to find transitional objects in the people around her, as well as in inanimate objects, and by perceiving herself as a doll, to be animated by someone external to herself.

Coppolillo (1967) described the analysis of a twenty-six-year-old man who, though superficially successful and charming, demonstrated an inability to form deep or lasting relationships with friends, as well as impulsive homosexual urges and an intense need for real gratification from the analyst. This need was manifested by preoccupation with words themselves, the couch, the warmth of the room, all to the exclusion of the analyst's ideas or person. It was only after this pervasive problem had been analyzed that treatment could progress. This patient's mother had been so intrusive and seductive that separation could not occur. In the analysis reconstruction showed that the mother continuously inserted herself as a real object into the child's life whenever he became involved with a transitional object. Coppolillo emphasizes the importance to the child of the transitional mode of experiencing reality, a concept broader than that of the transitional object itself (see Rose, chapter 22), and described by Winnicott (1953) as "the third part of the life of a human being, a part that we cannot ignore ... and intermediate area of experiencing to which inner reality and external life contribute." It is this ego-state that a child uses in imaginative play alone and that can be so effectively interrupted by an intrusive, seductive. controlling mother.

Marian Tolpin (1971) describes how the transitional object provides the child a gratification unavailable from the real mother of the postinfancy period. The transitional object can "re-evoke the lost soothing of symbiotic fusion." This soothing function is gradually internalized during normal development. When the process is impaired, the individual is left without a mental representation for external regulation of the soothing process. The "transmuting internalizations" of all the maternal functions are impaired, and the cohesiveness of the self is never fully developed.

My patient displayed this phenomenon in her pervasive dependence on others to augment her sense of self, modeling herself on girl friends, and using them to make decisions for her. She also would fantasize that I was an intimate part of her, augmenting her often depleted self-esteem by thinking of my status or accomplishments. During a conversation with three girl friends, Miss B. felt unimportant and inferior when the girls were talking of their ambitions and plans for the future, and of the special qualities of their boyfriends. She felt empty and worthless until she began to imagine that I was very important and respected; immediately she felt better about herself.

Miss B's symptomatology shows the extent to which she related to significant figures in her life as transitional objects rather than real people. She perceived me as a transitional object, not only to insure the availability of the object whenever needed, but also to make it possible to turn "it" off when it made demands or became threatening. In fact, this proved a major source of resistance, since Miss B. dreaded involving herself in a relationship in which she could lose her individuality and sense of self. If she allowed the object to be a real person, fully differentiated from herself, then she would become the used object, totally loved and cared for, but then subject to dissolution and total loss of self at the whim of her master. The subtle but pervasive manner in which object relations and sense of self are altered by the prolongation of the "transitional state" (Winnicott 1953) becomes apparent in Miss B, and was especially prominent in the transference.

CONCLUSIONS

Some of the determinants of regression to the use of a transitional object are related to a prolongation of the symbiotic state in childhood, and to a mother-child relationship in which the mother insinuates herself into the child's awareness and totally controls the process of coping with separation. This is not the total perpetuation of a symbiosis, but a state in which separation and reunion, which occur repeatedly, must be totally controlled because the painful affect of loss and loneliness is unbearable

This set of circumstances seems related to development of frustration tolerance in later life. It helps us to understand a characteristic type of object relation and a particular deficiency in the sense of the self and in the state of narcissistic investment of libido. It thus has important bearing on the entire development of the adult ego.

REFERENCES

Arlow, Jacob (1960). Fantasy systems in twins. *Psychoanalytic Quarterly* 29:175-199.

Busch, F., Nagera, H., et al. (1973). Primary transitional objects. *Journal of Child Psychiatry* 12:193-214.

Coppolillo, Henry P. (1967). Maturational aspects of the transitional phenomenon. *International Journal of Psycho-Analysis* 43:237-245.

Gaddini, Renata, and Gaddini, Eugenio (1970). Transitional objects and the process of individuation. *Journal of the American Academy of Child Psychiatry* 9:347-365.

Greenacre, Phyllis (1970). The transitional object and the fetish. *International Journal of Psycho-Analysis* 51:447-455.

Spiegel, Nancy Tow (1968). An infantile fetish and its persistence into young womanhood. *Psychoanalytic Quarterly* 37:635-636.

Stevenson, Olive (1954). The first treasured possession. *Psychoanalytic Study of the Child* 9:199-217.

Tolpin, Marion (1971). On the beginnings of a cohesive self: an application of the concept of transmuting internalization to the study of the transitional object and signal anxiety. *Psychoanalytic Study of the Child* 26:316-354.

Winnicott, D. W. (1953). Transitional objects and transitional phenomena. *International Journal of Psycho-Analysis* 34:89-97.

CHAPTER 16

The theory of transitional objects has provided productive access to the vicissitudes of the ego in its development toward independence from the nurturing mother. Winnicott views the transitional object as the usual transition, the first "not-me object" forming a bridge between child and mother. His writings suggest, for example, that, in children, songs, repetitive babblings, and even the psychiatrist himself may represent less concrete representatives of the more tangible blanket.

Joseph Solomon wishes to extend this concept. First, observation of child-rearing practices in other cultures suggests that the transitional object, so prevalent in this civilization, is actually an adaptation. In some cultures which allow prolonged body contact between mother and child, the typical transitional object is neither seen nor discussed. Second, intellectual functions, ideas, or even symptoms may take over the role of the transitional object. The child may seek contact with the mother by accepting the attitudes she communicates and may cling to these as transitional substitute objects. Since they never reach resolution, in circular style they form the basis for the sort of self-contained psychic system discussed in this chapter. Though such systems present a difficult therapeutic task, Solomon proposes several techniques for their management.

J.C.S., L.B.

TRANSITIONAL PHENOMENA AND OBSESSIVE-COMPULSIVE STATES

Joseph C. Solomon

Winnicott's idea that the transitional object acts as a link to object relationships is a major contribution, especially because it lends itself to further development. There are some instances when the transitional object can become an *end in itself* and when it may assume diverse forms. This is of particular importance in the understanding of obsessive-compulsive adult personalities.

From within Winnicott's frame of reference, the world of childhood, I should like first to review some of my work with the performance of children in play therapy. I found that children fall into three main groups: some show progressive systems, some stereotyped systems, and some disruptive systems. While the patterns may overlap to an extent, they generally remain true to form. I shall briefly describe each type.

PROGRESSIVE SYSTEMS

In the progressive system or pattern, obstacles become challenges rather than threats. A snag or problem will be dealt with successfully because previous obstacles were mastered. In other words, the child possesses confidence. He has the inner resource of a stockpile of coping mechanisms which cushions oncoming stress. Progressive play sessions are characterized by an easy working through of conflict situations. When there are hostile feelings, these are readily released with a

Editor's note: Dr. Joseph Solomon, an early student of Winnicott's ideas, died before his contribution to this volume could be revised and completed. Because many of his theoretical ideas are worthy of serious consideration and have practical clinical application, the editors have decided to include them in their present form.

minimum of guilt and are often played out as a fun game. Here, transitional objects extend into the world of grown-ups, mediating an approach rather than an escape. When the therapist tries to keep the play anonymous, the child often identifies himself with a play figure and can readily accept actions as his own.

Another type of progressive system, pathological in nature, is a premature propulsion into a later phase of development. Play patterns may appear as denials of the wish to be little. These children cannot wait to grow up because it is too painful to be little—when you are big you can defeat the threatening world. This hastened growth can be organized into a system of pseudoprogression bordering on stereotyped patterning.

STEREOTYPED SYSTEMS

In contrast to progressive systems, other play patterns seem aimed at making time stand still. Repetitive activities, ostensibly without goal or direction, are characteristic. We can distinguish at least two kinds of stereotype: repetition, which suggests the child seeks an answer to questions without answers, and a play pattern, presumably purposeless or meaningless, which repeats itself again and again without variation.

Essentially, stereotyped patterning serves to ignore or bypass confusing or conflictual messages which impinge on the nervous system. In animal experiments, compulsive or repetitive patterns occur, with exposure to a confusion of conflicting stimuli. The animal reacts either with a single repetitive response regardless of the stimuli or with failure to attain its goal.

Let us distinguish between the *content* and the *process* of stereotyped play. A child who repeatedly covers a fire engine with blocks may be telling a story about having been frightened by a fire engine. He masters the situation in his own way. But additionally, the play pattern may also represent the displacement onto the fire engine of deep-seated turmoil around conflicts in family or school, causing stress, pain, and fear. On the other hand, a stereotyped play pattern, such as repeatedly running a car back and forth, may involve a total inability to engage in communicative play.

Stereotyped play is the basis for ritualistic behavior in children and adults. I refer to self-imposed ritualistic behavior, which differs in some ways from the cultural rituals and ceremonies imposed upon individuals during critical developmental phases. The latter behavior resembles superstitious actions and religious practices in which repetitive patterns are invested with magical abilities to ward off danger and control the environment. Stereotyped play similarly serves to control unwanted drives. It consists in a set of actions which results from rearrangements of information systems in the mind of the child and serves to contain aggressive or sexual impulses. The stereotyped action becomes a bland substitute for the hidden impulses. Thus, behavior can be decoded in this manner: "You see, I am such a good boy so that you'll not know what a brat I really am." As a form of control of the inner and outer world, the stereotype may be saying, "If everything is all right out there, then everything will be all right in me" or, conversely, "If I can control everything in me, everything will be in control out there."

I should like to emphasize the static quality of the stereotype as contrasted with a dynamic progressive style. In the progressive system an active communication exists between therapist and patient. In the stereotyped system, however, there is a distinct distance between the two. This seems to indicate a fixation, or a tenacious hold on the "bridge."

DISRUPTIVE SYSTEMS

The disruptive pattern appears as a result of a failure to control inner forces. If this were all, then the disruptive action would be merely a breakthrough of turbulent forces held in check by stereotyped action. It is not that simple. Disruptive behavior with its repetitive nature has an active quality of its own, which suggests that it may be another form of psychic system.

Some children are characteristically unable to maintain sustained directional play. After a short time, they smash the house of blocks they have just built or resort to other destructive action, such as throwing objects, spilling water, or breaking toys. They may stop productive play communication and retire to a corner to suck a thumb, or may retreat to the bathroom. On one level, we can say that these disruptive actions are reflections of turbulence in the child's home; he controls actively what he experienced passively. A child disrupts his own activities because he has experienced disruption. Accustomed to constant interruptions by criticism and disapproval, he internalizes the familiar pattern. It is his bridge to reality.

Activity is also relevant to a consideration of disruptive systems. The infant-mother relationship is not always quiet and peaceful. The baby enjoys rocking, carrying, and jouncing. A quiet crib may be threatening when he is separated from his mother. The child may feel an intensified quality in the mother when there is action.

The mother-child equilibrium can be affected by activity, and the activity itself can come to represent the presence of the mother. From this vantage point, when all is peaceful, the compulsion to disrupt may indicate that the action is an attempt to create the maternal imago and thus deal with separation anxiety. By the same token, when all is peaceful, the compulsion to disrupt points toward survival and quiet— toward death.

ORALITY AND FETISHISM

Thumbsucking and nailbiting are prototypes of transitional objects, substitute gratification, and psychic systems. In parts of the world where babies are carried about, there is practically no thumbsucking. When the mother is absent, the child can form a closed circuit that excludes mother. This could represent a transition but it also can remain as a lasting fixation. In the latter case, thumbsucking should not be seen as a wish for the mother, but as a displaced dependency which *excludes* the mother. It forms a closed circuit in the self. Thus, the child attains a measure of self-sufficiency and builds a primordial, self-contained system. However, the dependency remains, displaced onto thumb or finger, and later to the teddy bear or security blanket.

Fetishism, often described as a magical restitution of a threatened loss of the penis, may have its pregenital origin in a threatened loss of the mother. Here both survival and erotic powers are transferred to the object. This same power to protect, and to ward off danger, is invested in the rosary, the mezzuzah and in other amulets and icons. All these devices represent stereotyped systems, to which the child and later the adult cling. The need for these substitute objects varies with the level of the threat: dependency, for example, becomes intensified when these objects are libidinized, sources of pleasures in themselves.

The sense of certainty the child experiences while sucking his thumb or engaging in stereotyped play can be transformed subsequently into a tenacious hold upon ideas. Thus, repeated motor actions can become compulsions, and repeated ideas can become obsessions. Ideas can be treated as things or possessions belonging to the individual, and become a part of the self. Witness the little child who has "ideas of his own." A resistant patient once said, "My thoughts are the toys of my childhood. If I give them to you, you will take them and break them."

We are familiar with people who have "one-track minds" or are "set in their ways." These rigid and often unrealistic individuals process their behavior to fit their tenaciously guarded ideas. These ideas may not be destructive—in fact, there are many dedicated individuals who perform useful service to the community through their devotion to a constellation of ideas, a "cause." On the other hand history is full of bigots, zealots, and tyrants whose devotion to single purposes has been only detrimental to mankind. They demonstrate a distorted vicissitude of transitional object development.

THE PRIMORDIAL SYSTEM

I once suggested that the first ego system consists of a recognition or awareness of one's existence. The child becomes aware of his mother, who in turn becomes aware of him. The primordial system is one of basic harmony, in which the child equilibrates with the mother who has equilibrated with him. Not only is this the precursor of harmonious object relations, but also of harmony within the self. With a high measure of this internal harmony, a challenge presented by the oedipal triangle (the triadic relationship) can be mastered without difficulty. The child's storehouse of mastered experience, the ego or ego bank, enables him to solve, or resolve, a new experience, just as he did in the earlier critical learning periods, e.g., weaning.

When there is a reasonably well-formed equilibrium, the traumatic experiences of group relationships, puberty, and adulthood offer less of a serious threat. Life proceeds without an excess of burdensome or traumatic experience. Thus, the harmony within the self extends to the family, to the group, and later to society. The transitional state can serve as a bridge between various developmental stages.

Thumbsucking is a good example of a substitute for mothering. Instead of obtaining gratification from the mother, the child finds pleasure in sucking his thumb. The child sucks as if the mother were present. The security blanket, stuffed animals, and favorite toys become derivative maternal substitutes. A dearth of mothering can lead to a "hunger" which can then result in a state of near parasitism or prolonged dependency. It should be stressed that dependency has many vicissitudes. In a child's development, the feeling of completeness that arises from a stable equilibrium contributes to the development of a feeling of body intactness. During the male child's phallic phase of development, this intactness involves the presence of a penis. In a sense, this is an inheritance from the original mothering experience. The presence of a penis is equivalent to, and a derivative of, the presence of the mother. (The mother-penis equation is well-documented in the psychoanalytic literature.)

THE FATHERING ROLE

Thus far I have stressed the mother. But what of the father? From the dyadic point of view, he has the capacity to disturb the mother-child equilibrium.* He can act as an intruder into the symbiosis. To balance the disturbed equilibrium, there can be an increase in mothering need. In terms of the oedipal triangle, an intensification of affinity to the mother and a stance hostile to the father develop. In boys this is clear, but in girls the maternal functions can be invested in the father, the mother emerging as the intruding figure. In most cultures, fatherliness embodies strength for protection from outside intruders and the capacity to control unbridled impulse. Fatherliness defines society, the outside world. It is a symbol of purpose, goal, and determination. In some homes, however, fatherliness is embodied in the mother. This may lead to confusion in the child's gender identity.

A consistent father representation is incorporated into the ego, influencing its structure in a manner reminiscent of the Le Chatelier principle in physical chemistry. This principle states that when a new ingredient is added to a given system, the system rearranges itself to accommodate it. The process of ego formation is facilitated when the father authority is reasonable, considerate, and endowed with feelings of loyalty and solidarity. He catalyzes the representation of the outside world.

People in whom hunger for mothering has never been satisfied are permanently dependent. They can only fail to cross the bridge. I have described them as "those who go through life with the umbilical cord in one's hand looking for a place to plug it in." The need for mothering can manifest itself by constant attempts to latch onto people, either as individuals or in groups (e.g., the joiner). This is the root of promiscuity and infidelity. Mothering needs are satisfied vicariously by gratifying those needs in others.

As pointed out earlier, a substitute mother need not be a person. The investment of maternal qualities in things establishes distance from the original mother imago. In fact, distance can in itself become a maternal substitute. Then too, it is not difficult to find those whose mother substitute is money. Needless to say, money is represented differently in each of us. It provides security, which means that there will always be a mothering blanket. Money also implies power, and power masculinity, reiterating the mother-penis equivalence.

---

* *Editor's note:* The father can promote the mother-child equilibrium, not only by providing substitute mothering, but also by supporting the mother and serving as an object against whom aggressive discharges can be directed.

FIXED IDEAS

Some adults adhere to fixed ideas* with all the tenacity of the infant adhering to his thumb. As stated previously, concurrent with the establishment of fixed ideas or patterns there exists a distance from external objects. As the baby with his thumb manages without his mother, these people can manage in isolation while they cling to their fixed thoughts. Although they clamor for closeness, they do not allow it. Distance becomes an integral part of their inner lives and forms a system together with obsessional ideas or compulsive acts. This gestalt then behaves as a mothering system. These people are difficult to modify therapeutically because of the tenaciousness of their systems. They seem fixated on a fetishistic "bridge," while keeping their distance from external reality.

Obsessive-compulsive neurotics are particularly fixated on their mothering substitutes but everyone manifests some degree of this phenomenon. We all have our characteristics or eccentricities, our pet superstitions, charms, and specific ways of doing things. These are transitional object derivatives that serve as stabilizers or gyroscopes to keep ourselves on an even keel, to dispel uncertainty and to avert danger.

MASOCHISTIC PATTERNS

Many people search for an immediate maternal substitute but instead find pain and suffering. Rarely, however, is pain the primary motive. The maternal gratification of the compulsive eater is one of immediate satisfaction; obesity may be the unwanted result. Alcoholism and drug addiction are analogous, with their instantaneous relief and ultimate self-destruction. People using these and other action patterns, such as stealing or gambling, are characteristically unable to learn from experience. They are driven to reenact their old systems again and again, as though a template were laid at the fixation point to replicate new editions on the same pattern.

It is hard to comprehend the fixed action patterns of the masochist, where pain seems an end in itself. Organisms turn away from discomfort

---

Editor's note: Dr. Solomon has explored these ideas in a paper on delusion formation and fixed ideas. The relevance for an understanding of psychotic processes is clear. Furthermore it is interesting to relate the pathology of obsessional states with that of the psychoses, considering Dr. Solomon's discussion of fixed ideas. This may shed light on some of the difficulty encountered while attempting a therapeutic modification.

and pain, and toward pleasure, relief, and comfort; but pain and suffering are intertwined in the lifestyle of the masochist; his substitutive or fetishistic state is the masochism itself. Masochism is like hanging onto a high barbed wire fence afraid to let go. The pain of holding on is tolerated in the face of death.

Stereotyped activity is a device for attaining tranquility or certainty from turbulence and uncertainty. But side by side with this tranquility is the need to engage in disruptive or self-defeating behavior. This stereotyped and disruptive pattern suggests that in the face of uncertainty the subject seeks a quiet maternal substitute, which, indeed, is not available. In seeking mother, he finds inconsistency and turmoil. The mothering which the patient derived from his family was disruptive. Some masochistic individuals clearly epitomize the formula "You hate me, therefore I hate myself; now you love me because we both agree."

I have stressed the process by which some people develop fixed ideas or actions, but I have not mentioned the content of these ideas or the symbolic meaning of the repetitive actions. These constitute an intrinsic part of every analysis. In my opinion, however, they are not as important as some believe, for fixed ideas and actions do not disappear by content analysis alone. It is as though the patient perpetually remains on the bridge, unable to reach his goal. One element is the desire to carry out the parental unconscious wishes, essentially an act of compliance to the superego, acting as an anti-ego and appearing as self-effacement. In addition, neighborhood and cultural influences become involved. In these instances, the mothering derivatives stem from a compliant attitude to both parents and peers, yet also often from defiance of authority.

CERTAINTY-UNCERTAINTY

Let us return to the fixed idea that everything must remain uncertain. This schema motivates the individual to reach for something certain. This certainty, according to our thesis, should be a derivative of the original mothering. If it is associated with memory traces or fantasies of uncertainty, then the cycle will continually repeat itself, an oscillating or reverberating circuit by which the individual quests for certainty, finds uncertainty, and then initiates a new search for certainty. Thus, the ruminative thinking of the toddler phase is perpetuated by the persistence of uncertainty. Subsequently, fixed ideas can be invested at higher libidinal levels. For example, to impress others some people flaunt their ideas in a phallic, exhibitionistic manner. Some use their ideas in an anal-sadistic way to smear or besmirch others, and some "spiritualize" their ideas with a religious maternal investment.

These patients show two kinds of patterning. When there is external turbulence or chaos in their lives, they tend to be rigid in their ways, to show compulsive behavior, and to adhere to fixed or obsessional ideas. When external harmony exists, they develop a disrupting internal turbulence or chaos, acquire physical symptoms, or leave tasks or activities unfinished. These patterns are actually two sides of the same coin. Whether there is external chaos and internal rigidity or exterior calm and internal chaos, the theme is the same; there must be a sense of turmoil. This turmoil reflects an attempt to come to terms with a sadistic, orally introjected mother, an attempt to seek in perception a bridge to reality.

A MATTER OF LIFE AND DEATH

The obsessive-compulsive individual uses the substitute object, or fetishistic object, as a matter of life and death. The pattern is fixed, repetitive, and unchangeable. It is probably indicative of an early training in which not the act or thought but the child is considered bad. The punishment imposed by a relentless superego is ultimately death. Little wonder such people have tenuous object relations and are wrapped up in their inner worlds. Perfectionism is their watchword, and during adversity they act as if they anticipate capital punishment. These individuals seem to be wrapped in a cocoon, a security blanket of fixed ideas, repetitive actions, and individual idiosyncracies, with little communication to the outer world. They are alive, but distant from the world of reality.

THERAPEUTIC CONSIDERATIONS

It is important to know the original elements that entered the patient's life when he constructed his cocoon. These invariably include failure of the transitional object to bridge the gap from internal perception to outer reality. There are two main therapeutic tasks: (a) to tease away the defensive, fetishistic cocoon and (b) to encourage the establishment of a true transitional world in the person of the therapist. Therapeutic failures occur when too much effort is devoted to the origins of content and less to the patient's use of disclosures to prevent object closeness. The therapist can become "victimized" by the patient's tendencies to cling to his symptoms, to display his suffering, to punish his parents, or to defeat his therapist. A successful analysis allows the patient to emerge from his cocoon and spread his wings in a world closer to objective reality. It is not always easy. When, for a lifetime, life has been a threat, it is difficult to see it as a challenge.

CHAPTER 17

Winnicott's concept of potential space has been expanded by Anni Bergman; in chapter 10 she illustrated the varied course of developmental and transitional space in normal infants. In a further elaboration, Masud Khan now examines the use of the secret as a potential space. At the same time, we are presented a vivid example of how Winnicott could work with severely ill patients. Khan uses a therapeutic stance derived from an understanding of play and the role of the nonintrusive mother in creating a holding, facilitating, nurturing environment. As Khan says, the model is also the squiggle game that Winnicott used for child consultations. In it the potential space of a piece of paper becomes a shared space "where both Winnicott and the child mutually act, toward that significant moment when the experience of the child can be interpreted to the child."

The secret was also of interest to Phyllis Greenacre. She saw it as Janus-faced, with a progressive role in normal development and a regressive fetishistic aspect. She described how it could express a considerable amount of passive aggression. As fetish, it can freeze an individual's development, binding him in his illusions. As transitional phenomenon, the secret can furnish an inner resting place for resisting an intrusive mother or, in the analytic situation, an intrusive therapist. Here Khan demonstrates how a barrier to progress was surmounted in therapy by his capacity to share, sensitively and unobtrusively, the patient's secret use of his waiting room; ultimately she was able to share it.

L.B

SECRET AS POTENTIAL SPACE

M. Masud R. Khan

Be silent!
of Nothing,
ever,
to anyone—
there
in the embers
time
is singing.
—Osip Mandel'shtam

In our clinical work, sometimes, it is more important to sustain a person in living than to rid him of his illness. Winnicott summed this up in his statement, "absence of psycho-neurotic illness may be health, but it is not life" (1967, p. 100).

The demand for *life*, and if that is not possible, for *not living*, is made upon us by the patient and is not a bias of our restitutive omnipotence as therapists. When a patient makes this demand upon us, we have every right to *refuse* it, but not to confuse it. The patient is willing to stay ill and suffer its consequences so long as he or she is *living* or *not living*. If we try to subvert his life by a cure he either escapes us or gives up the right to be alive and ill and enters into a complicity with us which we mistake for "treatment alliance." Gilles Deleuze (1973), in spite of his mocking acerbity, raises an important issue. He argues that Melanie Klein establishes a contract with her patients in which the patients bring their intense experiences of living and she translates these into fantasies for them. He argues that Winnicott takes the psychoanalytic process to that limit where this contract is no longer viable. It becomes more than a mere question of translating the vécu into fantasies or interpreting it. What transpires with Winnicott is to reach that point when he has to share with the patient his experience. Deleuze asks whether this is a question of sympathy, empathy, or identification. He concludes: "What we feel is rather the necessity of a relationship which is neither legal, contractual or institutional."

Of course the philosophers are always wiser and more just than we are; they are not harassed by the ordinary daily humiliations of having to fail a person in his demands. The *word* is by its very nature inexhaustably munificent and more understanding than the *act*. Yet Deleuze is right: "Il faut y aller, il faut partager son état." But to share and partake of another's predicament implies time and space. What is the nature of *this* time and space with such persons?

Philosophically to comprehend and share "des états vécus" of a dead genius like Nietzsche, whom Deleuze so insightfully writes about in the context I quote him from, is one thing: to make oneself available for *use* (to cite Winnicott's concept) to the *living* Nietzsche was another matter altogether. None succeeded.

On January 4, 1889, Nietzsche wrote to George Brandes from Turin:

> To my friend Georg! Once you discovered me, it was no great feat to find me: the difficulty now is to lose me . . . the crucified. [Nietzsche 1889, p. 345]

If Deleuze were to make the retort that we analysts are all too adept at *losing* those who do not fit our machinery of cure it would be hard to refute him.

Still I believe it is becoming clinically possible for us to meet the *need* of such persons who insist on *living* outside contractual or institutional relationships.

During the course of any psychoanalytic treatment we witness a patient inhabit and fluctuate through many spaces—inside/outside, subjective/objective—and we share these with him. The total analytic situation meets the various demands of the patient in his different states through three modalities: the analytic process, the analytic relation (transference), and the analytic setting. The analytic process actualizes through interpretation and deals with the hidden meaning (Freud), the absent meaning (Green), and the potential meaning (Khan) of the patient's communications. It is here that the analyst is par excellence the "supplementary ego" (Heimann 1956) of the patient. The transference relationship organizes that affectivity in the patient which enables him to project the roles of significant figures from his past onto the analyst, in the here and now of the analytic situation. In recent decades two more functions have been added to the analyst's role in the transference relationship, namely those of *holding* (Winnicott) and *containing* (Bion). The use of the analytic setting by the patient has come under scrutiny only recently, largely through the research of Winnicott and Balint.

In classical analysis, a patient's capacity to use the analytic setting was taken for granted, and most of the analytic literature is devoted to discussions of a patient's use or abuse of the analytic process and the transference relationship. The research of Winnicott (1955), Balint (1968), and Milner (1969) have progressively sensitized us to the fact that a patient in certain states of distress and disturbance may be able to use only the analytic space, while he finds himself incapable of using the analytic process or the transference relationship.

In my clinical experience, patients use the analytic space in two distinct ways: as concrete space to be in and as potential space, where they sustain moods and larval psychic experiences which their ego-capacities as yet cannot actualize. I am borrowing the concept of *potential space* from Winnicott. In his paper "The Location of Cultural Experience" (1967) he states:

> From the beginning the baby has maximally intense experiences *in the potential space between the subjective object and the object objectively perceived*, perceived, between me-extensions and the not-me. This potential space is at the interplay between there being nothing but me and there being objects and phenomena outside omnipotent control.
>
> Every baby has his or her own favourable or unfavourable experience here. Dependence is maximal. The potential space happens only *in relation to a feeling of confidence* on the part of the baby, that is, confidence related to the dependability of the mother-figure or environmental elements, confidence being the evidence of dependability that is becoming introjected. [p. 100]

Winnicott himself has not examined the analytic setting in terms of this hypothesis. Yet it seems to me that his squiggle-game consultations give us a vivid account of how a child uses paper as potential space in order to be privately alone with Winnicott. And this potential space of the paper is a *shared* space, where both Winnicott and the child *mutually act* toward that "significant moment" when the experience of the child can be interpreted to him (cf. Winnicott 1970).

The most interesting clinical example of how a patient creates a secret potential space is given to us by Marion Milner (1969) in her "*The Hands of the Living God.*" Milner recounts how her patient, Susan, had made a drawing the night before her first consultation. The patient had not mentioned or shown this drawing to Milner during some ten years of analysis. In her discussion of Susan's drawings, Milner does not elaborate upon the necessity for Susan, at first, to draw in secret privacy outside the analytic setting. In contrast to Winnicott's squiggle-game, drawings *with* the children, Susan, when she had first started to draw, could share her drawings with Milner only *after* the event. Susan's use of the potential space of the paper is an essential part of her "self-cure," to use Milner's phrase. Something from the total analytic experience is suspended by Susan, to be actualized later in the potential space of the paper. I am borrowing from André Green's new slant (1973) on Freud's concept of deferred action. Green postulates:

> One major capacity of the psychic structure is the capacity to cut off, to suspend an experience, while it is still going on. This is not for the purpose of observing the experience as in the conscious mental functioning, but to shut off the awareness of it in order to recreate it, in one's own way later on. It is important to see that this cutting off or inner splitting is a precondition for the establishment of further links by association. We should distinguish the moment of the experience and the moment in which it becomes meaningful.

It seems to me that for Susan, at first, the *experience* of herself in the analytic situation became meaningful only as a *secret*. The secret of her drawing in her own isolate privacy. The potential space of the paper captures and articulates this *secret*. I shall now give some clinical material to show how a very young girl created a *secret* and used it as the potential space where she could continue to be, quite apart from her inner life or familial existence, in the outside world.

A colleague had urgently asked me to see a young woman because according to him she was having a psychotic breakdown. This patient, whom I shall call Caroline, arrived in a most confused and agitated state. All she could tell me in the first consultation was how her husband had jilted her in a most brutal and humiliating manner a week earlier. He had now left her to live with another woman. She kept repeating "He has destroyed me!" and her crying was both intense and incessant. I was very struck by her utter incapacity to relate to me. She had hardly looked at me once during some two hours of consultation, even though she was sitting facing me. I had been told by the referring consultant that she was a doctor and for the past week had been unable to work. Alongside the acute feeling that she could not relate to me, there grew in me across the time of the consultation a sentient conviction that Caroline felt safe and viable in the space of my consultation room. It was this latter conviction that persuaded me to say to Caroline that I was willing to take her in analytic treatment if she so wished. Caroline accepted my offer with a blank absence of response.

Caroline turned up for her sessions five times a week with a punctuality almost frightening. The absence of resistance left me clueless as to what was happening to her, inside or outside analysis. Her mood-swings were dangerously volatile. Fortunately I had been able to find a physician of great ability to look after Caroline medically. It would have been impossible for me to hold Caroline in analysis or in life without the medicating care provided by my physician colleague. Caroline was not a silent patient. She either cried vehemently, moaning "My husband has destroyed me," or would arrive in a manic state and talk wildly about everything and everybody in her environment but herself. After some three months of analysis I knew no more about who Caroline was than I had after the first consultation.

It was very tempting to interpret her absence or, to use André Green's more telling phrase, her suspension of experience, as resistance, either from anxiety or hostile suspiciousness. There was a distinct flavor of secretiveness to all her behavior in analysis, and I chose to respect it, both as her right and as her privacy.

Then one day an accident happened. At a traffic light Caroline banged her car into another in front of her. She had not noticed the lights changing. A most courteous gentleman had emerged from the other car to look into the damage done. Caroline was so resourceless in the situation that he offered to meet her for lunch the next day and arrange matters. He was much taken by her. Caroline is a plump and pleasant-looking girl of some twenty-seven years of age, and there is an ebullient helplessness in her general way of being that is rather attractive. Within a week Caroline was living in the care of her new friend in his house. This was indeed a great relief and respite both for her physician and for me. Her mood-swings had been so excessive that we had started to think seriously of hospitalizing her. The newfound friend made this unnecessary. He was deeply devoted to her and had the patience of Job with her mad antics. The moment Caroline started this relationship quite a different person emerged from her being.

Caroline had been married for some six years and lived most docilely with an outrageously cruel and delinquent young husband. Now Caroline herself began to act out and test the love and care of her friend with a vehement vengefulness. She mistrusted his motives and was violently rageful. She put him into the most embarrassing social situations. Fortunately for everyone concerned, her friend had an inexhaustible capacity to contain and tolerate her nuisances. In analysis her cry now changed from "I have been destroyed by my husband" to "I have lost myself somewhere in my life." It is not my intention to discuss this phase of her treatment here. Gradually Caroline began to personalize into a coherent being and her moods became related to her actions.

It was at this stage, when she had been in treatment for some nine months, that one day she arrived for her session and before lying down paused and said to me: "I know now what is the matter with me! I have hidden myself." She lay down and continued: "I have never told you what I did at three and a half years of age." She recounted how one day when she was that age she had taken two silver candlesticks from her mother's dining room and buried them in the garden. There had been a lot of searching around for them. Police had been called and eventually the insurance had paid up the price. They were an expensive item. She had a sense of all that was going on in the house about the candles but said nothing. Some five months after this event the parents had moved to a new house in a different city. The whole episode had been forgotten. Then one day when she was nine years of age her parents while on vacation had returned with her for a visit to the old house, of which they were very fond. The new occupants of the house were friends of her parents. When everyone was having tea Caroline had gone into the garden, dug out the candlesticks and returned them to her parents. She concluded her account laughingly: "Real hell broke loose and my father gave me a big thrashing."

In the weeks following this communication Caroline was able to give a detailed account of the familial circumstances surrounding her act. When she was three her mother had given birth to premature twins after suffering a toxaemia of pregnancy. The whole climate in the home had changed. A nurse had been employed to look after the twins, both girls. The mother had sunk into a severe depression and was for years unable to take an active part in the running of the family. The parents hadn't even taken a vacation until their visit to the old house the summer the mother started to work again. It was then that the patient had dug up the candlesticks and given them back to her parents.

From the very beginning of her treatment, I had from choice allowed Caroline the privacy of her antics, inside and outside analysis. There was a definite risk involved which I felt it was her need and demand that I take by providing clinical coverage and holding (in terms of time and space) so that she could *transcribe* whatever she was reaching after in her chaotic and bewildered way. What aggravated this situation further was Caroline's incapacity for work during this phase; she had to give up her job, and hence was stranded with herself all day long. Her friend went to work early and returned late in the evening. Because of her confused mental state I could get no true picture of her daily existence; not only was each session an isolated *happening* each day, with no before and after, but it was also a clutter of bizarre bits and pieces of her random perceptions and volatile affects. Yet I had this sure feeling Caroline was making a very private *use* of the analytic space, and gradually even of me as a person. But she kept it all strictly to herself.

Once she told me about the candlestick episode everything changed in her manner of talking in analysis. She had taken some three sessions to tell all the story. This was the first time Caroline was able to sustain continuity of theme from one session to the next. What was even more important was that I began to have some inkling into her way of *using* me. I interpreted to her that by burying the candlesticks she had found a way of *absenting* herself from the changed and traumatizing familial environment. I deliberately used the word *absenting* rather than *hiding*. Here I was exploiting a concept of André Green's (1973). I interpreted that the candlesticks symbolized all the good nourishing experiences of her infancy and early childhood from good enough mothering. She then split off these experiences and *absented* them from the ongoing life of the family, in which she felt precarious and could merely exist, and which threatened to destroy even the goodness of her past relation with her mother. There was a distinct precocity in her capacity to use such a self-protective maneuver at this early age. The burying of the candlesticks created a secret where she could continue in suspended animation a part of her which she could no longer live and share with her parents, especially her mother. The *secret* encapsulated her own *absent* self.

Caroline responded to my interpretation by telling me of repetitive psychosomatic illnesses between the age of five and nine. These illnesses had kept her away from school. She said she never missed going to school during these illnesses, even though she was an active, sportive, and gregarious child at school. She added: "I had to withdraw every now and then and be with myself it seems." To which I said: "To be with yourself and with your secret at the same time."

It was when we were working in this area of her creating a secret where she could suspend a part of herself that Caroline asked me: "Why have you never interpreted that over the past two months? Almost every Friday I have forgotten something in the waiting room or don't you know of it?" I told her that I knew of it all right, since my staff always had informed me, and I had instructed them to return whatever item it was to her on Monday when she would return to analysis. She quizzed me: "Why didn't you tell me?" And I answered: "Because you never told me yourself and I respected your secret play with the waiting room and my staff." She became pensive and started to cry quietly. I think it was the first time I had seen Caroline cry in a session where the affect was related to what was being said or experienced. After a while I interpreted to her that I had registered the fact that she had started to leave things behind during the phase in which she had become very suspicious that her man-friend was trying to control her life. I interpreted further that I had understood it to mean that she was using the space of the waiting room to leave behind over the weekend some object that stood for a very private bit of herself. Thus a bit of her was safely there for her to collect on Monday, also saving her friend from whatever anger or rage might erupt from this part of her. I told her also that now, knowing about the candlestick episode, I would say that she was using my waiting room, as she had used the garden in her childhood, to find a place where she could leave a bit of herself in secret. The reason, I added, that she had not used the consultation room was that I might have noticed the "left object" straight away and she would have had to take it with her or, if I found it later, that I would sabotage her secret by interpreting it. She couldn't take that risk.

From this point onward her whole mode of communicating in the sessions changed. I was surprised to witness in her a joyous capacity to recall and narrate experiences from all areas and phases of her life with a sparkling vividness. I am not concerned with that material in this chapter. Briefly, the story as it emerged was that she had four buoyant carefree years, from nine to thirteen years of age. Then the twins had fallen ill with a crippling illness that took years to remedy. During this period Caroline became a devoted ally of her mother in the nursing of her sisters. Just as that was ending she met her future husband and *capitulated* to him. She had used that phrase. He was truly evil and she became his willing victim. She had given up all hope of personal life shared with someone. This had ended with his brutal jilting of her and her breakdown.

The argument of this chapter is that a person can *hide* himself into symptoms or he can *absent* himself into a secret. Here the secret provides a potential space where an absence is sustained in suspended animation. Like the antisocial tendency (Winnicott 1956), the secret carried a hope that one day the person would be able to emerge out of it, be found and met, and thus become a whole person, sharing life with others. I am grateful to Pontalis for drawing my attention to a passage in Freud's letter to Fliess on December 1896:

As you know, I am working on the assumption that our psychical mechanism has come about by a process of stratification: the material present in the shape of memory-traces is from time to time subjected to a rearrangement in accordance with fresh circumstances—is, as it were, transcribed. Thus what is essentially new in my theory is the thesis that memory is present not once but several times over, that it is registered in various species of "signs." [Freud 1954, p. 173]

What, however, has been even more enlightening for me toward an understanding of the function of a secret is Laplanche and Pontalis's (1973) commentary on the letter:

This idea might lead one to the view that all phenomena met with in psycho-analysis are placed under the sign of retroactivity, or even of retroactive *illusion*. This is what Jung means when he talks of retrospective fantasies: according to Jung, the adult reinterprets his past in his fantasies, which constitute so many symbolic expressions of his current problems. On this view reinterpretation is a way for the subject to escape from the present "demands of reality" into an imaginary past.

Seen from another angle, the idea of deferred action may also suggest a conception of temporality which was brought to the fore by philosophers and later adopted by the various tendencies of existential psycho-analysis: consciousness constitutes its own past, constantly subjecting its meaning to revision in conformity with its "project." [p. 112]

This discussion helps me to understand retrospectively a certain quality that characterized Caroline's behavior before she told me of her secret. Her way of talking randomly struck me often as rather mad. I could interpret all sorts of fantasies into it but in fact it was meaningless. There was no retroactive elaboration, psychically or symbolically, of any experience. Now I can begin to see how Caroline's secret had helped her consciousness *escape* its own past.

She lived in the instant here and now of explosive affects and random behavior. I can see now that what is hidden inside or repressed lends itself to endless rearrangements and even retroactive *illusion*. But what is absented into a secret stays out of reach for any sort of further elaboration. Hence I now consider erroneous my remark that the candlesticks *symbolized* early good relationship to her mother. What was important for Caroline was the *act* of burying them and not any symbolic meaning they may have had. This *act* concretized and encapsulated into a secret the point at which her growth in *mutuality* with her mother had been disrupted. The potential space of the secret imprisoned that fact and kept it frozen. But it also disabled Caroline from being able to elaborate or correct it in terms of new experience. The location of a secret of this type in psychic topography is that it is neither inside nor outside a person. A person cannot say: "I have a secret inside me." They are the secret, yet their ongoing life does not partake of it. In analysis what Caroline could report was either the bric-a-brac of daily existence or nothing. And to have treated her incapacity as resistance would have engendered only reactive guilt in her. This is a very specific issue with such patients: their tendency toward compliance makes them overreceptive to any interpretation that makes them feel guilty. Hence my quote from Deleuze, who rightly protests the translation of lived life into mere fantasies. Such interpretation of fantasies creates a pseudopsychic reality, to which the patient gets addicted. This leads to those interminable deep analyses which we often hear about these days.

Clinically, it is only if we succeed in gradually creating an atmosphere of *mutuality* with these patients that they can share their secret with us. This sharing of the secret amounts to that "experience of mutuality" Winnicott (1970) calls the essence of the mother's capacity to adapt to that baby's need. What had enabled Caroline to share her secret was my capacity to contain and hold all the confusion and risk her behavior perpetrated inside and outside analysis over the first eight months, as well as my capacity to allow her to *use* the waiting room in a private way for the weekend gap in analysis.

Lastly, I want to suggest that the creation of a secret creates a *gap* (Green 1973) in the person's psyche which is reactively screened with all sorts of bizarre events—intrapsychic or interpersonal. We as clinicians are then required to discriminate between the true experience of such persons and their reactive behavior. In Deleuze's phrase, these patients have to be enabled to *share* their experience with us, not merely report on it in terms of fantasies or through symptomatic gestures. What was important for Caroline when she left things behind, like her umbrella or a packet of chocolates or a book, was the *act* of leaving them. It was this *act* I held for her and unobtrusively shared until she was ready to share it mutually.

I have tried to give a clinical example of how a child absented herself into a secret when her ongoing life with her mother broke down, and how she gradually linked up with it in her analysis. Secret is only one way of encapsulating such experiences. Pseudologia fantastica often provides similar potential space to a person. And sometimes even repetitively forgotten dreams during analysis have this function.

I have found in the autobiography of Carl Jung, *Memories, Dreams, Reflections,* an interesting corroboration of my hypothesis that the secret can provide a space in which the threatened ongoing life of a child can be sustained intact. Jung recounts how in his childhood when he started to associate with his "rustic schoolmates," he found that they alienated him from himself. The years from seven to nine were full of turbulent inner crisis for Jung. Then at the age of ten "my disunion with myself and uncertainty in the world at large led to an action which at the time was quite incomprehensible to me." What Jung did was to carve a manikin on two inches of his ruler, wrap it in wool, place a stone by it, and put all these in a case which he hid in "the forbidden attic" of his house. He wrote letters to the manikin in a secret language, and would from time to time clamber into the loft unnoticed to leave them there with the manikin. Jung concludes his narrative:

> The meaning of these actions, or how I might explain them, never worried me. I contented myself with the feeling of newly-won security, and was satisfied to possess something that no-one knew and no-one could get at. It was an inviolable secret which must never be betrayed, for the safety of my life depended on it. Why that was so I did not ask myself. It simply was so.
> This possession of a secret had a very powerful formative influence on my character: I consider it the essential factor of my boyhood. [pp. 34–35]

REFERENCES

Balint, M. (1968). *The Basic Fault.* London: Tavistock.

Deleuze, G. (1973). Pensée nomade. *Nietzsche Aujourd'hui.* 10/18.

Freud, S. (1954). *The Origins of Psycho-Analysis: Letters to Wilhelm Fliess.* London: Imago.

Green, A. (1973). Introduction to the discussion on the genetic point of view. Unpublished manuscript.

——— (1973). Le double et l'absent. *Critique* 312.

Heimann, P. (1956). Dynamics of transference interpretation. *International Journal of Psycho-Analysis* 37.

Jung, C. J. (1963). *Memories, Dreams, Reflections.* London: Collins and Routledge and Kegan Paul.

Khan, M. M. R. (1974). The hermeneutic triangle. *Scientific Bulletin.*

Laplanche, G., and Pontalis, J-B. (1973). *The Language of Psycho-Analysis.* London: Hogarth Press.

Mandel'shtam, O. (1973). *Selected Poems.* Cambridge, England: River Press.

Milner, M. (1969). *The Hands of the Living God.* London: Hogarth Press.

Nietzsche, F. (1889). *Selected Letters of Friedrich Nietzsche*. Chicago: Chicago University Press.

Winnicott, D. W. (1955). Varieties of transference. In *Collected Papers*. London: Tavistock, 1958.

————— (1956). The anti-social tendency. In *Collected Papers*. London: Tavistock, 1958.

————— (1967). The location of cultural experience. In *Playing and Reality*. New York: Basic Books, 1971.

————— (1970). The mother-infant experience of mutuality. In *Parenthood: Its Psychology and Psychopathology*. Boston: Little, Brown.

CHAPTER 18

David Parrish studies the concept of a twin as both a transitional object and a transitional phenomenon. Presenting his clinical data within a developmental framework, he discusses the problems of twins in the context of the differentiation of self- and object-representations, internalization, identification, and separation. He considers the work of Stevenson and Busch in terms of the first and second transitional objects. These latter, occurring after the age of two, are more related to toys and obviously arise in infants with a more advanced ego organization. Here Parrish uses Busch's criteria to determine whether the twin in his case functioned as a transitional object.

Winnicott held that transitional objects can be animate and human as well as inanimate. Thus the mother as well as siblings and pets are possible transitional objects. In chapter 19 Volkan and Kavanaugh consider cats in this light, while in chapter 13 Ralph Greenson presents several instances in which patients used their analysts for this function. Transitional processes with animate objects are more silent, more camouflaged, and hence, less observable than with inanimate. Further, animate transitional objects are less subject to control. For example, while a teddy bear can be carried about and taken to bed with little difficulty, this is less possible with a dog or cat, and even less so with a sibling or mother. A transitional phenomenon would of course provide even greater plasticity than an inanimate object; yet in his observations Busch could find little he could assign to this category. Of course, such transitional phenomena as fantasies or secrets would be the least observable structures of all, and their absence from Busch's observations should not surprise us. Regarding the choice between animate or inanimate transitional objects, Abrams and Neubauer indicate in chapter 9 that it can be constitutionally determined. As to what determines the choice between objects and phenomena, however, we can at present only speculate. Parrish, aware of these problems, establishes that the twin was used first as a transitional object and later evolved into a transitional fantasy, allowing more flexibility and control.

L.B.

TRANSITIONAL OBJECTS AND PHENOMENA
IN A CASE OF TWINSHIP

David Parrish

Under certain circumstances various elements of a twinship can be related to transitional objects and phenomena.[1] Thus far the literature has not taken this into account. This chapter, based on the analysis of dizygotic twins, was conceptualized in the light of a review and reappraisal of transitional phenomena (Coppolillo 1967, 1976; Horton, Louy, and Coppolillo 1974), transitional object designation (Stevenson 1954, Greenacre 1970, Gaddini and Gaddini 1970, Busch et al. 1973), identification (Leonard 1961, Meissner 1970, 1971, and 1972), denial and separateness (Modell 1961), and internalization and externalization (Loewald 1962, 1970, Schaefer 1968).

Winnicott (1953) commented that the interrelating of "inner reality" and "outer reality," though a lifelong task, is one that has priority in childhood. The establishment of proper illusion is essential to this interrelating. The transitional object, seemingly representing and belonging to both the mother and the self, participates in this illusion. It is labeled neither completely real nor completely unreal, neither all me nor all not-me; hence it occupies an "intermediate area." Winnicott stated that any thought, idea, concept, object, or person[2] may function as a transitional object provided it is experienced in this intermediate area. He used the term *transitional phenomenon* for nonsubstantive forms filling the same function. While transitional phenomena are more difficult to observe, Winnicott clearly was describing subtle and widespread phenomena not limited to the experience of early childhood.

Before discussing secondary transitional objects and phenomena it is necessary to examine the earlier papers on primary and secondary transitional objects. Stevenson (1954) separated transitional objects into primary (first objects) and secondary (toys), suggesting that characteristics of secondary transitional objects include "personification of the object and projection onto it of human emotions." Busch et al. (1973)

argued that primary transitional objects ("the first transitional object") appear within or near the first year of life; secondary transitional objects ("the second transitional object") are established after the age of two. An attempt was made to differentiate the primary transitional object from transient objects. The first transitional object must have a duration of at least one year, possess a soothing quality that allays anxiety, must not directly meet an oral or libidinal need, must be selected by the child rather than provided by the parents, and finally, cannot be part of the child's body.

CLINICAL STUDY: CASE HISTORY

A careful examination of the patient's history, his behavior during the analysis and the transference neurosis indicated the presence of a fixated transitional relationship that originated with his dominant twin. This transitional relationship formed an extensive and central pathogenic element that extended from childhood through adolescence into adulthood. It finally emerged in a new edition in the analytic transference. Consequently, the main focus will be on historical elements and analytic material pertinent to the formation and resolution of his regressive transitional objects and phenomena.

The patient, a dizygotic twin, was a twenty-five-year-old, unmarried male graduate student who requested analysis for treatment of depression and anxiety secondary to his attempts to separate from his fraternal twin brother, whom he described as dominant. The diagnosis was neurotic depression. While some of his characteristics suggest a narcissistic personality organization, the degree of object constancy and the extent and efficiency of his secondary autonomous ego functions were more consistent with a neurotic formulation.

The problem of twinship pervaded his entire life. His brother had been born ten minutes before him, ten minutes that seemed "like ten years." Convinced that his brother occupied a position of ascendancy, he spent his entire life "trying to catch up." Because of this dependent relationship with his brother, his attitude toward competition and individuation was intensely ambivalent, first with his twin and later with peers: "He led the way and I would follow. If I became more successful than my brother, I had the feeling that I would be left alone."

Despite marked physical differences during early infancy and childhood, the mother treated his brother and him identically, even calling the patient a nickname which fused their two names. Later in childhood she began to favor the patient's brother.

The mother, a cool, narcissistic career woman, was often absent from the home, leaving the care of the twins to a nursemaid. He gave no history of a primary transitional object such as a blanket or diaper. His early toys were shared with his brother; he recalled episodes of play with their wooden animals. During this play the brothers communicated in a language of their own. Later the patient and his twin shared a flute, even though this was not dictated by economic necessity. His earliest memories included awareness of a playmate and constant companion; but only at the age of five did he realize that this was his twin. Brief periods of separation from his brother during visits to different relatives elicited anxiety. When the patient was ten, he suffered a ruptured appendix and had a prolonged hospitalization and convalescence. This separation from his twin brother left him "desolate and depressed."

During childhood and into adolescence, the patient sought his brother as a playmate more frequently than his brother sought him. As mentioned earlier, he allowed his brother to precede him in new activities, a practice that persisted into his adult life. His brother was first to masturbate, to date, to have heterosexual experience, and to marry. This constant awareness of his "older" brother helped him to feel consoled and secure. The brother, however, was frequently sadistic, beating him and taking his male friends and girl friends for himself. There were times when the patient could defend himself and temporarily overcame his brother. However, he said that when he became aware that he was winning, he felt "anxious and had to give up." Most of the patient's friendships as a child and adolescent were mediated through his brother. When the patient encountered a situation in which he wished to accomplish something his brother had not, it was first necessary to fantasize that his brother was doing it or that he was carrying out the activity in the guise of his brother. This practice continued into adulthood.

The parents augmented the patient's dependence on his twin through a family myth in which the brother was more artistic, socially adept, and academically successful. The patient was characterized by the parents as "weak, submissive, and inept." Although not the case, this depressing negative image was tenacious, providing a focal point on which his parents could project their hopes and failures. This mythic system played an important role in the choice of symptoms and the development of character traits, i.e., masochism, passivity, and depression as well as a pattern of alternating successes and failures. These failures were shown to the parents, while his successes were kept from them. This need to appear unsuccessful, to avoid an overt rivalry with his twin, extended into adulthood. If he received A's in school, he reported C's to his mother and brother to avoid their criticism and the subsequent feelings of guilt and fear. During the analysis he became aware that this fear was similar to the feeling he experienced when his brother overpowered and choked him.

Throughout his life the patient had made repeated attempts to separate from his brother, attempts which invariably failed and which resulted in increasing depression and passivity. Two years before the patient's analysis, the twin brother received a brief inpatient psychiatric treatment, an event which intensified the patient's anxiety and depression; he thought he would also "crack up" and require psychiatric hospitalization. The patient was strongly threatened by his twin's illness and fantasied that he had caused his brother's condition by kicking him in the head in utero.

CLINICAL STUDY: ANALYTIC MATERIAL

Initially, the patient saw the analyst as possessing the characteristics of his previous therapist, and anticipated even greater support and direction. He had sent his former therapist a pen as a gift, and had received no acknowledgment. Somehow the analyst was expected to know of this gift and comment on it. This was only one of numerous early examples of how he saw categories of people as stereotyped, lacking individuality. A tendency to view separate people as halves of dyads was particularly evident with males, although present to a lesser degree with females; it was most pronounced when associated with the need to reject the people involved. The patient projected his own feelings onto these dyadic individuals. He saw his graduate school professors as halves of dyads, and unsatisfactory girl friends were exactly like other unsatisfactory girl friends. Early in the analysis, he was surprised and puzzled when he suddenly became aware that the analyst did not have horn-rimmed glasses and short hair like his previous therapist. Not only did the patient unconsciously expect others to have physical counterparts, but on a more conscious basis he expected them to have relationships similar to the one he had with his twin. In addition, he would perceive that one of the "pair" was dominant. While the patient had some conscious expectation that all relationships would have these dyadic qualities he retained a certain mistrust of this expectation; this gave it the not completely "real" yet not completely "unreal" paradoxical characteristic of an experience in the "intermediate area."

Later transference development cast the therapist as a "twin-analyst" (Joseph 1960) who appeared in dreams and associations possessing characteristics similar to his bullying, dominant twin brother. During this phase, the patient reported a dream in which he was rowing a boat, accompanied by a girl friend. The twin-analyst rowed up in another boat and began seductive overtures toward the girl, attempting to take her away from the patient the same way his brother might have. The patient refused to surrender the girl friend and a chase ensued. He alternated between giving her up and embarking on renewed attempts to escape with her. Finally he did escape and took the girl with him. He felt a rage mixed with despair.

Increasingly the analyst was used in fantasy and dream material as an intermediary to new activity and friendships, just as his twin brother had been used. Gradually the patient shifted the analyst into the position of a soothing benevolent twin, a twin who allowed him a measure of autonomy, individuality, and consolation. This change in the transference was evident in a dream in which he invited the analyst to a dinner party at his home. The patient and his girl friend were hosts who occupied the center of attention and admiration. The patient commented, "I wanted you to see me with an attractive girl, someone you might pick for me." His associations to this dream made it clear that he had begun to see the analyst as someone who supported the expression of his libidinal and aggressive drives. Now he could have a girl of his own.

As the analysis continued he began to see physical and personality differences in others as signs of identity and individuality. Prior to the analysis, differences were seen as defects (large front teeth, aquiline noses, coarse pubic hair in girls) which disqualified the individuals as desirable, idealized twin partners.

With the resolution of the patient's attachment to his brother and the reduction of fixated transitional objects and phenomena, considerable oedipal material was uncovered. It became clear that certain elements of the twinship had come to represent and defend against feared oedipal wishes. At this stage, dream material represented the analyst as a forbidding and castrating father, the father who had "abandoned" him at the age of ten, when the parents were divorced. Later the analyst was transformed into a tolerant, encouraging father who allowed him further autonomy.

When the termination date was set, the patient, under the pressure of threatened loss, reverted to using the analyst as a supporting but no longer intrusive intermediary object; he used the analytic sessions as soothing, secure experiences. New feeling about these sessions were reported: "After a long day at school I now look forward to coming to my analytic hour. It's restful and peaceful here and I get energy to face the next day. It's like coming to a comfortable home after work."

Months before termination of the analysis, he made a trip to Europe and the city where he had spent the first eighteen years of his life. "I visited places in England and France where I had gone with my family. I had some unhappy times at some of these places. However, it seemed different this time because I was able to enjoy those places for myself." He was able to internalize some of his earlier experiences as a result of this trip and separate them futher from the internalized introject of his twin brother. When he returned, the phase of transference regression had ceased. Within a short time his analysis was terminated, coincident with his successful graduation from school and his departure from the city to follow a course of further training.

CLINICAL STUDY:
CHARACTERISTICS OF TRANSITIONAL
OBJECTS AND PHENOMENA

The transitional forms manifested by this patient satisfy some of the criteria outlined by Winnicott (1953) for (primary) transitional objects. However, their characteristics qualify them more precisely as secondary transitional objects (Stevenson 1954).

Coppolillo (1967), Fintzy (1971), and Volkan (1973) have presented borderline or markedly ego defective cases, in which transitional relationships were pathological. The transitional forms were therefore immature and more easily identifiable in terms of the (primary) transitional objects described by Winnicott. This analytic case material was from a neurotic whose transitional objects and phenomena were more mature, though fixated. The clear identification of them as secondary transitional forms is based on the qualities ascribed to transitional relationships in a later phase of development, i.e., they are chosen after two years of age. The patient's strong early attachment to his brother extended beyond symbiotic boundaries to constitute a not-me possession that occupied the position of an intermediate experience and territory in his relation to outside objects, both animate and inanimate. The other, internal twin functioned also in the role of a toy, a toy that was personified with qualities of the two personalities. This internal representation also existed as an extension and projection of the patient's own body ego. The patient's twin brother, as well as his internalized imago, became the focus for the continual projection of the patient's own affects. From childhood, separation from his brother resulted in marked anxiety and depression, which attested to the significance and strength of this attachment. The acceptance of his twin as a transitional relationship resulted in an object that was animate, age-equal, reciprocal, and intrusive. This choice interfered with the development of the patient's identity and autonomy. Throughout his life the patient used the internalized imago of his twin to mediate between self and not-self. (A further discussion of the role of the dominant twin in the formation of the patient's secondary transitional object will be presented in a later section.)

In the course of the analysis the patient began to substitute the analyst for his twin and treated the analyst as a secondary transitional object, albeit an interfering and fixated one. The process of differentiation was initiated by helping the patient become more aware of his fusion with his brother. To hasten the separation process, the analyst needed to function as a transitional form that was progressive rather than, as his twin had been, fixated. By persistently delineating his relation to other objects and to the analyst and by stressing their individual characteristics, the movement from fixated to progressive transitional relationship was augmented. For example, when the patient received a low grade from one professor in school he fantasied that professors in other courses were brothers who would come to know of his failure and also give him low marks. It was necessary for the analyst to indicate that this was most unlikely, since they had different names and different physical characteristics. He gradually understood how this fantasy was related to his experience with the twinship, where their identities were fused in the intermediate area, where he and his brother shared knowledge.

DISCUSSION

Intensification of the primary intertwin relationship has been noted by many observers, and has been associated with extended, often severe disturbances in personality development. The single child, excessively dependent upon the mother, is frequently unable to complete the separation of mother and child imagoes; twins, excessively dependent upon each other, are also subject to confusion of self-imagoes. The analytic material present here was particularly pertinent to these problems. The patient's persistent use of his twin, in fantasy and reality, to relate to new objects and activities and to maintain illusions of unity as well as separateness had extended through childhood into his adult life. The twin undergoing analysis possessed a marked impairment of his self-image and a limited separate identity. In effect, a partial fusion of self- and object-representation with diffuse ego boundaries existed. At times the twinship preempted the relationship with the mother, interfering with normal formation and resolution of the oedipal complex. Further-more, the narcissistic and anaclitic object choice hampered object constancy and mature relationships. While the patient's relationship with his brother had the appearance of a constricting, symbiotic object relationship, there were important differences: despite his impairments, the patient had the capacity for a limited love of objects perceived as separate from the self; also, he could maintain these love relationships in the face of limitations and frustrations.

In more normal development, the soothing illusions that accompany the successful negotiation of previous psychosexual and ego stages provide a secure platform for movement into later phases. However, the patient's illusion of the me/not-me aspect of his twinship, while characteristic of the transitional objects and phenomena, served regressive rather than progressive purposes. Robert Dorn, discussing Leonard's "Identification in Twins" (1961) commented: "The twin relationship sets up a twenty-four hour opportunity for an animated transitional object—one that sometimes 'intrudes' whether he is wanted or not" (p. 310). Leonard replied by pointing out that the twin does not adequately serve the function Winnicott proposed, as one twin cannot be controlled by the other and, further, cannot be the passive recipient of love and aggression. Thus, the other twin, acting as a transitional object, functions in a fixated, regressive manner in contrast to the usual inanimate, phase-specific transitional objects and phenomena which, as first described by Winnicott, promote development. Adding to the problem of the other twin's interpenetration is the difficulty that arises when the early transitional form is animate; it then resembles the original primary object, the mother. In this type of relationship, a blocking of individuation is likely to occur. The infant needs even more autonomy to select his own transitional object, an inanimate not-me possession, which can then be available for externalization and cathexis of the object and narcissistic libido formerly attached to maternal soothing functions. The infant creates an intermediate form which serves a soothing function and facilitates the process Winnicott describes as "keeping inner and outer reality separate yet inter-related." A continuum exists between pure subjective creativity and that which is objectively perceived.

In the transference, the analyst came to represent, at different stages, two distinct forms of twin representation. Initially he was viewed as a controlling, dominant, and sadistic twin, directly related to the personality of the patient's twin brother. This was illustrated in the boating dream, in which the analyst-twin (Joseph 1960) attempted to take away the patient's girl friend, a replication of a series of previous experiences with his dominating twin brother. In the later dream, in which the analyst was a dinner guest of the patient and his girl friend, the patient portrayed the analyst as a person who supported and encouraged his sexual and aggressive drives. This shift was mirrored in the transference, for the analyst-twin was now seen as less controlling, less intrusive, and more supportive. Both transference forms were used by the patient as intermediate objects—bridges to new activities and personal relationships—in much the same way as the patient had utilized his twin. The transformation from one transference form to the other was facilitated by his awareness of the fusion between him and his partner and the persistent delineation of differentiating characteristics both in the subject (the patient) and objects. Here the analyst offered himself as a transitional object, controllable by virtue of his nonintrusiveness and availability for transference expression. In addition he became a real object for the focus of affects, which did not repeat the interpenetration of the earlier twinship.

This process facilitated a "taking in" of those externalized soothing and reassuring experience gestalts necessary for the production of anxiety regulating and drive modulating internal structure. The externalization-internalization processes that accompanied corrective transitional object and phenomenon formation and function in the analysis provided an introject that was less likely to be used for defensive purposes, permanent regressive movement, or premature projection. It was also less likely to be as drive-dependent as the twin transitional relationship.

The altered introject was placed closer to the ego core and was consequently more available for the initiation of normal identification processes. The first phase of the analyst-twin transference relates to the function of a regressive transitional object, while the second phase indicates how progressive transitional objects and phenomena can promote separation and growth of psychic structure.

Does it not seem probable that the passive twin—more often than the dominant twin—would use the other as a transitional object? The material from this analysis suggests this may be the case. However, further research into this area is indicated. An issue resulting from the work of Stevenson (1954) and Busch et al. (1973) may be raised again: Did the twin transitional relationship represent a primary or a secondary transitional object? This is an important question, which applies to the genetic, structural, dynamic, and adaptive qualities of transitional objects. For an infant to acquire a normal animate transitional object in the first year of life, the object must necessarily be not only "available but finely attuned to both sides of the baby's individuation process" (Greenacre 1969, p. 148), a role a mother might fulfill but certainly not an age-equal partner. The acquisition of a twin as a transitional object in the first year would require a state of object cognition, including evocative memory and established object constancy and permanence, which is more compatible with psychic development at twenty-four months of age or later. A consideration of these criteria would place these transitional forms in the secondary transitional object category. (I might stress that the concept of the secondary transitional object is an extension of Winnicott's original concept, and occurs at a later developmental phase.)

When this patient's transitional object was carried beyond childhood, it served mainly defensive operations and infantile aims. It had become regressive by virtue of fixation, a fixation brought about by the other twin's intrusiveness, overstimulation and reciprocity of sameness. This transitional object challenged the illusion of individuality and autonomy. The connection of subject to object interfered with a more complete acceptance of separate external objects, reinforcing narcissistic and anaclitic fixations. These defects in the development of illusions of self and not-self reduced the striving for autonomy as well as the experiences of frustration that are a necessary prelude to the formation of object relations. As a result of the characteristics of this animate transitional object (marked availability, reciprocity, overstimulation, and intrusiveness),[3] it was not available as an efficient introject. Because it occupied a position so peripheral to the ego core, it was constantly caught up in the hyperaccelerated process of externalization and internalization.

During the phase of transference resolution, when a termination date had been set, there appeared to be a regression in the twin-parent-analyst complex in the direction of the primary transitional relationship. The combination of controlled regression and threat of loss induced the patient to use the analytic situation and elements of the transference in a more soothing and anxiety regulating manner. As indicated in the clinical material, the patient returned to an earlier stage of adaptation represented by the emergence and persistence of pregenital aims and demands. He became aware of his infantile dependence, but was temporarily unable to interrupt it. Through further internalization of anxiety regulating structure and the organization of more stable and adaptive identifications, the patient was able to reestablish and consolidate his earlier gains.

With this in mind, I would like once again to raise the question initially proposed by Kahne (1967) in noting the neglect accorded transitional objects and phenomena: "Are we not overlooking extraordinary implications concerning the early precursors of displacement and transference?" (p. 250).

THEORETICAL CONSIDERATIONS

Certain heuristic considerations emerge from all this. If the concepts of primary and secondary transitional objects and phenomena are to be of clinical and theoretical use an effort must be made to understand them and integrate them with the current concepts of internalization and externalization. This leads to the question of the eventual fate of the transitional objects and phenomena, a question raised most recently by Tolpin (1971). In 1953, Winnicott said they are gradually decathected and lose their meaning: "It does not go inside, neither is it forgotten, mourned or repressed."[4] But how can such an intensely cathected object, so central to psychic maturation, be decathected without mourning and relegated to Winnicott's "limbo"? Kahne has asked what mental agency or agencies are involved in decathexis and later, when reappearance of the transitional object takes place, recathexis. Tolpin (1971), differing with Winnicott, proposed that "the *soothing functions* of the transitional object do, in fact, 'go inside' and, precisely because of this, the treasured possession is neither missed, mourned, repressed or forgotten; it is no longer needed" (p. 320). A more important question is, how does this internalization take place?

Tolpin stated that internalization is brought about through a process whereby attributes and functions of the whole object are fractionally decathected and gradually internalized to promote the development of a cohesive self. The internalization of the maternal cathexes that have been attached to transitional objects and phenomena result in the formation of an early transitory form of ego organization, providing for anxiety regulating structure and the organization of drives.

Are the mechanisms for the internalization of primary transitional objects and phenomena the same as those for the internalization of secondary ones? Since there are different psychic capabilities at the times these two manifestations appear, one would expect different modes of internalization. Primary transitional objects and phenomena would seem to involve aspects of primary externalization and internalization described by Loewald (1962). He stated that in primary externalization the infant represents the establishment of externality, while primary internalization represents the culturation of internality. Loewald further commented: "On this level, then, we cannot speak of externalization (projection) and internalization as defenses (against inner conflict or external deprivation); we must speak of them as boundary creating processes and as processes of differentiation of an undifferentiated state" (p. 493). Nevertheless, it would seem that emerging inner and outer conflicts could strongly influence these primary functions. Since internalization and externalization of secondary transitional objects and phenomena occur against a backdrop of a sufficient degree of object cognition and evocative memory to support object constancy, the ego defense mechanisms of introjection and projection seem to be involved.

Consider the fate of the internalized object with specific reference to the secondary transitional object. Schafer (1968) felt that the fate of internalized objects came to be represented in the nature of the psychic integration. He determined three possible transformations of the internalized object: (1) introjects and "primary process presences" (2) identifications, and (3) forms recognizable as external to the subjective self. The first representation relates primarily to defense, the second and third to the production of growth. It would seem that the internalization of regressive secondary transitional objects and phenomena could result in the formation of functionally inadequate introjects that arrest further development, while the internalization of progressive ones could be involved in the formation of introjects leading to identifications and to forms recognizable as separate from the self.

The work of Stierlin (1973) further illuminates the construction and function of secondary transitional objects and phenomena. He identified three interpersonal dimensions of internalization: interpersonal intensity, exclusiveness of dependency, and the state of psychological boundaries. These dimensions are important considerations in a "relational dialectic" focusing on the object to be internalized rather than on the internalizing object. Where the secondary transitional object is animate and intrusive, the internalization process would result in a marked counterorganizing effect. Here the *dominant other*—be it the other twin or the mother—as a transitional object or phenomenon restricts and delimits the separation process. On first impression, these three dimensions—interpersonal intensity, exclusiveness of dependence, and state of psychological boundaries—appear primarily a function of the subject. However, consideration of the nature of the infant's psychic apparatus at two years of age, when subject-object differences are minimized, emphasizes the importance of the object itself, as well as its mode of relating.

In the twinship studied, the patient experienced a great emotional intensity generated by the overstimulation of the "together-together" relationship. Regressive hyperdependence and difficulty in the maintenance of psychological boundaries were derived from his subjugation to the dominant partner. These factors exerted strong centripetal pressures and had a marked bearing on the process of internalization as well as on the balance of the introjective-projective processes related to the give and take interaction between subject and object.

At this point, we can consider more specifically the possible effects of internalizing a secondary transitional object that is fixated and, in this case, intrusive, reciprocal, and poorly differentiated from the subject. Meissner (1971) conceptualized the transitional objects and phenomena as models for the development of object relations and stated that the process of internalization employs introjection to replace transitional relationships. These internal alterations of the self, taking the form of introjects, attain a "quasi-autonomous status" providing gratification of instinctual and drive dependent activity formerly derived from transitional objects and phenomena. Meissner placed introjection somewhere between the primitive oral narcissistic union of incorporation and the identification and autonomous identity associated with more mature forms of object relatedness. Introjects derived from schematically fixated secondary transitional objects and phenomena will hamper the movement away from regressively oriented defenses, primary-process, and drive-dependent orientations. These introjects block the formation of identification associated with the secondary process as well as block drive-dependent formations of secondary ego autonomy.

CONCLUSION

The context of a twinship has been used to examine the genesis and structure of a fixated transtional object in a submissive twin. The early portion of the patient's development involved a substantive transitional form—his twin brother as transitional object. Later in life, with a limited contact with his twin, the transitional process continued primarily as a mental representation (transitional phenomenon). Techniques have been described for effecting a resolution of this fixation within the analytic setting. Consideration has been given to the nature of the internalization process for primary and secondary transitional objects and phenomena, with respect to both their growth inducing properties when progressive, and their growth inhibiting functions when regressive.

NOTES

1. While considerable confusion has from time to time been evidenced regarding the terms *transitional object* and *transitional phenomenon,* in this

chapter the terms should be construed as substantive and non-substantive forms, respectively, of the overall concept of the transitional process.

2. "I should mention that sometimes there is no transitional object except the mother herself" (Winnicott 1953, p. 91). "I do adapt quite a little to individual expectations . . . Yet I am all the time maneuvering into position for standard analysis. . . . For me this means communicating with the patient from the position in which the transference neurosis (or psychosis) puts me. In this position I have some of the characteristics of a transitional phenomenon, since although I represent the early reality principle, and it is I who must keep my eye on the clock, I am nevertheless a subjective object for the patient" (Winnicott 1965, p. 166).

3. The research of Gaddini and Gaddini (1970) indicates that where the mother is intrusive and everpresent, there is little push for the infant to develop symbolic representation, creative thinking, and phase-specific transitional objects and phenomena.

4. Winnicott's later papers (1965, 1966) as well as a personal communication between Giovacchini (1974) and Winnicott support the contention that Winnicott came to the position that the transitional object was finally internalized.

REFERENCES

Busch, F., Nagera, H., NcNight, J., and Pezzarossi, G. (1973). Primary transitional objects. *Journal of the American Academy of Child Psychiatry* 12:193–214.

Coppolillo, H. (1967). Maturational aspects of the transitional phenomena. *International Journal of Psycho-Analysis* 48:237–246.

——— (1976): The transitional phenomenon revisited. *Journal of Amercan Academy of Child Psychiatry* 15:36–48.

Dorn, R. See Leonard, M. (1961).

Fintzy, F. (1971). Viscissitudes of the transitional object in a borderline child. *International Journal of Psycho-Analysis.* 51:107–114.

Gaddini, R., and Gaddini, N. (1970). The transitional object and the process of individuation: a study of three different social groups. *Journal of American Academy of Child Psychiatry* 9:347–365.

Giovacchini, P. (1974). Personal communication.

Greenacre, P. (1969). The fetish and the transitional object. *Psycho-Analytic Study of the Child* 24:249–264.

——— (1970). The transitional object and the fetish with special reference to illusion. *International Journal of Psycho-Analysis.* 52:447–456.

Horton, P., Louy, J., and Coppolillo, H. (1974). Personality disorders and transitional relatedness. *Archives of General Psychiatry* 30:618–622.

Joseph, E. (1960). The psychology of twins: a report. *Psychoanalytic Quarterly* 29:158–166.

Kahne, M. (1967). On the persistence of transitional phenomena into adult life. *International Journal of Psycho-Analysis* 48:247–258.

Leonard, M. (1961). Problems of identification and ego development in twins. *Psychoanalytic Study of the Child* 16:300–312.

Loewald, H. (1962). Internalization, separation, mourning and the superego. *Psychoanalytic Quarterly* 31:483–504.

—— (1970). Psychoanalytic theory and the psychoanalytic process. *Psychoanalytic Study of the Child* 25:45–68.

Meissner, W. (1970). Notes on identification, I: Origins in Freud. *Psychoanalytic Quarterly* 39:563–589.

—— (1971). Notes on identification, II: clarification of related concepts. *Psychoanalytic Quarterly* 40:277–302.

—— (1972). Notes on identification, III: the concept of identification. *Psychoanalytic Quarterly* 41:224–260.

Modell, A. (1961). Denial and the sense of separateness. *Journal of the American Psychoanalytic Association* 9:533–547.

Schafer, R. (1968). *Aspects of Internalization.* New York: International Universities Press.

Stevenson, O. (1954). The first treasured possession. *Psychoanalytic Study of the Child* 9:199–217.

Stierlin, H. (1973). Interpersonal aspects of internalizations. *International Journal of Psycho-Analysis* 54:203–214.

Tolpin, M. (1971). On the beginning of a cohesive self: an application of the concept of transmuting internalization to the study of the transitional object and separation anxiety. *Psychoanalytic Study of the Child* 26:316–353.

Volkan, V. (1973). Transitional fantasies in the analysis of a narcissistic personality. *Journal of the American Psychoanalytic Association* 21:351–376.

Winnicott, D. (1953). Transitional objects and transitional phenomena. *International Journal of Psycho-Analysis* 34:89–97.

—— (1965). The maturational processes and the facilitating environment. New York: International Universities Press.

—— (1966). The location of cultural experience. *International Journal of Psycho-Analysis* 48:368–372.

—— (1971). *Playing and Reality.* New York: Basic Books.

CHAPTER 19

Vamik Volkan and James Kavanaugh have worked extensively with borderline and narcissistic patients. Following Arnold Modell, they have used the transitional object concept to illuminate the patient's struggle toward individuation and separation. They regard these patients as functioning at an early transitional object phase, which they tend to equate with symbiosis. The first task of the therapist is to help the patient progress from modes of relating which are rigid, clinging, and fetishistic to those possessing a later transitional object quality.

Winnicott showed how, in the normal child, transitional objects and phenomena function as bridges to and from external reality. We should remember that many of his patients were borderline and that his concepts were developed from and applied in their treatment. Volkan and Kavanaugh demonstrate how three patients "used cats as reactivated transitional objects in working for resolution of symbiotic transference and more mature object relationships." They show also how the cat symbols have condensed within them representations from different developmental stages, bridging from the transitional object to the fetish as well.

Winnicott mentioned pets as animate transitional objects; Parrish (chapter 18) offers twins as another example. Clearly these objects are not subject to the type of control such inanimate objects as teddy bears are. Nor is the plasticity of representation as great as can be achieved with transitional phenomena, as instanced in the case, previously reported by Volkan, of a patient who used fantasies as transitional phenomena.

L.B.

THE CAT PEOPLE

Vamik D. Volkan

James G. Kavanaugh

Some adults with borderline personality organization may utilize reactivated transitional objects. During their psychoanalytic treatment, this reactivation usually appears when they are dealing actively with the resolution of psychic separation from mother/analyst and with the expansion of the realities of the outer world. Three cases reported here utilized a cat as a reactivated transitional object. Much current literature on the transitional object emphasizes an enlargement of its role as a link between not-me and mother-me, and views it also in terms of object relations.

> [The] symbolic magic ... of the transitional object is extremely primitive. Belonging to the earliest period in life, it offers an illusory bridge—or bridges; it comforts and fortifies the young venturer in taking his first steps into the expanding realities of the outer world ... It offers a cushion against distress of frustration before reality testing is at all secure, and provides dosages of omnipotence according to infant needs. [Greenacre 1969]

This bridge is chosen by the infant from available objects on the basis of texture, odor, visibility, movability, etc. (Winnicott 1953). In this sense, one may theoretically consider this link contaminated with primitive symbolism; but it can be assumed from a practical viewpoint that the object becomes an actual link in the infant's experiences. Modell (1968, 1970) applied the watershed concept, maintaining that the link has a progressive as well as a regressive side, corresponding to acceptance and nonacceptance of external objects. In this it resembles the Janus-faced fetish, a bisexual symbol which serves as a link between denial and acceptance of sexual differences.

REVIEW OF THE LITERATURE

Modell's study of the transitional object from the standpoint of object relations theory and the watershed concept elucidates the object relations of the transitional object's user. The normally developing child uses the progressive side to illuminate the presence of external objects so that he may eventually differentiate himself from them psychically. However, because of his illusion of absolute control over the transitional object, he may "turn it off" and regress to the security of objectless darkness, where he need not face the external. Modell suggests that the object relations of borderline individuals are arrested at this level, and that transitional object relations can exist in adult life when there is fixation in or regression to an early type of relationship. Such fixation or regression allows the patient to perceive his analyst as an independent entity, nevertheless invested "almost entirely with qualities emanating from the patient" (Modell 1963). Although Modell criticizes the use of the term *symbiotic* because it implies that the object's emotional attitude toward the subject is irrelevant, the transitional object relationship he describes is, in a broad sense, equivalent to the symbiotic object relationship described in the psychoanalytic literature.

Kahne (1967) studied the persistence of transitional phenomena and objects into adulthood. He believed transitional objects are revived "under circumstances in which there was a threat to the ego of separation from an important contemporary object," and that the existence of derivatives of such phenomena in adult life is not per se an indication of neurosis or psychosis. "The fact of persistence of unmodified transitional phenomena may, however, signal the existence of serious disturbances in object relations and reality sense in such persons."

After Modell, Fintzy (1971) hypothesized the covert persistence into adult life of an actual Januslike transitional object. By using its progressive side, the borderline individual may maintain a normal facade outside of therapy. Volkan (1973) demonstrated the clinical validity of the views of Modell and Fintzy with analytic material from a narcissistic patient. This patient had special transitional fantasies instead of tangible transitional objects; he saw them as autonomous and was addicted to them, but maintained dominion over them. This sustained his illusion of being in control of his entire external world.

The special use of nonhuman objects by borderline or schizophrenic persons has been clinically investigated (Searles 1960). Searles later (1963) emphasized how the nonhuman environment (including animals) can displace components of the child's essentially mother-directed feelings; and Burnham (1969) described how very regressed patients cling to or avoid particular objects. The nonhuman objects put to significant use by extremely regressed patients are not all transitional objects; however, Volkan (1976) sees some of them as transitional objects, either reactivated or released for the first time from their covert existence. Borderline patients become addicted to these objects, which soothe anxiety and buffer frustrations of reality testing. Volkan studied how these reactivated transitional objects permit psychic distancing between the patient and the external object: "The lantern has one opaque and one transparent side; when the opaque side is turned toward the outside world the outside world is wiped out in darkness, but the other side illuminates it so that it can be known." The person who exercises control over these objects may also have the illusion of being able to distance external objects—defined by Volkan as entities not uncontaminated but, rather, tinged with the person's externalization or projections. An "external object" is thus in part "subjectively created by the subject" (Modell 1975).

Kernberg (1966) shows that borderline personality organization in the adult is fixated at a level where libidinally and aggressively tinged self- and object-images are kept apart by primitive splitting, even though the individual can differentiate self-images from object-images, except in intimate relationships such as the analytic transference. He feels safer when he can externalize the aggressively tinged self- and object-images (those generally referred to as "all bad") onto external objects. His comfort is not stable, however; what has been externalized continues to threaten the "all good" images kept within. Clinical work shows, moreover, that "all good" and "all bad" units may change locus. Volkan (1975) demonstrates how these patients utilize certain nonhuman objects to cushion themselves from external objects contaminated with "all bad" self- and object-constellations, and to separate the "caring" external object from the "dangerous." In the patient's illusion of control over these objects, and in their use of "cushions," Volkan saw a reproduction of the way the infant uses the transitional object before he is fully able to test reality. Reactivation of these transitional objects—or variations on the theme of transitional objects (Fintzy 1971)—is best observed in treatment when transference progresses beyond a dominantly symbiotic object relationship toward a more mature one.

The adult borderline patient using an inanimate object as a reactivated transitional object can also condense higher-level meaning in it; it may become a bridge between subjective psychic reality and objective external reality at the lower level, while on a higher level the patient's more differentiated and integrated ego-parts use it as a fetish. Gray areas remain. Greenacre (1969, 1970) examined how childhood and adult fetishes resemble the transitional object yet differ from it. Volkan (1972, 1976) differentiated them from the pathological mourner's linking objects. Even Winnicott (1953) suggested a spectrum between the transitional object and the fetish, the latter described "in terms of a persistence of a specific object or type of object dating from infantile experience in the transitional field, linked with the delusion of a maternal phallus."

We should know what a patient's use of inanimate objects means to him at each point in treatment. The clinical examples that follow illustrate how three patients used cats as reactivated transitional objects while working for resolution of symbiotic transference, and toward more mature object relationships.

We called these borderline patients "cat people," using the term Sandford (1966) applied to her patient Elsie, and Volkan (1976) to Samantha. Elsie, who used cats as transitional objects, greatly resembled a cat herself. Samantha, a schizophrenic, *became* her cats in her involvement with them.

THREE CAT PEOPLE

These three patients were addicted to cats and used them for solace; sleep arrived only when the cat was snuggled into bed with the patient. This attachment marked the point in treatment where each was engaged in resolving a symbiotic transference. The cat was a reactivated transitional object, used to acknowledge external reality. These adult women with advanced functions did not use their transitional objects as infants do. They not only condensed a certain fetishistic element in them as they reactivated the transitional objects, but their egos were able to observe the transference relationship, the resolution of symbiotic relatedness. Thus, the clinical picture they presented was considerably more complex than that of an infant experiencing the same kind of resolution during the normal, phase-specific period of its life.

Margaret
Margaret, a nineteen-year-old Southern white girl, found herself one night seated on an overland bus beside a middle-aged black man who repeatedly ran his hands over her body in the darkness. Since there were

others on the bus, any noisy protest would have stopped him; but she could not say no, since she felt he was underprivileged and needy. In her own apartment, she gathered around her a group of emotionally deprived and "needy" people whom she was unable to deny anything. She felt a sense of mission about their needs, and obligation to make them whole; paradoxically, she used them for her own ends. As her five-year analysis progressed, we uncovered the genetic meaning of her inability to say no to needy people; they represented the depressed mother of her first years of life. Her symptoms expressed a fusion with the early mother, whom she hoped to make whole so that she herself could break out of the symbiotic relationship that bound them together.

Margaret was the third child of a middle class family. Her mother had an identical twin. Allegedly their mother had been injured while delivering the two infants, and, in spite of the fact that her death did not occur until they were ten, it was attributed to childbirth. Margaret's mother never fully accepted her own mother's death and endlessly sought her return. She always felt "incomplete" without her twin sister and lived near her, even after both were married. Margaret was conceived during a time when the mother was obliged to live far from her twin, suffering from a depression that continued during the first years of Margaret's life. When Margaret arrived, her mother consciously thought of her not only as her lost mother but as her "lost" sister. The mother's inability to achieve true individuation in spite of her many interests and achievements accounted for many peculiarities in her daughter's object relationships. Subsequently, Margaret's four siblings—two older and two younger than she—paired off, leaving Margaret with her mother. They were so close that when Margaret was ill they often rested on the bed side by side with their bodies curved reciprocally. When Margaret became a psychoanalytic patient, she felt that she could communicate with her mother and her analyst by means of "waves," "osmosis," or "a third eye."

It should be noted that outside the area of intimacy with the representatives of her depressed early mother (as in the transference) in her daily life this patient could differentiate her self-representation from object representations, and one external object from another. However, when under stress, she tended to regress to more symbiotic relationships. She had the habit of rolling the lint between her fingers into soft little balls which she called "fuzz balls"; these she fingered to soothe herself and to protect herself from the frustrations of reality testing. She had begun doing this at the disappearance of the blanket she carried about with her at age four or five. These reminders of her soothing blanket were under absolute control and she took pleasure as she grew up in chewing gum and sniffing at her soiled underwear while she toyed with the fuzz balls. Later, just fingering them was sufficient to reduce her tensions. She began to steal after her blanket disappeared; Winnicott (1953) had indicated that stealing can be connected with the transitional object. Margaret discontinued her stealing only when this conduct was adequately analyzed.

It is beyond the scope of this chapter to detail fully the course of Margaret's treatment, but it is interesting that she brought her fuzz balls to her psychoanalytic sessions, concealing them at first in her purse or between her fingers. A few months before entering analysis, she stole a cat from a child on the street and named it for her father, although it was a female, thus contaminating it with bisexual fetishistic qualities. It was not until a year of analysis had passed, however, that the cat became a reactivated transitional object. By then the analyst represented the early depressed mother. There was a hypertrophy of introjective-projective relatedness, or merging, with the analyst. Margaret merged with the analyst/mother, separated, and merged again. She was aware of this and tried to advance from this type of object relations. Her struggle to work through separation from her mother, and the concomitant pull back to symbiosis with her, manifested itself in a series of dreams. At this point the cat became a "special fuzz ball" and a bridge between not-me and mother-me. She not only became addicted to her cat, but in her hours on the couch she was excessively preoccupied with it. She could not sleep without it; she made the cat curl around her body on the bed in the way her mother had done when they "twinned" together and lost the boundaries between themselves. Now the cat was seen as having human characteristics: in its absence from the apartment Margaret was at times uncomfortable or even frightened.

The meaning of the cat as a link between not-me and mother-me was interpreted after Margaret had a dream of killing her mother, and another of searching for the meaning of integrity. These dreams were followed by others, the contents of which she was unable to recall, but to which she felt tied "by an umbilical cord." On the couch she felt the sensation of "floating in the air"; the couch itself seemed to float into position beneath her. She wanted to move away from the couch/analyst, but at the same time she wanted to cling to it. She fingered her fuzz balls more than ever, and she kicked her cat as if to kill it. Both the patient and her analyst continued to observe her attempts to separate from the early mother; the fuzz balls and the cat represented a link with this mother. Margaret began to leave a little heap of fuzz balls behind her at each analytic session, although she was not aware that she did this. The analyst collected them in an ashtray for more than a month until Margaret realized what she had been doing. She said the fuzz balls were no longer a solace, that she no longer needed them or the cat. For safety's sake, however, she kept some of the soft balls on hand, and a month later she tried to relax by masturbating with the fuzz balls between her fingers. This was unsuccessful, and she collected all the fuzz balls, flushed them down the toilet—and said good-bye to her mother. Of course, this dramatic event did not bring about a psychic separation from her mother once and for all, but did represent a major turning point in her treatment.

Jane
Jane was a twenty-one-year-old college student when she began psychoanalytic therapy, four visits a week. After a year and a half, she switched to the couch and remained in treatment for a total of six years before a successful termination was reached. When she came into treatment following an acute psychotic episode, she presented a confused and confusing picture, with an inability to differentiate between her self- and object-representations. Later, however, she evidenced a borderline character organization dominated by primitive splitting; her objects, though partly differentiated from her self-representations and from each other, were separated into the "all good" and the "all bad." She pronounced all objects, animate and inanimate, either "benign" or "aggressive."

She was the second child of a couple whose firstborn, a year and a half older than Jane, was congenitally deformed and expected to die in infancy. Indeed, she did die, in her mother's arms on the way to the hospital, when Jane was two. The mother, who had expressed great anxiety at the frailty of her first child, was unable either to grieve appropriately over its death, or to give her remaining daughter adequate mothering. Also, during the time she was nursing Jane she had an infection of the breast. In the first dream Jane reported in treatment, she was being fed a huge bowl of oatmeal, and then fell into it, choking until her panic awakened her. In one series of repeating dreams, she saw herself in the midst of a circle of chairs, all empty except for one occupied by her mother. Jane would convulse while her mother laughed at her. In analysis, these repeating dreams were understood as unsuccessful attempts to shake herself out of a symbiotic relationship to her mother.

When she was five, her father began to play sexual games with her. He would show her his erect penis, make her touch and fondle it, and would kiss her genital area; there was no actual intercourse however. Their "secret," at the oedipal level, resulted in Jane's regression and aided the preservation of the earlier symbiotic core and kept primitive object relationships alive. The incestuous relationship continued until the patient had her first menstrual period, when Jane's father approached her in her bedroom and kissed her breast so hard she screamed. He never touched her sexually again.

Social class differences were felt strongly in Jane's family, who lived in a traditional Southern community; the mother, a social climber herself, pressured Jane socially. She was sent to a college traditionally acceptable to families of wealth, but had to work as a waitress to meet her expenses. The psychosis appeared a few months before graduation, which represented an independence and individuation for which she was psychically unprepared.

Jane's preoccupation with a cat, like Margaret's, marked an attempt in the transference to separate from the mother representation. Volkan (1975) describes this aspect of her treatment elsewhere. Important movements in her relatedness to her immediate environment occurred concomitantly. She began to think of leaving home and finding an apartment for herself; at this point the family cat, Miss Kitty, became the most important object. She filled her therapeutic sessions with talk about it. She feared being poisoned by her mother as she attempted to separate physically and psychically from her; she also saw the analyst as dangerous to her. At times the cat became a total representation of herself, and she thought it too might be poisoned by her mother. More frequently, however, the cat was a bridge between Jane and her mother. She spoke of it as "a root into my mother." Although this statement made symbolic reference to the cat as a penis, the cat's principal significance, as events demonstrated, was in its use as a transitional object; this consideration facilitated the analytic working through of this phase of treatment. The main problem at the time was not the acceptance of her sexuality (with or without a penis) but her emergence from a symbiotic core.

When Jane moved into her own apartment, she felt incomplete and was preoccupied with fantasies about feeding her analyst and having union with him in this feeding. She also continued to be preoccupied with her cat, which she took to her apartment several months after leaving home. Then she was no longer alone, since she shared her home with part of her early mother/analyst and the part of herself "rooted" into her mother/analyst. At night she slept with the cat in bed; she could not sleep without it.

As Jane worked through her attempt to differentiate herself further from the mother/analyst and to achieve individuation, the magic of the cat as a bridge between the internal and the external dimmed. She felt that the cat was ailing, so she took it to a veterinarian and talked him into performing a hysterectomy on it, in spite of the fact that she knew, even without his warning, that the cat would not survive. Her associations to the cat at this time were reduced to breasts and nipples. An artist, she drew a picture of Miss Kitty lying on her back, displaying conspicuous udders with swollen teats. When, as expected, the cat died from the surgery, the next day she asked her analyst, "Did you know that part of me wanted Miss Kitty to die?" She experienced sadness but did not mourn in the adult sense.

Some months later Jane acquired another cat, which she placed in bed between herself and a young man with whom she had become intimate. She fantasized biting the boy's nipples and thought of him as her mother. At this time, she was more aware of the cat as a higher-level symbol, her penis, but on a lower level she continued to treat it as a transitional object, using it as a bridge to the external object. Through her relationship with the young man via the cat, she not only began to find her sexuality, but to achieve a view of herself as an entity apart from the external world around her.

Tarik the cat

Although the two patients described could usually discriminate between what was internal and external, each retained a "part" that lacked this power of discrimination. Thus it was necessary in treatment to advance this "part." At the time they were unwinding the symbiotic core, they activated a transitional object—in each case a cat—and inserted it between internal and external reality. Although the cats, with their playful softness, were pacifiers, we focus here on the utility of reactivated transitional objects in expanding outer reality.

Since Margaret had used transitional objects (fuzz balls) from childhood, her cat was in effect a special fuzz ball; in the history of the treatment of these patients and their concomitant daily life, the phenomenology of fetishism associated with cats does not stand out clearly. At this time, both patients exhibited the intensely oral sets from which it is more typical for a transitional object to appear. Margaret manifested a hypertrophy of introjective-projective relatedness that included the analyst and even merged with him. In the case of Jane, oral elements exhibited themselves even more openly. As in Kahne's patients (1967), in whom transitional phenomena persisted into adult life, "the phenomena and objects associated with them when seen in adults echo the infantile ego's attempt at mastery of the tensions involved in the earliest object differentiation." Treatment allowed the progressive sides of the "watershed" to prevail. The following vignette graphically illustrates the watershed characteristic of the use of the cat as a reactivated transitional object, and the ways in which therapy may maximize the use of this progressive side.

Like Jane and Margaret, Annabel, another young college student in her early twenties, became preoccupied with a cat when she was involved in separating intrapsychically from her mother/therapist. As she worked through this situation, she performed activities as if they were exercises devoted in her daily life to doing things on her own, without need of an external ego that represented her early mother. These attempts caused anxiety, and she would fall back into a symbiotic object relationship. After the therapist thought she had "exercised" long enough, he told her the story of the way in which Tarik, the Muslim warrior, conquered Spain. After Tarik and his men reached the shores of Spain from North Africa in 711 A.D., he ordered the ships on which they had made the passage burned so that any retreat (regression) was cut off. This move left only two possible outcomes: the invaders either would be engulfed in the sea (symbiosis) or would through conquest earn new territories. The patient, who was intelligent, understood the analogy in terms of her problem in maturation. A few months after hearing the story, she spoke of wanting a cat, and did eventually find a kitten. For a few months she was greatly preoccupied with it, spent time with it before going to bed at night, and kept it by her side when she had visitors, particularly a boy who was paying her some attention. She seemed to need it in intimate relationships with others, and panicked when it climbed a tree and was lost to her until rescued by neighbors.

This young woman had retained a teddy bear from her childhood, a transitional object without which she could not fall asleep. It was even necessary for her to take the teddy bear with her when she slept away from home. Her father had killed himself when she was a pubertal child and she had "linking objects" (Volkan 1972) to tie her to him. Thus, before using the kitten as a reactivated transitional object, she had a history of using a variation of the transitional object—a linking object. Now the kitten began to seem as important as the teddy bear. After a few months this patient confided to her therapist that before she had named the kitten "Tarik" she had gone to the library and read up on the historical figure of that name; the kitten represented her wish to struggle forward toward new territories of reality after the regressive possibility of retreat and surrender—after her "bridges burned behind her." When she understood the role her kitten played in this forward effort, her investment in it diminished and most of its magic disappeared.

ON CATS AND "ALL GOOD" AND "ALL BAD" SELF- AND OBJECT-REPRESENTATIONS

Our clinical account of the way in which three women used pet cats as reactivated transitional objects is not intended to specify these animals as uniquely suitable for an adult's transitional object; other objects could, of course, be substituted to the same psychological end. However, cats met the requirements of these three patients in interesting ways, having other qualities as well as the tactile appeal favored by infants in selecting transitional objects.

Individuals with borderline personalities have polarized self- and object-representational constellations; they therefore tend to polarize external objects as these objects are contaminated with the externalization of the individual's intrapsychic representations. As Jane explained so graphically, all of her objects were either benign or aggressive. Can we consider that the reactivated transitional object of the borderline patient, which contains elements both of the self and of external reality while serving as a bridge between them, must also be experienced as either "all good" or "all bad"? This is a theoretical issue that warrants further investigation. The magic symbolism of the infant's transitional object is for him the first not-me, mother-me, and the link between them as well. Thus the child selects the object according to its sensory (tactile, olfactory, visual, auditory) appeal. Possibly the reactivated transitional object may be selected with even greater unconscious recognition of symbolic suitability.

The cat has been close to mankind throughout history. The Egyptians, said to be the first to domesticate *Felis catus*, evolved a cult of cat worship before the Twelfth Dynasty (c. 2000 B.C.), and its influence reached into all social strata. Herodotus (c. 485-425 B.C.) left vivid descriptions of the great red granite temple at Bubastis, a temple sacred to the cat (Godolphin 1942). Cat goddesses were worshiped in effigy as Bastet, who was represented as having a human form and the head of a cat; she was loved and revered as the highest expression of femininity and maternity. Herodotus equated her with the Greek Artemis. Egyptians gave all cats the greatest respect; it was a capital offense to kill one, and they were mummified and mourned at death in extravagant rituals, occupying a unique place in the religion of Egypt for more than two thousand years.

Nevertheless, the cat has been seen also as an embodiment of evil, an omen of bad luck, the devil's messenger whose glowing eyes not only penetrate the darkness but provide a glimpse into a sinister world. When men feared witches and demons they associated cats with them as agents of dark powers and nameless horrors (Russell 1972), and this dread is reflected in law and within the church. Many a forlorn old woman was tortured to confess that her cat was her link to Lucifer and the instrument of baleful charms and spells.

Among man's pets, only the cat refuses to be dominated. As a kitten it is universally appealing; in maturity it seems tantalizingly remote and self-contained. It gives affection, but not on demand, acting unpredictably and according to its own needs. A resemblance is to be found in the child's early attempts to deal with the mother as a differentiated but not fully differentiated object: she is divine in power, "all good" when relieving tensions, but "all bad" when failing to do so. The omnipotence of the infant, moreover, allows him to shift from being a helpless supplicant (the kitten) to being a raging, devouring destroyer, a voracious big cat. We suggest that the feline nature suits the representation of the me/not-me, and the link between them at this level of human functioning. The experiences with cats in childhood usually remain little more than references to these animals in slang, in advertising slogans, as caricatures in cartoons, and as team "totems"; yet the original power of the image continues to lurk behind these banal manifestations. Only a small distance separates the cat's "domesticated" role in the everyday mix of symbolism and reality, from the role it played in the psychic disturbances of the three "Cat People."

REFERENCES

Burnham, D. L. (1969). Schizophrenia and object relations. In *Schizophrenia and the Need-Fear Dilemma*, ed. D. L. Burnham, A. I. Gladstone, and R. W. Gibson. New York: International Universities Press.

Fintzy, P. T. (1971). Vicissitudes of the transitional object in a borderline child. *International Journal of Psycho-Analysis* 52:107–114.

Godolphin, F. R. B. (1942). *The Greek Historians*, vol. 1, p. 147. New York: Random House.

Greenacre, P. (1969). The fetish and the transitional object. *Psychoanalytic Study of the Child* 24:144–164.

——— (1970). The transitional object and the fetish with special reference to the role of illusion. *International Journal of Psycho-Analysis* 51:447–456.

Kahne, M. J. (1967). On the persistence of transitional phenomena into adult life. *International Journal of Psycho-Analysis* 48:247–258.

Kernberg, O. F. (1966). Borderline personality organization. *Journal of the American Psychoanalytic Association* 15:641–685.

Modell, A. H. (1963). Primitive object relationships and the predisposition to schizophrenia. *International Journal of Psycho-Analysis* 44:282–292.

——— (1968). *Object Love and Reality: An Introduction to a Psychoanalytic Theory of Object Relations*, pp. 33, 40. New York: International Universities Press.

——— (1970). The transitional object and the creative act. *Psychoanalytic Quarterly* 39:240–250.

——— (1975). The ego and the id fifty years later. *International Journal of Psycho-Analysis* 56:57–68.

Russell, J. B. (1972). *Witchcraft in the Middle Ages*. Ithaca, N.Y.: Cornell University Press.

Sandford, B. (1966). A patient and her cats. *Psychoanalytic Forum* 1:170–176.

Searles, H. F. (1960). *The Non-Human Environment in Normal Development and in Schizophrenia*. New York: International Universities Press.

——— (1963). The place of neutral therapist-responses in psychotherapy with schizophrenic patients. *International Journal of Psycho-Analysis* 44:42–56.

Volkan, V. D. (1972). The "linking objects" of pathological mourners. *Archives of General Psychiatry* 27:215–221.

——— (1973). Transitional fantasies in the analysis of a narcissistic personality. *Journal of the American Psychoanalytic Association* 21:351–376.

——— (1975). Cosmic laughter—a study of primitive splitting. In *Tactics and Techniques in Psychoanalytic Therapy*, vol. 2, ed. P. Giovacchini. New York: Jason Aronson.

——— (1976). *Primitive Internalized Object Relations*, p. 201. New York: International Universities Press.

Winnicott, D. W. (1953). Transitional objects and transitional phenomena. *International Journal of Psycho-Analysis* 34:89–97.

CHAPTER 20

In the previous chapter Volkan and Kavanaugh observed in the use of pets a continuum ranging from transitional to fetishistic objects. Robert Dickes reexamines this problem of differentiation from the perspective of his 1963 study of fetishes and transitional objects. He narrows his original differences with Winnicott by concluding that some transitional objects—those used as aids to normal development—may be transitional in nature. However, he differs again by labeling transitional those objects Winnicott would have called comforters. He can thus deny Winnicott's dictum that the child is attached to them more than to his mother; the child can give them up, Dickes believes, without too much fuss. But these are objects more like toys than like Winnicott's "soothing" objects; to the latter the child is addicted, becoming more attached to them in times of stress than to the mother. Only these would Winnicott have called true transitional objects; Dickes regards them as fetishes. He demonstrates parental involvement in the child's choice of these objects, and connects them to the perversion of fetishism.

Deciding what is and what is not a transitional object is most difficult, particularly when we depend mainly on observation. Winnicott defined the transitional object in terms of its noninstinctual use, and specifically excluded all attachments in which drive discharge, sexual or aggressive, is primary. This issue, dealt with by both Judith Kestenberg and Renata Gaddini in this volume, has been discussed elsewhere, most extensively in the work of Phyllis Greenacre.

To reiterate: a transitional object is not just any object to which a child happens to be attached. For example, a psychotic child spinning a ball for hours on end in a corner of a room possesses a psychotic fetish, not a transitional object. As the child moves toward health, the object gains a more transitional quality. Dickes demonstrates the difficulties of observational studies in making clear distinctions when he presents intrapsychic data showing the parent's role in the choice of fetishes. However, the essence of the transitional object lies for Winnicott in the child's use of illusion to create the object, and in the good enough mother who allows this. Hence Winnicott would probably have agreed with

Dickes that in the cases presented here, where parents have been intrusive, sexualizing the objects, and playing a major role in their selection, we are dealing not with transitional objects but with pathological fetishes. It is evident that further research is necessary: both the observational sort represented here by Kestenberg, Gaddini, and Abrams and Neubauer and the clinical, as represented by Volkan and Dickes.

L.B.

PARENTS, TRANSITIONAL OBJECTS, AND CHILDHOOD FETISHES

Robert Dickes

That there has been little emphasis in the literature on the role of parents in the perpetuation and misuse of the transitional object and in the production of fetishism is surprising. That ample evidence of such parental involvement is readily apparent in the clinical material makes it even more so. In an earlier publication (1963) I commented on this neglect, noting that the only report principally concerning itself with the specific role of parents in fostering the development of fetishism and other perversions was made by Liten et al. (1956). Other authors stressing parental contributions include O. Sperling (1956) and M. Sperling (1963). In this chapter, I wish to focus attention on the active parental participation in the child's choice of the transitional object and in the creation of the child's deviant behavior with inanimate objects, as well as on the connections between the transitional object and the childhood fetish. It is, however, necessary first to clarify the characteristics of the transitional object and the childhood fetish, since disagreement does exist concerning their meaning and developmental significance.

M. Wulff (1946) was among the first to describe the special objects which infants and very young children invest with intense feeling and upon which they become so dependent. He considered an exaggerated attachment to these objects a manifestation of childhood fetishism. Wulff quoted two previous case reports, one by Friedjung in 1927, the other by E. Sterba in 1941. Friedjung mentioned a boy of sixteen months who needed to play with his mother's stocking or brassiere before he could fall asleep. When Friedjung accidentally discovered this, the grandmother described how the child flirted with the stocking in an animalistic manner, emphasizing a sexual and therefore fetishistic element in the boy's attachment.

Wulff also described a boy of four or five who used a "magic blanket." His mother reported that ever since he was weaned he had prized a soft woolen coverlet even more than he prized his mother or father. The mother noticed that when he was given the coverlet she could disappear. It was all the same to him. This description conforms to one of Winnicott's definitions of the transitional object.

Another case involved a boy of fifteen months who was attached to a bib named "Hoppa." This he would use during a rhythmic tiptoe dance in which he moved his entire body backward and forward in a manner that could be interpreted as having sexual connotations. "Hoppa" was lost when the boy was about two and a half years old. At four, his mother gave him a handkerchief, which he took to bed; this often pressed against his genitals, saying that in this way it could not be lost. The practice expressed a castration fear. Objects similar to those described by Wulff as childhood fetishes were also mentioned by Winnicott (1953), who renamed them *transitional objects*. The designation has been widely accepted, as has his conviction that the use of these objects is essentially healthy. Concerning this, Winnicott wrote: "There is a difference between my point of view and that of Wulff which is reflected in my use of this special term and his use of the term 'fetish object'. . . . I am not able to find in his article sufficient room for the consideration of the child's transitional object as a healthy early experience. Yet I do consider that transitional phenomena are healthy and universal." Winnicott emphasized this definition of the transitional object by citing a patient who at the age of one year adopted a toy rabbit and cuddled it until he was five or six. Winnicott described it as a comforter but indicated that it had never had the true quality of a transitional object: "It was never, as a true transitional object would have been, more important than the mother, an almost inseparable part of the infant." This description fits that of the magic blanket mentioned by Wulff and further defines the transitional object.

The presumed normality of the transitional object was reemphasized by Stevenson (1954). Her information was obtained by letter, questionnaire, or brief interview but not from the psychoanalytic situation. In spite of what seems to be clear evidence of pathology in some of her case reports, Stevenson maintained that "the transitional objects are an entirely healthy and normal manifestation of the beginnings of the reconciliation between reality and fantasy." Winnicott agreed and wrote a preface to Stevenson's article. However, in my opinion these conclusions are contradicted by the case material. A few of her examples may be cited.

Roy, a seven year old boy, had a duster called "Say" which he took everywhere, including school and Sunday school. If the teacher asked him to put the duster away he would do so, but only for a moment. He would pick it up again almost immediately, as noted by Stevenson: "As if compulsively—he is holding 'Say' again." The youngster was described also as a rather nervous, disobedient little boy, a trial to his mother, who had actually wondered whether she should take him to a psychologist. Although Stevenson thought the idea was precipitated by the tactless remarks of the neighbors, a recommendation that a child have treatment is not usually made by neighbors unless they have good reason to offer the advice.

Another child, Jean, was given a toy bunny while still in her pram. A year later the bunny disintegrated and she was offered in its place a wooly, cuddly dog. When this dog in turn fell to bits, the child kept the piece that smelled nicest to her. At six, she still took her "piece" to school every day and slept with it under her nose. When Stevenson visited her home, Jean sat sniffing the piece of fur, which even after long use carried the distinctive smell of a rather heavy, feminine perfume. Stevenson did not consider the behavior unusual nor did she question the odor of the piece of fur. However, children do not usually walk about smelling bits of a disintegrated toy dog. Furthermore, there is a hint of parental involvement in the persistent odor of the perfume.

Greenacre (1969, 1970), writing in accord with Winnicott, considered the transitional object virtually ubiquitous and commented that its presence did not forecast an abnormal development. It is noteworthy that Greenacre did not dispute Winnicott's definition of the transitional object as an object of greater importance than the mother. She considered it the first not-me object and wrote: "Perhaps the crux of the function of the transitional object lies in its being a tangible object which is neither just infant nor just mother." It seems to me that in this statement Greenacre arrived at a different conceptualization. On the basis of Winnicott's statements, the first possession or not-me object cannot be considered transitional until it meets the special criterion mentioned earlier. According to Winnicott, the first not-me object or the first possession must develop in importance until it is more than a comforter and exceeds the mother in importance.

Viewed in Winnicott's terms, M. Sperling's (1963) comments (to which Greenacre took exception) become more intelligible. She wrote: "It seems to me that Winnicott has created much confusion by referring to these phenomena and these objects as transitional. I believe they are pathological manifestations of a specific disturbance in object relationship. Winnicott's concepts are not only fallacious but dangerous, because they lead to erroneous assessment of the meaning and function of fetishistic childhood phenomena and childhood fetishism." Here the transitional object is confounded with the childhood fetish. Nor did Sperling separately consider the role of the first not-me object or first possession, *not yet a transitional object*. Even Winnicott himself did not sufficiently elaborate these distinctions.

I believe it possible to reconcile these conflicting points of view by clarifying the use of inanimate objects by infants and children. This involves considering both the developmental aspects of the early use of an object and its final evolution into a typical transitional object. Winnicott's comments (1953) on the first not-me possession are appropriate here. He related it to the newborn's fist-in-mouth activities eventually leading to an attachment to a teddy or other toy; the terms *transitional object* and *transitional phenomena*, he wrote, "should be used to designate the intermediate area of experience between the thumb and the teddy bear. By this definition an infant's babbling or the way an older child goes over a repertory of songs and tunes while preparing for sleep come within the intermediate area for transitional phenomena, along with the use made of objects that are not part of the infant's body yet are not fully recognized as belonging to external reality."

Winnicott then provided a list of transitional phenomena which included behavior as well as objects utilized in such activities as sucking a bit of cloth or babbling. From these activities one object or phenomenon emerges which becomes vitally important to the infant at sleep time. This, according to Winnicott, becomes the transitional object, more important even than the mother. Unfortunately, he further restricted this approach, which accommodated a wide range of developmental behavior, and refused to designate as transitional anything which did not transcend the mother in importance. This narrowing of the definition of the transitional object to an area of pathological behavior is a disservice to the broader approach. The definition is further confused by Winnicott's attempt to distinguish between a comforter and a soother. A certain man had as a child a series of valued objects, the last of which was a soft green jersey with a red tie. This Winnicott described as a soother, a "sedative" which always worked, and characterized it as "a typical example of what I am calling a *'transitional object'* " (italics his). His definition was once again modified to a less extreme position in which the mother was not exceeded in importance. The approach has its advantages.

Normally many children have objects that acquire special importance as a defense against anxiety which is often first noted at bedtime. I commented (1970) that most children, after a suitable period, become mature enough to discard their special objects. In health, there is a gradual extension of interests which can be maintained, even when depression or anxiety might arise. In these cases the special object is no longer needed to overcome the affective reactions. The object is thus devalued and is no longer of central importance. This type of relationship to an inanimate object should be included within the spectrum for transitional objects.

An extreme relationship to such objects involves the supplanting of the parent by the toy or Teddy or blanket. This appears pathological and, in my experience, only occurs when mothering is poor. At this extreme end, little or no distinction exists between so-called transitional object and the childhood fetish as described by Wulff. In fact, Winnicott's only recorded objection to calling these objects fetishes was that a consideration of children's special relationships to inanimate objects should leave room for healthy early experience.

The evidence noted in the literature points to a *spectrum* composed at one end of children who use inanimate objects for their normal enjoyment and at the other of children who use them in a grossly pathological manner. Between these two extremes is a great middle group of children who use toys or other objects to relieve the anxiety and depression caused by separations from the mother, especially at sleep time. These children, however, are never so reliant on their objects that normal development falters. I suggest that the terms *transitional phenomenon* and *transitional object* be reserved for use with this large group who do not value their prized possession above their caretakers. Encompassed here is a whole range of behavior not seen in children who do value a "possession" above their mothers. These latter children use their prized possessions in the fetishistic manner described by Wulff, M. Sperling, and myself. The use of the terms *transitional phenomenon* and *transitional object* with this group should be avoided. This approach should help to resolve the differences of opinion indicated by Sperling and Greenacre. Most interactions with inanimate objects are healthy, so long as there is no interference with the appropriate maturation of interactional processes with the caretakers.

The abnormal use of an inanimate object is in my experience based upon a pathological interaction between mother and child that can lead to the development of a greater or lesser degree of childhood fetishism. The milder version may well be exemplified by Roy, reported upon so briefly by Stevenson. Such children often use their objects in sexual and aggressive ways. Parents notoriously fail to report this type of behavior since they are so involved in the child's activity.

My own observations (1963) and those already mentioned along with some culled from the papers of Mittelman (1955) and Buxbaum (1960) (who did not note the involvement of the caretakers) indicate that not only do the parents play an important role in the creation of the full-fledged transitional object or childhood fetish but that in doing so, *they set the stage for the development of adult fetishism.* I pointed out that the parents of children who utilize inanimate objects as transitional objects in Winnicott's extreme sense or as childhood fetishes do this to refocus the child's developing object cathexis, both sexual and aggressive, onto inanimate objects instead of onto themselves. This is done to decrease *parental* anxiety as well as infant anxiety. At the same time, the parents' own sexual and aggressive needs are gratified. It is no wonder that parents often conceal these matters and that parental contributions to the child's use of inanimate objects are often overlooked.

Parental involvement is also present in less pathological situations. Winnicott commented that the infant chooses the transitional object. This is only partly true. The choice of a transitional object which travels everywhere cannot be made without the mother's approval. The first not-me object develops from the accidental object, the corner of the blanket or other regularly present objects (Gaddini, chapter 8) which supplant a body part such as the thumb. This first not-me object is then used by the child as a pacifier; but it is not yet a transitional object. It is the mother who notices that the object quiets the child, thus relieving her of the burden of the infant's anxiety or rage. The power of the infant's emotional state manifested in its crying can drive many mothers to attempt anything that will quiet the child. These women then turn to the use of inanimate objects as intermediaries between themselves and their children. The amount of inanimate object dependence which is fostered varies from mother to mother. Those who ultimately allow themselves to be supplanted by an inanimate object are poor mothers who usually insist that it is all the child's doing. Yet it is the mother who supplies and cares for the object, gives it to the distressed child, and takes it along wherever the child goes. An example will explain further.

A young woman brought her son to another child's birthday party. While the children played happily, the mothers sat in a group talking. Suddenly, one of them said "I left Billy's whistle [!] in the car. He'll feel terrible without it." She almost ran to where the children were playing to ask her son whether he missed the whistle. Her anxiety was quickly communicated to the child, who began to cry. The mother then said rather apologetically that she had to find Billy's whistle, since he was so unhappy without it. Of course it was the mother who became unhappy and insisted on the presence of the whistle. Thus it was possible to observe, in process, the enhancement of an object by a parent.

Another example illustrates how a mother can use an inanimate object to refocus a child's drives from herself onto a toy. A boy was frustrated in his wishes to have more candy than his mother allowed. When he burst out in rage at her, she gave him his "Wah Wah" instead of managing the issue directly and dealing with the results of her restriction. "Wah Wah" was a rather strange and shapeless homemade doll that showed considerable wear and tear. The woman then told her son that he was making "Wah Wah" unhappy, that this wasn't nice. He should love "Wah Wah." The child banged the doll around a few times and then cuddled it. The candy was quite forgotten. Here again we can see how a mother can enhance the value of an inanimate object in place of herself. Eventually, the parent no longer has to teach the child to focus on the toy for its needs instead of the parent. We then have the object which goes everywhere, an attachment which is pathological.

It is clear enough that many children possess favored toys without significant parental preference. These objects, however, are interchangeable with other toys and, though they are discarded quite readily, the children can take them along wherever they go. However, these are not critical nor are they regularly substituted for important interpersonal exchanges with the parents. This, I believe, is well within the broad span of normality; the parental stake is minimal. It is different, however, in those instances in which the object assumes undue importance and is not discarded at an appropriate age. The parents are definitely involved in the process, and the object is used by the child not only for his needs but for the parents' as well.

I am aware of the child's own investment in the overvalued object and of the complex significance of the object to the child. The primary goal in this chapter, however, is to emphasize the significance of parental participation. It is my belief that advanced stages of object enhancement can occur only with parental participation. I refer here to the childhood fetish as a precursor of the adult fetish and to the entire sequence that begins with the first not-me object and leads to fetishism. This sequence extends from the not-me object to the first possession and then on to the true transitional object that fulfills so many purposes, only some of which are healthy.

The analysis of a woman demonstrated this clearly. Unhappily married, she had two children. The first was born during a time when her marriage was still successful. The second child, however, a boy, was born after the parents separated. He was considered an unnecessary burden, and the mother had much unexpressed hatred for the child. She was unable to bear any of the child's demands and continually avoided confrontation with even the normal demands of childhood, let alone the many unreasonable demands that stemmed from his general insecurity and the knowledge of his mother's ambivalence. The boy often cried bitterly and accused his mother of hating him.

The existence of the transitional object was not known until the patient's mothering abilities began to improve during the course of the analysis. In her associations, she mentioned that she had forgotten to bring her little boy's Raggedy Andy along when they visited her parents. Though upsetting to the little boy, this represented the inception of the mother's willingness to deal directly with his needs. Eventually the precursors of the Raggedy Andy doll were uncovered. The mother realized that an empty bottle quieted the child at bedtime and used this method to avoid any struggle concerning falling asleep. The bottle was then succeeded by rubber, nipple-shaped pacifiers which were less cumbersome. Soon a whole collection of pacifiers was available, each for a different occasion. They were all carried in a ritualistic manner wherever they went. The mother made this ceremony a pleasurable event, thus reinforcing the value of these objects to the child. It is important to stress that this was done for the mother, not for the child, who had no choice but to join in the developing sequence. When people began to comment on the pacifiers, the embarrassed mother offered the Raggedy Andy doll instead. She rewarded its use and punished the child if he resorted to the pacifiers.

Did the child's Raggedy Andy represent a childhood fetish more than an ordinary transitional object? Two distinctions are crucial. As stated, once the object assumes more importance than the mother, the boundary between normal and pathological has been crossed. My observations suggest that children with this degree of dependence on inanimate objects use these objects in a sexual fashion.

Usually it is difficult to elicit this information. The patient I have described did not reveal these events until several months following the mention of the doll. She required some resolution of her own sexual problems before she could let herself be fully aware of how her son treated the doll. Actually his behavior paralleled that of the previously described children; he used the doll for masturbatory purposes. The regular sexual use of an inanimate object characterizes the object as a fetish and the child as a fetishist. Even though the structure of childhood perversion is less complex than in the adult, the similarities seem sufficient to justify the label.

Many authors overlook any relationship between transitional objects and fetishes, and separate childhood fetishism from adult fetishism. This seems an artificial dichotomy. I have suggested previously (1963) that the evolvement of the fetishist and the selection of the fetish is a complex developmental process. Numerous factors including preoedipal experiences play a vital role in the production of this symptom complex. The fetish does not arise de novo in the adult, nor does it appear only in the phallic phase. Even in the young child the fetish has its precursors, sometimes in transitional objects not used in fetishistic ways. In some cases, however, even the earliest object may be used for sexual purposes, a type of behavior resembling fetishism. Thus there exists a continuum from the earliest objects through transitional objects to childhood and adult fetishes. However, since many object to ascribing fetishistic behavior to the infant and the child, the question arises, What is fetishism?

Freud (1905) took a rather broad point of view. He commented that an inanimate object or a part of the body is substituted for a sexual object. Fetishism was therefore considered a deviation in the choice of the sexual object, the first of which is the mother or, rather, her breast and face. Freud also believed that a certain element of fetishism was normal, adding that the overevaluation of the beloved extends to everything associated with her. As Romeo said to Juliet, "Oh that I were a glove upon the hand. . . ." A state close to full-fledged fetishism was attributed to those whose love objects must fulfill such special criteria as peculiar hair color or nose type. Thus, Freud suggested a broad spectrum of fetishistic behavior, ranging from the normal to the severely pathological.

Lexicographers' definitions parallel Freud's ideas. Hinsie and Shatzky (1953) pointed out that the fetish stands as a substitute for the loved person, while Webster (1957) defined it as any object given special or unreasoning devotion. Neither Freud nor the standard dictionaries restrict their definitions to a view that regards only perverse adult activity as fetishistic. This permits a conceptual approach in which the earliest object and the transitional object are parts of a series that can ultimately lead to an adult fetish. Because of its focus on early development, this view calls our attention to the role of parents, who through their influence on the infant and child can produce childhood as well as adult fetishistic behavior. It is a role frequently overlooked and ignored in a manner suggesting suppression, if not actual repression. This is especially true in situations involving direct parental seduction.

Some years ago a young woman was presented to me at a clinical conference. The police had brought her to the hospital emergency room several days previous. Extremely agitated, quite disheveled, and screaming for help, she had arrived at the police station hysterically clutching a doll. The police said she had demanded that her father be arrested for rape. Instead of investigating the story, they brought her to the hospital. The resident on duty took the doll away in spite of her vehement objections and sent her to a closed ward for unmanageable, homicidal, and suicidal patients. She was presented as a case of schizophrenia. Delusions of rape was the evidence.

I questioned the young woman, found no evidence of a thought disorder or affect disturbance, and then checked the details of the rape story. They led me to suspect that her story was true. I then asked the staff if they had corroborated the story with family members; this had not been done. After the conference her story was confirmed by a brother and an aunt who lived with the family. The aunt also indicated that the girl's father frequently molested her niece. Nothing was done about this because they were all afraid the man would kill them if they said anything. The patient's mother was also aware of her husband's behavior. When questioned about this and asked why she didn't interfere, she laughed and said her husband always made passes at young girls, that it didn't mean anything. She couldn't understand all the fuss.

Little was revealed concerning the doll. The mother said that her daughter always kept it with her, that she was silly about it, talking to it as a person. Her mother did remember giving it to her when she was little to "shut her up, she cried so much." Without meaning to, the mother made it abundantly clear that she had neglected her child. The little girl had been left alone for long periods of time and had even gone without food. The doll was her only support and stood in the place of a mother. One can only guess at all the ways in which she used her doll since this was not pursued by the staff and the patient had been discharged. This unfortunate young woman and others like her, victimized by such parents, receive little support in our culture. It was difficult to find a suitable placement for her and, typically, nothing was done about her father. Some even felt that, since the facts were known, the patient could return safely to her home.

Dunton and Bemporad's case report (1969) of an eight-year-old boy demonstrates a marked parental involvement in a fetishistic symptom. When the boy was referred for treatment by the school authorities, the teacher had called him a "goofy kid." He hit himself in the stomach, fell down in the classroom for no apparent reason, licked the classroom walls, and asked to go to the bathroom every five or ten minutes. The parents evidently did not object to this behavior; only after the referral by the school authorities did they complain that their son walked around in the nude and played with his penis. They also described how he invented names for his penis, such as Smarko and Schmartgo, and talked of a fantasyland called Schmakoland.

At first the parents did not mention that the boy used his mother's feet in a fetishistic manner. The mother then revealed with embarrassment that the boy would sneak up on her, remove her shoes and lick her feet. She maintained that she discouraged the act, but Dunton and Bemporad in the lengthy case report (which, unfortunately, had to be condensed for publication) correctly pointed out that she was careful not to wear stockings in order to have her feet readily available. By the time her son was five or six years old, erections, masturbation, and wild shouting accompanied the act of licking her feet. While the mother claimed she specifically prohibited the behavior, he still engaged in the practice when he was eight. His mother said nothing about it, even to his therapist. Whenever she did talk about the sexual interplay, she blamed it on the boy.

However, the facts of the developmental history tell a different story. Although the mother stated that the baby loved to play with her feet during his first year, she acknowledged that she encouraged it. She would lie in bed watching TV while the baby gave her a foot massage. Later the child was rewarded with money for licking her feet, and by the age of five or six the full-fledged act was established.

This child's pathological practice would be impossible without parental instigation and seduction. The crucial nature of the mother's role became apparent when the youngster's fetishistic behavior decreased. She resisted with many rationalizations suggestions by the therapist that would help to stop the activity, and, at least once—after her son had improved somewhat—she paid him money to massage her feet. She said that it was harmless and didn't matter. Unfortunately, treatment had to be interrupted.

A telephone call to the mother several months later revealed that the patient was "doing well and had no symptoms." In view of the parents' unreliability, this is questionable. The child had been blamed for inventing Schmako when actually his father had done so. His mother had tried to undermine the treatment. Sexual relations between the parents were rare, and the child had become the focus of the mother's sexuality. As with many such cases, a truly successful therapy for the child would require therapy for the parents as well.

SUMMARY

Childhood fetishes have been described as objects which children invest with intense feelings and toward which they display unusual behavior. This includes valuing the object more than the mother and using the objects for the discharge of sexual and aggressive tensions.

Winnicott took exception to the term *fetish* on the grounds that it left no room for consideration of the healthy aspects of the overvalued object, suggesting the term *transitional object*. Not all agree, however. This is related to an ambiguity about the transitional object. Winnicott stated that the object must be more important than the mother, an almost inseparable part of the infant, before it can be called a transitional object. However, he also wrote that the terms *transitional object* and *transitional phenomenon* should be used to designate the intermediate area of experience between a body part and an inanimate object. This experience is then externalized onto one object or phenomenon which becomes important to the child. This definition contradicts the narrower one according to which the object must be more important than the mother. I consider the broader definition more compatible with normal development and more useful in reconciling the various points of view concerning the significance of the transitional object and its relation to normal development.

Evidence points to the existence of a spectrum composed at one end of children who make no special use of inanimate objects other than for their enjoyment and at the other end of those who use inanimate objects in a grossly pathological manner. Between these extremes is the great middle group, children who use a toy or object to relieve anxiety and discharge tension, but never rely on objects to such an extent that normal development fails. I have suggested that the term *transitional object* be reserved for these children, who never value their prized possession more than their mothers. Children who do esteem their prized possession excessively show a pathological use of these objects. This is based upon a disturbed interaction between mother and child which can lead to the development of childhood fetishism. These children use their objects for sexual purposes quite regularly. Parents notoriously fail to report these sexual and aggressive usages since they are involved in creating the abnormal behavior. The role of the parents is significant even in the less extreme cases that fall within the normal range.

Winnicott believed that the child chooses the transitional object; this is only partly true. A child does not select a toy and take it everywhere without a mother who supplies the toy, cares for it, and brings it along when the family travels. These objects serve the mother's needs as much as the child's. Some parents teach their children to rely on these objects for comfort and gratification, thereby avoiding direct interaction with the parents. In a number of cases parents seduce their children and offer sexual gratification via their body parts or inanimate objects. Consequently, treatment should include the parent as well as the child.

REFERENCES

Buxbaum, E. (1960). Hair pulling and fetishism. *Psychoanalytic Study of the Child* 15:243-261.

Dickes, R. (1963). Fetishistic behavior: a contribution to its complex development and significance. *Journal of the American Psychoanalytic Association* 11:303-330.

——— (1970). Psychodynamics of fetishism. *Medical Aspects of Human Sexuality* 4:39-52.

Dunton, H. D., and Bemporad, J. (1969). Foot fetishism in an eight-year-old boy. *Bulletin of the Association for Psychoanalytic Medicine* 9:53-58.

Freud, A. (1965). *Normality and Pathology in Childhood: Assessments of Development.* New York: International Universities Press.

Freud, S. (1905). Three essays on sexuality. *Standard Edition* 7:125-244.

——— (1927). Fetishism. *Standard Edition* 21:149-159.

Greenacre, P. (1969). The fetish and the transitional object. *Psychoanalytic Study of the Child* 24:144-164.

——— (1970). The transitional object and the fetish with special reference to the role of illusion. *International Journal of Psycho-Analysis* 51:447-456.

Hinsie, L. E., and Shatzky, J. (1953). *Psychiatric Dictionary.* 2nd ed. New York: Oxford University Press.

Liten, E. N., Griffin, M. E., and Johnson, A. M. (1956). Parental influence in unusual sexual behavior in children. *Psychoanalytic Quarterly* 25:37-56.

Mittelmann, B. (1955). Motor patterns and genital behavior: fetishism. *Psychoanalytic Study of the Child* 10:241-264.

Shakespeare, W. (1938). Romeo and Juliet. In *Complete Works,* vol. 3 London: Nonesuch Press.

Sperling, M. (1959). A study of deviate sexual behavior in children by the method of simultaneous analysis of mother and child. In *Dynamic Psychopathology in Childhood,* ed. L. Jessner and E. Pavensted, pp. 221-242. New York: Grune and Stratton.

——— (1963). Fetishism in children. *Psychoanalytic Quarterly* 32:374-392.

Sperling, O. (1956). Psychodynamics of group perversions. *Psychoanalytic Quarterly* 25:56-66.

Stevenson, O. (1954). The first treasured possession. *Psychoanalytic Study of the Child* 10:215-241.

Webster's New International Dictionary (1957). 2nd ed. Springfield, Mass.: Merriam.

Winnicott, D. W. (1953). Transitional objects and transitional phenomena. *International Journal of Psycho-Analysis* 34:89-97.

Wulff, M. (1946). Fetishism and object choice in early childhood. *Psychoanalytic Quarterly* 15:450-471.

CHAPTER 21

Giovacchini focuses on the lack of internalization of the nurturing modality in cases where mothering has not been good enough. The resultant ego defect is traced in the therapy of several patients with schizophrenia and affective psychosis. He ties this to the lack of stability of the self-representations, and points out the specific vulnerabilities of these patients to disruption as well as their need for pathological primitive defense. Tolpin has indicated that the transitional object does not just fade away and diffuse into the cultural field as Winnicott had first thought; she believes that in normal development its soothing functions are structuralized by Kohut's process of transmuting internalization. In this volume, Kaminer and Parrish consider aspects of this problem.

Giovacchini considers as well the impact of his patient's delusions on his own sense of identity as an analyst and relates this to countertransference distortions which he had to cope with during his work with these seriously disturbed patients.

L.B.

THE IMPACT OF DELUSION AND THE DELUSION OF IMPACT: EGO DEFECT AND THE TRANSITIONAL PHENOMENON

Peter L. Giovacchini

The treatment of severely disturbed patients focuses upon early developmental phases. I will direct my attention to both clinical and technical issues as well as to developmental disturbances, which I believe particularly significant in understanding some of the difficulties experienced in the treatment of delusional and deeply disturbed patients. The vicissitudes of the transitional process as described by Winnicott (1953) are particularly significant in helping us explain the difficult transferences and the puzzling manifestations of psychopathology we encounter.

PERCEPTION OF REALITY
AND DEVELOPMENTAL VICISSITUDES

Such patients highlight the fact that the effects of early trauma are selective. Though the sense of reality is sufficiently defective to allow delusional distortions of the external world, other aspects of the perceptual system, especially those directed to the inner psychic world can be unusually sensitive and discriminating.

Severely disturbed patients reflect their psychopathology in object relationships and in the formation of introjects that will later be amalgamated in the ego's executive apparatus in order to construct both adaptations and defenses.

Inadequate mothering, regardless of its quality, leads generally to the defective endopsychic registration of the nurturing function. The internalization of a modality which leads to the sense of security that one will be cared for regardless of the actual presence of the nurturing source is, in essence, what Winnicott (1953) described as primary psychic creativity and the transitional phenomenon. Early trauma interferes with this process; emotional development is, so to speak, distorted, which is manifested in the patient's perception of reality and general functioning. The former often leads to viewing reality delusionally and oneself and others as fragmented and incompletely separated, the latter to failure of adaptation and, in certain circumstances, to inhibition of creativity.

Nevertheless, the comparative lack of ego structure may result in what might be considered a fluidity, enabling the patient to be in tune with both inner psychic elements and aspects of the external world that would ordinarily go unnoticed. The patient's need to introject rescuing experiences may make him particularly sensitive to selective attributes of object relationships which may be either consonant with or disruptive to his needs.

In some instances, the patient's self-representation may be so vulnerable that often he has to believe he has rescued himself, that is, he clings to the delusion that he is self-sufficient and needs no one. To admit dependence is to permit others to intrude upon his minimal autonomy, clearly a repetition of the assaultive infantile traumatic environment. The patient attempts to reconstruct a situation similar to the developmental task of autonomously forming an introject of the nurturing function, a development which is itself the very definition of the transitional process. Projected into the surrounding world this introject represents the transitional object.

Insofar as psychopathology is based upon an intrusive traumatic infantile environment, the patient is exquisitely susceptible to any transaction which might impinge upon his precariously structured self-representation. The psychoanalytic process aims at preserving and promoting autonomy. Thus, regardless of how seriously disturbed such patients may be, many adapt quite well to analysis since it is designed not to impose values, not to manipulate or manage one's life. In other words, it is dedicated to releasing the patient's developmental potential. Analysis fosters whatever initiative the patient may have retained from his traumatic childhood in order to reestablish, or establish, his primary psychic creativity and to successfully negotiate the transitional process.

DELUSION: PERVASIVENESS AND IMPACT

I do not want to give the impression that psychotic patients with an unusual grasp of analysis are easy to treat. They are not. They present special difficulties which, if unrecognized, can totally disrupt analysis, which will then fail them just as in childhood their environment failed them. This does not mean, however, that there is something intrinsic in their psychopathology that would cause them to fail in analysis with every therapist. On the other hand, this does not require the analyst to have unique personality characteristics and sensitivity beyond those usually found in analysts. Perhaps the only feature that deserves emphasis is the analyst's willingness to continue analyzing even though, because of countertransference difficulties, he may temporarily have lost sight of his professional role (see Green, chapter 11). Furthermore, the type of countertransference difficulties to be described are almost ubiquitous and not necessarily indicative of specific psychopathology or an idiosyncratic orientation.

I wish to discuss the disruptive effects of delusional material, material indicative of defenses based upon structural psychopathology, on analysis. Under what circumstances do analysts find themselves stymied by the patient's delusions and then decide that such patients are untreatable? I wish to present some clinical situations that include both schizophrenic and affective psychoses.

A scientist, in his late twenties, spent most of his interviews describing in tremendous detail his attempts at what he called soul traveling. By this he meant that some persons are able to separate their souls from their bodies and travel anywhere they wish, but their ultimate goal is to reach certain planes located at different heights according to some kind of spiritual hierarchy. I need not go into the intricacies of his system, but its obvious goal was the attainment of total omnipotence. Anyone with a literary bent could pull this patient's material together and undoubtedly fill up several volumes of passable science fiction.

He was appallingly naive and had suspended entirely his extensive knowledge of scientific methodology. I wish to concentrate upon the structure of the delusions here, since they could be considered concrete expressions of defensive psychic operations designed to protect the patient's vulnerable self-representation.

Since his construction of the universe was based upon some known principles, it was in some measure testable. He subdivided the universe into a spiritual and a material universe. For him, the spiritual replaced the material universe and since the essence of spiritual mastery was omnipotence, his achievements would include predicting the future. He has himself not yet achieved such omnipotent abilities, but the various persons he talked to through telepathic communication had. As an aside, I was surprised to learn that there are actually local and national organizations involved in soul traveling. The members achieve different degrees, somewhat like Masons, based upon their attainment of various spiritual levels and "soul planes." In other words, his delusional system received considerable support from the external world and in that particular sector he would be considered eminently normal.

To repeat, the patient presented his universe as if it were testable in terms of my material universe. One of the masters telepathically told him that several different things would happen to him, about six in all, by the end of the year. All failed to materialize. My first inclination was to review the situation with him and to use this as evidence that he had made many unwarranted assumptions. I felt inclined to engage him in a discussion of scientific method to help him regain some of his lost reality sense.

Unable to suppress all of my feelings, I asked him, against my better judgment, what he felt about the reliability of all the assumptions of omnipotence he had assigned various spiritual forces and deified persons in his soul-traveling universe. I should have known better and been able to predict his obvious response. Of course, he was not the least abashed by the failure of the materialization of the predictions. The master that had made the predictions had negative karma toward him as a residue from a previous existence. I cannot tell you exactly what karma is, although he has repeatedly explained it to me. It has something to do with forces and feelings which can lead to positive or negative consequences for the person possessing it or for the person toward whom it is directed. I suspect it can be reduced to primal feelings of love and hate, but in any case the patient was using such concepts as karma and reincarnation to supply a retrospective explanation for the failure of his predictions. In fact, it seemed as if this failure served to strengthen further his belief in his system.

I was nonplussed. I should not have been irked, except perhaps at myself, because, as we all know, one cannot deal directly with the content of a delusion. The paranoid patient is especially adept at using any kind of data, supporting or, to us, nonsupporting, to reinforce his delusional beliefs. I believe that my irritation may have, to some measure, stemmed from certain specific characteristics of this patient that most patients do not have.

He is a scientist and truly an expert in scientific method. In any other area he would have been the first to emphasize that any hypothesis is meaningless unless it is phrased in such a fashion that it is capable of disproof.

The tremendous discrepancy between his scientific identity and the delusional system and the degree to which I identified with his scientific identity caused me to feel uncomfortably irritated with him. The fact that I had responded in a fashion that was contrary to my theoretical (scientific) orientation only served to increase my irritation because, in a sense, I was behaving like the patient. I had flaunted basic principles, principles which I held in high esteem. I denied a part of myself as had the patient with his delusional system. He considered his system scientific and had forsaken conventional science. I will return to what amounts to an identification with the patient's psychosis later.

Although this patient spoke of many interesting things, for his was a colorful delusion, in an intelligent and engaging manner, there was very little entertainment value to his associations and I often found them uninteresting. They were hard to listen to.

I was puzzled about this until I had a particularly significant glimpse of him one afternoon in my waiting room. He was sitting with a book in his hand, not reading it, just holding it by his side. His face had the most desolate, isolated look I have ever seen. He looked truly miserable but in a quiet, desperate fashion. He seemed entirely alone. I then learned that his wife was very depressed. There was practically no relationship between the two of them because he was always "off" somewhere, reading the master's writings, doing his spiritual exercises, carefully noting his physical reactions in order to regulate his cancer-dissolving diet and other activities involving his delusional system. He had even stopped working because he could not devote such a large block of time to a job. In fact, he was unable to work. He was completely blocked in his creativity, whereas prior to his delusions he was quite productive.

His wife, who in no way shared his views, felt totally left out. She could not eat with him because his faddist, ascetic diet did not permit him to eat ordinary foods. For some reason, which I never understood completely, he could not permit himself sexual relations. Apparently he had to attain some level of spiritual development which he had not yet achieved. His wife would not participate in any social activities because she felt embarrassed about her husband, since he would not eat or drink anything offered at a social gathering and would try to convert other guests to his dietary practices and spiritual beliefs. He proselytized.

The picture that emerged was of an empty, joyless life for him and his wife. I felt sympathy for the spouse, whom I saw as a depressed woman whose whole life was directed toward keeping her eccentric "nutty" husband from doing something that would cause her humiliation or possibly even endanger her financial security. She was afraid that he would irresponsibly donate or invest large sums of money. He had, prior to seeking therapy, lost sizable sums by using systems of investment unique to him, and so far as I know, unrelated to any accepted economic principles.

I am emphasizing that his delusion was pervasive. It extended into all activities and it was this pervasiveness that made the atmosphere in the consultation room heavy and oppressive. More than anything, I felt the joylessness of his life, the total lack of anything in it that I could consider pleasurable. There were no frenzied feelings of depression or abject misery, only dull and colorless sermons. Consequently, I felt weighed down and, at times, reacted to his associations as if he were pounding me, the blows becoming increasingly stronger.

I felt his impact and my natural inclination was to respond to him as his wife did, that is, to pull him out of his delusional system. She would constantly keep after him, calling him when he would start his spiritual exercises or when he would get a blank trancelike expression on his face indicative of a reverie in which he believed his soul had left his body. I, of course, could not use such methods. The only recourse I would have had would have been to argue with him.

The patient provoked his wife into treating him like a naughty little boy constantly getting into mischief. In analysis, he was becoming similarly provocative and this represented an important transference orientation. He was extremely ambivalent, clinging to his delusional system and, at the same time, pleading to be brought back into the world of material reality. However, for many reasons he was terrified of reality and had to retreat into a delusion in which everything was under complete control, in which he could omnipotently regulate all activities and feel himself magnificently invulnerable.

As this picture of the patient and our relationship gradually emerged, my understanding made it easier for me to deal with him. Still, disturbing elements remained which make the treatment of psychotic patients difficult. These are related to the all-embracing, pervasive quality of some delusions, which tempts the analyst to abandon his therapeutic stance. Before discussing the various facets of the analytic interaction with such patients, I wish to present material from a patient who had a similar impact upon the therapeutic relationship. Here it took a different form.

This patient, a middle-aged, lonely widower, was markedly paranoid. He heard persecutory voices from time to time and was constantly getting himself into trouble because he attempted to fight his persecutors. For example, he would make innumerable telephone calls harassing the administrative personnel of a hospital he had once been confined in because of his psychosis. He felt mistreated and the calls were his method of "telling them off" and seeking revenge.

Our relationship was friendly. He wanted me to side with him, two against the world. He is an eloquent speaker and a very intelligent, sensitive, and perceptive person. In order to tempt me into being his co-conspirator, he would expound viewpoints, make analyses, and lecture about topics that I found extremely interesting.

One evening the patient called me at home. He was in a state of frenzy bordering on panic. Apparently he had called a hospital official and vented his anger to the point where his speech became obscene. This official called the police and a policeman paid him a visit. This time he was simply warned but was told that the next time he would be put in jail. I was not pleased with his calling me at home, but in view of his distraught condition and the obvious relief he gained from sharing this traumatic experience with me, I decided not to pursue the matter further.

The patient then constantly tried to manipulate me into situations in which I would rescue him. He sometimes succeeded. I was able to control situations in which he asked me to call or write someone by simply refusing, and he understood my reasons for doing so. He did not resent my refusals and respected my attempts to avoid participation in his external world.

It was interesting to note how everyone became irritated with him, not just the people he had been harassing. The operators on my telephone service were both amused and annoyed by him. My wife and children resented his calls although he was always courteous and respectful.

I reached my peak of annoyance when finally he was put in jail. I had told him that I would absolutely not get involved again and, if he found himself in trouble, he would have to depend on his own resources. Shortly after he was arrested, I received a telephone call from the court psychiatrist, who happened to be one of my former students. Before I could say anything beyond the usual amenities, he reassured me that he would do anything *I* wanted concerning the patient. In contrast to others who dealt with my patient, this psychiatrist, a big friendly warm type, liked him. I had on one occasion done something for this student which was more than would have been expected of me. I had, in effect, rescued him, and now he felt impelled to return the favor. I explained the situation thoroughly to him, and although he accepted everything I said intellectually, I could still feel that he wanted to render some service beyond his official duties. He made good this wish by persuading the judge that the patient was a worthy individual who would not repeat his mischievous behavior since he could be controlled by psychotherapy. The judge released him with the provision that he make no more harassing telephone calls and that he remain in treatment.

I began to feel as if the world were working against me. I had not, however, completely incorporated my patient's paranoia, since at times the situation struck me as comic. The latter view gave way to irritation when the patient tried to persuade me to serve as a mediator with a former homosexual partner with whom he had had an altercation. Not only would this have been therapeutically unfeasible; I simply did not want to intercede.

One might wonder why I found such situations so irksome. After all, I could do as I pleased; I was not going to be forced to do anything I did not want to. True, I could not prevent others from calling me, but I could have presented the patient with an ultimatum, which eventually I did, rather than letting myself get upset. Apparently he had succeeded in stirring certain disruptive feelings in me, as had also the scientist patient, feelings which I believe many analysts share. Perhaps making them explicit may cause us to feel more charitable in our assessments of the treatability of psychotic patients.

The scientist patient created an atmosphere that was completely filled with his delusions. It infused all of his perceptions and activities in the outer world as well as completely occupying the consultation room. It was omnipresent and pervasive. I could almost feel its heaviness and was burdened by its oppressiveness. Its joylessness only added to my distress.

As I have mentioned, at times I felt impelled to shake some sense into him. The repetitive, monotonous recounting of the innumerable details and omnipotent aspects of his delusional system had a maddening effect. I was feeling the impact of this all-pervasive delusion and had fantasies of being completely engulfed and inundated by his material. I was perhaps reacting with a *counterdelusion of impact*. Some analysts have described similar feelings, expressed somatically, toward patients. They may feel pressure, usually on the chest or head; in contrast, I did not respond somatically except for, on occasion, a feeling of general tension.

The effect the second patient had on me was similar, although he created different technical problems. His material was as pervasive as that of the scientist, but it was not dull and monotonous. Nor did I feel inclined to argue with him. I had no urge to impose my reality upon him; on the contrary, his sessions were interesting and, if anything, I ran the risk of becoming too involved. Still, within the context of his sessions, no matter how seductive his material may have been, it was not difficult to maintain an analytic orientation. The transference projections were easily discernible; he had idealized me by projecting omnipotent grandiose feelings and was trying to please me by presenting himself as a very interesting and sensitive person. He also wanted to effect a symbiotic fusion; we could then megalomanically control the universe. One could work with this material analytically.

Complications arose when the patient tried to bring *the analysis into the delusional outer world* he had constructed. The scientist, in contrast, brought *the delusional outer world into the analysis.* In either case, I felt the impact of their attempts and reacted adversely.

My response of a delusion of impact is a somewhat dramatic and exaggerated expression of my reactions. I was not, of course, delusional in the traditional sense. I had most of my faculties and, at one level, found all of this quite interesting: interesting and disturbing enough to impel me to write this article, an activity which has mustered more secondary process and enabled me to pull together what had been a number of disparate observations. Still, the fact that the label, delusion of impact, still continues to be appealing must in itself be of some significance.

Myerson (1973) emphasizes how the patient's modus vivendi can lead to impasses in analysis which demand special, although not nonanalytic technical responses. Kernberg (1972) and Khan (1960) refer to particular aspects of patients suffering from severe psychopathology that create difficulties in treatment if not specifically understood; even then, it may not be possible to transcend them. Milner (1969) presents a detailed account of the analysis of a severely disturbed schizoid woman who many analysts would undoubtedly have considered too disruptive for analysis. Milner was able to overcome certain technical difficulties by encouraging the patient to bring drawings to her as equivalents to free associations. Thus she was able to maintain the analytic setting. Winnicott (1949) discusses how patients tend to repeat in analysis the assaultive intrusions, the "impingements" of early object relationships, and how the analyst may respond with a disruptive discomfort to feeling impinged upon. In all these articles, the authors directly or indirectly refer to maneuvers that the analyst can resort to in order to regain comfort and to be able to function from an analytic perspective.

The discomforts emphasized here represent potentially disruptive countertransference reactions that are outcomes of the loss of an analytic stance. These patients threatened my analytic identity and I felt uncomfortable.

To threaten one's identity or to make the functional aspects of the identity sense inoperative must lead to an existential crisis. It may not exactly reach crisislike proportions, but one must feel to some extent confused and impotent (see Erikson 1959). My subjective reaction to these attempts to paralyze my analytic activity was to feel submerged—the dominant manifestation of my delusion of impact. I felt submerged, much as patients who have identity problems do when there is an overwhelming, intrusive mother-imago (Giovacchini 1964) and they have not successfully experienced the transitional situation. It is easy, under these circumstances, to regard the treatment situation as impossible and to rationalize that the patient is untreatable. This often may be the case, but "untreatable" actually means untreatable by a particular analyst, or even by most analysts. The patient is unanalyzable only if *all* analysts react in the same fashion.

A professional identity contributes significantly to self-esteem. It is a valued aspect of the ego-ideal. Analysts generally feel uncomfortable when, for whatever reason, they are unable to continue functioning in their analytic capacity. In situations where the analyst's inner conflicts do not prevent him from functioning analytically, one may scrutinize particular aspects of the transference-countertransference interaction and focus upon the content of the patient's productions. The scientist patient, besides threatening my analytic identity, was also denigrating specific aspects of my ego-ideal. His proposing, even though he was a scientist, that his delusional system was scientific, meant to me that he was attacking science, an area I hold in high esteem. An unawareness of what the patient is doing makes it easier to give in to the temptation to argue in order to protect and often to justify one's value systems (see Giovacchini 1972, 1975).

The scientist had to bring me back into the analytic frame of reference, thereby illustrating maneuvers that stem from the patient. Recall my reactions when he used his failed predictions as further proof of the validity of his delusion; I abandoned my analytic stance. He threatened my analytic identity by the continuing and unshakeable pervasiveness of his delusion, offending my ego-ideal with the absurdity of his contentions. I responded by emphasizing that he was clinging to omnipotence, that his need for magic had apparently obscured his good judgment. Later, I realized that my exaggerated reaction was in part due to the tremendous letdown I experienced.

When he first told me about the predictions, six months prior to their expected materialization, I had some trepidation. Prophesies such as moving his home and leaving analysis could easily become self-fulfilling. Consequently, I was relieved when they did not come true. I must confess I also felt somewhat smug and saw myself sitting back in my chair like a mother hen clucking, "See, I told you so." Consequently, when he explained the lack of fulfillment of the predictions as the outcome of negative karma, I was suddenly deflated. My world could no longer be maintained as superior to his; it collapsed.

After my retort, which was in fact a rebuke, the patient's demeanor completely changed. His voice, in contrast to its usual monotonous quality, became emotional. With considerable affect, he agreed that he had a tremendous need for magic and that indeed he was clinging to omnipotence and magical salvation. He had to replace what he called the world of material reality by a world filled with karma. He emphasized how cruel and dangerous he found my world and how vulnerable, helpless, afraid, and devastatingly miserable he felt. He was justifying himself, but, interestingly enough, he was being solicitous toward me. He was indirectly telling me, "Come on, Doctor, wake up! Can't you see how weak I am—can't you see through all of this—can't you see how I desperately need to cling to some type of salvation? You cannot take this away from me now. Be an analyst—help me not need all this and then I will determine whether I want to give up these beliefs. Right now I have no choice." At least, that is the way I heard him, and I do not believe that I have embellished what he was communicating, as one might out of guilt.

Initially, I felt foolish and somewhat ashamed of myself. Afterwards, however, I experienced some exhilaration because now I could once more look at the patient from an analytic perspective. I had been properly reprimanded, but both the patient and I survived the situation. I had, in addition, regained my analytic identity and could look at his delusion as an important adaptation which helped him to maintain a defensive equilibrium. I also surmised that at some time in the future when I would begin to feel anew the impact of the patient's material, I would once more transgress. He probably would need to remind me that I am an analyst, refueling me for the analytic task.

Actually, nothing dramatic happened. On occasion, I slipped into a mild debate about the validity of some of his assertions, but my challenge usually brought some relevant material to the surface, material relating to anxiety about his vulnerable self-representation and a destructive maternal imago which threatened to devour him. Insofar as he could project the latter into me and then make me weak and impotent by his pervasive delusion, he felt relatively safe. Gradually, the elements of his delusion were traced to intrapsychic structures or superstructures used to render frightening introjects harmless. The patient is still in treatment and this process is continuing.

The situation with the paranoid patient was quite different and required the second type of maneuver. I, rather than the patient, had to make a confrontation in order to preserve the analysis. Whereas the first patient helped me regain my analytic identity, I had to do something that would cause the patient to regain his identity as analysand. Of course, this would help me function comfortably as an analyst. It did not necessitate any difficult or subtle interventions; I simply told the patient that I would not continue to be involved with his life outside the consultation room. As far as I was concerned, there was no external world—everything he told me was a product of his imagination, something he had constructed, like a fantasy, a dream, or a delusion. Or at least it would be considered this way. The patient understood my reasons and agreed to abide by my wishes.

After several months of a relatively serene analysis, he called me in order to put in a good word for him with a person he had once offended. I was furious, told him so, and hung up. Later, I felt I had overreacted due to something personal that had been stirred up. But I mastered it and the patient has made no further demands. Undoubtedly he will, but I now believe I can enforce the condition I laid down without becoming upset. I have also learned that provoking me was his method of defeating me, a need that is the product of his psychopathology and that as such should not be mixed up with my personal feelings.

IMPACT OF AFFECTIVE PSYCHOSIS

The patients just described conducted themselves in a reserved, well-mannered fashion. Their overt behavior was not disruptive or threatening. By contrast, one sometimes encounters patients whose behavior is extremely agitated, perhaps bordering on violence. Paradoxically, if analysis is attempted they prove less disturbing than the more subtle schizophrenic patients discussed here.

The patient I will describe suffered from an agitated depression which led to total helplessness. She was disturbed enough to be considered psychotic, and had been given a course of electric shock therapy.

Such patients are commonly seen in hospitals and clinics but rarely in an analyst's office. Their behavior is so disruptive that they are summarily rejected for analytic treatment. The impact they create is so obvious that the analyst is reluctant to become involved. Still, since this impact is so obvious and, from a developmental viewpoint, they are further advanced than schizophrenics, one wonders whether the difficulties they create in treatment cannot in fact be surmounted.

A psychiatrist referred a postmenopausal woman to me for "consultation." It was obvious that he could no longer stand her and was looking for a way out. Perhaps he hoped I would simply take her off his hands. I had no wish to see her but agreed to do so for reasons that are not relevant here. To my surprise, I learned that the only way I could relate to her was by strictly adhering to the analytic method. The patient, in turn, demonstrated to me how early developmental phases imperfectly and ambivalently structured the nurturing modality (the transitional phenomenon) so as to render her almost violently helpless.

When I first saw the patient (a fifty-year-old woman) in my waiting room, she was pacing back and forth with an anguished stare while her husband was sitting relatively calm. Seeing me, she grabbed her husband's hand and started rushing into the consultation room. I let her pass but stood on the threshold of the door when her husband attempted to pass. I told him that I had to speak to his wife alone. She howled, but he seemed to understand and retreated back into the waiting room.

She began by assailing me for not letting her husband in. I had to admit him because she was so confused she could tell me nothing. She could not survive without her husband's support.

I replied that I wanted to understand her confusion. It would be especially difficult for me to deal with two minds, so I preferred to see her alone. She then screamed something about my having to help her; in a rapid, staccato fashion, she poured out a tremendous amount of personal history. I will not enumerate these details here as they are neither relevant to my thesis nor necessary to an understanding of the treatment process.

The patient was standing throughout this narrative, or rather was dancing around, shifting her posture, and going through the motions of walking—marking time. I motioned her to the couch. She protested that she could not lie down as she was lying down already. The upper part of her body seemed relaxed, but she kept banging her feet together by alternately adducting and abducting her legs. She now screamed, "Aren't you going to give me drugs?" I answered, "Apparently you want me to fail you in the same way as my predecessors." She then calmly said, "I have been taking Marplan for fourteen years and now look at me." Her mood suddenly changed and she howled, "Tell me what to say." I chuckled, "It is really amazing how adept you are at asking me to do things I cannot do," and then referred to her demands about seeing her husband, prescribing drugs, and now structuring the interview according to my preconceived notions. She then made additional demands, ranging from asking me to tell her how to get to my office to how she would be able to pay my fees. I kept absolutely silent, feeling more comfortable saying nothing than attempting an obvious interpretation or asking an "analytic question" such as inquiring as to her motives for asking such questions. She kept jumping up from the couch, staring at me, and insisting that I answer her. I did not believe I was being silent simply to resist her demands; I felt she was controlling me whether I replied or not, but it was easier for me not to reply and I therefore felt less controlled. I also felt it was in her best interest to let her express her need to control me.

The patient persisted in her demands. Again she insisted I see her husband. I felt that I had to define the analytic situation incontrovertibly and assert my analytic identity, even if I were to lose the patient. Consequently, I told her I would see her husband, but once he walked through the door, she would leave and could never return. I believe I said this in a nonchallenging fashion and with perhaps a tone of regret. She immediately relaxed and once again lay down. Our time was up, however, and as I ushered her to the door, she renewed her agitation. She clutched her chest, moaned, and stated she was suffering from a terrible, sharp pain. I replied that perhaps she was feeling the pain of separation. She whimpered that she has this pain all the time. I then said that she was trying to defeat and confuse me.

As I opened the door to the waiting room, the husband moved toward me and gently asked me for a report on his wife's condition. I stated that I could not talk to him about his wife's condition but she would be able to explain what was necessary. She protested loudly that she was too confused and then proceeded to tell him that I wanted to analyze her, and that this would entail daily visits; she then told him my fee and that I felt she was trying to drive everyone crazy. I thought I detected an enlightened and approving facial gesture on the husband's part in reaction to my interpretation. He said nothing and started leading her out. She screamed she could not go home and wanted to spend the rest of the day with me. He gently led her away.

During the first session, she demanded to know why I did not take notes. I replied I was too busy listening to her. Several sessions later she repeated this question. I reminded her she had already asked that question. She did not remember. I was surprised because she had apparently remembered everything else I had said. I then repeated my response. In a calm, much deeper voice, she said, "I can only take in the bad things."

It became easy to converse with two different aspects of the patient's character: one I refer to as her helpless, vulnerable self; the other as her capable, competent self. Prior to her depression she had been a highly competent business woman and even now she experienced this part of the self in dreams whose manifest content usually referred to successful accomplishments.

The patient continues in treatment and the course is stormy. I need not elaborate, because I wish to emphasize only how her primitive orientation, her infantile fixations, threatened the establishment of an analytic relationship (one which many would have considered absurd even to consider). By contrast, even though the patient's demeanor produced a definite impact on me and threatened my analytic identity, I felt that the only way I could relate to her was within an analytic frame of reference.

This patient's behavior was incomparably more disruptive than that of the schizophrenic patients. She tried hard to make me experience her helplessness and misery, and was often successful. Her maneuvering seemed directed toward my relinquishing my analytic stance and rescuing her. Still, in spite of all her turmoil, it was not impossible to maintain the analytic setting. This might have been easier because I knew all else had failed—what did I have to lose? I believe also that there are intrinsic aspects of her character that account for her having created less impact than the schizophrenic patients.

She lamented that once she had been an effective, functioning person but that now she was just a "vegetable"; but even this denoted some structure and organization, because she said it a little humorously, adding "Not even a good vegetable." To me this meant that she had at one time constructed a stable identity which I was glimpsing even now. Consequently, when she projected disruptive aspects of her self-representation into me, my analytic identity did not feel threatened.

The fact that the patient had once achieved an identity, regardless of how defensively constructed it might have been, could have made her less covetous of mine. Furthermore, patients suffering severe characterological problems tend to project amorphous and destructive aspects of their self-representation into the analyst. Insofar as patients suffering from affective disorders retain some aspects of a former identity, their projections, as they reflect the way they view themselves, are less pervasive and have less of an impact than do those of schizophrenic patients whose identity sense is less organized.

Depressed patients view objects ambivalently, that is, in terms of their loving or destructive potential. Schizophrenics relate in terms of total annihilation or omnipotent salvation, whereas in the analytic relationship the depressed patient is able to perceive the analyst as a relatively well-structured person.

My depressed patient attacked discrete aspects of my analytic identity with her demands. The schizophrenic patients, on the other hand, tended to inundate me totally, attacking the analytic and all other aspects of my identity.

DEVELOPMENTAL ANTECEDENTS AND CLINICAL ASSESSMENT

The transference manifestations of these severely disturbed patients emphasized structural factors and ego defects due to faulty development. As I have stressed, this had a special impact on the therapist, whose various ego systems (i.e., self-representation and ego-ideal) were involved.

I wish to present a view of psychic development by Winnicott (1953) which I find particularly useful in the treatment of psychotic patients and patients suffering severe characterological psychopathology. It will be recalled that Winnicott believed that the infant who had experienced a successful mothering relationship finally reached a stage at which he believed he had created the gratifying breast. This stage, referred to as the transitional situation, is supported by optimal mothering. Insofar as the nurturing source provides immediate gratification, the infant can maintain the illusion that he has created his own gratification. The external world is congruent with his needs; the mothering aspect need therefore not be distinguished as separate. Winnicott calls this process primary psychic creativity.

One can think in terms of the infant's belief that the introject of the gratifying breast was formed by the inner world. The infant also constructs an immediately surrounding space over which he maintains omnipotent control, a space different from the more distant segments of the external world, which he has no control over and therefore prefers to ignore. The projection of the part-object breast onto objects in this space, a space that is essentially an extension of the ego boundary, leads to the formation of the transitional objects.

The infant at these early developmental phases does not of course believe anything; nor does he know anything about breasts as breasts or part-objects. To ascribe an illusion of creating to a neonate is patently absurd. These are words the adult uses to make intelligible certain observations made of adult patients who have undergone a transference-regression which demonstrates primitive psychic processes and development. Most likely, the infant is merely aware of vague states of comfort and discomfort and senses something about the directional nature of events related to the reestablishment of homeostasis.

Much of what Winnicott has described seems to be expressed in terms of a metaphor, but an extremely important metaphor. The transitional situation and primary psychic creativity, in my mind, refer to the structuring of an introject of the *nurturing modality*. Insofar as mothering has been synchronous with the child's needs, the mothering experience is smoothly incorporated within the ego. The infant, because he does not feel intruded upon, is forced neither to acknowledge the external world nor to defend himself against it.

A gratifying experience somehow promotes structuralization or creates favorable conditions allowing maturational processes to proceed. The perceptual system achieves a broader range of activity, and a wider variety of stimuli can be integrated within the ego. The stable incorporation of a gratifying source is beneficial to the development of all ego systems.

When the child develops beyond being a simple physiological, reflex organism, a good feed does not necessarily lead to sleep. True, homeostasis is reestablished, but this does not connote a lack of psychic activity. A homeostatic state is one of equilibrium—nondisruptive and optimal for psychic growth. An initially global ego can become differentiated into a variety of subsystems.

The acquisition of an inner nurturing modality provides the psyche with an internal regulator. It must also be emphasized that this transitional process is an outcome of the healthy resolution of the symbiotic phase. A successfully traversed symbiotic phase, besides resulting in the construction of a nurturing introject, leads also to a solidification of the self-representation as structuralization proceeds in the direction of object relationships.

With further ego synthesis, the self-representation incorporates the nurturing modality and, as already stated, the child begins to perceive himself as adequate and capable of taking care of himself. Again, I am dealing in metaphors, imputing to the child concepts to be found only at later stages of emotional development. The child does not "think" about these matters at all, but his capacity to be unconcerned about comfort and survival contributes to a primal state of security which is elaborated later in life.

From a theoretical perspective, it can be stated that after emergence from maternal symbiosis, the ego acquires or consolidates new structures. The early self-representation is enhanced by the incorporation of the nurturing modality, and the psyche, because of internal security, can turn to the outer world and external objects for further helpful experiences. The child can integrate the beneficial aspects of relationships, which causes expansions and structuralization of perceptual, integrative, and executive ego systems. This in turn leads to increased security, self-esteem, and confidence.

As the psyche continues to differentiate, the child (and, later, the adult) derives pleasure in his ability to take care of himself. Knowing that inner needs can be met causes further involvement with external objects. The ego can project valued parts of the self and this results in intimate, mutually rewarding relationships.

To project good things into someone else is an act of generosity, since the person is, in a sense, "giving away" something that is valued. The external object is then valued not only because of what is projected but because the projection enables him to discover parts of the external object that he can value and cherish.

Something similar happens during creative activity, the optimal outcome of primary psychic creativity. There is in the creative act a projection of something valued which stems from the transitional situation insofar as the subject believes this aspect of himself to be self-created, without antecedent in the external world. Most frequently, what is created is a unique and novel arrangement and positioning of external percepts into combinations having no counterparts in reality. Actually, to speak of projection here is a very loose use of the term because usually there is no external object—no person. Still, the creator experiences what is happening to him as a projection; he is putting parts of himself into what he feels to be an outside situation, whether something concrete or an abstract idea.

In psychopathology, absence of constructive experiences during early childhood leads to lacunae in the ego's executive system. The inability to structure the transitional state through the achievement of primary psychic creativity will be reflected in the patient's integration and will influence the nature of future psychopathology.

The schizophrenic patients demonstrated a total lack of confidence in their abilities to sustain themselves. This can be conceptualized as a developmental fixation where primary psychic creativity has occurred only minimally and the transitional situation has been weakly established. The psychotic symptoms, manifested by the construction of an omnipotent delusional world in the scientist and by controlling the external world by paranoid projections in the other patient, represent overcompensatory defensive adaptations to the terrifying state of defenseless helplessness, inadequacy, and overwhelming vulnerability. Both patients were able, through their delusions, to deny the absence of inner resources, of the nurturing, protective modality.

The extent of this denial was highlighted when the scientist patient, because of analysis, was no longer able to maintain his megalomanic delusional system. He then had to effect a massive withdrawal from a threatening and destructive world, one he was unable to manage. At first he regressed to a state of extreme dependency and infantilism in which he gave up all adult characteristics, remaining in bed and preoccupying himself exclusively with food. When this situation became intolerable to his family, he had to be hospitalized. He then withdrew further into a catatonic stupor, so classical that he demonstrated the phenomenon of waxy flexibility. Gradually, he was able to relate cautiously to some of the safer aspects of his environment without his delusions, and after several weeks returned home and resumed his analysis.

The scientist patient had perhaps been able to achieve some primary psychic creativity, a structured position from which he had regressed. I assume this because in the past he had made professional contributions which were considered ingenious and creative. This capacity had become regressively distorted in his delusions, but not destroyed, since the delusions had colorful and what might be considered creatively organized elements.

The paranoid patient, as is common, had delusions of being poisoned. Food for him was often perceived as dangerous and he occasionally fasted. During his treatment he had generalized this attitude and found the world hostilely withholding or destructively giving. This viewpoint determined his general paranoid attitude and his reactive behavior.

The introject of maternal nurture was a destructive introject. The transitional state did not lead to the acquisition of the transitional object, nor was it smoothly incorporated into the psyche as an aspect of the self-representation. It was projected instead into the external world rather than into the area specified by Winnicott, and, as the patient's behavior indicated, he then needed to control the world. As I have indicated, this created special problems in treatment, as he tried to involve me with his reality. He did not confine his need for control in the space between himself and reality—the space in which the transitional process is characteristically located.

My depressed patient revealed her helplessness openly instead of constructing a delusionally elaborated superstructure. She also referred to a past characterized by initiative and confidence. The regressive elements of her psychosis were clearly evident.

Affective psychoses presumably have progressed further on the developmental scale than have schizophrenics, and despite my patient's disruptive and unrealistic behavior she seems to support this viewpoint. Her prepsychotic orientation was characterized by realistic achievement. Her successful activities had a frenetic, compulsive quality which betrayed their defensive nature; nonetheless, they were reality-syntonic rather than delusional.

Apparently, this woman had experienced infantile trauma of an intrusive, assaultive nature which caused her to establish an ambivalent introject of the nurturing modality. She maintained equilibrium by incorporating its positive aspects in her adaptations to the outer world and, by virtue of her strength and competence, was able to control the destructive elements. To achieve this balance she hypercathected the transitional area, which was precariously and defensively established. Her good, "autonomous," adaptation protected her from her destructive, helpless inner core, which was either repressed or split off.

With psychotic breakdown, this equilibrium disintegrated. Her good competent self was submerged and her behavior preponderantly, but not exclusively, reflected her destructive helpless apsects. It was curious that her dreams were pleasant (see Grolnick, chapter 14) and depicted situations in which she was admired and functioned effectively. Apparently she could reveal her good side only at night in her dreams.

Some patients project valued parts of the self into the analyst along with the projection of hateful introjects (Giovacchini 1975). The patient credits the analyst with the ability to keep destructive and benign, helpful introjects separate. My depressed patient, by contrast, had to hide her competent self. Whenever she revealed some element which referred to self-reliance and initiative, she would immediately withdraw and then moan, scream, or otherwise emphasize her helplessness, which she referred to as her bad side. Basically, she was frightened that I would be envious and covetous, that I might "steal" the valued aspects of the self-representation. These aspects she hid protectively, a defensiveness, incidentally, that had its genetic antecedents among her numerous siblings (she is the youngest of eleven children). This concealment of positive aspects of the self I believe common among depressed patients.

The security of the self-representation depends upon the internalization of the nurturing modality, one which in this case was ambivalently constructed. The security of my patient's resources was threatened by the destructive component of her ambivalence. How she perceived herself, that is, her identity, was reflected in her lack of confidence in her ability to function. Thus, Winnicott's concepts (1953) of primary psychic creativity and the transitional situation and process are relevant to the construction of the self-representation, a psychic structure central in the psychopathology of patients suffering from psychoses and severe character disorders.

REFERENCES

Erikson, E. H. (1959). Identity and the life cycle. In *Psychological Issues* 1. New York: International Universities Press.

Giovacchini, P. (1964). The submerged ego. *International Journal of Psycho-Analysis* 43:371-380.

—— (1972). Countertransference problems. *International Journal of Psychoanalytic Psychotherapy* 1:112-127.

—— (1975). *Tactics and Techniques in Psychoanalytic Treatment: Countertransference Aspects*, vol. 2. New York: Jason Aronson.

Kernberg, O. (1972). Treatment of borderline patients. In *Tactics and Techniques in Psychoanalytic Treatment*, vol. 1, ed. P. Giovacchini, pp. 254-291. New York: Jason Aronson.

Khan, M. M. R. (1960). Clinical aspects of the schizoid personality: affects and techniques. *International Journal of Psycho-Analysis* 41:430-437.

Milner, M. (1969). *The Hands of the Living God*. New York: International Universities Press.

Myerson, P. (1973). The establishment and the disruption of the psycho-analytic modus vivendi. *International Journal of Psycho-Analysis* 54:133-143.
Winnicott, D. W. (1949). Mind and its relation to the psyche-soma. In *Collected Papers: Through Paediatrics to Psycho-Analysis*, pp. 243-254. New York: Basic Books, 1958.
——— (1953). The transitional object and transitional phenomena. *International Journal of Psycho-Analysis* 34:89-97.

CHAPTER 22

In this chapter, Gilbert Rose continues his long-standing interest in the creative process. He conceptualizes a transitional process that outlives the transitional object and underlies the creativity of everyday life. The creative imagination serves as a bridge from the self to the world of objects. Thus Rose presents a view of man living within an open system. Reality is reconstituted as the result of a dynamic dialectic of the experiences of fusion and separation. Crucial for the capacity of the ego to test reality is the ability to "de-differentiate, abstract and reintegrate, in the service of mastery." The implication is that where there is a decreased capacity to use these transitional processes, there will be a decreased ability to test reality within a weaker, more rigid ego.

This view of psychic systems as open and in flux grows out of ego psychology and contemporary ideas of the nature of reality. Rose shows that the ego core and a sense of identity lends stability to the flux inherent in this system. This idea is developed further in his consideration of Edward Munch's lithograph, "The Cry." There it is demonstrated that the transitional object role is more conspicuous where the ego core is weak and the sense of identity is unstable. This is analogous to the developmental period from the last half of the first year of life until age three. To some degree, this parallels Volkan's clinical work, where he has shown the development of "reactivated" transitional objects as his borderline patients are on the verge of achieving a mature level of object relations with true separation.

L.B.

THE CREATIVITY OF EVERYDAY LIFE

Gilbert J. Rose

"Thinking and art," wrote Martin Buber (1963) "supplement each other . . . like the electric poles between which the spark jumps." The critical gap across which the spark of life must pass has been pictured by Michelangelo as the vital space between the finger of the Creator and Man. This vital space sketches also the interval between individuation and fusion, self and otherness. This is the arena of reality construction: the area of the transitional process.

Making use of universal themes around birth and death, bodily forms and fusions, Man performs his human task, journeying in the transitional area between degrees of narcissistic fusion and separateness, creating the unique form of his own identity to become what he is in a world from which he abstracts what will constitute, for him, his reality.

The consensus about what constitutes reality has broken down in the past generation. Not only are Hartmann's "average expectable environment" and Winnicott's "good enough mothering" seen as grossly simplifying assumptions, but external reality, itself, is seen more as a dynamic oscillation between figure and ground than as a steady background for the projection of mental figures (Wallerstein 1973). The realities with which psychoanalysis concerns itself are as much man-made constructs as are literary and poetic visions of reality (Schafer 1970).

Rapid technological and social changes have led to profound changes in reality perception. There is now a more basic realization that the sense of reality is not formed by an "objective" reality impinging upon the mind but by the singling out of specific elements from a totality and electing them to become "real" (Novey 1955). A recent paper (Lichtenstein 1973) defined *society* as an instrument for the imposition and maintenance of a consensus of the real, and *revolution* as the passing of this power to a new group; it also was suggested that id, ego and superego functions were shifting in response to changes in our world of reality, in order to support the feeling of being real, intact, and authentic in a world perceived as impersonal, destructive, and degrading.

The revolution in world view is largely due to atomic physics, which has destroyed the idea of a geometrically perfect universe in infinite space where immutable matter obeys immutable laws. Instead of perfect geometry, physical continuity and continuous evolution, we have a chaos of probabilities, physical discontinuity, and change by leaps. The idea of continuity was an illusion created by the imperfection of our senses. The world is fluid and nothing constant: matter is discontinuous and moves by leaps of energy, matter and energy are equivalent, time is relative, time and space are continuous, space is finite, the universe is curved and four-dimensional. Reason is superior to observation and experiment and it, too, is fallible.

Modern abstract art reflects this dislocated universe with fractured planes, without continuity or solidity, in which space and time blend in plastic relativity. The body scheme, transformed by ultramicroscopic histology into a restless composition of molecular elements, is portrayed by Ernst's human-animal combinations, Dali's gelatinous people, Moore's person from within. Abstract art pictures the destroyed old-world order and attempts to build new unities (Marti-Ibanez 1968).

The traditional, Aristotelian all-or-none logic of dichotomy covers only the small field of subject-predicate relations and is not an adequate framework for considering man's relationship to his world.[1] The categories of experience are not a universal a priori, and even the object-subject separation is not absolute. Classic Western philosophy from Plato to Descartes and Kant notwithstanding, man is not primarily a spectator on his world but is, for biological reasons, actively creating it and being created by it in a mutual interaction.

The central problem in all fields of reality is dynamic interaction, with the organism viewed as an open system in exchange with its environment (von Bertalanffy 1968). This new image of man emphasizes immanent activity instead of passive reception and outer-directed reactivity.[2]

We are in a more or less fluid interaction with our environment on various levels. Forms are configurations or levels of balance in these interactions. They create order where otherwise there would be chaos or void. Each culture provides its own forms. They transform the passive world of impressions into the building blocks of "reality," creating particular and irreducible basic relations between "inside" and "outside," the I and the world (Cassirer 1953).

Myth, art, language, and science all suppress and pass over certain parts of the immediate factuality and constitute reality from several unique directions. Have the other latent, immanent meanings inherent in the pluralism of reality then been repressed or denied? Perhaps we might say that, from the point of view of the integrative function of the ego, the healthy obverse of repression and denial is abstraction.

Let us amplify this to avoid misunderstanding. Repression, denial, and abstraction all delete certain stimuli from awareness and in so doing lessen the burden on the integrative function of the ego. Repression and denial are mechanisms of defense which aid the ego in dealing with conflict and avoiding anxiety by opposing, respectively, internal and external events. They thus bring about a partial detachment from internal and external reality.

However, abstraction is essentially conflict-free and unconnected with anxiety. It consists of a preconscious withdrawal of attention cathexes from certain aspects of a myriad reality and a hypercathexis of others which then become manifest. By aiding in the formation of new reality configurations, abstraction acts in the service of the reality principle. But in constituting reality in this manner from a particular direction many elements are necessarily passed over. When we suggest that abstraction is the healthy obverse of repression and denial we mean to indicate that the ego, working nondefensively and conflict-free, can form and entertain novel reality configurations without anxiety and its attendant defenses.

Such a view is a necessary consequence of a shift from id to ego psychology. While the id has to do with common elements, the ego has to do with differences. Since the idea of what constitutes reality is apparently neither universal nor immutable, this idea must be a construct of the ego. Id psychology has taught us to be aware of the psychopathology of everyday life in the sense of the ubiquity of the Unconscious. Ego psychology highlights the creativity of everyday functioning in the sense of the multiplicity of ways in which reality may be constituted—individually, culturally, conceptually. From the point of view of reality construction, the function of myth, religion, art, language, and science is not, for example, escape through wishful distortion of the world, but orientation in it—a system of ideas to envisage one's relationship to society, the world, life and death—all in the service of the reality principle.

Man's sense of space and time is intimately related to the culture he shares and the language he speaks. Every language highlights some aspects of reality and overlooks others. In Arabic there are five to six thousand terms describing concrete aspects of camels, yet not one gives us a general biological concept (Cassirer 1953). The Aivilik Eskimos, on the other hand, have at least twelve different terms for various winds (Hall 1966).

The Sapir-Whorf hypothesis states that language is an arrangement of the stream of sensory experience which results in a certain picture of the universe; it determines what our reality will be. The Indo-European languages represent a provisional analysis of reality. Just as any number of non-Euclidean geometries can give internally coherent accounts of space configurations, there are many tongues other than the Indo-European which, by aeons of evolution, have arrived at different but equally coherent provisional analyses of reality.

Much of our own language and thought, except for relativity theory, imposes two grand cosmic forms, space and time, upon the universe. While obviously time and space do exist for the Hopis, the Hopi language does not refer to space or time as such. Its tenseless verbs indicate the degree of objectivity or subjectivity, i.e., what type of validity, the speaker intends his statement to have: whether a report of an event (our own past tense), an expectation (our future), or a generalization about events.

Chichewa, an East African language, has two past tenses: one for past events with present result or influence, and one for past without present result or influence. Coeur d'Alene, an American Indian language, requires speakers to discriminate among three causal processes, denoted by three causal verb forms. Our own verb form concept of cause, meaning "makes to happen," seems simplistic by comparison.

Abundant anthropological data seem to support the proposition that various cultures put differing emphasis on sight, hearing, and smell and thus develop and inhabit different perceptual realities. The interested reader is referred to the relevant literature for specifics, but the following examples, from Whorf (1956), are presented only to suggest the scope of the cultural variation. In contrast to the acoustic sensitivity of Germans and Dutch (double doors and thick walls), the Japanese (paper walls) screen out acoustic stimuli and are undisturbed by quantities of sound. In the West, man perceives objects but not spaces in between. In Japan, spaces are perceived and revered, and given a special term, *ma*, meaning intervening interval. The Aivilik Eskimos integrate time and space as one thing and live in acoustic-olfactory space rather than visual space (Hall 1966).

Man's sense of space and time are closely related to his sense of self. A particular culture may inhibit or encourage various sensory components of the self—visual, kinesthetic, tactile. One's reality is created out of the forms provided by the sense of self as it develops within a given culture.

What of the sense of self? It is likewise a matter of dynamic equilibrium, or relative inner constancy amid external change.[3] Out of the multitude of conscious and unconscious, realistic and distorted images which the child has had of himself, and the various bodily states and feelings he has experienced, the ego builds up a more or less constant and enduring self-image. Along with it, an enduring schema of individuals other than himself is constructed from the impressions, images and experiences he has had with these people. From the latter half of the first year through the third, the child gradually develops a conception of himself as separate from the mother and other external objects.

Despite the endless current of change in subjective reality, the continuous ebb and flow of differentiation underlying psychic life, there is normally an overall experience of inner continuity. The self, "primary identity," and "ego core" are various ways of trying to conceptualize this.

The self, acting as a constant frame of reference, receives energy charges from the pool of intermittent self representations. Disparate units become integrated into workable forms in the light of early identifications and the evolving ability to test reality (Spiegel 1959). One's identity theme is like the unchanging form of a musical theme throughout the transformation and variations which unfold in time (Lichtenstein 1965).[4]

Early identifications and bodily self representations, as well as the reality testing and integrative functions of the ego are a cluster of forces which make for a sense of uniqueness and stability in the midst of the continuous ebb and flow of differentiation. Taken together they might be conceptualized as ego core (Rose 1964). The construction of reality, arising from ego core, and the maintenance of identity, resting on primary identity, both constantly relate and reconcile continuity to change. They act like horizontal and vertical stabilizers of an aircraft. They approximate a cross-section and longitudinal section of the Self from an ego point of view.

Winnicott emphasized that the transitional object serves as a bridge between the familiar and the disturbingly unfamiliar, thus facilitating the acceptance of the new. It is a temporary construction to aid the infant in the early stages of the development of the sense of reality and identity, and in the separation from the mother. It has thus been called the "larval representation of the self" (Greenacre 1969). It is dispensed with when self and objects are sufficiently differentiated from each other that separation from an object does not threaten a loss of self. It disappears through the gradual shrinkage or conversion into a toy, play, fantasy, or creative form, and permeates the "cultural field"—that "whole intermediate territory" between inner reality and external world (Winnicott 1953).

Stages of development and disappearance of the transitional object have been described. A future artist's relationship with his transitional object may be the forerunner of his later capacity for controlled illusion (Rosen 1964). The transitional object may become elaborated into enduring collective alternates (Weissman 1971), those figures and forms, centering around early personal experiences, which combine the potential artist's sensitivity and responsiveness (Greenacre 1957). The transitional object may reflect early oral and separation-individuation trauma, and may become refined into transitional fantasies which become externalized as creative work —which thus serves the defensive continuing purpose of mastery of separation-individuation problems (Hamilton 1974). The analyst may serve as a transitional object, and be related to the imaginary companion (Greenacre 1969). Dreams and dreaming may serve as transitional objects in analysis (Grolnick chapter 14). Transitional phenomena may be divided into accessory objects, intermediate objects and "true" transitional objects (Kestenberg 1971). One might refer to the transitional object "level" as a "major resting place" or "important way station" on the road between fusion and object constancy (Grolnick).

However valuable these distinctions, I prefer to treat the transitional process as a confluence of self- and object-centered interests which underlies and outlasts the transitional object. The transitional object is but an early, concrete manifestation of the transitional process. While the transitional object disappears, the transitional process remains as a way of describing how the mind constitutes itself and its umwelt in dynamic interaction with the outside.

To be sure, transitional phenomena have been traditionally associated with the "intense experiencing that belongs to the arts and to religion and to imaginative living, and to creative scientific work" (Winnicott 1953). Thus, transitional phenomena lend themselves readily to the terminology of the mystical tradition, Buber's "intercourse with the being of the unknown" being a fair example.

If, however, we wish to bring out the garden-variety creativity of everyday ego functioning, the clinical-pathological tradition serves no better than the mystical. Hartmann's reference (1956) to the "equilibrium" we each establish between "our world" and "the objective knowledge of reality" helps normalize the process. It avoids the pejorative connotations of projective identification, regression in the service of the ego, narcissistic fusion, depressive anxiety, restitution, and the like. However, in my opinion, it suggests something akin to peaceful coexistence between two sovereign political powers. Such a relative noninterference in each other's internal affairs is, of course, more illusory than actual.

With the model of the organism as an open system the transitional process becomes more an expression of the dynamic between a breathing self and a changing reality—each shaping the other to create a unique *umwelt* in a synchronous, contemporary totality. The differentiation of self and reality being a continuing and mutual everyday process, the transitional process is an attempt to convey the essential quality of its mobility. But that label, too, being only a form of expression, is, like all forms, inescapably static.[5]

Freud's model (1925) of the active process of perception had the perceptual system advancing and withdrawing after each sampling of the outside world. The environment provides constant stimulus nutriment leading to the development of cortical structure and the building of mental presentations. Certain ego functions, including perception and reality testing, search for these presentations in the external world. Perceptual scanning continues to provide more stimulus nutriment for the development of further mental presentations, and further scanning seeks to find them again in the external world.

While this remains central to the idea of the transitional process, we would now stress other elements as well: the temporary suspension of the boundaries between self and object representation, the two-way traffic between rhythmic body imagery and outer forms, the sufferance of illusion, further mixing, testing, and abstracting to form bridges made of inner and outer elements. The bridge itself may not necessarily be an actual product: perception, thought, and object relations might all be considered as having transitional, bridging functions.[6] Likewise, work.

We know that the transitional object is needed near the beginning of the second year when the infant is starting to walk and talk and develop a sense of reality and identity. It helps to foster the separation from the mother and outside objects and the development of an autonomous self. It serves as a bridge between a fluid interior and a more or less expectably stable exterior. When the self is more or less firmly established, it disappears.

But the process of which it was an early manifestation retains its importance. It bridges a self which is by now more or less stable and an exterior which comes to appear notoriously fluid. The idea that reality is fixed is itself a necessary delusion of childhood; it provides the stability within which many new sensations may become organized and within which emerging functions may mature under protection. Unlike the good enough, constant mother of childhood, a static given "out there," reality comes to be seen increasingly as multidimensional; at times like the present, the world may once again appear disturbingly unfamiliar.

The burgeoning of information and the proliferation of possibilities of all kinds, unsecured from guiding values, may threaten the adult, too, with traumatic overstimulation or hound him into defensive insensibility. As in its early form as the transitional object, the transitional process in its developed form as the creative imagination remains an essential instrument of adaptation. It samples the pluralism of reality, withdraws and readvances, attempting to abstract coherent configurations composed of both self and nonself elements. They bridge the out-there with the in-here in new ideas or images. In contrast to repression and denial, these abstractions offer new perspectives from which to explore and enhance rather than circumscribe the appreciation of reality.

Intrapsychically, irrespective of its objective merit, the new perspective abstracted from self and world may retain for its author some private, defensive functions, perhaps akin to the early transitional object. Works of equal value may derive from varying degrees of differentiation of self and object representations within the ego and vary from person to person and within the same person over a period of time. There is little anecdotal material on which to hazard inferences and even less analytic data. Yeats said that he refashioned himself in the process of writing,[7] but for Sylvia Plath it was apparently a process of depletion. For her each extrusion of a new poem externalized relatively unneutralized aggression from a poorly differentiated self-object core and left her feeling suicidal again (Orgel 1974). Joseph Conrad would interrupt a work which was personally threatening and undertake another which would appear to master the threat; only then could the first be resumed (Armstrong 1971).

A particularly dramatic example of creative work which represented a transitional object for its author is supplied by the life of the painter Edvard Munch. After he developed a visual scotoma from an intraocular hemorrhage he portrayed this blind spot as a dark area of color integrated into the composition of a painting. A series of paintings done at this time contain this blindspot and record the progress of its disappearance during the course of recovery. Munch also painted his own eyelashes as vertical striations on a picture of his dead sister. Following a psychotic period he withdrew from people but could scarcely part with his pictures, which became his main love objects. Occasionally he would also beat a painting with a whip if dissatisfied with it, claiming that this "horse treatment" improved its character (Steinberg and Weiss 1954).

All art forms have the effect of reviving the metaphoric power of words and forms, refreshing the senses and waking the mind to the continuous ebb and flow of differentiation within itself and outside. They bring us into a new relationship with reality or actually reconstitute it in some new way. But is this not what the ego is doing unconsciously all the time in its moment-by-moment functioning? An art form is the process of mind slowed down, enlarged, and abstracted to the point where we can glimpse some of its inner workings almost in vivo, as it were, and just within reach.

I conceive of the creativity of everyday life as residing in the power of the ego to de-differentiate, abstract, and reintegrate in the service of mastery. In a series of earlier papers (Rose, 1963,1964,1966,1971), I describe this as an oscillating movement of ego boundary expansions and constrictions, trial fusions, and rapid scans of space and time, followed by reseparations, corrections and discriminations. Both growth and creative imagination are seen as resulting from and facilitating the ebb and flow of losing and refinding oneself personally and endlessly in space-time. This pendulumlike movement while fashioning one's own identity and structuring reality in wider integrations and higher differentiations is often accompanied by unconscious birth fantasies harking back to initial emergences from narcissistic fusion states (Rose 1969, 1971). One may describe this as an alternating cathexis between ego core and boundaries in normal growth, identity formation, reality construction, and creative imagination. Or one may, as I do in the present chapter, refer to the essential *bridging* nature of the transitional process.

The bridge itself is perhaps nowhere better portrayed than in Edvard Munch's lithograph "The Cry" (Figure 1). The precipitating "day residue" experience behind the composition was related by Munch on a number of occasions. He had been walking with two friends when the sun set and the sky suddenly became bloody red. He stopped, while his two friends walked on, and feeling dead tired and trembling with fright he leaned against the railing, looking at the flaming clouds that hung like blood and a sword over the fjord. In the picture, which took shape only gradually, a terrified figure, mouth agape, covers his ears and turns from a bloody landscape and sky swirling around him. The reverberating world seems to give voice to the silent scream.

The pictorial evolution of this scene has been traced by Reinhold Heller (1973). Among other artistic influences, the dynamic perspective of van Gogh is evident in the sharply receding railing, which is used to accentuate the emotional force of the main figure's isolation. By analyzing Munch's drawings allegorizing his father's death, Heller interprets the radically foreshortened pathway as a walkway to death. He supports this by taking into account certain Norwegian idiomatic

Edvard Munch, *The Cry* (1895). Lithograph. Courtesy of Rosenwald Collection, National Gallery, Washington D.C.

expressions. The picture as a whole is traced from a self-portrait, "Despair," done in the same year as the memory on the bridge (1892), and is seen as portraying the horror of loss of self.

Analytic intuition would agree with this. Done in a prepsychotic period of his life, the picture has been analytically interpreted as representing both the artist's threat of being engulfed by his environment and dissolving into it, as well as a shoring up of the body boundaries against this threat; the shocking sight at age five of the death of his mother of a pulmonary hemorrhage may well have impelled this as well as other work (Steinberg and Weiss 1954). One might add that primal scene connotations are perhaps present as well.

What deserves emphasis in this paper is the bridge. Its floor is wavy, but its railing, against which Munch had leaned in the memory, is the only solid, thick, straight form in the picture. As in the memory, it is the railing of the bridge which provides the firm support for the struggle that is being depicted. As was mentioned, the foreshortened bridge dramatizes the figure's emotional isolation. Indeed, he appears to be fleeing from the sight of the whole picture in which he is the main character, as well as from the sound of his own scream. But at the same time, it is the strong formal structure of the bridge's railing which holds him firmly attached to the two receding figures in the background.

While he and the other two figures on the bridge together make up a human triangle, they and the span of bridge between them also constitute but one side of another traingle: a large, formal triangle whose other two arms are made up of the turbulent sky and the landscape—all bounding a central, seemingly tranquil sea. These formal arrangements, a bridge which is a medium of both flight and attachment, itself part of a central triangle of land, sea and sky, serve to express the emotional turbulence and keep it integrated within the composition of the picture as a whole.

I suggest that the bridge might be taken as a forceful representation of the transitional process at a particular moment when it is endangered by an incipient psychotic state. Centrifugal forces in the transitional process nearly overpower centripetal ones, threatening the interdependence of self and reality and the loss of both. Inner and outer worlds are trembling on the brink of rupturing their connection. The reliability of the bridge in holding them together is rendered in ambiguous terms, contrasting the strength of its railing with the frailty of its floor.

The conflict on the bridge is a dynamic, pictorial presentation of a personal crisis in the universal dialectic of self and reality; I-and-Thou. It is largely the autonomous, conflict-free artistic ego which manages to contain the intensity of the struggle within the pictorial composition—

and, I would guess, to contain the psychosis of Edvard Munch as well. The dual current of repulsion and attraction, contraction and expansion, is dramatized and captured; the solitude of alienation versus the terror of fusion is expressed and aesthetically resolved in an orchestration of form and content centering on an imaginary transitional bridge.

May not such an artistic creation be as faithful an intimation of the problem of dynamic interaction between any ego and reality as the traditional clinical and philosophic ways of categorizing experience? May not the aesthetic synthesis reflect the oscillating current of de-differentiation and reintegration of any ego's everyday functioning—creating and rediscovering personal and collective meanings which bridge the two fluidities of inner and outer reality?

When Martin Buber writes that "thinking and art supplement each other . . . like the electric poles between which the spark jumps," it now appears to me both harsh and charitable—as though thinking were no art, as if art could be thoughtless.

Likewise with such faintly moralistic polarities as the triumph of autonomy over the regressive temptations of fusion. Again Martin Buber: "If I am I because I am I, and You are You because You are You, then I am I, and You are You. But if I am I because You are You, and You are You because I am I, then I am not I and You are not You."

But what if self-object boundaries, like perception, thought, and forms of art, breathe and grow and change in the transitional process of everyday creativity?

Then: I am I because I am I as well as because You are You. And You are You because You are You as well as because I am I.

We keep being both more and less than what we had supposed, as each remains himself, surely, but not only.

SUMMARY

The idea of the transitional process arises out of the importance that modern conceptual models place on shifting boundaries as opposed to stable structures. Primary and secondary processes, for example, are now thought to exist as a continuum, interacting on all intrapsychic levels, rather than as a pair of opposites on separate levels; reality is no longer seen as a steady backdrop but as a dynamic oscillation of figure and ground; and the organism as a whole is viewed as an open system continuously engaged in mutual development with the outside.

The term *transitional process* is used in this chapter to indicate (1) that the dynamic equilibrium between a relatively fluid self and reality is not limited to the transitional object of childhood but continues into adulthood; (2) that the adaptation of everyday life and the originality of creative imagination both represent a continuing "transitional" interplay between self and reality; (3) that in the light of the transitional process, adaptation may be thought of as creative, and creative imagination as adaptive and (4) that in both, an individual abstracts and maintains an *umwelt* of his own—a synchronous and contemporary but necessarily selective reality.

NOTES

1. Bohr's principle of complementarity reflects that the mind must grasp that totality transcends the logic of dichotomy; it must entertain and accept propositions which, by logical standards, are "irreconcilable," e.g., that light is both a wave phenomenon and a stream of impulses. It has been claimed that the structure of our logic is essentially determined by the binary hemisphere architecture of the brain, and that our central nervous system is constructed like a digital rather than analog computer; the neurones work according to the all-or-none law of physiology in terms of yes-or-no decisions. The profound concordance between our cerebral structure and what we perceive of reality was pointed out by early Gestaltists: "All experienced order in space is a true representation of corresponding order in the underlying dynamic context of the physiological process" (Kohler 1929).

2. This can be expressed in many ways, including psychoanalytic reconstruction of the child's building of the "world"; perception— Gombrich's "the innocent eye sees nothing" (1961); Von Uexkull's *Umwelt* (1934), in which each species reacts to only a small number of characteristics of his environment and treats the others as nonexistent, thus making the sense of space and time dependent on the organization of the perceiving organism; Cassirer's "symbolic forms" and culture-dependent categories (1953); and von Humboldt's and Whorf's (1956) evidence of linguistic factors in the formation of the experienced universe, thus making our world outlook dependent on our mother tongue, and vice versa.

3. The Caterpillar took the hookah out of its mouth and addressed Alice in Wonderland: "Who are *you*?" Alice replied: "I—I hardly know, Sir, just at present—at least I know who I *was* when I got up this morning, but I think I must have changed several times since then."

4. Before it became an object of psychological inquiry, identity was a biological concept. At the turn of the century it was recognized that the living animal refuses to form antibodies which could be harmful to its own tissues. What is carried out by the immunologic apparatus is, on a

psychological level, a function of the ego; impairments of psychological self-recognition are ego disorders.

5. Henri Bergson (1911) wrote that our logical thought is no more capable of presenting the true nature of life than can the pebble on a beach display the form of the wave that brought it there. Like Heraclitus, and the spirit of contemporary science, he felt that the reality is movement; but here the logical intellect can form a clear idea only of a succession of immobile positions along the course of what is, in reality, a continuously flowing arc. Our concepts, he said, were only static snapshots of a reality perpetually in transition.

6. That this involves as yet unsolved problems in the theory of narcissism and its development is apparent. A way of approaching it might be through the transformations between primary and secondary processes, but this is beyond the scope of this chapter and will be dealt with in another context.

7. "The friends that have it I do wrong
   Whenever I remake a song,
   Should know what issue is at stake:
   It is myself that I remake."
   W. B. Yeats

REFERENCES

Armstrong, R. M. (1971). Joseph Conrad: the conflict of command. *Psychoanalytic Study of the Child* 26:485-534.

Bergson, H. (1911). *Creative Evolution*. New York: Modern Library, 1944.

Bertalanffy, L. von (1968). *General Systems Theory*. New York: Braziller.

Buber, M. (1963). Man and his image-work. Translated by M. Friedman. *Portfolio* 7:88-99.

Cassirer, E. (1953). *The Philosophy of Symbolic Forms*. New Haven: Yale University Press.

Freud, S. (1925). Negation. *Standard Edition* 19:235-239.

Gombrich, E. H. (1961). *Art and Illusion*. Princeton, N.J.: Princeton University Press.

Greenacre, P. (1957). The childhood of the artist. *Psychoanalytic Study of the Child* 12:47-72.

——— (1969). The fetish and the transitional object. *Psychoanalytic Study of the Child* 24:144-164.

Hall, E. T. (1966). *The Hidden Dimension*. Garden City, New York: Doubleday.

Hamilton, J. W. (1975). Transitional fantasies and the creative process. *Psychoanalytic Study of Society* 6:53-71.

Hartmann, H. (1956). Notes on the reality principle. In *Essays on Ego Psychology*. New York: International Universities Press.

Heller, R. (1973). *Edvard Munch: The Scream*. New York: Viking.

Kestenberg, J. (1971). From organ-object-imagery to self and object representations. In *Separation-Individuation: Essays in Honor of Margaret S. Mahler*, pp. 75-99. New York: International Universities Press.

Kohler, W. (1929). *Gestalt Psychology*. New York: Liveright.

Lichtenstein, H. (1965). Towards a metapsychological definition of the concept of self. *International Journal of Psycho-Analysis* 46:117-128. Also in Lichtenstein, *The Dilemma of Human Identity*. New York: Jason Aronson, 1977.

————— (1973). The challenge to psychoanalytic psychotherapy in a world in crisis. *International Journal of Psychoanalytic Psychotherapy* 2:149-174. Also in Lichtenstein, *The Dilemma of Human Identity*. New York: Jason Aronson, 1977.

Marti-Ibanez, F. (1968). Atomic science and modern art. *MD*, November 1968, pp. 9-16.

Novey, S. (1955). Some philosophical speculations about the concept of the genital character. *International Journal of Psycho-Analysis* 36:88-94.

Orgel, S. (1974). Sylvia Plath: fusion with the victim and suicide. *Psychoanalytic Quarterly* 43:262-287.

Rose, G. J. (1963). Body ego and creative imagination. *Journal of the American Psychoanalytic Association* 11:775-789.

————— (1964). Creative imagination in terms of ego "core" and boundaries. *International Journal of Psycho-Analysis* 45:75-84.

————— (1966). Body ego and reality. *International Journal of Psycho-Analysis* 47:502-509.

————— (1969). Transference birth fantasies and narcissism. *Journal of the American Psychoanalytic Association* 17:1015-1029.

————— (1971). Narcissistic fusion states and creativity. In *The Unconscious Today: Essays in Honor of Max Schur*, pp. 495-505. New York: International Universities Press.

Rosen, V. (1964). Some effects of artistic talent on character style. *Psychoanalytic Quarterly* 33:1-24. Also in Rosen, *Style, Character and Languague*. New York: Jason Aronson, 1977.

Schafer, R. (1970). The psychoanalytic vision of reality. *International Journal of Psycho-Analysis* 51:279-297.

Spiegel, L. A. (1959). The self, the sense of self, and perception. *Psychoanalytic Study of the Child* 14:81-109.

Steinberg, S., and Weiss, J. (1954). The art of Edvard Munch and its function in his mental life. *Psychoanalytic Quarterly* 23:409-423.

Von Uexkull, J. (1934). A stroll through the worlds of animals and men. In *Instinctive Behavior*, translated and edited by C. H. Schiller. New York: International Universities Press.

Wallerstein, R. (1973). Psychoanalytic perspectives on the problem of reality. *Journal of the American Psychoanalytic Association* 21:5-33.

Weissman, P. (1971). The artist and his objects. *International Journal of Psycho-Analysis* 52:401-406.

Whorf, B. L. (1956). *Language, Thought and Reality: Selected Writings of Benjamin Lee Whorf*, ed. J. B. Carroll. Cambridge, Mass.: MIT Press.
Winnicott, D. W. (1953). Transitional objects and transitional phenomena. *International Journal of Psycho-Analysis* 34:89-97.

CHAPTER 23

D.W. Winnicott's intriguing ideas about illusion, play, and creativity seem uniquely suited to a role in psychoanalytic and aesthetic criticism. In this chapter, Rosemary Dinnage attempts a new approach to psychoanalytic criticism, stressing the similarity between Winnicott's view of experience and that of the neo-Kantian idealists Ernst Cassirer and Susanne Langer. On this view, the ultimate reality of a constructed work of art or an analytic reconstruction is unique. It exists only in the virtual, potential, or illusory metaphorical space between the artist and his audience, or between the analyst and his patient. Sensorimotor, presymbolic, and preverbal experiences intertwine with cognitive and affective meaning.

Mrs. Dinnage calls for a new and closer alliance between the creative critic and the creative psychoanalyst. They can work together, she believes, in attaining a deeper understanding and appreciation of the wellsprings of art and creativity.

Analysts today are in a better position to appreciate the uniqueness of an individual or of a creative work of art. By applying the more recent theoretical additions—structural, developmental, and adaptive—we can better avoid the reductivist stereotypes inherent in the use of dynamic formulae in which content analysis supersedes or excludes the more formal organization.

S.G., L.B.

A BIT OF LIGHT

Rosemary Dinnage

For us all, as for himself, the artist is repeatedly winning brilliant battles in a war to which, however, there is no final outcome.
—D. W. Winnicott, *Collected Papers*

Hence we are not raindrops, soon dried by the wind; we make gardens blow and forests roar; we come up differently for ever and ever.
—Virginia Woolf, *The Waves*

"I have got my picture into a very beautiful state," wrote Constable in 1832; "I have kept my brightness without my spottiness, and I have preserved God Almighty's daylight."[1] His aim, as he wrote elsewhere, was to give "one brief moment caught from fleeting time a lasting and sober existence."[2] Piaget, in his account of the early development of imitation and make-believe in children, describes his two-year-old daughter Lucienne playing: how she "took" a bird from the pattern on the wallpaper and gave it to her mother, and then a flower—and then "there was the same garden ... with a sunbeam that she pretended to bring; she then gave her mother *'a bit of light.'* "[3]

"Creativity," whether in the artist, child, or any of us, is a popular idea at the moment, applied to everything from advertising to happy marriage; but with the longing for it goes a fear, which has ancient roots, of finding out too much about it (when Winnicott wrote —and in a paper entitled "Creativity and its Origins"— that "it is not of course that anyone will ever be able to explain the creative impulse, and it is unlikely that anyone would ever want to do so,"[4] it was rather a serious Winnicottian joke). I would like to argue that, for various reasons, imaginative powers, and especially their great artistic products, were misrepresented in Freud's model of mind; that Winnicott's ideas give us indications of how they may be restored to their central place; that his ideas are supported by similar lines of thought from other disciplines, and above all by what artists have said about their own experiences of writing, painting, or composing. The link I want to make is between Constable's painting and Lucienne's game with "a bit of light."

It is a truism to say that psychoanalysis is uneasy in the presence of art; the debate about the problem is an old one, and among recent books I would refer to Jack J. Spector's *The Aesthetics of Freud* and Frederick Crews' *Out of My System*, both of which conclude with reluctance that Freudian theory fails at just this point. Many creative people have fought shy of psychoanalytic ideas for this reason, feeling that they themselves deal in an order of reality that would not be respected. By throwing light on the earliest use of the symbolic mode, and thus on its later use in play, make-believe and art, the implications of Winnicott's work enable psychoanalysis to correct a bias not only epistemologically shaky but also distorting in its implications.

Though his views varied at different times, essentially for Freud culture was imposed rather than enjoyed, adopted rather than spontaneous. He sets art apart from the rationality of "real" life; the *natural* satisfactions of constructing social, moral, or artistic patterns are left out. The model of a mind divided into "lower" and "higher" compartments can be misleading: crude and chaotic primary process refined by secondary elaboration, base desires sublimated into higher ones, regression down into chaos and painful upward progress to culture. The wicked but exciting hell of the primary stands below, and above, in a rather dishonest heaven, are art, culture, religion, morality. It is doubtful whether among all the struggles and pain recorded in artists' letters, journals, and conversations any reflection of this divided outlook can be found.

Defense, loss, substitution appear in this account of art, but not the extraordinary *trustfulness* that permits it to be created at all, and persevered in against all odds. What are the experiences that give the artist such certainty that what he is doing is worthwhile—an irrational certainty that may prove to contain rationality of the highest order? We are like overworked cab horses, wrote van Gogh, and

> you'd rather live in a meadow with the sun, a river and other horses for company....We are paying a hard price to be a link in the chain of artists, in health, in youth, in liberty, none of which we enjoy, any more than the cab horse that hauls a coachful of people out to enjoy the

spring....Like me, you have been suffering to see your youth pass away like a puff of smoke; but if it grows again, and comes to life in what you make, nothing is lost.... Take some pains then to get well, for we shall need your health.[5]

When he analysed dreams, Freud did, almost in spite of himself, find artistic patterns intrinsic to the very nature of thought. But because the dream processes—condensations, junction of contraries, concretization of ideas, patterns of imagery and elaboration of metaphors, in other words, the basic *symbolic laws* of the imagination—could be observed in illness and in sleep, they were for him something "not really true." Symbolic knowing was placed in direct opposition to rationality and there in psychoanalytic theory it still stands, waiting to be reinstated as the most natural and undivided way of apprehending experience. "We are all suffering from Freud's flight to sanity," Winnicott has said.[6]

In his isolated position Freud, of course, could have got lost if he had not clung to a very literal distinction between fact and fantasy. He was ambivalent, besides, toward artists and writers—"meaning is but little to these men; all they care for is line, shape, agreement of contours. They are given up to the *Lustprinzip.*"[7] Irony came naturally to him, but make-believe he distrusted, and any art that could move him without explanation. Even more important, as Lionel Trilling has pointed out, is the fact that psychoanalysis developed as an offshoot of medicine. Since patients come to the analyst, he points out, because they are hindered by obsessions that are out of touch with the current day-to-day reality, a tacit agreement is made with the analyst that for practical purposes this commonsense reality shall be their only reference point. So there were for Freud, says Trilling, "the polar extremes of reality and illusion. Reality is an honorific word, and it means what is *there;* illusion is a pejorative word, and it means a response to what is *not there.*"[8] Consequently art has—rather uneasily—been put into the "not really true" pigeonhole along with phobia, daydream, and hallucination. It is an old and recurring fallacy in aesthetic theory: we think of Bacon's dismissal of poetry—it "submits the shewes of things to the desires of the Minde, whereas reason doth buckle and bowe the Minde unto the Nature of things."

Yet, of course, the cultural, imaginative and moral realities we live by are our own constructions, are "taken" not "given" truths; and the illusive tricks of the arts are used to delve deeper into truths of feeling and knowing. Logic and chaos, "reality" and its disguises, do not stand in strict opposition; mental life is actually unified, a spontaneous patterning of metaphor following implicit symbolic laws. The patterns worked into dreams and written into poetry are the most direct and natural kind of logic, as well as the most satisfying.

Perhaps speculation about the root of Freud's distrust of imaginative pleasure may be taken a little further still. We know that he was a devoted collector of small antiques: "those things cheer me," he wrote in a letter;[9] and a colleague has reported that he would sometimes stroke one while he talked.[10] That he was aware of their symbolic connections is demonstrated by a patient's account of Freud's showing him some pieces from the collection to help explain dream symbols.[11] And yet it was not this private aesthetic experience that prompted Freud's speculations on art, but more "public" experience, such as the contemplation of Michelangelo's *Moses* and Leonardo's *Virgin and St. Anne.* Might it not be that if he had put his own precious collection of transitional objects, bridging the two worlds of reason and imagination, under the psychoanalytic microscope, he could have been in danger of paralyzing his own creativity?

The concept that we have to reconsider then, is that of "illusion"; the artist, Freud wrote, triumphs "thanks to artistic illusion";[12] art "does not seek to be anything but an illusion."[13] Winnicott's legacy is that we can discard Freud's simpler view, and readopt the more subtle one which as children and artists we intuitively understand. I turn back to Constable for an illustration; he writes that he has

> a small picture by De Hooge, of which a sunbeam, and that alone, may well be considered the subject; but it shines through a window on the wall of a clean little Dutch room, from which it is reflected on the return of the wall and other objects with extreme elegance, and *a degree of truth perfectly illusive* [my italics].[14]

Here a "bit of light" is preserved in paint, preserved again both through Constable's looking at it and in his words, and borrowed yet again for my argument; a chain of artists, as van Gogh wrote, is involved, and each or any of us is a link, the passengers just as much as the cab horse. And each deals in illusion to establish the necessary degree of truth.

If we now look at art in terms of a history of imaginative and symbolic activity in the individual, we may see some possible solutions to problems in aesthetic experience. The work of art need not seem a *saltus naturae*, awe-inspiring but inexplicable; the child can be seen to be father to the creative man. The lines between major and minor art and the ordinary person's creativity need not be absolute. Nor need the involvement of maker and percipient be totally separate, but can be seen to spring from the same deep satisfaction in finding the symbolic patterns of feeling that underlie confusion. Solutions to other problems, such as "where" art is ("out there" or in the percipient's mind), might suggest themselves. The vicissitudes of the imagination in art, dreams, play, and ritual can be seen to have natural laws and logic of their own; Winnicott's exposition of the beginnings of creativity shows that there is no discontinuity between the earliest and maturest kinds of creating, nor between the maker and taker of art: both had once to cooperate with the perceptual chaos of infancy in order to invent a stable world, and that apprenticeship stays crucially linked to both creating and perceiving.

In reconsidering the Freudian view of art, then, we start from the battered toys and bits of blanket that Winnicott describes: objects that are "real," in Freud's sense, with private and irrelevant histories of their own, and also real in the way that Constable's and Lucienne's illuminations are real (the former, though not the latter, preserved concretely through the use of a medium, of which I shall say more later). I am not concerned with them in a clinical context, but with identifying a junction point between inner and outer realities, where a distinct and separate object is also a newly created one, because it concurs so precisely with what is needed—from which, if this first sense of *causing* is richly fed, creativity grows. Winnicott sketches a history of how this happens, and even more important, legitimizes a dimension for psychoanalytic theory in which art can exist—in which Freud's antiques *did* exist for him.

I need not recapitulate Winnicott's ideas here; those that I know about are embodied in my quotations from writers and artists, but I will cite the few sentences essential to my argument. The baby, he says,

> develops a vague expectation that has origin in an unformulated need. The adaptive mother presents an object or a manipulation that meets the baby's needs, and so the baby *begins to need just that which the mother presents*. In this way the baby comes to feel *confident in being able to create objects and to create the actual world.*[15]

And second:

> I think of the process as if two lines came from opposite directions, liable to come near each other. If they overlap there is a moment of *illusion*—a bit of experience which the infant can take as either his hallucination *or* a thing belonging to external reality....In this way he starts to build up a capacity to conjure up what is actually available.[16]

The child recognizes something in the outside world that he did not even know he was expecting; and with the sense of "that's *it!*" grows the sense of "and I am *I*." He has, and has not, created it; *has*, in the language of art and symbol, because the timely concurrence of object without and expectancy within brought something to life in the inner world; *has not*, in everyday terms, because the object is in fact independent. From this intersection of child and mother, expectancy and arrival, the ability to recreate the world develops: first the ability to honor it in all its externality, and then the arrogance to say—Paul Klee speaks for the artist—"In its present shape it is not the only possible world."

A history of imagination in each individual life would start, therefore, from the first demarcation of self against object, and continue through the increasingly complex perceptual transactions that end in the average man's taking his existence for granted in a world of objects, but which in the artist are never finished. Spanning the self/other boundary line is the intermediate area that permits objective and personal truth to interact, as the artist interacts with his material; and the richness or impoverishment of this area, where objects are recreated and recombined symbolically, depends on the way the outer world coincides with imaginative expectation in early life: on the *fit* between inner constructions and the behavior of things outside. If objects are unpredictable, too much absent or present, the experience of solid identity and of traffic with them fluctuates. If ideas and expectations in the mind coincide frequently and comfortably with things from outside, the growing human being knows and retains the experience of *making* his world—of exercising the curious human trick of meeting fact halfway and re-creating it into a different kind of time. So such a history would begin with the first awareness of a not-self and the first symbolic games with it, and end with the artist, who subordinates the rest of his life to its recreation. In between come the jerry-built creations of daydreaming, the rhythmic satisfaction of ritual, and the raw poetic commentary of sleep dreaming.

The key to the making of things, then, is *concurrence:* when what the child expects and what the world offers intersect, the object is both found and created at the same moment. (Minimal art, conceptual art, "found" art, and other contemporary experiments are obviously concerned with this intersection point.) Thus, when writing poetry, says Robert Frost,

the initial delight is in the surprise of remembering something I didn't know I knew. I am in a place, in a situation, as if I had materialized from or risen out of the ground. There is a glad recognition of the long lost and the rest follows. Step by step the wonder of unexpected supply keeps growing. . . .

The wonder of unexpected supply is what Winnicott, like other children, was experiencing when

> I woke up on Christmas morning and found I possessed a blue cart made in Switzerland, like those that the people there use for bringing home wood. How did my parents know that this was exactly what I wanted? Certainly I did not know that such heavenly carts existed. Of course, they knew because of their capacity to feel my feelings. . . .[17]

When we think of this concurrence, this instant of recognition, we may be reminded of Coleridge's "in looking at nature . . . I have always an obscure feeling, as if that new phenomenon were the dim awaking of a forgotten or hidden truth of my inner nature"; of Keats's "poetry should appear almost a Remembrance"; or of Aristotle's description of the source of pleasure in representation—the perceiver exclaims, "Ah, that is he!" In a newspaper interview recently, an actor said: "Acting is nothing but reminding people." And no one interested in Winnicott's ideas, I imagine, will be unaware of the passage in the second book of Wordsworth's *Prelude*, where he compares the very young baby with the poet, "creator and receiver both," his mind "working in alliance with the works which it beholds" ("He seems to have read my books," Winnicott said when I pointed this out to him).

The opposite of concurrence, of the cooperation between outside "thereness" and inner expectation, is the sense of total unrecognizability, entire strangeness, which is nightmare and madness. In its dream form it is a figure who looks familiar and turning round, has a stranger's face:

> He said that the worst sadness happened a long time ago and he then told me about his first separation from his mother. . . . He told me: "Mother went away. I and my brother had to live by ourselves. We were sent to stay with my aunt and uncle. The awful thing that happened there was that I would see my mother cooking in her blue dress and I would run up to her but when I got there she would suddenly change and it would be my aunt in a different colored dress."
> . . . He then drew a mirage and took a holiday from the subject of hallucinations by giving the scientific explanation of a mirage. His uncle had told him all about it. "You see lovely blue trees when there are really no trees there."[18]

This was a mirage mother, not a mirror: delusion, not illusion. In myth form it might be the African story of the mother who weaned her child by painting a demon's face on her water jug, and then

> whenever the child attempted to follow her she would turn, hiding her own face behind the painted jug. And whenever the child looked at it, he was frightened, in fact, he was terrified: "That's not my mother!" he would exclaim, "That's a horrible *mushi* (demon)!" and run back to the village.[19]

In literature it is the world of Kafka and of Beckett; of Hopkins' "when I compare myself, my being-myself, with anything else whatever, all things alike, all in the same degree, rebuff me with blank unlikeness";[20] of Heathcliff's frenzied search for the dead Catherine, when he digs up her coffin—"I could *almost* see her, and yet I *could not!*";[21] of Camus'

> What does this sudden awakening mean, in this dark room, with the sounds of a city that has suddenly become foreign to me? And everything is foreign to me, everything, without a single person who belongs to me.... My home is neither here nor elsewhere. And the world has become merely an unknown landscape....[22]

In psychosis, finally, even the reality of absence has gone: there is only a substanceless, unpredictable world of "fleetingly-improvised people" (Schreber's words). The imagination proliferates without any correction from factual realities; the symbolic dimension, the transitional "as-if" that marries fantasy to fact and matter, is lost. The psychotic's greatest deprivation is the ability to pretend.

If the child, therefore, is terrifyingly weaned to objects that refuse to concur with his expectations, if the world turns too horrible a masked face, he may become mad, or unimaginative. The artist, however, has been compelled toward the obsessions and sacrifices of his life by special experiences both of the world's concurrence and of its refusal to concur: behind the remaking, there is some empty socket to be filled. With the extra strength that he also has, he can look at the mask, leave the recognizable behind in order to be at home in homelessness. He "sees lovely blue trees": and makes them exist. Even if at other times he is mad, when he is writing or painting he knows what kinds of reality his construction does, and does not, possess: its own intrinsic energy and lawfulness ensure this, and rule out confusion. The imaginative summoning up of objects will be the spring of his existence: his deepest experiences will be the arrival in him of the object (inspiration), and the absence of it (desolation). The balance, in his imagination, between good "thereness" and desolating "not-thereness" is poised finely enough to drive him to remake the world: but remake it with confidence and with a unique fidelity to its real nature, not according to his personal whim.

But first he was a child; and I return to Piaget's Lucienne, who understands the status of "illusion":

> "The dark's lovely. You can take everything you want in the dark, and put it back afterwards." —Did you dream last night? —"Yes, I dreamt a boat was flying. I saw it in the dark. It came with the light. I took it for a minute and then I put it back. It went away with the dark."[23]

Piaget's account of the origins of imagination is worth briefly tracing because it forms an important parallel to Winnicott's; the theme of his early books accords with Winnicott when the latter wrote, "From birth the human being is concerned with the problem of the relationship between what is objectively perceived and what is subjectively conceived of."[24] Piaget's concepts of *assimilation* and *accommodation* are processes that alternate and balance each other: the child assimilates the world, or takes in what suits his needs, and he learns to accommodate to it, to conform to *its* requirements. The world at first "presents neither permanent objects, nor objective space, nor time interconnecting events as such, nor causality external to the personal actions";[25] but as the baby grows, the increasing division between self and not-self keeps pace exactly with the separation between rudimentary getting (assimilation) and rudimentary giving (accommodation). The outside world gradually solidifies into permanence and separateness, and so, also, realistic accommodation to its exigencies makes it manageable; and assimilation of it, beginning in sucking and grasping, comes to mean understanding it.

Mental life begins, therefore, "neither with knowledge of the self nor of things as such but with knowledge of their interaction."[26] But the child inhabits "a universe constantly becoming more external to the self, and an intellectual activity progressing internally."[27] The intellect cleaves the original single world in two—objects out there, self in here. As the child assimilates this growing knowledge of out-thereness and grasps its separateness, the definition of his own identity proceeds, as figure is defined by ground. The world divides into *I* and *it*, *then* and *now*, *there* and *here*, *because* and *therefore*; and on the borderline is the *as-if* with which we are concerned.

Originally, Piaget says, the world presents itself as depending on the child's own activity, "alternatively made and unmade";[28] in Winnicott's account, what is crucial is the direction that this first sense of *causing* takes, this idea of the self as a center of power and creativity; and its fate

depends on the benignity of the environment, which responds—or not—
to his calls and gestures. When eventually the outside world, acquiring
laws of its own, ceases to seem dependent on the child's volition, it has
become a structure in which the child recognizes he is only a "thing
among things, an event among events."[29] This great act of intellect is
what most deeply impresses Piaget, rather than the intermediate stages
toward it, and he is inclined to treat it as a once-and-for-all happening;
but the artist's creative imagination repeats over and over again the
transactions with the external world which in most people are early
settled and forgotten.

So when the out-there world agrees with his expectations, the child
learns to feel powerful; it seems he is *making* that world. When it shows its
harsh and separate independence—though not too often or too
painfully—he learns that he is not literally making but "making"; he
starts to understand play, invention, and symbol. Even the conventions
of illusion, far from being sophisticated artistic products, are visible as
early as the earliest make-believe: the baby's gesture or laugh, the
stylizing of his mimicry, says he is pretending—it becomes symbol, in
Susanne Langer's words, an "act of *reference* rather than of representation."[30] The "voluntary suspension of disbelief," the use of illusion, are as
natural as smiling.

In a later account Piaget plots the development of play, through
stories, imaginary companions, elaborate make-believe dramas, all
developing out of the very first games of "causing" and "recognizing,"
"together" and "apart." Ritual and imitation are worked into the play
formulations that precede art: the self that is securely outlined against its
background is free to be *as if* something else. Imitation, for Piaget, follows
directly from the conservation of objects—it is one of the first things *done*
with the bits that have coalesced into a stable world, and at the same time
a means of fixing that stability. In Susanne Langer's words again,
"miming is the natural symbolism by which we represent objects to our
minds"; it is rehearsed, interiorized; encompasses people, things, places,
moods; and goes into the making of art. Giacometti speaks here:

> For a long time I'd had in my mind the memory of a Chinese dog I'd seen
> somewhere. And then one day I was walking along the rue de Vanves
> in the rain, close to the walls of the buildings, with my head down,
> feeling a little sad perhaps, and I felt like a dog just then. So I made that
> sculpture.[31]

Winnicott's transitional phenomenon allows us to include action and
movement—as in imitation, mime, drama, dance, and ritual—in the
realm of "illusion."

Of course in this comparison of play with art there is also the essential difference: the artist's use of a medium—the demand of one color or note or word for another, the potential form in one particular grain of wood, or the tone of one particular instrument. Just as the child learns in the end to accommodate to the intransigence of the object and let himself be no more than "a thing among things, an event among events," so the artist respects the stringency of his medium; and real works of art are made when the laws of the imagination, the inner world, work in accommodation to those of the material. (The art medium can discipline the sick imagination in psychosis, too: Schreber wrote that his piano playing was the only thing that silenced his malign voices, and "every attempt at 'representing' me by the 'creation of a false feeling' and suchlike is doomed to end in failure because of the real feeling one can put into piano playing.")[32] The artist's creative arrogance is only achieved after a struggle with the externality of the medium; the mediocre artist is the one who has engaged himself less seriously with it; he says "it is not the only possible world" too soon, before he has really known it in its present shape. "One starts," says van Gogh, "with a hopeless struggle to follow nature; one ends by calmly creating from one palette, and nature agrees with it, and follows." Nature is only tamed into this agreement by patience and humility. Constable did not say "let there be light," but: "I have preserved God Almighty's daylight."

Cooperating with his medium, therefore, the artist fuses his inner world with the one outside. Susanne Langer—whose account of symbolization as the "essential act of mind," and of art as the natural symbol for experience, complements Winnicott's account from the philosophical point of view, as Piaget's gives it descriptive backing— writes of the "nameless value" of the object that first joins these two worlds:

> To project feelings into outer objects is the first way of symbolizing and thus of *conceiving* those feelings. This activity belongs to about the earliest period of childhood that memory can recover. The conception of "self" ... may possibly depend on this process of symbolically epitomizing our feelings.[33]

The artist differs from the ordinary man only

> by virtue of his intuitive recognition of forms symbolic of feeling, and his tendency to project emotive knowledge into such objective forms. In handling his own creation, composing a symbol of human emotion, he learns from the perceptible reality before him possibilities of subjective experience that he has not known in his personal life.[34]

For a comparison from the child's life, we might think of Jung's account of the tiny figure he carved (at the age of eleven) and hid away in an attic:

> I colored him black with ink, sawed him off the ruler, and put him in the pencil-case, where I made him a little bed. . . . No one could discover my secret and destroy it. I felt safe, and the tormenting sense of being at odds with myself was gone.[35] [see Khan, chapter 17, p. 269]

So the apprehension of the "perceptible reality before him" directly feeds back solidity into the apprehender. The artist (and the artist in each person) fits inner—but communicable—feeling into what arrives from outside; and this piece of world, vanished and yet still stamped on the page, stays alive in its own right, a junction for the two kinds of reality. Objects—a blue toy cart, Giacometti's "Chinese dog"—acquire *numen* because they concur with feeling, embodying realness and reflecting it back. Finally the artist can say, with van Gogh: "That white board must become something." He is at just the same junction of thing and idea, fact and possibility, as the child playing. He travels in a circle: from the baby's objectless universe, knowing neither self nor object but only their interaction, to the first re-cognitions, and the godlike illusion of creating; through the long process of uncentering, relinquishing godship and becoming an object himself; and from this apprenticeship, joining some remnant of the godlike energy to humility before his chosen fragment of world—a white board, a lump of stone, a pattern of rhymes. Through that submission to the uncompromising separateness of things he retains the godlike power in earnest; he makes "something that was not and now *is*."[36] And arrives where he began—at the intersection between inner and outer worlds, between himself and his artifact.

Both Freud and Winnicott himself expressed some fear about exposing the roots of art; I do not think there is any need for it. Making and perceiving these things are mysteries, but they are natural, too; we know them in our ordinary selves, but easily lose them; and when we revere the man who brings them back to us—not a magician but a man of fearful honesty and obstinacy—we are revering ourselves too, and our renewed scope, and our amazing finds. My attempt has been to show that "truth" and "illusion" are less simple than Freud assumed when he laid the epistemological foundations of psychoanalysis; to link Constable's "degree of truth perfectly illusive" with Winnicott's "the enrichment of fantasy with the world's riches depends on the experience of illusion.;[37] and to follow the fate of the mind's object—as it is made and destroyed, lost and found again in the "wonder of unexpected supply," as it fits or jars against its independent counterpart outside the self, and as it is played with and elaborated as a symbol from the earliest age and fused with natural rhythms and patterns to make art.

NOTES

1. C. R. Leslie, *Memoirs of the Life of John Constable* (1st publ. 1843), p. 240.
2. John Constable, *Various Subjects of Landscape* (1832), introduction.
3. Jean Piaget, *Play, Dreams and Imitation in Childhood* (1st transl. 1951), p. 119.
4. D. W. Winnicott, *Playing and Reality* (London, 1971), p. 69.
5. Vincent van Gogh, *Letters.*
6. D. W. Winnicott, Review of Jung's *Memories, Dreams, Reflections.*
7. E. Jones, *The Life and Work of Sigmund Freud* (1st publ. 1953), vol. 3, p. 412.
8. Lionel Trilling: *The Liberal Imagination* (1st publ. 1950), p. 44.
9. Sigmund Freud, *The Origins of Psychoanalysis: Letters to Wilhelm Fliess 1887-1902* (London, 1954), letter of Aug. 6th, 1899.
10. Hans Sachs, *Freud, Master and Friend* (1944). Quoted in J. Spector, *The Aesthetics of Freud*, p. 11.
11. Joseph Wortis, "Fragments of a Freudian Analysis," *American Journal of Orthopsychiatry* 10 (1940) .
12. Quoted in Trilling (see note 8 above).
13. *Ibid.*
14. C. R. Leslie, *Memoirs of the Life of John Constable*, p. 228.
15. D. W. Winnicott, *The Maturational Processes and the Facilitating Environment* (1st publ. 1965), p. 62.
16. D. W. Winnicott, *Collected Papers*, p. 152.
17. D. W. Winnicott, *The Maturational Process and the Facilitating Environment* (1st publ. 1965), p. 70.
18. D. W. Winnicott, *Collected Papers*, p. 111.
19. Werner Muensterberger, *Psychoanalytic Study of Society* 2(1962):161-185.
20. G. M. Hopkins, *Comments on the Spiritual Exercises of St. Ignatius Loyola.*
21. Emily Brontë, *Wuthering Heights*, ch. 29.
22. Albert Camus, *Carnets 1935-1942*, p. 95.
23. Jean Piaget, *Play, Dreams and Imitation in Childhood*, p. 256.
24. D. W. Winnicott, *Playing and Reality*, p. 11.
25. Jean Piaget, *The Child's Construction of Reality* (1st transl. 1955), p. xii.
26. *Ibid.*, p. 354.
27. *Ibid.*, p. 356.
28. *Ibid.*
29. *Ibid.*, p. xiii.
30. Susanne Langer, *Philosophy in a New Key* (1942), p. 156.

378

ROSEMARY DINNAGE

31. James Lord, *A Giacometti Portrait* (New York, n.d.), p. 21.
32. D. P. Schreber, *Memoirs of My Nervous Illness* (ed. Ida MacAlpine and Richard A. Hunter, 1955), p. 144.
33. Susanne Langer, *Philosophy in a New Key*, p. 124.
34. Susanne Langer, *Feeling and Form* (1953), p. 390.
35. C. G. Jung, *Memories, Dreams, Reflections* (1st publ. in England 1963), p. 36.
36. André Malraux, *Voices of Silence* (1st publ. in England 1954), p. 461.
37. D. W. Winnicott, *Collected Papers*, p. 153.

CHAPTER 24

Simon Grolnick has spent two summers studying and teaching in Tuscan Italy. In this chapter he and Alfonz Lengyel, an archaeologist, show how the Etruscans used their art to cope with death and its inevitable separations. The authors examine Etruscan funerary monuments and analyze their images in the light of what is known about this mysterious people and the transitional object concept.

Actually, much here is applicable as well to other cultures. Treasured objects are often placed with the dead to reduce separation anxiety. It is frequently believed that these objects aid his journey to the land of the dead. The trip itself resembles the birth passage, with new life beginning on the other side. Volkan has written of "linking objects" (*Archives of General Psychiatry* 27:215–221), mementoes to which mourners remain deeply attached; these are used as transitional objects and serve to undo separation.

L.B.

ETRUSCAN BURIAL SYMBOLS AND
THE TRANSITIONAL PROCESS

Simon A. Grolnick
Alfonz Lengyel

And so, as Kinsmen, met a Night—
We talked between the Rooms—
Until the Moss had reached our lips—
And covered up our names—
Emily Dickinson, "I Died for Beauty"

Sepulchral art and its symbols lend themselves to interpretation based on D.W. Winnicott's concepts of transitional objects and phenomena (1951, 1971). Such an art was produced by the chthonically inclined culture of the Etruscans, whose dualistic after life, especially the part D. H. Lawrence has termed "its grisly underground hell and its horrors," comprises a nightmare world. Using this arena, we suggest that the transitional object functions of straddling and stabilizing the self-object, waking-sleeping, and concrete-abstract polarities are both analagous and developmentally related to man's persistent attempt to bridge, with his burial art and symbols, the interface between life and death. It seems to us that a complex continuum exists between the bedtime rituals of infants and children and the rituals and art of a culture's burial practices. The child's comforting transitional object is used to allay the separation anxiety signaled both by sleep and later by the idea of death. At the adult level, when there is an insufficiently developed internal soother (Tolpin 1971), a general regression due to illness, or fear of the reality of death, the individual and the culture reach for the solace of familiar objects. These can be functionally, symbolically, and often iconographically reminiscent of the transitional or fetishistic objects of early childhood.

SLEEP AND DEATH SYMBOLS

The fundamental symbolic relationship between sleep and death should first be reiterated. Recall that Hypnos and Thanatos were brothers in Greek mythology and that *cemetery* means "sleeping place" in Greek; that we close the staring eyes of the dead to shut out the light; that the depressive yearns for a long and final "rest." The oscillation between sleep and death symbolism is graphically illustrated by certain forms of marble sarcophagi available to wealthy medieval and early Renaissance Europeans. "Gisants" were fully dressed, plump, healthy appearing recumbent, "sleeping" figures. However, following the plague, the "transi" tomb became a popular form of sarcophagus lid carving. It depicted the shrouded or naked deceased in an actual state of decay. The sculpture demonstrated embalming scars and stitching, sometimes rotted open, with invading vermin, snakes, or frogs (Cohen 1973; Figure 1). They were experienced as "memento mori," moralistic reminders and warnings that death is real. Paradoxically, however, these nightmare figures provided solace for the living by substituting for the dead. Similarly, a patient reported by one of us (chapter 14) experienced a dreamless night as terrifying, and experienced his dreams as if they were stepping stones across a void. A nightmare was helpful—something to hold on to.

Fig. 1. Transi Tomb of Peter Niderwirt (d. 1522). Copyright 1973 by the Regents of the University of California; reprinted by permission of the University of California Press.

We often fear sleep as if it were death and reassure ourselves that death is only sleep.[1] In a sense, we die every night. The conscious and unconscious symbolic equation of death and sleep suggests that sleep and death rituals should demonstrate similar characteristics and functions. It is our aim to describe these similarities, taking for granted the multiple determination and complexity of each symbolic area.

THE LANGUAGE OF THE GRAVE

Children hold transitional or, sometimes, fetishistic objects to accompany them through the dark lonely night; stories are told, lullabies sung, and prayers recited. In a parallel manner, early graves contained the deceased's familiar, treasured objects.[2] Eventually these evolved into art forms with mythological themes, the "bedtime stories" that accompanied the dead on their eternal voyage to the river Lethe. J. J. Bachofen, in his pioneering *Essay on Ancient Mortuary Symbolism* (1859), wrote in his chapter on symbol and myth:

> The static symbol and its mythical unfolding are the speech and writing, the language of the tombs. The higher meditations inspired by the riddle of death, the grief and consolation, the hope and fear, the foreboding and joyful anticipation, are expressed only in art.... Only the symbol can combine the most disparate elements into a unitary impression. [pp. 49, 50]

Images of the bedtime story, a parental "have pleasant dreams," and the cuddled stuffed animal replace the parent during the dark night. Analogously, art images and objects began to adorn the tomb.

E.H. Gombrich referred to the practice of sacrificing slaves to accompany powerful men in their tombs:

> Later, these horrors were considered either too cruel or too costly, and art came to the rescue. Instead of real servants, the great ones of this earth were given images as substitutes. The pictures and models found in Egyptian tombs were connected with the idea of providing the souls with the helpmates in the other world. [Gombrich 1958, p. 35][3]

A hierarchy of substitutes has met societal loss and guilt concerning the practice of sacrificing wives, children, or slaves as companions in the other world. On Eddystone Island in the Solomons, the widow is kept in isolation and treated as if dead. James (1957) sees the widow's vigil at the

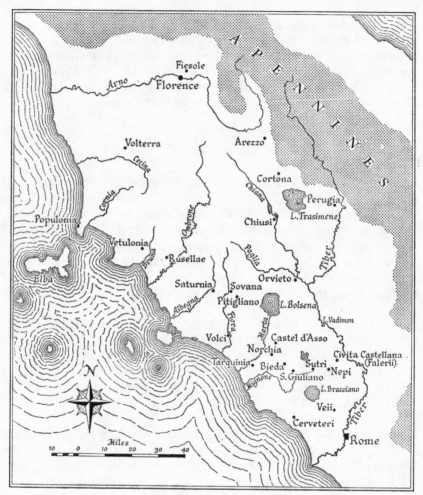

Fig. 2. Map of Etruria. From *The Etruscans in the Ancient World*, by Otto-Wilhelm von Vacano. London: Edward Arnold Ltd.

grave as a survival of these early practices. (A mother's "vigil" at the crib before sleep is a related phenomenon.) In Greek times the practice of women sacrificing their hair to the dead was so common a Greek word meaning to cut one's hair was used as a synonym for "to mourn over" (Panofsky 1964, p. 20).[4] Thus, the animate/inanimate world of ritual and art images is used to provide substitutes to assuage adult loss and separations as transitional objects do for each of us during infancy. The culture of the tomb bears further witness to this stabilizing function.

THE ETRUSCANS

Ernst Cassirer in *An Essay on Man* (1944) and Mircea Eliade in *The Sacred and the Profane* (1957) describe the profound philosophical and psychological changes that occur as man moves from a sacred to a more secular world. Man's original conceptual awareness of death was the profoundest blow to his sense of magical power. A defensive omnipotence followed, a denial of death by the magical, animistic, mystical aspects of religion. However, scientific challenge to religion then created the need for new alternatives, which can be conceptualized as substitutes—a culture's transitional objects, or more accurately, transitional and fetishistic object derivatives and symbols (Muensterberger 1962). As we have stated, the dangers of illness, invasion, and societal death that faced the Etruscans provide an arena for the application of our theses. This will lead us to a consideration of the specific iconography of an Etruscan mirror, the Volterra type of cinerary urn or ash chest, and the frescoes in the burial chambers in Tarquinia. But first, a short tour to place the Etruscan culture in an artistic, historical, and religious perspective.

The Etruscans lived between the Arno and the Tiber on the west coast of Italy—roughly, modern Tuscany (see Figure 2). They inhabited this area from the ninth to the first or second century B.C., reaching the acme of their civilization around the sixth or fifth century B.C. Then malaria, the Gauls, and the Romans precipitated their ultimate downfall as a society. Three major theories have developed concerning their provenance. Briefly, they are:

1. Orientalists accept Herodotus' description of a migration from Lydia in Asia Minor.
2. Autochthonists believe them to be the direct descendants of prehistoric tribes in Italy.
3. Environmentalists hold that the Etruscans are a mixed people, partly indigenous and partly immigrant. They maintain that the amalgamating powers of the environment and of common existence later produced an Etruscan identity.

This last theory seems the most plausible, and can be supported by aesthetic analysis of Etruscan artifacts. Objects discovered in Etruscan graves point to Villanovan, Umbrian, oriental, and Greek origins. However, not even an analysis of the blood types of fossil bones discovered in Etruscan graves can definitively answer the riddle of their origins.

The Etruscans were seafarers and farmers, and built powerful hilltop cities loosely organized into federations reminiscent of the city states of medieval Italy. Both their religion and art were created by multiple influences, Italic, Greek, Roman, and Near Eastern. It is important to stress that the Etruscans lived within a highly sacred space and time. In the underground the dead lived on, while on the surface the land was divided ritually into a *pars familiaris* and a *pars sinistras* (comparable to the familiar safe area and the forbidden dangerous area of the agoraphobic). The heavens were sectioned into sixteen parts, each signifying a different degree of good or bad fortune. Babylonian liver augury found a ready home in Etruria, and haruspicy (liver divination) was practiced for the Romans by Etruscan priests even into the Christian era.

The European earth-mother religion is expressed in the chthonic aspects of the Etruscan weltanshauung.[5] Frazer (1915, p. 287) noted that the tombs were identified not by the paternal lineage but by the maternal. No Etruscan building built above ground remains; these were not built for eternity. The tomb culture and its art provided a sufficient sense of contact with the infinite and the permanent. Apparently neither the above-ground Homeric or Christian view of a heavenly vault or dome nor its architectural equivalent was prominent in the telluric Etruscan world. There, underground spirits were ritually fed through the *mundus*, a covered cistern placed in the center of the town. Their cleverly vaulted tombs paradoxically opened into the bowels of the earth.

Tomb architects realized their apogee in the City of the Dead at Cerverteri, the present name for the Etruscan Caere, where it is still possible to stroll the streets of the dead. These run between bulky and grassy domes repeating the area's hills. The Etruscans often built on terrain comprising two adjacent hills overlooking the sea, one for the city and the other for the burial grounds. The living were linked to the dead by these twin hills. Tombs were filled with sarcophagi containing the ashes or bones of the dead, but also with both the actual possessions of the deceased and articles representing these. Male (phallic) and female (triangular pediment-shaped) symbols at the entrance identified the sex of the deceased.

These tombs existed for the Etruscans in the interface between death and life. The Etruscan world of a terrifying hell and the actual danger of societal and individual extinction from illness and invasion provided powerful separation and castration fears. Illustrative of this hell are the many sarcophagi which portray winged devils called *Lasae*. The Greek Charon is a relatively benign ferryman on the river Styx; in the Etruscan hagiology he becomes a frightening image, ready to crack the skull of any transgressor.

ETRUSCAN NIGHTMARES—THE SEA MONSTERS

A short voyage into the world of the Etruscan marine depths will illustrate further. The Etruscans portrayed a variety of fish-tailed monsters in their funereal art. The fanciful nature of these imaginative hybrid sea demons is derived in part from Greek mythology, but their artistic exegesis demonstrates a typically sinister, Etruscan character.

In archaic times, the hippocamp and varied types of mermen were favorite Etruscan sea creatures. During the period of Etruscan decline, more complicated hybrid animals were introduced by inventive Etruscan sculptors. Various Scylla monster figures were among the new motifs, no doubt as a result of an increasing Greek mythological influence. However, hybrid animal figures without Greek connections also appeared, such as sea panthers, sea dogs, sea wolves, and sea gryphons.

Significantly, the hippocamp appeared in Etruscan art more frequently than in Greek (Shepard 1940, p. 33). This swimming man-fish with outstretched arms was represented especially frequently in Etruscan funereal art. It is quite possible that on one level it symbolized the soul's journey to the underworld. Bronze braziers decorated with figures of hippocamps were discovered amid tomb furniture. These braziers could have been symbolic of a new source of light illuminating the dark passage leading to the other world.

Other sea monsters were frequently used decoratively on wall paintings (especially those on the gable space of tombs), and on urns, sarcophagi, toilette boxes, mirrors, and even Etrusco-Italic coins. These monsters appeared as winged, anthropomorphic, zoomorphic, or heteromorphic figures (Shepard 1940, p. 69). Since only a few of these Etruscan monsters had Greek or Roman mythological significance, it seems reasonable to connect them with the Etruscan belief in the journey of the soul to the other world. One mode of travel was swimming or riding the back of a sea monster. These interesting compromise figures are related to the comforting nighttime animal companions of the very young child. The hybrid sea monster combines the bridging qualities of the mythological nightmare and the reassuring companion or steed. In *The Magic Years*, Selma Fraiberg describes the "laughing tiger" of a two-and-a-half-year-old boy, calling this imaginary companion "the direct descendant of the savage and ferocious beasts who destroy the sleep of small children" [1959, p. 17].)

SOME EXISTENTIAL INFLUENCES ON ETRUSCAN ART

With the conquest of the city of Veii by the Roman dictator Marcus Furius Camillus in 396 B.C., the bell began to toll. The fear, death, and separation anxiety that had always permeated Etruscan psychology intensified significantly. The special poignancy that surrounds this doomed race is suggested by the Athrpa mirror (Figure 3), a well-known (and typical) Etruscan hand mirror interpreted by Von Vacano (1960).

Engraved on the back of this fine mirror are two tragic mythological couples, Aphrodite (Venus) and Adonis, and Atalanta and Meleager, while the figure of the wild boar, prominent in both myths, haunts the picture. In the center, a winged goddess of fate holds a hammer and is about to drive in a nail representing the passage of time and the acceptance of divine fate. Von Vacano refers to the mirror's Greek style and content, but cites its Etruscan atmosphere. Meleager is murdered by his mother, and Adonis is fated to be repeatedly slain by the tusks of a boar, year after year, and to be constantly shuttled between Aphrodite and Persephone, the goddess of the underworld. The figures seem to sense imminent death. Agnes Carr Vaugn (1964) aptly comments in *Those Mysterious Etruscans:* "The emphasis on the scene is not on reunion; it is on the sadness of separation." But perhaps some of the beauty of this moving scene lies in its capacity to freeze an image lying in the oscillating interface of separation and union (or reunion).

Etruscan fearfulness was intensified with the placing of the first nails in the Etruscan coffin. Sybille von Cles-Reden (1955), in her psychologically minded study *The Buried People,* refers to this change:

> As the realm of the chthonic gods came increasingly to be regarded as a place of sorrow and terror in the later centuries of their existence as a nation, we find the same excessive development of formalism, the same anxious attachment to innumerable rites of exorcism, on the exact fulfillment of which salvation depended. [p. 80]

Similarly, D.H. Lawrence (1932), after describing a fifth century B.C. tomb in Tarquinia as perfectly charming, wrote: "Then suddenly we came to the Tomb of Orcus, or Hell, which is given the 4th century B.C. as a date, and the whole thing utterly changes. You get a great, gloomy, clumsy, rambling sort of underworld, damp and horrid" (p. 74). Later on, "All the motion is gone; the figures are stuck there without any vital flow between them. There is no touch," (p. 74). Lawrence had said of the earlier Etruscans that "they know the gods in their very fingertips," (p. 47), that they "did not think about religion. . . . They felt the symbols and

Fig. 3. The Athrpa Mirror, c. 320 B.C. Diameter 7¾ in. From *The Etruscans in the Ancient World,* by Otto-Wilhelm von Vacano. London: Edward Arnold Ltd.

danced the sacred dances. For they were always kept in *touch*, physically, with the mysteries" (p. 52).

It would seem that generalized fear became so intense that the capacity for creative work was crippled, and that rigid adherence and "clinging to" (rather than "touching") rituals developed. This is reminiscent of the maladaptive developmental line that moves from normal transitional objects and phenomena to fetishism (Bak 1974, Roiphe and Galenson 1975). Under the excessive stress of the danger of body- and self-annihilation, the loss of body and genital integrity as well as separation from a symbiotic union, a childhood transitional object can be treated in a fetishistic manner (Muensterberger 1962, Greenacre 1969, Weissman 1971). That this is not an either-or process is explained by Weissman: "The normal transitional object may evolve into a hybrid form and the combined qualities of the fetish object may prevail over its feature as a created object; conversely, during a remission of pathological regression the qualities of the created object may supersede its fetishistic aspects."

Etruscan art became rigidified and Romanized at the same time. Its more spontaneous, expressive folk-art qualities began to disappear. The Roman persecutor prevailed, terrorized, and dominated the identity and products of the culture. Presumably this mechanism occurred in each Etruscan artist.[7]

ETRUSCAN ASH CHESTS

At this point, a detailed study of Etruscan Volterran style inhumation and cinerary sarcophagi should help to link this cultural evolvement more solidly with the developmental line of transitional objects/phenomena and fetishism. Essentially, these vessels consist of an alabaster, terra cotta, or lime-stone chest, with a lid supporting the semirecumbent figure of the deceased, leaning with his or her left elbow on a group of neatly piled, square, flat pillows. The right hand holds a ritual symbolic object.[8] The *illusion* evoked is that of the dead person attending a banquet, with hints of finality revealed by the symbolic object and his staring eyes, which seem to look out onto an infinite horizon (Figure 7). Panofsky feels that this Etruscan contribution to burial art provides a "real three-dimensional" and "less perishable and more aseptic" substitute for the gruesomeness of the corpse itself, i.e. a "realistic" illusion (Gombrich 1960).

Staring but not seeing, robust but dead—such images place these works of art in the world of illusion; they are symbols of a transitional world, reminiscences of infant and sleep experiences. The figures, spirits of stone, were sealed into an eternity of darkness, banqueting in death. Here form and content unite to become a balanced, bridging art symbol (Rothenberg 1975).[9]

A more detailed study of these semirecumbent figures reveals much. Often the fingers of the left hand rest in the folds of a robe or a head scarf; occasionally they are inserted in the concavity of an inverted libation plate. In both instances the index and little fingers are frequently displayed in the characteristic devil horns *(mano cornuta)* position, a symbolic warding off of the evil eye.[10] The juxtaposition of implied dangers (the evil eye, the demons of the underworld) and a magical gesture combined with the grasping of a textured cloth or a plate suggests the anxiety-relieving, soothing transitional object.

The treatment of the right hand can be understood similarly. It is stylized, but occasionally refers to the occupation or interests of the deceased. The held object could be a libation plate, a cornucopia or "rhyton" (in the shape of a sheep's body filled with fruit), a pomegranate (fertility symbol), a bronze mirror (especially in females), or, during the later Romanization, a scroll or book. The patera, however, is the most frequently utilized symbol. D.H. Lawrence (1932) describes its meaning in his luxuriant style, unfortunately not quoting his sources:

> The sacred *patera* or *mundum*, the round saucer with the raised knob in the centre, . . . represents the round germ of heaven and earth. It stands for the plasm, also, of the living cell, with its nucleus, which is the indivisible God of the beginning, and which remains alive and unbroken to the end. . . . [pp. 29,30][11]

The shape of the patera conforms to an image of the breast, as well as to ancient cosmic symbols representing the unity of the vast elements of the universe; it is also closely related to egg symbolism. It does resemble a food vessel, but representations of it have not been found with other Etruscan utensils. Most likely it served an essentially ritualistic function. Another plausible explanation for this multivalent symbol is that it represents a money disc, as it does in the Egyptian Book of the Dead (Radan 1975). In Greek mythology, when a shade approached the shores of the river Styx, it was necessary to have a small coin or *obolus* before entering Charon's boat (Roheim 1946). Otherwise the waiting time was no less than a hundred years. Whatever it was, the patera held by the deceased seems illusory in itself, at once concrete *and* symbolic, a food vessel *and* a cosmic symbol.

Both the tomb and sarcophagus are representatives and vehicles of transit between this world and the other. The ash chests are decorated

Fig. 4. Tufa cinerary urn (third century B.C.). Departure scene with patera, right hand. Figs. 4-6 courtesy Museo Archaeologico, Volterra, Italy.

Fig. 5. Alabaster cinerary urn (third to second century B.C.) The Calydonian boar hunt with patera, right hand.

Fig. 6. Alabaster cinerary urn (third century B.C.). The death of Eteocles and Polynices with patera, right hand.

Fig. 7. Volterra tomb with cinerary urns in situ. In the Museo Archaeologico, Florence, Italy. Copyright Leonard von Matt (Photographer).

with varied mythological themes. These include the Rape of Proserpina, Actaeon attacked by his devouring dogs, Perseus rescuing Andromeda from the monster, Cadmus contending with the Dragon of Mars, Oedipus slaying Laius, the Seven before Thebes, the fatal combat of Polynices and Eteocles, the Rape of Helen, the death of Politis, the murder of Clytemnestra by her son Orestes, and Orestes persecuted by the Furies. These tragic themes are preponderant; however, other urns do represent more pleasant subjects. They often picture the parting with the deceased at the funeral or the journey by sea, horseback, or chariot to the other world, while certain urns, especially admired by Lawrence, portray ordinary Etruscans in everyday pursuits.

The most frequent image, however, is that of the banqueting, semirecumbent Etruscan figure atop his own ashes contained in an urn that portrays tragic mythological crises or the transition between this world and the next. The upper figure comprise generative, death-denying, comforting, and familiar protective symbols, while in the lower section, mythological scenes tell stories of tragedy, of earth visits of the heavenly gods, or describe man's bridging journey to heaven.

CANOPIC URNS

The Etruscan cinerary urns are relatives of the Canopic urns of the Villanovans, an Iron Age Italic people who antedated the Etruscans. Canopic urns were stone vehicles for the voyage of the soul to another world and point to Pythagorean concepts of transmigration. They were hollow, primitive human figures which contained the ashes of the deceased (Figure 8). At times they took the form of a house; the ashes of the deceased concretely represented the soul in its bodily habitation. The Canopic figure urns were buried in the ground, seeds which grow in the depths of mother earth and which would lead to a spiritual rebirth.

They are also testimonies to the competing cremation and inhumation practices in Central Europe during this period. The Pythagorean transmigration of the soul mediated by the fire of cremation intensified the need to visualize the deceased with a concrete identity in the other world. These urns as such were artistically created body spaces containing the souls of the dead. They combined both concrete and abstract entities into a complex symbolism. The representation (in this case, symbols of the mind and body) helps to reassure the living of both their own and the lost one's continuity and ultimate reappearance, an attempt to externalize representations of the constant self-object. This resembles the use of the treasured blanket, stuffed animal, or doll of the one to two year old. The transitional object substitutes for the lost object (mother) as well as stabilizes various parts of the child's body image (Kestenberg and Weinstein, chapter 5), and provides continuity for the journey through the Stygian darkness.[12] That some of these Canopic urns take a doll form, and that Etruscan children were usually buried with their toys seems relevant to our thesis.

LIEBESTOD IMAGES AND THE EROTISM OF THE TOMB

George Dennis (1848), the father of British Etruscology, described the sensual aspects of Etuscan tomb sculpture:

One of these urns bears the effigies of a wedded pair reclining on it, as on the banqueting couch. Both are half draped, and decorated with ornaments. She lies on his bosom, while he has one hand on hers, the other holding a *patera*,—a specimen of Etruscan connubials highly

Fig. 8. Canopic urns (sixth century B.C.) of Villanovan origin. Courtesy Museo Archaeologico, Volterra, Italy.

edifying. The relief below displays a furious combat, a contrast, perhaps, intentionally introduced to show the turmoil and struggle of this life, as opposed to the blissful repose of a future existence, which the Etruscans could only express by scenes of sensual pleasure. [p. 343]

Other urns, including those of inhumation size, portray couples staring longingly into each other's eyes while in eternal embrace. There is no need for the patera here, as each stone partner is the "substitute." (These connubial urns, incidentally, have supplied additional evidence of the importance of the female in Etruscan society. The Greeks were horrified that Etruscan women dined with men under the same coverlet. Such Romans as Timaeus, Plautus, and Herodotus wrote of the decadence of Etruscan women, and Roman historians attributed the eventual degradation of the Etruscan civilization to their hedonistic attitudes.)

The nudity and occasional overt representation of sexual intercourse and sodomy in tomb paintings can be understood historically in terms of their primitive Etruscan origins, alloyed with an oriental, spiritual sensuality. In both primitive and oriental cultures, sexual symbolism often represented values of a more abstract nature. But let us examine some aspects of Etruscan sensuality as portrayed on other urns and in the colorful Tarquinia frescoes.

A couple lying side by side on a lid of a sarcophagus exhibited at the museum at Vulci is covered with a blanket showing the outlines of an intimate clinging embrace. (It has been interpreted by Scullard in The Etruscan Cities and Rome [1967] as representing the sleep of death.) The Boston Museum of Fine Arts houses two examples of sarcophagus lids depicting an embracing, blanketed nude couple (Figures 9, 10). The lids were fashioned in the idealized Hellenistic style. The Boston Museum of Art Catalogue (1963, p. 186) describes the reclining couples as reflecting the typical Etruscan delight in realistic detail, but this ignores the expressive force of this motif. Sensual union, though somewhat idealized, seems to fill the space of death, providing an "under the covers," textured, sensual, multidetermined symbol, with transitional-object qualities, to deal with the separation intrinsic to death.

An Etruscan terra cotta sarcophagus in the Villa Giulia, dated sixth century B.C., bears an "archaic" couple under the same cover reclining on the top of the sarcophagus. The woman is fully dressed while the torso of the man is nude. Superficially this has its decadent aspects. Yet perhaps the image can be understood as the earth-mother with her naked child, united by the covering blanket. Even more suggestive of this theme is a cinerary urn in the Museum of Volterra (Figure 11). On its lid is a fully dressed couple carved in reclining position. Publications using it as an illustration describe them as husband and wife; but on closer inspection the face of the woman appears as much that of the mother as of the wife. The man's eyes stare into the distance, the woman's devotedly into her partner's face.[13] The totality evokes the quality of a tender maternal farewell. Again, union and separateness are balanced in both form and content. E. H. Gombrich, in his basic study *Art and Illusion* (1960) cites a relevant passage from Euripides. A dying Alcestis is mourned by her husband Admetus. He anticipates the commission of a funereal effigy of his beloved:

> And represented by the skillful hands
> Of craftsmen, on the bed thy body shall

Fig. 9 (left). Sarcophagus of Peperino. From Vulci, marble lid. Husband and wife (fourth century B.C.). Courtesy Museum of Fine Arts, Boston. On loan from Boston Athenaeum.
Fig. 10 (right). Alabaster sarcophagus lid: husband and wife (third century B.C.). Courtesy Museum of Fine Arts, Boston. Gift of Mrs. Gardner Brewer.

Be laid; whereon I shall fall in embrace
And clasp my hands around it, call thy name
And fancy in my arms my darling wife
To hold, holding her not; perhaps I grant,
Illusory delight, yet my soul's burden
Thus should I lighten. . . .

THE PHALLUS AND THE TRANSITIONAL OBJECT

Representations of erotic and conjugal union in the setting of the tomb have referents not only in sexual love, but in union at a mother-child or symbiotic level. Sexual love and phallic or vaginal objects can provide as much a self-object meaning as a genital one. Many writers on primitive religion have arrived at analogous conclusions. The pre-Freudian anthropologists and pioneers of symbolism knew that primitive man used his sexual organs to express feelings and to signify the "higher" issues of his life, the sense of the seasons, biological rhythms, birth and rebirth, and, ultimately, concepts of mystical union. As the sexual organs came to be covered with clothing by individual and collective superegos, it became necessary for Freud to show us the erotic and underpinnings of our creations and habits. Thus in primitive societies the phallus itself was used as a symbol for other things, while in more sophisticated cultures other things were used to symbolize the phallus. Of course this is actually a reciprocal psychocultural mechanism, one level reinforcing the other, with the resultant symbolism capable of meeting the world of the transitional experience (Rose, chapter 22).[14]

The Marind-anim of Dutch South New Guinea have practiced an orgiastic puberty rite which is illustrative. A young couple openly have intercourse atop a platform of heavy logs. Following this, the supports are pulled away, the platform collapses and the two young people are extracted, cut up, roasted, and then eaten (Campbell 1959). Sexual union and death are equated, but the final act is a primitive incorporation or fusion with the dead. This serves as a symbolic rite aiding the passage through adolescence.

Róheim in his 1942 article "Transition Rites" convincingly shows that the uniting effect of the phallus can be traced to the period now known as separation-individuation:

There is anxiety in the transition period between separation and aggregation. One mechanism for dealing with the anxiety is the rebirth symbolism of the transition period whose functional significance is to represent it as a danger successfully overcome. The other mechanisms are all based on withdrawal of libido from the object. One important formula is: "You have lost your mother and have not yet got your wives, but you have your penis"—the magic wand that bridges the gulf of the transition period. The rites center about the penis and penis symbols *(tjurunga)*; for the initiate it is essentially a phallic ritual. [p. 356]

Later in the same article Róheim continues his discussion of the puberty rites of Australian tribes. He writes of

the repetition of the separation (foreskin, tooth, hair) in which the trauma is dealt with on a narcissistic object level; that is, instead of the original object we have its narcissistic equivalent (a part of the body), and this paves the way towards new ties or a symbolic unconscious renewal of old ones. Thus the guardian may keep the foreskin or tooth, establishing a bond between the young man and male society, or it is given back to the mother. Also, an intermediate cathexis is formed: the foreskin is cut off, but it then acquires a protective value; or the youth while separated from the woman is endowed with a supernatural penis *(tjurunga)*. [p. 369]

Fig. 11. Conjugal couple, cinerary urn lid. Courtesy Museo Archaeologico, Volterra, Italy. Note *mano cornuto*, devil's horn position of man's left hand.

Róheim's thinking, as well as Imre Hermann's, clearly anticipated Winnicott's conceptualizations.

Male followers of the Phrygian earth goddess, Cybele, castrated themselves during sexual-religious orgiastic states and then, as eunuchs, united with the cult and devoted their lives to higher pursuits. Their severed organs were wrapped up and buried in the earth or in underground chambers sacred to Cybele. They recalled her dead lover, Attis, to life and "hastened the general resurrection of nature" (Frazer 1915).

Bachofen (1859) was aware of the early oral and maternal referents involved in phallic and genital symbolism. In his *Essay on Mortuary Symbolism*, he included this passage in his discussion of the Orphic, Bacchic mystery egg:

> The phallic god, striving toward the fertilization of matter is not the original datum; rather, he himself springs from the darkness of the maternal womb. He stands as a son to feminine matter; bursting the shell of the egg, he discloses the mystery of phallic masculinity that had hitherto been hidden within it, and the mother herself rejoices in him as in her own demon. The phallic god cannot be thought of separately from feminine materiality. [p. 29]

THE TOMB OF THE BULLS IN TARQUINIA

Sybill von Cles Reden (1955) wrote of the Tomb of the Bulls in Tarquinia:

> It is indeed curiously disturbing to find a place of mourning decorated in the style of a place of sensual enjoyment. Yet there is something to admire in this grand denial of death by simply amalgamating it with life; and this is a characteristic feature of the Tyrrhenian people [the Etruscans] in their prime. [pp. 57-58]

Frescoes in the Tomb of the Bulls portray human figures performing anal coitus. This is repeated on several sarcophagi discovered elsewhere, as on a Tarquinian urn from the seventh century B.C.; there the love-making couple is shown in an oriental style. One of the erotic fresco scenes from the Tomb of the Bulls depicts two males and a female. One male is in the canine position, the female lying supine on his back; the other male, in a standing position, holds the legs of the female partner on his shoulders while penetrating her anally. This can be seen as the desire for eternal fusion, expressed in phallic and pregenital (here anal) terms.

Apparently the anthropologist, the sepulchral artist, and the psycho-analytic observer all sense the complementary relationship between separation-individuation and phallic themes. The work of Roiphe and Galenson (1972), which delineates a phase of genital awareness within the separation-individuation continuum, provides a developmental foundation for this construct. At the derivative level we are considering, a developmentally based process is implied in which genital and phallic symbols have meanings originating in the period of separation-individuation.

Man is reassured in the orgasm of sexual union that he has both a psychic unity and a separateness, that he is both dead and alive, that he possesses both his own genital and that of his partner. In this physical-mystical experience, a supreme illusion occurs that takes into account the paradoxes of existence. The act of union was used symbolically in protoreligious rituals; as in the transitional object–fetish interface in the child, there is an assertion of a separation-union, as well as an affirmation of phallicity, genitality, and the total body image.

CLARIFICATION

These ideas involve the question of whether an early developmental concept, transitional and fetishistic objects, is more than historical once an oedipal organization of the mental apparatus has appeared. It is our view that developmental and maturational systems do not "fix" in an Eleatic sense, that the Heraclitean flow back and forth across the primary-process–secondary-process, concrete-abstract, perception-fantasy, and self-object interfaces not only allows for, but actually defines, the presence of the transitional experience throughout development, i.e., until death itself. Gilbert Rose's "The Creativity of Everyday Life" (chapter 22) is an eloquent exposition of this point of view.

Phyllis Greenacre (1969) discusses the intrapsychic events that take place "before the dawn of clear (mental) memory":

Actual events from so early a time may leave residual patterns of sensory response and reaction. These appear sometimes fused with or incorporated into later memories and fantasies and sometimes as rather stark body reactions, to be re-enacted under the influence of the transference relationship—if one considers this to include the basic rapport between the analyst and analysand merging into but not exclusively limited to the transference neurosis which is constellated around the oedipus complex. I would regard these reactions as a special form of body memory which may take on a primitive form of communication. [p. 159]

The experience evoked by an art form, especially one associated directly with sleep and its symbolic twin, death (and their underlying terrors of separation, mutilation, and castration), can stir up preverbal memory traces, as can the analytic situation. In a separation-oriented, secularized Western society, patches are needed on our always imperfect psychic structure. A legacy of phallic and umbilical stumps in our self and object representations has led to the "fetishism of everyday life," i.e., the cigarette, the cocktail glass, the compulsively carried book or newspaper. These can represent externalizations of transitional experiences associated with separation and castration anxiety. When an artist offers his work, we can "have our cake and eat it," i.e., be provided with a reparative patch that does not preclude a simultaneous uniting and integrating creative experience.

THE ONTOGENESIS OF THE SYMBOL

A consideration of the intermediary process from the transitional experience and its cathected objects and phenomena to the establishment of both primary and secondary (unconscious) symbols (Piaget 1951) and of object constancy should help to place within a conceptual framework, the adult capacity to undergo a transitional-object–stage experience. David Beres (1965) has written of the "substitute object" which developmentally precedes the transitional object. He would probably include Harlow's surrogate mother and the blanket, as it might be used by the child younger than six months. Beres feels that as the capacity for representation increases, followed by tentative self and object differentiation and reality testing, the substitute object becomes the transitional object. The developmental line branches toward the eventual capacity for symbol formation and its analogue, object constancy. Earlier, Werner and Kaplan in *Symbol Formation* took Winnicott's concepts into account:

From a developmental point of view, there is an early stage at which the distinction or difference between symbol and referential object has not been clearly established; in other words, there are phenomena which are neither objects per se nor symbols per se but partake of both.

In terms of the development of symbols, the so-called "transitional objects" again seem to be of critical significance. In this regard, it is noteworthy that among the therapists who have utilized such objects in their patients' experiences to guide their patients towards "reality" some speak of "transitional objects" and others talk of (real) symbols. In fact, it is likely that these "objects" are transitional forms—prior to differentiation—of both true objects and true symbols. From the point of view of the development of symbolization, therefore, we may designate them as *protosymbols* (in contrast with representational symbols, in which there is duality between vehicle and referent). . . . Just as one moves through the transitional objects to true objects, that is, objects that are familiar, comprehensible and stable, so too does one move—in ontogenesis as well in the redevelopment of reality—from protosymbols to true symbols, symbols confounded neither with the objects they represent nor with the "mother"—or others—with whom one shares the objects. [pp. 75, 76]

Werner and Kaplan agree with clinical observations that there is a two-way continuum between advanced symbolic forms and their earlier versions:

Protosymbols may be transformed into true symbols by progressive differentiation of vehicle and referential meaning; true symbols may regress to protosymbols through dedifferentiation of vehicle and referent. [p. 17]

The concept of the protosymbolic form has been referred to and developed in the literature by Lorenzer and Orban (chapter 28), Balkanyi (1968), and Volkan and Kavanagh (chapter 19). These progressive and regressive movements correspond to the fluctuating modes of human relatedness, from the transitional mode to the true object relationship with its implied reasonable amount of object constancy and self-object differentiation.

TRANSITIONAL SOURCES

This concept of a fluctuating continuum between the transitional object and the symbol is provided more weight by recent attempts to show that transitional objects don't just "fade away," but become structured and provide a more stable inner comfort (Tolpin 1971). The protosymbol-symbol continuum is a system with varying degrees of both stability and flexibility in each individual. A symbol or, specifically, an art symbol serves a semantic function (associative meaning); yet, if it is rich and has been provided multiple determination and ambiguity on the part of the creator (the artist within a specific culture), it can evoke more concrete, synesthetic, nondiscursive, sensorimotor forms, as well as the "textural" qualities of the transitional experiences that are in epigenetic sequence and linkage with it. This allows us to "hold" it and to "savor" it—it stays with us!

A religious art symbol, the plaster saint (surely a vestige of the pagan idol) can be worshiped and touched. A nun in St. Catherine's Church in Siena, Italy, despaired over the tendency of some "foolish" followers of her patroness to worship and genuflect in front of the door of a broom closet they presumed was the entrance to a more sacred chamber. Concomitantly, the symbolic "pause that refreshes" is most frequently not mere time itself; it usually requires the warmth of a column of smoke suffusing in and out of the lungs, or the tingly, down-and-up sensations of a carbonated drink.

Mircea Eliade says in his *The Sacred and the Profane* that "history cannot basically modify the structure of an archaic symbolism. History adds new meanings but they do not destroy the structure of the symbol." And John Cuthbert Lawson, in demonstrating the pagan origins of the Christian saints in Greece, stated in 1909 that "in effect paganism was not uprooted to make room for the planting of Christianity, but served as an old stock of which a new vigourous branch, capable instead of fairer fruit, but owing its very vitality to alien sap, might be engrafted." Both statements imply that although semantic levels evoked by language, art, or nature might resonate via "horizontal" associations, from abstract symbols down to the more concrete "symbolic equations" (Segal 1957), they do so through transitional experiences and transitional object representations (protosymbolic representations) still "alive" deep within the ego-id continuum. Via this system, prelogical needs can be experienced, expressed, or externalized into new creative enterprise. Of course for early experiences to enter later consciousness, they must pass through the symbolic system of the ego; a transitional-object–related experience must appear in symbolic form to appear in consciousness. However, its associated transitional traces in the preconscious and unconscious depths of the ego-superego-id continuum can provide opportunities for nondiscursive, preverbal discharge. The process that leads from sensorimotor forms through intermediate forms to verbal and nonverbal symbolic forms (Lorenzer and Orban, chapter 28) is, to some degree a two-way street. "Revisits" can occur during structural regression and creative experiencing.

This warrants, however, the word of caution provided in Erik Erikson's fine essay "The Ontogeny of Ritualization." There he traces the hierarchical steps from a child's to a culture's rituals:

I am not suggesting a simple causal relationship between the infantile stage and the adult institution, in the sense that adult rituals "only" satisfy persisting infantile needs in disguise; rather, they support (among other things) what Hartmann has called "adaptation by a detour through regression." The image of the Ancestor of the God sought on a mature level is by no means "only" a replica of the mother's inclined face or the father's powerful countenance; nor is the idea of Justice "only" an externalization of a childish bad conscience. . . . In all epigenetic development, however, a ritual element, once evolved, must be progressively reintegrated on each higher level, so that it will become an essential part of all subsequent stages. [p. 613]

The word *symbol* etymologically implies a unity, a connecting of separate parts; it stems from the Greek *syn* + *ballein*, meaning "to throw together." This connecting function was elaborated by Deri (1974): "Symbols always arise from the wish to bridge over something or somebody in another reality, *to reach the directly unreachable.*" Hanna Segal in her essay, "Notes on Symbol Formation" writes that "the process of symbol formation is . . . a continuous process of bringing together and integrating the internal with the external, the subject with the object, and earlier experiences with the later ones."

The burial symbols and art associated with religious ritual demonstrate the derivatives of uniting-separating transitional experiences even more manifestly than the average symbolic art form *precisely because* these symbols are created within the interface of life and death. Here, separation-death danger provides an inordinate anxiety level that requires intense self, object, and body image stabilization and comfort via an adaptive detour that includes a resort to previous transitional experiences.

CONCLUSION

The evocative symbols bridging subject and object are developmentally derived from an earlier "protosymbolic" phase in which only partial differentiation exists among the triangular components—the symbol, its referent, and the symbolizer. This protosymbolic phase corresponds to Winnicott's transitional object and phenomenon, externalizations of what can be designated *the transitional process* (Rose, chapter 22).

As development progresses, this experience is organized more complexly. However, the art symbol can reveal the derivatives of its transitional-object ancestry. This would be especially so for the burial art symbol, which straddles the interfaces both of the here and now of wakefulness and life and of the void and separateness of sleep and death. There is a correspondence between a child's nighttime transitional objects, rituals, and bedtime stories, and the symbols, art, and mythological themes associated with a society's burial practices.

The chthonic Etruscan civilization had an affinity for the tomb and the afterlife, possessed a terrifying hell, and underwent intense separation and annihilation anxiety. The Etruscan art produced in the period of decline is viewed as influenced by this anxiety. The resulting rigidification of art is interpreted in terms of Greenacre's fetishistic process concept. In addition, the phallus–transitional object linkage helps explain the use in the tomb of genital symbolism in representing referents at more abstract, mystical, and at the same time, symbiotic levels of union.

It is hoped that studies which have identified the source of the motivation for the creative impulse in separation and castration anxiety will be supplemented by a more specific consideration of transitional object and phenomena origins, meanings, and derivatives in our art forms and their internal symbols. Detailed studies of sepulchral art and the mourning process and its rituals during various cultural epochs could provide a paradigm for a further understanding of the transitional experience. Conversely, an enriched psychoanalytic and observational knowledge of this aspect of development should enhance our comprehension of both the form and the meaning of the art that man has created to ward off, symbolize, and imaginatively master his eternal nemesis, the final separation, death.

NOTES

1. Our aging pets are "put to sleep," not put to death.
2. Róheim (1946) described the Rumanian practice of placing towels and pieces of cloth into coffins. They are called "bridge," referring to the belief they became bridges that carried the dead across obstacles in the other world (p. 161).
3. Gombrich (1975) reminds us that "it should not be forgotten that the Egyptian belief in an afterlife was a 'real belief'. " The progression from delusion to illusion in religion, the wafer=body to the wafer as symbolic of body, parallels the individual's development from concrete to symbolic thought.
4. Volkan's "linking objects" concept (1972) is relevant here. These are mementoes of the deceased that are like transitional objects, only more fetishistic. They are clung to in an obligatory manner by pathological mourners.
5. The extent to which Etruscan afterlife was an underworld womb concept is affirmed by the Etruscan creation myth of Tages. A creature

with a child's body, Tages possessed the wizened face and white hair of an old man. When uncovered by a ploughman near Tarquinia, Tages recited the ritual books (the Etruscan bible), and returned to his earth-mother, the underworld.

6. It should be stressed that the Etruscans cannot be considered a primitive tribe or as practicing a truly primitive religion. However, many protoreligious, magical, or ritualistic customs certainly prevailed. Vestiges of Etruscan religious practices and of the names of Etruscan gods persisted in Tuscan folklore as late as the nineteenth century (Leland 1891).

7. The usurpation by one culture of another's creativity and style following invasion could be explained strictly on sociological or behavioral terms. However, it would seem that collective intrapsychic processes should be taken into account. Though acculturation per se can change a nation's basic aesthetic style in the course of a century or two, there are exceptions to the rule; e.g., the Romans created pseudonyms for Greek gods, but allowed them to retain their essential identity.

8. These urns have been studied in the psychoanalytic literature by Eisenbud (1965). He cited the hand-breast symbolism involved in a series of archaeological artifacts from ancient fertility symbols held in the hand, through the Etruscan *patera* the egg, pomegranate and bird symbolism in European art. Eisenbud considered only the specific symbolism of the held object, not the work of art as a whole. Presymbolic and transitional object factors were not discussed.

9. Shakespeare wrote of this in "The Phoenix and the Turtle": "Love hath reason, Reason none/ if what parts, can so remain." (*The Riverside Shakespeare* 1974, p. 1797).

10. The evil eye was prominent in the Etruscan world. To combat it, amulets called *bullae* were worn. They consisted of a small bubble-shaped locket (Budge 1930, pp. 14, 15).

11. Lawrence was always fascinated by mystical experiences and death, and hence, by the Etruscans. Excited by bridging concepts, he compares the Etruscan bridge at Vulci with a rainbow. In the novel *The Rainbow* (1915) the multihued ribbon extends from sepulchral miners' tunnels (he was born in a Welsh mining town) to the heavens.

12. John Donne's poem "The Funeral" strikingly presents a related theme. The narrator is steeped in yearning and a morbid sadness after being rejected by his lover. He begins:

> Whoever comes to shroud me, do not harm
>   Nor question much
> That subtle wreath of hair which crowns my arm;
> The mystery, the sign you must not touch,
>   For 'tis my outward soul,
> Viceroy to that, which then to heaven being gone,
>   Will leave this to control,
> And keep these limbs, her provinces, from dissolution.

For if the sinewy thread my brain lets fall
Through every part
Can tie those parts and make me one of all. . . .

This wreath of hair that serves as an "outward soul," whose threads can "tie these parts" ("her provinces"), has transitional-object qualities. The imagery is reminiscent of the poetically woven gems of Emily Dickinson, an avid reader of Donne; these were left in her drawer, to be her substitutive self, for all eternity (see Miller, chapter 27). The last line quoted points to a comforting compromise between having and having not; but the final phrase shows the fragility of this compromise: "That since you would save none of me, I bury some of you." "The Relic" and "The Funeral" were both written in the year 1633. "The Relic" is addressed to the man who will disinter the poet:

And he that digs it, spies
A bracelet of bright hair about the bone,
Will he not let us alone,
And think that there a loving couple lies,
Who thought that this device might be some way
To make their souls, at the last busy day,
Meet at this grave, and make a little stay?

Again, the uniting bracelet of hair joins self and object symbolically; but it also provides the possibility that during the busy (Judgment) day, the dispersed parts of the body and the soul will again be reunited in a "little stay" (eternity). In "The Ecstasy" (also 1633) he wrote of this:

But as all several souls contain
Mixture of things, they know not what,
Love these mixed souls doth mix again,
And makes both one, each this and that.

13. Dr. George Radan (personal communication) points out that this placing of eye axes is probably an Etruscan imitation of Greek stelae of the fifth century, "where such symbolism shows that the dead see the living and maintain contact, but the reverse is not so."

14. A similar process at a somewhat different level is alluded to in B. Z. Goldberg's *The Sacred Fire*: "The erotic symbol in religion was naturally a concomitant of the erotic religious thought. In fact, the two were elements of the same formative process. The thought affected the symbol, and the symbol influenced the idea. We should therefore expect the development of erotic symbolism to follow that of erotic thought. Just as man originally saw the generative process not by sexes but in the actual union, so did he seek to symbolize the generative force by the actual union of the sex organs" (p. 115).

REFERENCES

Bachofen, J. (1859). *Myth, Religion and Mother Right*. Princeton: Princeton University Press, 1967.

Bak, R. (1974). Distortions of the concept of fetishism. In *Psychoanalytic*

Study of the Child 29:191-214.

Balkanyi, C. (1968). Language, verbalization and superego: some thoughts on the development of the sense of rules. *International Journal of Psycho-Analysis* 49:712-719.

Beres, D. (1965). Symbol and object. *Bulletin of the Menninger Clinic* 29:2-23.

Budge, E. A. (1930). *Amulets and Talismans.* New York: MacMillan, 1970.

Campbell, J. (1959). *The Masks of God. Primitive Mythology.* New York: Viking, 1970.

Cassirer, E. (1944). *An Essay on Man.* New Haven: Yale University Press.

Cohen, K. (1973). *Metamorphosis of a Death Symbol: The Transi Tomb in the Late Middle Ages and the Renaissance.* Berkeley: University of California Press.

Dennis, G. (1848). *The Cities and Cemeteries of Etruria.* Vol. 2. London: John Muray.

Deri, S. (1974). Symbolization in psychoanalysis and schicksalsanalysis: a revised theory of symbolization. In *Separatdruck aus Szondiana IX*, pp. 35-52. Vienna: Verlag, Hans Huber.

Dickinson, E. (1960). *The Complete Poems of Emily Dickinson.* Ed. Thomas H. Johnson. Boston: Little Brown.

Donne, J. (1633). The funeral. In *The Norton Anthology of Poetry.* New York: Norton, 1970.

Eisenbud, J. (1965). The hand and breast with special reference to obsessional neurosis. *Psychoanalytic Quarterly* 34:219-248.

Eliade, M. (1957). *The Sacred and the Profane.* New York: Harcourt, Brace and World.

Erikson, E. (1966). The ontogeny of ritualization. In *Psychoanalysis, A General Psychology.* New York: International Universities Press.

Euripides (1955). Alcestis. In *The Complete Greek Tragedies*, vol. 3, ed. David Grene and Richmond Lattimore. Chicago: University of Chicago Press.

Fraiberg, S. (1959). *The Magic Years.* New York: Scribner.

Frazer, J. (1915). *The Golden Bough.* 3rd ed. Vol. 2. New York: St. Martin's Press, 1966.

Goldberg, B. Z. (1930). *The Sacred Fire: The Story of Sex in Religion.* New York: Liveright, 1970.

Gombrich, E. H. (1958). *The Story of Art.* London: Phaidon Press.

——— (1960). *Art and Illusion.* Princeton: Princeton University Press.

——— (1975). Personal communication.

Greenacre, P. (1969). The fetish and the transitional object. In *Psychoanalytic Study of the Child* 24:144-164.

James, E. O. (1957). *Prehistoric Religion.* New York: Praeger.

Langer, S. (1942). *Philosophy in a New Key.* Cambridge: Harvard University Press, 1973.

Lawrence, D. H. (1915). *The Rainbow.* New York: Viking, 1961.

——— (1932). Etruscan Places. In *D. H. Lawrence and Italy.* New York: Viking, 1972.

Lawson, J. C. (1909). *Modern Greek Folklore and Ancient Greek Religion.* New Hyde Park, N.Y.: University Books, 1964.

410 SIMON A. GROLNICK AND ALFONZ LENGYEL

Leland, C. (1891). *Etruscan Roman Remains in Popular Tradition*. London: T. Fisher Unwin.

Muensterberger, W. (1962). The creative process: its relation to object loss and fetishism. In *Psychoanalytic Study of Society* 2:161-185.

Panofsky, E. (1964). *Tomb Sculpture: Four Lectures on Its Changing Aspects from Ancient Egypt to Bernini*. New York: Abrams.

Piaget, J. (1951). *Play, Dreams and Imitation in Childhood*. New York: Norton, 1962.

Radan, G. (1975). Personal communication.

Read, H. (1965). *Icon and Idea: The Function of Art in the Development of Human Consciousness*. New York: Schocken.

Róheim, G. (1942). Transition rites. *Psychoanalytic Quarterly* 11:336-374.

——— (1946). Charon and the obolos. *Psychiatric Quarterly* 20:160-196.

Roiphe, H., and Galenson, E. (1972). Early genital activity and the castration complex. *Psychoanalytic Quarterly* 41:334-347.

——— (1975). Some observations on transitional object and infantile fetish. *Psychoanalytic Quarterly* 44:206-231.

Rothenberg, A. (1975). Cognitive processes in creation. To be published in *Creative Processes*, ed. Michael Krausz. London: Clarendon Press.

Scullard, H. H. (1967). *The Etruscan Cities and Rome*. Ithaca: Cornell University Press.

Segal, H. (1957). Notes on symbol formation. *International Journal of Psycho-Analysis* 38:391-397.

Shakespeare, W. (1601). The phoenix and the turtle. In *The Riverside Shakespeare*. Boston: Houghton Mifflin, 1974.

Shepard, K. (1940). *Fish-Tailed Monsters in Greek and Etruscan Art*. New York: Privately published.

Tolpin, M. (1971). On the beginnings of a cohesive self: an application of the concept of transmuting internalization to the study of the transitional object and signal anxiety. *Psychoanalytic Study of the Child* 26:316-354.

Vaugn, A. C. (1964). *Those Mysterious Etruscans*. London: Robert Hale, 1966.

Volkan, V. (1972). The linking objects of pathological mourners. *Archives of General Psychiatry* 27:215-221.

Von Cles-Reden, S. (1955). *The Buried People. A Study of the Etruscan World*. (Das Versunkene Volk). London: Rupert Hart-Davis.

Von Vacano, O. W. (1960). *The Etruscans in the Ancient World*. London: Edward Arnold.

Weissman, P. (1971). The artist and his objects. *International Journal of Psycho-Analysis* 52:401-406.

Werner, H., and Kaplan, B. (1963). *Symbol Formation*. New York: Wiley.

Winnicott, D. W. (1951). Transitional objects and transitional phenomena. In *Collected Papers: Through Pediatrics to Psychoanalysis*, pp. 229-242. New York: Basic Books, 1958.

——— (1971). The place where we live. In *Playing and Reality*. New York: Basic Books.

CHAPTER 25

In chapter 10, Anni Bergman described the spatial relations affecting the mother-child dyad throughout development. With language and speech, as with vision, it is possible for the child to separate and yet remain close to the mother—to feel "I am not alone."

Winnicott indicated that the infant's vocalization could be used as a transitional phenomenon. In this sense, the sounds or their patterned expression would be used to undo separation from the mother. Here, using data from linguistics, Martin Weich discusses the infant's developing language function. He introduces the terms *transitional language, language fetish,* and *language constancy,* all of which aid conceptualization of the infant's language development and the nature of object relations. Weich sees the internalization of the language function associated with transitional language much as does Tolpin in her paper on structuralization of the soothing function of the transitional object.

In chapter 26, Emilie Sobel shows how certain poetic forms derive from transitional language.

L.B.

TRANSITIONAL LANGUAGE

Martin J. Weich

Everything of importance has been said before by somebody who did not discover it.
—Alfred North Whitehead, 1917

Winnicott, in his classic "Transitional Objects and Transitional Phenomena" (1953), subsumed the infant's use of sounds and words under the broad category of transitional phenomena. With the exception of McDonald's paper dealing with transitional tunes (1970) and Griffith and Ritvo's examination of echolalia (1967), others have made only brief or indirect reference to these phenomena (Ekstein 1965, Balkanyi 1964, 1968, Tolpin 1971, Greenson 1954, Greenacre 1969). Some writers have cited language, a medium inherent in the analytic situation, as an illustration of the persistence into adult life of problems stemming from early vicissitudes in the use of transitional objects and phenomena (Kahne 1967, Greenacre 1969, Volkan 1973, Modell 1970, Greenbaum chapter 12, Grolnick chapter 14). However, the child's use of language as a transitional phenomenon and its subsequent effects upon language development—in fact, its being required for language development at all—has not been discussed.

One reason for this neglect may be that Winnicott tended to stress the physical concreteness of the transitional object, along with the sensory modalities of touch, smell, vision, and taste, while he paid little attention to the auditory sphere. Then, by relegating the fate of the transitional object to its disappearance and diffusion over the whole cultural field, he neglected to consider its transformation into psychic structure.

Tolpin (1971) made an initial attempt to fill this gap by applying Kohut's concept of transmuting internalization (1971) to the study of the transitional objects and phenomena. Transmuting internalization is an intrapsychic process which accounts for the eventual replacement of lost functions of the object image. In the setting of optimal frustration, a particle of inner psychological structure assumes the functions which the object used to perform for the child. Thus the object's function is preserved and precipitated in a manner reminiscent of Freud's description (1923) of the character of the ego as a precipitate of abandoned object cathexes. Tolpin emphasizes the fate of the transitional object as a self-soothing psychic structure, disagreeing with Winnicott's assertion that the transitional object does not "go inside," but loses meaning and becomes diffused over the whole cultural field (see also McDonald 1970).

This chapter will consider the development of infant language highlighting its function as a transitional phenomenon. Previously (1968), I attempted to illustrate the broad unfolding of the language function in the context of the changing levels of object relations by examining the concepts *transitional language, language fetish* and *language constancy.* Clinical examples of adults using words to soothe themselves and keep themselves company like children's teddy bears were offered to suggest that words could act as transitional phenomena persisting into adult life. Recent observations in linguistics have pointed to a period of early language development during which words initially act as transitional objects. The child seems to carry the word with him as if he owns it. He repeats it to soothe and reassure himself, as though the word were there whenever he needed it. At this stage of development, words have not yet attained the status of true representational symbols; they are used as objects as well as symbols. Transitional language also seems to be the first creative use of language by the child. Its internalization as psychic structure then prepares the way for the next stage in language development—two-word utterances or simple sentences.

EARLY LANGUAGE DEVELOPMENT

The process by which the child's expressions for conveying messages becomes increasingly verbal takes place as follows: Out of the matrix of body movements and vocal intonational patterns, an increasing articulation of speech units ("vocables") occurs, with the gradual subordination of intonation and gesture to speech symbols (Werner and Kaplan 1963). More specifically, this prelinguistic development proceeds from undifferentiated crying to differentiated crying and cooing by the third month. Babbling is seen by the fourth month, lallation (imitation of the infant's accidentally produced sounds) between the sixth and the twelfth. Echolalia (imitation of the sounds of others) begins at nine months. Early linguistic units make their appearance as one-word utterances between about twelve and eighteen months, with two-word utterances generally occurring between seventeen and twenty-two months (Eisenson et al. 1964).

During prelinguistic stages, when the infant uses intonation and gesture to express himself, his various attitudes (wishes, demands, etc.) are more or less syncretically fused, undifferentiated, and poorly controlled, with the exception of smiling and early babbling activity. Considerable progress is seen in the development of one-word utterances with an increase in variety of forms, variation of intonations, differentiation of attitudes, adoption of vocal patterns resembling adult forms, and the differentiation of the various components of a referential situation (i.e., reference to a state of affairs involving such components of a situation as self, other, and object of discourse).

EARLY LANGUAGE DEVELOPMENT AND OBJECT RELATIONS

The link between language development and the development of object relations is now well accepted. Greenson (1950) describes how children initially treat words as objects. Ekstein and Caruth (1969) see thought and language development proceeding in a manner that parallels developing object relations: from autism through complete fusion, to greater degrees of differentiation and individuation within the symbiotic sac, until an optimal separation has been achieved. Greenson in addition describes how speech provides a means of retaining a connection to the mother as well as separating from her. Children replace sucking at the breast with introjection of the mother's sounds. With the use of language they replace passivity and mother-attachment with activity and mother-identification. Echolalia appears, with its imitation of accent, tone, and rhythm as well as words. Ekstein (1965), Ekstein and Caruth (1969), Shapiro (1973), Meltzer (1974), Griffith and Ritvo (1967), and others have attempted to describe phases in the echolalic, imitative responses of psychotic and autistic children by examining their language in relation to the therapist (object) and his language. The therapist attempts to identify and repair the damaged link in the developmental continuity of both object relations and language. This is an attempt, consistent with Mahler's observations (1961), at aiding the child's progress from the syncretic, sensorimotor, affective, immediate response to a delayed, abstract, conceptualized response indicating the capacity to evoke a mental representation of the absent object. Mahler describes the breakdown in psychotic children of the ego's capacity to create the relatively complex intrapsychic image of the human symbiotic object. In these children there is the loss of a precarious mental representation of a symbiotic object excessively linked to need satisfaction. Distinctions have been made between echoing (echolalia), a rigid, parrotlike repetition of the examiner's words (Shapiro 1973); advanced echolalia, verbalization by the child of the therapist's actions (echopraxia); and delayed echolalia, the child's imitation of the therapist's words in the absence of the therapist (Ekstein 1965). Ekstein considers echolalia as a primitive form of imitation due to a failure in the achievement of permanent introjections and identifications; however, he sees delayed echolalia as a primitive form of mental representation. Griffith and Ritvo (1967) then introduced the term *negative echolalia* to describe the negative restatement by a psychotic child of the therapist's positive statement. Using Winnicott's formulations and adhering to Ekstein's view of echolalia as the auditory substitute for the transitional phenomenon, they considered negative echolalia a transitional phenomenon in that the little girl's response represented her negative transformation (coming from inside) of the therapist's positive statement (the external object).

THE DEVELOPMENT OF LANGUAGE AS A TRANSITIONAL PHENOMENON

In light of some recent observations in the field of children's language, and in concert with efforts by analysts to expand, refine, and integrate the concept of transitional objects and phenomena, it is important to note the following.

1. The acquisition of language as a transitional phenomenon, which I have termed *transitional language*, represents a crucial development in the unfolding of the language function
2. Transitional language develops gradually, reaching maturity *between* the time of acquisition of one-word and two-word utterances
3. Transitional language represents the earliest creative use of language[1]
4. The absence of the internalization of the use of language as a transitional phenomenon interferes with (and is characteristic of) the language function in schizophrenic children

The concept of transitional objects and phenomena represents an intermediate phase of object relations, which occurs during separation-individuation and in which transitional objects and phenomena (including sounds and words as well as teddy bears) gradually contribute to the formation of the psychic structure that helps lay the early foundations of a cohesive self (see also Kohut 1971, Tolpin 1971). Tolpin, using the blanket as the transitional object, describes this process:

> When the infantile psyche "transfers" the mother's narcissistically cathected soothing functions to the blanket, this inanimate object becomes the treasured "not-me" possession that preserves the soothing effects of the lost symbiotic merger. With [it] the child can then dose himself with more soothing than even the "good enough" mother can provide.—The psyche [thus] establishes an auxiliary pathway for the acquisition of tension-reducing mental structure. As soothing experiences with the mother are first prolonged and then gradually internalized with the help of the auxiliary soother, by the process of fractionated cathexis and decathexis which characterizes its use, the functions of the transitional object also "go inside"—the metapsychological basis for the fate of the "out-grown" blanket. [p. 347]

Before language acquires the function of a transitional phenomenon and undergoes the process described above, sounds and early words have a tension-discharge function. They pass through an autoerotic stage in which they are regarded much as a pacifier. The child is attached to his own sounds and indulges in a form of self-echoing. Then as he cathects his mother's soothing voice, he begins to imitate her sounds and words and the stage of the one-word utterance makes its appearance. At this point, these parrotlike, repetitious, imitative utterances (echolalia) require reinforcement from environmental stimuli. They are very unstable mental representations until the appearance of the delayed form of echolalia, which seems to represent a primitive verbal form of a transitional phenomenon. The maturation of transitional language occurs approximately between sixteen to eighteen months, somewhere between the stages of the one-word and the two-word utterance. It prepares the way for a major leap in language function—the full-fledged articulation of experience with the aid of words in sentence form. Whereas one-word utterances can be regarded as names which have a global rather than a circumscribed reference, two-word utterances begin to show transformations into words in the referential sense. They have a syntagmatic role, showing more differentiation and increasing delineation and specification of reference. Then there is a progression toward differentiation between object or thing and action (Werner and Kaplan

1963). Fraiberg (1969) notes that "somewhere around the middle of the second year of life, the child's vocabulary will tell us that he, too, can evoke the image of a small range of objects having relative autonomy from need states as well as exteroceptive experience." With Piaget, she considers eighteen months the baseline for "evocation of the thing" and writes that "evocation of the image of the absent mother" appears shortly before eighteen months (see also Beres 1965).

In certain respects speech serves as an indicator of the consolidation of certain internalized capacities, or mental representations of language competence, which, prior to speech, were unstable and hence not translatable into spoken words. Two-word utterances are a combining in speech of references to both action and object. This reveals an internalized schema that can be expressed in words. This schema, which could only be implied during the period of one-word utterances, involves the capacity to hold a complete event (i.e., agent and action) in mind.

In order to examine the use of language as a matured transitional phenomenon, a discussion of some important new observations by the linguist Lois Bloom, as reported in her *One Word At A Time* (1973), should be helpful. Bloom refutes the claim of many that one-word utterances are holophrastic[2] and thus presyntactic. Actually, children often mouth extended strings of unintelligible sounds, jargon, or "mature babbling." These are attempts to reproduce or mimic adult patterns of sentence intonation. The child can utter a sequence of connected sounds considerably longer than a single word. These utterances are usually not systematic, nor are they phonemically structured in relation to one another. Immature memory and physiology could explain these constraints; however, Bloom's observations of her daughter at the age of sixteen months strongly indicate that immature memory and speech capacity were not involved.

At sixteen months, the child began to use the expression *wida* (pronounced "weeda") with other words, e.g., "da da weeda," "mama weeda," "no weeda," "more weeda," "uh oh weeda." For a three-week period, "weeda" occurred more often than any other word (including person names); it rarely occurred in isolation; and it dropped from use just as suddenly as it had appeared. Other features characterizing its use—context and the child's accompanying behavior—could not be correlated with speech events in which "weeda" occurred, and its appearance in the child's speech was noticed and questioned by all who knew her, even by strangers. Bloom concluded that "weeda" referred to anything and everything, and therefore meant nothing. This highlighted the fact that the absence of sentences was not attributable to memory or motor immaturity. "Weeda" almost never occurred alone and it was always the final word, so that the child apparently was aware of word order. The term had obvious meaning for her, but this meaning could not be determined.

A similar occurrence in the speech of other children can easily go unnoticed, or be considered jargon or baby-talk. After three weeks, at seventeen months of age, "weeda" disappeared and never occurred again. Gradually, by twenty-two months, two-word utterances appeared (Bloom 1973).[3] This combining of words is a new and major development of patterned speech. Videotapes of the "weeda" period provided an opportunity for futher observation. The child would make frequent excursions away from the mother to other rooms, carrying her teddy bear and occasionally uttering her "weeda" combinations. She would often return to her mother (as if for refueling), remain for a few minutes, say some words (including the "weeda" groups), and then be off again. It was as if she would dose herself with her "weeda" combinations. "Weeda" seemed her companion, which she carried about as she carried her teddy bear.

Tolpin (1971) provides a related clinical vignette. A mother told her child, "I'll see you in the morning when the clock rings." Upon awaking from a dream around midnight, the child happily called out "clockring." Tolpin's example illustrates the echolalic, holding-on nature of a child's verbalization; it reduces the anxiety occasioned by separation from the mother. While two words were uttered, their meaning parroted the last two words of the mother's message (while distorting her meaning) to express his wishes for reunion with her. This may resemble the psychotic child's use of delayed echolalia, but it seems to compare more with the "weeda" phenomenon, with its spontaneous, creative use of mother's words to soothe and assist him in her absence.

In the early development of symbols, there is a stage where the distinction between the symbol and the referential object has not yet been clearly established. Thus "weeda" seems a case of Werner and Kaplan's designation of transitional objects as protosymbols (1963; see also Lorenzer, chapter 28). These are transitional forms of both true objects and true symbols—in contrast to representational symbols, where there is a separation between the symbolic vehicle and the referent. "Weeda" derives from the language sounds of the environment (i.e., mother), which are creatively transformed by the child, leading to an idiosyncratic significance. It is a precursor of the use of speech for symbolic communication. "Weeda" seems to be that missing link necessary for the continued development of a healthy language function.

It linguistically indicates the early experience of internalization of the transitional self-object.

It is this experience which is consistently lacking in the schizophrenic child's object relations and language. His speech is of the echolalic variety, imitative and sterile. It seems burdened by the primary functions of appeal and holding on, and is dominated by the need to revert to reunion and communion rather than progress to communication (see Ekstein and Caruth 1969, p. 134). The schizophrenic child fails to internalize the symbiotic merger with the mother, a process which would have furthered individuation. "Weeda," on the other hand, indicates a creative[4] and independent activity reflecting the child's efforts to separate and differentiate from maternal regulating functions. It facilitates the process of self-regulation and, eventually, of self-regard.

Schizophrenic children and borderline adults may manipulate words as transitional phenomena because they "have attained a degree of mature language function and, when they become ill, present a mixture of regression from and restitution to, their previous attained levels of differentiation and integration" (Burnham 1974, p. 406). Neologisms in the schizophrenic reaction represent regression, disruption, fragmentation, and de-differentiation of the language function, whereas, in the child who develops normally, the neologism (e.g., "weeda") is creative, constructive, and adaptive. It furthers separation-individuation and is indicative of increasing speech differentiation.

The internalization of this phase of language comprises the wellspring from which emerges the healthy, creative use of language, and, when lacking or defectively negotiated, may reflect pseudocreativity or schizophrenic attempts at creativity.

I have received some corroboration of the "weeda" phenomenon in a nineteen-month-old boy in the one-word utterance stage. His mother, a psychologist, informed me that he had been displaying increasing separation anxiety and that his vocabulary seemed to increase during these periods. In particular, she noticed that he began to use the word *hot* more frequently, in a variety of contexts which had nothing to do with the meaning of the word. She said that he seemed to carry the word around with him to keep him company when he was not in her presence.

Balkanyi (1964) has arrived at a conclusion similar to mine regarding the child's arbitrarily investing with idiosyncratic meaning heard sound-groups. She believes that a sound group may become the nucleus of a created fantasy figure and that the created name acts as a transitional object (p. 67).

It is my impression that clichés, which Stein (1958) has discussed in regard to adult analyses, probably have their origin in the echolalic period of language development when the child repeatedly used the mother's words. Stein stressed their defensive function in response to the analyst's interpretation. However, the separation anxiety inherent in being faced with new knowledge about one's self suggests another function of the cliché—a regression to holding-on language behavior, a primitive form of identification with the analyst, aimed at reuniting with him. Clichés may act as "language fetishes" and bear some relationship to lucky stone fetishes (see Greenacre 1960, Muensterberger 1962). They too are carried about and used by children and adults during periods of anxiety and stress.

Although Winnicott and others have noted the function of language as a transitional phenomenon, the detailed unfolding of this function and its necessary part in language development has not previously been described. In this chapter, observations of children's speech have provided a basis for discussing the development of infant language and its function as a transitional phenomenon; this in turn has led to the suggestion that its internalization as psychic structure prepares the way for further stages of language development. Correlations and comparisons of early transitional language can be made with the speech of schizophrenic children. Also, transitional language may represent the first creative use of language by the child. Such repetitive, non-creative language forms as the cliché may, correspondingly, have their developmental origins in fetishistic phenomena and the stage of echolalia.

The consideration of language as a transitional phenomenon and as, in a pathological sense, a fetishistic phenomenon, should ultimately elucidate certain aspects of child-parent and patient-therapist dialogue, as well as successful and unsuccessful aspects of literary and poetic creation.

NOTES

1. The normal creative use of language seems to stem from the transitional language phase of language development, whereas the artist's creative use of language may also have fetishistic implications. Creative language and its connection to language fetishism will be discussed in a future communication.
2. In holophrastic speech, although only one utterance can be expressed, the child is capable of conceiving full sentences.
3. The linguistic implications, while related to language development, are not relevant to my present aims.

4. The creative implications of transitional language are illustrated in Sobel's study of the poetry of Gerard Manley Hopkins (chapter 26).

REFERENCES

Balkanyi, C. (1964). On verbalization. *International Journal of Psycho-Analysis* 45:64–74.

——— (1968). Language, verbalization and superego: some thoughts on the development of the sense of rules. *International Journal of Psycho-Analysis* 49:712–718.

Beres, D. (1965). Symbol and object. *Bulletin of the Menninger Clinic* 29:3–23.

Bloom, L. (1973). *One Word At A Time*. The Hague: Mouton.

Burnham, D. (1974). A discussion of the paper by Donald Meltzer on mutism in infantile autism, schizophrenia and manic-depressive states: the correlations of clinical psychopathology and linguistics. *International Journal of Psycho-Analysis* 55:405–406.

Eisenson, J., Aver, J., and Irwin, J. (1964). *The Psychology of Communication*. New York: Appleton-Century-Crofts.

Ekstein, R. (1965). Historical notes concerning psychoanalysis and early language development. *Journal of the American Psychoanalytic Association* 13:707–730.

Ekstein, R., and Caruth, E. (1969). Levels of verbal communication in the schizophrenic child's struggle against, for and with the world of objects. *Psychoanalytic Study of the Child* 24:115–137.

Fraiberg, S. (1969). Libidinal object constancy and mental representation. *Psychoanalytic Study of the Child* 24:9–47.

Freud, S. (1923). The ego and the id. *Standard Edition* 19:3–66.

Greenacre, P. (1960). Further notes on fetishism. *Psychoanalytic Study of the Child* 15:191–207.

——— (1969). The fetish and the transitional object. *Psychoanalytic Study of the Child* 24:144–164.

Greenson, R. (1950). The mother tongue and the mother. *International Journal of Psycho-Analysis* 31:1–6.

——— (1954). About the sound "mm". *Psychoanalytic Quarterly* 23:234–239.

Griffith, R., and Ritvo, E. (1967). Echolalia: concerning the dynamics of the syndrome. *Journal of the American Academy of Child Psychiatry* 6:184–193.

Kahne, M. (1967). On the persistence of transitional phenomena into adult life. *International Journal of Psycho-Analysis* 48:247–258.

Kohut, H. (1971). *The Analysis of the Self: A Systematic Approach to the Psychoanalytic Treatment of Narcissistic Personality Disorders*. New York: International Universities Press.

Mahler, M. (1961). On sadness and grief in infancy and childhood. *Journal of the American Psychoanalytic Association* 16:332–351.

McDonald, M. (1970). Transitional tunes and musical development. *Psychoanalytic Study of the Child* 25:503–520.

Meltzer, D. (1974). Mutism in infantile autism, schizophrenia and manic-depressive states: the correlation of clinical psychopathology and linguistics. *International Journal of Psycho-Analysis* 55: 397–404.

Modell, A. (1970). The transitional object and the creative act. *Psychoanalytic Quarterly* 39:240–250.

Muensterberger, W. (1962). The creative process: its relation to object loss and fetishism. *Psychoanalytic Study of Society* 2:161–185.

Shapiro, T. (1973). Language development in young schizophrenic children. *Psychoanalysis and Contemporary Science* 2:175–187.

Stein, M. (1958). The cliché: a phenomenon of resistance. *Journal of the American Psychoanalytic Association* 6:263–277.

Tolpin, M. (1971). On the beginnings of a cohesive self: an application of the concept of transmuting internalization to the study of the transitional object and signal anxiety. *Psychoanalytic Study of the Child* 26: 316–354.

Volkan, V. (1973). Transitional fantasies in the analysis of a narcissistic personality. *Journal of the American Psychoanalytic Association* 21:351–376.

Weich, M. (1968). Language and object relations: toward the development of language constancy. Presented at the fall meetings of the American Psychoanalytic Association, December 21, 1968.

Werner, H., and Kaplan, B. (1963). *Symbol Formation* New York: Wiley.

Whitehead, A.N. (1917). *The Organization of Thought, Educational and Scientific.* London: Williams and Vorgate.

Winnicott, D. W. (1953). Transitional objects and transitional phenomena. *International Journal of Psycho-Analysis* 34:89-97.

CHAPTER 26

In this chapter and the next the transitional phenomena concept is applied to the poetic process. Emilie Sobel analyzes the poetry of Gerard Manley Hopkins to show how a poet's use of language, rhythm, and imagery is rooted in a transitional mode of experience involving access to the presymbolic period of childhood. Winnicott himself suggested that the infant's babbling and humming were potential transitional phenomena; Sobel, drawing on Kestenberg's work, shows the influences on creativity of play and oral rhythms derived from the nursing situation. Where Martin Weich uses his concept of transitional language to help us understand the child's developing communicative function, Sobel uses it to enrich our affective comprehension of poetry.

Winnicott saw a basis for adult creativity in the infant's capacity to form transitional objects. In chapter 22 Gilbert Rose elaborates this insight, suggesting the "transitional process" as the essence of the "creativity of everyday life." Similarly, Modell has described how primitive symbolic forms analogous to transitional objects were created in paleolithic art. In these primitive symbols—termed *protosymbols*—there is only a partial separation between the symbol and the referential object. Such hybrid forms were created by Hopkins through a deliberate fusion of object and symbol. Whatever the unconscious connections or genetic meanings, he used conscious, logical modes to organize the sounds, rhythms, imagery, and forms derived from preverbal times.

L.B.

RHYTHM, SOUND AND IMAGERY IN THE POETRY
OF GERARD MANLEY HOPKINS

Emilie Sobel

How does Phyllis Greenacre's well-known and evocative statement that creativity involves "continuous access to childhood" help us understand the poetic use of language, rhythm and imagery? I will suggest that it implies access to a presymbolic intermediary mode of experiencing reality that originates in periods of childhood predating the achievement of logical thought and object constancy. The ramifications of this access include the poet's use of the vehicle of language, of sound itself, and of rhythm. Each of these will be considered separately to illustrate the form of poetry and how this form itself utilizes the verbal and cognitive modalities that derive from early childhood. Imagery will also be viewed as embodying a content which recapitulates the same early aspects of development. Selections discussed will be from the work of Gerard Manley Hopkins, a "poet's poet" who uses all the devices of poetry to their maximum; in this sense he can serve as an "everypoet."

Greenacre's idea of continued access to childhood bypasses certain problems with the concept of "regression in service of the ego." The diffusion of the outgrown transitional object "over the whole cultural field," Winnicott (1951) has suggested, is a universal experience (though intensified in the artist). The poetic or artistic product serves as illusory replacement and substitution for early object loss caused by separation (Muensterberger 1962), and in its creation the artist operates in a space transitional between inner and outer reality. In this context, the notion of "access" will be taken up as a concept having heuristic value and not implying the pathology suggested by the term *regression*.

Gerard Manley Hopkins was a Jesuit priest and teacher of classics whose religious devotion and asceticism were so complete as to lead him to give up voluntarily the writing of poetry during certain periods of his life. However, he was able to produce highly unconventional poetry and held idiosyncratic poetic and nature theories that led to the invention of his own metric system. Hopkins entered the Jesuit novitiate in 1868 and in 1889 died, unacclaimed as a poet, at the age of forty-five. Nor was his poetry accepted when, in 1918, it was finally published.

He believed that poetry must try to "inscape"[1] reality. He wished, in his words, to make meanings "explode." To accomplish this, he made maximum use of assonance, alliteration, end rhyme, internal rhyme, obscure syntax, and a kind of consonantal rhyme or chime which he borrowed from Welsh poetry. The result was an elliptical compression and condensation which his friend, the poet Robert Bridges, found highly disturbing. Hopkins was one of the first modernists, and although in many ways his language is a paradigm for contemporary poetry, it would be a mistake to think of him in the narrow sense of his modernism. A study of Hopkins can cast light on the essential characteristics of all poetry. With Hopkins, the flora and fauna of poetry are so flagrantly displayed that they can be examined with ease.

The following is an example of the apparent syntactic and logical chaos into which we plunge when we enter the poetry of Hopkins.

> When will you ever, Peace, wild wooddove shy wings shut,
> Your round me roaming end, and under be my boughs
> [Peace, 1879]

Peace, an essentially inward experience, becomes a bird and roams in Hopkins' psychological space as it flies in nature. As if that were not enough, it has shy wings. Untangling this imagery, one can discern the poet's mental state as he poeticizes. He is not operating in the realm of what is objectively perceived; neither is he completely subjective. In fact, he seems to be in that transitional area between inner and outer which Winnicott (1951) found in young children before they attain to object constancy. To demonstrate the poet's "access" to this phase of development, I will discuss Hopkins' sound, his rhythm, his imagery, and, finally, his language.

Hopkins' use of sound. Hopkins held that the chief end of all things is to glorify God, that everything glorified God by existing as its own unique, individual self. He held with Duns Scotus—and against Aquinas—that form, not matter, was the principle of individuation. It is this inner form, uniqueness, or "inscape" that he constantly tries to express, that led him to innovate with the English language and to consider sound a way of "instressing" uniqueness. In discursive prose speech, sound is an aspect of language which, unimportant in itself, is in the service of conveying meaning. For Hopkins, sound is an essential aspect of total expression; patterns of sound, like music carry no direct reference to the external

world nor to internal states. They are autonomous like musical sounds—
the inscape of uniqueness of pattern stands by itself. According to J. Hillis
Miller (1963), Hopkins held to an etymological hypothesis: words will be
similar in meaning if they are similar in sound. In his early diaries, he
often lists words of similar sounds and then comments on their similarity
of meaning: "Grind, gride, gird, grit, groat, grate, greet, crush, crash,
krotein, etc. (meaning to strike, rub, particularly together)."
The outcome of this practice can be seen in his mature poetry, for
example in Verse 8 of the Wreck of the Deutschland. Here it is clear how
inseparable sound, stress, meaning, and the saying-of-it are for Hopkins.

> —— Oh,
> We lash with the best or worst
> Word last! How a lush-kept plush-capped sloe
> Will, mouthed to flesh-burst,
> Gush! — flush the man, the being of it, sour or sweet,
> Brim, in a flash, full! — Hither then, last or first,
> To hero of Calvary, Christ's feet —

Never ask if meaning it, wanting it, warned of it—men go. Sound here,
along with rhythm, is a vehicle which converts language into a kind of
music, and for Hopkins music carries a fusion of inner and outer reality
that syntax can only dissect.
Leavis (1932) says of the "lash with the best or worst" passage that
Hopkins' "association of inner spiritual emotional stress, with physical
reverberations, nervous and muscular tensions, contributes to a sense of
mystical identification." Translated into the terms of this chapter,
"mystical identification" can be understood within the framework of the
relationship between language development and early object relations.
The earliest language sounds are a means of connecting to and
identifying with the mother (Greenson 1950).
The childhood use of sounds as transitional objects is now documented
in the literature (Winnicott 1951; Weich, chapter 25). However, it was M.
M. Lewis in his classic work on infant speech (1930) who may have set a
precedent when he compared the child's babbling to a rudimentary work
of art. Transcending the satisfaction of primary needs, babbling is play
within the medium of language. It is expressive. The pattern of an
experience, says Lewis, and the pattern of the accompanying cry become
fused. In babbling—the essentially aesthetic use of language—
symbolization is not the intent of the sounds; they are attempts to
actually reinstate the experience for the very satisfaction that the
reinstatement provides. This contrasts with the more practical use of

language in goal-directed behavior. The young child's babbling aspires to repeat an experience which, though no longer occurring in actuality, nevertheless needs to be expressed, or as Hopkins would say, "instressed," for its own sake. This primitive attempt at understanding occurs prior to the capacity for representation. When used by the mature poet, the medium of sound breaks through the symbolic function of language, yet still, within the modality of words, *reinstates* rather than *represents* an experience.

Hopkins actually longed to grasp or master the experience of the Trinity, God, and the Virgin Mary. Theological treatises and symbolic ritual represent religious experience in a discursive or symbolic manner and could not accomplish this. Hopkins wanted to possess his object. There was no way for him to master, reinstate, or have the experience-God, except to somehow instress it through the medium of sounds. Consider the following passage:

> Stanching, quenching ocean of a motionable mind;
> Ground of being, and granite of it: past all
>   Grasp of God, throned behind
> Death with a sovereignty that heeds but hides, bodes but abides. . . .
>   [*Wreck of the Deutschland*, Verse 32]

Or:

> Since, tho' he is under the world's splendour and wonder,
>   His mystery must be instressed, stressed;
> For I greet him the days I meet him, and bless when I understand.
>   [*Wreck of the Deutschland*, Verse 5]

Hopkins tries to grasp God with his words, not merely symbolize him. With his sounds, he reaches out toward experiences which are beyond the grasp of the rational mind. The *g* sounds in the passage leading up to "grasp of God" do, in a sense, grab God in the grip of that *g*, even as God expands beyond death, out of human reach or the reach of the "motionable mind." The *s* sounds in the next passage seem to stress the very fact of stressing. Here is another fine example of word piled upon word, an augmentation of pure sound:

> Earnest, earthless, equal, attuneable, vaulty, voluminous, . .
>   stupendous
> Evening strains to be time's vast, womb-of-all, home-of-all,
>   hearse-of-all night.

Her fond yellow hornlight wound to the west, her wild
hollow hoarlight hung to the height. . . .
[Spelt from Sibyl's Leaves, 1885]

We actually experience an expansion of consciousness, until, at the end of the passage, we are with Hopkins at the horizon of his experience. It is difficult to describe discursively where that is, but we can travel there with him and experience his vast voluminous night. The sound of the *h* in "hung to the height," the *w* in "wound to the west," the beginning *e-a-r* in *earthless* and *earnest* contribute as much to the experience of space as does the image that is cast upon the imagination. *H* followed by vowel sounds, the breathiness of that combination, and the weightlessness do hang one to the height in a gravity-defying way. Consonant sounds, on the other hand, add more to weighted matter and gravity. The long expansive sound of a word like *vaulty* requires a longer trip in time than a more constricted word. In addition, the *au* in *vaulty* takes us around a bit of verbal curve, and before that trip is over, Hopkins carries us through *voluminous* and *stupendous*, and on and on until the reader is in "time's vast . . . night." For the poet, sound and sense are interrelated but are by no means concretely equivalent.

In his discussion of the transitional object, Winnicott mentions that the infant is not omnipotent with his first "not me" possession, but controls it by active manipulation. For the poet, manipulating sound is an analogous function. Language and its sounds become a mode of mastering his experience, by its construction and reconstruction. Sound is the transmutable, malleable material with which the poet works.

Rhythm in Hopkins. Rhythm provides an undeniable and important contribution to the altered state of consciousness poetry can evoke. Rhythm is essential to poetry; does this suggest that poetry recapitulates earlier and biologically more primitive states than does prose? Biological rhythmicity, in fact, is among the most basic and earliest facts of human life. Darwin spoke of man coming forth from the sea, retaining tidal rhythm in touch with the lunar cycle. There is also a continuous geophysical action on man. Biological rhythmicity is a fact confirmed by electrocardiogram and electrodermatogram readings. Meerloo (1969) even speculates that the rhythmic sound world of the intrauterine environment may possibly affect subsequent development. He hypothesizes that amniotic fluid conducts the sounds of the 70 frequency maternal heartbeat and the 140 frequency fetal heartbeat, creating a complex prenatal rhythmic sound world. Meerloo also speaks of the "milk dance" in the nursing dyad, and Kestenberg discusses the motoric interaction between mother and nursing child (1967).

Later on in childhood there are many varieties of autoerotic rhythmic movements, such as rocking, bouncing, babbling, etc. In general, there is an innate biological rhythmicity—excitation and discharge which the organism brings to the environment as a natural endowment. Meerloo asks what happens when maternal schedules intrude upon the biological rhythm of the infant. It is also interesting to ask what happens when secondary thought processes begin to intrude upon more primitive rhythmical organizations. Kestenberg (1967) discusses this in her studies of movement patterns in early development:

> Rhythms of tension flow are sequences of fluency and restraint in the state of the muscles in various parts of the body. They are apparatus for discharge of drives through motor channels. In successive developmental phases, regulations of tension flow . . . come under the regulation of the ego. [1967, p. 86]

She mentions Kris's study of laughter, in which he says the id has "no expressive behavior of its own. Only ego controls can alter primitive forms of rhythmicity into mimetic expressiveness" (1967, p. 3). Thus secondary process allows the binding of free flowing cathexis. Kestenberg (1969) quotes Freud: "as the child grows up, fantasies provide content and add purpose, so to speak, to forms of excitation and discharge." Thus, according to Kestenberg, an antagonistic rhythm is created by the inhibition, and the expression, of flow of libido. Children, for example, overshoot in movement. They spill and fall. The mechanism of secondary process regulation is faulty. A sudden release of laughter (Kris) or a sudden shower of tears are examples of totally unregulated free flow. Pleasure consists in a free flowing of libido. Inhibition is provided by "methods of flow regulation which help to organize motor discharge" and range "from neurophysiological apparatus that decrease repetition and promote flow stabilization to ego controlled modulation of flow intensity" (1967, p. 51).

To carry this conceptualization into the area of poetry and language, discursive prose can be seen as a product of "ego controlled modulation of flow intensity."[2] Poetry, which Ezra Pound (1930) describes as a more highly energized form of speech, might modulate the intensity of flowing libidinal discharge along a continuum from neurophysiological apparatus of regulation to ego controlled modulation. It can therefore place a foot in either camp, that is, express primitive rhythmicity and flow, while at the same time modulating them through the use of secondary process and fantasy.

No poet better illustrates the use of a rhythmic mode than Gerard Manly Hopkins. Most conventional poetry is written in iambics, a measured quantification of alternating slacks and stresses. Hopkins was an innovator and made one of the first modern departures from iambic pentameter. Though he was not accepted by his contemporaries, actually the time was ripe for this departure. Bridges himself had declared that in English poetry rhymed verse and Miltonic blank verse were exhausted. In America, Amy Lowell, leader of the American Imagists, proposed the exchange of meter for what she called "organic rhythm," which she explained by reference to the give and take of breathing. Hopkins employs what he calls "sprung rhythm," a counting only of stresses while slacks remain free. He considered it more "natural" than iambic or anapestic meter.[3] When read aloud, his poetry produces a powerful kinesthetic beat, somewhat akin to the early Anglo-Saxon poems in the oral-formulaic tradition. Hopkins aimed at creating an elaborate system of interrelated reverberations in his poetry (a verbal analogy to music), but surely some aspects of his poetry originated in a presymbolic zone of mental functioning close to the sensorimotor intelligence of childhood. Here rhythmic-intonational patterns accomplish some of the work later taken over by the linguistic apparatus in syntactical speech. Werner and Kaplan (1963) assert that rhythmic-intonational patterns are precursors of linguistic connectives. The first connectives that emerge in ontogenesis are conjunctions binding two events in either space or time: they are *and* and *then*. *If, when,* and *because* do not emerge until a more advanced logical relationship is possible. Rhythmic-intonational patterning, however, is earlier than either of these modes of binding together diverse events [pp. 175-178]. Inner and outer events can mesh in a rhythmic connective web, facilitating the creation of transitional phenomena where linguistic connectives alone would not allow the same degree of fusion of ideas.

The imagery of Hopkins. The imagery employed by Hopkins dramatically bears out Greenacre's concept of "access to childhood" and specifically involves the creation of transitional phenomena. Tarachow (1963) echoes Jacobson's general thesis that within the dual unity of mother and child separation from original environment entails object loss. He asserts that the origin of thinking "depends on the disruption of the symbiotic tie to the mother." What is torn asunder, however, can be rejoined at a new level of integration, by language. As discussed earlier, sounds are uttered during the "babbling" state to reinstate the experience of having the mother nearby. Later, as secondary process develops, pure sound and pure imagery can be shaped by logic and language. Representation becomes possible and object relations can be conducted in absentia, not only through imagery but through presymbolic mental representation as well. Secondary elaborations can be used, as Muensterberger states in his paper on the creative process (1962), to ward off fear of separation and avoid the "inevitable disillusionment that is an integral part of the adaptive process (p. 167). Muensterberger believes that image formation and representation serve to deny separation anxiety.[4] The artist, "allowing himself to reexperience the early pain of separation, reenacts a withdrawal with introjects which he then reprojects and makes visible, audible or touchable in a new form" (p. 183). These introjects, reprojected, result in poetic creations such as Hopkins' "wild wooddove" and his ubiquitous Christ and Virgin Mary figures, as we shall see.

Hopkins entered a Jesuit novitiate and suffered great deprivation, as do all Jesuit aspirants, during an initiation period of several years. Following the Spiritual Exercises of St. Ignatius Loyola, he was encouraged to give up objects in the real world in favor of withdrawal and contemplation. One can see the rebirth of lost objects in the figures of Christ and the Virgin Mary in his poetry. Christ, Mary, God, and the Holy Ghost are presented so as to evoke the preoedipal mother and the phallic stage father—with both of whom he longed to reunite. Much of the phenomenology of these figures can be specifically tied to the preoedipal transitional object period, as I will demonstrate. They are, however, then reworked by the vicissitudes of the phallic stage of development.

Greenacre speaks of a dual phase of the artist's childhood (1956). In discussing experiences of awe, she says there are "two periods of special sensations of exhilaration and upsurges of intense animation." These are the latter part of the second year and the phallic phase of the fourth or fifth year. She speculates that creative activity "may carry the whole gamut of mixed libidinal phase pressures, genital and pregenital."

This general thesis, that creative activity may carry the whole gamut of libidinal phase pressures, can be elaborated as follows: the earliest experience of objectless autism, where emergent body boundaries are blurred and the rudimentary body image merges with the near object (Kestenberg 1967, p. 87), is the experience of nursing. The breast looms in front of him, cutting off his vision from anything lying beyond. This powerful experience of looming, enveloping size, becomes a total visual experience to the boundaryless infant. It has been suggested that this is related to Lewin's dream screen and that perhaps it is an origin of mystical or oceanic experiences. From then on, says Kestenberg (1967),

> there is a continuous yearning for closeness to the object and throughout life the periphery of the body retains a double representa-

tion of self and need satisfying object. . . . The near space . . . belongs to the body image as well as the outside space.

The images of Hopkins are replete with experiences of expanding and contracting body boundaries. Consider "God's Grandeur" (1877):

The world is charged with the grandeur of God.
    It will flame out, like shining from shook foil;
    It gathers to a greatness, like the ooze of oil
Crushed . . .

which concludes:

. . . though the last lights off the black West went
    Oh, morning, at the brown brink eastward, springs —
Because the Holy Ghost over the bent
    World broods with warm breast and with ah! bright wings.

This image, a "Holy Ghost over the bent world broods," plays havoc with size constancy and horizons. The brooding ghost with its breast and wings seems to cover and hover over the whole world. Another poem illustrates this as well: night "whelms, whelms, whelms and will end us." Remember too, the ever expanding horizon of "Earnest, earthless, equal attuneable" quoted earlier. A line from another poem, "The Blessed Virgin Compared to the Air We Breathe" (1885), "Give God's infinity, dwindled to infancy," conveys the same blurring of boundaries and body image, as does this line from *Wreck of the Deutschland*, "I am soft sift in an hourglass-adrift."

During the phallic-oedipal period, "the whole body is invigorated to feats of jumping, leaping and dreams of flying. . . . Even awareness of shapes and forms in the surroundings reflect the inner body feelings" (Greenacre 1956, p. 20). Related to this is Piaget's idea that there is a lack of size constancy in early childhood, a lack corresponding to intense sensual experiencing and egocentric perspective. The child's concept of space at this time demonstrates the importance of proximity over other values such as means and ends. Within the still egocentric perspective, this leads to "false absolutes" based on large size that predominate over other values and contribute to a sense of awe. Some of the images in the early part of "God's Grandeur" suggest the surprise-filled world of the young child, where a flame can "flame out," where shining awes and delights, where oozy substances spread under pressure from the child's finger and change shape, etc. It is a magical world charged with the omnipotence of protective adults. In the phallic-oedipal period, the child's total experience is eroticized, and awe and wonder become specifically related to phallic attributes.

As the child enters this phallic stage, he begins to identify space itself with his love object and has a "love affair with the world" (Greenacre). Preoedipal merging with the mother and outer space is replaced by an exploring love affair with the peripheral and ever expanding horizon. The phallic-stage love affair, in which the child attempts to "surrender to, be engulfed by, fill and conquer space" (Kestenberg 1967, p. 120) as well as somehow incorporate the love object is illustrated well by Hopkins' 1885 poem entitled "The Blessed Virgin Compared to the Air We Breathe."

> Wild air, world mothering air
> Nestling me everywhere....
>
> This needful, never spent
> And nursing element;
> My more than meat and drink
> My meal at every wink;
> This air, which by life's law,
> My lung must draw and draw,
> Now to but breathe its praise,
> Of Her who not only
> Gave God's infinity
> Dwindled to infancy
> Welcome in womb and breast,
> Birth and milk and all the rest....
>
> Mary Immaculate,
> Merely a woman yet,
> Whose presence, power is
> Great as no goddesses....

Here, identification with the love object is based on fantasies of incorporation and the projection of object representations. Air is a medium external to the self and transcending the self boundaries, yet it may become part of the self (Fenichel 1953). The very idea of incorporation implies a distance between subject and object, and the fantasy here is an attempt to bridge that distance rather than an attempt to merge with the mother, which occurs at an earlier time. At this stage of development, there is a distance between inner and outer to overcome, but not as yet a complete separation. During this early state, transitional phenomena concretely create the illusion that the child has his mother nearby. In another part of this poem, Mary, as the air we breathe, does wrap around the child, thus creating the illusion that he is engulfed by the preoedipal mother. This is apparent in the following:

> I see that we are wound,
> With mercy round and round,
> As if with air; the same
> Is Mary, more by name,
> She wild web, wondrous robe,
> Mantles the guilty globe. . . .

and in the last lines of the poem:

> World mothering air, air wild,
> Wound with thee, in thee isled,
> Fold home, fast fold thy child.

These lines are derived from the time of development during which transitional phenomena occur. Earlier, in the line "God's infinity, dwindled to infancy," the phallic stage father had entered, only to merge with the representation of the preoedipal mother and the concomitant experience of awe.

Hopkins's unbiquitous Virgin Mary images nowhere more graphically illustrate the phallic-oedipal masculine awe of pregnancy than do these lines from "May Magnificat" (1878):

> All things rising, all things sizing
> Mary sees, sympathizing
> With that world of good,
> Nature's motherhood
>   Their magnifying of each its kind
>   With delight calls to mind
>   How she did in her stored
>   Magnify the Lord.

Here the awe and delight is literally tied up with the concept of size. Images of an awe inspiring God-Christ who literally takes on giant proportions are replete throughout the *Wreck of the Deutschland*, where, eulogizing after the famous shipwreck, Hopkins conceives of the whole tragedy as a harvest of souls by a mighty, compassionate God. Consider this description of Christ:

Our passion-plunged giant risen
The Christ of the Father compassionate, fetched in the storm
of his strides.
The girth of it and the wharf of it and the wall .. ;
Grasp God, throned behind
Death with a sovereignty that heeds but hides, bodes but
abides.

Here is an object, God—large enough to be throned behind death itself, heeding and hiding. This heeding and hiding, etc. is reminiscent of the peek-a-boo games which occur at a time when there is no object constancy, when appearance and disappearance of the object excites the child. Here, at the phallic stage, the incompletely introjected object, along with its vicissitudes, is projected in his grandeur. Again, in the following image from the *Deutschland*, the phallic stage father reappears, now with the terror of his disapproving face:

The frown of his face
Before me, the hurtle of hell
Behind, where, where was a, where was a place?

Thus, at a stage of development roughly corresponding to the phallic stage, the child begins to achieve object constancy through introjecting the parental imago. Yet this period coincides with periods of logical development (Piaget 1954) at which space, time, and causality are not objective structures. As Piaget describes it, before maturity, the child is in a dilemma in regard to projective space, time, and causal relations. The dominance of sensorimotor immediacy, in which he is unaware of himself and in which reality is distorted by the demand of proximities, is the egocentric dilemma. The child is involved in unconnected false absolutes. The first causal conceptions, for example, are drawn from the completely subjective consciousness of the activity of the self. In logic, transduction or reasoning from particular to particular precedes deduction. The child distorts the spatial field so that all displacements are perceived as linked to himself as the center. He can't locate them in an objective system that includes his own body. In general, he takes appearance for reality. Representation gradually becomes more possible as objectivity develops. During the preschool stages, even though object relations are becoming more stable, the field is still distorted by the immature schemata with which the child constructs his spatial, temporal, and causal reality. The internalization of the father then takes place within an as yet unstable logical autonomy. The parental imago, then, as a representation, is projected into a hypothetical psychological space so inconstant that it can reach giant proportions and span far horizons. The image can be "throned" behind death, but at the same time dwindle to infancy. It is omnipotent and abstract, yet very concrete, as the beginning lines of the *Deutschland* will illustrate

> Thou mastering me
> God! giver of breath and bread;
> World's strand, sway of the sea;
> Lord of living and dead;
> Thou has bound bones and veins in me, fastened me
>   flesh,
> And after it almost unmade, what with dread,
>   Thy doing: and dost thou touch me afresh?
> Over again I feel thy finger and find thee.

Here the omnipotent object has the power literally to make and unmake him. There is God's mastery and power, yet Hopkins can find him by feeling the touch of his finger. Thus, Hopkins does as the child does with his transitional object. He creates and manipulates it with the illusion that it, being omnipotent, also manipulates and masters him. Kohut has pointed out that there is a gradual withdrawal of cathexis from the imago of archaic unconditional perfection which continues throughout childhood. In poetry we see the recapitulation of that childhood period when the transition from omnipotent to real objects takes place. We see the creation of transitional phenomena: hybrids which bridge the increasing distance between inner and outer reality.

Hopkins' use of language and symbol. "The Windhover" was written by Hopkins in 1877 and dedicated "To Christ, our Lord." In a letter to Bridges, he called it the best thing he had ever written. This poem, with its alliterative riotousness, is the essence of Hopkins. It can serve here to illustrate Hopkins' unique use of language.

> I caught this morning morning's minion, king-
>   dom of daylight's dauphin, dapple-dawn-drawn Falcon, in
>   his riding
> Of the rolling level underneath him steady air, and
>   striding
> High there, how he rung upon the rein of a wimpling wing
> In his ecstasy! then off, off forth on swing,
>   As a skate's heel sweeps smooth on a bow-bend: the hurl
>   and gliding

> Rebuffed the big wind. My heart is hiding
> Stirred for a bird,—the achieve of, the mastery of the
>   thing!

John Pick (1966) has said that this poem is an onomatopoeic recreation of the flight of the windhover. The poem moves with the rhythm of flight and it "starts with a swirl, soars, whirls again and again and then banks with the wind." In short, the poem does what the bird does. In our earlier example, the peace bird was flying in Hopkins' psychological space; but here the poem itself is flying. The movement and word formations contribute to and participate in the subject matter as much as does the content. J. Hillis Miller (1963), who made an extensive study of Hopkins' journals, points out that Hopkins wants us to believe that all words have an intimate participation in the nature of what they name. "The adjectives name qualities in things which are both objective and subjective. Reality has simultaneously the dynamic activity and instress of verbs, the solidity and substantiality of nouns and the sensual vividness of adjectives." For Hopkins, language was not an autonomous vehicle for the symbolization and representation of a separate material reality, but was rather a participant along with the world of nature in a new reality of his own creation.

Yvor Winters (1957) criticized "The Windhover," claiming the poem goes beyond poetic license when Hopkins assumes that a bird performing his everyday locomotion can have the attribute of ecstasy—the poet feels ecstasy, he says, not the bird. This criticism is not to the point, however. Hopkins did not make the distinction between inner and outer that language directed toward communication would demand. The bird, and Hopkins' state of mind, cannot be so clearly distinguished here as they would if the bird were intended to symbolize Hopkins' feelings.

Again, for Hopkins language was not a medium for the representation of reality but rather participates in and presents reality. Beres (1970) differentiates between *presentation* to the senses and *representation* in the absence of direct stimulation of the senses. Susanne Langer makes a similar distinction between presentational symbolism, which involves simultaneous, integral presentation in a total structure of meaning, and discursive symbolism (1942, p. 47). Presentational symbols have no negatives—"hence the possibility of presenting opposites simultaneously" (p. 267). In presenting reality, language is not, then, truly symbolic but rather presymbolic, or, if you will, protosymbolic. This form of language has its origin in early childhood and is well described by Roderique, as quoted by Werner and Kaplan (1963). As the symbol-referent relationship becomes increasingly differentiated, there are four moments—self, other, symbol, and object:

At the early state at which the distinction between symbol and referential object has not yet been clearly established there are phenomena which are neither objects per se nor symbols per se but partake of both.

In terms of the development of symbols, the so-called "transitional objects" again seem to be of critical significance. These objects are transitional forms—prior to differentiation of both true objects and true symbols. From the point of view of the development of symbolization we may designate them as protosymbols. [p. 76]

This protosymbolic function of language thrives in Hopkins, and perhaps, to a greater or lesser degree, in all poets. In any case, Hopkins liked to build up groups of words into single linguistic units, combining adjectives, verbs, and nouns in an idiosyncratic array. The result is an entity possessing the functions of all the major parts of speech without their clear assignment to discrete words. "Comprehensibility, grammar and a clear logical form may be sacrificed to the attainment of strongly marked pattern" (Miller 1963). The minimal use of prepositions, copulas, etc. carries the maximum in possible overtones, contexts, and meanings, both conscious and unconscious. At the same time, the strict bifurcation between inner and outer realities, between action and subject, symbol and referent that a more syntactical speech reflects, is eliminated. Werner and Kaplan describe the very early speech of the young child in much the same manner. All parts of speech may perform the combined functions of noun, verb and adjective simultaneously, reflecting the global state of the child's experience. The mature work of Hopkins consists of a highly developed, technically contrived generality and therefore is not equivalent to the global speech of the child, which is developmentally immature. The parallel between the two is, however, striking.

When using a fully syntactical, lexicalizable form of language, an adult reflects a level of cognitive development at which he is independent of sensorimotor concreteness, space, time and causality having become constant structures. Within the framework of psychoanalysis, discursive speech and a fully developed logic presuppose internalized structures and a considerable degree of secondary process development. The logic of subject and predicate, for example, is related to the fact that self representation and object representation have become polarized. In early language development, subject and predicate are fused into one and two word utterances. This is commensurate with a lack of differentiation between the self and the object world. Within this milieu, transitional objects are created.

Such objects as Hopkins' wild wooddove or windhover are hybrid creatures. They belong wholly to neither material nor psychological reality. Yvor Winters finds Hopkins' analogy between the windhover and Christ denigrating, reasoning that his own pedigreed airedales, beautiful in motion too, are creatures on the same level of creation as the bird. While the bird is beautiful in flight, it is too much of a leap of faith to use a bird as a representation of Christ. But again, Winters misses the point. True symbolism does not emerge here, in the sense of a strict isomorphism between symbol and referent. Rather, a transitional object derivative is created in which the bird in flight inspires awe, and Christ inspires awe; they are equivalent objects in the sense that they both exist in an equivalent transitional area of experience. In "Peace, wild wooddove shy wings shut . . . , Hopkins does not state that peace *is* a wooddove; as a matter of fact, the explicit copula is omitted. There is more of a quality of fusion than in true symbolism. But this is not the total concrete equation of wooddove and peace that would be found in schizophrenic thought; what we have here is protosymbolic. We would not find Hopkins out trying to catch a wooddove because he wanted to have peace.

Hopkins' compression and elliptical syntax as well as his contextual embeddedness of words in a rhythmic melodic medium rather than in a logical relationship is a type of language intermediate between unconscious primary process thinking (Bleuler's "autistic thought") and the secondary process. It is akin to Piaget's (1955) egocentric language. This kind of language could be regarded as "regressive," but it represents a wellspring of creative activity, for the "simultaneous function" (Kurt Goldstein), "Janusian thinking" (Rothenberg 1971), or the "presentation of opposites simultaneously" (Langer 1942). In a holophrastic, syncretic, global medium, illusory experience is possible. Dystaxia and ellipsis facilitate creation of transitional phenomena, since redundancy is minimal and diverse meanings are brought into closer proximity than would be possible in a more fully syntactical language.

Conclusion. Dylan Thomas (1934) said that "Freud cast light on a little of the darkness that he had exposed. Benefitting by the sight of the light and the knowledge of hidden nakedness, poetry must drag further into the clean nakedness of light more even of the hidden causes than Freud could realize." It is interesting as well, to look for and bring to the light of scholarship some of the early childhood origins of poetic creation itself. Exactly how childhood is preserved in the poet has raised the question of "access" to childhood versus "regression in the service of the ego" (Kris). We conclude, with Brenner (1968), that "normal modes of ego functioning are not wholly free of the archaic, infantile features which characterize pathological manifestations without being considered pathological." Poetry is a manifestation of man's ongoing "process," life, which rarely sees the naked light of day. The difference between the poet and everyone else may be a matter of motivation, range and talent, the capacity to utilize that "access" to childhood states we all have; this is the basis of the "shared illusion" we experience in art appreciation.

NOTES

1. Hopkins coined this term. To inscape something is to express its uniqueness and individuation.
2. It has even been thought of as a *superego* modulation. Fenichel (1945) pointed out that "sensations that form the basis of the superego begin with the auditory stimuli of words." Isakower (1939) also elaborated a similar view, saying that there is a close connection between the linguistic and logical concept "right-wrong" and the moral concept of "good-bad." It is irresistible to quote Hopkins in this very context as he plays out the sounds of right-wrong in "Spelt from Sibyl's Leaves": ". . . all on two spools; part pen pack/Now her all in two flocks, two folds- black, white; right wrong; reckon but, reck but, mind/ But these two; ware of a world where but these two tell, each off the other; of a rack/Where, selfwrung, selfstrung, sheathe- and shelterless, thoughts against thoughts in groans grind."
3. It may seem paradoxical here to speak of a highly contrived metrical system as close to sensorimotor intelligence or primary process. However, as Leavis (1932) points out, although Hopkins' journals are filled with elaborate descriptions and justifications of sprung rhythm, "He could not himself be reconciled to his originality without subterfuge. His prosodic account in terms of logoaedic rhythm, counterpoint rhythm, sprung rhythm, rocking feet and outriding feet will help no one to read his verse. . . . The real prescription that Hopkins gives to 'take breath and read it with the ears' is more to the point." I think this statement of Leavis not only gives an idea of how it is to be read but how it may have been written as well. During the actual creation of the poems Hopkins was operating in spontaneous attunement with his own rhythmicity and fantasy. Later he elaborated a theory of poetry to justify his unconventional means of expression.
4. This whole concept goes back to Imre Hermann, who first referred to thought as an intermediary object. His paper "Sich Anklammern—Auf Suche gehen" is central to these concepts (personal communication, Werner Muensterberger).

REFERENCES

Beres, David (1970). The concept of mental representation. *International Journal of Psycho-Analysis* 51:1.

Brenner, C. (1968). Archaic features of ego functioning. *International Journal of Psycho-Analysis* 49:428.

Fenichel, O. (1945). *The Psychoanalytic Theory of Neurosis.* New York: Norton.

——— (1953). Respiratory introjection. In *Collected Papers of O. Fenichel,* pp. 221–240.

Greenacre, P. (1956). Experiences of awe in childhood. *Psychoanalytic Study of the Child* 11:9–29.

Greenson, R. R. (1950). The mother tongue and the mother. *International Journal of Psycho-Analysis* 31.

Isakower, O. (1939). On the exceptional position of the auditory sphere. *International Journal of Psycho-Analysis* 20.

Kestenberg, J. S. (1965). The role of movement patterns in development. I: Rhythms of movement. II: Flow of tension and effort. *Psychoanalytic Quarterly* 34:1–36; 34:517–563.

——— (1967). The role of movement patterns in development. III: The control of shape. *Psychoanalytic Quarterly* 36:356–409. (All of these are reproduced in the unabridged republication of the Dance Notation Bureau. Pagination follows this publication).

Kohut, Heinz (1971). *The Analysis of the Self.* New York: International Universities Press, pp. 1–34.

Langer, Susanne K. (1942). *Philosophy in a New Key.* Cambridge: Harvard University Press.

Leavis, F. R. (1932). Gerard Manley Hopkins: new bearings in English poetry. Ann Arbor: University of Michigan Press (1960); Chatto and Windus, 1932. Reprinted in *Hopkins,* ed. Geoffrey Hartman. Englewood Cliffs, N. J.: Prentice Hall, 1966.

Lewis, M. M. (1930). Babbling. In *The World of the Child,* ed. Toby Talbot. Garden City, N.Y.: Anchor Books.

Miller, J. Hillis (1963). The universal chiming. In *The Disappearance of God: Five Nineteenth Century Writers,* pp. 276–317. Cambridge: Harvard University Press. Reprinted in *Hopkins,* ed. Geoffrey Hartman. Englewood Cliffs, N. J.: Prentice Hall, 1966.

Meerloo, Joost A. M. (1969). The universal language of rhythm. In *Poetry Therapy,* ed. J. Leedy. Philadelphia: Lippincott.

Muensterberger, Werner (1962). The creative process, its relation to object loss and fetishism. *Psychoanalytic Study of Society* 2:161–185.

Piaget, Jean (1954). *The Construction of Reality in the Child.* New York: Basic Books.

——— (1955). *The Language and Thought of the Child.* New York: Meridian Books.

Pick, John (1966). *Gerald Manley Hopkins, Priest and Poet.* New York: Oxford University Press.

—— (1966). *A Hopkins Reader*. New York: Image Books Edition, Oxford University Press.

Pound, Ezra (1930). How to read. In *Literary Essays of Ezra Pound*. Norfolk, Conn.: New Directions.

Rothenberg, A. (1971). The process of Janusian thinking in creativity. *Archives of General Psychiatry* 24, March.

Thomas, Dylan (1934). *New Verse* 11:9.

Tarachow, Sydney (1963). *An Introduction to Psychotherapy*. New York: International Universities Press.

Werner, Heinz, and Kaplan, Bernard (1963). *Symbol Formation*. New York: Wiley.

Winnicott, D. W. (1951). Transitional objects and transitional phenomena. In *Collected Papers*, pp. 229–242. New York: Basic Books, 1958.

Winters, Yvor (1951). Gerard Manley Hopkins. In *Hopkins,* ed. Geoffrey Hartman. Englewood Cliffs, N. J.: Prentice Hall, 1966.

CHAPTER 27

Ruth Miller, a poet as well as a literary critic, has studied Emily Dickinson from the perspective of one directly involved in poetic creation. She sentimentalizes neither the creative process nor her subject; instead she indicates how hard Emily Dickinson worked within her total commitment to poetry.

Miller sees Dickinson's poems as transitional objects, in the sense that they provided bridges to the world and became for her a sort of "litmus test of reality."

These poems not only traverse the space between inner and outer but also cross the boundaries of time, linking Dickinson to future generations and immortality. In a related manner, Volkan has described the "linking objects" by which mourners seek, via fantasy and possession, to preserve contact with the lost object. Grolnick and Lengyel (chapter 24) write of burial objects fulfilling something of the same function. Both focus on the bridge across a transitional space or time, often expressed in metaphors of geographic distance—crossing a river, flying to Heaven. This transitional space is a derivative of the protosymbolic space associated with Winnicott's intermediate area (see chapters 3 and 10).

However, not only does Dickinson utilize the poems themselves as transitional object derivatives, but, as alluded to so sensitively by Miller, the *internal* poetic images balance the oscillating and unstable equilibrium between the double agonies of isolation and fusion. Concrete and abstract images of space and time are adjusted to decrease anxiety. We can see here that the poet's use of transitional language (see Weich, chapter 25) and images has similarities to the fetishistic utilization of a transitional object, when it relieves primitive separation anxiety and defends against the sense of self and body fragmentation and annihilation. Thus, under certain circumstances, the poem, with its use of paradoxical images and its capacity to tune the tensions between the concrete and the abstract, can function as its traditional counterpart, the dream (see Grolnick, chapter 14).

L.B.

POETRY AS A TRANSITIONAL OBJECT

Ruth Miller

We concede to poets their lifetime of reflection and study, their concentration on the writing of poems; we must accept, therefore, without surprise or envy, that usually they take little part in the practical world, the world wherein we perform concrete actions in the light of specific goals in accordance with known or at least predictable effects. Certainly poets may be quite able to inhabit the conventional arenas of reality; certainly they may perform well their commonplace tasks; but their essential act remains always withdrawal into the privacy of their desk space to compose, to wrestle with vocabulary and syntax and structure, to attempt to place onto the paper a rendering of thoughts and feelings that have grabbed them, and they, dog-teeth firm, they will not let go until a transmutation of the pulling force into communicating verse takes place.

The poetic process requires that poets construct for themselves a metaphysics of reality, an eschatology, an ontology, a symbology—a logos of soul—and this takes time. If poets are to find their discoveries in books, they must read. If they are to create their own theology, their own sociology, their own psychology, to fabricate a humanism for which there is no copy, this takes time. Emily Dickinson was just such a poet. She devoted her life to her craft:

#657

I dwell in Possibility—
A fairer House than Prose—
More numerous of Windows—
Superior—for Doors—

Of Chambers as the Cedars—
Impregnable of Eye—
And for an Everlasting Roof
The Gambrels of the Sky—

        Of Visitors—the fairest—
        For Occupation—This—
        The spreading wide my narrow Hands
        To gather Paradise—[1]

Her conception of the art of poetry is that held by typical romanticizers,
inhabitants of the nineteenth century, inhabitants as well of the
fifteenth century—that time when mystics treasured their transmuta-
tions of experience as intuitions of the soul. Emily Dickinson's Paradise is
that of poetic accomplishment; her occupation is the concrete task of
creating poems; her visitors are the Muses, and her place of dwelling,
personified as a house, is Nature.
    We may suspect that Emily Dickinson whiled away her days sitting on
a garden bench gazing at a mimosa tree. But, if she did, she was also
organizing those pink flowers in bud and blossom into a space that fit the
green fronds, and the lawns; her observing eyes were also locating her
acre on a middle space of wind and clouds and sun and sky; and her
intuitions were arranging this location to fit the universe, the cosmos,
the heavens and the will of God.

                            # 742

        Four Trees—upon a solitary Acre—
        Without Design
        Or Order, or Apparent Action—
        Maintain—

        The Sun—upon a Morning meets them—
        The Wind—
        No nearer Neighbor—have they—
        But God—

        The Acre gives them—Place—
        They—Him—Attention of Passer by—
        Of Shadow, or of Squirrel, haply—
        Or Boy—

        What Deed is Theirs unto the General Nature—
        What Plan
        They severally—retard—or further—
        Unknown—

Just as the acre gives location to the trees, so do the trees give place, geographic identity to the acre; and as they arouse the attention of a man strolling by, or of a squirrel briskly rushing from tree to tree, they may perhaps be arousing some notice in Nature, they may be participating in a larger general plan; but what that plan is, whether the four trees advance or slow down the plan, is not known to the poet.

Emily Dickinson was on quest for the truth about Nature, herself, and God. When her reason bid her retrench, retreat, reduce her vision, compress her discoveries and her beliefs into a form of words, a crystallization of perception, when her spirit drove her to write poems rather than remain in the mystic state of transcendence of reality, she was taking upon herself so large a task it may have shaken her soul and distempered her mind. But that task so conceived took time, a lifetime of devotion to reflection, to contemplation and to writing. She withdrew into the confines of her house and garden where for many years she strove to content herself with her self-appointed mission, working on her poetry, always revising, rewriting, renewing her speculations, sharpening her observations, and refining the verses. Inside her ample room, which held a few pieces of genteel furniture—a handsome bed, a writing table, and a bureau into which she carefully placed her perfected manuscripts—her spirit took motion beyond the limits of the real space. Through her windows she wandered on vast meadows, climbed the slopes to mountain peaks, fled down to the sea or soared beyond the sky.

Here she is striving to present with particularity and concrete clarity the way in which that large phenomenon of the sun setting manifests itself to the small yet observant human eye:

716

The Day undressed—Herself—
Her Garter—was of Gold—
Her Petticoat—of Purple plain—
Her Dimities—as old

Exactly—as the World—
And yet the newest Star—
Enrolled upon the Hemisphere
Be wrinkled—much as Her—

Too near to God—to pray—
Too near to Heaven—to fear—
The Lady of the Occident
Retired without a care—

> Her Candle so expire
> The flickering be seen
> On Ball of Mast in Bosporus—
> And Dome—and Window Pane—

The poem begins on the smallest level of the commonplace experience of a lady going off to bed. The edging of gold on the horizon is her garter; the clouds falling to the horizon are her purple petticoats; her intimate apparel, white underwear—dimities—is the last light. The wrinkled skin of this lady, older than the world, has the twinkling brightness of the first star. Does the lady fall asleep as we are wont to do, with prayers? with anxiety? The transition from the light of the star to the expiring light of her candle brings us back to the homey metaphor and we hear that she falls asleep placid and content, and her candle, typical of what all maiden ladies in New England placed on their night tables, expires in its own good time, making a flickering light that extends (way out again) to the mast of a ship in the harbor of the Bosporus, past a great church dome and back again to Emily Dickinson's own window pane.

Let us not construe Emily Dickinson's determination to confine herself to her privacy as sickness or defend it as New England spinsterhood. Well, it scarcely matters what we decide. The poems are all we have, and all we need to understand; from them we know that no matter how close she kept herself, her mind's eye opened always onto infinite space, as the poem above demonstrates. I daresay poets who travel up and down the world may write crabbed and crimped verse; this poet who for nearly twenty years roamed within the acre of her father's house and property, and when that became too broad a distance, walked upstairs and down, through the dining room to the greenhouse and back, up to the bedrooms, along the corridor to her sister's room, her mother's room, or to the attic and cupola above, this poet wrote stanzas structured on time and space and multitudes of place and men. As she sat staring through the glass or walked straightly within the hedge of thick pines, she allowed her bees to fly about, her birds to take flight, her little skiffs to sail on the surface of tumultuous waters, her cherub companions to stroll along the marble floors of heaven. Her imagination reached out always. Meditating on the grave, gazing at the mound of soil, she wrote of horses that traversed eternities of space, bearing a corpse to the right hand of God.

279

> Tie the Strings to my Life, My Lord,
> Then, I am ready to go!

Just a look at the Horses—
Rapid! That will do!

Put me in on the firmest side—
So I shall never fall—
For we must ride to the Judgment—
And it's partly, down Hill—

But never I mind the steepest—
And never I mind the Sea—
Held fast in Everlasting Race—
By my own Choice, and Thee—

Goodbye to the Life I used to live—
And the World I used to know—
And kiss the Hills, for me, just once—
Then—I am ready to go!

It was her poems that tried out the world. She sent 581 poems to friends, to relatives, to potential publishers, to slight acquaintances; she sent many many letters containing highly poetical passages, or quatrains, or scattered bits of verse. In her life-span of fifty-six years she sent 1,049 letters. Poems and letters frequently accompanied small gifts, tiny mementoes, flowers, colorful leaves, even weeds that struck her fancy. Here is a typical poem she tucked into a gift of flowers:

903

I hide myself within my flower,
That fading from your Vase,
You, unsuspecting, feel for me—
Almost a loneliness.

And this poem was hastily scrawled on a slip of paper wrapped around a stub of a pencil and sent to Samuel Bowles, a dear friend:

921

If it had no pencil
Would it try mine—
Worn—now—and *dull*—sweet,
Writing much to thee.

> If it had no word,
> Would it make the Daisy,
> Most as big as I was,
> When it plucked me?

To Bowles, Emily Dickinson frequently spoke of herself as "Daisy," the homely commonplace little flower as distinct from the exotics he seemed to her always to prefer.

Emily Dickinson spent fifteen years inside her house but she reached out always beyond her self-appointed place, reached out via the delivery man and the mails to the real world. The poems were her transitional objects, for she meant always to enter the world of men and affairs and tested out the nature of that world by reassuring herself first that outsiders would respond agreeably to her verse; if the poems were well received, she might then trust herself.

We know now that she found the way barred to her, for her poems were rejected, her letters not understood; she was made a figure of fun and gossip, and gradually gave up trying to gain acceptance as a poet. She curtailed her letter friendships, consoling herself with the inviolate conviction that these very poems would eventually reach out beyond the neighborhood, beyond the circle of acquaintances, and meet the eyes of strangers who would understand and receive her with joy and welcome. The poems became in her view the link between herself and generations to follow.

883

> The Poets light but Lamps—
> Themselves—go out—
> The Wicks they stimulate—
> If vital Light
>
> Inhere as do the Suns—
> Each Age a Lens
> Disseminating their—
> Circumference—

Assuming the poetic fire to be authentic, it will remain after the death of the poet and travel to subsequent generations just as sunlight-fire travels eras of time after the first emission. Embedded in this metaphor is the interesting notion that true, the poem must have vital light, and true again, each age must have the proper lens to perceive, to concentrate, to disseminate that light. In a word: good poets need good readers. Emily Dickinson was well aware of the difficulties of the craft; the labor of composition did not deter her. She was utterly certain that her gift, rejected by her peers, would be cherished by her progeny.

675

Essential Oils—are wrung—
The Attar from the Rose
Be not expressed by Suns—alone—
It is the gift of Screws—

The General Rose—decay—
But this—in Lady's Drawer
Make Summer—When the Lady lie
In Ceaseless Rosemary—

This poem too speaks of the need for hard application to the task of writing: the metaphor derives from the activity of the perfumer, pressing the rose petals bit by bit in order to extract the oil. What is lingering in the lady's drawer is not sachet but packets and packets of poems.

Emily Dickinson was the second of three children; she had an older brother, Austin, and a younger sister, Lavinia. As she matured she found herself fascinated with the art of poetry, and contented herself with little schooling but read widely—not wisely, but well enough for her. Mainly she wrote, refining the skill of crafting poems by imitating those she saw published week by week in newspapers, magazines, and popular anthologies. She too wanted to be a published poet. She besieged two family friends, Samuel Bowles, editor of the *Springfield Republican,* and Josiah Holland, poet and literary editor associated with the *Republican* and later with *Scribner's Monthly,* striving endlessly to convince them, Bowles especially, to publish her verse. She was refused again and again but her importunities did bear fruit, though frugal, when five small lyrics finally made their way into print, suffering Bowles's corrections and alterations in the process. The anonymity of the publication troubled her also, for she longed for recognition. The following poem confirms this desire:

174

At last, to be identified!
At last, the lamps upon thy side
The rest of Life to *see!*

Past Midnight! Past the Morning Star!
Past Sunrise!
Ah, What leagues there *were*
Between our feet, and Day!

The poem shows a perhaps inordinate belief in the significance of identity through publication, but, so it was. To Emily Dickinson it meant she would have place in her time and immortality for all time. I make the point to allay the suspicion that Dickinson was an amateur or dilletante, a spinster who indulged herself with poesy. She was deadly serious and totally committed.

I am well aware that in this essay I devote a good deal of space to dispelling the myths grown up around one of our greatest American poets. But the myths after all tell what sentimental Americans like to believe is true about their poets, especially their lady poets comfortably tucked way in shy corners, too timid to seek public eyes, shy and sweet alyssum, martyred for the sake of a lost beloved. This sells books. But Emily Dickinson tells us in her poems what she knows to be the truth about herself and her poetry. She knew she was a damn good poet and she was sore as the devil that no one anywhere agreed with her.

The manner in which she was finally convinced that Bowles would not encourage or support her career in any way came about in a manner that totally destroyed her love for him, and for a time, her pride and her poise. The following article appeared in the *Springfield Republican* in 1860:

When Should We Write?

There is another kind of writing only too common, appealing to the sympathies of the reader without recommending itself to his subject. It may be called the literature of misery. The writers are chiefly women, gifted women may be, full of thought and feeling and fancy, but poor, lonely and unhappy. Also that suffering is so seldom healthful. It may be a valuable discipline in the end, but for the time being it too often clouds, withers, distorts. It is so difficult to see objects distinctly through a mist of tears. The sketch or poem is usually the writer's photograph in miniature. It reveals a countenance we would gladly brighten, but not by exposing it to the gaze of a worthless world. We know that grief enriches the soul, but seldom is this manifest until after its first intensity is past. We should say to our suffering friends, write not from the fullness of a present sorrow. It is in most cases only after the storm is passed that we may look for those peaceable fruits that nourished by showers, grow ripe and luscious in the sun. There are those indeed who so far triumph over their own personal experiences as to mould them into priceless gifts to the world of literature and art. Like the eider duck bending over her famished young, they give us their heart's blood and we find it then a refreshing draught. But there are marked exceptions. Ordinarily the lacerated bosom must first be healed, 'ere it can gladden other natures with the overflowings of a healthful life.

This published address to her, as she interpreted it, was an almost mortal blow to Emily Dickinson; she understood that Bowles had decided at last to say in print what he was unable to bring himself to say directly to her face. Among the papers and poems she left behind at her death, we can trace clearly the traumatic effect this article had on her. In a letter, referred to by biographers as the "second Master letter," these sentences occur:

> If you saw a bullet hit a Bird—and he told you he wasn't shot—you might weep at his courtesy, but you would certainly doubt his word.

> One drop more from the gash that stains your Daisy's bosom—then would you believe?[2]

The imagery resounds with echoes from the article. And there are dozens of poems left behind that lose their obscurity once we read them in the light of this event. "I cried at Pity—not at Pain—" begins one; "Good Morning—Midnight—" is another. Here is the prototype of them all:

412

I read my sentence—steadily—
Reviewed it with my eyes,
To see that I made no mistake,
In it's extremest clause—
The Date, and manner, of the shame—
And then the Pious Form
That "God have mercy" on the Soul
The Jury voted Him—
I made my soul familiar—with her extremity—
That at the last, it should not be a novel Agony—
But she, and Death, acquainted—
Meet tranquilly, as friends—

Salute, and pass, without a Hint—
And there, the Matter ends—

Emily Dickinson refers time and again to a single experience that taught
her living death.

But she was resilient. To make a test of the validity of Bowles's
judgment Emily Dickinson eventually sent a selection of her poems to
Thomas Wentworth Higginson, the literary editor for the *Atlantic
Monthly*. In the April 1862 issue there had appeared an article entitled
"Letter to a Young Contributor," explaining what poets ought to write
about, how they should train themselves, what constitutes proper style,
and so on. Emily Dickinson sent four poems to this new "Master" and
inquired of him: "Are you too deeply occupied to say if my Verse is alive?"
On April 17 Higginson wrote to his own editor, James T. Fields:

I foresee that "Young Contributors" will send me worse things than
ever now. Two such specimens of verse as came yesterday & day
before—fortunately *not*—to be forwarded for publication!

To his mother he wrote:

I have more wonderful effusions than ever sent me to read with
request for advice, which is hard to give. Louise was quite
overwhelmed with two which came in two successive days.

Higginson's advice to Emily Dickinson is well known: she should "delay
to publish." And that rejection confirmed the opinion of Samuel Bowles.
The literary judgments were made within two years of each other and it
was at this stage that Emily Dickinson withdrew from the world. She was
angry, bitter, disillusioned. She had sent out her poems to feel the safety
of the way into the world before risking the journey. Rejected, she
retreated, found her way back to a protected place, but never ceased to
send, hoping always that one day her cage door, her prison door,
eventually her coffin lid, would open. She maintained a correspondence
with Higginson, posing as his "pupil" though she wrote far more
frequently and at greater length than did he. Over the years she sent him
102 poems, not one of which he ever recommended for publication
anywhere. He did come to her funeral, and he did, under pressure, accept
the task of editing a tiny collection of her poems, which the family wished
to send out to their friends as a memento. But when he came to edit at a
later date a large anthology of American poetry he did not include any
poem by Emily Dickinson.

All of this is very sad. All of this is true.

I call the poems her transitional object, not in the sense that she takes a little bit of home with her as she enters among strangers, but as a test of the safety for herself among strangers. They were a type of litmus test of reality. Emily Dickinson continued to the end of her life using her poems as a link to the world; acceptance, approval, would enable her to come in person.

But they were never accepted, never approved. She contracted her actual space to a minimum, reduced her options, and wrote on. As she became convinced, and conceded that the judgment of the world was final, she began to write poems to herself about herself. She peered into her soul. And the poems of this period were a type of transitional object between her body, her heart, and her soul. They traversed, as it were, an interior distance; as vast as the distance between Amherst and Heaven was the space between Emily Dickinson's face, her heart, her soul and Christ and immortality. To this period we may trace the poems that pass from self-pity to self-containment, celebrating the strength of the self, the impregnability of the spirit, the mounting exaltation of the soul.

Let us examine a cycle of poems to show their relationship to this experience. First, a concrete poem describing a phenomenon in nature— the transformation of the caterpillar:

173

A fuzzy fellow, without feet,
Yet doth exceeding run!
Of velvet, is his Countenance,
And his Complexion, dun!

Sometime, he dwelleth in the grass!
Sometime upon a bough,
From which he doth descend in plush
Upon the Passer-by!

All this in summer.
But when winds alarm the Forest Folk,
He taketh *Damask* Residence -
And struts in sewing silk!

Then, finer than a Lady,
Emerges in the spring!
A Feather on each shoulder!
You'd scarce recognize him!

By Men, yclept Caterpillar!
By me! But who am I,
To tell the pretty secret
Of the Butterfly!

This is a simple, uncomplicated poem describing with precision the butterfly that emerges from a cocoon. There is, certainly if we choose to discover it there is, an implication of the mask for Emily Dickinson herself, who will one day metamorphose into the psyche of poetry.

Next is a poem about a bird, with the transformation that occurs from silence to sound, from the garden walk to the outreaches of the sky:

760

Most she touched me by her muteness —
Most she won me by the way
She presented her small figure —
Plea itself — for Charity —

Were a Crumb my whole possession —
Were there famine in the land —
Were it my resource from starving —
Could I such a plea withstand —

Not upon her knee to thank me
Sank this Beggar from the Sky —
But the Crumb partook — departed —
And returned On High —

I supposed — when sudden
Such a Praise began
'Twas as Space sat singing
To herself — and men —

'Twas the Winged Beggar —
Afterward I learned
To her Benefactor
Making Gratitude

Now Emily Dickinson reveals how severely she suffers from her rejection; the imagery of food and flight remains, but here even that crumb is diminished, a gnat's dinner as compressed as the space traversed:

612

It would have starved a Gnat —
To live so small as I —
And yet I was a living Child —
With Food's necessity

Upon me —like a Claw —
I could no more remove
Than I could coax a Leech away —
Or make a Dragon — move —

Nor like the Gnat — had I —
The privilege to fly
And seek a Dinner for myself —
How mightier He — than I —

Nor like Himself — the Art
Upon the Window Pane
To gad my little Being out —
And not begin — again —

She compares herself to a gnat and finds herself lesser, less in her need
for sustenance and less powerful in her control over her destiny. She
cannot do away with this need, it is an organic necessity; she cannot go
out and get her own sustenance nor can she destroy herself, as can the
insect. She is helpless and hopeless, unable to alter her destiny one iota.
It's a scary poem, and so I suppose are the many others written at this
time describing graves and corpses with meticulous detail—compared to
these, in fact, the gnat is a pleasant poem. Still, Emily Dickinson is looking
clear-eyed at her nature and her destiny. She is gazing through her
window, reflecting upon herself in relation to the tiniest of all insects,
scarcely visible, this gnat. In the poem that follows the poet is looking
through a glass, but it is a mirror and she is staring at herself:

#458

Like Eyes that looked on Wastes —
Incredulous of Ought
But Blank — and steady Wilderness —
Diversified by Night —

Just Infinites of Nought —
As far as it could see —
So looked the face I looked upon —
So looked itself — on Me —

I offered it no Help —
Because the Cause was Mine —
The Misery a Compact
As hopeless — as divine —

Neither — would be absolved —
Neither would be a Queen
Without the Other — Therefore —
We perish — tho' We reign —

It is a bleak outlook, this wasteland, that contains nothing of what ought
to be; her eyes stare at a blank wilderness that changes only into blank
blackness and with a shock we realize the eyes are staring at a face which
has been so described, a bleak face, her own face. Nor can she help it: her
image, her self, are locked in a compact of misery not merely endless but
innately a part of the choice she has made—a divine compact to become a
poet. She chose it, it is a holy covenant, it is a hopeless quest for this place
and time, and although she knows she is a poet, a "Queen," the price is
heavy, it is to be paid with failure, she will perish. The divine royalty may
one day be vindicated but not in her lifetime.

When Emily Dickinson begins to heal, the interior spaces widen and
the mirror attains to a larger perception. She begins to see beyond her
posture and place:

822

This Consciousness that is aware
Of Neighbors and the Sun
Will be the one aware of Death
And that itself alone

Is traversing the interval
Experience between
And most profound experiment
Appointed unto Men —

How adequate unto itself
Its properties shall be

Itself unto itself and none
Shall make discovery.

Adventure most unto itself
The Soul condemned to be —
Attended by a single Hound
Its own identity.

750

Growth of Man — like Growth of Nature —
Gravitates within —
Atmosphere, and Sun endorse it —
But it stir — alone —

Each — its difficult Ideal
Must achieve — Itself —
Through the solitary prowess
Of a Silent Life —

Effort — is the sole condition —
Patience of Itself —
Patience of opposing forces —
And intact Belief —

Looking on — is the Department
Of its Audience —
But Transaction — is assisted
By no Countenance —

And now, the final poem of this series demonstrating the path to healing
as it coincides with an increase in poise, ultimately to transform into a
celebration of self. This psychological restoration coincides with an
increasing awareness of the depth of interior space, and this in turn
parallels abstract space. The poem is more generalized and yet it is the
same persona, viewing herself as no longer confined to the quarter-inch
beating space against the window pane, but elevated to a position
impregnable and defiant.

721

Behind Me — dips Eternity —
Before Me — Immortality —

Myself — the Term between —
Death but the Drift of Eastern Gray,
Dissolving into Dawn away,
Before the West begin —

'Tis Kingdoms — afterward — they say —
In perfect — pauseless Monarchy —
Whose Prince — is Son of None —
Himself — His Dateless Dynasty —
Himself — Himself diversify —
In Duplicate divine —

'Tis Miracle before Me — then —
'Tis Miracle behind — between —
A Crescent in the Sea —
With Midnight to the North of Her —
And Midnight to the South of Her —
And Maelstrom — in the Sky —

Thus she satisfied herself; thus she quieted her longings; thus she
understood her isolation: she was the mortal simulacrum of Christ.

At some time during this warfare with her nerves Emily Dickinson
began to make small collections of her poems, choosing twenty or so that
in her view belonged together, representing the best that was in her. She
copied these selections onto fine paper and sewed the pages together at
the spine, creating little volumes that she placed carefully into her bureau
drawer, where they would await discovery in the coming generations.

530

You cannot put a Fire out
A Thing that can ignite
Can go, itself, without a Fan —
Upon the slowest Night —

You cannot fold a Flood —
And put it in a Drawer —
Because the Winds would find it out —
And tell your Cedar Floor —

I submit that these fascicles were for the poet the transitional object
designed to link herself and posterity. And I suggest further that these

were for the poet the transitional object designed by her to forge the link between Emily Dickinson and immortality. The poem quoted earlier, # 279, "Tie the Strings to my Life, My Lord," serves as an emblem for the work of fascicle-making. She personifies herself as a little package, importunes God to put the finishing touches on her, then to pick her up and place her into the carriage bound for everlasting continuity.

The expansion of place encountered in the earlier poems gives way to expansion in time (subsequent generations) in the later poems. We may, if we choose, chart the course of the development of this poet:

Emily Dickinson ⟶ POEMS ⟶ People ⟶ Failure
Emily Dickinson ⟶ POEMS ⟶ Self ⟶ Satisfaction
Emily Dickinson ⟶ FASCICLES ⟶ Posterity ⟶ Fulfillment

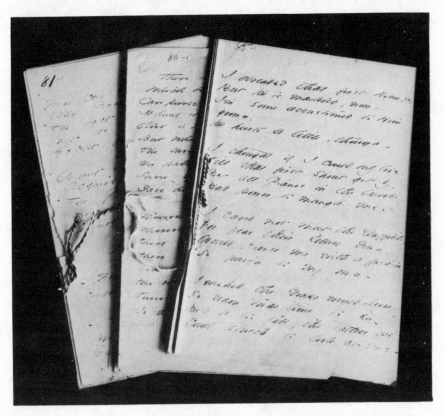

Photograph of three of Emily Dickinson's fascicles. Courtesy of Frost Library, Amherst College.

She left behind her forty-six fascicles well-arranged and neatly placed. Each small volume contained examples of every type of poem she had written; a publisher needed only to pick up one, any one of her fascicles, set up the type, and he would be able to present a complete sampling of the skill of this poet. There were poems of nature, lyrics of suffering and sorrow, bardic avowals of belief in Christ and immortality, occasional verses, elegies, and celebrations.

To Emily Dickinson, the packets functioned as the bridge between the poet and people. Often, at the opening of a fascicle, the poems render concrete space, natural geographic place. And as we proceed through the packet we feel the spaces interiorize, become more abstract, yet retaining the sense of the concrete, serving now as the springboard to some philosophic lesson. Or we may find that we proceed through the narration of a private experience that is devastating, to a time of healing, moving from sense perception to the passions of the heart to the knowledge of the soul, concluding on a note of exaltation or triumph or affirmation or placidity—in a word, resolution.

Here are two sunrise-sunset poems that demonstrate well the shift in emphasis from this more personalized, concrete rendering of the real world to one more abstract and generalized:

318

I'll tell you how the Sun rose —
A Ribbon at a time —
The Steeples swam in Amethyst —
The news, like Squirrels, ran —
The Hills untied their Bonnets —
The Bobolinks — begun —
Then I said softly to myself —
"That must have been the Sun"!
But how he set — I know not —
There seemed a purple stile
That little Yellow boys and girls
Were climbing all the while —
Till when they reached the other side,
A Dominie in Gray —
Put gently up the evening Bars —
And led the flock away.

1033

Said Death to Passion
"Give of thine an Acre unto me."

Said Passion, through contracting Breaths
"A Thousand Times Thee Nay."

Bore Death from Passion
All His East
He—sovereign as the Sun
Resituated in the West
And the Debate was done.

Both poems describe the sunset but in the first it is as if children were walking over a purple stile to reach their grey-robed nurse; in the second it is as if passion (the myriad reds, golds, and purples in the sunset sky) contended with Death (darkness and night)—losing, of course.

Once Emily Dickinson decided to confine herself to her dwelling, she did not change her mind. Doubtless she would have liked to end her isolation, but that which drove her in remained in force. As late as 1881 she sent a tiny collection of verse to an editor, hoping he would honor an old declaration of interest in her poems made to her friend Helen Hunt Jackson, but his reaction was no different from that of Bowles and Higginson two decades earlier, more cool, more impersonal, but equally adamant.

When Emily Dickinson began to have fainting spells toward the end of her life she refused medical care, stipulating that the doctor might look in on her from the doorway of her bedroom, but that was all. She died of Bright's disease on May 15, 1886.

Within the year, her family was busily preparing for publication the first small selection of her poems, as a memento for friends and relatives. The volume was a huge success. William Dean Howells, probably the most influential literary critic of that era, said:

In the stanzas...there is a still, solemn, rapt movement of thought and music together that is of exquisite charm...the love poems are of the same piercingly introspective cast as those differently named. The same force of imagination is in them....They are [the short poems] each a compassed whole, a sharply finished point, and there is evidence, circumstantial and direct, that the author spared no pains in the perfect expression of her ideals.

Two further volumes followed. And there followed then books and books, studies, biographies, monographs, new collections; one might say America grew up to Emily Dickinson. Her intuition of her value, of her ability, and of her excellence as a poet was confirmed by posterity.

Today in any anthology Emily Dickinson stands with Walt Whitman as the great American poets of the nineteenth century. In an anthology of major American writers spanning the period from 1619 to the modern era, Emily Dickinson is given place as one of twelve. She has been vindicated by those generations she always said would pronounce the final judgment.

And the poems serve in their old capacity. They are the means whereby we make our way back through the nineteenth century renaissance in American letters, back to the petite woman sitting alone in her upstairs bedroom; the poems take us through her face and figure into her heart. Only the poems can tell us what she felt and thought about. Only as we read them do we know her. They are our transitional object, linking us and the poet.

NOTES

1. All poems are quoted from *The Poems of Emily Dickinson*, ed. Thomas H. Johnson. Cambridge, Mass.: Harvard University Press, 1951, 1955.

2. *The Letters of Emily Dickinson*, ed. Thomas H. Johnson and Theodora Ward. Cambridge Mass.: Harvard University Press, 1958. Letter 233, p. 273.

CHAPTER 28

Evaluating Winnicott's thesis that the transitional object represents the first possession, Lorenzer and Orban reason that as the infant is in the undifferentiated phase, and as there is no self established, there can be no first possession. What is possessed must belong to someone: no self, no possession. Unlike Winnicott, they deemphasize early subjectivity as the essence of transitional object formation, and, like Flew (chapter 29), they are troubled by the third world concept.

Their concern is the sensorimotor interface with the representational, and they stress the interactions with the external world that lead to more stable "interaction forms" analogous to Piaget's schemata. The transitional object is seen as one moment of these interaction forms, crystallizing as differentiation takes place, and then contributing to further differentiation and development.

Their discussion approaches that of Metcalf and Spitz (chapter 7) in terms of conceptualizing the transitional object as another psychic organizer—an indicator of a certain level of self-object differentiation, and a catalyst to that very process. In addition, and by virtue of this role, the transitional object contributes to early protosymbolic and language formation as well as to the establishment of body boundaries.

L.B.

TRANSITIONAL OBJECTS AND PHENOMENA: SOCIALIZATION AND SYMBOLIZATION

Alfred Lorenzer
Peter Orban

In attempting to bridge the gap between psychoanalytic experience and critical social theory (i.e., historical materialism), it is obvious that not all concepts and theoretical formulations derived from psychoanalytic insight are equally useful. Indeed, it is exactly this bridging or mediation that needs careful consideration in order to do justice to the entire spectrum of psychoanalytic experience; nothing may be left out. On the other hand, no psychoanalytic concept or idea can be transposed without some alteration. The conceptual framework of a theory of "subjective structure" derived from psychoanalysis must stand out against the ahistorical and nonhistorical categories of psychoanalysis, corresponding to the total social theoretical framework. In any case, to preserve the "abbreviations" of psychoanalytic concepts when they are viewed from the perspective of critical social theory, a conceptual mediator will be required.

However, differences do exist, and the task of transposing concepts closely related to certain "behavioristic-positivistic" hypotheses will be greater (and the yield smaller) than with others. In this chapter special attention will be given to the concepts behind Winnicott's model of "transitional objects" and "transitional phenomena." This does not mean that a series of a priori assumptions implicit in Winnicott's conceptual formulations will not require critical scrutiny. It is obvious that such phrases and assertions as

The infant has
A constitution.
Innate developmental tendencies ('conflict-free area in ego').
Motility and sensitivity.
Instincts, themselves involved in the developmental tendency, with changing zone-dominance. [Winnicott 1956, p. 303]

Translated by Ruediger Schroeer

ALFRED LORENZER AND PETER ORBAN

are reason enough to reexamine whether and in what way these ahistorically based assumptions concerning the composition of individual structures permeate the Winnicott model. These quoted assertions collide sharply with fundamentals derived from historical materialist principles. Neither innate developmental tendencies (influenced by life experiences), nor instincts (drives), nor perceptual skills can be seen as ahistorical constants. Furthermore, it is difficult to accept a conflict-free zone, within which the constitution of particular personality structures—the always conflictual confrontation of "inner nature" and social practice—would be removed from social norms. A personality theory developed out of a critical social theory must see the composition of an individual structure entirely as a practical, dialectical "process of production." Correspondingly, the subjective and objective cannot be thought of as opposites in a sit venia verbo, "naive" way as in the following quote:

> I am not specifically studying the first object of object relationships. I am concerned with the first possession, and with the intermediate area between the subjective and that which is objectively perceived. [Winnicott 1951, p. 231]

Further, to speak of the first possession which does not belong to the self is inadmissable. All these assumptions overlook the basic problem that "subjects" are produced within social processes. They also overlook the fact that the "self" cannot exist before the infantile organism comes to terms with the society into which it is born.

That this is not a matter of hair-splitting or interpretive pedantry is demonstrated by the following quote:

> I think there is use for a term for the root of symbolism in time, a term that describes the infant's journey from the purely subjective to objectivity; and it seems to me that the transitional object (piece of blanket, etc.) is what we see of this journey of progress towards experiencing." [Winnicott 1951, p. 234]

A historical and materialist socialization theory demands an opposing formulation: for one thing, there is no such thing as a "pure subjectivity" from which we can proceed to objectivity. Instead, the development of subjectivity *runs parallel* to the development of an external world. Initially both processes are so closely related, opposite sides of the same coin, that at this early point they do not allow a conceptual separation. We can speak of an infant's subjectivity only *after* an external world has developed, when the original presubjective, organismic nondifferentiation has been differentiated, through a long developmental process, into self-representations on one hand and object-representations on the other. If one looks at this process more closely, then our disagreement with Winnicott becomes more obvious, as we must regard the development of the child as a line leading from purely physiological *objectivity* (beginning with the prenatal child and mother organism) to *subjectivity* in the sense of many subject-subject interactions, which can be achieved only after the infantile period has been terminated.

Now, those familiar with Winnicott's works might maintain that a false issue has been raised. However, no interpretation of the last quote can change the core of Winnicott's thought and hide what we have stressed, the "journey of the constitution of self and object representations," which was the central problem of Winnicott's work. Nevertheless, these questionable assumptions do not preclude an interpretation of Winnicott's discoveries from the perspective of social criticism. This criticism should not diminish the worth of Winnicott's discoveries, so long as the influence of the criticized assumptions are carefully teased out. Winnicott's findings not only lend themselves readily to a socialization concept, but actually clarify an important point in child development and thereby achieve even further significance. This will be demonstrated later. We note next Winnicott's description;

> I have introduced the terms 'transitional object' and 'transitional phenomena' for designation of the intermediate area of experience, between the thumb and the teddy bear, between the oral erotism and true object relationship, between primary creative activity and projection of what has already been introjected.... [Winnicott 1951, p. 230]

In these few lines, the close tie between objects that are part of the body and those that are not, on the one hand, and between object and phenomenon, on the other, is suggested. This is also clear in the following list:

1. with the other hand the baby takes an external object, say a part of a sheet or blanket, into the mouth along with the fingers; or
2. somehow or other the bit of cloth is held and sucked, or not actually sucked. The objects used naturally include napkins and (later) handkerchiefs, and this depends on what is readily and reliably available; or
3. the baby starts from early months to pluck wool and use it for the caressing part of the activity. Less commonly, the wool is swallowed, even causing trouble; or

4. mouthing, accompanied by sounds of 'mum-mum,' babbling, anal noises, the first musical notes and so on....
All these things I am calling *transitional phenomena*. [Winnicott 1951, pp. 231-232]

That Winnicott views transitional phenomena and transitional objects as produced and as steps in the development of a subjective structure, despite his loyalty to the traditional biological or positivistic viewpoints criticized above, is suggested in the following remarks:

In another language, the breast is created by the infant over and over again out of the infant's capacity to love or (one can say) out of need. A subjective phenomenon develops in the baby which we call the mother's breast. [Winnicott 1951, p. 238-239]

A footnote regarding the "mother breast" deserves special attention. It not only clarifies the psychical nature of phenomenon and object, but also extends this association to the situation, the scene:

I include the whole technique of mothering. When it is said that the first object is the breast, the word "breast" is used, I believe, to stand for the technique of mothering as well as for the actual flesh. [Winnicott 1951, p. 239]

We will come back to this.

Let us point out again that the link between phenomenon and object is one of the important features of the theory of the transitional object and the transitional phenomenon. The importance of this discovery becomes even more conspicuous if we take the situational moment of the development of the scene between "inner reality and the outer world" out of the shadow of the two often concretized areas of "inner" and "reality" and realize once again that the differentiation between self and not-self during the child's development, that is, between area one (inner world) and area two (outer) world, grows out of an undifferentiated third area (see Flew, chapter 29).

Placing Winnicott on materialist feet requires a consideration of his interpretation of the third area:

The third part of the life of a human being, a part that we cannot ignore, [is] an intermediate area of *experiencing*, to which inner reality and external life both contribute. [Winnicott 1951, p. 230]

The inner and outer do not *make up* this intermediate area; instead they *differentiate themselves out of it*—through a switchboard representing the functional circles—into transitional objects and phenomena.

For a full appreciation of this process, we must take an overview of infant development as a socialization process. We shall begin with that early situation in which, during the mother's pregnancy, the fetal system enters into a stimulus-response relationship with the mother organism. Both organisms contribute to a mutual adaptation. They adjust to each other and thereby the infant organism becomes regulated. At first this interaction consists of an organic, physiological, stimulus-response complex. Later, after birth, differentiation occurs, and the interaction is between mother and child, within the mother-child dyad. Much later the development ends in interactions between one subject and other subjects, the infant's experiential objects. It readily follows from the above, that this interplay acquires its form as a result of each 1, 2, 3 and further interactions. In short, the regulatory system, in view of the self-adjustment of the whole ensemble, is—and cannot be anything but—the blueprint for interaction.

Because this structure building is always the result of a defined form of practice (interaction *is* practice), we must explore briefly the intervening factors. Socially determined practices in the mother-child dyad must be seen in the following manner: as the special ways in which activities and interchanges take place between mother and child, or in short, as the special *gestalt* in which interaction between the mother and child occurs.

It is in the nature of the embryo's first life expressions that these interactions occur as intrauterine, interorganismic exchanges, initially nothing else but the cooperation between a developing physiological system and another organism which contains the embryo, and upon which the latter is totally dependent. Postnatally, these interactions run their course within the orality of the child, and this in the endeavors of the feeding mother to guarantee the child's survival. This social interaction, the offering of nurture, can occur in a loving, indifferent, nervous, anxious, neurotic (non-accepting), or aggressive manner. The child reacts by taking the nurture in what ever manner it is offered.

The description we have offered is not inconsequential. What from our "view from the outside," appears as cooperation *between* a "mother" and a "child," is for the embryological or infant organism a sequence of changing circumstances within an undifferentiated continuum. Within this continuum, no inner and outer, and no mother or self as yet exist. Instead, there is only a stimulus-response field with no firm boundaries. Within this field, the form of the stimulus-response circuit and the shape of the interactions give rise to weighty consequences; the "infantile reaction system" changes with every completed interaction, since the infant organism represents an unfolding, self-developing system.

To summarize: in the process of primary socialization, the reactions of the child and mother work together to develop what might be called a blueprint; this occurs in utero. This blueprint is the precursor, the departure point, the foundation of the individual experiential structure. It is the *organizer* of the development of drives insofar as the embryological and infant "responses" are ways to satisfy bodily requirements. These become bodily needs which are related to others (objects) and thus, to the drives. They have been shaped concretely into a "determinate interaction-form"[1] during the past interactions (Lorenzer 1972).

The beginning of an infant's world can be characterized as follows: the continuity (which becomes a psychic structure through practical experiences) of the interaction-form always precedes the separation between internal and external worlds. As drastically as the organization of the initial stimulus-response complex changes during the transition from a physiological-organismic basis to an organization of experiences (stored up in the central-nervous system) and finally to conscious life experiences, *all differentiation proceeds according to the blueprint of the sensorimotor complexes.*

A dramatic developmental change occurs with the introduction of language, that is, with the linking of the sensorimotor complexes by way of speech and acoustical motor complexes. Thus, the basic elements of "experiencing" and "acting" change from interaction forms to symbolic interaction forms. A successful differentiation system emerges from the stimulus-response unit; eventually, two poles of a developed experience become differentiated—self-representations and object-representations. To clarify once again: both the "inner area" and the world of "outer reality" have their roots in the primary-narcissistic nondifferentiation of the interaction-forms. This nondifferentiation still survives, while the interaction-forms are given a name; thus, during the transition to symbolic interaction forms, these interaction forms are "introduced into speech."

It is clear that the concept of unconscious interaction-forms refers to that nondifferentiation which is Winnicott's basic assumption: nondifferentiation out of which transitional objects and transitional phenomena emerge. It presents itself, on Winnicott's theory, as (a) the—still undifferentiated—unity of self and object (human) and (b) the—still undifferentiated—unity of phenomena and objects (things).

Further elaboration is unnecessary to bring Winnicott's idea into agreement with our concept of interaction-forms. We want only to point out that without the questionable basic assumption of three areas, that is, an a priori coexistence of "subjectivity" and "objectivity" resulting in an intermediate area, the functioning of the transitional objects and phenomena becomes even more obvious: as an indicator of an unfolding of the steps toward the individuation of both inner and outer areas, as structures crystallized out of the nondifferentiation for the first time. The transitional object does not as yet clearly represent a separation into self and object, nor is it an outer object (Winnicott 1951) or a part of the self. Yet it is a "possession." It is a possession, however, only in as far as it becomes a *part* of the child (even though not yet differentiated) and thereby invests the child with a particle of subjectivity: it does not represent a *belonging to me* for the child.

From this viewpoint the functions of transitional objects become clear. Transitional objects are still part of the situation into which the child grows and in which his experiences, particularly his conscious experiences, are presumed to occur. Transitional objects are those first things in the child's awareness which he can use in the situation (which does not include the self) through his initial disposition and effective experience. They are small, manageable, cathected particles from the bridge between things belonging to the body and things at the not-child pole (not yet independently experienced nor recognized as "objects") of the stimulus-response circle of interactions (i.e., the not-child pole of the specific interaction-form, which is "realized" in concrete interaction).

In order to emphasize the agreement between the concept of interaction forms and Winnicott's concepts, the following quotes referring to his theoretical premise will be helpful:

1. The infant assumes rights over the object. . . . Nevertheless some abrogation of omnipotence is a feature from the start.
2. The object is affectionately cuddled as well as excitedly loved and mutilated.
3. It must never be changed, unless changed by the infant.
4. It must survive instinctual loving, and also hating, and, if it be a feature, pure aggression.
5. Yet it must seem to the infant to give warmth, or to move, or to have texture, or to do something that seems to show it has vitality or reality of its own.
6. It comes from without from our point of view, but not so from the point of view of the baby. Neither does it come from within; it is not an hallucination.

7. Its fate is to be gradually allowed to be decathected, so that in the course of years it becomes not so much forgotten as relegated to limbo. [Winnicott 1951, p. 233]

In short, *the transitional object is a part of the scene, the realization of one moment of the interaction-form, which is able to become independent and concrete and in the light of which the emergence of self and object can be elaborated and demonstrated.*

In relation to the transitional object the infant passes from (magical) omnipotent control to control by manipulation. . . . [Winnicott 1951, p. 236]

If the tension resulting from the need to experience the interaction passively (interaction regulated by particular forms of interaction) and to make active use of the transitional object has been treated here with special emphasis, then it is because the function of transitional object and transitional phenomenon with regard to the constitution of subjectivity may be understood directly under this heading.

We noted above the constitution of subjectivity in the differentiation of subject and object out of the narcissistic nondifferentiation during the first phase of socialization, with its particular interaction-forms. We also pointed out that the transitional object and transitional phenomenon represent a distinct turning point within the developmental process. A question arises, however, concerning the energy which propels this process after differentiation.

Let us attempt a brief outline. Undoubtedly the first differentiation within the intrauterine unity results not in a distinction between inner and outer, but in a disturbance of the continuity of pleasure. Stimuli elicit reactions. For example, tapping on the abdomen of a pregnant woman leads to movement by the fetus. The first indicator and the disturbance of the continuity of gratification follows the sequence: pleasure-unpleasure-pleasure. This means either continuity-disturbance or continuity-repair of continuity. A memory "retains" this first indicator, which could be compared to a dog-eared page in a book: when smoothed out, it does not return to its original state.

Out of the temporal distinction grows (in both the intrauterine and extrauterine situations) the *spatial* separation into "inner" and "outer." This is determined by the sequence of pleasure-unpleasure-pleasure; i.e., the change from a satisfying continuity to uncomfortable disturbances is registered along the boundaries later recognized as body boundaries. These stimulus-sensitive zones per se do not allow the differentiation between "inner" and "outer" processes. This is so because the continuous activities always include in the interaction that which is internal and never exclude that which is external—until eventually, by means of available transitional objects and transitional phenomena, the interaction can be actively tested and mastered. Only the *active* removal of unpleasure, the manipulation of the transitional object as a defense against depressive anxiety, permits not only the localization of change from unpleasure to pleasure at the body boundaries but also the relating of this exchange to the inner-outer dimension. The manipulation of the transitional object, as a transitional phenomenon, provides practical information about the connection between the removal of unpleasure and the active changing of the interaction field at points which we may later recognize as situated on both sides of the dividing line between the subject and object worlds. The manipulation leads to individuation, which is an important step toward a concrete extraction of a world of "objects" from the thus far undifferentiated stimulus-response field of the interaction forms.

If we correct Winnicott's untenable separation between the self and the outer world *before* the formation of the transitional objects and transitional phenomena, the inverted sequence is reversed by viewing the *beginning* differentiation of the homogeneous experiential sphere into a "self and outer world"; then the following quote gains additional significance:

> Such an object (a blanket, a piece of cloth or a piece of satin) can acquire important meaning and can become an intermediary between the self and not-self. Usually while falling asleep, the baby holds such a play thing in its arms (I named it a transitional object) and at the same time sucks on two fingers or on its thumb and possibly caresses the underlying lip or nose. This situation is a private one. It occurs while the baby falls asleep, when the baby feels depressed or anxious and can continue to occur into the later childhood years or can continue into adulthood. All this is part of a normal emotional development. Here one has the opportunity of studying the beginning of affective behavior. [Winnicott 1956, p. 36]

How close Winnicott came to this view becomes clear when we examine his statement about the relationship between transitional objects and the order of symbols. If the transitional object and the transitional phenomenon are the first practical attempts at differentiation, i.e., if we view them as the beginning of a polarizing of the interaction-forms, then we are dealing with preverbal, presymbolic stages. This is exactly Winnicott's point when he writes:

It is true that the piece of blanket (or whatever it is) is symbolical of some part-object, such as the breast. Nevertheless the point of it is not its symbolic value so much as its actuality. Its not being the breast (or the mother) is as important as the fact that it stands for the breast (or mother). [Winnicott 1951, p. 233]

In view of this, it is difficult to dispute the significance of transitional objects and transitional phenomena in symbol formation (see Deri, chapter 4). Not until transitional objects and transitional phenomena have been recognized as presymbolic determinants can their function with respect to symbolization be understood.

An addition is necessary to clarify the position from which we saw Winnicott's concept of transitional objects and transitional phenomena as precursors of symbol development. As we explained, the change of certain specific interaction-forms into symbolic interaction-forms results from the fact that those specific interaction-forms were given "names." The introduction of the word *mama* can serve us as a model situation. The mother (or the mother figure) says the word and "points" to the situation. She does not indicate, in terms of the baby's awareness, *herself* (since the object world has not yet been differentiated this would not be possible), but the interaction-form at the moment, i.e., the realized interaction-form. When a child mimics speech, he connects the experienced concrete interaction-form with a speech complex. The child takes the sound sequence *mama* as an acoustical expression of an interaction presently taking place. This link makes it possible to direct sensorimotor complexes (the interaction forms) through the intervention of a second representational system: the interactional experiences can be removed from the matrix of a system, and can be acted upon through factors independent of the situation. It is for this reason that we can contemplate and discuss our acts independently of the situational arrangement; i.e., we can engage in "trial actions." The symbolic operations occur in two tracks: the acting occurs on the sensorimotor level and the "trial actions" on the speech motoric-acoustical level. In each case, however, the other system is also activated.

By contrast, the operation with transitional objects occurs along a *single* track. Transitional objects are mere "parts" of the real relational situation. However, they are "parts" that are "taken out," that can be manipulated actively. Even before a second system has been activated, through the properties of the situation, *pars pro toto*, a "proxy" can be produced. Insofar as this happens—happens *actively*—the formation of transitional objects and transitional phenomena functions as an important predecessor, as an initial step in the development of verbal symbols. And just because the formation of transitional objects and transitional phenomena is an essential distributional factor in the differentiation of interaction-forms, the linkage of sensorimotor and acoustic complexes with the transitional object must occur openly before, as well as after, the introduction of speech.

In this regard we point to Winnicott's observation: "As the infant starts to use organized sounds (mum, ta, da) there may appear a 'word' for the transitional object" (Winnicott 1951, p. 232). A provision for the active handling of a "part of the situation" is the successful development of comparatively conflict-free interaction-forms, i.e., sensorimotor complexes of satisfying interaction. When this goes awry, transitional objects do not develop. These assumptions are in harmony with the observations of Provence and Ritvo (1961). Having studied children in foundling homes, they arrived at this conclusion:

> The use of toys and play materials was poorly developed. . . . Another person, a toy, his own body, all things he could be expected to reach out for were poorly invested and rarely approached [p. 191]. . . . The hand to mouth maneuver appeared at the expected time but after a few days or a few weeks of some thumb or finger sucking, this behavior disappeared [p. 196]. . . . Even though they appear to get some pleasure from the toys, there is no evidence of displeasure when the toys are removed. [p. 198]

It goes without saying that disturbances at this stage lead to deficiencies at higher levels. It is only when conflict-free consistent interaction-forms (Lorenzer 1974) exist that symbolic interaction-forms can develop; speech signs become emotionally relevant only as symbolic interaction forms.

> In the normally developing infant the mama, dada, baba sounds appear at around six to seven months of age and become specific names for the parents during the last three months of the first year. In the institutional infant the mama, dada sounds could be elicited, though with much effort, at the expected time, but they did not become the names of people and were not used for communication or social interchange. [Provence and Ritvo 1961, p. 192]

In these children, the anchoring of the speech-acoustical complexes in the sensorimotor complexes by way of the evolving interaction-forms is nonexistent. Transitional objects and transitional phenomena are the route to this process.

NOTE

1. The concept *interaction-forms* describes those elements of the personality structure which result from realistic interactions, beginning with the intrauterine state of the maternal and the fetal organisms. This entails the "echo" of the orchestration between the child's physiological reactions regulated by needfulness and, on the other side, the socially determined maternal pattern.

REFERENCES

Lorenzer, A. (1972). Zur *Begruendung einer materialistischen Socialisationatheorie* (Toward the establishment of a materialistic socialization theory). Frankfurt.

——— (1974). *Die Wahrheit der psychoanalytischen Erkenntnis* (The truth of psychoanalytic knowledge). Frankfurt.

Provence, S., and Ritvo, S. (1961). Effects of deprivation in institutionalized infants. In *Psychoanalytic Study of the Child* 16:189-205.

Winnicott, D. W. (1951). Transitional objects and transitional phenomena. In *Collected Papers*, pp. 229-242. New York: Basic Books, 1958.

——— (1956). Primary maternal preoccupation. In *Collected Papers*, p. 303. New York: Basic Books, 1958.

CHAPTER 29

Because Winnicott's observations have rather obvious philosophical implications, we thought the views of a rationalist philosopher of science would be helpful in clarifying the essence of transitional objects and phenomena. Antony Flew's response is sceptical. However, his textual and conceptual analysis touches on many of the misconceptions and ambiguities which have sometimes blocked the fruitful clinical application of Winnicott's ideas. By and large, Alfred Flarsheim's discussion of Flew's chapter represents the developmental point of view shared by most psychoanalysts.

Many of Flew's comments are addressed to all analysts, as well as to Winnicott particularly. Flew attacks untidy theoretical propositions, adultomorphic conceptions, and overgeneralization. He cites the importance of attention to basic definitions and warns of the dangers of reductionism and jargon. For example, Flew asks what Winnicott means by *illusion*; this is a basic question deserving extensive study. Flarsheim's answer highlights the expansion of perception and the mixing of inner and outer reality, whereas Flew emphasizes misperception and failure in reality testing. Flew does not seem to appreciate the importance of the role of illusion in child and adult development. We do agree, however, with his conclusion that Winnicott is not primarily interested in *objects* as transitional, but in the *use of the object*. It is the child's intrapsychic development that is in transition.

Flew stresses the important fact that all three of Winnicott's worlds are representational and intrapsychic (Karl Popper's World 2). It is interesting to note, however, that Alfred Lorenzer and Peter Orban (chapter 28) see the earliest transitional object as mediating the sensorimotor and representational worlds. In this sense, perhaps Flew would allow that Winnicott's transitional object overlaps the world of actuality (Popper's World 1) in its very earliest functions.

L.B.

TRANSITIONAL OBJECTS AND TRANSITIONAL PHENOMENA: COMMENTS AND INTERPRETATIONS

Antony Flew

1. By tradition philosophical papers begin, as the life of Socrates ended, with an *Apology*. I begin with a confession instead. When the editors asked me to contribute to the present volume I knew Dr. D. W. Winnicott's work only very slightly, and that entirely by reputation. I had not read *Playing and Reality*, nor even his Pelican *The Child, the Family and the Outside World*, much less the *Collected Papers: Through Paediatrics to Psycho-Analysis*.[1] I presume my invitation came because the editors had seen one or another of my previous essays in the philosophy of psychoanalysis.[2]

Now that I have done my belated homework, it seems that my previous ignorance has been in one way an advantage. For it has forced me to recognize an extraordinary disproportion: between the degree of interest being shown here and now in Winnicott's suggestions about "transitional objects" and "transitional phenomena," and the amount and nature of what he himself actually said in the four most relevant papers in *Playing and Reality (PR)*: "Transitional Objects and Transitional Phenomena" (TOTP), "The Location of Cultural Experience" (LCE), "The Place Where We Live" (PL), and "Mirror-role of Mother and Family in Child Development" (MMFCD). To appreciate this disproportion is a step toward seeing what and how much is still to be done before the suggestions first made in 1951 (in the first version of TOTP) become a body or bodies of testable and tested theory.

Before considering these suggestions, and to illustrate this disproportion, I myself have two suggestions to help explain how it may have arisen. The first is occasioned by some wise words of Alexandre Koyré. In one of the classics of the history of ideas, *From the Closed World to the Infinite Universe*, he observes that " 'influence' is not a simple, but on the contrary, a very complex, bilateral relation. We are not influenced by everything we read or learn. In one sense, and perhaps the deepest, we ourselves determine the influences we are submitting to; our intellectual ancestors are by no means given to, but are freely chosen by, us. At least to a large extent" (1958, pp. 5-6).

The point for us is that some part of the explanation of the impact of "Transitional Objects and Transitional Phenomena" must surely lie in the antecedent concerns and beliefs of those who have been impressed and excited by it; and, consequently, their response may well be to something which is not all, or even not at all, to be discovered by a detached study of that original paper. The history of ideas, as Koyré and his colleagues know, and show, is full of examples of work whose influence, or lack of influence, has for reasons of this kind been anomalous.

My second suggestion is that Winnicott—whom I, of course, never had the privilege of knowing—may have been one of those who have so much more to give in personal contact than in writing, especially theoretical writing. For any English-speaking philosopher of my generation the example of this phenomenon which leaps to mind is that of John Anderson of Sydney. Many of Australia's finest philosophers were his pupils. They continue to express their great admiration for and gratitude to their teacher. Yet Anderson's philosophical remains seem to most of those who never knew him inferior to anything produced by any of these leading pupils. That Winnicott was another though less extreme instance of this Anderson phenomenon is perhaps evidenced by the hints of a great flair for understanding individual children which I think I see in many of Winnicott's case reports.

2. If there is anything in either of my first two suggestions, then it becomes more necessary than ever to begin by discovering what is actually said in TOTP. This should leave us in the position to see what if anything has to be added before we have some theory ready to test. Insofar as the second suggestion applies, these additions must presumably come from those who had direct personal acquaintance with Winnicott himself, and with his practical work. Insofar as the first suggestion applies, it must be up to others to develop whatever possibly very different ideas Winnicott's writings happen to suggest to them.

(a) So now, what, for Winnicott, is a transitional object; what are his transitional phenomena; and what are those transitions transitions between? Well, transitional objects are a kind of material thing; but a kind defined by reference, not to any shared physical characteristics, but to their similar use: "after a few months infants of either sex become fond of playing with dolls. . . . most mothers allow their infants some special object and expect them to become, as it were, addicted to such objects" (TOTP, p. 1). Again: "Perhaps some soft object or other type of object has been found and used by the infant, and this then becomes what I am calling a transitional object. This object goes on being important. The parents get to know its value and carry it round when travelling. The mother lets it get dirty and even smelly, knowing that by washing it she introduces a break in continuity in the infant's experience, a break which may destroy the meaning and value of the object to the infant" (TOTP, p. 4). The point that the concern is with the use of such objects rather than with their often engaging but sometimes rather regrettable physical characteristics is underlined in the Introduction to *PR*: "What I am referring to in this part of my work is not the cloth or the teddy bear that the baby uses—not so much the object used as the use of the object" (pp. xi-xii).

So far, so very good. Transitional objects so defined surely deserve study. They are most important not only to infants but also to young, and to not so very young, talking children. Hence they are important too to the families of all these children. I myself think here especially—and very warmly—of two of our own family favorites. There is the woolly elephant, who once spent weeks with his head down in a jug of water, "because Elly is terribly thirsty and needs a drink." There is the brushed nylon white seal, who passed not just weeks but months choked by bandages, "because Sealey has muggly tum"—an extraordinarily persistent, yet elusive and indeterminate, affliction of the stomach. Since transitional objects certainly do have great temporary importance, it becomes necessary to inquire whether what we might call the transitional object life of a person as a child ever or always has some continuing influence on adult life. Nevertheless, even if it never did, it would still be well worth studying for its own sake. It would still be a considerable part of everyone's life. And the psychologist of all men must echo Terence: "I am a man, and reckon nothing human alien to me."

Having thus established what transitional objects are, we can now notice one or two slightly unfortunate further remarks. In the same Introduction Winnicott insists that "in considering the place of these phenomena in the life of the child one must recognize the central position of Winnie the Pooh" and "gladly add[s] a reference to the Peanuts cartoons by Schulz" (PR, p. xi).

For anyone familiar with A. A. Milne's enchanting books, what that author is describing does indeed constitute an ideal illustration of what Winnicott starts to talk about. Certainly these books, and those cartoons, circulate well beyond the English-speaking countries of their origin. I treasure, for instance, my photograph of a bas-relief of Pooh and Piglet taken in the street of the same name in Warsaw in 1966.[4] Nevertheless, although many children in many countries do know Pooh and his fellows, it is a parochial error thus to assert that something which has been and remains very far short of universal occupies "the central position . . . in the life of the child."

Furthermore: while Pooh and Piglet and the rest were transitional objects for Christopher Robin, they cannot by Winnicott's own definition be transitional objects for other children, except insofar as those other children happen to possess their own appropriate dolls. The point is, that Winnicott has provided only for physical and not also for imaginary transitional objects. That this is a considered intention, not a casual slip, becomes quite clear when he compares "the transitional object concept with Melanie Klein's (1934) concept of the internal object. The transitional object is *not an internal object* (which is a mental concept)— it is a possession. Yet it is not (for the infant) an external object either" (TOTP, p. 9; italics original).

A second lapse occurs in his first "clinical description of a transitional object," the case of a firstborn son: "From twelve months he adopted a rabbit which he would cuddle, and his affectionate regard for the rabbit eventually transferred to real rabbits. This particular rabbit lasted till he was five or six years old. It could be described as a *comforter*, but it never had the true quality of a transitional object. It was never, as a true transitional object would have been, more important than the mother, and almost inseparable part of the infant" (TOTP, p. 7).

It is unfortunate that the very first example offered in the form of a clinical description should, apparently, be not really an example of an authentic transitional object. It is far more unfortunate that the further stipulation being thus belatedly added to the original definition should be such as totally to transform, and almost totally to depopulate, the newly established category of transitional objects. Yet these surely are the consequences; unless, that is, being "more important than the mother" is to be construed in some weak and never specified technical sense. For very few of the well-loved rag dolls, traditional teddy bears, or trendy plastic wizards, which do satisfy the requirements repeated in the first paragraph of the present subsection, could also meet this extra demand. Their loss, that is to say, would occasion in the child neither a bigger public display nor a bigger internal upset than would the loss of the mother. If, on the other hand, it is really something other and much weaker than this which is meant, then it is misleading so to misuse the expression "more important than the mother," and that without any warning explanation.

(b) Once we have got straight about what are to rate as transitional objects there should not, we might have expected, be any difficulty in identifying corresponding transitional phenomena. They must be, surely, those in which transitional objects are involved as such: a child's adopting something as a transitional object; the child's treating and reacting to it accordingly; the effects of all this on that same child then and perhaps later, and even as an adult; the effects then and perhaps also later on other people; and so on.

This is not, however, what Winnicott wants. Despite some initial reluctance to offer any description at all, it emerges that transitional phenomena are not to be defined in terms of transitional objects. There are to be some transitional phenomena in which no transitional objects are involved. This last point is the more worth emphasizing since Winnicott himself never makes it explicit.

The initial reluctance to deploy any examples, or, in effect, to say anything at all, appears in his Introduction. He writes: "I find myself continuing to be reluctant to give examples. . . . Examples can start to pin down specimens and begin a process of classification of an unnatural and arbitrary kind, whereas the thing which I am referring to is universal and has infinite variety. It is rather similar to the description of the human face. . . . The fact remains that no two faces are exactly alike and very few are even similar. Two faces may be similar when at rest but as soon as there is animation they become different. However, in spite of my reluctance I do not wish to neglect completely this kind of contribution" (PR, p. xii).

Certainly we must sympathize with a hesitation to embark upon what might well prove a premature exercise in systematic classification—one, that is, which picked on the wrong principles of division, and which might therefore inhibit the development of a proper understanding of the phenomena. Certainly too, if we have any knowledge of and feeling for the history of philosophy, we must also empathize with such Heracliteans as the legendary Cratylus, who proclaimed that nothing can be said about a world which seems to be ever changing and infinitely various. Yet this conclusion, though perhaps tempting, is wrong. As we all know, it is possible both to pick out, and to indicate to others, what it is we want to talk about. Nor does the fact—if it is a fact—that no two particular possible subjects of discourse, and hence no two individual members of any general class, are identical, preclude that there are respects in which these same individuals are similar. Every human face, for instance, may be, especially in animation, different from every other and not identical with any. But this does not prevent there being specifiable similarities and specifiable differences between individual faces. Even here there are—as again we all know—possibilities as well as difficulties, both of ordinary verbal description, and of sophisticated Identikit operations.[5]

That Winnicott does not want to define transitional phenomena in terms of transitional objects becomes clear: first, when he says that "an infant's babbling and the way in which an older child goes over a repertory of songs and tunes while preparing for sleep come within the intermediate area as transitional phenomena, along with the use made of objects that are not part of the infant's body yet are not fully recognized as belonging to external reality"; and then when he proceeds to speak of "an intermediate area of *experiencing* to which inner reality and external life both contribute" (TOTP, p. 2; italics original). The first of these two passages is introduced with the words "By this definition," though no definition either has been or will be provided. If, however, "an infant's babbling and the way in which an older child goes over a repertory of songs and tunes while preparing for sleep" rate as transitional phenomena, then transitional objects cannot be essential to transitional phenomena. The key word now becomes not *object* but *transitional*.

(c) This increases the load on our third fundamental question: What are the transitions transitions between? I suggest, albeit with less than complete conviction, that the best answer is that they are: "between a baby's inability and his growing ability to recognize and accept reality"; "between primary creativity and objective perception based on reality-testing"; or in reverse order, "between external or shared reality and the true dream" (TOTP, pp. 3, 11, and 25).

If this were all, then all would be tolerably well. But there are difficulties. As "an application of the theory" Winnicott says: "It is not the object, of course, that is transitional. The object represents the infant's transition from a state of being merged with the mother to the state of being in relation to the mother as something outside and separate." (TOTP, pp. 14-15). The difficulty is that a person's mother is at most only one element in the "external or shared reality" revealed by "objective perception based on reality testing." The solution is, presumably, that she is the one element which Winnicott here wants to emphasize as overwhelmingly important.

Again, Winnicott speaks of the intermediate area of experience, "between the thumb and the teddy bear, between the oral erotism and the true object-relationship, between primary creative activity and projection of what has already been introjected, between primary unawareness of indebtedness and the acknowledgement of indebtedness. . ." (TOTP, p. 2). On my interpretation the first phrase of this passage has simply to be dismissed as a mistake. For, since the teddy bear is a paradigm transitional object, the poles which the transitions are transitions between surely cannot be: the one, something else; and the other, the having of such an object. The second phrase too, and perhaps the third as well, suggests that the transition is after all between the oral erotism and the having of transitional objects. For on the very next page Winnicott speaks of "the little child's teddy bear"—it seems indiscriminately along with "the infant's . . . fist (thumb, fingers)"—as "the first object of object relationships." (At times Winnicott's concepts, if not their objects, do seem to belong to a Heraclitean world of flux!)

3. I have now gone as far as I can with the elucidation of Winnicott's new technical terms—*transitional object* and *transitional phenomenon*. This has left us with something perhaps slightly tidier, and marginally more self-aware, than his original offerings.

Certainly any further adjustment would involve a departure from Winnicott's ideas. My own immediate recommendation for a move ahead would be to define *transitional phenomena* in terms of transitional objects, and in such a way as to ensure that, if anything not involving a transitional object were admitted as a transitional phenomenon, this should be allowed only on the basis of some very specific and firmly known resemblance between that phenomenon and phenomena in which transitional objects are manifestly central.

I believe that, in spreading his net for transitional phenomena much too widely much too soon, Winnicott made a mistake of a sort which has been characteristic of psychoanalytic theory from its earliest days. This present sort of mistake has, I think, been almost as characteristic as another, mentioned earlier. That was recklessly, without any properly comprehensive inquiry, so to extend local generalizations that they were confidently proclaimed as covering all mankind in every place and period. This was done—and indeed still is—notwithstanding that these favored generalizations were based on a clinical experience confined to some one contemporary culture. By drawing attention to transitional objects Winnicott did a service. These objects are very important for children. (In that weak sense it is also true to say that they must be important in the development of children. To say this is not, however, to say—what may, of course, be true—that every child's transitional object life has some abiding influence upon that child's future career as an adult).

So far, so good. But Winnicott depreciates his own first service when he at once submerges the new notion of transitional objects under his blanket concept of transitional phenomena; which may or may not involve such special and interesting objects. The mistake, as I see it, begins with the introduction of a useful but still limited notion—useful indeed because limited. This is in itself fine. The trouble comes when—before you have even started to get to grips with whatever falls within the scope of that original limited notion—you proceed so enormously to extend in one way or another its range of application that of its original meaning only the probably now unwarranted overtones remain.

(a) What Winnicott offers as the "original hypothesis" is, however, directly concerned with what he later picks out as transitional objects. He begins: "It is well known that infants as soon as they are born tend to use fist, fingers, thumbs, in stimulation of the oral erotogenic zone . . . . It is also well known that after a few months infants of either sex become fond of playing with dolls. . . ." His proposition is: "There is a relationship between these two sets of phenomena. . . . , and a study of the development from the earlier into the later can be profitable, and can make use of important clinical material that has been somewhat neglected" (TOTP, p. 1).

So far as it goes that too is, no doubt, excellent. Yet it is scarcely what Sir Karl Popper has in mind when he speaks of "bold conjectures."[6] Nor, it is well to emphasize at once, does it even allude to any possibilities that the transitional object life of the child may in some ways condition its future career as an adult. It is not looking forward at all.

(b) Winnicott next proceeds to introduce the expressions *transitional objects* and *transitional phenomena*. He gives the unsatisfactory definition of the latter already quoted, and faulted, in my earlier subsection (2)(c). Almost immediately transitional objects begin to take second place to transitional phenomena. It is through the former that Winnicott's theorizing makes both its first contact with reality and its first appeal to our attention. Yet it is his wide-ranging hints about the latter which are thought to endow that theorizing with general, even philosophical, significance.

"My claim," he writes, "is that the third part of the life of a human being, a part that we cannot ignore, is an intermediate area of *experiencing* to which inner reality and external life both contribute. . . . I am therefore studying the substance of *illusion*, that which is allowed to the infant, and which in adult life is inherent in art and religion, and yet becomes the hallmark of madness when an adult puts too powerful a claim on the credulity of others, forcing them to acknowledge a sharing of illusion which is not their own" (TOTP, pp. 2, 3: italics original).

Now this, as the English auto rally drivers say, is going a bit quick. It is going a bit quick in its move from the transitional objects of infancy and childhood to the third part of the whole life of a human being. It is also going a bit quick in what it says or suggests about that putative third element. A slower, and sounder, progression from the transitional objects of infancy and childhood to this third element in the later life of the child grown adult would involve direct studies, or at least reference to direct studies, not only of infants and children, but also of adults. Winnicott's "original hypothesis" points only to the scarcely deniable relationship between the use of "fist, fingers, thumbs in stimulation of the oral erotogenic zone" and the almost immediately consequent becoming "fond of playing with dolls" and becoming "as it were, addicted to such objects."

What we need if we are to go on from these childhood addictions to features of adult life is some suggestions on how what features of these early addictions are causally related to what features of later life, and also some reason for thinking that these suggestions, or some others of the same kind, are true. We cannot overlook the point that similarities between aspects of childhood and aspects of adult life are not in themselves a sufficient reason for concluding that there are causal connections between the one and the other. We must have, and have some reason to have, suggestions that—for instance—certain sorts of child behavior, or certain ways of treating children, ensure, or at least make it likely, that the consequent adults will be either above or below average, prone to this or that kind of illusion, or whatever. Without any such suggestions, or any reason for holding that some such suggestions must be true, the study of transitional phenomena in the adult is just a separate subject from the study of transitional objects and transitional phenomena in infancy and childhood.

What Winnicott says or suggests about his third world is also unpromising: "I am therefore studying the substance of *illusion* . . . which . . . becomes the hallmark of madness when an adult puts too powerful a claim on the credulity of others, forcing them to acknowledge a sharing of illusion which is not their own. We can share a respect for *illusory experience*, and if we wish . . . form a group on the basis of similarity of our illusory experiences. This is a natural root of grouping among human beings" (TOTP, p. 3; italics original).

It is self-defeating to suggest that all the beliefs of a sane man are really just as much illusions as those characteristic of a mad man. The whole point of saying that something is an illusion is to contrast it with something which is not. Of course all sane men in fact nourish some illusions. But, if and insofar as sanity and madness are to be distinguished by reference to differences of belief, then the defining beliefs of the sane man must be not illusory but true; and those typical of the mad man, illusory and false.[7] (If anyone wants to urge that in some special psychological sense all beliefs equally must be illusions, then he should be reminded that Winnicott himself described his own third world by contrast with the reality of the universe around us: "I am here staking a claim for an intermediate state between a baby's inability and his growing ability to recognize and accept reality"—TOTP, p. 3.)

Winnicott claims in the same passage that "the substance of illusion . . . in adult life is inherent in art and religion." Far be it from me, as a vice-president of the Rationalist Press Association, to dissent from the Freudian conviction that religious beliefs are illusions. But it is not similarly true to say that illusion is inherent in all art and art appreciation. Certainly you may say that the enjoyment of fiction, whether in print or on stage or screen, presupposes some sort of "willing suspension of disbelief" and hence, perhaps, illusion. But it cannot be said that most sculptors and graphic artists are trying to produce representations which might, even momentarily, deceive, or that their public are, however briefly, under misapprehensions about what it is that they are looking at. Cézanne and Picasso were not attempting, and failing, to produce successful trompe l'oeil. Tilman Riemenschneider and Michelangelo were not trying, and failing, to deceive us, as we may well be deceived by the waxwork policeman at Madame Tussaud's. (Once again the patient defender may appeal to some made-to-measure sense. This time it has to be a factitious sense of the word *illusion*, one which does not necessarily involve anything so vulgarly definite as a false belief. And once again the patient defender must be reminded that the third world of transitional phenomena is supposed to be located and defined by reference to misappreciation of the truth about the universe around us.)

(c) Winnicott twice suggests that the peculiarly Roman Catholic doctrine of transubstantiation belongs to his new world of transitional phenomena. In the Introduction he writes: "this which may be described as an intermediate area has found recognition in the work of philosophers. In theology it takes special shape in the eternal controversy over transubstantiation" (*PR*, p. xi). The second passage begins: "It seems that symbolism can be properly studied only in the process of the growth of an individual, and that it has at the very best a variable meaning. For instance . . . consider the wafer of the Blessed Sacrament, which is symbolic of the body of Christ. . . . For the Roman Catholic community it *is* the body, and for the Protestant community it is a *substitute*, a reminder, and is essentially not, in fact, actually the body itself. Yet in both cases it is a symbol" (TOTP, p. 6).

A first thing to mention briefly, and get out of the way, is the statement "that symbolism can be properly studied only in the process of the growth of an individual." No doubt this would be the natural and fitting way to study symbolism for someone with the particular professional interests and training of Winnicott. But I can find no reason given why this must be the only proper way. We do not have to believe the cobbler when he says, Nothing like leather.

Second, Winnicott's argument does not prove his point that the word *symbolism* has a "variable meaning"—though this is not to say that is has not. For the fact that one party believes that this is the real thing, and that the other believes that it is not, has no tendency to show that it cannot also be for both parties, and in one and the same sense, a symbol. In World War II some believed that Stalingrad was strategically important, and some believed that Stalin's commitment to hold it at all costs sprang mainly from the personal and sentimental associations it had for him.[8] But all agreed that it was a symbol, in the *Concise Oxford Dictionary* sense: "something regarded . . . as typifying or representing or recalling something" else—in this case Soviet power, Great Russian patriotism, or what have you.

Third, in this increasingly secular age we must display the nerve of the doctrine of transubstantiation decisively.[9] The authoritative Tridentine definition is to be found in the second Canon "On the sacrament of the most holy Eucharist." This Canon anathematizes anyone who "shall say that in the most holy sacrament of the Eucharist the substance of bread and wine remains . . ., and who shall deny that marvellous and singular conversion of the whole substance of the bread into the body, and of the whole substance of the wine into the blood, with the appearances of bread and wine remaining; which conversion the Catholic Church most aptly calls transubstantiation."[10]

It is essential to grasp that it is a defining characteristic of the miracle alleged to occur in every properly conducted Mass that no discernible change occurs. Thomas Hobbes knew exactly what he was talking about when he attacked and derided this distinctively Roman Catholic dogma. In one of the most splendidly outrageous passages in his splendidly outrageous masterpiece, *Leviathan*, that "monster of Malmesbury" wrote: "The Egyptian conjurers, that are said to have turned their rods to serpents, and the water into blood, are thought but to have deluded the senses of the spectators by a false show of things, yet are esteemed enchanters. But what should we have thought of them, if there had appeared in their rods nothing like a serpent, and in the water enchanted nothing like blood, nor anything else but water; but that they had faced down the King, that there were serpents that looked like rods, and that it was blood that seemed water. That had been both enchantment, and lying. And yet in this daily act of the priest they do the very same, by turning the holy words into the manner of a charm, which produceth nothing new to the sense. But they face us down, that it hath turned the bread into a man; nay more, into a God."[11]

Fourth, what Winnicott himself actually says about transubstantiation as a transitional phenomenon is not much. The two passages already quoted, which are all that *Playing and Reality* has to offer on this doctrine, add up to little more than a rather indeterminate hint. Nevertheless it can be a very valuable hint. For this dogma could be well employed as a textbook example to illustrate something which is important, and true of a great many religious beliefs. The dogma as defined, that is, can be illuminatingly seen as a compromise formation. The compromise is a compromise between illusion and reality. Winnicott might have said of it, as he said of play in his paper "The Location of Cultural Experience," that it is "in fact neither a matter of inner psychic reality nor a matter of external reality" (LCE, p. 96).

My own perhaps different thesis is that we can see the doctrine of transubstantiation as having evolved in this sort of way and as retaining its appeal for similar reasons. There has been among Christians from time immemorial a practice, thought to have been instituted by the Master himself, of taking a symbolic meal together. The symbolism is a symbol of a shared allegiance; and, no doubt, of much else besides. In the earliest days it seems to have been a real as well as a symbolic meal. Now, some literal-minded enthusiasts want to maintain that the wine and the bread are not just real bread and real wine, which are also and more importantly symbols of the body and the blood of their Redeemer. They want to maintain that the Master is really present at every such ceremonial meal, that the wine really is "his blood which was shed for you," that the bread really is "his body that was broken for you." Unfortunately, intractable reality keeps breaking in. The bread and wine visibly, tangibly, and in every other actually or possibly discernible way, remain unchanged, bread and wine.

The solution is a compromise, between illusion and reality, between the belief that the enthusiast so desperately longs to hold, and the reality which cannot be denied. This particular compromise emerges through a highly sophisticated formulation. It draws resources from the treasury of Greek philosophy in a fashion that must make Aristotle turn in his grave. To say this is, of course, to take for granted that the doctrine is either false or in some way incoherent. That is a judgment requiring argumentative support—which, on another occasion, I would gladly provide. But here and now I have to indicate that transubstantiation is not the only religious doctrine to which the present notion of compromise formation might be applied.

Consider, for instance, the belief in life after death. The realities are the familiar, undeniable and undenied, facts of death. The illusion is the illusion of immortality. Typically, if not quite always, the compromise formations presuppose that the real person, or at least an element in the person, is incorporeal. To speak of the doctrine as a compromise between illusion and reality is again to take it for granted that it is either false or in some way incoherent. But in this second case I have argued elsewhere for that conclusion.[12]

4. The present article concentrates upon the first and, it seems, most seminal paper in *Playing and Reality*. Before leaving the field to others, who I hope will be able to be more constructive, I want to comment on two related points arising primarily from Winnicott's later papers.

(a) In the Introduction he writes: "I am drawing attention to the *paradox* involved in the use by the infant of what I have called the transitional object." He goes on to appeal for this paradox to "be accepted and tolerated and respected, and for it not to be resolved," since "the price of this is the loss of the value of the paradox itself" (PR, p. xiii).

My trouble with Winnicott's promised paradox is that it seems to me artificial. I also remain at a loss to see what we stand to gain by not resolving it, and that in very short order. Winnicott presents this trophy in "The Use of an Object". He writes: "The essential feature in the concept of transitional objects and phenomena . . . is the paradox, and the acceptance of the paradox: the baby creates the object, but the object was there waiting to be created and to become a cathected object. . . . In the rules of the game we all know that we will never challenge the baby to elicit an answer to the question: did you create that or did you find it?" (UO, p. 89).

Certainly there could be little profit in putting to a child, much less to an infant, the question Winnicott suggests. (My somewhat oblique phrasing is designed to take account of the fact that the obvious and true answer to the question as he actually formulates it here would be, presumably, either "I found it" or "you, or someone else, gave it to me.") But this paradox collapses when we recall the last clause of the sentence immediately preceding the first to be quoted in the present subsection (4a): "what I am referring to . . . is not . . . the teddy bear that the baby uses—not so much the object used as the use of the object" (PR, pp. xi-xii). What the baby creates is not the object but its use. By choosing to employ this particular object in this particular way the baby transforms that object into a transitional object; and hence, if you must, creates the transitional object as such.

(b) Winnicott sometimes talks of his third world in terms which may suggest that it should be identified with Popper's World 3. For instance, Winnicott in his Introduction says: "This area of individual development and experience seems to have been neglected while attention was focused on psychic reality, which is personal and inner, and its relation to external or shared reality. Cultural experience has not found its true place in the theory used by analysts . . ." (PR, p. xi). Later he explains that he has been using "the term cultural experience as an extension of the idea of transitional phenomena. . . . The accent is indeed on experience. In

using the word culture I am thinking of the inherited tradition . . . the
common pool . . . into which individuals and groups of people may
contribute, and from which we may all draw *if we have somewhere to put what
we find*" (LCE, p. 99: italics original).

Certainly the aforementioned "external or shared reality" and "psychic
reality" of Winnicott do correspond pretty well with Popper's World 1
and World 2, respectively. Popper says (his italics): "We can call the
physical world 'world 1,' the world of our conscious experiences 'world 2,'
and the world of the logical *contents* of books, libraries, computer
memories, and suchlike 'world 3'."[13] Yet the residual members of the two
triads are not so easily identified. For Winnicott in the second passage is
obviously contemplating literary rather than scientific, technical, or
logical works; while such cultural objects as pieces of sculpture and
paintings belong for Popper unequivocally in his World 1, and so too do
copies of books and musical scores (as opposed to their semantic
contents). Winnicott did not, I suggest, think very closely, or in any
detail, about the philosophy and theory of art and culture—as witness his
easy but erroneous assumption that all art and art appreciation involves
illusion. (See section 3b above.)

It is in part, but only in part, in consequence of this that it is so difficult
to make out what is going on in his inquiries in "The Location of Cultural
Experience" and "The Place Where We Live." The better our understanding of what Winnicott thinks he is doing, the more we shall be
surprised—and disturbed—to discover that there is as much correspondence as there is between his three fundamental categories and those of
Popper. Since the aims and interests of the two men are so diametrically
different we should expect to find little or no correspondence at all. So
just what is Winnicott up to here? At the risk of appearing frivolous, we
must be prepared to ask why, if while reading *Troilus and Cressida* in bed we
are asked what we are doing and where we are (if anywhere at all), it is
unacceptable to respond: in bed, reading *Troilus and Cressida* (PL, p. 105).

The answer is, I believe, that Winnicott is trying to draw some sort of
map of the mind or map of experience: "The accent is indeed on
experience." It would have been much easier to assess his success, and
perhaps to repair any failures, had he thought to spell out the aims and
rules of this game. Above all I wish to be told why the *experience* of
transitional phenomena apparently belongs to a third world somehow
intermediate between, on the one hand, "external or shared reality" (the
physical world), and, on the other hand, "psychic reality" ("the world of
our conscious experience"). Why does it not belong, as it seems to me it
obviously must, to the second of the original two? Worlds, as Ockham
might have said, are not to be multiplied beyond necessity.[14]

We can get some weak and flickering light on what is going on, and I think wrong, if we remember that the Freudian concept of the mental, unlike the Cartesian, is one which does not essentially involve consciousness.[15] So a truly Freudian map of the mind cannot be confined, as any Cartesian chart would have to be, to all but only varieties of consciousness. This Winnicott seems sometimes to have overlooked. One result is the confusion just noticed over the proper principles of division between his own proposed third world and the world of psychic reality. (Perhaps too the word *experience* is here being employed, at a high cost, to include some phenomena which do not involve consciousness.)

There also seems to be a further and more fundamental confusion: between, on the one hand, a requirement of a new—as some would say— phenomenological trichotomy, which is to divide the Gaul of the Freudian mind into three parts; and, on the other hand, the quite different requirements of an ontological classification, which is to divide the contents of the public world into ultimate categories of things—as well as to separate that public world from the essentially private sphere of "psychic reality." It is this latter kind of ultimate ontological classification in which Popper is engaged when he produces his trichotomy. It is the former, the mapping of regions of the Freudian mind, with which Winnicott is professionally concerned. A failure clearly to see, and clearly to say, what this different and peculiar exercise must involve leads to confusion between his and the Popperian type of undertaking.

5. The upshot of my study of what is actually said about transitional objects and transitional phenomena in *Playing and Reality*, especially in the paper using that phrase as its title, is dispiriting. I now withdraw from the field, leaving it to others, who, whether through their personal knowledge of Winnicott or however, must surely be ready with more positive contributions than I. What, please, is the no doubt deeply motivated psychic blindness which inhibits me from joining the chorus of welcome, which Winnicott graciously acknowledges (*PR*, p. 40), "in psychoanalytic circles and in the general psychiatric world in respect of [the] description of transitional phenomena"?

NOTES

1. The first of these was published by Tavistock (London, 1971), the second by Penguin Books (Harmondsworth, 1964), and the third again by Tavistock (London, 1958). The second is in the main a conflation of

materials which appeared originally in either *The Child and the Family* or *The Child and the Outside World*, both from Tavistock (London, 1957). Since my page references to *Playing and Reality* are to the Tavistock edition rather than to that issues simultaneously by Basic Books in New York, and in case the pagination of the two editions differs, I also indicate the chapters in which these pages occur.

2. These were: (a) "Motives and the Unconscious" in H. Feigl and M. Scriven (eds.), *The Foundations of Science and the Concepts of Psychology and Psychoanalysis* (Minneapolis: University of Minnesota Press, 1956), to be reprinted in a collection edited by Dr. Emmett Wilson which should by now have appeared in New York; (b) "Philosophy and Psychopathology" in S. Hook (ed.)*Psychoanalysis, Scientific Method and Philosophy* (New York: New York University Press, 1959); and (c) "Psychoanalysis and the Philosophical Problem of Freewill" in C. Hanly and M. Lazerowitz (eds.) *Psychoanalysis and Philosophy* (New York: International Universities Press, 1970). I hope to be able in the not too distant future to include revised versions of the first and the third of these in a collection of my own papers.

3. Harper and Row (New York and London, 1958), pp. 5-6. The original 1957 edition was from the Johns Hopkins University Press.

4. Although Christopher Robin like his parents evidently belonged to a social class nowadays detested by sociologists and all other such left-thinking people in Britain, these memorials looked as if they had been erected during what a Warsaw historian then described to me as "the period of People's Poland."

5. The two essentials are that we must be able both to pick out individuals as subjects of discourse and to discern respects in which these individuals are either similar or different. Given these essentials we can proceed to speak also of classes of individuals—classes, that is, membership in which is determined by similarities in some particular respect or respects. A stronger grasp of these fundamentals may perhaps be achieved by considering the curious awkwardness of John Locke's answer to the question why a language could not consist only of proper names for particular individuals. In his *Essay Concerning Human Understanding* Locke observes: "All things that exist being particulars, it may perhaps be thought reasonable that words, which ought to be conformed to things, should be so too, I mean in their signification, but yet we find the quite contrary. The far greatest part of words that make all languages are general terms; which has not been the effect of neglect or chance, but of reason and necessity" (III[ii]1). It has indeed. Yet Locke himself labours through three subsequent sections without ever seizing the crucial point. This crux is that a language consisting only of proper names would enable us only to indicate, without providing us with any means of saying anything about, possible subjects of discourse.

6. Popper's own best account of his philosophy of science is surely "Science: Conjectures and Refutations" in his *Conjectures and Refutations*

(London: Routledge and Kegan Paul, 1963). An excellent introduction to all his thought is Bryan Magee's *Popper* (London: Collins Fontana, 1973).

7. There are very good reasons for insisting that mental disease, and perhaps madness too, should be seen as a matter of incapacity rather than either abnormality or false belief. See my *Crime or Disease?* (New York: Barnes and Noble, 1973; London: Macmillan, 1973).

8. Stalingrad is the city now known—but for how much longer?—as Volgograd. It had been renamed Stalingrad in honor of the part he played in holding it for the Bolsheviks during the Civil War. When once I suggested to Sir Isaiah Berlin, mischievously, that I still insisted on calling it Stalingrad, he declared that for him it always had been, was, and would be, Tsaritsyn.

9. But not only in this age, for even in the late sixteen-hundreds a future Archbishop of Canterbury made it very clear in a public controversy on this theme that he did not, in the most literal sense, know what he was talking about. See, for instance, my *Hume's Philosophy of Belief* (New York: Humanities Press, 1961; London: Routledge and Kegan Paul, 1961).

10. H. Denzinger (ed.) *Encheiridion Symbolorum* (Freiberg im Breisgau: Herder, twenty-ninth revised edition, 1953), §884. The translation is mine.

11. Chapter 44. I have modernized the spelling and punctuation.

12. See, for instance, the Introduction to Antony Flew (ed.) *Body, Mind and Death* (New York: Collier-Macmillan, 1964); or, recovering much the same ground, the article "Immortality" in P. Edwards (ed.) *Encyclopaedia of Philosophy* (New York: Free Press of Glencoe and Collier-Macmillan, 1967).

13. *Objective Knowledge* (Oxford: Clarendon Press, 1972), p. 74. Popper's italics.

14. Perhaps he did; the usually quoted maxim "*Entia* non sunt multiplicanda praeter necessitatem" (italics mine) is apparently not to be found in his extant works.

15. I tried to explain this observation more fully, and to justify it, in my paper "Motives and the Unconscious," mentioned in Note 2 above. See especially Part II, section 3.

CHAPTER 30

DISCUSSION OF ANTONY FLEW

Alfred Flarsheim

Winnicott's concept of the transitional object has become so familiar that it is already a fundamental part of our thinking. Some of us even take it for granted, regarding it as established beyond question or criticism. Therefore the paper by Anthony Flew serves us well by encouraging a new look at Winnicott's underlying assumptions, and their place in our overall conceptual system. Flew's paper prevents us from becoming complacent.

In spite of their wide acceptance, the concepts of transitional objects and transitional phenomena have often been misunderstood, and even distorted. I once heard a child-care worker say that she was on her way to the teddy bear department of a toy store to buy a transitional object for a child! Flew devotes several pages of his discussion to a correction of this distortion. He points out that the *use of the object* as well as the object itself must be emphasized, and that "transitional objects are a kind of material thing; but a kind defined by reference not to any shared physical characteristics, but to their similar use." This is an extremely cogent aspect of the concept that we too often forget.

Flew asks why transitional objects and phenomena have found such widespread acceptance among psychoanalysts. He suggests two possible reasons: (1) that on the basis of previous experience analysts were prepared to welcome this concept and (2) that there might be something in Winnicott's personal teaching style that is not apparent in his writings.

In discussing his first reason, Flew says that some part of the explanation of the impact of Winnicott's paper "Transitional Objects and Transitional Phenomena" must surely lie in the antecedent concerns and beliefs of those who have been impressed and excited by the paper, and "consequently" their response to the paper may be to "something which is not all, or even not at all, to be discovered by a detached study of the paper." I am not sure that I can see the relationship between the two parts of this statement linked by the word *consequently.* The antecedent concerns here were predominantly clinical. A gap existed in our understanding, a gap which seemed quite obvious once it was pointed out. We welcomed an hypothesis which could fill it and broaden the range of clinical phenomena our concepts could explain.

And now Flew's second point, Winnicott's personality: It was the immediate clinical utility of Winnicott's theoretical and clinical writing that so impressed me that I went to London in order first to study under him and then to have analysis from him. One of the questions that I asked myself when I read Flew's paper was, therefore, how can it be that two people reading the same material can acquire such opposite impressions? I then decided to discuss Flew's arguments in the sequence in which he presents them to attempt to answer my own question by seeking to understand the basis of his opinion. While doing this I was able to acquire a fuller comprehension of the relations between ego processes and the transitional object, transitional phenomena, the transitional area, and the way in which the so-called intermediate area of experience furthers our understanding of transference in neurotic and psychotic patients.

My first impression of Flew's essay was that he finds the concept of transitional phenomena difficult to integrate with his other thinking. While he refers to many classical philosophical writings on the characteristics of human personality, there is one essential area that he neglects: i.e., the stress on the principle of developmental continuity that is so important clinically. Transitional phenomena are part of the continuum from autoerotism through narcissism to object relatedness. Essentially it is this development which is under discussion, as well as the residuals in human nature of each stage of this process.

In Freud's time it was difficult to conceptualize a developmental genetic continuity between the instincts and impulses of the toddler-age child and the sexual impulses of adults. In our time what is often ignored is the genetic developmental continuity between earliest infancy, even the prenatal state, and subsequent developmental stages. Flew seems to get stuck just here. Freud has referred to the unborn baby as a "completely narcissistic creature." It is easy to see that the fetus has no object relationships, no concept of an outer world. Some time following birth the child becomes aware of an outer world separate from the self; this results from a developmental process. Adult psychology and psychopathology show important derivatives of the phase of life during which ego boundaries are in the process of formation.

A. A. Milne's *Winnie the Pooh* stories are typical derivatives of these early developmental stages. Flew feels that Winnicott generalizes too widely from a particular group of English-speaking children to society as a whole when he refers to "the central position of *Winnie the Pooh* in the life of all children." I do not believe that Winnicott means here that children everywhere encounter these stories. It is rather that Milne's imagery is central to the life of all children, no matter how it is expressed in different societies. Winnicott merely gives Milne priority for having recognized and written about transitional phenomena.

Flew then criticizes Winnicott's statement that "a true transitional object" is "more important than the mother, an almost inseparable part of the infant," and points out that the loss of a transitional object would not cause a bigger public uproar or a bigger internal upset than would the loss of the mother. I think that Flew is correct here, but an explanation is necessary. What Winnicott intended was that the transitional object is experienced by the child as more important than the mother when the relationship with the mother is intact and so secure that it can be taken for granted.

Flew then discusses Winnicott's use of the phrase *transitional phenomena* in contrast to *transitional objects*. He points out that not only material objects but activities as well can be classified as "transitional" and reaches the important conclusion that "the key word . . . becomes not *object* but *transitional.*" Then he asks, "What are the transitions transitions between?" He refers to the teddy bear as the "paradigm transitional object," but here the important point remains, it is not the object, the teddy bear, that is transitional but rather the *meaning of the object* to the developing infant. Here the principle of developmental continuity can be helpful. The word *transition* implies change, and the change to which Winnicott is referring is a gradual developmental change. *At any one time* the term *intermediate* conveys Winnicott's meaning more exactly than does the word *transitional.* Our question then becomes, What are transitional phenomena intermediate between? This leads to Flew's criticism of Winnicott's use of the term *illusion.*

Flew suggests that "similarities between aspects of childhood and aspects of adult life are not in themselves a sufficient reason for concluding that there are causal connections between the one and the other." He is criticizing Winnicott's hypothesis that there is an intermediate area between the purely objective and that which is perceived externally, the area of transitional phenomena in infancy and of the artistic, religious, and creative experiencing of the adult. He quotes Winnicott's statements that illusory experiences can be shared, but that it is "a hallmark of madness when an adult puts too powerful a claim on the credulity of others, forcing them to acknowledge a sharing of illusion which is not their own," and that in healthy persons shared illusory experiences are "a natural root of grouping among human beings." Flew feels that 'it is self-defeating to suggest that all the beliefs of a sane man are really just as much illusions as those characteristic of a mad man." And later he says the "third world" (the intermediate world) of

transitional phenomena and illusion is "supposed to be located and
defined by reference to misappreciation of the truth about the universe
around us." When Winnicott uses the word *illusion* he does not imply a
"misappreciation" of the external world. It is rather that illusion refers to
an *expanded perception*, in which primary and secondary process both take
part, whereas primary process alone refers to inner reality and secondary
process concerns the effects on the psychic apparatus of the perception of
external reality.

In terms of aesthetic experience, "illusion" includes sublimation. This
also helps us resolve Flew's criticism of Winnicott's discussion of the
relationship between transitional phenomena and symbolism. Flew
criticizes the use of the term *illusion* with reference to the symbolic
meaning of transubstantiation. He says that there must be "a
compromise, between illusion and reality." Actually there is no conflict
here, as Winnicott's use of the word *illusion* is broader than a
"misappreciation of external reality." It includes what Flew mentions as
"a compromise." *Webster's Unabridged Dictionary*, Second Edition, defines
illusion as "a perception which fails to give the true character of an object
perceived" and states that the term is often used synonymously with the
word *delusion*. Still, I believe that the term *illusion* does include greater
respect for and acknowledgment of the actual characteristics of the
external object than is implied by the term *delusion*. *The American College
Dictionary*, 1957, defines *illusion* in psychology as "a perception of a thing
which misrepresents it or gives it qualities not present in reality." This is
helpful. Certainly a continuum exists, but what Winnicott referred to is
the enrichment of the perception of external reality that can derive from
its integration with internal reality. This can be contrasted with
hallucination on the one hand and with a totally unimaginative
perception of the external world on the other. *The intermediate area of
transitional objects and phenomena is the same as the area of integration between internal
and external reality.*

In his paper "Primitive Emotional Development" (1945) Winnicott
defines the word *illusion* as he uses it. He says there that the "moment of
illusion" is one in which the infant, child, or adult feels an identity
between that which he is capable of hallucinating and that which exists in
the outside world. Illusion, in this sense, is necessary for emotionally
meaningful contact with the outside world, and therefore becomes a
precondition for ego development, integration, and maturation.

Flew criticizes Winnicott's contention that there is a paradox in
attitude toward a transitional object that should not be resolved. The
paradox is that from the adult point of view the object has real existence
in the outside world but from the infant's point of view the object is *both*

an external object *and* also self-created, in the sense that a hallucination is self-created. It is just this dual significance that designates the object as "transitional" or intermediate. The same considerations apply to the adult's cultural experience. A "cultural object," such as a piece of sculpture, a painting, or a musical score, belongs to the physical world, which Flew calls Popper's World I. When used with "creative illusion," the object becomes a bridge between the internal world and the external world, and has "transitional" significance. Flew says, "At the risk of appearing frivolous, we must be prepared to ask why, if while reading *Troilus and Cressida* in bed we are asked what we are doing and where we are (if anywhere at all), it is unacceptable to respond: In bed, reading *Troilus and Cressida*." And Flew answers this question himself earlier, when he points out that by choosing to employ an object in a particular way one can transform the meaning of that object, and thus create a transitional object.

Then Flew asks again whether the concept of a transitional area of experiencing is methodologically unsound. He points out that we can postulate two areas, the first being external or shared reality, the physical world, and the second psychic reality, the world of our conscious experience. Are these not sufficient? Why a third area of experiencing? The answer, of course, is that it is the area of illusion, consisting of the *integration* of the two worlds—external perception on the one hand and dream and hallucination on the other—that enriches life experience.

For the clinician, perhaps the most important consequence of understanding the concept of the transitional area is that it provides a continuum on which to classify transference reactions. In the center of the continuum is the most satisfactory type of treatment situation, in which the patient finds himself feeling and reacting toward the therapist as though the therapist were some figure out of the patient's past, while remaining all the time aware of the present reality of his own identity, the identity of the therapist, and the realities of the treatment situation. It is this simultaneous awareness of two kinds of reality, namely the reality of his own feelings from his past and the reality of the current situation, that characterizes a transference reaction of a kind that we can expect to be resolved in the course of treatment. The word "illusion" is appropriate to describe this kind of transference reaction. The two ends of the continuum contrast with the center. At one end the patient can see the therapist only as a receptacle for a projected part of the patient's inner world, and is cut off from awareness of the actual realities of his own identity as well as that of the therapist. We call this a delusional transference. At the other end of the continuum the patient perceives only the external realities of himself, the therapist, and the interview situation, and is cut off from awareness of his inner world of feeling and fantasy. From a clinical point of view this kind of one-sided perception presents therapeutic difficulties which are equal to, and in some instances greater than, those in the delusional transference.

Anthony Flew concludes his essay with the statement that "the upshot of my study about what is actually said about transitional objects and transitional phenomena . . . is dispiriting." Here I think he does himself an injustice, because he has provided a very valuable stimulus for us to examine our understanding of the concept of transitional phenomena, a concept of vast clinical importance. Therefore, far from being dispiriting, Flew's contribution is in effect inspiring.

REFERENCE

Winnicott, D. W. (1945). Primitive emotional development. In *Collected Papers*. New York: Basic Books, 1958.

CHAPTER 31

THE CONCEPT OF THE TRANSITIONAL OBJECT

Leonard Barkin

Winnicott's observations of transitional objects and transitional phenomena were both basic and original. Once he pointed to the data, it became apparent to us all that a common piece of behavior had been overlooked. Genius sometimes reveals itself in discovering the obvious. Winnicott did more: he explored and explained his observations, and developed theoretical conceptions to apply them, not only to child development, but also to pathology, therapeutic technique, and the origins of culture.

BASIC FORMULATIONS

Winnicott immediately related the concept of transitional objects and phenomena to developmental stages (1951). He indicates that infants "as soon as they are born tend to use fist, finger, and thumbs in stimulation of the oral erotogenic zone, in satisfaction of the instincts of that zone, and also in quiet union" (p. 1). He then states that "after a few months infants of either sex become fond of playing with dolls, and that most mothers *allow* their infants some special object and *expect them* to become...*addicted* to such objects, the first not-me possession, an attachment to a teddy, a doll or soft toy, or to a hard toy" (p. 7, my italics). He says that "something is important here other than oral excitement and satisfaction though this may be the basis of everything else." Some of these important other things include:

1. The nature of the object
2. The infant's capacity to recognize the object as "not-me"
3. The place of the object—outside, inside or at the border
4. The infant's capacity to create, think up, devise, originate, produce an object
5. The initiation of an affectionate type of object relationship (p. 2).

He then introduces the terms *transitional objects* and *transitional phenomena*, roughly relating them to what has preceded, but not exactly: "I have introduced the terms 'transitional objects' and 'transitional phenomena' for the designation of the *intermediate area of experience*, between the thumb and the teddy bear, between the oral erotism and the true object relationship, between primary creativity and the projection of what has already been introjected, between primary unawareness of indebtedness and the acknowledgment of indebtedness (say: 'Ta.')" (p. 2, my italics). While *transitional* relates to the object, it more specifically describes the infant that is in the transitional state to self- and object-representation differentiation, from symbiosis to separation and individuation, from part to whole object relating, traversing a path (viewed from another angle) from narcissistic to object love. By definition, then, the transitional object is neither inner nor outer but rather partakes of both, i.e., is at the border between them, in an intermediate area. Winnicott delineates an interface concept analogous to the concept of an intrapsychic compromise formation. We should not think of it as a simple or concrete amalgamation, as it encompasses the inner and outer worlds and depends on the complexities of ego development. At this early stage of the developmental continuum, we recognize that inner and outer are not distinct, and that ego functions are in a state of developmental flux. Winnicott focuses on this, recognizing both the child's growing reality sense and the infant's primitive state and implicit "inability" to test reality. The intermediate area is a space in which the infant both *creates* and *experiences* illusions, and is allowed to do so, in the service of his attempts to cope with separation. While the initial unit is a fused mother-child, Winnicott is interested not only in the poorly demarcated part object breast, but also, and primarily, in the *use* to which the transitional object is put and the child's role in the process of creating this primitive symbol, or pre-symbol, for the breast.

WINNICOTT'S EXAMPLES

While Winnicott (1951) calls the transitional object the first possession, he indicates that there may be series of such objects often in a developmental line of increasing organization and complexity, though he does not provide a methodical delineation. For example, in describing transitional phenomena he refers to the "infant's babbling and the way in which an older child goes over a repertory of songs and tunes while preparing for sleep" (p. 2). *Transitional phenomena*, then, is a term used to describe activities or the mental products of those activities, e.g., singing or the tunes themselves. At another point he presents a typical case of transitional object formation, a child who "adopted the end of the blanket where the stitching finished.... When he was a year old he was able to substitute for the end of the blanket a soft green jersey with a red tie.... This was not a 'comforter' but a 'soother.' It was a sedative that always worked...a typical example of what I am calling a transitional object" (p. 17). This child sucked his thumb from the early weeks of life to the age of three or four.

Again we note a series, and while the object perhaps was still concretistic, it was becoming more distant from the immediate experience of the nursing situation and life in the crib. I also call attention to this "typical" example of early thumbsucking which continues. The child may have a number of transitional objects at one time: one child I observed used a blanket primarily, but would use her mother's hats if the blanket were unavailable.

Coming back to Winnicott's example, this child developed normally as an adult, marrying and separating from his mother. His brother by contrast had an aberrant development, remained quite attached to his mother, and never married. The brother "never sucked his thumb or his fingers. He had a very strong and early *attachment to* (the mother) *herself*, as a person, and it was her actual person that he needed." He developed an attachment to a toy rabbit when a year old, and this was eventually transferred to real rabbits. This latter attachment lasted until he was five or six. But this was a *comforter*, not a true transitional object or *soother* that would become, in Winnicott's words, more important than the mother (p. 7). Interestingly enough, at the age of seven months he developed asthma.

These cases are important for a number of reasons. Winnicott is making the point that not all object attachments are transitional, that there are specific criteria concerning the use of the object that define its transitional nature. He makes it a sine qua non for the transitional object that the child, at times, be more attached to it than to the mother. Another facet of the above cases is the question of thumbsucking and the development of asthma, issues dealt with in a later section.

Another criterion of transitional objects is that there must be some *separation* from the mother before the child using his creative capacity and illusion, undoes the separation and reestablishes the symbiotic union (Gaddini and Gaddini 1970). Also, Winnicott (1971) showed that there must be a history of successful *use* of the object either for going to sleep or when the child is tired or entering strange situations. It must truly "soothe." Apparently this was not so for the brother. Winnicott noted in addition that "sometimes there is no transitional object other than the mother herself" and that the "sequence may be broken or maintained in a hidden way." Thus it may be difficult for an observer to make a simple determination as to whether an object attachment is transitional or not. Other variables include the older brother's developing an object attachment (comforter) at one year, changing it, and keeping the new object for years, until five or six. This we would now say is not an unusual course for transitional objects, and Busch (1974) found, much to his surprise, that many transitional object attachments developing in the first year lasted as long as five or six years. (Greenacre [1970] noted that they last until latency.) However, the basic thrust observed by Winnicott is that a healthy child who has had a successful symbiotic phase will be able to enjoy the transition state and will be able to make use of the transitional object for progressive adaptive use (Greenacre 1969, 1970). This will not be true for the disturbed child. The benefits of age appropriate symbiosis and the capacity to reestablish it are linked ultimately with a more successful separation from the mother.

THE NATURE OF THE OBJECT

The nature of the transitional object is related to its origin in the early stage of life, to the ambience of the crib, the nursing situation, oral erotism, and autoerotic behavior. As the child sucks and plays, what is mouthed and the skin and cloth textures available to him become interrelated and connected. It was noted that the objects seem to be engaged in two clusters: at six months, and then at two years of age (Busch 1974, Stevenson 1954). The former Busch called the first transitional object; the latter, the second. By and large all the six months objects were soft, easily mouthable, and treated primarily with affection. The children would bury their faces in them at times, suggesting that more than the mouth and mouthing is involved, that the areas around the mouth are important as well (Busch 1974). The imagery is certainly reminiscent of a child snuggling at its mother's breast (Greenacre 1960). Later objects might be hard, but these would be obtained usually by boys, with girls continuing to acquire softer objects; both sexes, however, would use them similarly. While both Winnicott and Greenacre (1969) thought odors important in maintaining the continuity of the object, Busch (1974) found textures more crucial. When the texture of a blanket was changed by washing, it was rejected. Gaddini (chapter 8) found that the objects chosen by a series of children seemed most related to the nursing blanket character: smoother, related to cotton in the summer, and furrier, related to wool in the winter.

The object can be either animate or inanimate. Among the former, more difficult to control, are the human, e.g., mother, siblings, and friends, as well as the nonhuman, e.g., pets. The inanimate include such well-known examples as teddy bears and blankets. As already mentioned, the object should be chosen by the child, must be non-me in part, and not part of the child's own body, e.g., the thumb. Similarly, pacifiers start out certainly as being presented from the outside, and there is more libidinal discharge with them; hence they would not qualify. The transitional objects should be created in a "neutral area" (Winnicott 1951), and this is one of the criteria for delimiting them from distortions in their use. They soothe rather than stimulate. Objects used for masturbatory purposes would clearly, then, not qualify as transitional.

Busch (1974), in trying to establish which object attachments are transitional, used duration of attachment as one of his criteria, establishing one year as the minimum amount of time. To me this seems arbitrary, though with more observational research and long term follow-up it might prove a valuable insight. Also, Busch states (as does Kahne 1967, speaking of adults) that he found little evidence of transitional phenomena. The problem is complicated by the possibility of both subtle breaks in continuity and of silent sequences, phenomena equally difficult to observe. Hence, transitional phenomena—repetitive activities or the products of such activites, e.g., babbling, words, tunes, caressing, tapping, mannerisms—might not be readily apparent; such inner processes as fantasizing and dreaming are obviously even less so. We can take as an example of a repetitive activity the one Busch himself gives (p. 225) of a child who used the blanket as "part of a compulsive ritual in going to sleep." I would suggest that this "compulsive ritual"— arranging the blanket, a pacifier, and a teddy in special positions—might well be a transitional phenomenon.

DEVELOPMENTAL LINES

Anna Freud (1965) introduced the basic concept of developmental lines. This is necessary for understanding the evolution of any psychic structure and allows us to avoid reductionism and to provide a sound basis for clinical assessment—especially in evaluating levels of functioning while taking into account maturational, structural, regressive, and progressive trends. Anna Freud indicates that the developmental line seems to work best with the classical libidinal phases, which also roughly correlate with the age of the developing child, in spite of much overlapping. While we can tease out many such strands for longitudinal study, we are aware that all are interconnected as the child develops from the matrix of the undifferentiated phase. What happens in an adult can never be directly equated with the process in a child except by analogy, no matter what the level of regression or ego impairment. The issue can be restated: when we discuss a case we might say that the patient is regressed to the oral phase, and there is a tendency to think of a global ego regression to the oral phase of development, i.e., as if there were a global ego regression paralleling in instinctual regression. This has its roots in early analytic theorizing. However, as Arlow and Brenner (1964) state, this is a fallacy we will avoid if we apply the structural theory. A modern ego psychology depends on differentials in ego-superego and developmental progressions, on arrests and regressions as well as libidinal phase.

The concept of *derivative structure* enables us to discuss a mental structure at different developmental levels, maintaining the continuity of the form and function, though these may change in different matrices. In this way we can deepen our understanding while avoiding simplistic reductionist fallacies. It is in this sense that we view transitional objects and phenomena profitably in their changing forms and functions and distortions throughout life. Within this context, transitional objects and phenomena themselves become externalizations of the transitional processes (Rose, chapter 22). At this level we are involved with the creative imagination and all the ego functions contributing to it which lead to the formation of transitional objects and phenomena. Each of these ego functions has a developmental history of its own.

With regard to the developmental sequence of transitional objects and phenomena, Anna Freud (1965) describes it under the heading "From the Body to the Toy and from Play to Work" and sees the process commencing with autoerotic and erotic play activities, which also involve the "mother's body (usually in connection with feeding)." (See also Tolpin 1971.) In her view, the "properties" of the "mother's and the child's body are then transferred to some soft substance...the infant's first plaything, the transitional object...which is cathected with narcissistic and object libido." She then describes how the child's clinging is replaced by a cathexis, first to soft objects generally, and then to one object—a symbolic object which, cuddled and maltreated alternately, nevertheless survives the child's ambivalent handling.

Anna Freud feels that the transitional object continues to be used primarily as an aid to sleep and its regressive modes. The child is drawn later to materials which do not "possess object status" but will instead be used by the ego to express fantasies. She indicates that daydreaming develops when play with toys fades. Games originate in the phallic-oedipal stage, when mutuality is possible. She dates hobbies from the latency period, and places them "halfway between play and work."

Let us pause for the moment and note again that this developmental line is a sequence of play activities which not only become more complex as the child's ego functions mature but which will also become less dependent on material things. Anna Freud's conceptualization of play in the nursing situation corresponds to that of Winnicott, Kestenberg and Weinstein (chapter 6), and Gaddini (chapter 8), among others.

It is possible to place the transitional object more directly in the developmental line of object relations and follow its *use* throughout life (see, e.g., Kestenberg 1971 for a thorough, elegant discussion of this issue). Mahler had indicated there is a lifelong struggle to deal with the problem of separation. As psychic structures and needs change, the transitional object or phenomenon can play a continuing though derivative role. This has been discussed from a series of vantage points: the vicissitudes with development (Kestenberg 1971); the appearance in adults (Kahne 1967, Coppolillo 1967); the phenomenology in aging (Berezin 1973); in connection with funerary symbols (Grolnick and Lengyel, chapter 24); and applications to therapy (Greenson, chapter 13; Volkan 1973; Volkan and Kavanaugh, chapter 19; Searles 1975; Solomon, chapter 16; Giovacchini, chapter 21).

There is a parallel and related development in the nature of transitional phenomena, which become more complex as the ego develops. The possibilities and the activities themselves are more varied, e.g., fantasizing, daydreaming, hobbies. Included in the object line are precursor objects and substitute objects, followed by transitional objects (as the first treasured possession, as the first imaginary companion, and as an indicator of primitive symbolic functioning). A transitional object may develop into an infantile fetish (Roiphe and Galenson 1973) or prosthetic object (Bak 1974) and be carried into adulthood as a true fetish. All these "objects" can appear with associated phenomena expressing a related meaning, as with transitional phenomena and fetishistic phenomena.

PRECURSOR OBJECTS

The use of precursors to transitional object during the stage of symbiosis was suggested by Winnicott and elaborated in studies by Gaddini (chapter 8, 1970). These objects are utilized in a presymbolic phase for consolation and to restore the homeostasis inherent in the symbiotic dyad. The objects described include parts of the mother's or child's body (thumb, tongue), or other objects provided the child by the mother (pacifier, bottle). They can be divided into two groups: the earliest are placed into the mouth; the later are related more to skin contact and tactile perception. Those in the latter group can develop into transitional objects, though there is an overlapping in the categories as well as subsequent changes in role as development proceeds. Gaddini (chapter 8) has studied the use of precursor objects in the symbiotic period and found that if objects presented from the outside (such as pacifiers) or other sucking activities (such as using the thumb) were interfered with, there would be a disturbance in the normal development of transitional objects and a secondary disturbance of the psychosomatic equilibrium with the presence of dermatoses, rocking, rumination, and colic. In a series of cases of asthmatic children she found an absence of transitional objects.

The concept of precursor objects (e.g., pacifiers) is an important one by virtue of their early role in maintaining homeostasis and their contribution to successful symbiosis. Also, they remain something for the infant "to fall back on" before transitional objects are developed. This has been shown above in Winnicott's case of the boy with the successful soother, in contrast to his brother, who never sucked his thumb. Later on, thumbs, fingers, and pacifiers may still continue to play an accessory role to the transitional object.

To some degree, this is equivalent to saying that interference with the early autoerotic satisfaction and homeostatic mechanisms will result not only in disturbances in instinctual and structural progression, but also in the allied development of equilibratory ego apparatuses, one constituent of which is the transitional object. Undoubtedly this developmental line starts in the first month, the autistic phase, in which physiologic mechanisms, sensorimotor and reflex in nature predominate, and in which myelinization is quite limited. It seems most appropriate to speak of anlage here. While we must remember that the mother is of greatest assistance to the child in establishing homeostatic and tension control regulation, from the dawn of life accessory factors are present. Freud's speculation of the hallucinatory wish is one such thesis which relates to binding of tensions and the formation of regulating structure. Beres (1960) implicitly cautions us that we must not conceptualize the hallucinatory wish as that associated with later developmental phases, and even asks us to question whether the infant's mind is sufficiently developed to create such a relatively complex structure (see Deri, chapter 4). Yet it is appealing to consider such activities of the mind, which include dreaming (Grolnick, chapter 14) in a series leading and contributing to transitional objects and structures—precursor objects, substitutes, transitional objects and phenomena—on the road to internalization and object constancy.

ACCESSORY AND INTERMEDIATE OBJECTS

While considering the aim of reestablishing the symbiotic state via organ-object imagery fusion, Judith Kestenberg (1971) has also attempted to differentiate the transitional object from other object use in the infant's surround. Accessory objects are "people who assist the mother in the care of the infant," such as a nurse or sibling, but whose images link with the expectation of reappearance of the mother. Intermediate objects are those objects that are part of the two way traffic between mother and child—food, bodily products such as urine and feces, toys, or even people. They serve more transiently, in the here and now, whereas the transitional object links past, present, and future.

SUBSTITUTE OBJECTS

The concept of substitute objects can be approached at two levels, the descriptive phenomenological level to be discussed now, and that of symbolic abstraction, to be discussed later. The use of the substitute object overlaps with the precursor and leads into the transitional. Tolpin (1971), disagreeing with Bowlby's assertion (1969) that the transitional object has no meaning and no value apart from its role as substitute object for the unavailable mother, points out that it continues to have a function even in her presence. More relevant is that if the mother is gone long enough, as Winnicott noted (1951), the transitional object ceases to have any function. If by substitute we mean that the child responds to the object fully as the missing mother (Beres 1965), an equation seen in Lorenz' experiments with imprinting in goslings (1971) or the use by infant monkeys of a cloth mother in Harlow's emperiments (1960), then again, on a phenomenological basis, the transitional object must be differentiated from the substitute—i.e., on the need for the continuing function of the good enough mother for there to be a transitional object at all.

INSIDE/OUTSIDE

Saying the object is created by the child does not preclude some contribution from the outside. Obviously the objects in the child's environment are presented to him. But he chooses and he symbolizes (or more accurately, presymbolizes) and uses the object. I studied one child quite intensively in a research nursery directed by Drs. Eleanor Galenson and Herman Roiphe. This eight-month-old girl developed a persisting attachment to a blanket and several hats, the latter being used in an accessory manner. They clearly possessed a soothing quality, and she would use them when tired, when she went into strange situations, at stressful times, and when falling asleep. The mother told how the child was attached to a musical toy. The grandmother had been a singer and often danced with and sang to the little girl. She may even have given her the toy. This was the family's preferred object, but the child chose the others, clearly her own "choice."

While what I have just described can be considered the more usual pattern, whether transitional object formation can proceed from the outside is a question difficult to answer from observations in the preverbal period. A clearer differentiation can be made in the verbal phase.

There is also a question as to whether what starts out as a precursor might not end up as a transitional object, i.e., whether a change of function can occur with further development. Mahler (1975) says that the bottle can become a transitional object. Ordinarily, the bottle would be characterized as a precursor object, playing a major role as a direct source of oral need satisfaction and libidinal gratification, especially prior to weaning, but usually continuing for some time after. Like the pacifier, it is presented to the child from the outside and is not his own creation.

In addition, the clinical work of Buxbaum (1960) and Fintzy (1971) should be considered. Buxbaum, in treating two cases of hair pulling in latency children, provided them with an object (called an intermediary object) which was accepted by them and utilized by them as a transition in the development of object relations. Fintzy has described a similar use of an object in a borderline child. While such examples are not exactly comparable to the latter half of the first year of life, and while they at first seem more related to distortions in transitional object use than to the "pure" transitional object, it seems that what starts out as a distortion, a fetish, or an object with fetishistic reference can develop and be used by the child increasingly in a manner gradually approaching that of the transitional object in Winnicott's sense (see also Furer 1964, Roiphe 1973, Volkan 1973).

ROLE OF SEPARATION

The relationship of separation and childrearing practices in various cultures to the formation of transitional object has hardly been studied. We can, however, say this much: separate sleeping and room arrangements in our culture increase the stress on children, thus requiring them to adapt by developing transitional objects. The Gaddinis (1970) have reported in a study of urban middle and rural lower class families that the frequency of the transitional object diminished among the latter when there was less space and the mothers and other family members were in more frequent physical contact with the child. Busch (1974) emphasized the absence the mother at bedtime as being important in transitional object formation. However, Muensterberger (1962) has described cultures in which increased dependency is encouraged, in which there are fewer transitional objects, but in which increased magic, less separation, and increased fetishism develop. Another observation which has yet to be followed up was made by Bettelheim (1969), who was struck by the fact that the children in the Israeli Kibbutzim demonstrate a striking lack of transitional objects.

I would agree with Busch (1974) that, contrary to Tolpin's suggestion (1971), physical growth alone in the six-month-old child is not enough to lead to the progression from the symbiotic state. Busch (1974) has emphasized the role of the parents' expectations of the child, i.e., their making more demands of him, especially for delay and independent functioning. In addition, he has directly related the development of recognition memory of the mother at six months to transitional object formation, so that "the mother, even if cathected as a self-object, is increasingly recognized as being outside the infant's control and a willing partner in his omnipotent narcissistic state." This is adumbrated by Winnicott in his statements about the child's ongoing developing of reality testing, as well as in his comment that from the beginning "there is some abrogation of omnipotence."

However, I think it important to spell out the relation of perceptual, memory, and representational functions to the capacity for symbolization, affect, and the creative process, with reference to transitional object formation in the context of object relations and the attainment of object constancy. This I will do later, when we come to consider the many possible fates of the transitional object, of its rudimentary forms and its distortions.

THE INTERMEDIATE AREA

Winnicott (1971) has described the "third world" in various ways. He said that "the intermediate area. . .is allowed to the infant between primary creativity and objective perception based on reality testing" (p. 11), and that it is an "area or experience, unchallenged in respect of its belonging to inner or outer (shared) reality. . .throughout life in the intense experiencing that belongs to the arts and to religion and to imaginative living, and to creative scientific work" (p. 11). Here, then, it is related to the role of illusion in the creation of the transitional object, with a decathexis of the transitional object as cultural interests develop. In addition, he describes it as being in "direct continuity with the play area of a child lost in play," and necessary in infancy "for the initiation of a relationship between the child and the world." Here play is seen as leading to positive cultural experience in the presence of good enough mothering, a thought which, while no doubt related to the concept of sublimation, has a different emphasis. Additionally there is an adaptive aspect in which illusion helps throughout life with the "task of reality acceptance that is never completed. . .no human being is free from the strain of relating inner and outer reality, and. . .relief from this strain is provided by an intermediate area of experience. . .which is not challenged (arts, religion, etc.)" (p. 13). It is also seen as "the potential space between the baby and the mother," a "hypothetical area that exists (but cannot exist) between the baby and the object" (p. 107), an area "in which because of trust the child may creatively play" (p. 104).

Intermediate area and potential space, then, are metaphorical terms that Winnicott uses as equivalents, associating them with the adaptive use of illusion which emerges in the earliest experiences of play, and which continues throughout life in cultural pursuits and everyday creativity (Rose, chapter 22). The need for basic trust and good enough mothering relates here to creative play and to transitional object formation, partially to undo the separation between child and mother, and to provide a resting place to relieve the strain. To some degree there is a relationship, with good enough mothering leading the way to drive neutralization, ego structuralization, and sublimation via the intermediate area, and a reciprocal interplay. It must be stressed that Winnicott is concerned with intrapsychic process when he speaks of the relationship of inner and outer. Hence the third world is an inner world, and the locus is not an actual space that can be concretized and measured. Though there are important related issues in development concerning the relative space between mother and child (see Bergman, chapter 10), this is not the essence of Winnicott's intermediate area concept.

Flew (chapter 29) questions the third area concept along several lines, one aspect of which is the question as to whether it is possible for illusion to be used to adapt to reality (see also Flarsheim, chapter 30; Rose, chapter 22; Greenacre 1970; Beres 1960; Modell 1970). The problem is related more to the role of the creative imagination or transitional processes in reality testing and adaptation than to the question Flew stresses, of how a loss of reality sense in an illusion can allow for better adaptation. There is a progressive aspect in the use of illusion that enables the child to consolidate perceptions and augment its autonomy, resulting in a better reality sense. Thus the creative imagination is a tool which can lead to invention and mastery (Greenacre 1959), just one of the possible outcomes of transitional object development.

THE FATE OF THE TRANSITIONAL OBJECT

Winnicott (1951) said that the fate of the transitional object is

> to be gradually allowed to be decathected so in the course of years it becomes not so much forgotten as relegated to limbo...that in health the transitional object does not "go inside" nor does the feeling about it necessarily undergo repression. It is not forgotten and it is not mourned. It loses meaning, and this is because the transitional phenomena have become spread out over the whole intermediate territory between "inner psychic reality" and the "external world as perceived by two persons in common," that is to say over the whole cultural field. [p. 5]

On this view, the transitional object does not become internalized as structure but, by virtue of its location in the intermediate area and its relation to play, it then "fades away" as other cultural interests take over. By and large, Greenacre (1970) went along with this when she said that it is relinquished "until only a small piece of it remains...a kind of obsolescent memento of the past." However, she describes a line of development similar to that described by Anna Freud, a line branching off in various directions: to toys; to daytime play; to representation in a creative work; or to a fantasy which serves as a "bedtime comfort," essentially a transitional phenomenon. Silverman (1977) has described an adolescent patient who created stories in order to put himself to sleep. Such nighttime rituals as counting sheep can have a similar function.

But isn't Winnicott implying structure formation when he states that "patterns set in infancy may persist into childhood" or that "a need for a specific object or a behavior pattern that started at a very early date may reappear at a later age when deprivation threatens"? Tolpin (1971) utilized Kohut's concept of transmuting internalization to delineate the progressive, piece-by-piece internalization of maternal functions, leading to the structuralization of a "self-soothing" function. Hence, according to Tolpin, it does "go inside," if there is good enough mothering: the transitional object becomes part of the idealized maternal imago and a component of tension-regulating structure as it contributes to formation of a "cohesive self." If this internalization does not take place, then an archaic transitional self-object will be required. It is because the functions are internalized that the transitional object is not mourned.

A comment made by Winnicott (1951) in reference to the intermediate area (see above) seems relevant to this discussion: "No human being is free from the strain of relating inner and outer reality." Volkan (1973) described a narcissistic patient whose "blankets" were soothing fantasies that had not been successfully internalized. They were chosen with the aim of mastering separation and loneliness and as bridges to the external world. See Grolnick (chapter 14) for a patient's similar use of dreams; Volkan and Kavanaugh (chapter 19) indicate how pet cats in adults may serve on an early level of symbolization as *reanimated* transitional objects.

Rosen (1964) indicates another potential fate of the transitional object when he links it to character and life style. Though he discusses it in relationship to the special sensory endowment of the artistically gifted adolescent, we can wonder whether this applies to the ordinary children of ordinary devoted mothers. Certainly Kaminer's discussion (chapter 15) of his patient suggests that the vicissitudes of the early relationship to the transitional object do influence the quality and directions of personality type and the "textures" of life style. This implies that the facets of transitional objects and phenomena are internalized, fully or partially, into both self- and object-representations, as well as in the ego-ideal and superego. On the other hand, it is possible that what initially is a transitional object might become a transitional phenomenon (Parrish, chapter 18).

ADDICTION TO THE OBJECT

One of the paradoxes and mysteries in the functioning of the transitional object is that it promotes autonomy while reestablishing the symbiosis; indeed, the child behaves as if he were addicted to the object, preferring the transitional object to the mother during certain times of stress. Tolpin (1971) denies that this takes place. However, Busch (1974) observed that it was a frequent occurrence, and that many of the mothers he observed were quite distressed by the child's preference for the transitional object. Dickes (chapter 20, 1963)) and Sperling (1963) argue that this is a sign of a pathological outcome. Initially, in 1963, both, following Wulff (1946), felt that any such object attachment in childhood could be considered pathological and fetishistic. Dickes has since modified his views, maintaining now that fetishistic objects are particularly those to which the child seems addicted (Winnicott's true transitional objects or soothers); a healthy transitional relationship of a child to an object is to be found where the child is less attached, being able to give it up more easily, as though it were a toy (Winnicott's definition of the comforter). The problem cannot be dealt with solely as a matter of definition or example, however. Tolpin (1971) has suggested that the answer lies in the creation of the object by the child. As such it allows the distressed child himself to adaptively utilize illusion and thereby obtain the soothing required by a recreation of the lost symbiosis. In addition, the transitional object does not administer narcissistic wounds, is portable, and is more easily subjected to omnipotent thought, control and tactile manipulation. However, the transitional object is not chosen at all times of stress in preference to the mother; nor is it accurate to say the child cares more for the object than for the mother. The object is conceptualized as auxiliary to her, and not as a primary object as is the mother to the child. It represents the idealized maternal imago or part object breast, and the mother's supportive tension-regulating functions. Further, because the transitional object is created in a neutral way and remains relatively conflict free, it is especially valuable and stabilizing whenever the maternal representation is still unstable, or when the soothing function has not been sufficiently internalized (Metcalf and Spitz, chapter 7; Rose 1964, chapter 22; Tolpin 1971; Giovacchini, chapter 21).

TRANSITIONAL OBJECT AND FETISH

Wulff (1946) categorized as fetishes a series of infantile object attachments but made no clear distinctions. Winnicott (1971) described the transitional object and its use in health. Dickes (chapter 20, 1963) had asked whether the transitional object was the child's creation or was presented to the child by the mother pathologically, in lieu of herself. On this view, the transitional object would not be a normal universal as Winnicott and Stevenson (1954) suggested. Sperling (1963) even categorized Winnicott's conceptions as "dangerous." Both she and Dickes felt that an overfrustrated, rejected or sexually overstimulated child experiencing marked trauma would turn from the not good enough mother to the inanimate object they likened to a fetish. The mother's encouraging the child to use the object would be more of the same, and the addiction developed would be a pathological tie. The object was portable and could be more easily utilized for magical manipulation and more easily controlled than the mother. It could be a substitute for aggressive and libidinal drive discharge, but at the same time the needed object and the dependent self would be preserved. The object would be called fetishistic, or an oral fetish, to distinguish it from a fetish standing for a phallus.

According to the Dickes-Sperling hypothesis, infants lacking good enough mothering should turn to toys. One study which clearly demonstrates the fallacy of the hypothesis is that made by Provence and Lipton (1962, see also Provence and Ritvo 1961). They found in a group of children with severe deprivation that no transitional objects were formed. While certain maturational processes proceeded normally, these could not be utilized by the child's developing ego, and development lagged. There was impaired grasping, dimished play with toys, and little body exploration. Ego deficiencies included body image, language, and symbolization. In addition, these children did not have the necessary neutralized aggressive thrust to propel development.

The question has been discussed by various writers: Greenacre (1970), Anna Freud (1965), and Bak (1974). All emphasized that the examples given by Sperling and Dickes were not of typical transitional objects, and that the cases chosen involved distortions of the concept. Bak, for example, noted that in a number of Sperling's cases the mother gave her the object, and that as it came from the outside (was the mother's creation) it could be classed as an intermediate object in Buxbaum's sense (1960). Greenacre (1969) has indicated that aggressive discharge was involved in the adult fetish where it is expressed as "congealed anger" related to castration panic. Further, the fetish represents a patch over a flaw in the body image and reality sense, a denial of castration. Greenacre (1960) has described fetishistic phenomena attachments related to the fetish, e.g., the amulet and the secret (see also Khan, chapter 17), but not to genital sexual performance. The secret, in my opinion, can range in meaning from a transitional phenomenon to a fetishistic phenomenon, and the latter can be used to categorize an activity, such as collecting, or thought or fantasy where the symbolization is phallic. Bach's categorization (1971) of a patient's imaginary companion as a transitional phenomenon that represented a phallus would therefore more correctly be called a fetishistic phenomenon. There can be a continuum as well as an oscillating complementary series expressed in the symbolization of transitional objects and phenomena, and fetishistic objects and phenomena. At the pathological end of this continuum are objects used by symbiotically disturbed children, objects characterized by Furer (1964) as psychotic fetishes (Bak 1974). Perhaps the repetitive motions of these children in their stereotyped activities can be described as psychotic fetishistic phenomena, or autistic phenomena, an attempt to structure a nurturing modality (Roiphe 1973).

When an attachment to an object in infancy is used to deal with castration anxiety and to reinforce the genital body image, the object has been designated an infantile fetish. Galenson and Roiphe (1971) have studied the last half of the second year of life, more or less coincident with Mahler's stage of rapprochement crisis, and found evidence of a preoedipal phallic phase with castration anxiety, i.e., with no oedipal conflict resonance, especially in girls, where it is also associated with a more depressive mood (see also Roiphe 1968). While there is still controversy (Bak 1974), there have been related supporting observations made by Mahler (1966). Contributing is the upsurge of aggression and such other anal phase phenomena as toilet training and the loss of stool and urine, as well as genital exposure illness, bodily trauma, and separations (Roiphe 1973). Transitions from transitional object to infantile fetish have been demonstrated (Roiphe and Galenson 1973).

It has been noted that there are more children using infantile fetishes than there are adult fetishists (A. Freud 1965, Roiphe and Galenson 1973). Hence, the problem of the infantile fetish may relate more to developmental issues than to the problem of adult fetishism (though the latter can be involved). It would be interesting to consider the formation of the second transitional object in relation to the infantile fetish.

Having dwelt on regression, distortions, arrests, and pathology, we may turn to kinder and, happily, more usual fates. Healthy development, abetted by the progressive and creative use of transitional objects and phenomena, will now be considered.

CREATIVE FUNCTION

Winnicott's view of the creative function is linked to the process of undoing the separation between mother and child as differentiation begins. Illusion is utilized adaptively to bridge the "baby's inability and growing ability to recognize and accept reality." He adds that "In favorable circumstances the potential space becomes filled with the products of the baby's own creative imagination." The emphasis is on a developing complex ego function itself dependent on other ego functions which are in various stages of development. The focus is on *process* rather than product (Beres 1960). Works of art themselves are not the issue, but rather the relationship between playing and the formation of transitional objects and phenomena, which lead to shared and symbolic play and to cultural experience. Creative processes leading to transitional object formation have been termed *transitional processes* by Rose (chapter 22), and are thought of as surviving the initial transitional object functions. Then they continue contributing to the reality adaptation of the adult. Where mothering is not good enough such functioning will be impaired, along with the capacity to play, to symbolize, and to separate.

ANIMISM, OMNIPOTENT THINKING AND THE IMAGINARY COMPANION

Muensterberger (1962) has described how primitive and not so primitive man, with the development of shared fantasies and myths, has created objects with the aim of mastering reality through fantasy. Omnipotent thinking and animism play a role in endowing these "fetishes" with the power of the preoedipal mother. He directly alludes to the creative function of the child and a developmental line commencing with transitional object formation when he compares this process to a "drowsy infant holding on to substitute representatives of his immediate environment, *imaginary companions* be they his thumb, blanket, a pacifier or teddy bear" (my italics). Animism plays a role in breathing life into the inanimate world, and allows the child to regain the lost symbiosis. Clearly animistic thinking is still available within the creative imagination of the adult, where it continues the same functions, but now in derivative forms. We here approach the area of religion, where more "primitive" forms lead to so-called "higher," or more symbolic, forms. There is at the same time a relation to pathology, as in the obsessional symptoms explored by Solomon (chapter 16).

SYMBOLIZATION

The symbolizing process is another complex ego function inextricably interrelated to the development of memory, representation, boundary formation, reality testing, apperception, and synthetic function. Winnicott (1971) was, aware of this when he stated that "when symbolism is employed the infant is already clearly distinguishing between fantasy and fact, between inner objects and external objects, between primary creativity and perception" (p. 6), and that "there is use for a term for the root of symbolism in time, a term that describes the infant's journey from the purely subjective to objectivity" (p. 6).

According to Werner and Kaplan (1963), symbolic representation "implies some awareness, *however vague* that vehicle and referential object are not identical but are, in substance and form, two totally different entities (p. 16, my italics). They called *protosymbols* those vehicles which "present" meanings rather than "represent" them, and considered these important in that they could achieve true symbolic form by virtue of a continuing "progressive differentiation of vehicle and referential meaning." The "dynamic schematizing" activity for the transitional object vehicle could be described, then, as commencing in the primitive surround of the nursing situation and progressing as cognitive functioning and inner-outer differentiation proceed, with a marked advance indicated with the arrival of the first indicator, the smiling response. This anticipatory affective reaction is based on a sign Gestalt (Spitz and Wolf 1946; Spitz 1959; Metcalf and Spitz, chapter 7) and represents the first time that the infant will reliably react to a percept from the outside; as such it represents the beginning of reality testing. Soon after this, transitional object formation is first seen, along with separation anxiety, indicating mother-child differentiation (Metcalf and Spitz, chapter 7). However, substitute objects, precursors of the libidinal object, can easily function in the care of the child until the eighth month, when stranger anxiety, the second organizer, indicates that the libidinal object proper has been established (Spitz 1959)—another quantum leap in mental functioning. (See Mahler 1974 for a developmental overview.)

Memory is on a recognition basis in the presence of need, and evocative memory of the absent mother is only rudimentary in the late differentiation phase (McDevitt 1975, Fraiberg 1969). It has been suggested that the transitional object can function as a "prosthesis" for the maternal representation (Metcalf and Spitz, chapter 7), and that the retention of this image can be equated with primitive imagination (Rosen 1960). By eleven months, according to Piaget, the infant will search for the inanimate object which has been placed behind the screen. This has parallels in what is observed between mother and child (McDevitt 1975). The child remains dependent (though progressively less so) on the presence of the mother or mother substitute for evocation of her image until sixteen to eighteen months of age. Then the child is notably less dependent on the stimulation of the maternal object or inner need, and is on the verge of true symbolic representational thought. Nevertheless, by the late practicing phase, approximately fourteen months, the child has begun early symbolic play. To put it differently, before object constancy in the Piaget timetable (16-18 months) is established, early symbolic play is observed and has made its appearance in the absence of the mother (McDevitt 1975). It is also about this time (15 months) that the "no" response, Spitz's third organizer, is seen, and precursors of symbolic language are utilized.

Unless the infant can evoke the absent object, Beres (1965) would classify the object as substitute rather than symbolic. The substitute object is defined as being "in every sense equal to the original object; it does not represent the original one." Sarnoff (1970) has on the basis of clinical data indicated that the psychoanalytic symbol develops at twenty-four months. This concept depends on the presence of repression (following Jones 1916), including an unconscious referent, and must involve the delineation of self- and object-representations so that there is both the aspect of allusion in the symbol and differentiation between symbolizer, symbolic vehicle, and what is symbolized (Werner and Kaplan 1963). Beres (1965) says that the "transitional object starts out as a substitute for the breast and becomes in time a representation of the breast." Essentially, here a sign becomes a presentation on the way to becoming a representation, a symbol (see Grolnick and Lengyel, chapter 24).

Winnicott indicated that the "actuality" of the transitional object and its being neither breast nor mother is as important as its being a part object symbol. The fusion of "me/non-me" is inherent in the primitive symbolization of the transitional object. While the balance is tilted more toward the "me" and the presentational, it is the beginning separation and "non-me" aspects which I am emphasizing, and which here contribute to a rudimentary symbolic form.

The creation of the transitional object at a critical period serves as an *indicator* that a certain level of ego functioning has been attained. At the same time, it contributes to further symbolization and structuralization. In this sense it has been called a psychic organizer (Tolpin 1971, Metcalf and Spitz, chapter 7). I would note also the warm affective response to the first transitional object, the affect being another criteria for a psychic organizer. With ongoing development, the object will "accrue" other functions and meanings (Tolpin 1971) and other levels of symbolization may be condensed in its representations, e.g., supporting the body image, while at the same time the original function of undoing separation is maintained (Muensterberger 1962, Roiphe and Galenson 1973). Obviously the formation of transitional objects at age two involves issues other than the capacity for symbolization in normal children—e.g., *what* is symbolized and why.

A final aspect of development in relation to the symbolization process is the increasingly complex psychic products which can be structured and utilized as symbols in the service of the creative imagination, among them, "image, fantasy, thought and concept" (Beres 1960). Fantasies, for example, can become more complex in content and function and be utilized as transitional phenomena for refueling to help master stranger anxiety and to promote separation (described in a two-year-old in Sandler 1977). Silverman (1977) has described an adolescent patient who put himself to sleep by constructing stories, and Solomon (1960) has described fixed internal ideas as transitional objects (actually a transitional phenomenon). Searles (1975) and Solomon (chapter 16) have been able to apply the concept to symptoms; Natterson (1976), to the sense of self; and Grolnick (chapter 14), to dreaming.

We have tried in this volume to demonstrate that an understanding of the broad developmental line of transitional and fetishistic objects and phenomena has deep implications for future speculation and research on the creative process and symbolization, including language and symptom formation. It also provides the beginnings of an understanding of the links between the development of object relationships and the equilibrium that exists between the protosymbolic presentational world and the symbolic world.

The number and variety of studies and interpretations of the concept of transitional objects and phenomena testify not only to its complexity, but also to its wide applicability. We hope to have shown how an original observation of childhood development, the transitional object, is only the manifest aspect of an essential mode of our experiencing of the internal and external worlds: it is a crucial internalized component within a psychic structure conceptualized as dynamic in nature.

REFERENCES

Arlow, A., and Brenner, C. (1964). *Psychoanalytic Concepts and the Structural Theory.* New York: International Universities Press.

Bach, S. (1971). Notes on some imaginary companions. *Psychoanalytic Study of the Child* 26:159-173.

Bak, R. (1974). Distortions in the concept of fetishism. *Psychoanalytic Study of the Child* 29:191-214.

Beres, D. (1960). Perception, imagination, and reality. *International Journal of Psycho-Analysis* 41:327-334.

——— (1965). Symbol and object. *Bulletin of the Menninger Clinic* 29:2-23.

Berezin, M. (1973). Senescence and the phenomenology of separation-individuation. Panel: the experience of separation-individuation in infancy and its reverberations through the course of life: maturity, senescence, and sociological implications. Reported by Irving Sternschein. *Journal of the American Psychoanalytic Association* 21:633-645.

Bettelheim, B. (1969). *Children of the Dream.* New York: Macmillan.

Bowlby, J. (1969). *Attachment and Loss. Vol. I: Attachment*. New York: Basic Books.

Busch, F. (1974). Dimensions of the first transitional object. *Psychoanalytic Study of the Child* 29:215-229.

Buxbaum, E. (1960). Hair pulling and fetishism. *Psychoanalytic Study of the Child* 15:243-260.

Coppolillo, H. P. (1967). Maturational aspects of the transitional phenomena. *International Journal of Psycho-Analysis* 48:237-246.

Dickes, R. (1963). Fetishistic behavior: a contribution to its complex development and significance. *Journal of the American Psychoanalytic Association* 11:303-330.

Fintzy, R. T. (1971). Vicissitudes of the transitional object in a borderline child. *International Journal of Psycho-Analysis* 52:107-114.

Fraiberg, S. (1969). Libidinal object constancy and mental representation. *Psychoanalytic Study of the Child* 24:9-47.

Freud, A. (1965). *Normality and Pathology in Childhood*. New York: International Universities Press.

Furer, M. (1964). The development of a preschool symbiotic psychotic boy. *Psychoanalytic Study of the Child* 19:448-469.

Gaddini, R., and Gaddini, E. (1970). Transitional objects and the process of individuation. *Journal of the American Child Psychiatry* 9:347-365.

Galenson, E., and Roiphe, H. (1971). The impact of early sexual discovery on mood, defensive organization, and symbolization. *Psychoanalytic Study of the Child* 26:195-216.

——— (1972). Early genital activity and the castration complex. *Psychoanalytic Quarterly* 41:334-347.

——— (1975). Some observations on transitional object and infantile fetish. *Psychoanalytic Quarterly* 44:206-231.

Greenacre, P. (1953). Certain relationships between fetishism and the faulty development of the body image. *Psychoanalytic Study of the Child* 8:79-98.

——— (1959). Play in relation to creative imagination. In *Emotional Growth*, vol. 2, pp. 555-574. New York: International Universities Press, 1971.

——— (1960). Further notes on fetishism. *Psychoanalytic Study of the Child* 15:191-207.

——— (1969). The fetish and the transitional object. *Psychoanalytic Study of the Child* 24:144-164.

——— (1970). The transitional object and the fetish with special reference to the role of illusion. *International Journal of Psycho-Analysis* 51:442-456.

Harlow, H. (1960). Primary affectional patterns in primates. *American Journal of Orthopsychiatry* 30:676-684.

Kahne, M. (1967). On the persistence of transitional phenomena into adult life. *International Journal of Psycho-Analysis* 48:247-258.

Kestenberg, J. (1971). From organ-object imagery to self and object representations. In *Separation-Individuation*, ed. J. B. McDevitt and C. F. Settlage, pp. 75-99. New York: International Universities Press.

Kohut, H. (1971). *The Analysis of the Self: A Systematic Approach to the Psychoanalytic Treatment of Narcissistic Personality Disorders.* New York: International Universities Press.

Lorenz, K. (1971). *Studies in Animal and Human Behavior.* Cambridge: Harvard University Press.

Mahler, M. (1966). Notes on the development of basic moods: the depressive affect. In *Psychoanalysis—A General Psychology,* ed. R. M. Loewenstein, L. M. Newman, M. Schur, and A. J. Solnit. New York: International Universities Press.

——— (1974). Symbiosis and individuation: the psychological birth of the human infant. *Psychoanalytic Study of the Child* 29:89-106.

———, Pine, F., and Bergman, A. (1975). *The Psychological Birth of the Human Infant.* New York: Basic Books.

McDevitt, J. B. (1975). Separation-individuation and object constancy. *Journal of the American Psychoanalytic Association* 23:713-742.

Modell, A. (1968). *Object Love and Reality.* New York: International Universities Press.

——— (1970). The transitional object and the creative act. *Psychoanalytic Quarterly* 39:240-250.

Muensterberger, W. (1962). The creative process: its relation to object loss and fetishism. In *The Psychoanalytic Study of Society,* vol. 2. New York: International Universities Press.

Natterson, J. M. (1976). The self as a transitional object: its relationship to narcissism and homosexuality. *International Journal of Psychoanalytic Psychotherapy* 5:131-144.

Provence, S., and Ritvo, S. (1961). Effects of deprivation on institutionalized infants: disturbances in development of relationship to inanimate objects. *Psychoanalytic Study of the Child* 16:189-205.

———, and Lipton, R. (1962). *Infants in Institutions.* New York: International Universities Press.

Roiphe, H. (1968). On an early genital phase with an addendum on Genesis. *Psychoanalytic Study of the Child* 23:348-365.

——— (1973). Some thoughts on childhood psychosis, self and object. *Psychoanalytic Study of the Child* 28:131-146.

———, and Galenson, E. (1973). Infantile fetish. *Psychoanalytic Study of the Child* 28:147-166.

Rose, G. J. (1964). Creative imagination in terms of ego core and boundaries. *International Journal of Psycho-Analysis* 45:75-84.

Rosen, V. (1960). Some aspects of the role of imagination in the creative process. *Journal of the American Psychoanalytic Association* 8:229-251. Collected in *Style, Character and Language,* ed. S. Atkin and M. Jucovy, pp. 261-283. New York: Jason Aronson, 1977.

——— (1964). Some effects of artistic talent on character style. *Psychoanalytic Quarterly* 33:1-24. Collected in *Style, Character and Language,* ed. S. Atkin and M. Jucovy, pp. 331-352. New York: Jason Aronson, 1977.

Sandler, A. M. (1977). Beyond eight month anxiety. *International Journal of Psychoanalysis* 58:195-208.

Sarnoff, C. A. (1970). Symbols and symptoms: phytophobia in a two-year-old-girl. *Psychoanalytic Quarterly* 39:550-562.

Searles, H. (1960). *The Non-Human Environment.* New York: International Universities Press.

——— (1975). Transitional phenomena and therapeutic symbiosis. *International Journal of Psychoanalytic Psychotherapy* 5:145-204.

Silverman, J. (1977). Personal communication.

Solomon, J. C. (1962). Fixed idea as an internalized transitional object. *American Journal of Psychotherapy* 16.

Sperling, M. (1963). Fetishism in children. *Psychoanalytic Quarterly* 32:374-392.

Spitz, R. A. (1959). *A Genetic Field Theory of Ego Formation.* New York: International Universities Press.

———, and Wolf, K. M. (1946). The smiling response: a contribution to the ontogenesis of social relations. *Genetic Psychology Monographs* 34:57-125.

Stevenson, O. (1954). The first treasured possession. *Psychoanalytic Study of the Child* 9:199-217.

Tolpin, M. (1971). On the beginnings of a cohesive self. *Psychoanalytic Study of the Child* 26:316-352.

Volkan, V. (1973). Transitional fantasies in the analysis of a narcissistic personality. *Journal of the American Psychoanalytic Association* 21:351-376.

Werner, H., and Kaplan, B. (1963). *Symbol Formation.* New York: Wiley.

Winnicott, D. W. (1951). Transitional Objects and Transitional Phenomena. In *Through Paediatrics to Psycho-Analysis.* New York: Basic Books, 1975.

——— (1971). *Playing and Reality.* New York: Basic Books.

Wulff, M. (1946). Fetishism and object choice in early childhood. *Psychoanalytic Quarterly* 15:460-471.

EPILOGUE

Poets, artists, and philosophers have consciously or unconsciously known that the I and the Thou, matter and mind, affect and cognition, and symbol and referent are not optimally distributed, either as warring or as fixed polarities. To the extent polarities interplay paradoxically within a homeostasis, they can satisfy, comfort, and synthesize. When this occurs, we can better achieve a mental equilibrium, a creative activity, or, perhaps, even a work of art. The earliest paradox, the transitional object or phenomenon, imbued with endeared parts of the self and the mother, is suffused with affect. It is loved by the child with enthusiasm, attacked with impunity, sobbed into for comfort. These affective sources allow it to serve as an internalizable foundation for future derivative links between ourselves and the symbolizable environment, between one person's love and another's.

Transitional objects and phenomena do not, of themselves, "explain" creativity, talent, or art. Many constitutional factors, including the vicissitudes of perceptual and drive maturation and the form-building capacities of the ego, are involved. But what is delineated in this volume is an important developmental line, the *transitional process*, first indicated by the appearance of transitional objects and phenomena: our first loved primitive symbols. Involving the complex beginnings of maturation and development that lead to relationships and interplay between proto-dreams, protosymbols, and transitional objects and phenomena, this developmental line proceeds throughout our lives—coloring, influencing, and interacting with the objects and activities that render life not only tolerable but pleasurable. With healthy development, some of these dividends are the earliest illusionary recapturing of a lost symbiosis; the imaginary companion and its descendents; the ability to play and engage in nonfetishistic sexual foreplay; the nurturing and maintenance of hobbies; the capacity to experience nostalgia; and the creative use of the imagination.

Winnicott's concepts provide a base from which we can study the wellsprings of man's symbolizing capacity. His work carries the factor of our affective life directly into the arena of the epistemology of symbolism as developed by Cassirer, Langer, de Saussure, Piaget, Lacan, and others. At a time when workers in many fields are searching deeply into the mysteries of man's dream and symbol-making capacity, we now have a better opportunity to understand the *background* of the factors that determine whether individuals and cultures are able to create the affectively ambiguous symbols that support, synthesize, and at times inspire.

In addition, the use the transitional process makes of the human and nonhuman environments is a way of conceptualizing the developmental hierarchies of symbol formation that leads to new ideas concerning the therapeutic process. At this writing, psychoanalysts are beginning to realize that, given the contemporary patient, the psychoanalytic situation evokes far more than an interpretation of unconscious conflict. It is more than simply a place to deal with the analyst's or therapist's role as an oedipal-level transference figure. We are finding that the dramatic, illusionary nature of analytic interplay and the manifestations of the transference must take place within a facilitating environment, a facilitating analytic *setting*, to provide a fertile ambience for the ultimate building, or rebuilding, of the self and its capacity to create a richness of symbolic meaning. The more traditional function of psychoanalytic treatment, the interpretation of hidden or repressed meanings from the unconscious and the past, can proceed concurrently and dialectically. Without *both* processes, there is danger of substituting dead, affectless and nonsynthesizing symbols (intellectualized new understandings or reconstructions) for the often incapacitating "sick" or "neurotic" symbols (symptoms) developed by the patient.

Just as the archaeologist digs, uncovers and discovers the old, but begins immediately to construct new meanings that elucidate past, present, and even future man, so a psychoanalytic understanding of a patient, an artist, or a cultural phenomenon should move, in a temporal sense, both anteriorly and posteriorly. Winnicott's concept of the developmental processes involved in symbol formation, his framework for understanding illusion, and the capacity to maintain paradox provides a two-way bridging of the early and the later as well as of the inner and the outer. Above all, his evocative suggestions concerning the broad and subtle factors that influence the capacity to form an early incarnation of meaning within primitive, affective protosymbols provides a psychological basis for our never-ending attempts to resolve the problematic subject-object, affect-cognition splits. We hope the extensions of his concepts as elaborated in this volume will interest many in the related fields of philosophy, esthetics, semiology, linguistics, literature, and anthropology as well as provide a fresh and workable conceptualization of the symbolic and affective interchange within the psychoanalytic situation.

S. G.

GLOSSARY

Accessory Objects: "People who assist the mother in the care of the infant" and who "are frequently fused in memory with the image of the mother." These can be nurses, grandmothers, siblings, or the father. "Underneath the depression about the loss of a nurse or a grandmother, in infancy, there always lurks a latent feeling of loss of a symbiotic organ-object. Unlike the intermediate object [which see], the accessory object is held onto as a temporal link of the past with the future ('when Nannie goes, Mother will come')." Accessory objects are one of Judith Kestenberg's three principal infantile patterns of erecting symbiotic bridges between organs and objects. The other two are intermediate and transitional objects.

Kestenberg, J. (1971). From organ-object imagery to self and object-representations. In J. Kestenberg, *Children and Parents: Psychoanalytic Studies in Development*, pp. 215–234. New York: Jason Aronson, 1975.

Analytic Object: A metaphor referring to the communication and creative reconstruction occurring between analysand and analyst. Each comprises a union of two parts: what is lived or experienced, and what is communicated, each of which is the double of the other. The analytic object is the complementary union of these two doubles and is "neither internal (to the analysand or to the analyst) nor external (to either the one or the other)." Its early developmental counterpart appears in Winnicott's potential space between mother and infant. The term and the concept were first used by André Green (see chapter 11).

Green, A. (1975). The analyst, symbolism and absence. *International Journal of Psycho-Analysis* 56:1–22.

Analyzing Instrument: A metaphor derived from Freud to describe the essence of psychoanalytic communication. It is a composite of two complementary halves, one functioning in the analyst and the other in the patient. The analyst uses his unconscious "like a receptive organ towards the transmitting unconscious of the patient....as a telephone receiver is adjusted to the transmitting microphone" (see *Standard Edition*

12:109–120). It was Otto Isakower who first used the concreteness of this image to help the analyst tease out the intrapsychic process leading to the development of what ultimately becomes an autonomous ego skill. Theodore Greenbaum (chapter 12) tries to show the similarity of this empathic field to the sensitive attunement of the good enough mother with her child via the transitional process. (See *analytic object*.)

Clinging Instinct *(Sich-Anklammern)*: Term used by Imre Hermann in 1936 to describe an inherent need of the child to cling to the body of the maternal object. Its dialectical counterpart was designated the *going-in-search instinct*. Hermann considered it an innate developmental need that can later become endowed with libidinal or aggressive components. As such it is involved in the evolution of noninstinctual precursors of transitional objects, what Gaddini (chapter 8) has termed *skin contact and tactile precursor objects*. If not frustrated or highly instinctualized, this nonexcitatory clinging in its interplay with the going-in-search instinct seems to correspond to and adumbrate the potential space in which easy playing can eventually occur. When the ability to cling to the mother is frustrated, the infant seeks other objects to cling to. The degree of instinctualization and of anxiety will help to determine these objects as transitional or fetishistic.

Hermann, Imre (1936). Clinging–going in search: a contrasting pair of instincts and their relation to sadism and masochism. Translated in *Psychoanalytic Quarterly* 45:5–36.

Collective Alternates: An important aspect of the creative process in the potentially gifted infant. Because of the inherent intense receptivity and sensitivity to sensory impingement, the sights, sounds, smell, and feel of the objects and phenomena in the surround become endowed and embraced with object love derived from the primary object tie. In this sense, the infant artist's "love affair with the world" is mediated through the creation of a kaleidoscopic array of transitional phenomena and objects, his collective alternates. This has profound implications for the specific qualities of the artist's creativity as well as the unique qualities of his object relations. Phyllis Greenacre first described this phenomenon.

Greenacre, P. (1957). The childhood of the artist. *Psychoanalytic Study of the Child* 12:47–72; reprinted in *Emotional Growth*, vol. 2, pp. 479–505, International Universities Press, 1971.

Developmental Line of Transitional Objects and Phenomena: A concept elaborated by Anna Freud in her *Normality and Pathology in Development*. There are various longitudinal currents of development leading from earlier, more primitive infantile ego-id-superego structures and functions to more complex combinations, where new levels are reached at later stages. Anna Freud included Winnicott's concept of transitional objects and phenomena in a sequence she designated: From the Body to the Toy and from Play to Work.

We feel that the transitional process can be traced from the beginnings of self and object differentiation throughout the life cycle (see Rose, chapter 22). A modern ego psychology implies separate but interactive levels of development of narcissicism and object relations. It is possible to tease out conceptually a transitional object line that interacts with, mediates, and helps define the growth of a vital self and object world. However, the developmental line of the transitional process not only is a concept of object relations, but also includes the equilibrium between primary and secondary process mechanisms, concrete and abstract cognitive operations, presentational and representational memory, and protosymbolic and symbolic thinking.

Facilitating Environment: Related to *good enough mothering*. Maturational processes are promoted by an environment created by a mother who, though sensitive to her child's needs, is not perfect. Winnicott suggests that perfection is an ideal associated with machines, and that with the human adaptation to need, imperfections become "an essential quality in the environment that facilitates." It is important, however, that there be continuity of care, and that frustration is not so great as to be traumatic.

Fetish: An obligatory inanimate object utilized by an adult (usually male) to ensure genital sexual performance. A part of the body inappropriate for intercourse, such as the foot, may also be a fetish. Sometimes certain attributes of the object—a color, an odor—assume overriding importance. The basic fear of castration leads the fetishist to deny this possibility by splitting as well as by symbolic displacements, the fetish standing for a female phallus. This reinforces the fetishist's body image, diminishes castration anxiety, and allows sexual performance. While pregenital elements can be crucial in the predisposition to fetishism, the fetish itself is not a transitional object. Significant sexual or aggressive discharge in an object attachment disqualifies that object as transitional.

Fetishistic Objects and Phenomena: The emphasis here is usually on *pregenital*, either oral or anal, aspects of an object attachment; in this sense they could be called *pregenital fetishes*. Transitional objects are not fetishes because with the latter the primary focus is a repetitive and stereotyped substitutive process rather than normal growth and development. A clinical example in adults would be the various addictions. Whereas by the above definition *fetishistic* means "like a fetish, but not," the term is also applied where phallic phase phenomena *are* involved, as in "fetishistic phenomena." Hence it is important to examine the context in which the term appears. In either case, however, the use of the object does not correspond to that of the fetish in an actual perversion. What is called fetishistic here is not utilized in an obligatory way to ensure genital functioning, and where actual perversion has orgasm as its aim and is primarily an illness of men, such fetishistic phenomena as compulsive collecting or decorating and the use of amulets or charms can involve either men or women.

Good Enough Mother: Provides a facilitating environment promoting maturational processes. She makes it possible for maximal growth and development to occur by actively adapting to the infant's needs. But this adaptation gradually lessens as the infant's frustration tolerance increases. Now failures to respond, if not too frequent or severe, do not induce traumata but instead promote development. In fact, too close a correspondence between infantile need and maternal nurture can produce a failure of separation and promote regressive fusion rather than independence. Good enough in this realm is best. Anything "better" is "too good" and falls as short of the optimal as simple neglect or rejection. Winnicott's view of transitional object development is inextricably bound up with this concept: without the good enough mother the child is unable to acquire the creative capacity to develop true transitional objects and phenomena, a capacity indicating progressive growth and, circularly, good enough mothering.

Illusion: For the first time in psychoanalytic theory building, Winnicott has tried to trace the developmental line of illusion formation. Nineteenth century psychology saw the word *illusion* confined to "illusions of the senses, that is to say, to false or illusory perceptions" (Sully 1881). This definition would now be closer to our current usage of the word *delusion*. As the ego's capacity to experience illusory phenomena differentiates itself from the infant's delusional and hallucinatory world, reality testing, at first a crude device, gradually evolves into a function capable, in its own service, of suspending its own activity, of oscillation and even playfulness; ultimately the capacity for illusion, for "as if" and "let's pretend" can develop (of course the line between delusion and illusion is not clearly demarcated).

As cognitive development and object relations mature, the ego states of illusions, their contents, and our adaptive and creative use of them become increasingly complex. A developmental line intimately related to the transitional process is implied here. It begins with the earliest illusion (emerging from delusion) of the infant, that the breast is part of himself and yet is not.

Winnicott's view of illusion is within its healthy, nonpejorative connotation. The successful mix of the representational and perceptual world, and of the self and the object worlds, is the basis of future self-comfort, play, and creative experiencing. The capacity for illusion formation, for the "suspension of disbelief," is necessary for gratifying life experience, and represents a healthier, more adaptive solution than delusion, discomfort, and disillusionment.

It is interesting that, even in 1881, one of Freud's acknowledged progenitors (Freud 1900), James Sully, was aware of this aspect of illusion. Sully, influenced by the romantic movement as well as by contemporary science, was able to call illusion formation an occupation that is "quite natural to children, and to imaginative adults when they choose to throw the reins on the neck of their fantasy. Our luminous circle of rational perception is surrounded by a misty penumbra of illusion" (1881, p. 3).

Winnicott added a diachronic, developmental dimension to the understanding and appreciation of illusion. He established himself, in addition, within the philosophical and aesthetic tradition of Kant and Coleridge, and his ideas seem to mesh naturally with those of such modern aestheticians as E.H. Gombrich and Susanne Langer (see Dinnage, chapter 23).

Freud, S. (1900). Interpretation of dreams. *Standard Edition*. 4/5:60, 135 (n. 2), 501–502, 591.
Gombrich, E.H. (1961). *Art and Illusion*, 2nd ed. Princeton: Princeton University Press.
Langer, S. (1953). *Feeling and Form: A Theory of Art*. New York. Scribner.
Sully, J. (1881). *Illusions: A Psychological Study*. New York: Appleton.
Winnicott, D.W. (1971). *Playing and Reality*. New York: Basic Books.

Infantile Fetish: When an attachment to an object is used to deal with castration anxiety and to reinforce the genital body image, the object has been designated an infantile fetish. Roiphe and Galenson have studied such objects and found them in general harder than transitional objects, which tend to be furry and appear between eighteen and twenty months. Although the adult perversion of fetishism unfortunately is implied in the term, it is clear that while there may be such object attachments in the histories of fetishists, not all such attachments result in adult perversion; nor are we talking about adult sexual performance in

544 GLOSSARY

children. Bak thought it preferable, in order to avoid confusion, to call objects substituting for or reinforcing the body image in children "prosthetic objects." These may later (but need not) appear as fetishes in a developed adult perversion.

Bak, R. (1974). Distortions of the concept of fetishism. *Psychoanalytic Study of the Child.* 29:191–214.
Roiphe, H., and Galenson, E. (1973) The infantile fetish. *Psychoanalytic Study of the Child* 28:147–166.

Intermediate Objects: Characterize a stage in the progression from organ-object imagery to self- and object-representations. In Judith Kestenberg's words, intermediate objects are "food and bodily products associated with organ pleasure" that seem to belong to both infant and mother. Such objects "help to maintain the sense of dual unity in the absence of the object." When the infant loses his bodily products (food, feces, urine), these products relinquish their warm, living quality. To master the sense of loss, he reanimates them as "intermediate objects," associating them with the "inanimate things that he felt and saw in the intimate space he shared with his mother (fingering her clothing during feeding, feeling the texture of sheets, diapers, bath water and soap, etc.)." External objects, though never inside the child's body, can become associated with bodily products and be treated as intermediate objects. Such items include toys, utensils, pets, and even people. These are distinguished from transitional objects proper in that involvement with them is in the here and now, while for Kestenberg "transitional objects serve the preservation of the old, within the newness of the present, into the future. They not only evoke the illusion of unity with the mother but also unite body parts and integrate simultaneous, yet different needs." When a *person* is treated as an intermediate object, this use should be differentiated from an accessory object (which see). As Werner Muensterberger has pointed out (see chapter 1), Róheim used the term *intermediate object* to describe a stabilization of the transitional process. This corresponds to Winnicott's *transitional object*. In Hermann's paper on clinging–going-in-search, *intermediate object* is used in Kestenberg's sense.

Kestenberg, J. (1971). From organ-object imagery to self and object-representations. In *Children and Parents: Psychoanalytic Studies in Development*, pp. 215–234 New York: Jason Aronson, 1975.

Playing: Winnicott used the term in its progressive, creative, developmental sense. Play is the "work" of childhood, and for some becomes the work of psychotherapy. Optimally, it is an ego activity only minimally cathected with libidinal or aggressive energy. Playing takes place in the potential space between baby and mother, between therapist and patient. It facilitates growth, separation-individuation, communication, and symbol formation. Winnicott places himself in the tradition of those who have related play to the creative process, among them Schiller, Groos, Rank, and Huizinga. Free play, nursery play (games not rigidly regulated) extend the interplay between the feeding infant and the mother through the use of toys or playthings, the derivatives of transitional objects and phenomena. As described by Piaget, Kestenberg, Grolnick, and Metcalf and Spitz, there is a close relationship between ludic (play) symbols and dream symbols. This concept of play is easily extended to language development and the relatively new field of speech play. The Winnicott model for psychotherapy and psychoanalysis is play involving blocks, balls of wool, or a spoon and dish—in contrast in quality and ambience with the more structured chess game model of classical psychoanalysis.

Winnicott, D.W. (1971). *Playing and Reality*. New York: Basic Books.

Potential Space: The metaphorical space between infant and mother while differentiation of self- and object-representations is incomplete— or, more positively, while the infant is hatching from the dual unity or symbiotic membrane. It is within potential space that the transitional process occurs, and from which emerge transitional objects and phenomena and the capacity for illusion, play, and the creative imagination. Potential space meshes seamlessly with the developmental use of actual space, as shown in this volume by Anni Bergman and Susan Deri. The terms *intermediate area, third world,* and *third area* are earlier versions of Winnicott's more definitive concept.

Winnicott, D.W. (1971). *Playing and Reality*. New York: Basic Books.

Precursor Objects: Used by the child for consolation, these are the functional progenitors of the transitional object. Either inanimate objects provided by the mother or parts of the child's or the mother's body, they may include the child's tongue, hair, fingers, hand, pacifier, and bottle (if used as a pacifier), and the mother's hair, ears, or nevi. Renata Gaddini distinguishes the early "into-the-mouth precursor object" from the later "skin contact and tactile sensation precursor object." In the course of development, the into-the-mouth precursor object is given up, while the tactile precursor object can become the transitional object. The term, originally suggested by Winnicott, has been developed by Gaddini (chapter 8).

Primary Creativity: The child's earliest creative capacity, involving the use of illusion. Not to be taken for granted, this capacity is itself the result of experience with a good enough mother. An indicator of health, this capacity, though not identical with adult creativity, is related to it within a developmental line. It should be understood that primary creativity does not foreordain the creation of works of art. Nor does the capacity to create such works imply psychological health, as is often assumed in discussions that rely on a simplistic understanding and application of the sublimation concept. Finally, primary creativity is among the first evidences of a complex ego functioning and is related to an increasing ability to play and symbolize. The ultimate result is the capacity to enjoy and adapt via a creativity of everyday life (see Rose, chapter 22).

Primary Maternal Preoccupation: A special condition of the mother, approaching a "normal illness," in which the "ordinary devoted mother" develops an extraordinary involvement with and sensitivity to her infant and its needs. Occurring toward the end of the pregnancy and lasting a period of weeks after the child's birth, it involves a moderate withdrawal from the world outside the mother-child dyad. This reaction allows the mother to meet the child's needs and to offer a good enough environment promoting psychological and physical development.

Protosymbol: A primitive symbol in which the symbolic vehicle directly "presents" a meaning rather than "representing" it as would a true symbol. The protosymbol appears during the developmental process leading from substitute objects to the ultimate capacity for true symbol formation. Because the transitional object develops when there is only a partial differentiation of self- and object-representations, Werner and Kaplan consider it a protosymbol. It follows that the vicissitudes of transitional object development will be of critical importance in establishing the symbolic capacity and its qualities.

Werner, H., and Kaplan, B. (1963). *Symbol Formation: An Organismic-Developmental Approach to Language and the Expression of Thought.* New York: Wiley.

Psychic Organizer: A term borrowed from embryology by René Spitz to describe the intrapsychic products of the various currents of maturation and development at certain critical points. The establishment of these organizers is evidenced by reliable behavioral symptoms, or epiphenomena, of the process, such as the reciprocal smiling response, stranger anxiety, and the "no" response. These are designated *indicators.* Metcalf and Spitz show in chapter 7 that the transitional object functions as an additional, critical psychic organizer.

Spitz, R. (1965). *The First Year of Life: A Psychoanalytic Study of Normal and Deviant Development of Object Relations.* New York: International Universities Press.

Squiggle Game: In the squiggle game, Winnicott would make a spontaneous line drawing and invite the child being interviewed to turn it into something. The child would then make a squiggle for Winnicott to do the same. Winnicott developed this interactional game into a most perceptive diagnostic tool, combining in it elements of free play and association. It is conceptualized as occurring in the area of potential space.

Substitute Object: An object used by an animal or man simply to replace another object. This sign system can be stimulated at either pole only by a direct stimulus. The substitute object stands for, and in place of, but does not *represent* the original object. Here the organism cannot evoke the representation of the absent object, as it can with a symbolic object.

Beres, D. (1965). Symbol and object. *Bulletin of the Menninger Clinic* 29:2–23.

Transitional Language: A phase of the object-related developmental line of language formation as it proceeds from presentational to representational forms. Transitional words retain their "thingness" while beginning to have protosymbolic, referential significance (see *protosymbol*). From the speaker's standpoint, there is a lack of clear differentiation of symbol, referent, and self. The developmental line begins with words mouthed in a manner analagous to the infant use of such precursor objects as pacifiers (see *precursor objects*). Then, as outer words and inner language structure are increasingly connected, words come to resemble true transitional objects and begin to internalize their functions: hence, transitional language. First described by Martin Weich (see chapter 25), these words or phrases are "carried" by the child as if they were transitional objects. While the developmental line in question tends toward what might be termed *language constancy* (a truly symbolic referential language) in adults, a protosymbolic function may nevertheless be retained. This was perhaps implied in Roman Jakobson's division of language into referential and poetic functions, the latter designating language usage where the "shape" is the message: it can be exploited for its own sake. Transitional language in the adult can develop into speech play and poetry; such modern poets as Ezra Pound and Wallace Stevens, as well as Gerard Manley Hopkins (Sobel, chapter 26), have used words in a manner strongly reminiscent of transitional language.

Transitional Objects: The infant's first possessions. Winnicott saw their normal development as a sequence of mouthing activities followed by attachment primarily to such soft objects as blankets, dolls, and teddy bears. These attachments usually develop between four and twelve months and indicate the child's capacity to create, however protosymbolically, the mental concept of an object, thereby alleviating the normal developmental stress of separation-individuation. Transitional objects are often utilized when the infant is tired or going to sleep, or goes on a trip, leaving behind what is familiar. Winnicott felt an object was truly transitional if on occasion the child could be more attached to it than to the mother. It should be understood that this does not imply that the healthy child with a loved good enough mother cares for the object more than the mother. There is no competition in this optimal situation. What is meant is that, at times of inevitable conflict with the mother, the child has the ready capacity to utilize the (then "preferred") transitional object to create the illusion of her physical presence (see Metcalf and Spitz, chapter 7; Gaddini, chapter 8). At the same time, the object should not be *primarily* a source of instinctual gratification, though undoubtedly some instinctual discharge is involved. Furthermore, the infant's principal affective attitude toward the object is a loving one. While the object may represent the breast or feces, this is not Winnicott's major focus. Rather, he is stressing the creative use of illusion to bridge inner and outer, to fill a gap, and to undo separation in the service of normal growth and development. Although transitional objects can be distinguished from transitional phenomena (which see), the two categories no doubt represent a continuum.

Transitional Phenomena: Whereas transitional objects are tangible, portable objects, transitional phenomena are activities or products of activities: mannerisms, behavior patterns, images. Included are fantasizing as well as specific fantasies, and such repetitive motions as tapping and rocking. The important consideration is that they satisfy the criteria for transitional objects. Thus the *use* of any such phenomenon is critical: to determine whether a fantasy, for instance, is a transitional phenomenon, its function in the life of the individual would have to be understood. If it is "held," savored, and used to re-create an illusion of merging with the mother, if it serves the separation-individuation process, it may qualify as transitional. In derivative forms, transitional phenomena play a role throughout life. Both transitional phenomena and transitional objects are externalizations or crystallizations of the intrapsychic transitional process (which see).

Transitional Process: A term arising out of the importance modern conceptual models place on shifting boundaries as opposed to stable structures. Primary and secondary processes, for example, are considered continuous, as interacting on all intrapsychic levels rather than as a pair of opposites on separate levels; reality is no longer seen as a steady backdrop but rather as a dynamic oscillation of figure and ground; and the organism as a whole is viewed as an open system continuously engaged in mutual development with the outside. *Transitional process* was first used by Gilbert Rose to indicate that (1) the dynamic equilibrium between a relatively fluid self and reality is not limited to the transitional object of childhood but continues into adulthood; (2) the adaptation of everyday life and the originality of creative imagination represent a continuing "transitional" interplay between self and reality; (3) in the light of the transitional process, adaptation may be thought of as creative, and creative imagination as adaptive; and (4) in both, an individual abstracts and maintains an *umwelt* of his own—a synchronous and contemporary but necessarily selective reality (see Rose, chapter 22).

CONTRIBUTORS

SAMUEL ABRAMS, M.D.
Clinical Assistant Professor, Division of Psychoanalysis, Downstate Medical Center
Training and Supervising Analyst, Child and Adult Sections, Division of Psychoanalysis, Downstate Medical Center
Research Psychiatrist, Child Development Center

LEONARD BARKIN, M.D.
Clinical Assistant Professor (Psychiatry), Albert Einstein College of Medicine
Faculty Member, Division of Psychoanalysis, Downstate Medical Center

ANNI BERGMAN
Adjunct Professor of Psychology, City University of New York
Coauthor with Margaret Mahler and Fred Pine, *The Psychological Birth of the Human Infant*

SUSAN DERI, Dipl. in Medical Psychology (Hungarian Royal State College for Medical Psychology)
Formerly lecturer, Graduate School of Psychology of City College, New York
Faculty Member, National Psychological Association for Psychoanalysis
Author, *Introduction to the Theory and Practice of the Szondi Test*

ROBERT DICKES, M.D.
Chairman and Professor of Psychiatry, Department of Psychiatry, Downstate Medical Center
Training and Supervising Analyst, Division of Psychoanalysis, Downstate Medical Center
Director, Center for Sexual Dysfunction, Downstate Medical Center
Director, Infant Behavior Research Laboratory, Department of Psychiatry, Downstate Medical Center

ROSEMARY DINNAGE
Author, *The Handicapped Child*, Volumes I and II. She works for the *Times Literary Supplement* (London) and contributes to the *New Statesman*, *New York Review of Books*, and other journals.

ALFRED FLARSHEIM, M.D.
Clinical Associate Professor of Psychiatry, University of Illinois College of Medicine
Consultant, The Sonia Shankman Orthogenic School, University of Chicago

ANTONY FLEW, D. Litt. (Keele)
Professor of Philosophy, University of Reading, England
Author, *A New Approach to Psychical Research, Hume's Philosophy of Belief, God and Philosophy, Evolutionary Ethics, An Introduction to Western Philosophy, Crime or Disease?, Thinking Straight, The Presumption of Atheism,* and *Sociology, Equality and Education*
Editor, *Logic and Language* (First and Second Series), *Essays in Conceptual Analysis, Body, Mind and Death,* and *Malthus on Population*

RENATA GADDINI, M.D.
Professor of Mental Health, Lecturer in Child Psychiatry, Catholic University of Rome
Associate Professor of Pediatrics, Director of Mental Hygiene Unit, Department of Pediatrics, State University of Rome
Vice President, International College of Psychosomatic Medicine
Editorial Boards, *Neuropsichiatria Infantile* and *Psychiatry in Medicine*

PETER L. GIOVACCHINI, M.D.
Clinical Professor of Psychiatry, University of Illinois College of Medicine
Author, *Psychoanalysis of Character Disorders*
Coeditor, *Annals of Adolescent Psychiatry*
Editor, *Tactics and Techniques in Psychoanalytic Treatment,* Volumes I and II

ANDRÉ GREEN, M.D.
Formerly Chief of the Clinic of the Chair of Psychiatry (Paris)
Formerly Director of the Paris Psychoanalytic Institute
Coeditor, *The International Journal of Psycho-Analysis,* the *International Review of Psycho-Analysis,* and *Nouvelle Revue de Psychoanalyse*

THEODORE GREENBAUM, M.D.
Clinical Assistant Professor, Department of Psychiatry, Downstate Medical Center
Affiliated Staff, New York Psychoanalytic Institute
Faculty Member, Division of Psychoanalysis, Downstate Medical Center

RALPH R. GREENSON, M.D.
Clinical Professor of Psychiatry, UCLA School of Medicine
Training and Supervising Analyst, Los Angeles Psychoanalytic Institute

Formerly Chairman of the Advisory Board, Foundation for Research in Psychoanalysis

Author, *The Technique and Practice of Psychoanalysis*

SIMON A. GROLNICK, M.D.

Clinical Assistant Professor, Division of Psychoanalysis, Downstate Medical Center

Faculty Member, Division of Psychoanalysis, Downstate Medical Center

Psychiatric Director, Brooklyn Community Counseling Center

HENRY KAMINER, M.D.

Clinical Assistant Professor of Psychiatry, Rutgers Medical School

Faculty Member, Division of Psychoanalysis, Downstate Medical Center

Secretary, New Jersey District Branch, American Psychiatric Association

JAMES KAVANAUGH, M.D.

Assistant Professor of Psychiatry and Pediatrics, University of Virginia School of Medicine

JUDITH S. KESTENBERG, M.D.

Clinical Associate Professor of Psychiatry, Department of Psychiatry, Downstate Medical Center

Training Analyst, Child and Adult Sections, Division of Psychoanalysis, Downstate Medical Center

Director, Child Development Research, Codirector of the Center for Parents and Children, Child Development Research, Port Washington, N.Y.

Author, *Children and Parents*

M. MASUD. R. KHAN, M.A.

Editor, the *International Psycho-Analytic Library*

Coeditor, *Nouvelle Revue de Psychoanalyse*

Director, Freud Copyrights

Associate editor, the *International Journal of Psycho-Analysis* and the *International Review of Psycho-Analysis*

ALFONZ LENGYEL, Ph.D.

Professor of Archaeology and Director of the Classical Art and Archaeology Program, Northern Kentucky State College

President, Toscan-American Archaeological Research Association

Board of Directors, Mediterranean Fine Arts Research Association

ALFRED LORENZER

Professor of Socialization Theory, the J. W. Goethe University, Frankfort/Main

Author, *Sprachzerstörung und Rekonstruktion, Überden Gegenstand der Psycho-analysise oder: Sprache und Interaktion*

DAVID METCALF, M.D.
Director, Research and Research Training, Department of Psychiatry, University of Colorado, Medical Center
Institute Associate, Denver Institute

RUTH MILLER, Ph.D.
Professor of English and Comparative Literature, State University of New York at Stony Brook
Author, *The Poetry of Emily Dickinson*, for which she received the Melville Cane Award of the Poetry Society of America

MARION MILNER
Member, British Psychoanalytic Society
Author, *On Not Being Able to Paint, A Life of One's Own*, and *The Hands of the Living God: An Account of a Psycho-Analytic Treatment*

WERNER MUENSTERBERGER, Ph.D.
Clinical Associate Professor of Psychiatry, Department of Psychiatry, Downstate Medical Center
Fellow, Royal Anthropological Institute (England)
Editor-in-chief, *The Psychoanalytic Study of Society* and *Man and His Culture*

PETER B. NEUBAUER, M.D.
Director, Child Development Center, New York City
Chairman, Task Force I, Joint Commission on Mental Health of Children
Clinical Professor, Department of Psychiatry, Downstate Medical Center
President, Association for Child Psychoanalysis
Training and Supervising Analyst, Child and Adult Sections, Division of Psychoanalysis, Downstate Medical Center

PETER ORBAN
Author, *Sozialisation* and *Subjektivität*

DAVID PARRISH, M.D.
Director, Adolescent Department, Boulder Psychiatric Institute, Boulder, Colorado

GILBERT ROSE, M.D.
Clinical Associate Professor, Department of Psychiatry, Yale Medical School
Member, Faculty of the Western New England Institute for Psycho-analysis

EMILIE SOBEL, M.A., Psy.D.
Psychologist, Brooklyn Community Counseling Center

JOSEPH C. SOLOMON, M.D.
Former Clinical Professor of Psychiatry, University of California Medical School

RENÉ SPITZ, M.D.
Former Professor Emeritus, Department of Psychiatry, University of Colorado Medical Center
Author of numerous publications, including *No and Yes, The First Year of Life*, and *A Genetic Field Theory of Ego Formation*

VAMIK D. VOLKAN, M.D.
Professor of Psychiatry, University of Virginia Medical Center
Faculty Member, Washington Psychoanalytic Institute
Visiting Professor of Psychiatry, University of Ankara, Turkey
Author, *Primitive Internalized Object Relations*

MARTIN J. WEICH, M.D.
Clinical Assistant Professor of Psychiatry, Cornell University School of Medicine
Faculty Member, Division of Psychoanalysis, Downstate Medical Center

JOAN WEINSTEIN, M.S.W.
Participant in the Center for Parents and Children, Child Development Research, Port Washington, N.Y.
Social work consultant, Union Settlement Head Start

CLARE WINNICOTT
The widow of D. W. Winnicott, she is at present working on his biography.

NAME INDEX

SUBJECT INDEX

and self,
  dolls in representation of, 223-43
  oscillation between, 357, 358, 407
  role of transitional object function in creating, 478, 479
  and subject, oscillation between, 169
  objects-trouvés, 56, 370
obsessional rituals, 11, 12
obsessive compulsive states, 247, 255
  technique for treating, 254, 255
ocnophilia, 151, 159
odor, of object, 309, 516
Oedipal complex, 251, 277, 280
ontogenesis, symbols of, 286, 402, 419, 439-43, 480
orality, and fetish, 250, 528
oral triad, 104
organizer, psychic, and transitional object function, 103, 104, 133, 469, 476, 478, 532

oscillation between
  assimilation and accommodation, 373
  centripetal and centrifugal forces, 357
  certainty and uncertainty, 254
  clinging and searching, 150
  closeness and difference, 145-65
  concrete and abstract, 401
  creating and being created, 348
  de-differentiation and reintegration, 358-87
  differences and universals, 349
  ego core and ego boudaries, 355
  erotic symbol and erotic thought, 408
  fetish and transitional object, 289, 390

figure and ground, 347
form and content, 358
fusion and object constancy
  body imagery and outer forms, 353
  self and reality, 353, 357, 358, 359, 427
narcissistic fusion and separateness, 347
perception and dream, 509
phallic and separation themes, 436, 437
phallus and transitional object, 398, 528
primary and secondary process, 42, 401
sameness and change, 71
self and object, 357, 358, 401
self and object space, 145-65
separation and union, 388, 397
soma and psyche, 63, 109-31
subject and object, 169
subjectivity and objectivity, 46, 175, 379, 472
symbols and protosymbols, 403, 404
thinking and art, 358
transitional object and symbol, 403
outer forms and body imagery, 353

pacifiers, 78, 79, 115, 122, 314, 517, 520, 522
paradox, 41, 42, 46, 51, 218, 276, 497, 508
parents, contribution of, to fetishism, 312-17
  influence on development, 523
  transitional object needs, 312-18
part object, 171, 514
past, and present, linking of, and transitional object function, 52, 76, 90, 216, 468